ARKANSAS ODYSSEY

The Saga of Arkansas from Prehistoric Times to Present

A History by Michael B. Dougan

Rose Publishing Company, Inc., Publishers

LITTLE ROCK

Editor: Carol Griffee
Designer: Jim Cleveland
Cover Design: Jim Cleveland
Cover Photographs:
    Harvesting Apples, courtesy of Shiloh Museum
    Black Family at Rosboro, Clark County, courtesy of Special Collections Division,
    University of Arkansas Libraries
    Quapaw Bottle, courtesy of Kent C. Westbrook, M.D.
    Balloons on the Arkansas River, © Copyright 1993 by Tod Swiecichowski

Preparation of the manuscript was partially funded by a grant from the Arkansas Humanities Council.

Library of Congress Cataloging in Publication Data

Dougan, Michael Bruce

Arkansas Odyssey: The Saga of Arkansas from Prehistoric Times to Present

p. cm.
Includes bibliographical references
1. Arkansas — History. I. Title.
F411.D761993   LC Card Number: 88-62036   ISBN:0-914546-65-1

DEDICATION

*To my students, who have taught me
more than I have taught them.*

Foreword

This is a book marvelously rich in detail, and its author exposes to view facts that will surely surprise many readers: That, for instance, Abraham Lincoln was not even on the Arkansas ballot in the 1860 presidential election; that the Civil War, in the wilder parts of the Ozarks, continued for decades; that a vote against the 1868 Constitution was grounds for being denied the franchise in future elections; and that for ten years after the Civil War, only Republicans and blacks celebrated the Fourth of July. The work is as well sprinkled with entertaining anecdotes that reveal, for instance, that the Taensas Indian chief was accorded great respect and was followed around by three wives who agreed with everything he said; that in the nineteenth century, the warden of the state prison could whip prisoners legally but not curse them; that, in the early days of radio, stations in Arkansas often stopped operations in the summer; that in the early twentieth century, a move to close Little Rock saloons collapsed when Jewish saloon keepers insisted on their rights; and that in 1923, Arkansans owned more than 113,000 motor vehicles, more than half of which were Fords.

Factual variety and accuracy are, of course, necessary elements of good, useable history, but they are hardly sufficient. The nature of Professor Dougan's achievement lies not in giving Arkansans an enduring and readable chronicle of their past, though he has done that, but in providing them with an interpretive framework within which they can begin to comprehend its significance. The author, of course, demonstrates a truly admirable knowledge of the primary and secondary materials that bear on Arkansas history, but, more importantly, he has marshaled them in a way that is penetrating and distinctive. By returning again and again to a motif that seeks to understand Arkansas history as a continuing conflict between traditionalism and the forces of modernization, Professor Dougan compels his reader not simply to absorb and remember but to think and react as well. It is this engagement between author and audience that makes this book memorably unique.

In choosing to place his book among those that adhere to the modernization paradigm, Professor Dougan has rejected forthrightly the Marxist/Progressive tradition that, with a tedious tenacity, viewed significant historical events merely as the product of class struggle. This was not just a simple-minded approach to the world, though it certainly was that, but it left out of the account the rich texture of cultural connections between classes that make for a frequent intersection of their personal interests, and it encountered real difficulty in keeping the theory together when members of the same class found themselves divided by race or culture. Professor Dougan, of course, has not abandoned a "political" interpretation of Arkansas's past in favor of an arid recital of facts and events, and this is as it should be. No teacher who is serious about his students' education can escape the duty to organize his materials into patterns that try to make coherent sense of disparate data. In adopting the modernization model, the author assumes a posture that inevitably will involve him in political statements and the occasional expression of an ideological position. Modernization theory, in fact, evidently assumes that modernization is a good thing — Who, after all, would admit to not wanting to be modern — and so an ideology inheres in the approach. There will be persons of intelligence and good will who will not share all of the assumptions of the modernization school, especially the central role for government rather than free enterprise that it

posits as a necessity for discernible economic
and social progress. (Perhaps for this reason it
would not be far wrong to call the school "Marx-
ish.") But in choosing this way of organizing
and presenting the facts, Professor Dougan
adopts a tone and voice that leave plenty of
room for disagreement, for he never reserves
the moral high ground for himself or descends
to didactic preachments.

For all these reasons, and particularly for
bringing the general history of Arkansas into
the traditions of twentieth-century scholarship,
an aim that he expressly embraces in his preface, Michael Dougan has not just written an
excellent book: He has produced a true histori-
ographical event.

Morris S. Arnold

Preface

The noted critic Alain Robbe-Grillet once observed that, contrary to popular opinion, "nothing is more fantastic than accuracy."

After more than twenty years of struggling with this book, I have concluded that accuracy, the lowest level of historical understanding, is not achieved easily. Let an error appear once, and there becomes a better than even chance that it will be repeated again and again. Sometimes these errors are minor matters of dates or places; others, perhaps best described as myths, are omnipresent. Dozens of towns lay claim to having missed becoming the state capital by one vote; every county in the state wants to believe that both De Soto and Jesse James came its way.

Writing state history is particularly challenging. History is an objective study of the past, but too often state historians have engaged in provincial patriotism rather than scholarly analysis. They have tended to venerate their ancestors, ignore social and economic factors, leave out the poor and oppressed, minimize coverage of the twentieth century and eschew analysis in favor of a bland factual approach. The overriding objective in writing this book has been to bring Arkansas history in line with modern scholarship, beginning with the Indians and ending with the question of whether there is an enduring Arkansas.

Because we live in a federal republic, our varieties of experiences often differ from national and sometimes even regional norms. If this book proves anything, it is that Arkansas is not American history writ small.

My research has been extensive and eclectic. Besides endeavoring to examine published materials, I have looked into primary sources extensively. But history is more than the paper trail of the past. People have taught me

history. Margaret Ross, formerly of the *Arkansas Gazette*, indoctrinated me into the mysteries of nineteenth century politics at the onset of my scholarly career. The late T.J. Fakes of McCrory taught me about the Delta. Larry McNeil, a pioneer educator in Crittenden County, showed in his personal life how blacks endured the hardships of segregation. The late Mary Hudgens of Hot Springs was ever ready to help. The late Robert Walz of Southern Arkansas University got me started collecting and preserving historic photographs. And the list goes on. Oral history projects have brought me into contact with hundreds of persons from politicians to sharecroppers. Almost as important has been the land. There are the drainage ditches I know by name and number across the Delta, the best camping gravel bars on the Buffalo River, the lushness of a spring day on the Ouachita Trail and the suggestiveness of the first hint of fall in the air.

In reducing my research to writing, I have been guided by the advice of English historian C.V. Wedgwood, who said one should "go on reading until he hears them talking." I cannot claim that expertise with Indians and French, but I have endeavored to achieve that familiarity with the Americans of the last 200 years.

The formal credits that I owe are extensive. Sam Sizer, the first archivist at the University of Arkansas, suggested this book and said it could be done in six months. My wife, Carol, has been my constant critic. Carol Griffee supplied both facts and stories for the latter chapters as well as serving as the project editor. Melissa Rebenstorf also read the manuscript in the galley stage. Tom W. Dillard read and commented on the early drafts and directed me to additional research materials. Waddy W. Moore reviewed the manuscript before its final revision, offering his trenchant comments and moral support. In endeavoring to tell the Indian story correctly, I enlisted Hester Davis, Ann M. Early, Dan and Phyllis Morse and George Sabo III from the Arkansas Archeological Survey. Others who read portions of the book include Morris S. Arnold, Tom Baskett, Dee Brown, George Fisher, Tony Freyer, Carl Moneyhon, Bob Razer, Ted Wagnon and Miller Williams.

I am also in debt to the library staffs at the Arkansas History Commission, the University of Central Arkansas, The Newberry Library, Columbia University, the University of Arkansas and Arkansas State University. Over the years I have been assisted by a fellowship from The Newberry Library, a summer research grant from the National Endowment for the Humanities and leave from Arkansas State University. Generations of student typists have labored over the revisions, but the bulk of the work has been done by Sue Hogue, the Department of History office secretary, and Teresa Hinton.

Michael B. Dougan
The J. V. Bell House
Jonesboro, Arkansas

Introduction to Bibliographic Essays

The bibliographic essays that follow each chapter are designed primarily to guide the reader to readily available published sources. Thus they often do not necessarily reflect the research that went into preparing the chapters. That research directly and indirectly has occupied the last twenty years and has included examination of Arkansas materials at the National Archives, the Library of Congress, Duke University, Emory University, the University of Texas, the University of North Carolina, Louisiana State University, the Chicago Historical Society, The Newberry Library, Columbia University, the Arkansas History Commission, the University of Arkansas, the University of Arkansas at Little Rock and the cooperation of friends interested in the history of this state. A second source has been newspapers.

Extensive use has been made of the *Arkansas Gazette*, the Arkadelphia *Southern Standard* and the Washington *Telegraph*. Dozens of other papers have been examined as well. I have used numerous locally published pamphlets as well as documents and articles found in local historical society quarterlies. Finally, oral history has been of great use for the twentieth century.

List of Abbreviations Used for Journals:

AA: *Arkansas Archeologist*
AAdv: *Arkansas Advocate*
AB: *Arkansas Business*
AHQ: *Arkansas Historical Quarterly*
AL: *Arkansas Libraries*
ALR: *Arkansas Law Review*
AN: *Arkansas Naturalist*
APSR: *American Political Science Review*
AT: *Arkansas Times*
BCP: *Benton County Pioneer*
BPM: *Black Perspective in Music*
CCHQ: *Carroll County Historical Quarterly*
CrCHQ: *Craighead County Historical Quarterly*
FLASH: *Flashback*
FN: *Field Notes*
GrPHB: *Grand Prairie Historical Bulletin*
HERHS: *Heritage* (Hot Spring County)
ICC: *Independence County Chronicle*
JNH: *Journal of Negro History*

JSH: *Journal of Southern History*
LH: *Labor History*
LHQ: *Louisiana Historical Quarterly*
MSF: *Mid-South Folklore*
MVHR: *Mississippi Valley Historical Review* (now *Journal of American History*)
O: *Outlook*
OHR: *Ozark Historical Review*
OSJ: *Ozark Society Journal*
PAHA: *Publications of the Arkansas Historical Association*
PAPA: *Publications of the Arkansas Philological Association*
PCHR: *Pulaski County Historical Review*
PSQ: *Political Science Quarterly*
SEP: *Saturday Evening Post*
REC: *The Record* (Garland County)
UMS: *University of Missouri Studies*
WCH: *White County Heritage*

About the Author

Michael Bruce Dougan, Professor of History at Arkansas State University, in Jonesboro, Arkansas, grew up in Neosho, Missouri, just north of the Arkansas state line. He earned a bachelor of arts degree cum laude from Southwest Missouri State College (now University) in Springfield, Missouri. His graduate work was done at Emory University in Atlanta, Georgia, where he studied under the noted Civil War historian Bell I. Wiley. His master's thesis was a history of the Little Rock press during the Civil War, and his dissertation, "Confederate Arkansas: The People and Policies of a Frontier State in Wartime," winner of the Mrs. Simon Baruch University Award of the United Daughters of the Confederacy, was published by the University of Alabama Press in 1976.

A member of the faculty of the Arkansas State University since 1970, Dougan is the author of numerous articles and books. He and his wife, Carol, edited *By the Cypress Swamp: The Arkansas Stories of Octave Thanet* (1980). With Tom W. Dillard, he prepared *Arkansas History: A Selected Research Bibliography* (1984). He wrote an introduction and located new material for the re-publication of *Confederate Women of Arkansas, 1861-1865* (1993).

His honors include fellowships from the National Defense Education Act, the National Endowment for the Humanities and The Newberry Library. A past president of the Arkansas Historical Association, he was the 1980 winner of that group's Violet B. Gingles Award for his article on bridge and ferry law in Arkansas. In 1987 the Arkansas Women's History Institute presented him with the Susie Pryor Award for his article on the Arkansas Married Woman's Property Law.

He, his wife Carol and two cats have restored the J. V. Bell House, which is listed on the National Register of Historic Places. The home was featured in the 1992 publication *America's Painted Ladies*. Carol plays the cello with the Northeast Arkansas Symphony and is a noted pie maker. The Dougans enjoy in equal measure camping, gardening, antiques and opera.

About the Endpapers and the Artist, Carroll Cloar

In many striking ways, artist Carroll Cloar (1913-1993) stands as a metaphor for the Arkansas experience. Cloar's grandfather, Thomas Jefferson Cloar, got into a difficulty with a girl in Union City, Tennessee, and promptly decamped to Arkansas, where he bought land near Earle. On a neighbor's back porch he met his future wife, who was busy skinning a rabbit. Of their thirteen children, the last of whom was Carroll's father, only three survived infancy.

Carroll's father married the daughter of a one-eighth Quapaw who played the fiddle at parties and lived off trapping and hunting. After progress hit the Delta with the arrival of drainage, the family adapted. Brother Thomas Jefferson Cloar served on the St. Francis Levee Board, the most politically important institution in eastern Arkansas.

Young Carroll graduated from Southwestern College in Memphis in 1934, studied at the Memphis Academy of Arts in 1935 and at the Art Students League in New York from 1936 to 1938, where his goal was to be a cartoonist. His first lithographs appeared in 1939. He served in the Army Air Corps in World War II. By 1948, *Life* magazine featured his work, and in 1953 he returned to Memphis, where he lived for the remainder of his life. The 1977 collection of his work published by Memphis State University as *Hostile Butterflies and Other Paintings by Carroll Cloar* remains the best overview.

Once he found his style, Cloar destroyed his early works and focused on the material he knew best: the land and people of the Delta. A storyteller both visually and orally, he painted the past and present in an instantly recognizable style, superficially simple but full of nuances. People, white and black, were integrated into a distinctively Delta landscape. Although Cloar avoided the overt political and social messages common in the paintings of Thomas Hart Benton, at times he made strong social statements. In a 1970 painting entitled simply *Federal Compress*, a compress and its water tower loom large in the background while in the foreground a group of hunched-over cotton pickers seem to have bowed to a deity.

In the enigmatic title painting of his book, three people are chased by "hostile" butterflies. Although the uninitiated might dismiss the scene as improbable, a reliable witness, Emma Jean Stewart, who was once in the White River bottoms during a migration of Monarch butterflies, reports that a massive presence of butterflies is beautiful and threatening. Some of the artist's acquaintances find a personal meaning in the painting, for Cloar's artistic sensibilities set him apart from others in his family and in the community, Cloar created his own psychic butterflies. The painting can also stand as a metaphor for the way too many people shy away from Arkansas history, pursued by old ghosts and nascent fears that to others are no more threatening than butterflies.

The two endpaper drawings present important parts of the Arkansas heritage. The front papers, *Sunday Afternoon at Sweet Home, Arkansas,* show Cloar's extended family. The clothes — overalls, ties, hats and a college jacket — differentiate the lives of the disparate kin brought together for a ritual occasion. *The Candidate* shows the essential localism of politics, where a handshake is considered a vote.

The author thanks the artist's widow, Patricia S. Cloar, for permission to reproduce the drawings here.

Table of Contents

INTRODUCTION
The Geographical Imperative and Modernization as Themes in Arkansas History

CHAPTER I
Indians of Arkansas

CHAPTER II
Arkansas Under the French and Spanish

CHAPTER III
Creating an Arkansas: 1803-1835

CHAPTER IV
Flush Times and Hard Days

CHAPTER V
Settlements and Society

CHAPTER VI
Religion, Education and Reform

CHAPTER VII
Slavery: The Manners and Mores of a Southern Institution in a Frontier Community

CHAPTER VIII
The Making of a Southern State: 1850-1861

CHAPTER IX
A Divided State in Wartime

CHAPTER X
Reconstruction and Modernization

CHAPTER XI
Arkansas as a New South State

CHAPTER XII
The Populist Era

CHAPTER XIII
The Progressive Era

CHAPTER XIV
Confronting the Twentieth Century: Arkansas in the 1920s

CHAPTER XV
The Great Depression

CHAPTER XVI
World War II and Post-War Dilemmas

CHAPTER XVII
The Conflict of Integration and Modernization

CHAPTER XVIII
Developing an Arkansas Culture

CHAPTER XIX
The Promise and Problems of Modernization

Table of Illustrations

This book would not have been possible without the generous assistance of the following individuals and institutions. Credits have been shortened under each illustration to save space. The full credit requested by each institution is given below. Special thanks is given to the *Arkansas Democrat-Gazette* for use of *Arkansas Gazette* images.

Table of Vignettes

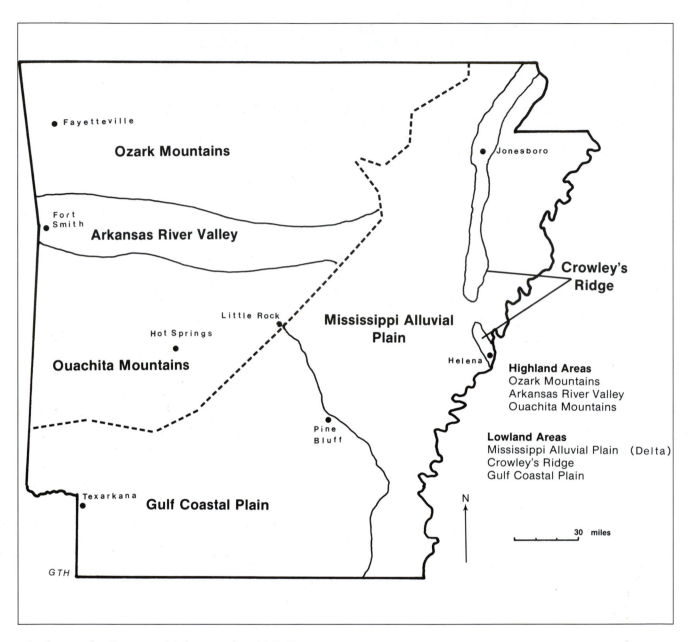

The Geographic Regions of Arkansas, Gerald T. Hanson

The Geographical Imperative and Modernization as Themes in Arkansas History

INTRODUCTION

History is the acts of people on a geographical stage set by nature. In the case of Arkansas no understanding of the political, economic or social aspects of the state's history can be reached without a clear reference to the physical environment and the ways in which it has shaped history. Man, not nature, shaped a state with boundaries that encompass parts of at least six natural divisions. Some of these divisions are readily apparent to the casual viewer; others are not. Indeed, geographers have failed to reach a consensus on just what the divisions are. For history the most immediate effect has been a cultural diversity paralleling the geographic variety.

THE EVOLUTION OF ARKANSAS

The land we call Arkansas evolved over a long period of time. The entire state was covered by water during the Paleozoic Period (600 million years ago). The Ouachitas were the first to rise, followed by the Ozarks. Not until the end of the Mesozoic (230 million years ago) did the Coastal Plain of the southwest and the Delta and the Mississippi stay permanently above sea level. Nature's forces continued working less spectacularly in leveling and rising, cutting and filling. Glaciers never reached Arkansas, but during cold periods, the drop in the ocean level expanded lowland areas. The essential features of the modern state were intact by one million years ago, although variations between wet and dry and hot and cold continued to alter flora and fauna. In more recent times man has been the agent for alteration, although not always successfully.

Superficially, Arkansas can be divided into two sharply contrasting sections: the uplands, consisting of the Ouachitas and Ozarks, both comprising 25,155 square miles covering 48 percent of the state, and the lowlands, where the Gulf Coastal Plain and the Mississippi Alluvial Delta contain 27,376 square miles or 52 percent of the land surface. This common oversimplification led to the belief that hillbillies and sharecroppers typified Arkansas.

This stereotype failed to explain cultural settlement patterns, and it did not account for the great local variations within the sections that often produced stark contrasts. By the twentieth century, Arkansas had elements of the American South, the Southwest and the Midwest. Finding an answer to why this confusion exists begins with looking at Arkansas's six natural divisions.

THE OZARK MOUNTAINS

No part of Arkansas has done more to define the Arkansas image than the eroded plateau called the Ozarks. Arkansas contains only the southern-most part of this variegated region that extends westward into Oklahoma, encompasses a third of Missouri and touches Illinois. Unfortunately, the Arkansas part of the Ozarks is the poorest.

Most early white settlers filtered south from Missouri, and only one railroad running through Fayetteville on its way to Fort Smith ever crossed the Mountains. The roads through the Mountains, notably U. S. Highway 71, have been a lasting source of complaints. The Mountains are beautiful, but as a

source of income to the state, this subsection has supported only hunters, lumbermen, tourists, moonshiners and marijuana growers, and more recently, Wal-Mart, chicken farms and trucking.

In the northern section of the Ozark Mountains in the northwestern part of the state is the Springfield Plateau. Its namesake and modern cultural center are across the state line in Missouri, although a series of cities along U.S. Highway 71 — Fayetteville, Springdale and Rogers — in Washington and Benton Counties in Arkansas are surging both economically and culturally. The Arkansas part of the Springfield Plateau encompasses about 12,000 square miles of limestone soils, rolling hills and numerous springs. It was prized highly as farmland by early white settlers. More recently, cattle, poultry and industry have flourished.

The White River generally separates the Springfield Plateau from its poorer cousin to the east, the Salem Plateau. With 31,000 square miles, this subsection lies almost entirely in Arkansas. One reason for the steepness of the terrain at Eureka Springs is that the city lies on the escarpment between the Springfield and Salem Plateaus. To the east are found such cities as Harrison, Mountain Home and the Plateau's namesake, Salem, the Fulton County seat. In contrast to the rich limestone soils in the Springfield Plateau, much of the Salem Plateau is rough, rocky and poor.

The Ozarks have been transformed greatly over time. Historic Indians used the area primarily for hunting, but white settlers in the nineteenth century cleared and farmed everything but the cedar glades, using methods that soon exhausted the soil. Massive emigration and land abandonment followed in the twentieth century. Just as the land was beginning to recover, cattlemen discovered the value of permanent pasture and Northerners discovered the lure of retirement homes. The threat of environmental destruction has appeared again, leaving the Ozarks with an uncertain future.

THE ARKANSAS RIVER VALLEY

Carved by the Arkansas River as it cut through the hills long ago, this Valley of varying width averaging about forty miles is an entire synclinorium or trough lying between the two well-defined groups of mountains — the Ozarks and the Ouachitas. Some physiographers and geographers decline to consider the Valley as a separate division and usually include it with the Ouachitas because its flora and soils are more closely related to that division than to the Ozarks. The Valley contains fertile soil, scenic beauty and good transportation with the result that it is home to some of the larger cities in Arkansas — Little Rock, Fort Smith, North Little Rock, Russellville and Conway.

The River itself rises in Colorado where the name is pronounced with the emphasis on the second syllable, AR-KAN-sas. All of the Arkansas part and most of the Oklahoma portion of the River was made permanently navigable in the 1960s at a cost of $1.2 billion. Water quality has improved since and the River is now suitable for municipal, agricultural and commercial uses.

THE OUACHITA MOUNTAINS

Another elevated portion of Arkansas is the Ouachita Mountains. Lying south of the Arkansas River Valley, these Mountains display extensive folding and faulting in a pattern of ridges invariably running east and west. The tree cover is far more likely to be pine than in the Ozarks, thus indicating a poorer soil. Numerous exotic minerals and rocks are found in the Ouachitas, including novaculite, used for making whetstones. One grade of novaculite actually is called "Arkansas." The Central Ouachitas are rich in quartz, which has been cherished by mystics throughout history as peace-giving. Unlike the Ozarks, most of the Ouachitas are within Arkansas, although the western terminus is in Oklahoma, where the Mountains are called the Kiamichis.

The Ouachita Mountains begin abruptly just south of the Arkansas River Valley. Mount Magazine in Logan County at 2,823 feet is the highest point in Arkansas. Ironically, until its ownership was transferred to the state for a park, the Mountain was located in a section of the Ozark National Forest. The Fourche Mountains come next, and are followed by the Central Ouachita Mountains that comprise the heart of the area. Though not the highest point in Arkansas, Rich Mountain near Mena generally is regarded as the most dangerous point in the state because of the number of small planes it has claimed. The Athens Piedmont of rolling hills suitable for farming lies on the southern edge of the division. Diamonds are found at the site of a defunct volcano at Murfreesboro in the Athens Piedmont.

These varied features make the Ouachitas an area of contrasts, for besides the highest points, it also has the Saline River swamps that measure only 300 feet above sea level and the hot springs in Hot Springs National Park. Culturally and economically much of the area's modern history parallels the Ozarks.

THE GULF COASTAL PLAIN

Most of the southern part of Arkansas is a section of the Gulf Coastal Plain, a land long covered by the waters of the Gulf of Mexico. The Gulf Coastal Plain stretches from Texarkana, which is divided by the Arkansas-Texas state line, to Ashley County and the pine forests that support Crossett and the

Georgia-Pacific Corporation.

Part of the Plain dates from the Cretaceous Period (135 million years ago), but the eastern section was formed much later during the Eocene Epoch (58 million years ago). The different dates of creation produced different soils. The rich river bottoms along the Red River and patches of Blacklands Prairie Soils (that show up in place names like Terre Noir Creek or Blacklands Township) were created first; the poor sandy soils growing only pine trees came later. In the nineteenth century, the prime lands were home to small farmers. Soil exhaustion overtook the small farmers in the twentieth century as the land reverted to forests cultivated by large-scale, out-of-state corporations. The discovery of oil near El Dorado created a special way of life not found elsewhere in Arkansas.

THE MISSISSIPPI ALLUVIAL PLAIN

The Mississippi Alluvial Plain, commonly called the Delta, takes its name from the River that forms Arkansas's eastern boundary and that over time deposited a variety of soils over the area. Until the introduction of modern flood control measures in the 1930s, the River changed its course with every flood. This is why Arkansas has been in court with Tennessee and Mississippi on numerous occasions trying to determine state boundaries that are supposed to be in accord with where the River ran in 1783. The uncertain course of the River was also responsible for the relocation of Arkansas Post and delay in settlement. As an example of both the power of the River and the confusion it could cause, an 1876 flood created Centennial Island when it detached 4,000 acres from the Tennessee mainland.

Besides the Mississippi, other rivers such as the Black, St. Francis, Cache, L'Anguille, White and Arkansas contribute to the Delta.

All left soil deposits along their watercourses and created sloughs, bayous and oxbow lakes. Because the depth of the soil deposits varied, the commonly held opinion that eastern Arkansas is flat is only relatively true. The lands adjacent to the River are higher than land a few miles inland. The soil patterns also vary. Prairies running north and south and made up of sand lay back from the rivers on the highest elevations. In addition, other prairie areas such as the Grand Prairie (Arkansas, Prairie and part of Lonoke Counties) contained a heavy clay subsoil that effectively resisted tree roots. The clay subsoil proved to be excellent for growing rice. Stuttgart is the economic and cultural center of the Grand Prairie, though rice has become a commodity that is grown throughout the Delta.

Beginning with the prehistoric Indians, people learned to adapt to the Mississippi River floods. Farmers cultivated the highest lands and in the nineteenth century ran cattle on the prairies. The land did not come into full use until the introduction of drainage in the twentieth century. The transformation of the Delta from swamp and prairie to the leveled, featureless farmland of today has been the most profound economic, social and ecological change in Arkansas history.

CROWLEY'S RIDGE

Eastern Arkansas also contains Crowley's Ridge, perhaps the most misunderstood section of Arkansas. Named for pioneer white settler Benjamin Crowley, this Ridge runs for 150 miles north from Helena. It varies in height from 250 to 500 feet above sea level and disappears briefly near Marianna. The existence of this Ridge in the middle of the Delta has led to much speculation. Some writers have claimed that it was created by the great New Madrid Earthquake of 1811-1812, while others have asserted that it blew in from China.

Alice French Describes the Delta, ca. 1887

The natural beauty of the Ozark Mountains and the Ouachita Mountains is recognized nationally. What has been lost to modernization is the beauty of the eastern Arkansas lowlands. Just before the coming of widespread lumbering and drainage, writer Alice French, who was known by her pen name of Octave Thanet, described the Delta in "The Mortgage on Jeffy" published in Scribner's *magazine, October 1887:*

They went by the Black River Road (*Alice French, ca. 1887*)
Author's Collection

There are few more beautiful sights than an Arkansas forest in late February; I mean a forest in the river-bottom, where every hollow is a cypress brake. Prickly joints of bamboo-brier make a kind of green hatching, like shadows in an etching, for a little space above the wet ground between the great trees. Utterly bare are the tree-branches, save for a few rusty shreds clinging to the cypress-tops, a few bunches of mistletoe on the sycamores, or a gleam of holly-leaves in the thicket; but scarlet berries flicker on purple limbs, the cane grows a fresher green, and in February, red shoots will be decking the maple-twigs, there will be ribbons of weeds which glitter like jewels, floating under the pools of water and ferns waving above, while the moss paints the silvery bark of the sycamores, white-oaks, and gum-trees on the north side as high as the branches, and higher, with an incomparable soft and vivid green. The white trunks show the brighter for their gray tops and for that background everywhere of innumerable shades of gray and purple and shell-red which the blurred lines of twigs and branches make against the horizon. . . . Yet beautiful as it is, there is something weird and dreary in its beauty — in those shadowy pools of water, masked by the tangle of brier and cane; in those tall trees that grow so thickly, and grow, I know, just as thickly for uncounted miles; in the shadows and mists which are instead of foliage; in the red streaks on the blunt edges of the cypress-roots and the stains on the girdled gum-trees, as if every blow of the axe had drawn blood — there is a touch of the sinister, even, and it would not be hard to conjure up a medieval devil or two behind such monstrous growth as those cypress knees.

Source: "The Mortgage of Jeffy," Scribner's *Magazine, II, (October 1887), 48-54*

Crowley's Ridge actually began as part of western Tennessee. The Mississippi River once turned westward near Cape Girardeau, Missouri and flowed in what is now the valley of the Black River before joining with the White and Arkansas Rivers and meeting the Ohio River below what is now Helena. New patterns were created when the Mississippi altered its course. Crowley's Ridge remained as an island, with the windblown soil (loess, pronounced 'les) and plant life of western Tennessee. In addition, altered drainage patterns east of the Ridge caused the St. Francis River waters to back up, thereby creating the alleged "Sunken Lands" that also have been credited to the earthquake in popular accounts.

Since lands lying next to Crowley's Ridge typically are lower than those near the rivers, early settlers often found the Ridge flanked by swamps. This explains why such cities as Paragould, Jonesboro, Wynne and Forrest City were established on the Ridge itself. The loess soils, deposited mostly on the western slope, are highly erodible: the first reported case of erosion was noted in 1859 near Helena. Despite the presence of loess, many gravel pits and some stone outcroppings can be found. Culturally, the Ridge resembled the Ozark-Ouachita pattern of small farms in the nineteenth century, but land clearing and drainage in the surrounding Delta altered the way of life after 1900.

THE CULTURAL MEANING OF ARKANSAS GEOGRAPHY

The creation of artificial boundaries by Washington politicians left Arkansas as a state with three orphaned sections. The Ozarks, with its northward orientation, has its natural capital at Springfield, Missouri. In addition, the richer Ozark lands in Missouri developed far more rapidly than those in Arkansas and received better state services, especially roads, from the wealthier state.

A second orphan is the Gulf Coastal Plain section that has its closest ties to Shreveport, Louisiana, in one direction, and Dallas, Texas, in another. The history of Texarkana, which straddles the Texas-Arkansas boundary line demonstrates the liabilities of being in an orphaned section in a poor state. The Texas side surged economically after World War II while the Arkansas side stagnated. Meanwhile, Dallas grew to such importance that it displaced St. Louis as Arkansas's financial and cultural center.

A somewhat different condition of orphanage prevailed in the Delta. Although much of the farmland lay within Arkansas, the economic capital came to reside safely above the high water mark on the east side of the Mississippi on the Chickasaw Bluffs at Memphis. The wealth of the Delta flowed to this site, leaving behind in Arkansas worn-out agricultural workers and some of the most extreme examples of poverty in America.

Yet another gravitational pull on Arkansas could be felt on the western border from Oklahoma. The prosperity associated with oil and natural gas in those areas created a magnet that many found hard to resist. Fort Smith, with its historic ties to the Indian Territory, physically and culturally resembles a Western rather than a Southern city.

With the outlying areas detached to other polarities, the "real Arkansas" consists only of a central region within a 100-mile radius of Little Rock. The influence exerted in modern times by newspapers and television is a triumph of politics over geography, for within that radius can be found fragments of all the geographic sections. The gravitational pull has never been strong, for Little Rock has failed to develop an identifiable industrial or financial base commensurate with its political status. Because the outlying areas are tied economically to outside polarities, the legislature has granted vast discretion to the counties.

Culturally, people both inside and outside the state remain confused about the nature and character of Arkansas. Many geographers and historians, faced with a state that consistently resisted categorization, simply left it out of their studies. People within the state have not been better placed to correct the misunderstandings. Although the state lacks political, economic or cultural unity, the nation at large found an Arkansas image compounded of the "Arkansas Traveler" of song and story, jokes about moonshiners and the absence of shoes, Delta sharecropping, Cummins Prison, the Ozark hill country and the Little Rock integration crisis of 1957.

Although diverse, all these factors unite in projecting the notion that Arkansas, which statistically ranks at or near the bottom in most surveys measuring state economic and educational status, stands for the failure of modernization.

INTERPRETING ARKANSAS THROUGH MODERNIZATION THEORY

In the past, historians have sought in vain for clues to define Arkansas's peculiar development. One much-emphasized feature has been the endurance of the frontier, for a combination of geographic and political reasons led the frontier to survive as a way of life in Arkansas far longer than in comparable states.

Another influence has been the strong gravitational pull of Southern sectionalism, present economically first in slavery and then in sharecropping, and which in the Civil War and the Little Rock integration crisis demonstrated a pervasive power in convincing fashion. Still others have seen Arkansas in the light of a colony, lacking assurance or self-sufficiency. Yet all of these factors, however true in part, are inadequate interpretive tools for viewing the whole of Arkansas history, not in the least because they represent often contradictory trends. Instead, Arkansas history in all its frontier, Southern and colonial features unites as part of the larger theme of modernization.

Arkansas history can best be viewed as a tug of war between two polar opposites, modernizers on one side and traditionalists on the other. Although the social, economic and political contexts vary, and many compromises and gradations mark the course of the struggle, the parameters of the conflict may be summarized briefly:

Modernizers

1. The primacy of science as a source of knowledge.
2. A strong commitment to education.
3. Economic fulfillment through rationalized agriculture and industrial development.
4. Work habits determined by the needs of the marketplace.
5. A democratic vision of society.
6. A belief in the equality of all persons before the law.
7. A belief in women's rights.
8. A belief in the need for people to grow and explore.
9. An active role for state government in bringing about change; taxing as necessary.

Traditionalists

1. The Bible as the source of all knowledge.
2. A weak commitment to education.
3. Economic fulfillment a lesser concern than self-sufficiency in agriculture; little interest in industry.
4. Personal pleasure more important

than efficiency.

5. A patriarchal and deferential vision of society.
6. A belief in white supremacy.
7. A belief in male superiority
8. Opposition to change and an emphasis on submission to the authority of the family.
9. A passive role for the state marked by a strong commitment to local self-government and a persistent opposition to taxes.

Modernization theory was developed by economists, sociologists and historians to explain the problems that Third World countries faced in industrializing.

Because Arkansas shares many of those conditions, as did all America in the nineteenth century, modernization theory best accounts for the diverse elements. At the same time, it avoids the rigidity inherent in Marxism and other ideologies, for modernization should be seen as a process continuing over time and subject to debate and reinterpretation both by supporters and opponents. The usefulness of the model is that, with these qualifications, it can be applied with equal success to the debate about banks in 1836, the struggle to establish a highway department in 1920 or the need to improve the educational system in 1991.

CONCLUSION

In contrast to the glib generalizations found in most American history textbooks, significant local and regional variations have produced ways of living more or less outside the ordinary American experience. The purpose of this book is to set forth those features and give meaning to one state's experience in both regional and national settings.

BIBLIOGRAPHIC ESSAY

A good introduction to the problems inherent in the physical aspects of the state is Gerald T. Hanson and Hubert B. Stroud, *Arkansas Geography: The Physical Landscape in the Historical and Cultural Setting* (Little Rock, 1981). A cogent argument for the significance of geography can be found in George H. Thompson, *Arkansas and the Reconstruction: The Influence of Geography, Economics and Personality*, (Port Washington, 1976). The first state-commissioned report was David Dale Owen, *First Report of a Geological Reconnaissance of the Northern Counties of Arkansas, Made During the Years 1857- 1858*, (Little Rock, 1858). Left incomplete at Owen's death was *Second Report of a Geological Reconnaissance of the Middle and Southern Counties of Arkansas, Made During the Years 1859 and 1860*, (Philadelphia, 1860). Work was resumed in the late 1880s under John C. Branner, and numerous published annual reports and surveys resulted. A recent addition, simply written and beautifully illustrated, is the Arkansas Department of Planning's *Arkansas Natural Area Plan*, (Little Rock, 1974; reprinted, 1977).

The New Madrid Earthquake has been the subject of myth and legend as well as scientific investigation. Little fault can be found with James Penick, Jr., *The New Madrid Earthquake of 1811-1812*, (Columbia, Mo., 1976), which supersedes Myron L. Fuller, *The New Madrid Earthquake*, (Washington, 1912). The most recent significant Supreme Court case, unusual in that the published legal record includes two foldout maps, is *Mississippi* v. *Arkansas*, 415 U. S. 289 (1973), fought about Luna Bar located opposite Chicot County.

The *History of the Organization and Operations of the Board of Directors, St. Francis Levee District of Arkansas, 1893-1945*, (West Memphis, n.d.) is almost the only published

work relating to one of the greatest transfor-
mations in Arkansas life.

Modernization theory was developed largely
as a means of analyzing emerging third world
nations. American historians have found it
increasingly useful. Richard D. Brown, *Mod-*
ernization: The Transformation of American
Life, 1600-1865, (New York, 1976) presents an
overall view. Richard Jensen, "Modernization
and Community History," *The Newberry*
Papers in Family and Community History, 78-
6 (January 1978) provided many leads.

Drawings of Arkansas Indians, ca. 1747. French explorer Dumont dit Montigny illustrated the text of his memoir with these drawings. **Top:** *The first, of three warriors, shows one on the left displaying the traditional weapons, the one on the right has a musket, and the one in the middle holds a peace pipe in one hand and a rattle in the other.* **Bottom:** *The second, of the women, shows a chief's wife on the left with her ornaments and a turkey feather fan, the girl on the right grinds corn, and the middle woman is dressed in turkey feathers.* **The Newberry Library.**

CHAPTER I

Indians of Arkansas

INTRODUCTION

Few American states are richer in pre-Columbian aboriginal archeological remains than Arkansas, but Indians played only a minor role in historic Arkansas and were displaced westward early in the nineteenth century. The existence of a huge gap between the riches revealed by archeology and the meager record found in history has led to a lack of understanding. Early white settlers were aware of the archeological heritage but lacked formal processes to evaluate it. Fanciful theories tying mound-building Indians to the Aztecs, Toltecs, or even the lost tribes of Israel captured the popular imagination.

American archeology has emerged within the last fifty years as a specialized discipline characterized by increasingly effective use of scientific methodology. This, combined since 1969 with federally mandated research required before site destruction, has created a body of knowledge that has not found its way to the public. It also has resulted in such a volume of data that interpretations become increasingly complex, making textbook generalizations risky.

Underlying these problems is the fact that Arkansas geography played a dominant role in defining many cultural possibilities. The different sections of Arkansas produced varied cultures that were no respecters of state boundaries created artificially in the nineteenth century. This has led to scholarly fragmentation, as in the case of the Caddo, a group centered on the Great Bend region of the Red River now contained within four states and studied by four different sets of state archeologists. The most essential overall feature about the Indian cultures of Arkansas was their isolation, for it was not until the arrival of De Soto that one force touched all of the different segments. The pre-history of Arkansas, therefore, was a piecemeal affair.

PALEO INDIANS

Sometime during the late Pleistocene geological period, Asiatic hunters, taking advantage of low water levels caused by glacier build-up, wandered into North America, possibly following moose and bears. These people were present in such numbers 11,500 years ago that modern researchers have been able to uncover enough skeletal remains to prove that they were the ancestors of the present day Indians and that they had reached Arkansas.

Early mankind found a region much different from that of today. The land was much cooler because glaciers were still as close as what is now the Great Lakes area. As the glaciers retreated, the northern pine and spruce followed, and oak and other hardwoods took their place. A number of large animals, now extinct, roamed the land. The mastodon browsed in the forest, the mammoth fed primarily on grass, and a giant catfish, a giant beaver, the ground sloth, the musk ox, the tapir and the horse lived here.

As the climate grew warmer, all these animals had problems adjusting. Dramatic artists often have implied that early man hunted these animals to extinction, and it is believed that these men hunted the mastodon and mammoth. In Arkansas, no connection has been proved between Paleo Indian artifacts and mastodon bones. Cautious modern scholars are far more willing to believe that climate changes—not hunters—led to the demise of these megafauna.

On arriving in Arkansas, Paleo Indian bands spread all over the land. They probably operated within a given territory in search of food. The earliest artifacts so far identified are stone spear points with fluted bases. Commonly misnamed arrowheads, these fluted points fall into two broad categories in America: Clovis and Folsom, both named for the locations at which they were first identified. Clovis points appear in Arkansas in a regional variation called Crowley's Ridge, and Folsom points bear the label Sedgwick.

Because almost all of the archeology finds associated with the Paleo Indians consist of randomly discovered points, little actually is known about their diet, clothing, housing or society. Analogy to other hunting bands known to anthropologists suggests they probably lived in groups of about twenty persons, hunted nomadically over a circular area, and used the spear as their primary tool.

Because of their limited technology, their numbers could not have been large. One band appears to have operated east of Crowley's Ridge, another to the west, and others in the Ouachitas, Ozarks and other sections.

DALTON INDIANS

A new style of tool-making appeared around 8,500 B. C. Known as Dalton, it included an improved spear point and also a variety of tools for woodworking and butchering. Fluting disappeared, and the new tools could be resharpened and recycled into other uses as they wore down. Some seem to have been only ceremonial. The invention of a wood-working tool, the stone adze, was perhaps the most significant advance, because it opened opportunities for making dugout canoes, building better housing, clearing land and carving wood. Dalton culture lasted for some thousand years in Arkansas, overlapping the end of the Paleo Indian period and the beginning of the Archaic years.

Technological improvements led to population increase. Almost a thousand Dalton sites have been recorded in northeastern Arkansas alone. Trade became important because Dalton groups in the lowlands depended on the Ozarks and Ouachitas for supplies of quality stones. Dalton Indians used cliff overhangs and caves for hunting camps and storage in the uplands. These sites appear to have been at least semi-permanent, focusing on a base camp from which small groups went forth continually to hunt, fish, gather and trade. What appears to be the first recorded cemetery in the New World, the Sloan site in northeastern Arkansas, contained some twelve to twenty-five graves and a wide variety of tools. Systematic burials, an indication of cultural advancement, usually presuppose the presence of religious ideas.

ARCHAIC PERIOD

Late Dalton culture overlapped with the beginnings of the Archaic period, which in Arkansas lasted for some 7,000 years. Archeologists divide Archaic into early, middle and late segments, based primarily on changes in stone patterns. Corner-notched and stemmed points were two Archaic hallmarks.

These improved tools became common in the early period, and the middle period coincided with a sharp weather change called the Hypsithermal from 7,000 to 3,000 B. C. During the recurring summer droughts the forest area shrank, grasslands spread and streams dried up or diminished. The Hypsithermal affected various parts of the state differently, apparently having the least impact on the southwest region.

Climatologists and archeologists do not agree about exactly what happened, but one theory holds that the prairie lands enlarged and that pine and juniper, both drought-resistant, dominated in the surviving forest. Animals dependent on acorns and other hardwood fruits greatly diminished in number, forcing the humans who relied on the supply of game to adopt new modes of living. Population relocated out of the lowlands, now often prairie, and settled along the streams, particularly along the edge of the Ozarks.

Different game, notably grassland animals such as the bison, could have become more important in the diet, and a wide variety of new tools, notably the side-notched grooved axe and the atlatl, a weighted throwing stick, marked the changes. The worst was over by around 4,000 B. C., and rainfall began to increase. The techniques that enabled man to survive in hard times now allowed for a greatly expanding population to reassert itself.

Late Archaic developments are demonstrated dramatically by finds at Poverty Point thirty miles south of the state line in Louisiana along Bayou Macon. The large number of artifacts recovered includes extensive bead work, vessels made of steatite (soapstone), marine shells, pieces of novaculite from the Hot Springs area, effigies of animals and clay cooking balls.

The high quality of the objects suggests that utilitarian needs were coupled with artistic considerations, which in turn required some leisure time. New stone tools included an improved atlatl; the plummet, a grooved stone entrapping weapon probably thrown at birds; improved axes and stone mortars for grinding vegetables. Indians at Poverty Point found the time and discipline to erect two major mounds and crescent-shaped earthworks set in parallel ridges. Poverty Point-type clay objects were used in Arkansas. Baskets, wooden objects and woven materials have been recovered from Ozark cliff shelters, but no Arkansas sites compare to Poverty Point in size or complexity.

Because novaculite, quartz crystals and other stones had become widely distributed by the late Archaic period, trade obviously had increased in importance. It also can be assumed that some specialization was taking place, although most objects were still made

King Crowley *(photographer unknown, ca. 1930) This fake with the furniture-caster eyes "unearthed" by Jonesboro jeweler and gunsmith Dentler Rowland was one of the major frauds in American Indian artifact history. A small collection of Rowland's work is located at the Arkansas State University Museum.* **Babcock Collection, University of Arkansas at Little Rock.**

King Crowley

A Jonesboro jeweler and gunsmith, Dentler Rowland, claimed in 1924 to have unearthed evidence of a lost Aztec civilization on Crowley's Ridge. Locally, Rowland's artifacts were accepted at face value. The largest, dubbed "King Crowley," a forty-pound stone statue with inset copper eyes and silver pupils, gold ear plugs and a copper "valentine" heart, was acquired by the Museum of Science and History at Little Rock; other museums bought smaller examples. Arkansas history books for fifty years invariably mentioned "King Crowley" as part of the Indian heritage of the state.

Despite favorable local testimony, experts were not impressed. Beginning in 1924, the Smithsonian Institution in Washington D.C. and various professional archeologists repeatedly denounced the objects as fakes, but public support for this Arkansas version of the Piltdown Man demonstrated that people tend to prefer the simple and dramatic to the complex and true.

Rowland did not limit his work to fake Indian relics. In addition to a petrified phallus, he claimed to have unearthed a creature that was half man and half monkey, presumably a stage in Darwin's evolutionary process. As for "King Crowley," once the pride of the state, it mysteriously disappeared in the late 1940s or 1950s and has not been seen since.

within the structure of a household economy. Food supplies exceeded population needs, for the luck of the hunt was being balanced by the first domestication of plants. Acorns were eaten, after being debittered by soaking, and gourds and squash arrived from Mexico. Only the seeds provided much food, but dried shells had practical and ceremonial uses.

The simple undifferentiated bands gave way to a clan organization linking several different families. These in turn made up a larger unit: the tribe. Head men and women doubtlessly rose to power, although group leadership through a council of elders proba-

bly predominated. Priests and medicine men (shaman) unquestionably fulfilled their specialized functions.

WOODLAND PERIOD

The late Archaic period began blending into what archeologists call Woodland around 500 B. C. The three basic hallmarks of Woodland were the use of pottery, extensive horticulture and more mound building. All three seem to have arisen slowly and seemingly without an overt outside influence. Each represented a step away from the hunter-gatherer mode of living.

The first key element was pottery. Indians made baskets of rushes and other ephemeral materials in earlier periods. But earthen pottery was infinitely superior both for food preparation and for storage. The cultural origins of pottery are uncertain, but the essential clay was available extensively in Arkansas. The first pots were made of clay mixed with sand in a process that took a month of drying under carefully controlled conditions before the pot could be fired at a temperature of 1,112 degrees Fahrenheit (600 degrees Centigrade) for one hour. Pottery making, therefore, was inconsistent with migratory living.

A second feature was expanded horticulture. Indians long had been gatherers of fruits and seeds, but gathering was being supplanted by the growing of desired items by the Woodland period. Early crops included the marsh elder and sunflower. More squash varieties arrived, but corn and beans were still missing. Agriculture tended to reduce mobility because crops needed attention and protection.

The third feature, mounds, arose spectacularly at Hopewell complexes in Ohio and Illinois and appeared in Arkansas. One theory for the existence of mounds is that they began as houses for the dead. When the house was full of bodies, dirt was piled on it. In time, the size of the mound became a status or genealogical symbol for the elite. One now-demolished mound at Helena revealed elaborate burials, including a copper and silver-covered panpipe and a number of ornately wrought beads. The mound also contained the bodies of men, women and children, suggesting to some that only the family of one leader lay buried there, but others concluded that the entire community was included.

The new complexity produced a number of local variations that largely reflected geographic conditions. A culture known as Fourche Maline in southwestern Arkansas arose after 1000 B. C. and lasted until A. D.

900. A conservative culture given to making plain, flat-based vessels, its people were dispersed in small villages and honored their dead with cremation burials. Their domain occupied a region given to inconsistent rain patterns, which doubtless retarded a dependence on agriculture or the rise of large communities.

Larger concentrations of populations arose in the rich hunting and agricultural lands of eastern Arkansas. Mound building flourished under a Middle Woodland culture called Marksville-Hopewell (A. D. 1-400) before declining under its successor, Late Woodland Baytown (A. D. 400-700). The new complexity both in pottery and mounds greatly increased the range of artifacts that archeologists could examine, thereby enriching the depth of interpretation.

Toward the end of the Baytown period, Indians living along Plum Bayou near the Arkansas River began the construction of a vast complex of seventeen mounds, apparently erected entirely for ceremonial purposes. Anachronistically called Toltec because of a fancied resemblance to a Central American site, this cultural flowering owed little to outside models and today is preserved as a state park.

MISSISSIPPIAN PERIOD

The last phase of prehistoric Indian activity centered along the Mississippi River. Arkansas Indians were influenced early in the period by the Coles Creek culture emanating from Louisiana. These Indians built flat-topped mounds that probably were used for ceremonial purposes, and they introduced a small, notched projectile point mounted on a shaft and fired from a bow. The "arrowhead" had arrived at last, greatly enhancing the hunter's capabilities. One Arkansas wood, the bois d'arc (Osage orange), soon became the bowmaker's choice, thus stimulating trade.

Even as the bow and arrow expanded the

hunter's output, agriculture became the dominant source of food. Corn was the first new crop. An easy plant to harvest and store, corn exhausted the soil's fertility, promoted tooth decay and led to an unbalanced diet. Two of those problems, soil infertility and dietary imbalance, were partially corrected when beans became common. The location of good farming land determined town locations as farming became primary.

Another striking development came with the introduction of shell-tempered pottery. Lime could be made by burning mussel shells, easily found in local streams. When added to clay, lime gave new strength to pottery. When it leached into cooked corn, it helped to correct a dietary deficiency. Cooking and storage vessels of increasingly elaborate design and specialized use appeared during this period. South of the Arkansas River, Indians tempered clay with crushed bones rather than shells and incised their pots after, rather than before, firing.

The new prosperity led to a wave of mound building, notably at Cahokia near St. Louis. Most of the new mounds were ceremonial. The Mississippian culture extended into Arkansas, immediately displacing Baytown and reaching as far west as Spiro, Oklahoma. Southern Arkansas drew its cultural strength from the Plaquemine culture in Louisiana, and the Caddo emerged from the older Fourche Maline tradition in the southwest. Both the Plaquemine and Caddo erected mounds, but the former still used theirs for burial.

The Caddo made small notched and barbed arrowpoints, often from novaculite, and were famous as bowmakers. Their highly decorated ceramics were much prized. In addition, they continued to retain their older dispersed settlement pattern even as they pushed their domain into the Ozarks, building mounds at Elkins, Siloam Springs and War Eagle. Evidence at the Crenshaw site indicates that these ferocious warriors appear to have collected the skulls of their victims as trophies.

The wattle and daub (stick and mud) house was commonplace in Mississippian villages, but the Caddo still built a conical farmstead covered with grass. A microcosm of Mississippian culture was revealed in excavations at Zebree, a Mississippi County site that subsequently was destroyed by the building of a drainage ditch. Shell beads were manufactured in this small village using drills made from rocks taken from the Crescent quarries near St. Louis. Hoes were made from chert (flint) outcroppings located in Union County, Illinois, and the first reported harpoons were recovered, indicating that Indians were tapping the rich fishing resource. The houses were rectangular with walls of cane matting. Community food was stored in pits, the largest of which could hold 110 bushels. A wide range of pottery was unearthed at Zebree and at other sites. Exotic designs included beakers and jars with handles, bowls with effigies and lip decorations, and bottles with both short and long necks.

A new social order came with the new agricultural prosperity. The elite grew in power as a paramount chief displaced the older council system. Astronomy, always important to agricultural societies, gave new power to the state. One mound at Cahokia, used to bury two chiefs, included sheets of rolled copper, 800 arrowheads, two bushels of mica, 20,000 shelled beads, as well as four headless males, and some seventy servants, many of whom were young females. Even at the Zebree village, evidence indicated that the elite got the red meat. Thus while Europeans were carrying stones to build their huge cathedrals, Arkansas Indians were busy bringing in dirt for their mounds.

A major disruption hit the Mississippi Valley around A. D. 1400. Cultural aggrandizement became open warfare, marked in stone possibly by the introduction of a special man-killing arrowhead called the Nodena point. Warfare increased the powers of chiefs as the hierarchical system grew more rigid. The most significant demographic result was the abandonment of the dispersed villages typified by Zebree. Some apparently fell victim to raids, but most probably were consolidated as the population concentrated in central locations. Some historians think that environmental changes played a major role in shaping the relocations because the fifteenth century was a time of disorder in all other parts of the world, too.

One Arkansas site perfectly suited to the new conditions was at Parkin. Strategically located on the St. Francis River with both good farmland and fishing, this site reached a high level of late Mississippian development. The elaborate pottery interred with the dead suggested a highly developed religious system. Yet whatever the prospects might have been, few of those living in 1541 would be able to enjoy it. Hernando De Soto, the Spanish conquistador, entered the Mississippi River Valley in the spring of that year. The prehistoric age ended, and rapid and destructive changes were in store for Arkansas's Indian inhabitants.

DE SOTO AND THE SPANISH

Christopher Columbus sailed in 1492 to discover a new world for European civilization. The Spanish first established themselves on the Caribbean islands and then explored the mainland. The resulting conquests of Mexico and Peru altered the European balance of power and produced wealth that far exceeded anything in Europe's imagination for those hardy surviving conquistadors. One of the men who came over poor and rose to riches and fame was Hernando De Soto. Arriving in the New World in 1519, De Soto participated in expeditions to Nicaragua in 1527, Guatemala and Yucatan in 1528, and he served as second in command to Pizarro in the conquest of Peru in 1533.

De Soto was convinced that North America would prove as rich as Peru, and he gained permission from the crown to explore Florida after being named Governor of Cuba. De Soto brought to the task all the wealth of experience the Spanish had learned in thirty years. His force of 600 men, twenty-four priests and twenty officers drew on the cream of New Spain's manpower, and past campaigns had shown the value of horses, fighting dogs, a drove of pigs and plenty of nails.

De Soto's force landed at Tampa Bay and began its search for riches on May 31, 1539. The Spanish believed that mineral wealth could be found only in the uplands and that a large native population would be there exploiting it. Instead, De Soto found that Indians were located on the best agricultural lands in the lowlands, and the hill country was largely uninhabited. Thus the frustrated Spanish followed their quest from tribe to tribe throughout the Southeast, occasionally encountering pronounced hostility. The diminished but still resolved army arrived by May 1541 on the banks of the Mississippi River and prepared to cross. While carpenters constructed four large wooden boats, the local Indians arrived punctually each day at three o'clock in 200 canoes and showered the Spanish with arrows. The actual crossing on June 19 was undisputed by local Indians.

Modern historians do not agree on who these Indians were and where the crossing took place. These questions arise because four different accounts of the De Soto expedition have survived, three being roughly contemporaneous; the last did not appear until more than fifty years after De Soto's death. Scholars attempting to fit the published accounts with geography and archeology have failed to arrive at consensus. The De Soto Commission in the late 1930s and the current authority, University of Georgia Professor Charles H. Hudson, differ widely on the key question of where De Soto crossed the Mississippi River.

The river crossing site is the key to interpreting De Soto's activities. Because the Span-

De Soto at the Mississippi River *(Howard Simon,* Arkansas Gazette Centennial Edition, *1936) Artist Howard Simon worked extensively in woodcuts, illustrating many books for his wife, novelist, Charlie May Simon. This picture apparently was printed in reverse, and viewers will find the scene more convincing if they try holding it up to a mirror.* **Arkansas Gazette.**

ish kept mileage records, their activities for the next two years trace back to the point at which they crossed the River. The De Soto Commission believed that the site was near Helena; the Hudson school places it farther north near Memphis. The second problem concerns the Indians. By one account, those attacking the Spanish crossing were from Pacaha; another source indicated that the warriors came from a "great lord named Aquixo."

Confusion about names in the various accounts arose persistently because the Spanish had to rely on interpreters.

After crossing the River, the Spanish stopped to dismantle their boats in order to reclaim the precious nails. Then they marched westward to Aquixo. This "beautifully situated" town was abandoned, so De Soto headed north toward the Casqui. They crossed what one chronicler called the worst swamp they

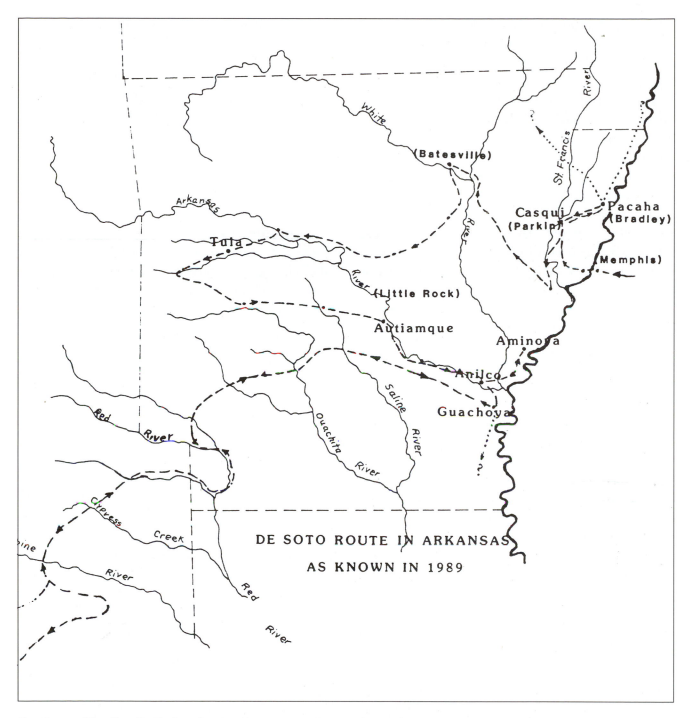

White

(Batesville)

St. Francis

Arkansas

Casqui
(Parkin)

Pacaha
(Bradley)

Tula

River

(Memphis)

(Little Rock)

Autiamque

Aminora

Anilco

Saline River

Guachoya

Ouachita River

Red River

?

Cypress

Creek

Red River

DE SOTO ROUTE IN ARKANSAS

AS KNOWN IN 1989

River

Professor Charles H. Hudson's 1989 Reconstruction of the DeSoto route.

had yet seen with water up to their knees and occasionally their waists. They arrived at the capital on June 30, after ascending the River of the Casqui. Hudson believes this site was present-day Parkin.

The Spanish were welcomed and asked by the chief if their god could make rain. De Soto answered affirmatively, and in two days, his men erected a giant cypress cross on top of a mound. Next the priests chanted the *Te Deum Laudamus* in a four-hour ceremony that attracted a crowd estimated at between

15,000 and 20,000 natives. The appearance of rain cemented the Spanish-Casqui alliance. Recent excavations at Parkin have revealed the base of a large charred post that could have been the cross as well as a sixteenth-century Spanish bell and glass bead.

De Soto had been given to understand that the Pacaha had gold, and because the Casqui were their bitter enemies, he evidently intended to use his new allies to his advantage. Thus a combined force left Casqui on June 26, moving east toward the Mississippi River. Although the Casqui chief had said it was a one-day trip, it took three days to make the journey.

Pacaha was a walled town with towers, surrounded by a ditch that connected to the "River Grande." Apparently much more powerful than Casqui, Pacaha controlled Quizquiz and Aquixo to the south. The Pacaha chose not to oppose the invaders but instead fled to an island sanctuary. De Soto prevented the Casqui from burning the town, but his allies did empty the wooden chests containing the Pacaha chief's ancestral ashes. They also liberated some of their own people who had been enslaved and lamed in order to prevent their flight.

Following the Pacaha to the island, De Soto pushed the Casqui into battle only to discover that they had feeble fighting qualities. Because the town was devoid of gold, De Soto would gain little by continuing the war, so he forced the two chiefs to negotiate a settlement in which the Casqui chief agreed to acknowledge the genealogical superiority of the Pacaha. As one Spanish account noted, "but neither the expression of their faces nor the look they bestowed upon each other were of true friendship."

Modern archeologists of the Hudson school believe that Pacaha was a Nodena phase site located in modern Crittenden County where Wapanocca Bayou joins the Mississippi River. De Soto stayed there a month to pursue his quest for precious minerals.

Apparently several expeditions went forth, two of which were described in some detail. One, to the northwest, was undertaken by a small Spanish party that traveled for eight days through a lightly inhabited area where the residents carried rush huts on their backs and lived off fish and game. Another expedition formed after eight "strangers and merchants" told De Soto that salt and precious metals were to be found some forty leagues (170 miles) northwest, presumably in the Ste. Francois Mountains.

De Soto dispatched two "diligent individuals," Hernado de Silvera and Pedro Moreno, to investigate these rumors and provided them with trade goods of pearls, chamois "and some vegetable things called frijoles." The men and their guides made an eleven-day journey through a "sterile and poorly populated" country before returning with some copper and salt. Interestingly, several Spanish artifacts have been recovered at a site north of Blytheville in Missouri.

The absence of a large population or evidence of riches convinced De Soto that these leads were not worth following, so he turned south, still convinced that people and riches went together. Leaving Pacaha on July 29, the expedition returned to Casqui and then moved south down the St. Francis River to what Hudson believes was the vicinity of present-day Madison, where the Indians ferried them across the River. Three days later, they arrived at Quiguate, reportedly the largest town visited on the entire trip. Here they were welcomed and occupied one third of the town. The Grant site in Lee County has been suggested as a possible location, and a hawk's bell and a matchlock gun support have been found at nearby Clay Hill.

Like Casqui and Pacaha, Quiguate was primarily an agricultural community devoid of mineral resources. After remaining a month and surveying the prospects, De Soto headed northwest for Coligua, a chiefdom he was told lay near the mountains. Instead of a road or trail, the party traversed four swamps in four days while moving through the lowlands separating the Cache and White Rivers. Coligua "was a pretty village," recalled one party member, and the Spanish took "much people and clothes, and a vast amount of provisions and much salt." Magness near Batesville is a possible location, and although the reports conflict, the Spanish may have encountered buffalo for the first time. Once again De Soto was frustrated; although mountains lay to the west, the natives reported that the Ozarks were inhabited only by primitive hunters.

De Soto headed south on September 6 and arrived at Calpista, "where there was an excellent salt spring which distilled very good salt in deposits." Liberty Valley near Bradford, twenty-nine miles south of Magness, could have been Calpista. On the 8th, the Spanish arrived at Palisema (Palisma) where, because the people lived in a dispersed settlement pattern, no great supplies of maize could be seized easily.

Nothing induced De Soto to move more than the necessity of provisioning his army, and after leaving Palisema (probably near Judsonia), the expedition continued on in a southwesterly direction, entering Quixila (Vilonia) on the 11th and Tutilcoya (Conway) on the 13th. Spurred by reports of a large chiefdom called Cayas, he proceeded up the River of the Cayas (Arkansas River), staying for almost three weeks at a Caya town called Tanico where he found nothing of value.

The Cayas reported the existence to the southwest of another large group known as the Tula but could not even offer an interpreter. This was a clear indication that De Soto was about to encounter a new cultural and linguistic group. In the march to Tula, De Soto encountered heavy opposition from this warlike people who flattened their heads and tattooed their bodies. Eventually, Tula (Blufton in Yell County) was taken, and with it came new stories of wealth to be found if the

Spanish would hurry on. Inasmuch as precious metals were believed to lie along the equator, De Soto decided to investigate further. His route took him west at first, probably to near Boles and Y City, but then he turned east and arrived at Quipana on October 22 and Quitamaya (Benton) on the 31st. On November 2, the Spanish reached Autiamque, a town located on the River of the Cayas, probably downstream from Little Rock. Here the party wintered, eating the Indians out of house and home.

Apparently De Soto had given up trying to find a large population in an upland setting, because he moved farther east to Anilco in the spring of 1542. A site perhaps located in Arkansas County, Anilco consisted of a large town dominated by a high mound housing the chief and containing 400 houses and rich corn resources. A second stop was at Guachoya, a strongly palisaded town to the south on the Mississippi River, whose inhabitants called the River by a different name from that used farther north. The nearby area proved to be swampy and uninhabited. De Soto, sickened by a fever, died and was buried secretly on May 21, 1542. Assuming Hudson's calculations to be correct, De Soto thus died within the boundaries of present-day Arkansas and not in Louisiana as the old accounts supposed.

Stranded in a hostile country and opposed by an Indian population that had been looted systematically, the Spanish under Luys de Moscoso de Alvarado decided to return to New Spain by heading overland in a southwesterly direction. Their route took them through the chiefdom of Chaguate on the Ouachita River somewhere between modern Arkadelphia and Malvern.

Contrary to popular opinion, the Spanish did not visit the Hot Springs area. Passing through the Caddoan chiefdom of Naguatex located in the Great Bend region of the Red River Valley, they probably reached the Trinity River in Texas, but the hostile climate and scarcity of Indians to rob left no choice but for the expedition to return to Arkansas.

They began backtracking in October and were in Anilco again by December. Those Indians were so demoralized by the first visit that they had failed to plant a corn crop and could not feed the Spanish. They did recommend generously that the Spanish visit Aminoya, a town probably near Old Town in Phillips County that consisted of two palisaded components. The Spanish, upon arriving at Aminoya, occupied one palisaded component and ransacked the other in order to build seven wooden boats. A late spring flood in June 1543 enabled them to make an easy departure, and they headed down the Mississippi on July 2. Each ship had a sail but the Spanish relied more on seven pairs of oars. Large fleets of Indian canoes persistently attacked the travelers, but this did not stop the Spanish from raiding an occasional river town.

AFTER THE DE SOTO VISIT

After De Soto's party left Arkansas, no written historical accounts described the area until the French arrived 130 years later. By then, all of the former centers of Mississippian occupation were uninhabited. What had happened to all those Indian towns and the miles of corn fields? The most probable answer is that De Soto's men planted the seeds of destruction largely from the diseases they left behind.

We do know that arrival of the Europeans led to massive outbreaks of decimating epidemics in other parts of the Americas. Smallpox was the worst killer; it allowed the Spanish to defeat the Aztecs. As an example of the disease's power, when it struck the Mandan Indian villages on the upper Missouri River in 1837, only 130 from a population of 2,000 survived. Measles, influenza, mumps, and every other disease new to America also struck the natives hard. In addition, it is possible that the Spanish brought malaria into the Mississippi River Valley. Carried by the ubiquitous mosquitoes, malaria was a slow killer, leaving its victims weak and subject to renewed attacks of chills and fevers and thus less able to defend themselves militarily.

The diseases apparently hit Arkansas Indians unequally. Communicable diseases made their greatest impact on a stationary, village-centered population such as the Mississippian culture in east Arkansas. The nomadic Indians on the fringes who ran away or the Caddo, who not only fiercely opposed the Spanish but also lived in a dispersed hamlet pattern, were spared. Cultural disintegration accompanied population loss. Those most likely to come in contact with the Spanish were the chiefs and priests. The decimation of the leadership played a key role in the overthrow of the Aztecs and was followed by cultural collapse as the people no longer believed in their religious or political systems.

Finally, the hard feelings already extant and exacerbated by De Soto's visit probably spurred new wars even as the warriors were dying. Had the Spanish established themselves, under their protection the population might have recovered in time. Instead, probably no single population in America suffered more than the Indians of Arkansas from their first contact with Europeans.

ARRIVAL OF THE FRENCH

Although the Spanish arrived first in the Mississippi Valley, nothing in the De Soto expedition accounts inspired a return visit. The Spanish kept up some trading contacts with the southeastern Indians because Spanish trade goods were reported common in the next century, and a seventeenth century Spanish bead was found in Little Rock, but Spain's dynamic impulse largely was expended. It was the French who entered the region next and first appreciated its possibilities.

In seeking a foothold in the New World, the

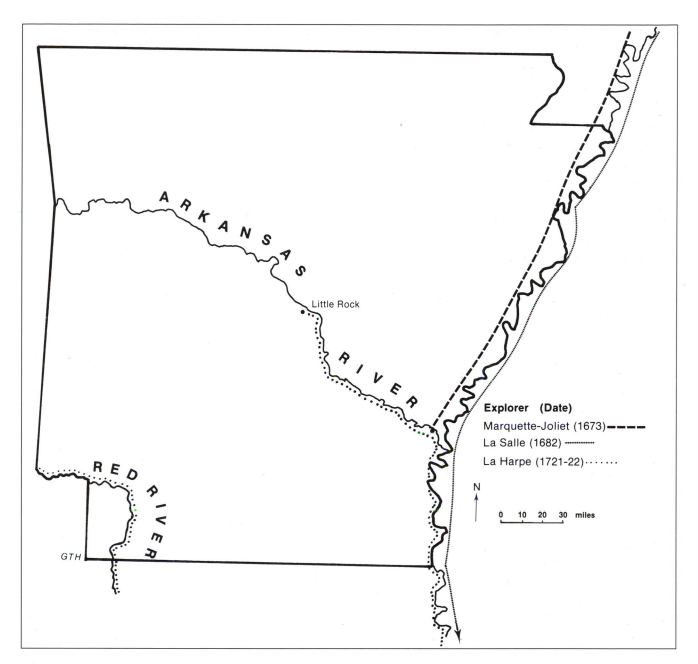

Early Explorers. **Gerald T. Hanson**

French had three objectives: the discovery of the long-sought Northwest Passage, the conversion of Indians to Catholicism and profits from trade, mostly in furs. These three elements often were at odds with one another, so that New France was riddled with cliques juggling to gain or keep royal approbation.

The French came upon the Great Lakes in the course of exploring the St. Lawrence. Indi-

ans there referred to a great river, and in hopes that it would lead westward to the Pacific, two explorers were sent to find it. Louis Joliet, a wagonmaker's son born in Quebec in 1645, had studied for the priesthood before dropping out to become a fur trader. He was still close to the dominant Jesuit order and thus found a fit companion in Father Jacques Marquette, who had been a missionary since the age of seventeen and could speak six Indian languages.

With two canoes, three *voyageurs* (boatmen) and a supply of smoked meat and corn, the party left on May 17, 1673, to find the Mississippi. Passing through the Straits of Michilimackinac and following Lake Michigan, they moved west to the Wisconsin River and into the Mississippi on June 17. For over a fortnight they encountered no signs of human life until they at last reached the summer villages of the Illinois Indians.

Near the site of modern Alton, Illinois, Marquette and Joliet passed the famous Piasa monster, a bluff painted red, black and green depicting a snake, a deer and a bird. While the Frenchmen were still recovering from the shock, the turbulent Missouri River entered, full of debris and muddy water. Continuing their journey, they noted the Ohio River and passed in silence all of the former centers of Mississippian culture before arriving near the mouth of the Arkansas River.

Here they encountered a group of Quapaw who made ready to attack until, at the last moment, a chief recognized the calumet (peace pipe) Marquette waved above his head. Then the hostile reception turned into a joyous greeting as the Indians escorted the party to what Joliet called the town of Akansea but which was better known as Kappa. The Quapaw spoke Siouan, which was not in Marquette's repertoire, but one Indian spoke a little of the Illinois tongue so that a limited conversation took place. The Frenchmen learned from the Quapaw that the River continued south and the Indians below had hatchets, knives and beads obtained in trade from the Spanish. Apparently they also learned that the Mitchigamea tribe of the Illinois Confederacy had a village somewhere on Black River in northeastern Arkansas. Having failed to achieve their objectives, the French returned to Canada. Joliet later explored the Hudson's Bay area, and Father Marquette died working with his missions.

As with the Spanish, problems of interpretation remained. Although both men kept records, only Joliet's map survived. Thus this account rests partly on obviously inaccurate later descriptions. It appears that Marquette and Joliet visited only the one village, but the map located several Indian towns. In addition, two conflicting accounts tell of their first arrival. However, it is certain that after 1673, the area known as Arkansas (after the Indian village name) began to influence French colonial policy.

The religious impulse that had burned so brightly in the beginning was waning by the late sixteenth century. Economic and imperialistic motives became increasingly dominant, and the man who foresaw those possibilities was Robert Cavalier, Sieur de la Salle. Coming to the New World as a fur trader, La Salle was in fact a visionary empire builder with a grand design for a New France stretching from Canada to the Gulf of Mexico.

His reach exceeded his grasp in two areas, however. First, the French government of Louis XIV was greatly over-extended in European wars and thus increasingly reluctant to support colonial adventures. Second, the Jesuit missionaries wanted to monopolize the fur trade for themselves and protect their Indian converts from the social degeneration associated with *coureurs de bois* (trappers and hunters) and the *voyageurs*. The royal governor, Count Frontenac, provided La Salle with initial support, but Frontenac's power was undermined and the greatest of New France's governors was recalled.

Even so, La Salle made a start, beginning with a royal grant to erect a fort on Lake Ontario and followed by permission to explore the west at his own expense in return for trading rights. In France, La Salle recruited a skilled lieutenant in Henri de Tonti. The son of an Italian refugee banker, de Tonti was reared in France and trained as a soldier. He lost his right hand in a grenade explosion and thereafter wore an iron or copper substitute

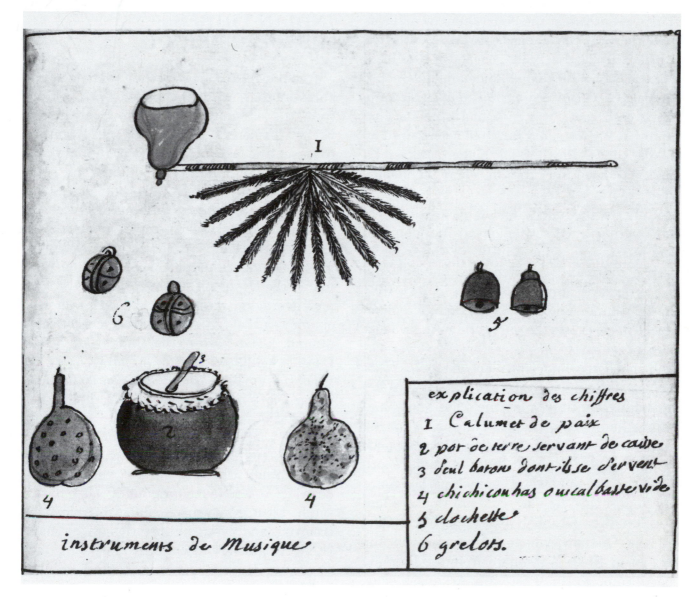

explication des chiffres
1 Calumet de paix
2 pot de terre servant de caise
3 deul baton dont ils se servent
4 chichicouhas ou calbasse vide
5 clochette
6 grelots.

instruments de Musique

Drawings of an Indian calumet (peace pipe), clay drum, drumstick, rattles made from dried gourds, hand bells and small bells, usually called Hawks Bells in trade. *Memoirs, Dumont dit Montigny, ca. 1747.* **The Newberry Library**

that gave him the nickname of "Iron Hand."

La Salle's first expedition started from Canada during the winter of 1679. Despite local opposition and disaffection within his party, La Salle reached into Illinois and erected the fort, christened Crevecoeur, near the future site of Peoria. Leaving de Tonti in charge, La Salle returned to France for more supplies. His financial affairs were in a tangle, however, and the men at the fort mutinied and deserted. Undeterred, La Salle equipped a new expedition and returned. Meanwhile, the friendly Illinois Indians had been ravaged by the Iroquois, who killed many, burned the villages and destroyed the crops.

It was not until 1682 that La Salle was able to get all of his forces together and proceed down the River. The trip was uneventful. At the Chickasaw Bluffs, the future site of Memphis, he erected a small fort named Prudhomme in honor of a company member who had gotten lost and delayed the departure.

They also visited the four Quapaw villages and those of the Taensas farther south. On April 9, 1682, La Salle reached the Gulf of Mexico, which he named Louisiana in honor of Louis XIV. On returning to Canada, La Salle discovered that Frontenac had been recalled and that his forts and furs had been seized by his enemies. Playing for bigger stakes, La Salle returned to France to report the significance of his new discoveries.

In Paris, La Salle unfolded his great plan of making a French settlement at the mouth of the Mississippi, thus controlling the trade of half a continent. Granted royal support, La Salle set forth from La Rochelle in July 1684 in four ships. A stop at Santo Domingo introduced disease into the party and in their quest for the mouth of the Mississippi, they overshot and ended up wandering along the Texas coast before landing at Matagorda Bay. After searching fruitlessly for the Mississippi and failing to find Spanish gold mines in Texas, La Salle was slain by a member of his own party.

Meanwhile, Henri de Tonti had come south from Canada in hopes of contacting the colony. Failing in this, he allowed Jean Couture and five others to establish a trading post in 1686 at the Quapaw village of Osotouy on the Arkansas River. A remnant from the La Salle party came to this Poste aux Arkansas bearing the news of the great explorer's death.

The Post became the first French settlement west of the Mississippi and for the next twenty years was their southernmost penetration. The Spanish from Mexico, alarmed by La Salle's plans, advanced on his Texas settlement only to find that smallpox and the Indians already had destroyed it. Yet the Spanish made no further effort to extend their physical control to the Mississippi. The Gulf continued to be up for grabs to whatever power chose to follow up on La Salle's pioneering effort. Meanwhile, Arkansas Post served to wed the Quapaw to the French alliance and extend the range of French interests.

INDIAN TRIBES: HISTORIC PERIOD

It is possible to identify the Indian relationships at the end of the seventeenth century from the accounts left by the Spanish and French explorers. During the next century, disease and warfare greatly reduced the already small number of Indians and some tribes lost their identities completely. The Quapaw lived at the beginning of the period on the Arkansas River near its juncture with the Mississippi. Southwestern Arkansas remained under the control of the Caddo. Both feared the Osage of Missouri, the "Little People" averaging more than six feet tall, who claimed all of Arkansas for their hunting ground. They drove the Caddo out of the Ozarks and harassed the Quapaw.

Of the smaller tribes, the Koras partially merged with the Choctaw; the Cahinnias, last recorded separately in 1771, moved to Louisiana as did the Ouachita, the "Cow River People," and both were absorbed into the Natchitoches tribe. The Tunica, who may have been from Arkansas originally, also moved south. Little is known about how these mergers occurred, and even the histories of the major tribes remain very incomplete.

The Quapaw

The historic Indians most associated with Arkansas were the Quapaw, but historians and archeologists disagree sharply about their origins. Many archeologists believe them to be the descendants of Mississippian residents present at the time of De Soto. This contention is supported by continuity between Mississippian and Quapaw pottery and other artifacts. On the other hand, Quapaw tradition and some historical data hold that the Quapaw were driven west by the Iroquois and arrived to find a loosely held or empty land.

As a northern tribe, they shared the Siouan language with other western tribes. By their

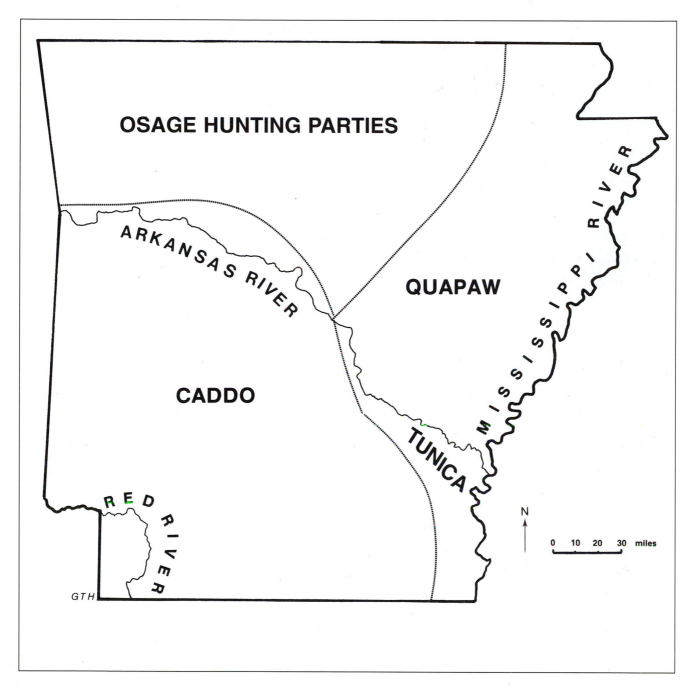

OSAGE HUNTING PARTIES

ARKANSAS RIVER

QUAPAW

CADDO

TUNICA

MISSISSIPPI RIVER

RED RIVER

GTH

N

0   10   20   30   miles

Indian Tribes of Arkansas, 1690. **Gerald T. Hanson**

tradition, when their fleeing remnants reached the Mississippi River, the Omahas went north, the Osage west and the Quapaw south, thereby becoming the "Downstream People." Chief Paheka in 1827 remembered a namesake as the leader in that move. When the French first arrived in 1673, one Quapaw village was still located on the east side of the Mississippi.

Because almost no archeology work has been done on the Quapaw, little is known about how they lived. Their four villages presumably were fortified and there are references to mounds, but not to the temple culture found farther south. Although the early French accounts mentioned extensive fields of corn, the Quapaw lived in a culture that

Charlie Quapaw. *This late nineteenth century photograph was taken after the Quapaw had resettled in northeastern Oklahoma.* **Kansas Collection, University of Kansas Libraries.**

emphasized hunting buffalo and deer. Their agriculture included watermelons, apples, peaches and tobacco, in addition to corn, squash and beans. The cultural relation between hunting and farming was demonstrated by Quapaw marriage rites: the man gave the woman an unclean leg of deer for her to prepare while she gave him a basket of corn symbolizing her agricultural duties.

At the time of the French arrival, the Quapaw probably numbered between 2,500 and 3,500 divided into four villages. Tourima and Osotouy were on the north bank of the Arkansas River, Tongigua was on the east side of the Mississippi, and Kappa was on the west bank some twenty miles up from the mouth of the Arkansas River. Each town was ruled politically by a hereditary chief. Tribal decisions were made collectively by the four chiefs. The villages contained rectangular houses consisting of a frame of poles arched at the top and covered with cypress bark and cane matting. Sleeping platforms were moved outside in the summer.

Impressed by their initial contact, the French called the Quapaw "the best formed Savages we have seen," or *les beau hommes*, the handsome men. Certainly the French had ample opportunity for observation because Quapaw men went naked or with only a breech cloth except in the winter, when they donned buffalo robes. The women wore only a deerskin skirt. As late as 1791, an American traveler noted that they "very innocently displayed their Navels, [although] the curious eye might have explored other parts which civilized Nations industriously conceal."

Little was recorded about Quapaw religion until late in the nineteenth century, long after the practices and beliefs had been abandoned. Apparently they worshiped a central life force and a wide variety of lesser spirits connected to the hunt and the crops, which in turn were tied into Quapaw clan names. Ritual and dance were important. One Frenchman considered lewd a dance in which men and women synchronized their poses and gestures with sexual desires. Magic and juggling were important: French traveler Jean Bernard Bossu told of a man whose trick consisted of swallowing a seventeen-inch stag's rib that he then pulled out of his stomach.

The Quapaw were often at war with their neighbors, primarily the Osage to the north and the Chickasaw to the east. Bossu told of a Quapaw raid to capture Caddo women and how he arranged a peace. In preparation for battle, the warriors consumed dog meat in the belief that it made the eaters strong and brave. Man's best friend also served the women who made a dog offering to the crops. The Quapaw used a manitou or good-luck charm. A dried dead crow or other useful animal generally was employed. The Quapaw painted themselves red and black and compensated for their inferior numbers by conducting surprise attacks. Prisoners were adopted into the tribe, enslaved, or killed. The Quapaw welcomed the French so that they could trade for superior weapons to off-set their small numbers. The price they paid for the French presence was smallpox, which reduced the number of warriors to fewer than 300 by 1699. In the process one village was abandoned, and Father St. Cosme wrote that at Kappa, "There was nothing to be seen but graves. All the children and a great number of the women were dead." The Quapaw never suffered so severe a loss again, but through diseases, warfare and alcohol addiction, their numbers continued to decline until only 215 individuals were considered Quapaw by the federal government at the end of the nineteenth century.

The Caddo

The Caddo, properly called the Cadhadacho Confederacy, consisted of three or more confederations containing some twenty-five tribes. Their nickname for allies, "Tejas," became the word Texas, and their people lived from Louisiana to west Texas. Much internal fighting took place because the Confederacy lacked strong central government.

Perhaps because the fierce opposition of the Caddo to De Soto limited their contact with whites or because of their diffuse settlement pattern, the Caddo passed through the 130-year period between the Spanish and the French largely intact. The western-most Caddo, the comparatively primitive Hasinai, may have made contact with the Spanish explorer Francisco Vasquez de Coronado in 1540-1542, and by the time of La Salle, the Caddo were in fairly constant contact with the Spanish in Mexico. They benefited by occupying a strategic middle ground between the French and Spanish for more than 100 years. Tribal members easily could be found by the eighteenth century who spoke one language or the other.

The Arkansas Caddo, living on the rich lands of the Red River Valley, were among the most advanced of the Confederacy's tribes. They continued to live in a dispersed settlement pattern and built rather curious houses: large bee-hive shaped cabins that stood some fifty feet high and held eight to twelve families. Fortunately, one French artist in 1691 sketched a Caddo settlement, and a post Civil War photograph also captured a late look at this house form. Before the general use of guns in the late eighteenth century, the Caddo were famous for high quality bows made of bois d'arc, their pottery was highly regarded and they were active salt merchants. Hunting was important, especially for the western tribes that followed the buffalo. There are conflicting reports about their trading skills, but Leclerc Milford, who visited Caddo country in the late eighteenth century, observed that, "It is dangerous to trade on account of their bad faith." Even so, he added, merchants persisted because the Caddo "are the best tanners of buffalo and beaver skins, of which they trap a quantity."

Warfare played an important role in Caddo life. The Tula encountered by De Soto were armed with lances and appeared especially warlike with their flattened heads, red body paint and elaborate tattooing. The Tula's opposition to De Soto may have influenced his decision to turn east. The term "red men" certainly described the Caddo, who were much given to red paint and named the Red River. During the late sixteenth century, the Caddo were losing wars to the more western tribes that had preceded them in acquiring and mastering the horse. Horses were reported to be common among them by the eighteenth century.

The Caddo appear to have been more developed religiously than the Quapaw. Theirs was a temple culture presided over by the priest who administered an eternal flame. The French explorer Jean Baptiste Lemoine de Bienville, the founder of New Orleans, reported a temple filled with idols. The Caddo built both temple and grave mounds. On occasion, perhaps during prolonged dry spells, a temple

A Caddo Camp. *(William S. Soule, ca. 1867-74) Although refugees in Indian Territory at the time, these Caddo perpetuated traditional building forms. The shed on the left with a bark roof was used as a cook house.* **Smithsonian Institution National Anthropological Archives.**

would be set afire and then buried. The resulting underground fire produced large volumes of smoke—and perhaps rain. Anticipating the 1980s "New Age" popularity of quartz, the Caddo deployed crystals to influence the weather. Flood stories were prominent in their cosmology, but in 1855, Indian scholar Henry Schoolcraft was told that the tribe issued out of the hot springs. The western Caddo used peyote in their religious rites, and probably all

Caddo medicine men used the drug in the eighteenth century.

As with the Quapaw, the decline of the Caddo came about from the introduction of European diseases. An epidemic of smallpox hit the nearby Natchitoches in 1718, reducing the number of warriors from 400 to eighty. Then it spread to the Caddo. Another outbreak in 1777 cut Caddo numbers in half, and only about 600 Caddo remained by 1820.

Artifacts from Arkansas Mounds. *(H. J. Lewis, ca. 1880) Archeologist Edward Palmer explored Toltec and other Indian sites accompanied by black artist H. J. Lewis. The collected artifacts ended up in the Smithsonian Institution in Washington, D. C. Earlier a number of fine objects had been displayed at the state capitol, but this collection was lost or stolen by 1869.* **University of Arkansas at Little Rock.**

Physical weakness invited attack. The Osage from Missouri raided and burned the central Caddo temple village on the Red River. A few years later when the Freeman-Curtis expedition visited the Caddo in 1806, their Caddo guides "proposed to visit it with a bottle of liquor, that they might take a drink and talk to the Great Spirit." Consolidation took place after the epidemics, ending in the creation of the modern Caddo tribe, which is made up of the original tribes of the Confederacy and probably some of their eastern neighbors.

The Taensas

To the east of the Caddo in Arkansas and Louisiana were the Taensas, a tribe with a brief history. Henri de Tonti contacted them in 1682, noting that the principal chief's cabin was located near a lake some leagues south of the Quapaw. The edifice was forty feet square with a domed roof about fifteen feet high. The chief was accorded great respect and was followed around by three wives who agreed with everything he said.

The Taensas suffered greatly from smallpox, which diminished their numbers from 700 warriors to forty. The cultural collapse that accompanied such losses for all tribes fortuitously was recorded by a European writer. First, the Taensas had to abandon the practice of strangling a number of tribal members at the chief's funeral, leaving that deceased dignitary unaccompanied on his trip to the next world. Second, the principal temple was struck by lighting and burned to the ground in March 1700. The enraged priest blamed the people and tried to get the women to throw their children into the fire to appease the god.

When the power of the Taensas waned, their bitter enemies to the east, the Chickasaw, began to make war on them for the purpose of selling the captives to the English as slaves. Forced to leave their traditional home, the Taensas relocated several times until they returned in the nineteenth century to northern Louisiana. The Tensas River, which takes its name from the tribe, became their final location, and it is likely that a number of obscure Arkansas tribes merged with them during the years of decline.

CONCLUSION

The Indian cultures that flourished in the prehistoric period left a network of trails, thousands of acres of cleared land and hundreds of sites ready for resettlement. This physical legacy, however, was not matched by a cultural influence. Arkansas did not have an Indian "problem" by the time of statehood in 1836. This ethnic discontinuity has isolated Arkansans from the Indian experience in America, and it has made people unreceptive to the preservation of the prehistoric legacy. From the late nineteenth century to the present, Arkansas's prehistoric remains have been scavenged by "pot hunters" and collectors. Often interested only in whole artifacts—which command high prices—they have discarded as irrelevant what would have been vital cultural information to the archaeologist. Thus many sites have been looted and destroyed, their stories lost, and the trophies sold out of state. Many Arkansas farmers acquired land-leveling equipment after World War II. Protruding spots that were sometimes Indian mounds have been sacrificed for bushels of soybeans. Few farmers have known enough to avoid disturbing such sites or to call in archeologists before proceeding.

It is doubtful that these destructive measures would have become so widespread if Arkansas had still possessed an Indian political constituency. Site loss reduces the possibility of understanding fully the story of the people who lived, hunted, fished and farmed for 97 percent of the time that human beings have known of Arkansas.

BIBLIOGRAPHIC ESSAY

One of the biggest gaps in Arkansas historiography is the failure to translate the fine technical work done by the Arkansas Archeological Survey into publicly accessible literature. The Arkansas Archeological Society publishes *The Arkansas Archeologist* and *Field Notes*, which are often too technical for the general reader, as are occasional research reports. An annotated list of articles and reports can be found in Tom W. Dillard and Michael B. Dougan, comps., *Arkansas History: A Selected Research Bibliography*, (Little Rock, 1984)

Archeological interpretations have changed considerably since Charles R. McGimsey, *Indians of Arkansas,* (Fayetteville, 1969). A simplistic account is M. P. Hoffman, *The First Arkansans*, *AN*, II (April, 1984), 1-27. The status of current research is found in Neal L. Trubowitz and Marvin D. Jeter, eds., *Arkansas Archeology in Review*, (Fayetteville, 1985). The most complete survey of any section is Dan F. and Phyllis A. Morse, *Archeology of the Central Mississippi Valley*, (New York, 1983). For the Toltec site, see Martha A. Rolingson, *Emerging Patterns of Plum Bayou Culture,* (Fayetteville, 1982).

The original sources for the De Soto expedition are in Edward G. Bourne, *Narratives of the Career of Hernando De Soto*, (New York, 1904), and John and Jeannette Varner, *The Florida of the Inca*, (Austin, 1951). The old interpretation of De Soto's route is presented in John Swanton, *Final Report of the United States De Soto Expedition Commis-*

sion, U. S. Congress, 76th Cong., 1st Session, House Document 71 (Washington, 1939). The revisionary view is sketched in Charles H. Hudson, "De Soto in Arkansas: A Brief synopsis," *FN*, No. 205, July/Aug. 1985, 3-12. The point of crossing and the northeastern Arkansas activities also are discussed in Morse and Morse, *Archeology of the Central Mississippi Valley.*

The French penetration was treated first by the legendary Francis Parkman, *La Salle and the Discovery of the Great West,* (Boston, 1869, and many subsequent editions). A more recent treatment, narrower in focus, is John A. Caruso, *The Mississippi Valley Frontier in the Age of French Exploration and Settlement,* (Indianapolis, 1966), which also includes chapters on the Caddo and Quapaw. S. D. Dickinson, trans., *New Travels in North America* by Jean Bernard Bossu, (Natchitoches, 1982) offers a translation with useful notes.

The Quapaw have been accorded a new history in W. David Baird, *The Quapaw Indians: A History of the Downstream People,* (Norman, Okla., 1980). The record of the historic Caddo can be found in John R. Swanton, *Source Material on the History and Ethnology of the Caddo Indiana,* Bureau of American Ethnology Bulletin 132 (Washington, 1942). Interesting material on the more obscure Arkansas tribes can be found in S. D. Dickinson, "Historic Tribes of the Ouachita Drainage System in Arkansas," *AA* XXI (1980), 1-11. The early history of Arkansas archeology and much more are in Marvin D. Jeter, ed., *Edward Palmer's Arkansaw Mounds* (Fayetteville, 1990).

Delta Swamp (*photographer and date unknown*) *The rivers and swamps of eastern Arkansas hampered overland travel. Indians and later settlers made pirogues out of local trees. It was possible to travel over most of Arkansas's flatlands in the Delta without touching land.* **University of Arkansas at Little Rock**

CHAPTER II

Arkansas under the French and Spanish

INTRODUCTION

On March 13, 1682, Robert Cavalier, Sieur de La Salle erected a wooden column containing a Christian cross and the arms of France at the Quapaw village of Kappa, thereby claiming possession of Arkansas for France. More or less permanent French possession really began four years later when Henri de Tonti, who had been granted land in Arkansas by La Salle, in turn made a grant to six *coureurs de bois*. That control lasted until the Spanish took over in 1764.

Between 1686 and 1803, Arkansas Post moved several times, withstood attacks by Indians and by the British, became the focus of a visionary plan of settlement and performed an unheralded but necessary function in French imperialist ambitions. The Post's lack of success in becoming a great trading center, a rich agricultural heartland or a famous fort was attributable primarily to Delta terrain. The military and the traders needed a site on or close to the Mississippi, and farmers needed to be safe from flooding. Arkansas Post, despite being placed in three different locations, remained caught on the horns of a geographic dilemma because any site close to the Mississippi posed too much of a flood hazard for farmers. Thus the Post left behind few enduring traces once French and Spanish control ended in 1803. Even so, this first European settlement in the Trans-Mississippi became a microcosm for parts of the Arkansas experience.

John Law, Duc d' Arkansas *(painter and date unknown) Considered a swindler, Law fled France with only a single diamond ring in his possession and died poor.* **Arkansas History Commission.**

THE DE TONTI PERIOD: 1686-1704

Henri de Tonti's grant to Jean Couture, Jacques Cardinal and four others rested on La Salle's grant to De Tonti. De Tonti bid for Jesuit support by designating 130 yards of frontage for a mission, but ambitions exceeded reality. When remnants of the La Salle party arrived at "Ville de Tonti," they found only a single log storehouse. One survivor reported that the traders had used up their supply of goods and "had almost as much need of our help as we had of theirs." Before proceeding on to Canada, the La Salle men left some powder and shot and took with them the few furs the traders had collected.

Arkansas Post failed to develop into a major station in the fur trade. The Quapaw had little experience trapping beaver and even less curing pelts for the market. In addition, southern beaver possessed inferior coats, and the extra cost of transportation to Montreal put Post traders at a serious competitive disadvantage. Then, late in the seventeenth century, New France became embroiled in major wars with the Iroquois, who promptly cut the trade routes. The Post's furs got to market only three times in six years.

One alternative trade route was due east via the Chickasaw to the new port of Charles Town, South Carolina, recently settled by the British. English and Scottish merchants and hunters pushed the British connection west late in the century. The English could offer better quality goods and higher prices, and the first English merchant was reported at Kappa by 1699. An opportunity for a life that was more free from restrictive monopolies and governmental and church interference was too much temptation for Jean Couture, and he deserted to the English. However, the others held on and the Quapaw, perhaps because they were such bitter rivals of the Chickasaw, remained loyal to their French connection.

Unable to compete with the English, the French government tightened its trade restrictions, largely at the expense of de Tonti. The veteran explorer visited the Quapaw in 1698, but only an illicit trade produced any profit. Jesuit missionaries to the Quapaw reported no French traders present in 1699. Meanwhile, the French, finally recovering their energies after La Salle's death, reentered the lower Valley. Le Moyne d'Iberville established Biloxi in 1699 and New Orleans in 1718.

This revival of La Salle's grand scheme did de Tonti little good, for now his commercial interests were squeezed at both ends. He applied to the crown for a monopoly on buffalo skins, an item too cheap to warrant shipping by canoe to Canada, but profitable enough if marketed by flatboat down the

Mississippi to New Orleans. However, d'Iberville saw to it that de Tonti's request was rejected while his own position was strengthened. The royal decision to support d'Iberville left de Tonti bankrupt, and when the veteran explorer died from yellow fever at Mobile in 1704, his claim to Arkansas had lapsed.

THE JOHN LAW COLONY

The abandonment proved to be short-lived, largely because the French mind had become inflamed with dreams of riches to be had from a French Peru located somewhere on the Arkansas River. Such riches were needed, for the government was bankrupt when Louis XIV died in 1715. Rather than retrench, the Regency, which ruled for the child Louis XV, endorsed the monetary theories of John Law, a Scottish financier.

In 1716, Law was given a charter for the Banque Royale under which the national debt was assigned to the bank in return for extraordinary privileges. The key to the Banque Royale agreement was that the national debts would be paid from revenues derived from opening the Mississippi River Valley. Thus the bank was tied directly to a number of Law's other enterprises: the Company of the West and the Companies of the Indies. All three in time became known collectively as the Mississippi Company. Given a twenty-five year monopoly on trade and all the supposed mineral wealth, the company prospered—on paper. A boom in company stocks led to riots in Paris and the coining of a new word, "millionaire," to reflect paper profits. Law, a national hero, was ennobled with the title of Duc d'Arkansas.

Law's ultimate success depended on the immediate discovery of great wealth in the Mississippi River Valley. Stories of precious metals were given credence in France, and when former Louisiana governor Antoine de

la Mothe Cadillac said such hopes were "a dream," he was hustled off to prison in the Bastille. Jean-Baptiste Bénard de la Harpe was the explorer chosen to find the wealth, and his party of seventeen men left New Orleans in three pirogues in 1719 to explore the Red River. He left in December 1721 on his second trip to explore the Arkansas River. His private instructions included orders to bring back a sample from the large jewel rock the company claimed existed up the Arkansas River.

At the Yazoo settlements in Mississippi, La Harpe was joined by Jean Benjamin dit (nicknamed) Montigny François Dumont, who became the official, albeit untrained, scientist of the expedition. In reporting on their reconnaissance of the Arkansas River, the two confessed that the "river on which we voyaged was nothing like that" described in the company's treasure map. They did describe a wide, clear stream entering the Arkansas River from the north, perhaps Cadron Creek, where one could weigh down a cloth one day, dry it, and shake out the gold on the next. French expectations were so high that even a golden stream was not enough. Some French publications remained convinced of the jewel rock, now described as a crystal column, but many stockholders gradually began to have misgivings.

Once questions arose about the profitability of Law's ventures, worried holders of bank notes began to cash them in. Because Law's bank operated without adequate reserves, his notes could not sustain a run. A series of decrees failed to stem the tide, and Law, besieged by a mob that now wanted to lynch him, fled France. His empire was in ruins, but like so many ventures, part of it had taken on a life of its own. Arkansas Post was reborn in the time between the downfall of Law and the collapse of his American ventures.

In addition to mineral wealth, Law had sought to develop the agricultural resources of the Valley. About 1,600 European settlers were sent over before the collapse. Some 100 of them arrived in Arkansas. Lieutenant Dumont dit Montigny laid out a formal town plan, and a garrison of seventeen soldiers under Lieutenant La Boulaye established a fort during the summer of 1721. The farmers, placed on Law's grant on the Grand Prairie, tried in vain to break the sod with their simple wooden tools. Despite sickness and acclimatization problems, about eighty people remained by November 1721. When news of Law's collapse reached America in March 1722, the population was down to forty-two, and they were saved from starvation only by a timely shipment of flour from the north.

By the following year, the colonists were living in two groups: fourteen men and a woman remained at the original site; the rest had moved five to nine miles up the River where the garrison was located. Included among them were six black slaves imported by another of Law's companies. The new location offered old Indian fields to farm that promised a productive harvest.

However, the whole system of development stopped once the effects of the Law bankruptcy became fully apparent. The French government cut the army in half and withdrew its Post garrison. Commerce on the River ground to a halt, and with it went the reason for having farmers at the Post. "Government economy," one historian has written, "destroyed John Law's colony at the moment when it had attained to success." Only three huts were located at the Post by 1723, and the colonists drifted south.

FRENCH CONTROL: 1722-1764

The French government resumed control of the Mississippi River Valley, but having no money to spend, proposed using missionaries in place of soldiers. In 1727, Father Paul du Poisson arrived to succor the Quapaw and the European inhabitants, whom he estimated to

number thirty. At first he was assisted by a lay brother, but this man died of heatstroke in 1729. While on his way to New Orleans, Father du Poisson had the misfortune to be at Fort Rosalie when the Natchez Indians massacred the population of 250 in a surprise attack. Arkansas's first resident priest died of decapitation.

The uprising convinced the French that missionaries were not enough. They also believed the English had encouraged the plot. The Quapaw, lamenting the slain priest, began open hostilities against the Natchez and their allies, bringing in four scalps taken from the Koras and the Yazoos. Eventually the French defeated the Natchez, whose last formal resistance occurred at a fort erected on the upper Saline River in Arkansas.

The French hardly could expect the Quapaw to defend the area without assistance, and in 1731, twelve men commanded by First Ensign de Coulange arrived to garrison the station, a move that prompted the Quapaw to wage war against the far more dangerous Chickasaw. Their forays led the Chickasaw to begin attacking Mississippi River traffic, which in turn caused the new royal governor, Jean Baptiste Le Moyne de Bienville, to plan a two-pronged offensive designed to inflict a major defeat on the recalcitrant Chickasaw. Major Pierre D'Artaquette moved down the River from Illinois with 140 regular soldiers supported by militia and Indians, picking up additional support from the Quapaw. He was supposed to wait for de Bienville coming upstream from New Orleans, but when his Indians grew restive, D'Artaquette decided to face the Chickasaw alone.

This decision proved fatal. His army was annihilated while more than 100 French were killed, and the commander and thirteen captives were roasted alive. When de Bienville finally arrived in Chickasaw country, his force was inadequate to meet the enemy and only a

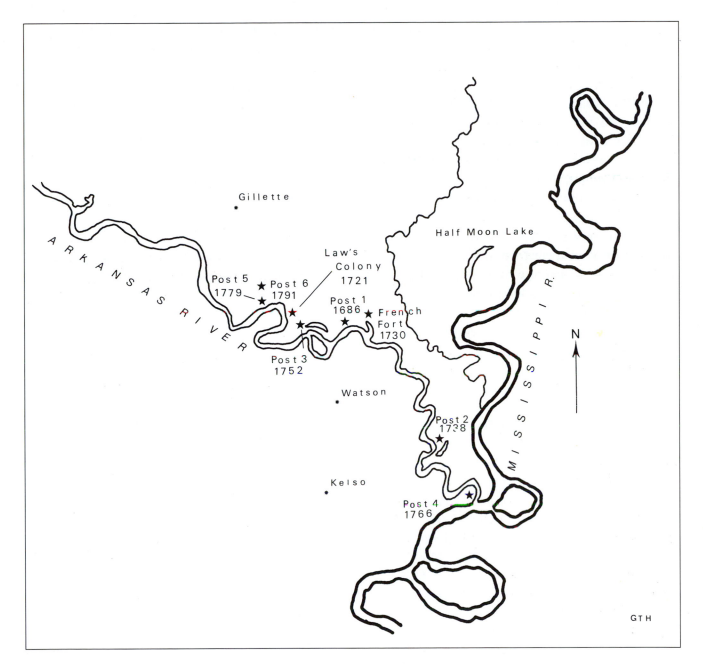

Map of the Sites of Arkansas Post. *The inability to find a suitable site that did not flood was the ultimate cause of the failure of the Post to thrive.* **Gerald T. Hanson**.

timely retreat to the shelter of the Choctaw saved him from a similar fate.

De Bienville reorganized his forces and renewed the offensive in 1737. Preliminary plans called for the attack to be made from a base camp at the point in Arkansas where the St. Francis River joined the Mississippi, near what is now Helena. The Quapaw were involved actively in the preparations and the feeding of the force de Bienville assembled in the fall of 1738. However, early rains made it difficult for the army to move, and the Indian allies grew restive and deserted. Eventually, all that the frustrated Frenchman could do was use his force to negotiate a settlement. The French then abandoned their St. Francis post and another across the River on the Chickasaw Bluffs (Memphis).

Meanwhile, Arkansas Post struggled on. First, Ensign de Coulange's blatant use of a government convoy for his private speculations led to his replacement in 1734 with a De Bienville relative, First Ensign Jean Ste. Thérèse de Langloiserie. He in turn was followed in 1739 by Lieutenant Jean François Tisserant de Montcharvaux, who reportedly drank too much.

The fort consisted during these years of four buildings: a log house, measuring eighteen by thirty-two feet, which housed the commandant and contained a kitchen with a mud fireplace; a magazine measuring eight by ten feet; a barracks at sixteen by forty feet, and a jail. Although the garrison served to protect the Quapaw who brought in scalps for payment, the force was too small to mount attacks, and the fort itself was reported to be perpetually in a ruinous condition. Even so, its very existence deterred the English and gave the French a presence on the Mississippi River that for the most part protected the western trade.

The intermittent aggression between the Quapaw and the Chickasaw often spilled over into the settlement. Cattle were killed and shipping raided. The only direct attack came on May 10, 1749, when Chickasaw chief Payah Matahah led a party of 150 warriors across the River. The Quapaw villages were unoccupied, so the Indians attacked the fort, killing six men and taking eight women and children prisoners. The fort itself, although partially burned, withstood the attack, and Payah Matahah was wounded severely in the assault. The next census indicated that the population had declined to only thirty-one settlers.

The threat of Chickasaw raids prompted the Quapaw to relocate up the Arkansas River and away from the Mississippi. Naturally, they hoped the fort would follow to give them protection. On the other hand, a fort too far up the River weakened the French presence on the Mississippi. The inability to find an

acceptable site led to a series of relocations. The first site chosen by de Tonti was near the Quapaw village of Osotouy at the foot of Little Prairie. The Law colony followed at this location, and it was there that the fort stood during the 1749 attack.

In order to accommodate the Quapaw, the Post was moved up the River to a site near Grand Prairie called *Ecores Rouges* (Red Bluffs) where the present national memorial is located. This fort was erected in 1751 by Lieutenant Paul Augustin le Pelletier de la Houssaye, who was given a five-year concession on the Indian trade in return for erecting the new buildings. Although safe from high water, the new location was not convenient to the Mississippi, and a new site was chosen in 1756 below the old Post location close to the White River cutoff.

A new interest in Arkansas developed during the 1740s. The French had long been rivals of the Spanish for control of the Caribbean and the Indian trade in the Southwest. Even though the French Bourbon family had come to occupy the throne of Spain in the eighteenth century, the colonial rivalries persisted.

One trade route to New Mexico lay up the Arkansas River, and two Post merchants, the brothers Pierre and Paul Mallet, visited Santa Fe in 1739. Their initial route had been via the Platte River to the Rocky Mountains and then south, but they returned via the Canadian and Arkansas Rivers, arriving at the Post in July 1740, where they created a great sensation. The overthrow of the Spanish trade monopoly by direct trade between the Post and Santa Fe terrified Spanish governmental officials as much as it delighted the provincials. Accordingly, the French government cautiously endorsed the trade, and the Spanish were determined to suppress it.

French hopes ran high in the beginning, and Santa Fe became a mecca for traders and runaways. When the Post commander made

Drowned Out. *This 1866 drawing from* Harper's Weekly *reflected recurring conditions in eastern Arkansas.*
University of Arkansas at Little Rock

an unauthorized trip to New Orleans in 1748 to protect his commercial interests, the Post's entire force—six soldiers and a corporal—deserted, taking with them not only the government's stores but the commander's private stock as well. The hope that the Post might serve as an intermediary trade center for a brisk Santa Fe trade proved illusionary when French traders found themselves arrested and their goods confiscated. When war broke out between the French and English, the last thing the French needed was difficulty with Spain. Thus the governor was ordered in 1754 to stop French traders. Lacking the troops to enforce the decree, he turned to the Quapaw chief, Guedetonguay, to fulfill that function.

When Jean-Bernard Bossu, a captain in the French marines, visited the Post in 1751, he noted that the fort was decayed and the Quapaw so weak that only 150 warriors remained. Quapaw weakness meant that when the fort was relocated and rebuilt by Lieutenant de La Houssaye in 1752, the French supplied a force of forty-one men and a new Jesuit missionary, Father Carette.

In addition, Guedetonguay and seventeen other minor chiefs were given the royal treatment during a visit to New Orleans. Such attention was deemed necessary because the Quapaw were becoming restive. Although the French were in alliance with both the Quapaw and the Osage, they were unable to restrain the more powerful Missouri tribe from making war on their weaker southern neighbors. The Quapaw demonstrated their unhappiness by making some temporary alliances with their ancient enemies, the Chickasaw, and by fighting the Illinois Indians, who were also French allies.

The rebuilt fort may have signaled a viable French presence on paper, but in the face of a Mississippi flood in early 1758, it was hardly impressive in reality. All the fort was under water, and one inhabitant survived by gathering within his eighteen-by-twenty-foot house his twenty pigs, four children, five slaves, the dog, cat and chickens. Left outside in ten inches of water was the cow.

The fort was rebuilt again in 1759, but time had run out for the French. The great decisive battle was fought on the Plains of Abraham outside Quebec, ending in Montcalm's death and defeat and terminating the French regime. The Peace of Paris in 1763 transferred Canada to the British, and France, anticipating its loss on November 3, 1762, completed the demolition of her American possessions by giving Louisiana to Spain. The word did not reach Arkansas until 1764. The Quapaw chiefs went to New Orleans to protest, but after the arrival of the first Spanish governor in 1766, the Post became Fuerte de Arkanzas at Los Arcos. One era had ended.

SPANISH CONTROL: 1764-1779

Spain's dynamic energies were long spent when it inherited its part of the fragmented French empire. The first Spanish governor at New Orleans was driven out, and not until General Alexandro O'Reilly reestablished control firmly in 1769 did Spanish rule become effective. During the first years of Spanish rule, the Post commanders, Le Gros de Grandcour (1764-1768), Alexandre de Clouet (1768-1770), and François Demasellière (1770), were French holdovers. A visible Spanish presence did not exist until the arrival of Captain Josef Orieta with six Spanish soldiers in 1770.

A great lethargy had settled over colonial New Spain, so it is not surprising that the new owners did not build a royal road tying the Post to Santa Fe or devote much energy to promoting permanent settlement in the Valley. Nor was much done to keep up the fort. The second Spanish commander, Captain Fernando de Leyba, declared that if the Osage attacked, they would be met in "open combat" because the fort had "more entrances than those who defend it have fingers." When his successor, the reappointed Orieta, practice-fired the Post cannon, the local natives were astonished, so long had it been since the military had put on such a display.

The first initiative for improving the Post came from Captain Balthazar de Villiers in 1778. After noting privately that the Post was "the most disagreeable hole in the universe," he pointed out to the authorities that the site had flooded each of the last four years, ruining the crops. The "*habitants* (French farmers) and the savages are very discouraged . . .

and desire that the post be transferred . . . "
De Villiers's plan was to move the fort back up
the River to its earlier location at the *Ecores
Rouges*, which he claimed was still close
enough to the Mississippi River to provide
security. In the spring of 1779 the flood
waters again covered the Post, reaching the
most elevated houses and causing the fort to
collapse in several places. De Villiers decided
to move. A new settlement was established at
the *Ecores Rouges* and with *habitant* labor, a
new fort, christened Post de Charles Trois
(Charles III) de Arkansas, was finished after
the end of the year.

THE REVOLUTIONARY WAR: 1779-1783

Some of the urgency for relocating came
from the arrival of American refugees fleeing
the war now raging east of the Mississippi.
Captain de Villiers was petitioned on February 2, 1778, by thirteen *confederes ameri-
cains* who sought sanctuary at the Post. De
Villiers gave them permission to stay until
the governor's will could be known. Others
followed, and by March when de Villiers sent
in a census, there were fifty Americans consisting of eight families and eleven bachelor
hunters. More arrived in August. Nine more
Americans from one family arrived from Illinois in the spring of 1780, and others came
from South Carolina. For the first time in
Arkansas history, the commandant felt justified in establishing the militia, which he
formed into two units, one French and one
American.

The settlement boom ended in 1779 when
Spain agreed to support France in the War of
the American Revolution. The Post suddenly
became one of Spain's most exposed positions
in the west, its twenty soldiers and a captain
being an easy target. East of the Mississippi
River the War had been a bitter and bloody
business. Many of the Indian tribes as well

as the hunters and merchants stayed loyal to
the English connection. Although Colonel
George Rogers Clark had secured the Illinois
country and Captain James Willing had captured Concordia, the Tories at Natchez had
staged a pro-British uprising and the Chickasaw remained active under the leadership
of James Colbert, a Scottish trader who had
reared a large family of half-breeds whom he
led into battle.

That all the newly arrived Americans might
not share Spain's new commitment to the
cause became apparent in early 1782 when
evidence came to light that two German soldiers and some of the Post's Americans
planned to betray the settlement to the
British. After the plot was exposed, the
accused were sent to New Orleans for trial.
Two soldiers and two Americans were later
executed. The resulting suspicion generated
so much distrust between the French and the
Americans that when another threat materialized, de Villiers called out his French militia
but only five "honest" Americans.

James Colbert assumed the offensive in the
last stages of the War in the west. Although
the British lost their major post at Pensacola
in May 1781, Colbert was able to disrupt traffic on the Mississippi River, on one occasion
capturing the wife of the lieutenant governor
of Illinois and her four sons. Spain responded
by reinforcing the Post with an additional
twelve men, and work on the fort continued.
Colbert's successes increased to the point that
he began crossing the Mississippi.

Four soldiers went up the St. Francis in
early 1783 to warn the hunters of an
impending attack. These men were
ambushed; one was killed and three captured. Then on April 17, 1783, at 2:30 a.m.,
Colbert, his family and the Chickasaw
attacked the fort. Two soldiers were killed
outright, and one officer, six soldiers and five
habitant families were captured. The fort
stood firm, and after firing perhaps 300 cannon rounds at the attackers, a daring coun-

terattack by the garrison and a few Quapaw routed Colbert, who, while swearing to return with his entire force, promptly took his prisoners and retreated across the Mississippi. One entry in the Spanish records indicated that the generous ration of brandy used to generate the enthusiasm for the attack cost 200 Spanish dollars.

Colbert's raids were prompted in part by the desire to win the freedom of the Natchez Tories, considered by the Spanish to be traitors. Although initially the Spanish refused to consider Colbert as a regular commander, calling him a rebel and a pirate, such recognition became necessary in order to get an exchange of prisoners. Negotiations opened in time, although in regard to settling Post accounts Colbert asserted that "you seem very much interested in charging me for too many articles for more than they are worth." Colbert's life ended when he fell from a horse while on his way to visit the British at St. Augustine. Peace returned to the Valley thereafter.

SPANISH CONTROL: 1783-1804

Captain de Villiers did not live to see the War's end in 1783, for he died June 19, 1782, in New Orleans after an operation to remove a tumor on his liver. Lieutenant Louis de Villars, who had been the officer taken captive by Colbert, succeeded him in command until Captain Jacobo Dubreuil arrived in January 1783. Colbert's attacks had served to remind the Spanish that the Post could not protect the Mississippi River when located at the *Ecores Rouges* site, and there was talk of closing the fort in favor of an east bank location if the Chickasaw Bluffs could be secured. However, the Spanish occupation there proved to be temporary and the Post remained. Its American inhabitants, still under suspicion for treason and now no longer needing protection, had largely departed. By 1791, the census reported a population of 107 persons living in twenty-seven households. Twenty-one were French families, five were German-American and only one was Spanish.

The derelict condition of the fort seems to have remained constant. By 1787, the River had eaten away the base of the fort, causing the garrison to be moved outside the walls, the commandant's house to be abandoned and the battery removed. Post commander Don Josef Vallière was unable to obtain authorization to rebuild from parsimonious Spanish officials. However, his successor in 1790, Captain Juan Ignacio Delinó, fared better. Largely through the labor of the local *habitants*, a new fort was christened *San Esteban* (St. Stephen) and succeeded Fort Charles III. Victor Collot described it as consisting in 1796 of "two ill-constructed huts, situated on the left, surrounded with great palisades, without ditch or parapet and containing four six-pounders."

The uncertainty concerning the fort continued. The Quapaw had diminished to the point where they were scarcely significant, either for hunting or for defending themselves from the Chickasaw or the Osage. The unoccupied status of eastern Arkansas thus tempted the Spanish to use these lands for political and strategic purposes. The Illinois Kaskashia were permitted in 1775 to settle on the White River in return for promising to expel the English traders. They remained only a year before returning north.

Some Delaware Indians located on the St. Francis in 1786, where their presence attracted American traders who crossed the Mississippi illegally to tap this market. The Spanish commander, Don Josef Vallière, sent an expedition up the River in 1788 to drive the traders away, calling out the militia at some unwanted expense to the government. The Delaware chose not to stay, and shortly thereafter they moved north to Missouri. Only a few Creeks were settled in Arkansas by 1796.

The Spanish had greater success luring dissident Americans. With the Proclamation Line of 1763 gone and with Revolutionary War veterans being paid in western land grants, westward expansion was all the rage. Spain, fearful of American intentions and nervous about a Louisiana version of the French Revolution, attempted to thwart expansion by claiming both sides of the River and closing the waterway to navigation.

At the same time, selected Americans were given special privileges. Daniel Boone, who helped found Kentucky, went bankrupt and relocated in Missouri, as did Moses Austin, the father of Texas hero Stephen F. Austin. Roughly halfway between the Post and the Missouri settlements, the Spanish in 1789 allowed Revolutionary War patriot George Morgan to found a new settlement called New Madrid. Located on a bend of the Mississippi, New Madrid kept tumbling into the Big Muddy but nevertheless boasted more than 600 inhabitants, largely French, moving in from Illinois.

As settlement grew north of Arkansas, another movement was underway in the south. The Spanish assigned Jean-Baptiste Filhiol, a French native and wartime captain, to assume command on the Ouachita River in 1782. Filhiol led a party of two families that poled their boats up the Mississippi, Red, Black (Louisiana) and Ouachita Rivers, finally reaching as far north as Écore á Fabri (Camden). After less than a year in Arkansas, he returned south and established his command at *Prairie des Canots*, the future site of Monroe, Louisiana. Filhiol's first survey indicated that his domain already contained 207 persons, mostly hunters. He was expected to encourage them in agriculture, moderate their drinking habits, supervise their trade with the Caddo and keep out interlopers.

The Spanish tried to keep the upper hand during the early 1790s. The new American government was still weak and the Spanish used bribes effectively to divide the Americans. General James Wilkinson, the ranking army officer in the west, was the foremost double agent and benefited through private trade concessions. The Spanish moved at the same time to stifle any internal discontent. Post merchant François Menard was probably the richest man in Arkansas in 1788, but his wealth gave him no immunity from arrest for the alleged crime of having told an Abenaqui chief that the future lay with the United States.

A new constitution in 1787 led to a stronger union. After the United States stabilized relations with England in Jay's Treaty, Spain retreated into a defensive posture. The Treaty of San Lorenzo (Pinckney's) in 1795 partially opened the Mississippi to American commerce and forced the final Spanish evacuation of the east bank. With the Chickasaw Bluffs and Natchez gone, the Post temporarily became more important. Under Captain Carlos de Villemont, whose eight-year assignment set a record for Post commandants, the garrison seems to have been supplied adequately. Captain Francisco Caso y Luengo assumed command in 1802, holding the fort until its evacuation in the spring of 1804.

SOCIETY AT THE POST

The Post of Arkansas remained economically and socially tied primarily to the fur trade throughout its long existence. The merchants at first traded with the Quapaw, the usual article of exchange being liquor. In addition, the fear of flooding in the 1760s had prevented the settlers from planting crops, leaving them dependent on the Quapaw for food. The French and Spanish governments took a dim view of the liquor trade, and one governor in 1769 actually proposed that the commandant assemble the Quapaw and "make a speech to them on the evils of drinking."

Trading relations were strained greatly during the administration of Captain Fernando de Leyba in 1771-1772, especially after he arrested Nicholas Labussière, a Post trader, on a charge of selling liquor to the Indians and other crimes. The enraged Quapaw threatened the Post and especially the captain with physical harm, but as a practicality, the Quapaw always could find English traders at Concordia ready to supply the potent beverage. One Englishman who intermarried into the tribe tried to seduce the Quapaw from their French alliance. The Quapaw expelled the man in 1773 after a great cannon display.

A new commandant, de Villiers, proposed relaxing the trade restrictions on liquor in 1779 by opening the sales to everybody. The free trader doubtlessly must have been shocked when the Post merchant community protested that the result would "expose *habitants* to the continual insults of the said savages" and requested that only one place be established where *eau de vie* would be dispensed. De Villiers acquiesced, but liquor was so common among the Quapaw that in 1786, three of the major chiefs asked the Spanish to stop all sales. Eventually, on October 17, 1787, Governor Esteban Miró's prohibition was published and legal sales were replaced with bootlegging. The Quapaw were so diminished in number by that time that their activities bore little relation to the Post's economic success.

The prospect of a monopoly on the Indian trade had been sufficient in 1751 to prompt Lieutenant Paul Augustin le Pelletier de La Houssaye to erect a new fort, but within a decade trade was described as negligible. The Quapaw were replaced by French hunters, those *coureurs de bois* of legend, who in government circles carried a bad name. "Most of those who live there," wrote Natchitoches Lieutenant Governor Athanase de Mézières of the men of Arkansas, "have either deserted from the troops and ships of the most Christian King or have committed robberies, rape, or homicide . . . "

Throughout the French and Spanish periods, little practical control could be exercised despite the strict regulations on paper, mostly because hunters stayed away from the Post except under dire necessity. According to the law, all were supposed to return to the Post every year to receive a passport; in actuality, some lived for up to twenty years in the camps without ever entering the Post. In 1749, for example, the Post contained thirty-one residents, but forty hunters with expired passports were reported on the Arkansas with others on the White and St. Francis Rivers.

Although most were anonymous and doubtless illiterate, one of these men, known by his nickname of Brindamár, emerges from the documents as a personality. A man of "gigantic frame and extraordinary strength," he became a "petty king" over the other hunters. His name appeared in the 1749 census at the head of the list of those who had failed to report. A few years later he was reported at Pointe Coupee where he seduced a man's wife into joining him. After the husband died—a death attributed to "the unexpected rashness of his wife"—the couple went to the Post to be married. Shortly thereafter, one of his followers killed him, an event Lieutenant Governor de Mézières considered "divine justice."

The active presence of these hunters in the west created animosities with the Osage, who probably became a greater threat than the Chickasaw after 1760. Aided and abetted by the rising St. Louis fur interests, the Osage were encouraged to war on the Quapaw in order to deny Arkansas interests access to the West. Thus, St. Louis grew and the Post stagnated. In 1770 the Spanish ordered all of the hunters to report to the Post. After seven Osage war parties successfully ransacked the far-flung camps in the spring, the hunters reluctantly acquiesced, in part because they now lacked the supplies needed to continue hunting. The

Francoeur brothers arrived in June accompanied by both women and children, the latter having no shirts. The commandant wanted them to go either to New Orleans to regularize their marital relations or for the authorities to send up a priest to perform the needed rites en masse on the about seventy children needing baptism.　Doubtless the commandant was more worried about this matter than the hunters themselves, for as Ouachita commandant Jean-Baptiste Filhiol observed, "Hardly do they know whether they are Christians."

The hunters, who were the most primitive of the Post's social classes, were tied economically to the merchants, who were the most advanced.　Under the laws and customs of the Valley, merchants advanced supplies the hunter needed and in return took a first mortgage lien on the furs, hides, beeswax and bear oil brought in. Some, like merchant François Menard, a long-time resident, acquired a goodly amount of property. His widow, who in 1791 was continuing the business, owned nine slaves, and if the census records are correct, used none of them in farming.

Merchants generally had close ties to New Orleans and the civilized world. Thus in 1752, the marriage contract between François Sarrazin and Françoise Lepine not only was consistent with Parisian notarial practice but also included clauses "in accordance with the custom received in the colony of Louisiana."

Unfortunately, the perpetual round of flooding and site relocation gave little opportunity or incentive to display wealth. Merchants were under the legal jurisdiction of the commandants, who at times were petty tyrants, especially if they were engaging in trade on the side. The persecution of François Menard for his alleged candid remarks about the future was not an exception.

French colonial authorities envisioned permanent settlement by *habitants*, but agriculture remained of secondary importance in the history of the Post. In its lower location, two development obstacles were flooding and the difficulty of cultivating the prairie soils. Flooding prompted settlers to put their houses on six-foot stakes, which the settlers hoped would be above flood waters, but it was impossible for them to protect their fields. In the 1758 flood, all crops were lost except those of the storekeeper Étienne Maurafat Layssard, who had constructed a levee around his garden, apparently the first flood control measure in Arkansas.

The local population grew slowly in the eighteenth century. The Post reported seven men, eight women, sixteen children, fourteen slaves, three horses, twenty-nine oxen, sixty cows and twenty pigs in 1748.　After the temporary increase at the time of the outbreak of the Revolutionary War, population remained stable.

In 1791, when the Spanish census reported 107 residents, only twenty-six claimed to be farmers, and they produced only 126 barrels of wheat and 1,815 of corn. Wheat, which grew readily, found an exponent in German farmer Michael Wolf, whose crops were "equal to that of the best departments of France." A 1793 Spanish visitor, Captain Pedro Rousseau, referred to "very beautiful fields of wheat," presumably those of Wolf. That Wolf was exceptional can be seen from Victor Collot's comment: "But with an administration so vicious as the present, Mr.　Wolf was compelled to display a constancy and firmness of character which are rarely to be found." Unfortunately, Wolf died before the 1798 census was taken.

Population increased more rapidly during the last decade of Spanish rule. In 1798, the census reported 341 whites, three times that of only seven years earlier. Tobacco had been introduced, but the corn harvest had decreased. Elsewhere in the Valley, cattle were becoming important and the Grand Prairie was especially well suited to their needs. However, repeated Indian depredations prevented any significant development. Perrin du Lac reported in 1802 that the *habitants* grew only enough corn for their oxen and horses.

Adventurous Americans began again to settle in Arkansas by the late 1790s. Unlike the typical French, these men were interested in obtaining legal title to their land. Thus in the last years of the Spanish regime, not only did a number of new settlers apply for land patents but many older ones took steps to confirm their existing holdings. Despite what the commandants and the settlers thought, none of these grants in Arkansas and only a few in Missouri complied with all the technicalities of Spanish law. One contemporary noted in reference to affairs in Arkansas that "Land situated so remote from population and commerce was held in very little estimation, [and was] scarcely worth paying the fees of office for the file papers."

With the local commandants willing to make what passed for grants, and with no one willing to challenge their actions, legal title was simply not a concern, even to the farmers. Thus in the will of merchant François Menard, who died in 1791, his notes and bonds, slaves and store merchandise were duly noted, but in referring to property he only listed a house in New Orleans on the Rue de la Madame Boisclare. Significantly, this will fulfilled all the technical requirements of the law, in marked contrast to the Spanish land grants.

Religion at the Post

Although the French and Spanish governments considered religion a civilizing and controlling influence that they hoped to apply to both Indians and hunters, efforts to establish a strong religious base in Arkansas failed. Jesuit Father Louis Carette, who arrived in 1750 and stayed for eight years, reported that in the absence of a chapel he was forced to use the commandant's dining room, which was not enclosed and lacked the proper atmosphere because "of the bad conduct and freedom of language of those who frequent it." On one occasion, a stray hen flew over the altar and upset the chalice, causing one person to exclaim, "There! The God's Shop is upset."

Eventually Carette departed in disgust, having, as Father Watrin observed, "labored to correct the morals of the French, but reaped hardly any fruit from his toil." When some Post females taken captive in 1749 were ransomed from the Chickasaw, an observer could find scarcely any distinction between them and the Indians except the women clung to their rosaries.

Only a few traveling priests visited the Post during the Spanish period. Although Madame de Clouet had attempted to endow a chapel at the Post and left some sacred ornaments, these disappeared. In 1770, Captain Demasellière wanted to convert the chapel, a one-room building "unadorned by any religious goods," into a shelter. What happened is unclear, but in 1794, Father Sebastien Flavien de Besançon, a French Capuchin refugee who stayed at the Post for perhaps three months, found no chapel or even a confessional. The Parish of Arcanzas was created two years later, and Pierre Janin, another French priest, became the first permanent resident since Carette. A chapel named St. Stephen was dedicated, but after Janin left in 1799, no priest replaced him.

The absence of a formal religious presence mattered little to most of the Post's inhabitants. The hunters were basically irreligious, and the merchants always could arrange to visit New Orleans. Church and state were closely tied under French and Spanish law. Father Carette had helped in legal matters, and doubtless the settlers would have welcomed to some extent an authority capable of counterbalancing the petty tyranny of the commandants. Evidence of true piety at the Post was hard to come by, and Louisiana presented more encouraging opportunities for priests than the handful of farmers gathered around the flood-prone Post.

Slavery at the Post

Slavery had been introduced with the Law colony, and from then on a handful of slaves seemed always to have been present. Most worked either for the traders or in agriculture. One was a blacksmith, and two, Luis and Sezar, carried out the delicate assignment of selling illegal liquor to the Abenaqui Indians for merchant Don Bentura Orueta. After drunken Abenaqui attacked the local Quapaw, an investigation revealed the source of the liquor. Because under law a master was legally responsible for the actions of his slaves, the merchant was arrested. Under Louisiana law it was also illegal for anyone to sell liquor to slaves unless they possessed written permission from the owner. In this and doubtless other particulars, the letter of the law carried little weight,

No records of slave marriages have been found for Arkansas, although slave births and deaths were reported. In 1798, the Post reported three free persons of mixed blood, all females and euphemistically listed as seamstresses (a term that elsewhere meant prostitutes), and it is probable that blacks and Quapaws had engaged in interbreeding. Running away apparently was not uncommon, for three of the fourteen slaves François Menard left to his wife had taken flight. Menard also provided for his illegitimate daughter, Constance, and doubtless the freedom the Post's mixed bloods enjoyed owed something to their origins.

Although masters were in the habit of underreporting their slaves in Louisiana, it is doubtful that many more than sixty slaves lived in Arkansas. Almost nothing is known about their lives, housing conditions or work. The only one who emerged in history with a

personality was Marie Jeanne (1788-1857). Manumitted on July 4, 1840, she was known to the Americans as Mary John and was a famous cook and tavern keeper at the Post until her death.

Arkansas Post as a Patriarchal Model

In contrast to free-wheeling American society, every aspect of formal Post life supported the idea of a patriarchal society. The town plan, which probably stayed similar despite the repeated relocations, consisted in 1793 of thirty houses "with galleries around, covered with shingles, which form two streets." The French peasant village remained an ideal, with formal authority being vested in the commandant and the priest, who in turn doubtless demurred to the *paterfamilias*.

That perceptive American, Washington Irving, caught the flavor of the place as late as the 1830s when he published "The Creole Village." In contrast to American bustle and development, "the Post was where art and nature stand still, and the world forgets to turn round." The old houses, "in the French taste," were now flimsy and in ruinous condition, and the wagons, plows, and other implements "were of ancient and inconvenient Gallic construction, like those brought from France in the primitive days of the colony. The very looks of the people reminded me of the villages of France."

French was still spoken, and the village girls dressed in "trim bodice and covered petticoat and little apron with its pockets to receive the hands when in an attitude of conversation; the colored kerchief wound tastefully round the head, with a coquettish knot perking above one ear; and the neat slipper and tight drawn stocking with its braid of narrow ribbon embracing the ankle . . . "

Perrin du Lac had observed in 1802 that during the off-season, hunters at the Post

Madame Chouteau's Home, St. Louis *(artist unknown) No homes of French colonial origin are known to have survived in Arkansas even though this was the common architectural form for almost a hundred years. William Montgomery, who ran the tavern at the Post and hosted the first meeting of the territorial legislature, purchased a building similar to the one pictured here, reportedly from a shadowy Frenchman named D'Armand. This became the main building at Montgomery's Point. The closest surviving examples of the form are found at Ste. Genevieve, Missouri.* **Author's Collection**

"pass their time in playing games, dancing, drinking, or doing nothing, similar in this as in other things to the savage peoples with whom they pass the greater part of their lives and whose habits and customs they acquire." The hunters were gone by the late 1830s, but Irving heard the fiddle and a scrap of an old French chanson, "doubtless a traditional song, brought over by the first French emigrants, and handed down from generation to generation."

The commandants were gone, and because the French in Arkansas gradually had been excluded from the new American legal structure, the patriarchal figure in the community was Frederick Notrebe. "His sway over his neighbors," Irving observed, "was merely one of the custom and convention, out of deference to his family." The community was too weak in numbers and insufficiently supplied with cultural institutions to resist the American onslaught. Gallicisms lingered longer in Missouri and survived in Louisiana, but in Arkansas, the name *Françoise Michel* was Americanized into Fannie Mitchell and the town of *Chemin Couvert* became Smackover.

CONCLUSION

In turning his back on Arkansas Post and floating on to the Mississippi and into the American mainstreams, Washington Irving ". . . cast back a wistful eye upon the moss-grown roofs and ancient elms of the village, and prayed that the inhabitants might long retain their happy ignorance, respect for the fiddle, and their contempt for the almighty dollar."

But it was not to to be. Ironically, in lamenting the Post, Irving had coined the phrase "almighty dollar," which best came to symbolize American life in the new century.

BIBLIOGRAPHIC ESSAY

Many aspects remain to be explored in the colonial history of Arkansas. Edmund R. Murphy, *Henry de Tonty, Fur Trader of the Mississippi,* (Baltimore, 1941), is a useful biography of the founder of Arkansas Various aspects of the Post's history are contained in Stanley Faye, "The Arkansas Post of Louisiana: French Domination," *LHHQ,* XXVII (July 1944), 629-716. Also useful is Morman W. Caldwell, "Tonty and the Beginning of Arkansas Post," *AHQ,* VIII (Autumn 1949), 189-205.

Colonial Arkansas 1686-1804: A Social and Cultural History by Morris S. Arnold (Fayetteville, 1991) is the social history of the settlement. See also, Morris S. Arnold *Unequal Laws Unto a Savage Race: European Legal Traditions in Arkansas, 1686-1836,* (Fayetteville, 1985) The question of the Post's location is discussed by Morris S. Arnold, "The Relocation of Arkansas Post to Ecores Rouges in 1779," *AHQ,* XLII (Winter 1983), 317-331, and additional details appear in Gilbert C. Din, "Arkansas Post in the American Revolution," *AHQ,* XL (Spring 1981), 3-30. Some post-war aspects of Spanish policy are covered in Stanley Faye, "Indian Guests at the Spanish Arkansas Post," *AHQ,* IV (Summer 1945), 93-108.

Orville W. Taylor, *Negro Slavery in Arkansas,* (Durham, 1958), briefly treats the colonial period. For the Post's best-known free woman of color, see Dorothy J. Core, "Mary John, A Remarkable Woman of Arkansas," *GrPHB,* XXI (October 1978), 16-19. Washington Irving's "The Creole Village: A Sketch from a Steamboat," first published in 1837, was collected in *The Crayon Papers* (various editions). Finally the physical history of the community along with much material on the later period, is found in Edwin C. Bearss and Leonard E. Brown, *Arkansas Post National Memorial, Arkansas, Structural History, Post of Arkansas, 1804-1893 and Civil War Troop Movement Maps, January 1863* (Washington, 1971).

MOUTH OF THE ARKANSAS.　　　DIE MÜNDUNG DES ARKANSAS.

Mouth of the Arkansas *(H. Lewis, 1846-47) Published in Germany, this picture shows houseboats, pirogues, rafts and steamboats together with an early view of the town of Napoleon. Note that already the river banks are being stripped of trees to fuel steamboats.* **Arkansas Territorial Restoration.**

Chapter III

Creating an Arkansas: 1803-1835

INTRODUCTION

Napoleon Bonaparte, flush with visions of a world empire, had forced the Spanish king to return the old French holdings in the New World. Keeping these outposts depended on achieving naval parity with England and reconquering Haiti. But yellow fever destroyed Napoleon's army in Haiti, and faced with American hostility and war with England, he sold Louisiana to the United States.

The United States Senate ratified the Louisiana Purchase on October 19, 1803. Actual French possession lasted only twenty days before the Americans took control of New Orleans on December 20, 1803, and in St. Louis on March 10, 1804. A reference to Arkansas Post appeared in American records for the first time on April 14, 1804, and the military commander remained in charge in the absence of civil government for at least a year.

The delayed arrival of the American officials foretold retarded economic, social and political development of Arkansas. Geography put major hindrances on settlement, prolonging frontier conditions. In contrast to some other Southern states, Indians were not an important factor, but plantation agriculture was slow to take root. Violence, common to all frontier regions, was perhaps excessive and certainly enduring.

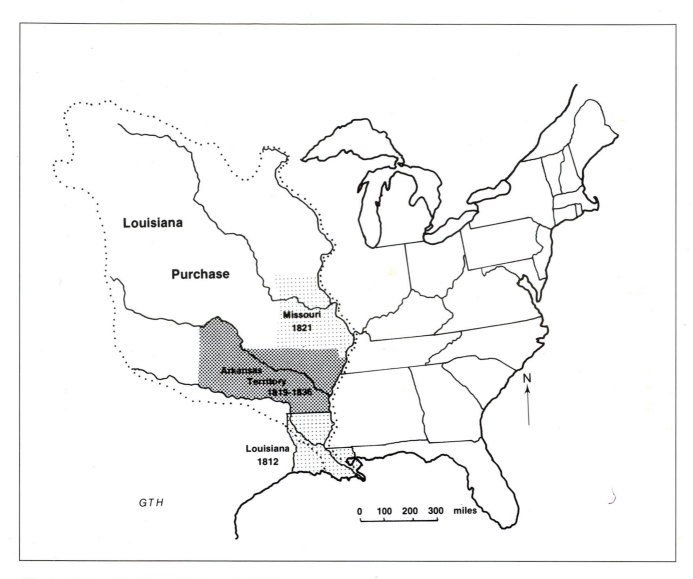

The Louisiana Purchase, 1803, Gerald T. Hanson.

EARLY SOCIETY

The passing of control from Spain to France and then to America did not alter the lives of the people of Arkansas immediately. At the time of the Louisiana Purchase only two places could be called settlements. One was Benjamin Foy's (Fooy's) trading site. The Spanish Camp de la Esperanza had been moved to the west bank of the Mississippi River and Anglicized to Hopefield. Although no rival to the better-situated Memphis, which later arose across the River on the Chickasaw Bluffs, it remained an important village throughout the nineteenth century. From it the United States government surveyed a road to Little Rock, and in the absence of a bridge, Hopefield became the ferry terminus for one of the leading routes into Arkansas.

The Post of Arkansas, the best-known settlement, consisted in 1819 of forty houses in the French style, which Governor James Miller called "but little better than a square of rail fence." Besides the *habitants*, Thomas Nuttall found "renegade Americans who have fled from honest society." In 1804, William Dunbar, a Mississippi planter and friend of

President Jefferson, reconnoitered the southern region, finding at Hot Springs a few huts and a small group of convalescents. Finally, a small Quapaw-French community was located up the Arkansas River at Little Rock, a name that appeared in print for the first time in 1805.

Hunters still predominated. The men—French, half-breeds and Americans—kept a small acreage near the Post or along one of the streams. They erected French colonial homes or crude log cabins with dirt floors and stick and mud chimneys, cleared a few acres to plant corn, and farmed lackadaisically during the spring and summer. As soon as the crops were in, they were off to hunt for the fall and winter. Deer skins and bear fat, their most important commodities, were sold to factors (middle men) working for New Orleans trading companies. Markets also existed for beeswax, otter, beaver, coon skins and buffalo meat.

The men wore buckskin suits and the women wore everything from bearskins to very revealing dresses. One hunter recalled that dancing was a major recreation: "We had some oald back down dances on the dirt floar and if any of us lost aney toe nales, thare never was any thing said about it." The fiddler at the Post knew only one tune, and to the scandal of newly arriving Americans, the French continued their fun on Sunday.

Civilized amenities were few. Governor Miller lived on bread, meat, grease and coffee and complained to his wife about the absence of butter. The ancient legal principle of self-help prevailed, and civilization in the form of officials, laws, mail service and surveyors was almost unknown. Because every civilized advance threatened their way of life, hunters were as stubborn as the Indians in trying to discourage immigration. Part of the bad reputation Arkansas carried could be attributed to the tall tales they told travelers.

Trade Regulation

Because the hunter-trappers were the inadvertent agents of advancing civilization, the federal government sought to exercise some control over their activities. Even in the seventeenth century it had been recognized that private trading with Indians often produced misunderstandings and led to wars. Colonial security came to rely on a coherent Indian policy regulating trade. This policy could be a useful weapon in diplomacy, acquiring new land, and "civilizing" Indians.

One manifestation of these assumptions was the existence in Arkansas from 1805 to 1810 of the Arkansas factory, a government trading post set up at the Post to secure the Indian trade of the Arkansas and White Rivers. The factory system met with strong opposition from private fur traders, and a lack of cooperation from the military and the inefficiency of the operation itself doomed the experiment. By the time the factory closed on September 1, 1810, white hunters had largely replaced the Quapaw.

While the majority of the people were living in a hunter's paradise, those who marketed the hunter's goods rose to positions of leadership in their communities. Benjamin Foy, a Dutch trader, prospered in Hopefield. Aaron Burr, whose Trans-Mississippi schemes eventually led to his arrest on treason charges, were among the notable visitors at Foy's home.

Even more entrepreneurial was Frederick Notrebe. An immigrant from France, Notrebe arrived in 1811, settling at the Post, where he served as factor for New Orleans companies. His economic activities made him the leader of the French community and involved him in politics. In contrast to the cabins of the hunters, Notrebe set a table with cut glass and silverware, hosted Washington Irving on his journey to Arkansas and impressed that fastidious traveler, G. W. Featherstonhaugh (pronounced Fanshaw). Notrebe was also an agent in the economic changes that overtook territorial Arkansas. Beginning in 1819, he became involved with New Orleans cotton agents and encouraged the introduction and production of the new white-bolled plant.

Cattle on the Frontier

Even before farming was well established, commercial cattle raising came to Arkansas. Cattle had been a part of the frontier since colonial days. In general, the cattle culture followed and overlapped with hunter-trapper culture. In the Mississippi River Valley, evidence of commercial cattle production first appeared in 1796. As early as 1807, reports indicate that livestock brought from Kentucky were grazed in Arkansas on public lands. The *Emigrant's Traveller's Guide* of 1834 indicated that prairie remnants in eastern Arkansas were considered choice cattle lands. Cattle were allowed to run free in the woods as well, eating the long, thin grasses that grew in the virgin forest. Canebrakes were also fertile feeding grounds, especially in the spring when tender tops emerged.

Controlled breeding was as unknown as permanent pasture, fences or veterinary care. When cattle were slaughtered, the meat was packed in salt and shipped down the Mississippi to New Orleans to go to the West Indies. The hides became important sources of leather for tanneries.

Salt: The First Industry

References to salt abound in De Soto expedition accounts, for prehistoric Indians used the salt springs and early European settlers continued the practice. With refrigeration still in the future, salt was needed in quantity for preserving meat. Imported salt sometimes sold for $20 to $35 a bushel, and, a resident wrote in 1826, "comes higher to the people of the Country, than any other article." Fortunately, Arkansas had salt resources.

One of the oldest salines in Arkansas was on Saline Bayou on the Ouachita River at Blaketown (Arkadelphia). There had been an earlier Indian operation on the site, and in 1811 John Hemphill developed it further. He had boiling kettles shipped in from New Orleans. These saline springs functioned under a variety of owners until the 1850s. Another early operation useful to the Arkansas Cherokee was near Dover on Illinois Bayou.

Perhaps the most valuable saline was located west of Fort Smith near the Grand River. In 1815, with the permission of the Osage who claimed the land, Major William Lovely authorized Bernard R. Mouille, Johnson Campbell and David Earheart to establish a works there. Known as the Campbell Salt Works, it flourished until Campbell was murdered in 1819. David Earheart and William G. Childers, the accused, were the first criminal defendants in the new Arkansas territorial court. Thomas Nuttall, the naturalist who visited the site in 1819, reported that at its peak, the enterprise produced 120 bushels a week from one well drilled through solid limestone.

After the collapse of the Campbell operation, John W. Flowers, a white man married to a Cherokee woman, set up a works near the junction of the Arkansas and Illinois Rivers with the permission of the Cherokee. Whites' complaints about the salt monopoly led the federal government to turn the site over to Mark and Richard Bean. The Beans bought the kettles used at Campbell's works and built a furnace protected from the weather by a log shed. According to an 1821 traveler, ". . . the Workes on Small Well with a few kittles about 55 gallons of water about three days in the Weake . . ." The firm charged $1 a bushel and supplied all the settlements along the upper Arkansas River. By 1822, the establishment consisted of a double log cabin, slave quarters, stables, two drying houses, salt warehouses, two long houses holding 100 iron kettles, outhouses, furnaces and a five-mile road leading to another warehouse on the Arkansas River. Output was thirty-five to forty bushels a day.

Although the Beans charged $1 a bushel at the warehouse, transportation costs pushed up the price for consumers. The Cherokee, never happy about a white salt works in their midst, complained that they paid $3 at Fort Smith and demanded the return of the salines. The federal government brushed aside these complaints and granted the Beans a three-year lease in 1822.

With the establishment of Fort Gibson on the Grand River and increasing white settlement in the area, the Beans anticipated an expanding market. They developed a new spring in 1825 and announced plans to open a road to the White River. Despite the disruptions caused by the Osage-Cherokee war, the salt business flourished. By 1828, the Beans had sixty kettles at one works and thirty at the other. The white influx had become so great that the legislature created Lovely County.

The Arkansas Cherokee brought the Beans' control to an abrupt halt when all whites were expelled from the area. In August 1828, Cherokee Walter Webber took over their works, and the smaller works of John Lasater, established in 1826, went to Samuel McKay. George H. Guess (Sequoyah), who had run a Cherokee salt works in Arkansas, opened a new saline, and the Cherokee reopened the old Campbell works. The Beans argued that they had been done an injustice, and in 1857, they received $15,000 in compensation from the federal government.

Other bitter struggles took place over salines. According to federal law, all salines were reserved to the government. However, in Sevier County in southwestern Arkansas, an unidentified saline went on the market. Two sets of buyers tried to gain possession: one led by a man already producing salt there and the other by "a united effort of disappointed Speculators, Our Territorial Secretary Mr. Critten-den, and a Mr. Chester Ashley of the Bar." Ownership of this spring remained unresolved for many years.

Despite its early prominence, salt did not remain important long. In 1840, Congress gave Arkansas twelve springs that the state could lease to private parties. Seven years later the state was permitted to sell them. By that time, national salt prices had plummeted because of new techniques of mining in Louisiana and Ohio and better transportation. The boiling method became obsolete, although it was revived during the Civil War. As the first industry, salt manufacturing was contemporaneous with the arrival of the frontier. The extensive use of slaves by the Beans presents another side of the peculiar institution.

Land Speculation

When the new lands of the Louisiana Purchase came under American control, interested individuals began to look for easy profits. Because the buying and selling of land was the major occupation for Americans, the first wave of settlers arriving in Arkansas was intent on enriching themselves as first-comers. One old hunter later remembered the arrival of civilization this way: "We about this time began to get some male contracts and soon after that some Law sutes mixed in." The lawyer, the surveyor, the land speculator and the politician began arriving in Arkansas.

In putting the new lands of Louisiana on the market, the government envisioned a grand plan of organized growth. Although often circumvented, elements of this plan were profoundly important to Arkansas. One feature was the institution of a systematic and comprehensive survey using physical descriptions scientifically given rather than the old English system of "metes and bounds" in which property descriptions depended on physical objects such as trees or creeks.

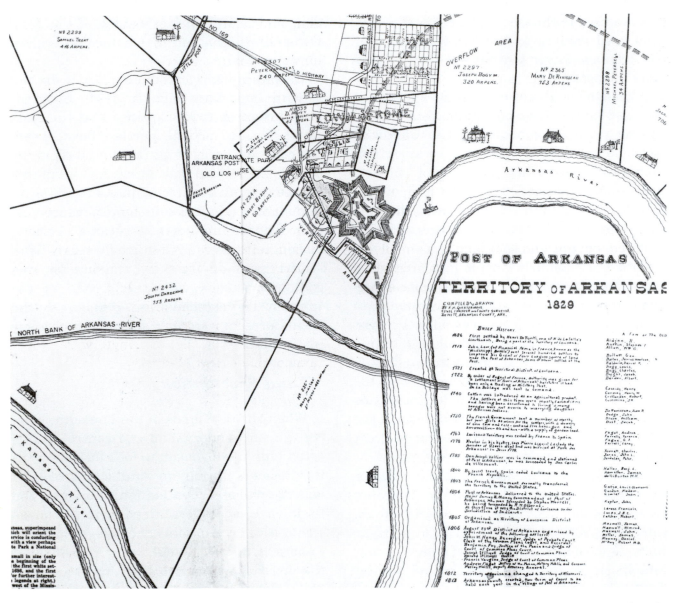

The Post of Arkansas (1829). *This modern copy of an old surveyor's map shows the old Post and the newer plotted towns of Rome and Arkansas. Note that French land holdings are given in arpents rather than acres. The original map is more interesting, but is too faint to photograph.* **University of Arkansas at Little Rock**

For the Louisiana survey, two government surveyors, P.K. Robbins and Joseph C. Brown, met where the baseline and the fifth principal meridian intersected, a point in a swamp in eastern Arkansas. It was from this point that most legal descriptions of property in the Louisiana Purchase were based. The spot is now a small state park at the juncture of Lee, Phillips and Monroe Counties, and a visit there graphically illustrates the difficult conditions faced by these surveyors and the early settlers. Most land titles in Arkansas are recorded by township, range and section, but older counties still have land measured in metes and bounds.

The first step in formal settlement was to regularize the old French and Spanish land titles. Because no grants in Arkansas and only thirteen in Missouri complied with all the French or Spanish rules, Congress modified the strict standards of the law by setting up a court in St. Louis to hear individual pleas.

Those without papers but with a proven history of residence could convert their French *arpents* (five-sixths of an acre) into American titles. A more fertile source for fraud, collusion, forgery and favoritism could hardly be imagined. One Arkansas resident estimated that perhaps only one claim out of twenty was legitimate.

Although most claims were filed in Missouri, some speculators extended their reach into Arkansas, and William Russell was equally at home in both areas. Russell, who surveyed, bought and sold land, was involved in one claim for more than a million acres. His numerous critics charged him with concealing public records for private use, secretly converting small grants into large ones, surveying bogus claims and withholding from landowners news of the confirmation of their grants in order to get their property.

In 1818, he platted the town of Rome just outside Arkansas Post, where it competed with William O. Allen and Nicholas Rightor's nearby site called Arkansas. Russell relied on Sylvanus Phillips, who came to Arkansas in 1797 and later founded the town of Helena, named after Phillips's daughter. Phillips's job was to watch over Russell's lands. Russell never paid the tax assessments, finding it cheaper to let the land go for taxes and have trusted agents buy it back at the subsequent sale.

Confirmed French and Spanish claims actually amounted to less than 1 percent of Arkansas's total land area, but the claims did include many prime commercial and agricultural sites. The news that the government was recognizing claims led a descendant of John Law to claim unsuccessfully all of Arkansas on the basis of Louis XV's long-forgotten grant. So many claims surfaced that in 1824 Congress gave Arkansas Territory's Superior Court jurisdiction over smaller claims. These claims brought James Bowie of Bowie knife fame to Arkansas, for he had a trunk full of forged papers, false affidavits, nonexistent witnesses and the active support of Chester Ashley and Robert Crittenden.

The second problem that upset the orderly course of settlement was the speculation in New Madrid certificates. On December 16, 1811, the New Madrid Earthquake, the worst American earthquake on record, hit the Mississippi River Valley. Because the area was sparsely settled, few persons actually witnessed the event, but earthquake stories became a fruitful source of folklore. To speculators the earthquake became a cause for rejoicing, for Congress granted 515 New Madrid certificates giving landowners whose property was damaged by the disaster the right to relocate elsewhere. Only twenty actually were used by the original grantees; the remainder fell into the hands of speculators. Little Rock and Hot Springs were both claimed under New Madrid certificates.

Squatters

The American government's inability to control westward expansion was nowhere more evident than in Arkansas. Thousands of families headed west, and with total disregard for land laws, picked out choice sites and erected crude cabins. In the early nineteenth century, occupancy generated no legal rights, so these squatters existed in a legal no-man's land. "A large proportion of the citizens of Arkansas are, or have been [squatters] at some period of their lives," the *Arkansas Gazette* asserted in 1838. In response to western pressures, Congress passed a series of pre-emption laws giving those living on the land the first chance to buy it. Other purchasers had to pay the squatter for the value of any improvements. In operation by 1830, these laws were not replaced by the Homestead Law until 1862.

CREATING A GOVERNMENT

The two major population centers on the Mississippi, New Orleans, the shipping point

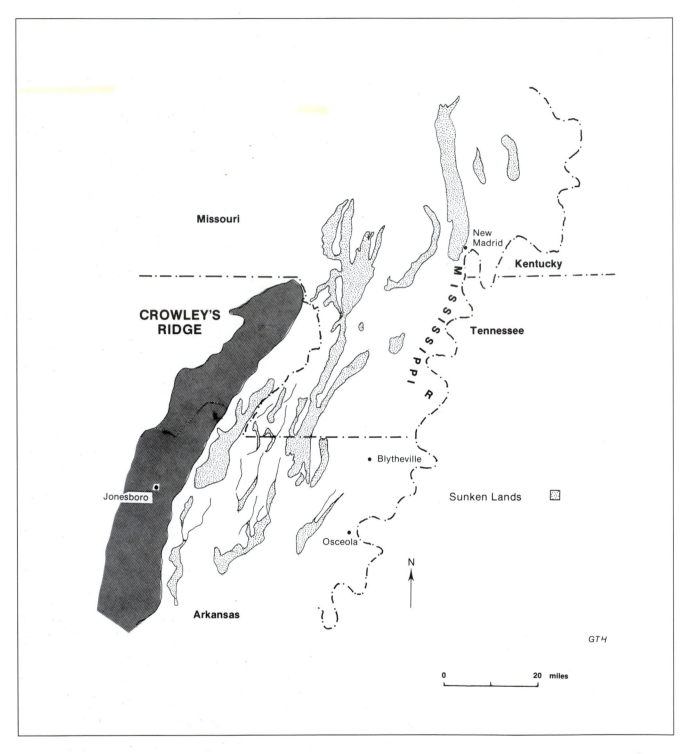

Missouri

New
Madrid

Kentucky

MISSISSIPPI R

**CROWLEY'S
RIDGE**

Tennessee

Jonesboro

• Blytheville

Sunken Lands

Osceola •

Arkansas

N

GTH

0   20 miles

The New Madrid Earthquake. *The New Madrid earthquakes began in 1811 when few people lived in this area. It was a continuation of a series of quakes which included rumblings in 1699, 1776, 1779, 1792, 1795 and 1804. These predecessor quakes were quite possibly even stronger, and some of the changes later credited to the New Madrid Quake probably came earlier.* **Gerald T. Hanson**

The New Madrid Earthquake

On December 15, 1811, John Bradbury, a Scottish naturalist, was headed down the Mississippi River with a party of boatmen. They were tied up for the night just upstream from the Chickasaw Bluffs (the future Memphis), and Bradbury was fast asleep when "a most tremendous noise" panicked the group. "All nature seemed running into chaos," he later wrote, as wild fowl fled, trees snapped and river banks tumbled into the water." Bradbury recorded twenty-seven shocks.

Called the New Madrid Earthquake, largely because New Madrid (Missouri) was the closest settlement, the quake actually began along the St. Francis River in Arkansas some sixty-five miles southwest of New Madrid. Bradbury was closer to the epicenter than the residents of the town of New Madrid, who were awakened by shaking houses and falling chimneys.

After the first December rumbling, jolts continued. One Louisville observer recorded 1,874 separate quakes between December and March. During this time the epicenter moved closer to New Madrid, and on February 7 the residents deserted what once had bid fair to become the metropolis of the middle Mississippi River. The houses had fallen, and possibly even the land on which the town stood had sunk by March.

Because so few persons were in the area of greatest damage and most of those who were there were illiterate, only a few firsthand accounts provide detailed information. Stories and legends grew apace, however, for the earthquake was felt all over North America, and reinforced the evangelical religious notion that the end of the world was at hand. Henry Schoolcraft, who took to poetry to record the quake, wrote:

The rivers they boiled like a pot over coals, And mortals fell prostrate, and prayed for their souls.

Actually, the 1811-1812 earthquake was merely a continuation in a series which included rumblings in 1699, 1776, 1779, 1792, 1795 and 1804. These predecessor quakes were quite possibly even stronger, and some of the changes later credited to the New Madrid Quake probably came earlier. In time, the quake was credited with causing the Mississippi River to flow backward, with creating the "Sunk Lands" in the St. Francis River Valley, in raising Crowley's Ridge, and creating Reelfoot Lake in Tennessee.

Minor jolts continued. Paragould began celebrating an Earthquake Days Festival in 1984 and New Madrid held earthquake inspired celebrations. Blytheville was less amused by a good rattling in 1985, and television stations began to run safety tips the next year.

If another quake of the magnitude of the New Madrid Quake of 1811 should hit the region, it would be the worst natural disaster in American history. Especially vulnerable are buildings of brick and concrete. Almost all of downtown Memphis would fall. The highways and interstate systems would be shattered and bridges destroyed. Massive gas line ruptures would threaten life and property. If the Mississippi River were already near flood stage, the destruction of levees could result in the flooding of perhaps a quarter of the state. Overall, the loss of life could run into the hundreds of thousands.

Despite its prominence as one of the great recorded natural events in American history, the New Madrid Earthquake had very little impact on the history of the region. Although minor tremors were felt off and on, and some timid folks, especially in the 1890s, decided to move elsewhere, the earthquake remained irrelevant to life until Iben Browning, a business consultant with some scientific pretensions, announced that another quake was due on December 3, 1990. Despite numerous scientific attacks on Browning's methodology, the public became truly alarmed. Local communities took disaster relief seriously and sales of earthquake policies soared. Jonesboro's city council, which had just gutted its building code to eliminate earthquake resistance, hastily reversed itself. Many residents stockpiled water, flashlight batteries, plastic bags and toilet paper. Timid folk even left the state. Days prior to the supposed event, every motel room near New Madrid was taken up by news persons ready to cover the projected disaster.

December 3, 1990, passed with nary a tremor, and the quake became the Great Non-Event of 1990. Nevertheless, the publicity did have a positive effect as few area residents could claim to be unaware of eastern Arkansas's natural heritage.

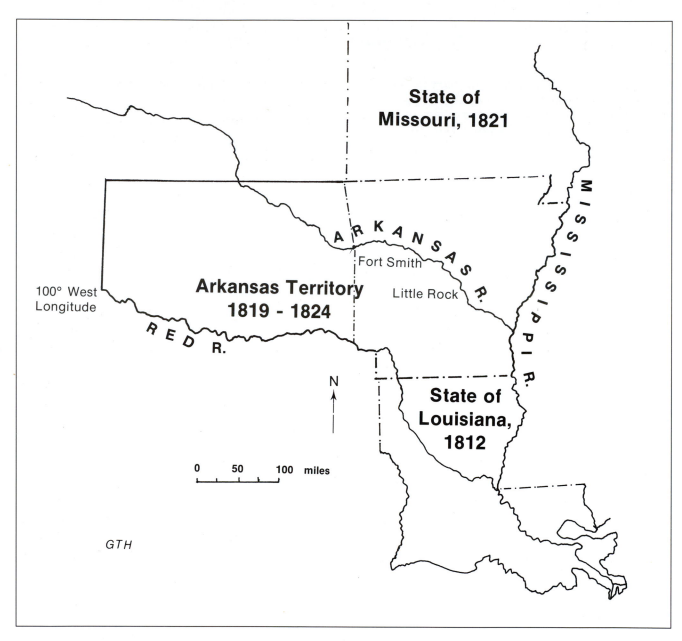

Arkansas Territory, 1819-1824. **Gerald T. Hanson**

for the Mississippi River Valley, and St. Louis, boasting a population of about a thousand and the center for the fur trade, fixed their boundaries with little regard for Arkansas, which contained only a small population of hunters.

The Territory of Orleans, the future state of Louisiana, began with the unsurveyed thirty-third parallel as the northern border. The remainder of the Louisiana Purchase was designated as the District of Louisiana and assigned to Governor William Henry Harrison of Indiana Territory. On March 3, 1805, the District received territorial status as the Territory of Louisiana. General James Wilkinson, subsequently exposed as a Spanish spy, was the first governor, and the judges of the federal court constituted the first territorial legislature.

The District of New Madrid, created at the same time, included all of Arkansas and southern Missouri. On June 27, 1806, the District was divided, and the southern half became the District of Arkansas, the first legal use of the name. Wilkinson was succeeded by Captain Merriwether Lewis of Lewis and Clark fame. After Lewis's death in 1809, a possible suicide resulting from his difficulties in governing the region, General Benjamin Howard was in charge until June 4, 1812, when Captain William Clark, the other half of the famous expedition, took over, and remained as governor until Arkansas embarked on a separate existence as a territory in 1819.

A number of changes took place during the time Arkansas was a part of the district. In 1812, the Territory of Orleans became the State of Louisiana, causing the old Louisiana to become the Territory of Missouri. By 1816, voters could elect both the upper and lower legislative houses and choose a nonvoting delegate to represent them in Congress.

In 1813, the Missouri legislature created Arkansas County with the Post as county seat. The northern boundary ran from the mouth of the Little Red River (Judsonia) due east to the Mississippi River; what was to become the northern remainder of the state was a part of New Madrid County. The next year Henry Cassidy was chosen to represent Arkansas County in the legislature. In 1814, Arkansas was assigned its own judge by Congress, and the following year Lawrence County was created out of the southern part of New Madrid County with a northern boundary line running north of the current state line. Lawrence County's seat of justice, Davidsonville, the site of the first post office in Arkansas, was served once a month by a horseman who traveled from Monroe Court House, Louisiana, via Arkansas Post (the second post office) and thence to St. Louis.

As Arkansas's population increased, three additional counties were created in 1818: Pulaski, Clark and Hempstead. By 1819, certain political forces in Missouri were agitating for statehood. As it then stood, Missouri was deemed too large for admission, so a movement developed to detach the southern counties. Evidence indicated that Arkansas residents were equally anxious to depart from Missouri. In November 1818, a Missouri newspaper reported Arkansas County in a "state of anarchy for months, having no sheriff in commission nor judge in attendance and although they have a population of nearly 10,000 souls, they remain without weight in our councils."

However, the sentiment was different in the New Madrid area. J. Hardeman Walker, a prominent politician, cattle baron and landowner, is credited with instigating the changes that show up in present-day maps as the "Missouri Bootheel." So defined, Missouri's proposed admission to the Union went before Congress.

The emergence of Arkansas Territory reflected less the needs of the people living in the area than it did the will of policy makers in Washington. Since the creation of the American Republic, sectionalism had been rampant with New England interests ready to sacrifice the frontier for commercial advantages with Spain or Great Britain. The Louisiana Purchase committed the new nation to westward expansion but did not resolve whether such expansion was to be in line with Northern or Southern cultural aspirations. In this emerging debate, one hotly contested issue was African slavery.

Although the slavery question achieved its greatest notoriety in the debate over the admission of Missouri, the granting of territorial status for Arkansas actually marked the onset of the struggle. New York Congressman John W. Taylor proposed that Arkansas be stopped from importing new slaves and should be required to emancipate those already there. At one point the House of Representatives accepted Taylor's proposal, but after a trip in and out of committee, the amendment disappeared. One strong argument used by pro-slavery men was that the Louisiana Pur-

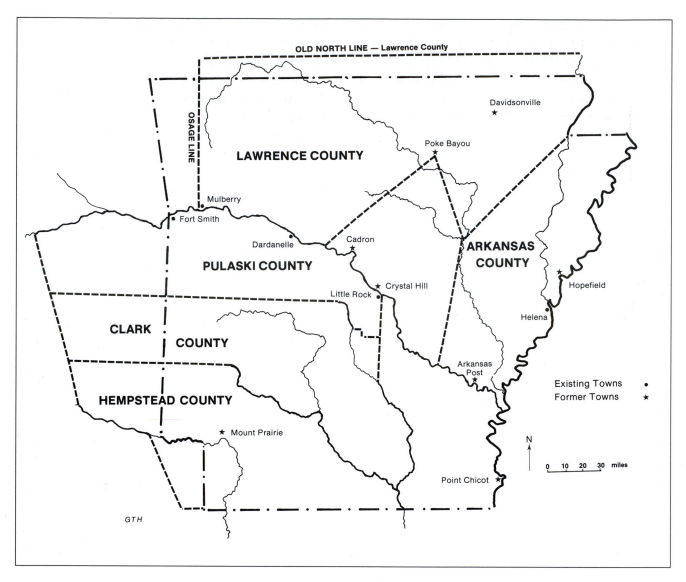

OLD NORTH LINE — Lawrence County

OSAGE LINE

LAWRENCE COUNTY

★ Davidsonville

★ Poke Bayou

Mulberry

• Fort Smith

Dardanelle •

Cadron

ARKANSAS COUNTY

PULASKI COUNTY

★ Crystal Hill

Little Rock

★ Hopefield

CLARK

COUNTY

Helena

Arkansas Post ★

HEMPSTEAD COUNTY

Existing Towns •
Former Towns ★

★ Mount Prairie

N

0 10 20 30 miles

Point Chicot ★

GTH

Arkansas's First Counties, 1813-1819. *Five counties were carved out by 1819. Some of these extended beyond our present state boundaries. Settlement was sparse and towns were small. All of these counties, except Arkansas, were named for notable American patriots.* **Gerald T. Hanson.**

chase Treaty guaranteed residents their property rights and that because slavery existed in Arkansas in 1803, it would be a violation of slave owners' rights to remove it in 1819.

Eventually Congress approved the creation of Arkansas Territory but the Missouri debate continued. The Missouri Compromise in 1820 resolved nothing, for it simply balanced Missouri with Maine. However, in fixing the Arkansas-Missouri border as the future northern limit on slavery in the Louisiana Purchase lands, the Missouri Compromise left Arkansas

as a border slave area with a possible northwest outlet to freedom.

The main government official in the Territory of Arkansas was the governor, appointed by the president for a three-year term. The governor also served as commander of the militia and superintendent of Indian affairs. The second major executive official was the secretary, appointed for a four-year term, who handled the official business of the Territory and served as acting governor in the event of that official's absence or death. The judicial system was made up of three presidentially appointed judges constituting the Superior Court with both original and appellate jurisdiction and other local courts established by the legislature. The first legislature consisted of the governor and judges, but the governor could allow the freeholders the right of election as soon as they indicated a desire for an elected body. The laws of Missouri were to continue in force until modified.

Forming the Territorial Government

The Arkansas Territory legally came into existence on July 4, 1819. The event seems to have passed without notice at the Post, for it was not until July 28, 1819, that the territorial secretary, in the continued absence of the governor, called the judges into session, and decreeing the laws of Missouri in effect, established the offices of auditor and treasurer and formed two judicial circuits.

This secretary, the single most controversial figure in early Arkansas history, was Robert Crittenden, aged twenty-two, the younger brother of Senator John J. Crittenden and a member of a prestigious Kentucky political family. To Albert Pike, a friend and admirer, young Crittenden was "a thoroughly well-bred Kentucky gentleman," and "sagacious and well informed." To critic, Judge Thomas P. Eskridge, he was "the agitator of faction, the instigator of crime, the promoter of duels, the corruptor of youth, the open and shameless gambler, [and] the inmate of the vilest and most debasing associations of profligacy."

In either event, Crittenden was a member of what that crusty agrarian philosopher of Virginia, John Taylor of Caroline, called the "paper aristocracy," men who used government office, patronage, land deals and sharp practices to launch their economic and political careers. Joining Crittenden were Judges Andrew Scott from Missouri Territory,

Charles Jouett of Michigan Territory and Robert P. Letcher of Kentucky. All were related to prominent politicians or had held office elsewhere before their appointments in Arkansas. Only Judge Scott remained in Arkansas for life.

After the first session of the legislature concluded with the governor still absent, acting governor Crittenden proceeded to fill the vacancies his session had created. James Woodson Bates and Neil McLane were assigned to the judicial circuits; William Trimble and Henry Cassidy became the circuit attorneys; George W. Scott, the judge's brother, was made auditor and James Scull was appointed treasurer. Crittenden then appointed the entire roster of county officials. In response to a petition from the freeholders on October 20, he elevated Arkansas to a territory of the second grade, thus allowing the voters to elect the next legislature and send a delegate to represent the Territory in Washington.

In the November 20, 1819, election for representative, James Woodson Bates defeated five other candidates. Bates, whom Albert Pike called a "polished, keen, brilliant writer," was another of the paper aristocracy. A student at Yale and a graduate of Princeton, Bates had moved from Virginia to Missouri. His brother, Frederick, had been secretary of three different territories, and another brother, Edward, became attorney general in the Lincoln administration.

Thus government in Arkansas was a going concern and the people had spoken when, at last, on December 26, 1819, Governor James Miller of New Hampshire arrived at Arkansas Post. Miller, a second choice for the appointment, was competent, deserving and needy. During the War of 1812, he had been a minor hero at the Battle of Lundy's Lane, where his response to a seemingly impossible order, "I'll try, Sir!" became the slogan of his success. Miller entered Arkansas on a large barge with flags flying. One had "Arkansaw" on it in large letters and "I'll try, Sir" interspersed in several places.

After his grand theatrical arrival, Miller immediately ran into difficulties with his very efficient secretary. Miller's first official act was to call for the newly elected legislature to meet on February 7, 1820. In examining federal territorial law, Miller concluded that Crittenden had erred in allowing the voters to choose the upper house. Unless an 1816 act applied to Arkansas, an 1812 law required an appointive upper house. The judges of the court disagreed over the meaning of the law, and Crittenden strongly defended his actions. In the end, Miller let the elected council meet but got the legislature to agree to share in any blame should his decision be overturned.

To the governor's embarrassment, Crittenden's interpretation was sustained. In addressing the legislature, Miller urged the adoption of a territorial law code and support of education. To advance the Territory economically, he pledged to ask the federal government for more roads and postal routes, favorable land policies and suitable Indian treaties.

If Governor Miller expected to preside over rapid and peaceful expansion, he misjudged the nature of the people. Problems appeared in the judiciary in early 1820. One of the three judges, Judge Jouett, had been absent almost his entire term. On May 1, 1820, he wrote to the president resigning his office saying that his family was sick and his wife would not remain in Arkansas. Judge Letcher returned to Kentucky (where he was subsequently a congressman and governor), creating a second vacancy on the court. One of the new appointees, John Thompson of Ohio, started for Arkansas but apparently heard such discouraging accounts of the unhealthiness of the region that he turned back. Eventually, Joseph Selden, a United States army major from Virginia, accepted Letcher's seat, and Benjamin Johnson of Kentucky, brother of Senator Richard M. Johnson, took Jouett's position.

The Arkansas Gazette

While the government was forming, William E. Woodruff, a New York-born printer, appeared at Arkansas Post. Woodruff was foreman of the Nashville *Clarion* when he learned that the new territory would be without the services of a printer. Buying a used wooden press, Woodruff started for Arkansas, arriving at the mouth of the White River cut-off on a New Orleans-bound keelboat. There he transferred his press to a pirogue and was poled up to the Post. Woodruff later recalled that he had to convince the nervous raftsmen that the press was not an infernal engine spewing out bullets.

On October 31, 1819, the fledgling printer set up shop in a two-room log cabin, where on November 20, 1819, he published the first issue of the *Arkansas Gazette*. It consisted of four pages, 18 1/2 inches long and 11 1/4 inches wide, with four columns to the page. What Woodruff planned was a nonpartisan paper promoting the new territory and receiving patronage. But inevitably the *Gazette* was drawn into controversy as the violent nature of frontier society asserted itself.

Early Duels

The first recorded duel in the Arkansas Territory occurred on March 10, 1820, between William O. Allen, a former military officer turned Arkansas Post lawyer, and Robert C. Oden, a lawyer recently arrived from Kentucky. The origins of the conflict are unclear, beginning by one account as a personal difficulty arising from a prank and by another account from political differences. Allen challenged Oden, and the two men met on a small island near the Post, where both were wounded and Allen died.

The appearance of dueling in Arkansas was to be expected. Since the Hamilton-Burr duel of 1804, the practice had been growing in popularity, especially among the elite of the western border. Thus the Allen-Oden duel enlisted George W. Scott, the United States Marshal and brother of Judge Scott, as Allen's second. In the eyes of the law, death by dueling was murder. Although a grand jury indictment was handed down against both Oden and the seconds, the charges were dismissed at the trial on various legal technicalities. The legislature on October 23, 1820, passed a strict law against dueling, but the practice continued. Ten more duels of significance occurred before statehood, and this resort to honor continued until after the Civil War.

The next duel highlighted the problems of enforcement. Judges Scott and Selden of the Superior Court had a personal difference over a game of whist. The men circumvented the law by fighting their duel on the east bank of the Mississippi opposite Helena, where Scott shot Selden dead on the spot. Scott's only punishment was the United States Senate's refusal to reappoint him to the bench in 1827.

Locating the Capital

The first territorial political issue was the selection of a permanent capital. The Post was unhealthy, not centrally located, subject to frequent flood, and perhaps most important, did not provide the possibility of great profits to be made from speculation. The legislature in the fall of 1820 heard about the prospective merits of Cadron and Little Rock. Little Rock was chosen because it was more centrally located, situated near richer farm land and had more powerful supporters. The governor signed the bill into law and set June 1, 1821, as the removal date.

The geographic advantages of the first rock escarpment on the Arkansas River were clear, but it was not certain who owned the site. Three New Madrid certificates held by William O'Hara, James Bryan and Stephen F. Austin were contested by two preemption claims held by William Lewis, Benjamin Murphy and later William Russell. The New

Madrid owners actively pursued their site for the capital, offering as inducements a public square, lots and a temporary building. A New Madrid claim was ranked under a preemption claim. William Russell advised the New Madrid men that he had purchased the preemption claims and he demanded $25,000 as settlement. The New Madrid party refused payment, and the case went to court. Meanwhile, Benjamin Murphy obtained from the Batesville land office another preemption certificate covering the area, and Russell, whose claim had no foundation at all, promptly purchased a half interest in it. Both sides distributed parts of their claims in order to bolster their influence. Crittenden and his friends Henry Conway, Joseph Hardin, Robert C. Oden, William Trimble and Townsend Dickinson labored with Russell. The New Madrid party enlisted Chester Ashley, a wily young lawyer from New York, and Governor Miller.

During the spring, with the question of ownership still unresolved, the government and its attendants moved up the River to what the O'Hara group called "Arkopolis" and that within three years would be called "The Rock." In June 1821, the Superior Court opened the new career of the territorial government by rendering a decision in the land claim. Because Judge Scott was a partner in the preemption claim, it was the newly arrived Benjamin Johnson who ruled that Russell did have access to the disputed land.

The prospect that Russell would take possession of the buildings in the disputed area led the New Madrid party to remove them. A painted and masked gang that was well fortified with whisky set to work with ropes and chains to carry the buildings over into the adjacent Quapaw lands. The one house they could not move was burned. Surveys showed that the two claims did not coincide exactly but overlapped. The New Madrid claimants controlled the location of the seat of government, and the preemptioners held the river frontage. The standoff led to compromise, and Little Rock began to develop.

Ironically, Roswell Beebe later discovered that both claims were invalid, and twenty years later a new title settlement had to be reached. Thus Little Rock became the capital as well as the county seat of Pulaski County. Curiously, in the twentieth century, numerous stories circulated of how a dozen or more towns missed becoming the capital by one vote. The original records reveal that only Cadron was ever mentioned and only briefly.

The Era of Personal Politics

The government in Little Rock remained remarkably like the old one at the Post. Despite his boasts, Governor Miller did not try very hard. Finding little evidence of civilization or hope of future success or glory, he virtually left Crittenden to run the show. Most of the leading men associated themselves with Crittenden and benefited from his patronage.

Arkansas's first book, *Laws of the Territory of Arkansas* was published at the Post in 1821 by William E. Woodruff, but shortly after its publication Woodruff followed the territorial government and moved the *Arkansas Gazette* to Little Rock. Fittingly, this book, a compilation of the laws carried over from Missouri and those enacted by the territorial legislature in 1819 and 1820, caused a controversy when Crittenden, believing Woodruff had charged too much for the work, refused full payment.

In 1821, James Woodson Bates announced he would be a candidate for reelection. Opposing Bates was Matthew Lyon, the former Vermont Congressman, whose jailing by the Federalist Party for violating the Sedition Act had made him a national hero. Lyon had moved to Kentucky, where he served in Congress for four terms (1803-1811), and in 1821 appeared in Arkansas, working as an Indian factor. The seventy-two-year-old veteran campaigned

vigorously but unsuccessfully. His canvass of Little Rock was a disaster, his mule having thrown him into a muddy bayou so that he arrived "a subject of much laughter by his companions and the town."

Lyon lost the election by sixty-one votes to the incumbent Bates but refused to accept the tally, blaming Crittenden for his defeat and charging him with various irregularities. Congress upheld Bates's election, and Lyon died the following year. Whether his charges were true cannot be ascertained, but this marked the first assertion that Arkansas was ruled by a clique, the most enduring battle cry in Arkansas political history.

The 1823 race produced four rivals for Bates's office: William Trimble, Thomas P. Eskridge, Henry W. Conway and Major William Bradford. Behind this opposition was the belief that Delegate Bates was negligent in protecting western Arkansas interests, particularly with respect to lands and Indian treaties. In addition, Bates and Conway had a discussion, the import of which was that Bates planned to marry and retire from public life in favor of Conway. But Bates's fiancee died, and the distraught delegate decided too late to seek a third term. By the time Bates's decision reached Arkansas, Conway already had announced with Crittenden's support. Both Eskridge and Trimble retired from the contest, making the race essentially between Bradford and Conway.

Major William "Old Billy" Bradford, the commander at Fort Smith, was at age fifty-one "a small, stern-looking man, an excellent disciplinarian and a gallant officer." Much involved in western Indian affairs, he ran as the defender of western interests, a theme consistent with Lyon's campaign two years earlier. Henry W. Conway, thirty-one, was the scion of another of those office-holding frontier families. His uncle, William Rector, was surveyor general of Missouri. When Conway came to Arkansas as receiver of public moneys for the Arkansas Land District, he was joined by a cousin, Ambrose Hundley Sevier, who began his career in Arkansas by serving as temporary clerk of the House of Representatives for the 1820 fall session.

The campaign revolved around charges that Conway headed a Missouri party, that Bates had been forced out of the race and who could best rid Arkansas of Indians. The *Gazette* continued to be officially neutral with its columns open to letters from both sides. Crittenden's support proved decisive, for Conway polled 1,300 votes to Bradford's 921.

Crittenden's power was now at its zenith. Governor Miller had ceased altogether trying to administer the government of the Territory, taking two long trips back to New Hampshire and leaving Crittenden as acting governor. Almost every political appointment depended on the secretary's good graces, and in two elections western discontent had been squelched. On December 31, 1824, Miller submitted his resignation. Although subsequently elected to Congress from New Hampshire, he also resigned that post to become customs collector for the port of Salem, Massachusetts, a good, safe job far from the hurly-burly that now erupted in Arkansas. Various Western politicians sought the governorship, including Crittenden, but President James Monroe appointed Pennsylvanian George Izard, a former Federalist and a military man.

Izard, whose name was pronounced with the accent on the second syllable, was born in England during the residence there of his father, Ralph, a rich South Carolina planter and notable Revolutionary War patriot. Preferring a foreign post, George apparently was not pleased with his assignment. While Izard was preparing to come to Arkansas, the Crittenden faction triumphed again as Conway won reelection by defeating Bates, the former delegate, 2,105 to 519. On May 31, 1825, Izard arrived in Little Rock, only to find the territorial secretary gone to Kentucky. So completely had the secretary swallowed up the government that the new governor found himself unable to become "acquainted with the Details of the Public Affairs in this Quarter." Izard's subsequent hostility to Crittenden began with this initial embarrassment.

In his opening move, Izard proposed to reorganize the territorial militia, a necessity in his view because the eastern Indians would be moving through the area to reach their new homes in the West. Very little came from the effort, militia duty being a drunken frolic, but most of the leading men received appointments as Arkansas "Colonels."

The governor soon was embroiled in a variety of feuds. He removed David Barber as subagent for Indian affairs, claiming Barber was negligent and intemperate, a charge Barber disputed. He clashed with Edward W. DuVal, the Cherokee agent, over the payment of Indian claims, and he became engaged in an enduring quarrel with Crittenden. In the fall of 1826, Crittenden planned a leave of absence to go to Washington to settle his government accounts, which apparently needed considerable explanation. Governor Izard decided to return to Philadelphia at the same time and opposed the secretary's plan.

Fearing that Izard intended to thwart his renomination as secretary, Crittenden waited until after the governor left and then he, too, departed, leaving Arkansas with no executive. A certain amount of newspaper criticism from the still disgruntled Bates became more serious when Delegate Conway proposed that in the absence of both the governor and the secretary another person be designated as acting governor. Crittenden saw this move as a betrayal, and a schism developed between the two leaders.

The Crittenden-Conway Dispute

On April 10, 1827, Conway announced that he would stand for reelection. One week later, Robert C. Oden entered the race with Critten-

Henry W. Conway *(artist unknown). Conway's portrait, reproduced in John Hallum's* Biographical and Pictorial History of Arkansas *(Albany, 1887) suggests the youth common to many early Arkansas leaders.*
University of Arkansas at Little Rock

den's support. "Probably a man of better talents than anyone in the territory," according to a contemporary, Oden had served as Pulaski County clerk, a lieutenant in the militia and attorney for the third judicial circuit. His public notoriety came from the killing of William O. Allen in the 1820 duel.

Oden's chief charge against Conway, supported by incriminating evidence, was that the delegate had borrowed $600 in government money for his private use out of funds intended for the Quapaw. Crittenden was the source of this information, and Conway's rejoinder was that the secretary had given his permission for the action. The charges and countercharges about the $600 grew heated as the public and private acts of many of the leading men of the territory were questioned.

Conway escaped official reprimand, but Governor Izard aided the Conway side by bringing suit against Crittenden supporter Thomas W. Newton, guilty of the same indiscretion. For the first time, the *Arkansas Gazette* took a stand in favor of Conway. Reportedly, Crittenden threatened to cut Woodruff's throat and "the nose of every printer in the place and pull down the printing office." With no access to the press, Oden was forced to go to Memphis to get his circulars printed. It was to no avail; Conway won reelection, 2,427 to 856. Crittenden was considered to be the real loser, for his place at the center of power was now broken.

The emotions unleashed by this election did not stop with voting. On September 4, 1827, Ambrose H. Sevier and Thomas W. Newton journeyed to Indian Territory, where they fought a bloodless duel. That was but a preliminary for a confrontation between Crittenden and Conway. On July 24, 1827, Conway wrote in the *Gazette* that Crittenden's charges against him were "wilfully and intentionally . . . false," and that Crittenden was "so destitute of principle, that he will resort to any measure, however base and grovelling in its nature, to accomplish his object." Crittenden's reply to this insult was a challenge to duel. The two men met on the east side of the Mississippi River opposite the White River cutoff on October 29, 1827, Conway was wounded seriously in the encounter and died on November 9, 1827, probably from an infection caused when Crittenden's bullet drove fragments of Conway's toothbrush into the wound.

Although Arkansas was saddened by Conway's death, the violent nature of territorial politics continued. On January 17, 1828, an inebriated minor Crittenden supporter, John T. Garrett, transformed his hatred of Chester Ashley, Crittenden's former law partner, into action by invading the *Gazette* office and opening fire. In the resulting foray, Ashley fired at Garrett but hit Woodruff, and Garrett apparently was shot with his own pistol. An inquest lasting for three days failed to issue an indictment, but Woodruff thought that Crittenden, in whose company Garrett had earlier been seen, had instigated the assault.

On December 17, 1827, a special election was held to fill Conway's seat. His cousin, Ambrose H. Sevier, in the words of one historian, "rode into Congress largely on his dead cousin's popularity." Even so, it was a hard ride, for Sevier's two opponents, Richard Searcy and Andrew Scott, polled 883 and 116 votes respectively, denying Sevier a majority of the votes cast.

On November 22, 1828, Governor Izard died in Little Rock. During his term of office the lines of factionalism formed around the breakup of the Crittenden clique. Many leading men, including Robert C. Oden and Thomas W. Newton, still supported Crittenden, but the Conway faction, aided by the ever-scheming and crafty Chester H. Ashley, emerged dominant. The Conway group had the

Robert Crittenden. *(artist unknown). Also found in Hallum's* History, *the original was a small oval which inspired both this steel engraving and the portrait now found at the Arkansas History Commission.* **Arkansas History Commission**

additional fortification of bringing into the system a string of nephews, cousins, in-laws and other assorted relatives. Having the only press in the Territory gave them a news monopoly.

Jacksonian Democracy

Izard's death coincided with the national rise to power of Andrew Jackson, whose "new broom to sweep clean" now threatened to overturn the patronage system in Arkansas. The outgoing president, John Quincy Adams, nominated Hutchins G. Burton, a former governor and congressman from North Carolina, for the vacant Arkansas governorship. The

Senate refused confirmation, leaving Crittenden as acting governor and giving Andrew Jackson a free hand to make his own choice. Given the inveterate opposition Jackson had faced from Senator John J. Crittenden, it was hardly likely that his brother, Robert Crittenden, would achieve his long-desired goal of becoming governor or even that he would keep the office of territorial secretary.

Jackson appointed John Pope of Kentucky as governor. A brother-in-law of ex-president Adams, the one-armed Pope had deserted his family to get on the Jackson bandwagon. His assignment to Arkansas was quite a come-down from the cabinet post he expected, but he accepted the honor and arrived in Little Rock on May 31, 1828. Before this, Jackson removed Crittenden from office, placing in his seat William Savin Fulton of Alabama. Fulton, born in Maryland in 1795 and a War of 1812 veteran, had been Jackson's military secretary during the Seminole Wars in Florida. Ten days before Pope arrived, the new secretary took up residence at the capital.

The Jacksonian Revolution had little other impact in Arkansas. In the 1829 election, Sevier stood for reelection and was opposed by the veteran Crittenden supporter, Richard Searcy. In a dull contest Sevier won 2,064 to 1,756. Part of Sevier's success in solidifying his position came from his record of accomplishment. An additional superior court judge had been added, the salaries of the legislators now were paid by the federal government and the appointive powers of the governor had been so greatly trimmed that the legislature now chose all officials except the auditor, treasurer and justices of the peace. In addition, Sevier claimed credit for various land laws that benefited Arkansas.

The feeling that progress was underway continued in the opening ceremonies of the Pope administration. Addressing the legislature, he urged a number of reforms. The militia needed strengthening, the territorial finances were not strong (scrip stood at 60 cents on the dollar) and better laws against gamblers and public violence were needed. But the validity of these suggestions was undone by Pope's personal character. Vainglorious, politically naive and an egotist, he compared Arkansas to a plantation and himself to the overseer. In a public speech he crowed: "While many other appointments of the President are condemned, all parties concur in conceding the office of Governor of Arkansas is well filled." Such a man was hardly prepared to cope with the tangled web of subtle plots and schemes that constituted territorial politics.

The first victim of the governor's folly was his own nephew and secretary, William Fontaine Pope, who undertook to correct a slur on his uncle's honor by challenging the author of the criticism, the young Charles Fenton Mercer Noland of Batesville, to a duel. The two men met on the Texas side of the Red River, where young Pope fell mortally wounded. Fortunately, the governor was well supplied with nephews, and he soon returned from Kentucky with another nephew-secretary, also named William F. Pope. This Pope managed to avoid the antagonism of politics and eventually left a memoir of the period.

The election of 1831 marked a change in territorial politics. Personality, the dominant mode to date, was being replaced by factional organization. Crittenden supported his friend Benjamin Desha in an unsuccessful race against Delegate Sevier, but at the same time made a successful effort to win control of the territorial legislature. The *Arkansas Gazette* monopoly had been broken by the establishment of Crittenden's *Arkansas Advocate*, and Crittenden now wanted his paper rather than Woodruff's to get the lucrative public printing business. Woodruff faced a hostile legislature and lost his contract, the mainstay of his income. The little "harrow-hearted Yankee" took the loss in bad grace, blasting the legislators for accepting "canvas hams" from Crittenden in return for votes. The confrontation grew violent when Woodruff, busily copying the House journal, was set upon by Dr. Nimrod Menefee, "the dueling surgeon," who knocked him senseless.

The legislators were asked to prop up Crittenden's sagging fortunes in another way. He had erected Little Rock's first mansion, which he now found himself unable to afford. The federal government had granted to Arkansas ten sections of public land, as yet unlocated, the sale of which was to finance the erection of a capitol building. All the speculators wanted to take the land off the territory's hands, including Chester Ashley, who offered to swap his house, and William McK. Ball, who offered $10,000 for the land. Crittenden offered his house and agreed to locate the ten sections on unimproved acreage.

When the legislature accepted his proposition, Woodruff successfully urged the governor to veto the bill, and the veto was sustained by only one vote in the Senate. Pope's veto of the Crittenden house exchange raised the level of political animosity, putting new pressures on Charles P. Bertrand, the editor of the *Advocate*. Fortunately, Crittenden had discovered Albert Pike, a Massachusetts native and former Harvard student, who was teaching school in western Arkansas. Crittenden set him to a higher task, that of fracturing the political relations between Pope, Sevier, Woodruff, Fulton and President Jackson.

All the skills the *Advocate* possessed were utilized in 1831 when Crittenden himself challenged Sevier. This race should have been the culmination of all the old feuds in an exciting battle to the death. But it was not to be. A decade of criticism and a complete lack of popularity in the western counties doomed Crittenden's effort. In Washington County, one Crittenden rally was broken up by the Sevier camp's distribution of free whisky. The usual election violence resulted, including a collision in Little Rock between the Pulaski County sheriff and candidate Sevier, who had drawn a knife during an election-day fight with some Crittenden men. The polls gave Sevier 4,476 votes to Crittenden's 2,520.

More successful was the *Advocate's* sniping attack on the coalition. The first crack came when Pope accused the *Gazette* of not being sufficiently warm in his defense and of overcharging for printing. Pope financed a new editor, John Steele, to found the *Political Intelligencer,* a pro-Pope paper, and gave him the "good fat job" of printing the digest of the laws. That Pope would dispense major patronage without consultation with Sevier and give it to a newcomer indebted only to him led to major tension between the territorial delegate and the governor. Then Secretary Fulton, who had suggested the swap for Crittenden's house in the first place, disagreed with the governor on the Ten Section Bill and used the *Gazette* to explain his position.

All parties turned to Washington for support, and Pope was in the worst position. Fulton, in his correspondence to Jackson, had made Pope out to be a Clay-lover and a critic of Jackson's bank policy. After his betrayal of Adams, Pope was of no further use to Jackson, and early in 1835, the president nominated Fulton to succeed him. After Pope retired to Kentucky, Steele, now no longer an editor, was reported associating with an outlaw gang.

One man who did not benefit from the fall of Governor Pope was Robert Crittenden. In debt and unable to make political headway in Arkansas, Crittenden wrote of moving to Mississippi. Ironically, he suddenly died in Vicksburg on December 18, 1834, after a seizure in court. Although only thirty-seven years old at the time of his death, his best political days were well behind him. The first politician in Arkansas, he was the guiding force for the early period. His faction, which after his death became the Whig Party, continued in Arkansas, providing an alternative to the Democrats for nearly twenty years. Its leader, Albert Pike, had been hand-picked by Crittenden.

The Statehood Movement

Meanwhile, the winds of political change were blowing from another direction. Before the mid-1830s, national politicians saw Arkansas only as an insignificant Territory and a possible dumping ground for dispossessed Indians. But as the implications of the Missouri Compromise became apparent, it was inevitable that Arkansas must enter the Union as a slave state and be paired with a Northern territory to preserve the tenuous sectional balance. The publication of *Walker's Appeal* in 1829, the founding of the *Liberator* by William L. Garrison in 1831, and Nat Turner's insurrection the same year heightened the national consciousness. Arkansas was close to the 40,000 population figure then required for statehood, and Michigan Territory was eager to join the Union.

Because only two Southern territories existed, Florida and Arkansas, it was Delegate Sevier's opinion that if Arkansas did not come in with Michigan, it might have to wait twenty-five years for another chance. Sensing a sectional rather than a local need, Sevier and Woodruff brought the Southern version of the slavery issue into play and began the statehood campaign.

The question of statehood occasionally had been mentioned in the press before, but usually with a realistic appraisal of the difficulties Arkansas would face from the loss of federal funds for roads, rivers and government expenses. The general sentiment had been to wait. When Sevier changed his mind on the subject, he caught the public unaware. Fairly soon, both Woodruff of the *Arkansas Gazette* and Pike of the Arkansas *Advocate* were on the statehood bandwagon, together with other politically minded men. The new governor, William S. Fulton, was not. He was opposed less to statehood per se than to the way it would be brought about. Michigan had taken the lead by holding a convention, drafting a constitution, and sending it to Wash-

ington, all without formal congressional approval. The pro-statehood party in Arkansas proposed to proceed by the same possibly illegal route.

Despite Fulton's scruples, the legislature debated summoning a convention. All was harmonious until the question of apportioning seats arose. Then the legislature forgot all factionalism and split sectionally, with the north and west demanding a formula based on the principle of white manhood suffrage and the east and south insisting upon counting slaves as in the federal three-fifths rule. After parliamentary maneuvering, a bill emerged giving the north and west twenty-seven delegates and the south and east twenty-five. With this compromise, the convention bill became law without the governor's signature.

On January 4, 1836, the delegates to the constitutional convention assembled in the Baptist Meeting House, moving to the Presbyterian Church two days later. Everything proceeded, as delegate David Walker of Washington County wrote, "in better feeling than I expected, yet the exciting question is not yet reported." That question was the renewal of the sectional battle. Later in the month when that issue was finally broached, disharmonious wrangling followed with plan and counterplan. Compromise prevailed in the end. In theory, the lower house would be based on white population, thus giving the north and west a majority, but in the Senate, both sides were to be equal and a center district consisting of Pulaski, White and Saline Counties would hold the balance of power. The convention adjourned on January 30, 1836.

The Proposed Constitution

The new constitution was an unexceptional product of the early nineteenth century's march toward democracy. Voters chose a governor for a four-year term who could not serve more than eight years in twelve; elected the legislature, with two-year terms in the lower house and four years in the upper and elected the justices of the peace on the county level. Almost all state offices were chosen by the legislature, including the secretary of state, auditor, treasurer, the supreme court, the circuit judges and circuit attorneys. Although the governor possessed veto power, a simple majority in each house was sufficient for an override.

Other important features of the constitution included authorizing banks, encouraging internal improvements, banning lotteries, requiring officeholders to acknowledge the existence of God, encouragement of "intellectual, scientific, and agricultural improvement" and creating a state militia. The legislature was forbidden to emancipate slaves without the consent of the owners. The slave trade within the state could be prohibited, slaveholders were obliged to treat their chattels "with humanity" and slaves accused of crimes were to be given trials with impartial juries and receive the same punishments as whites. Compared to other Southern constitutions, the Arkansas document showed an advance of democracy on the Southern frontier. Gone were property qualifications for voting, and the number of elected offices was increased. The legislature, viewed as the supreme agent of the *vox populi*, wielded the most power. However, no popular referendum was held on the constitution because the convention's approval was considered sufficient.

To present the new constitution to Congress, the convention chose C. F. M. Noland, although one delegate from Carroll County nominated "U. S. Mail" to do the job and supported this nominee through all seven ballots. The vote proved to be ironic, for Noland, fearing winter storms, chose a safe southern route to get to Washington and arrived a month later because of it. The mail containing an *Arkansas Gazette* "extra" publishing the constitution beat Noland by eight days and was used by the congressional committee in arranging Arkansas's admission to the Union.

Persisting sectional tensions made every statehood debate a potentially explosive political issue. The joint Michigan-Arkansas entry was no exception. Missouri's Senator Thomas Hart Benton, a Southerner, managed Michigan's case, while Pennsylvanian James Buchanan presided over Arkansas's destiny. Despite the pairing, objections surfaced. Some found the new constitutions illegally drawn because of a lack of congressional authorization. Anti-slavery men objected to the slavery clauses in the Arkansas document. Above all, the anti-Jackson men saw in the statehood move a Democratic way to gain additional electoral votes for Martin Van Buren. The road to final approval was strewn with parliamentary maneuvering, a twenty-five hour session of the House, and much bickering.

But the Jackson men were in control, and statehood passed on June 16, 1836. As editor Woodruff, now a firm supporter of Van Buren's presidency, noted: It was due "solely . . . to the friends of the Administration and of Messrs. Van Buren and Jackson." The Whigs "left no effort untried to prevent the passage of the bill" and thus deserved no political support in Arkansas. National politics would now enhance the local politics of personality, one reason being that the Van Buren vice-presidential nominee was Colonel Richard M. Johnson of Kentucky, whose brother, Benjamin, became the first federal district judge and whose nephew was Ambrose H. Sevier. With Pope gone and Crittenden dead, there could be no doubt that the Democratic faction would control the new state.

INDIAN REMOVAL

Accompanying Arkansas's march to statehood was the federal government's final solution to the problem of the southeastern Indian tribes and the local Quapaw. The largely empty lands of Arkansas tempted the more pressured southeastern tribes almost as much as it did land-hungry whites. Eventually, because the whites were overwhelming in number and militarily stronger, they won control of the region. Not only did the Cherokee and Choctaw find themselves victimized, but the native Quapaw, who had the best claim to permanence, were uprooted and nearly pushed to extinction.

Quapaw Removal

When the Americans took control of Louisiana, the Quapaw consisted of 575 men, women and children living in four villages, one of which contained Choctaw men with Quapaw wives. Anxious to conciliate the Indians, the government presented them with two hogsheads of tobacco and four barrels of whisky. Arkansas Post, renamed Fort Madison, received a garrison of a captain and sixteen soldiers. The Quapaw were not impressed and complained that the government ignored them.

At the outbreak of the War of 1812, federal troops stationed at Fort Madison were withdrawn, but some white settlers, fleeing possible danger elsewhere, took refuge at the Fort. According to the white squatters, the Quapaw and Choctaw were "daily in the habit of killing their cattle, hogs, and stealing horses, and committing personal abuse on the Inhabitants." While the whites called for restoring military protection, the government was considering plans to make the Trans-Mississippi the dumping ground for eastern Indians.

In May 1816, Missouri Governor William Clark sent David Musick and William Parker to order the white families living on the Quapaw lands to leave and scheduled a conference of Quapaw, Cherokee, and Osage chiefs. Nothing was decided at the conference, and as more Cherokees began to move west into Arkansas, the Osage responded to this invasion of the lands they considered

theirs by waging open warfare. The Quapaw sided with the Cherokee, and the desultory war occasioned great alarm among the few whites in Arkansas.

The government again addressed the western question in 1818. In order to obtain more lands to offer the eastern Indians, the government forced the Quapaw to give up all their claims to lands east of the Mississippi and north of the Arkansas River and their hunting lands in the west. What remained of their previous 30,000,000 acres was now a mere 2,000,000 located in southeastern Arkansas, the right to hunt in the west and a yearly annuity. Heckaton, one of the principal chiefs, got a military uniform to wear. Despite the loss of hunting land, the Quapaw had preserved a large area suitable for extensive agriculture.

The treaty proved to be little obstacle to white greed. In its first session, the Arkansas legislature petitioned the government to reduce the 2,000,000 acre tract to twelve square miles, and James Woodson Bates, the territorial delegate, pursued a consistently anti-Quapaw policy. Further, the government was late in paying the annuity, refused to provide a blacksmith, and when the Osage murdered three Quapaw hunters near Fort Smith, territorial secretary Crittenden instructed the Quapaw "to stay at home and tend their crops."

In addition, government surveyors misinterpreted the 1818 treaty and cut off some 800 square miles of Quapaw lands. When the discrepancy was pointed out, the government simply published a new version of the treaty, changing the language to coincide with the survey. The pressure increased in the following years. Crittenden, who called the Quapaw "a poor, indolent, miserable remnant of a nation, insignificant and inconsiderable," believed that they could be induced to sell out for $25,000. Congress took the suggestion that they be merged with the Caddo on the Red River and voted $7,500 for that purpose with the understanding that the Quapaw were anxious to resettle with the Caddo.

In fact, the Quapaw were determined to stay. In May 1824, Crittenden had met with the Indians, who reluctantly agreed to a reduction in their boundaries but insisted on staying. When word of the government's plans arrived, Crittenden recalled the Indians, and despite their pleas to remain, told them of the government's decision. In the formal agreement signed on November 15, 1824, the Quapaw gave up all their land, received no western land in recompense and were to merge with the Caddo. Secretary of War John C. Calhoun reputedly termed the treaty "the best ever made with an Indian tribe."

Although led to Louisiana by sub-agent Antoine Barraque, a French refugee whose wife was half Quapaw, the removal proved to be a disaster. The unsympathetic Caddo wanted no part of the Quapaw, and no arrangements had been made for their arrival. Established in three villages near the future site of Shreveport, the Quapaw planted their corn only to have two Red River floods wipe it out. Sixty died of starvation. One-fourth of the nation followed Saracen, a half-blood chief, back to Arkansas. The resulting scandal prompted Henry Conway to call for an investigation and the War Department to send relief supplies. Meanwhile, the tribe remained divided. The Saracen group petitioned to be allowed to become Americans, and when the Red River group was flooded out again, more Quapaw trickled back.

Although negotiations were reopened in 1830, when Heckaton journeyed all the way to Washington, the crisis remained unsolved. The Quapaw wanted to remain in Arkansas, but white farmers were expelling them from the newly reoccupied lands, while the ever hostile *Arkansas Gazette* furiously denounced them as "drunken vagabond savages." A new treaty in 1833 reassigned them to lands along the northwestern Arkansas border between the Senecas and Shawnees. Not all the Quapaws moved, as some preferred to stay in Arkansas and others were in Louisiana and later Texas. The reuniting of the various fragments of the Quapaw did not occur until the Arkansas Sesquicentennial in 1986.

Caddo Removal

Although the Caddo were one of the major tribes of early Arkansas, no Indian group played a smaller role in territorial and state affairs. The primary reason was that before 1800, the Osage already had expelled the Caddo from their villages north of Red River. Indeed, one Osage chief, He-sha-ke-he-ree, went by the English name of Caddo Killer. In 1819, the Caddo formed an alliance with the Choctaw to retaliate, but Governor Miller made the war party disperse.

White settlers so pressured the Caddo that on July 1, 1835, the tribe agreed to cede all their lands in Louisiana and Arkansas to the federal government and move west into Mexican-held Texas in exchange for $30,000. As with other Indian removals, tribal disintegration followed. By 1842, only 250 Caddo were reported left, and they were living in destitution with the Choctaw. In the early 1850s, the Caddo and some other peaceful and agricultural Indians settled on the Brazos River and prospered until encountering growing white hostility late in the decade. In 1859, the Caddo were removed a second time, this time north of the Red River into Indian Territory. During the Civil War many fled north to Union lines in Kansas, but the tribe regrouped after the War. By 1877, farming and stockraising were common, and one observer noted that "very few families are now living in the old grass houses." Some conservativism was still present, however, for Caddo John Wilson in the late nineteenth century was a leader in first the Ghost Dance movement and then in the Peyote religion.

INDIAN MIGRATIONS, 1800 - 1836

Ce - Cherokee
Cs - Chickasaw
Co - Choctaw
Cr - Creek

0   50 m.

Indian Migrations, 1800-1836. **Gerald T. Hanson.**

Cherokee Removal

The greatest controversy surrounded the Cherokee, a large tribe with an educated leadership, an advanced agriculture and eventually a written culture. The Cherokee began arriving in Arkansas in large numbers in 1817, forming that part of the nation known as "Cherokee West." Their settlements as defined by an 1817 treaty were restricted to northwestern Arkansas. Eventually more than 7,000 Indians settled in this area and engaged in both hunting and agriculture. In 1819, Nuttall compared their sturdy cabins and cleared fields to the slovenly practices of the French and Quapaw; only whisky was the Cherokee's big failing.

The lands occupied by the Cherokee also

were claimed as hunting grounds by the Osage, whose nearest settlement lay on the Verdigris River to the west. A fierce, strong and warlike people, the Osage promptly went to war with the Cherokee. The skirmishing back and forth, the ambushing of hunting parties and raids on the Quapaw made Arkansas a place of excitement and no small danger.

In response to the repeated cries of alarm, the government in 1817 sent engineer Major Stephen H. Long and commander Major William Bradford, who erected a military outpost at Belle Point. Named Fort Smith, the facility had a twisted history. The first fort was designed only for Bradford's some seventy men. When Colonel Matthew Arbuckle arrived in 1822 with additional men, the first fort was too small to serve. Accordingly, it was abandoned in 1824 in favor of a new establishment, subsequently known as Fort Gibson, on the Verdigris River farther west. In 1831, the army moved back to Fort Smith only to leave again three years later. Finally, in 1838, Fort Smith was reactivated and a permanent facility erected.

The Fort's purposes were twofold: policing the Indians and keeping the whites and Indians separated. There was certainly plenty to do to keep the military busy. One of Governor Miller's main tasks was to try to mediate the dispute between the Osage and Cherokee. To this end, he met at Dardanelle under the Council Oaks with the Cherokee and journeyed to the Verdigris to negotiate with the Osage. But it was all in vain. Osage cattle rustling continued to disturb the frontier, although Major Bradford courted popularity by managing to avoid calling the militia into service.

Meanwhile, white settlement into the west continued despite the flareups. The Osage ceded their claims in Arkansas in 1824. That left up in the air the Cherokee claim to land that was an outlet to the West guaranteed to them by previous treaties but which now was

being settled by whites. Arkansas created Lovely County northwest of Fort Smith in 1827. It was named in honor of William L. Lovely, who bought the land from the Osage that the government had promised to the Cherokee. The Cherokee hastened to protest this action, and Nu-tah-R-Tuhh wrote a letter "to the man who makes the paper talk every week at Little Rock" reciting the justice of the Cherokee position and observing that the Cherokee maintained a higher standard of living than the frontier whites. Because the federal government was anxious to move the Cherokee out of Georgia, away from a confrontation with the state government, and open the supposedly rich gold mines to white exploitation, the western Cherokee held a strong bargaining position.

In the end, a compromise was reached under which the Cherokee gave up their Arkansas lands in return for undisputed possession of their western claim. There was some opposition to the treaty in the Senate. Missouri's Thomas Hart Benton argued that because it bordered Mexico, Arkansas should be as large as possible, but a boundary line drawn due south from Missouri's western edge would result in a weak state. Although Sevier also opposed the treaty, there was little opposition in Arkansas, even in Lovely County, for residents were compensated with lands elsewhere. Accordingly, Lovely County was abolished in 1828, and the Cherokee moved west again from Arkansas. Dwight Mission, located on the west bank of Illinois Bayou and one of the earliest missionary education endeavors in the west, followed the Cherokee move.

Choctaw Removal

A different obstacle was presented south of the Arkansas River. Under an 1820 treaty, the Choctaw were to move from east of the Mississippi to western Arkansas, where they were given a reservation consisting of nearly one-third of the western part of the present state. There was considerable opposition to this treaty, beginning with Delegate Bates, who pointed out that the threatened area was the most populated part of Arkansas. Governor Miller, joining the chorus, estimated that one-third of the white population resided in the disputed area. That one of the commissioners for the Choctaw treaty was presidential hopeful Andrew Jackson was not forgotten subsequently in Arkansas. The unpopularity of the treaty also hurt the political career of James Woodson Bates.

In response to the pressure, Secretary of War John C. Calhoun promised a new treaty. Finally, in 1823, Congress appropriated money to buy out part of the Choctaw claims. This treaty made the western boundary of Arkansas a southern extension of the Missouri western line. Arkansas again protested, claiming that from 1,200 to 2,000 persons would still be dispossessed. Responding to pressure, Congress shifted the line forty miles west. In turn the Choctaw protested and won partial compensation. When James S. Conway, the surveyor, measured the line, he moved it even more to the west, taking additional land away from the Indians. The Choctaw eventually became suspicious of the survey, and after several false starts, discovered they had been swindled out of 136,204.02 acres. In 1886, the government reluctantly paid them a paltry 50 cents an acre.

Late in the Spanish period, miscellaneous bands of Delaware, Shawnee and Cherokee began filtering into Arkansas and settling along the eastern streams, frequently on old mounds. These settlements bore a bad reputation as whites charged the Indians with cattle stealing and robbery. During the 1820s and 1830s the Indians' titles were extinguished, and the tribes were moved farther west. An Izard County group of Indians forced out in 1833 was among the last formally expelled from the Territory. Usually the process was peaceful, but in one instance, the Miller County militia had to be called out to speed the removal of some of the Red River parties. Despite government policy, individual Indians either remained behind in Arkansas or came back across the border and settled. One 1844 petition from Saline County demanded that a Creek be expelled, asserting, among other things, that his ties to the county's free blacks were too close. Arkansas court records are surprisingly full of cases involving whites and Indians and many Arkansas families boast of a "Cherokee grandmother."

THE SIGNIFICANCE OF THE WESTERN BOUNDARY

Fixing Arkansas's western boundary and dispossessing the Indians did not end Arkansas's involvement with Indian affairs. The federal government's relocation plans for the eastern Indians led to a series of removals, which in the case of the Cherokee became known as the Trail of Tears. This uprooting was equally hard for the Creeks, relocated in 1827-1829 and in 1835-1836, and for the Choctaw, who passed through in 1831-1833 and in 1835. Sickness was a major problem among the poorer Indians, and the failure of government contractors to provide adequate food led to charges that the Indians stole from whites. On the other hand, many local whites made good money on these contracts by selling their agricultural surplus.

The location of so many wards of the government on the western border led to the development of the town of Fort Smith. Captain John Rogers, an early merchant, conceived of connections with Santa Fe, but in reality Fort Smith became a service center for the Indians, providing illegal whisky, gamblers and more prostitutes than any other town in Arkansas, as well as political employment for Indian agents, lawyers and other

Arkansas Counties, 1836. **Gerald T. Hanson.**

minor figures in the patronage game.

On the positive side, it was Fort Smith editor John F. Wheeler, brother-in-law of Cherokee leader Stand Watie, who cast the type when Sequoyah (George H. Guess), the former salt springs operator, created an alphabet and hence a written language for the Cherokee. Cherokee leader Elias Cornelius Boudinot practiced law and edited newspapers in Fayetteville and Little Rock. Sophie Sawyer's girls' school at Fayetteville drew heavily from a Cherokee clientele.

Among the numerous important nineteenth-century Arkansas politicians and society leaders who had extensive contacts among the civilized tribes were saltmakers Mark and Richard Bean; William M. Quesenbury, an early painter and poet; Cephas Washburn, a missionary to the Cherokee from 1828 to 1840 and later a minister in Arkansas; and Washburn's son, Edward, who painted the *Arkansas Traveler*. The prime significance of the Indian removals and the establishment of the western boundary was that it made Arkansas a small state by Western standards. Given the swampy nature of the eastern part, only the western acres attracted immigrants. A boundary line reaching to the plains—about 100 miles west of the current line—would have made Arkansas much more of a Western state, greatly enhanced the mineral resources, and eventually given Arkansas sufficient oil to rank among the leading states in the South. But without the western area, Arkansas was left with only a portion of the Ouachitas and the poorest part of the Ozarks. The Indians formed a permanent barrier to trade and westward expansion on the western border. No "Gateway to the West," such as Missouri boasted, would be Arkansas's lot. Instead, the boundary decisions crippled the Territory and thwarted the development of the state.

CONCLUSION

Arkansas became a territory and achieved statehood more for external than internal reasons. For political reasons it was decided that Arkansas would be a slave state and that decision brought about tragic consequences that have not been overcome even to this day. White settlement increased rapidly, but the location of the western boundary worked a hardship on future development. The decision to plant the Indians on the western border retarded economic development throughout the nineteenth century. Politically, Arkansas exhibited the violence and extreme partisanship typical of a western territory. Factional politics based on personality dominated, although substantive issues were nevertheless present. Perhaps most importantly, Arkansas began to be perceived in the national mind as a place remote from civilization. Headline events about duels and border skirmishes contributed to what in time would be called the Arkansas image problem.

BIBLIOGRAPHIC ESSAY

The basic documentary sources are in Clarence E. Carter, ed., *The Territorial Papers of the United States: The Territory of Arkansas,* XIX, XX, XXI (Washington, 1953-1954). Although Arkansas scholars have failed to study the cattle frontier, Frank L. Owsley, *Plain Folk of the Old South,* (Baton Rouge, 1949), a seminal book in Southern history, contains Arkansas references. Early commerce is discussed in Wayne Morris, "Traders and Factories on the Arkansas Frontier, 1805-1822," *AHQ,* XXII (Winter 1973), 312-336. Some early Hopefield history is recorded in David O. Demuth, "The Burning of Hopefield," *AHQ,* XXXVI (Summer 1977), 123-129; while Margaret S. Ross, "Cadron: An Early Town That Failed," XVI (Spring 1957), 3-27, sheds light on that settlement.

A detailed study of Arkansas land speculations is much needed, although evidence of activity is everywhere. Lonnie J. White, *Politics on the Southwestern Frontier: Arkansas Territory, 1819-1836,* (Memphis, 1964), and his numerous articles in the *AHQ* provide a modern overview. Margaret S. Ross, *Arkansas Gazette: The Early Years, 1819-1866,* (Little Rock, 1969), offers more than just an institutional history. Tom W. Dillard, "An Arduous Task to Perform: Organizing the Territorial Arkansas Militia," *AHQ,* XLI (Summer 1982), 174-190, shows how that institution failed. Few individuals left memoirs from this period, but William F. Pope, *Early Days in Arkansas, Being for the Most Part a Personal Recollection of an Old Settler,* (Little Rock, 1895), is entertaining although not always accurate.

Indian affairs have always fascinated students of history. Grant Foreman remains the standard authority, notably in "Indian Removal: The Emigration of the Five Civilized Tribes of Indians," (Norman, Okla., 1932). Also useful for the Arkansas scene is Ginger L. Ashcraft, "Antoine Barraque and His Involvement in Indian Affairs of Southeast Arkansas, 1816-1832," *AHQ*, XXXII (Autumn 1973), 226-240. The Arkansas Cherokee have received increasing attention. Robert P. Markham, "The Arkansas Cherokee," (Ph. D. diss., University of Oklahoma, 1972) is a useful over-all study. A valuable summary is Edward E. Dale, "Arkansas and the Cherokees," *AHQ*, VIII (Summer 1949), 95-114, and Ted R. Worley, "Arkansas and the 'Hostile' Indians, 1835-1838," *AHQ*, VI (Summer 1947), 155-164, showed how violence was manipulated for political purposes. Also valuable is Daniel F. Littlefield, Jr., and Lonnie E. Underhill, "The Cherokee Agency Reserve, 1828-1886," *AHQD*, XXXI (Summer 1972), 166-180.

Fort Smith has been a familiar theme. The best history is Ed Bearss and Arrell M. Gibson, *Fort Smith: Little Gibraltar on the Arkansas,* (Norman, Okla., 1969). Special studies of value include Elsa Vaught, "Captain John Rogers: Founder of Fort Smith," *AHQ*, XVII (Autumn 1958), 239-264; James N. Haskett, "The Final Chapters in the Story of the First Fort Smith," *AHQ*, XXV (Autumn 1966), 214-228, and for interpretation, W. David Baird, "Fort Smith and the Red Man," *AHQ*, XXX (Winter 1971), 337-348. Nearby Lovely County is treated in Ina Gabler, " Lovely's Purchase and Lovely County," *AHQ*, XIX (Spring 1960), 31-45. W. David Baird, "Arkansas' Choctaw Boundary: A Study of Justice Delayed," *AHQ*, XXVIII (Autumn 1969), 203-222, details one sordid aspect. Cephas Washburn, *Reminiscences of the Indians,* (Richmond, VA., 1869; reprinted, Van Buren, 1955) remains the essential memoir.

The State Bank *(artist and date unknown) Although this building was used only briefly as a bank, it served as an important source of office space until sometime after the Civil War.* **Arkansas History Commission**

Chapter IV

Flush Times and Hard Days

INTRODUCTION

The territorial period left a legacy of intensely personal politics. Factions contested every election, and newspapers served primarily to unite and inform a candidate's friends of the evil actions being taken on the other side.

Once Arkansas entered the Union, national issues came into play. From 1828 to 1836, the Democratic Party of Thomas Jefferson was captured by that wild Westerner, Andrew Jackson. His opponents, led by Henry Clay of Kentucky, formed the Whigs in opposition. With the rebirth of a national two-party system and with a two-faction system already in place in Arkansas, it was simply a matter of timing, family and luck that led the supporters of Robert Crittenden to become Whigs and the Sevier-Conway-Johnson connection to latch on to the Party then called Democracy.

Andrew Jackson was the kind of hero to catch the imagination of Arkansas voters, and that appeal was transferred to Martin Van Buren in the first presidential election in which Arkansans participated. However, the states' rights policies of the Jacksonians hurt Arkansas economically when most federal assistance for internal improvements stopped. In addition, Jackson had destroyed the Bank of the United States, which through its manipulation of credit had kept rein on the economy. By placing federal money in "pet banks," Jackson fueled an already overheated economy.

From 1836 to 1842, Arkansas experienced a high level of prosperity known in the Southwest as "Flush Times." After 1842, Arkansas was hit by a national depression compounded locally by the folly of the state creating two unsupervised wildcat banks. Their crash led to more than financial embarrassment: traditionalists captured power as Arkansas voters resolutely rejected modernization. The Mexican War and the California Gold Rush provided outlets for escape that many chose.

THE POLITICS OF PROSPERITY

For the first six years of statehood, Arkansas prospered as land values rose, cities were platted and immigrants hastened to find their destinies. In this atmosphere, the main political question was how best the state government could aid the development process.

Whigs

The state Whig Party traced its roots to friends and associates of Robert Crittenden. Nationally, Whigs stood for modernization, supporting the Bank of the United States in order to achieve a stable currency and controlled economic growth. Whigs believed that internal improvements financed by the federal government would bring the nation together through better communication and transportation. Henry Clay, the author of the "American System" and Party war horse, captured the imagination of the people. Many fathers bestowed his name on their male children. Typical Whig hallmarks were superior formal education, a commitment to economic development and conservative social behavior. More likely than Democrats to live in a frame or brick home, Whigs were often Presbyterian.

Arkansas Whigs came from two backgrounds. Those living in the northwest and central parts of the state were from the mer-

chant class. They dominated towns like Little Rock, Fayetteville and Batesville in city elections and drew additional support from progressive farmers. The other center of Whig strength was the planter class in the Delta and southwest. Unfortunately, intrastate factionalism and the lack of a common economic interest so afflicted the Whigs that, as one Party member commented, "sometimes the north has presented an unbroken front; and then again, the south; but never both at once."

Statistically, Whigs were richer than Democrats. Real estate holdings of sixty identifiable Whig leaders in 1850 exceeded those of ninety-seven comparable Democrats by about 200 percent ($8,260 compared to $3,387). Whigs also owned more slaves; 38 percent of the Whigs owned twenty or more slaves compared to 24 percent of the Democrats. Despite the Party's failure in Arkansas, Whiggery proved to be persistent, for it outlived its Party as a way of thought.

The Democrats

Andrew Jackson was an appealing but contradictory symbol for the Democratic Party in Arkansas. Although Jackson and his Party nationally appealed to small farmers and workingmen, Jackson himself and Arkansas leaders were actually speculators and planters. The Seviers, Conways and Johnsons owned extensive plantation lands, sent their children east to school and rode in carriages. Even Archibald Yell, who alone had the common touch and railed at speculators in his speeches, invested in Red River lands with James K. Polk of Tennessee, and with Whig David Walker, created the speculative town of Ozark in Franklin County. Nationally, Jacksonians retarded modernization by their adherence to a states' rights philosophy and by dismantling the national banking system. Locally, Democrats and Whigs were associated equally in the state banking experiment. Yet the national Democratic

Party did win support in Arkansas for its policy of Indian removal and by trying to deny abolitionists the use of the mails.

The Dynasty or "Family"

At the center of the Democratic Party in Arkansas stood a kinship connection known as the Dynasty or "Family." The Rectors and Conways were cousins, and Ambrose H. Sevier, whose mother was a Conway and whose grandmother was a Rector, married the daughter of Benjamin Johnson. Sevier, a New York paper noted, was "one of those rough and tumble geniuses which no country can produce but ours, and in ours, only the extreme western portion." Most "Family" members were not geniuses, but many shared that rough-and-tumble character. Occasionally, marriage crossed party lines, for Whig Congressman Thomas W. Newton was the father-in-law of Democratic editor Richard H. Johnson.

Family connection provided an entry into politics, usually at a young age, and Democrats benefited from the national Party's control of the White House at the time of Arkansas's admission to the Union and during most of the antebellum period.

The key to "Family" control lay in masterly inactivity. Debates on the tariff, slavery in the territories, public lands, banking policy, internal improvements and obnoxious foreigners were carried on with great vigor and no little sophistry, but without much meaning. Picnics and parades competed with irrelevant rhetoric while, behind the scenes, courthouse cliques made the important decisions. In comparison to other American states, Arkansas displayed a type of political control that was far more common fifty years earlier when deference to established leaders was the hallmark of voter attitudes rather than the tough, independent-minded agrarian democracy supposedly characteristic of the age of Andrew Jackson.

James Sevier Conway (photographer and date unknown) Conway was a surveyor of the southwestern boundary of Arkansas, a land speculator and the least politically inclined of the "Family." He was born in Tennessee and well educated by frontier standards. The state's first governor, he was a strong supporter of education, but had no luck influencing the legislature. After 1840, he retired to his plantation in the Red River Valley. **Arkansas History Commission**

The First State Elections

Once Arkansas became a state, voters could choose a governor and one congressman. The Democrats nominated James Sevier Conway for governor and Archibald Yell for Congress in 1836. Conway was a Red River Valley planter and Yell resided in Fayetteville. Their Whig opponents, Absalom Fowler and William Cummins, both Little Rock lawyers, lacked strong personal appeal. Yell carried the ticket, polling 6,094 votes to Cummins's 2,379, while the aristocratic Conway won by a less decisive margin of 1,831 over Fowler. The secret of Yell's success lay in his charismatic ability to out-shoot and out-pray his opponents, thereby receiving the vote of the common man.

The first legislature chose Arkansas's first two U.S. senators. Whig newspapers attempted to drive a wedge between the Democrats, but the distribution of offices already had been taken care of at a quiet meeting. William S. Fulton received one seat as the price for his cooperation with the statehood movement, and Ambrose H. Sevier had inherited the mantle of the fallen Henry W. Conway, killed in his duel with Critten-den. The legislature also chose the three Supreme Court judges: Townsend Dickinson, Daniel Ringo and Thomas J. Lacy, all with little opposition. William E. Woodruff became the state treasurer. In November, voters participated for the first time in a national election, and by 2,557 to 1,363, Arkansas's vote went to Democrat Martin Van Buren over the Whig Hugh Lawson White. Some reflected glory descended on Arkansas by the election of Kentucky's Colonel Richard Mentor Johnson, the brother of Federal District Judge Benjamin Johnson, as vice-president. More persons voted in the state election than in the presidential race, a pattern that continued long into Arkansas history.

Two-Party Politics

The election of Yell to Congress and Sevier to the Senate in 1836 actually gave them terms that expired on March 3, 1837. Sevier's problem was overcome by a reappointment by Governor Conway and his reelection at the next session of the legislature. Yell's case was more complicated. On June 5, 1837, the Governor called for a special election to be held July 3, 1837, to fill the vacancy. Although Yell won without opposition, Whigs argued that this election only permitted Yell to attend the current special session. Yell agreed to run again in October, and by defeating Whig John Ringgold of Batesville, made his third victorious statewide race in fourteen months, all for the same office.

Although Whigs did not capture a major state office, they did possess the power to embarrass the Democrats in the legislature. William E. Woodruff, the state treasurer, who because of the Panic of 1837 experienced great difficulties in collecting money due the state from the federal government, was harassed consistently by the Whigs. His defense, submitted as a communication to the legislature, was refused because of disrespectful language. Samuel C. Roane and William McK. Ball, the compilers of the new state code, experienced difficulty getting paid. There were significant objections to their work, for Roane and Ball had added laws from other states that they thought ought to be enforced in Arkansas, and Albert Pike, in editing the code, had deviated still further. Eventually the book was adopted, any laws to the contrary notwithstanding. However, the legislature took the printing of the code away from Woodruff and gave it to Albert Pike, even though Pike had to go to Boston to get the work done.

Yell chose not to seek reelection in 1838. Judge Edward Cross of Hempstead County, the brother-in-law of Chester Ashley's wife, defeated Whig William Cummins. Governor Conway two years later declined renomination, some said because he feared a challenge from Yell. At any rate, Yell was the Democratic gubernatorial nominee in 1840, winning without opposition, while Cross defeated Absalom Fowler. Nationally, 1840 was the year in which the Whigs nominated William Henry Harrison, who had been governor in 1804 when Arkansas was assigned to Indiana Territory. The Whigs made Harrison into a popular hero on the scale of Andrew Jackson, organizing a Tippecanoe Club in Little Rock and building a log cabin. A generous supply of hard cider insured a large crowd, but despite the brave show, Martin Van Buren carried Arkansas with 6,679 votes to Harrison's 5,160.

Nationally, the Panic of 1837 had been followed by a depression that spread gloom and doom over the Eastern states and was moving slowly west. It had not reached Arkansas when polling took place or the state might have gone Whig.

FLUSH TIMES

Arkansas prospered during the first years of statehood. Governor Conway in 1837 reported that the state had a surplus of $50,000. Modernizers called for using the money to establish what Chicot County Representative A. H. Davies styled the "University of Arkansas." Traditionalists retaliated by ridiculing the idea of higher education, indeed of tax-supported education at all, and the legislature voted a tax cut. The state did spend $45,000 constructing a state penitentiary located on a prominent hill just west of town, and the federal government contributed to the building boom by erecting a new fort at Fort Smith and an arsenal at Little Rock. The magnificently designed state bank building gave yet another notable public building to the capital as brick masons, plasterers and carpenters found ready employment.

The federal government continued some internal improvements. Captain Henry N. Shreve succeeded in 1838 in clearing a temporary channel through the Red River raft, a backup of logs and debris that heretofore had rendered the stream nearly useless for transportation by Arkansas planters. The result was a boom in Red River lands, for cotton could now be marketed directly to New Orleans. Finally, even if the state legislature remained in the control of traditionalists, it did let private parties have ready access to state incorporation. Each session brought forth new charters proposing the building of roads, railroads, canals, schools and manufacturing concerns.

Arkansas's First Banking Experiment

When Westerners surveyed their prospects in the early 1820s and 1830s, they almost invariably concluded that a want of ready capital retarded growth. America from colonial days had been capital shy, because men invested heavily in land with the expectation of future sales at a good profit. "Land poor," long a popular expression in Arkansas, meant that a man had more land than cash. On the frontier, the most speculative individuals pushed the cutting edge between profit and loss to a very fine point.

Thus, the crash of 1819 actually had spurred settlement in Arkansas when some Missouri prodigals found it expedient to leave their debts behind and seek prosperity in a new land. To generate a larger supply of money, speculators pushed for the creation of state banks that would both loan money on easy terms, and circumventing the federal Constitution, print bank notes that would increase the money supply. In the first session of the state legislature, Arkansas joined the ranks of those states that experimented in financial legerdemain.

The 1836 Constitution authorized the legislature to charter two banks. The first, "to provide long-term credit to farmers and planters," was the Real Estate Bank. The other, the State Bank, was designed for the state's merchant community. Both received state assistance in the form of direct cash subsidies bearing the faith and credit of the state. Yet both were exempt from any meaningful state control.

The Real Estate Bank

The Real Estate Bank began business with

Ambrose H. Sevier (*artist unknown*) *This drawing from Hallum's* Biographical and Pictorial History of Arkansas (*Albany, 1887*) *suggests the force of personality that Sevier exerted during his twenty years of power in Arkansas.* **University of Arkansas at Little Rock**

the proceeds from the sale of $1,500,000 in state bonds. In return for receiving this money, the Bank promised to pay the interest and principal as it came due. Senator Sevier forced the Smithsonian Institution in Washington, D.C., to purchase 500 of the thousand-dollar bonds, and another thousand were taken by the North American Bank and Trust Company of New York.

With $1,500,000 in hand, the main office opened in Little Rock on December 12, 1838, and branches went into business at Washington, Columbia, Helena and Van Buren. In addition to its state-supplied capital, the Bank sold stock. The main inducement for buying into the Bank was that one could bor-

row up to half the stock's value. From the beginning, no one doubted whom the Bank was intended to aid. A Chicot County representative wrote the bank bill, and of the 22,500 shares of stock, 6,286 shares (30 percent) went to twenty-eight Chicot County residents.

Under this planter-run bank, loans were easy to obtain and land was the usual security. Bank officials often failed to check closely on their customers. Very generous estimates on land values gave an inflated and unrealistic picture of individual worth. Senator Sevier, for instance, mortgaged 1,084 acres as security for a $15,000 loan. The appraisers rated his land at $32,000, but the tax assessor figured it at only $13,975.

The State Bank

The State Bank, as the name implied, was an entirely state-managed affair with its officers elected by the General Assembly. This institution faced considerable difficulty getting started. The first bond issue, advertised as paying 5 percent, failed to sell in a depressed bond market, so a second offering at 6 percent became necessary. In addition, the Bank was given all the money due the state from the sale of seminary lands, leasing of salt springs and the 5 percent of proceeds that the federal government returned to the state from the sale of federal land. A final bonus was an early version of revenue sharing: Arkansas's share of the federal surplus created when the Jackson administration paid off the national debt. State Treasurer William E. Woodruff's great difficulty in collecting these federal funds produced the first internal difficulties in the state's Democratic Party. Even so, the Bank went into operation with a central office in Little Rock and branches at Batesville, Fayetteville and Arkansas Post.

Banking Collapse

The timing of these two banking ventures had much to do with their disastrous collapse in 1839. In the beginning, both institutions were redeeming all their paper notes at face value in gold or silver. Because the amount of paper that both banks issued soon far exceeded their specie reserves, they relied on customer good will and a certain amount of manipulation in order to avoid runs. One way to encourage the use of notes was to have them issued by one branch and distributed at others, thereby making redemption expensive.

Such techniques were of no use in the hard times that beset the nation in 1839. Before 1836, the Bank of the United States, a federally chartered institution, had kept close rein on state banks, virtually dictating how much paper money they could issue. Andrew Jackson, who destroyed the Bank, began the disastrous policy of placing federal money in selected local institutions. These "pet banks" then used these new resources to increase the money supply, fueling the Flush Times of the old Southwest and bringing eager would-be planters to Arkansas to speculate, invest and borrow.

In order to give speculators credit, Arkansas's banks were first created, then unsoundly managed and finally allowed to engage in wildcat money production. When an alarmed Jackson finally responded with the Specie Circular requiring gold or silver for federal land payments, a run started that brought financial ruin to the overextended.

The first to fall was the State Bank. The Bank had debts of almost $2,000,000 by 1839. As public confidence in banking sagged, holders of Bank notes presented them for conversion to specie. The Arkansas Post branch suspended specie payment on October 31, 1839, and the other branches and the main bank followed. Instead of retrenching, the Bank began to issue even more paper money. By 1843 some $750,000 in Bank notes were in circula-

tion. Without the backing of hard currency, the public refused to accept them except at large discounts, eventually as low as 30 cents on the dollar.

An 1842 investigation revealed that the Bank had made unsound loans and could not pay the interest on the state bonds as required by law. In addition, at Fayetteville cashier William McK. Ball hid the account books. When they finally were discovered, some pages were missing, as was Ball, who under the cover of darkness ran his slaves off to Texas and started a new life for himself farther west.

The state banking system was declared insolvent in 1843 and placed in the hands of receivers, who then attempted to collect on a few of the old debts. Many more then joined the rush to Texas. Between September 21 and October 24 of 1843, more than 300 suits were filed against the Bank's principal officers in Little Rock. Efforts to collect continued throughout the antebellum era. By November 2, 1855, 400 suits were filed in Batesville alone. Lawsuits failed to recover the losses, and by October 1858, only $740,338.68 had been collected from a debt of $1,112,172.49.

Part of the problem was that the depression sent commodity prices and land values plummeting even as the money supply dried up. The expensive brick structure in Little Rock erected to house the main bank cost $28,000 and sold for $200; the Batesville office, valued at $2,000, went for $25. Overall, the Bank had $66,500 invested in fixtures and buildings; it realized only $1,200 from the liquidation.

The collapse of the Real Estate Bank paralleled that of the State Bank. Two days after the State Bank suspended specie payment, the Real Estate Bank followed suit. It also printed even more paper money, going from $153,910 to $328,400 in just two months. By May 1840, the Bank had issued $759,000 in notes, which were discounted 40 percent.

Meanwhile, as customers were unable to pay the Bank, it had difficulty making its payments. On January 1, 1840, in a desperate effort to stay afloat, the Bank illegally sold 500 state thousand-dollar bonds to the North American Bank and Trust Co. for $121,336 in specie.

This small amount of gold and silver failed to help, and in July 1841, the Real Estate Bank closed its doors. Meanwhile, the New York bank sold the state bonds to London banker James Holford for $325,000. These bonds, commonly called the Holford Bonds, became one of the most controversial issues in Arkansas for the rest of the century.

Unlike the State Bank, which was controlled by the General Assembly, the Real Estate Bank was largely free from state interference even though the state was liable for its debts. In taking bankruptcy in 1841, the board of the Bank turned the institution's affairs over to receivers of their own choosing. Thus the Bank continued to do business in such a way as to bring little embarrassment to its creditors while paying nothing on the money owed the state. By 1848, the Bank was listing liabilities of more than $2,500,000 and assets of only $900,000.

While receiver Albert Pike was building a splendid mansion, others, especially from the yeoman class, were growing restive. A most dramatic episode occurred in 1837 in the first session of the legislature to meet in the new Capitol. During a debate on a bill to increase the bounty paid on wolves, J.J. Anthony, an obscure Randolph County representative, proposed that Speaker John Wilson, who was also president of the Real Estate Bank, certify each pelt. Speaker Wilson responded by ruling the motion out of order and telling Anthony to take his seat. When Anthony refused, Wilson left the chair, drew his Bowie knife, and rushed on to the floor. In the struggle that followed, Anthony used his knife to wound Wilson, but Wilson knocked Anthony down and then plunged his knife into the fallen legislator, killing him on the spot. "It is not the first time he has insulted me," Wilson proclaimed as he christened the Capitol in blood.

Bank critics refused to let the matter die, and Wilson, expelled from the legislature, was acquitted of murder in a trial at Benton that many considered a farce. Thereafter he moved to Pike County and in 1842 was back in the legislature. During another debate on the Bank, Dr. Lorenzo Gibson, a leading Whig, offered remarks that again infuriated Wilson, who once more sprang forth armed. This time a large body of men gathered around both men, and bloodshed was averted.

It was hard to make a political issue out of the Bank troubles, for Real Estate Bank officials consisted of eighty-three Democrats and fifty-six Whigs. Nevertheless, small farmers whose land and future taxes constituted the bulwark of the faith and credit of the state felt betrayed by their leaders. Archibald Yell, who drew his support largely from this class, began criticizing the Banks in 1842 when, as governor, he complained that their reports were "too often calculated to mislead and deceive." Others continued to agitate, but it was not until 1855 that state officials wrestled control from Real Estate Bank receivers and began a serious plan of liquidation, a policy that voters repudiated in the 1860 gubernatorial election.

Meanwhile, the depression that had hit the East earlier arrived full force in Arkansas. "Distress, ruin, and embarrassment pervade every village, neighborhood, and family," the *Arkansas Gazette* reported. Unwilling to be deprived of their property, armed men in Phillips County prevented a sheriff's sale. Many chose not to fight, and converting what they could to cash, headed west for Texas.

In the wake of the collapse, the state legislature in 1844 adopted the first amendment to the constitution: "No bank or banking institution shall be hereafter incorporated, or established in the State." Besides banning banks, others talked of repudiating the debt. State tax revenues dropped so sharply with hard times that taxes failed to pay even normal expenses. Although the state was liable for the bonds that were properly issued, Governor Yell pointed out that the Holford Bonds had been sold for less than face value in violation of the law and were a "fraud upon the State and stockholders." Yell promised to "resist all attempts from any quarter for the collection of either principal or interest." Yet Yell was unwilling to push matters, and many simply hoped for a miracle to get the state free from its entangling debt. The new amendment was one major obstacle.

After the Panic of 1837, most states abandoned experiments in public banking but allowed private parties operating under state law to engage in "free" banking. Arkansas would not allow this, so the state remained capital starved, with the traditionalists in firm control. Another example of the new attitude came when Yell refused to appoint a state geologist, thus denying the public accurate information about Arkansas's resources.

The banking amendment and the failure to appoint a geologist reflected a new reality. Progress had been tried, and it had failed. Those who supported the Banks had become embarrassed financially and had imposed on others by involving the state government in their speculative ventures.

HARD TIMES POLITICS

The economic downturn that came too late to affect the 1840 elections surfaced in 1842 when Congressman Cross drew not only the opposition of Whig William Cummins but that of dissident Democrat Lemuel Evans. Evans, a maverick Jacksonian, failed to keep Cross from winning and then joined the ranks of those leaving for Texas. At home, Democrats who had defended the Bank found it rough going. Newly elected "tenderfoot Democrats," as Ambrose Sevier called

them, had the temerity to inquire into the Bank failures. Because such a course was likely to prove embarrassing to Sevier, he was reelected quickly before committee investigations revealed that the Senator had converted Bank money to his private use and loaned Bank funds to some Arkansans in New York. Sevier, who had marketed the Real Estate Bonds in the East, paid himself and a colleague $5,000 for this work and then hired an agent for an additional $5,000. By the time the report came out, Sevier was on his way back to Washington and the Whigs had lost a potent political weapon.

The political defense of Sevier was in the hands of William E. Woodruff of the *Arkansas Gazette*. The legislature had become increasingly hostile to the New York native, and besides investigating Sevier, this nominally Democratic body gave the state printing to the Whig *Times and Advocate*. In addition, a judgment remained against Woodruff for his alleged mishandling of state funds while treasurer. Disgusted by legislative hostility and resentful of Party neglect, Woodruff, claiming that his financial needs were pressing, sold the *Gazette* to the Whig Benjamin Borden in 1842.

The Whigs made political capital as the Democrats pooled their funds and started a new paper. Solon Borland, a sometime Memphis editor, doctor, and lawyer, arrived from Louisville to edit the *Arkansas Banner*.

Borland, the author of the state's first medical treatise, stuck verbal needles into Whig editor Borden, who replied in kind. When Borden called Borland's courage "that virtue to which he has the least claims, Borland assaulted Borden on the streets of Little Rock. As Woodruff reported to Senator Fulton, "the doctor used Ben. pretty roughly" having beaten his face into a jelly, and "bro't the claret with every blow." The two men then met in a duel west of Fort Smith. At the command of fire, Borden's pistol accidentally discharged into the ground. Borland then took careful

Chester Ashley and His Wife, Mary Ashley *(photographer and date unknown) The personality of this wily speculator and devious politician is muted in this domestic photograph. The two look like characters from a Charles Dickens novel.* **University of Arkansas at Little Rock**

son's son, Robert Ward, for Congress. Nominated by a state convention in which only sixteen of the forty-two counties were represented, Conway and Johnson encountered opposition from independents Richard C. Byrd and Lewis B. Tully. To heal the split, the Party called a new convention at which both Conway and Johnson withdrew, and Dr. Daniel J. Chapman and Archibald Yell took their respective places. When Chapman withdrew because of illness, Thomas S. Drew took his place. Both new candidates represented the yeoman interest, for Drew, although a political infant, was at that time from the northern part of the state.

The 1844 contest was the highwater mark of the two-party system in Arkansas. Both Whigs and Democrats were now as fully formed as they were ever to be. Issues in state government about banking and retrenchment had arisen, and the 1844 presidential candidates, Henry Clay for the Whigs and James K. Polk, "Young Hickory," for the Democrats, inspired loyalty. Both had Arkansas ties: Clay's brother was an Arkansas minister, and Polk owned land in the Red River Valley.

The 1844 election marked the first statewide exposure for Chester Ashley. This prince of speculators, whose land deals were both legendary and dubious, had heretofore been a cautious participant in politics. C.F.M. Noland suggested this reticence was attributable to some hold that his enemy Wharton

aim and felled his opponent with a bullet just four inches from the heart. Borden's wound was not fatal and both men returned to Little Rock to continue their war of words.

In 1844, state Whigs nominated Dr. Lorenzo Gibson for governor and David Walker for Congress against the divided Democrats. The Dynasty choices for office were Elias N. Conway for governor and Judge Benjamin John-

Rector held over Ashley. But with Rector dead, Ashley emerged in the campaign as a presidential elector. His Whig counterpart, Alfred Arrington, although an eloquent speaker and later a noted novelist, was a defrocked Methodist minister with a sordid sexual reputation.

Ashley's hopes of advancement rose rapidly in August when incumbent Senator Fulton died, supposedly from having slept in a freshly painted room. Because both Yell and Ashley wanted the Senate seat, the fall campaign took on a new intensity. Ashley's most potent friend was William E. Woodruff, and as the legislature and not the voters chose the senators, Yell's charisma gave him no particular advantage. While Ashley was carrying the state for Polk and Drew was winning with less than a majority of the votes, Yell was conducting his most famous campaign, outsinging Walker at a revival one moment, winning a shooting contest the next and handily defeating him in the end.

The victorious Democrats gave Ashley the remainder of Fulton's Senate term, supposedly upon on strength of his promise not to seek reelection in 1846 when the term expired. Sevier was vindicated by the removal of his censure voted by a previous legislature and had tendered to him a statement of thanks for his conduct of the Bank affairs. Editor Borland became adjutant general of the militia. Only Woodruff, who was unable to get his financial affairs adjusted, failed to benefit.

It was apparent by 1845 that both Yell and Ashley had eyes on the 1846 Senate race. Borland was solidly in the Yell camp, but Ashley had no success in luring Governor Drew over to his side. On the other hand, Ashley did obtain the appointment of Woodruff as postmaster despite Yell's hostility. Woodruff returned the favor by beginning the publication of a new paper, the *Arkansas State Democrat*.

Arkansas in the Mexican War

The outbreak of the Mexican War in May 1846 momentarily pushed politics into the background. Arkansas was called on to furnish one cavalry regiment for service in Mexico and to provide troops for the frontier to free existing forces. Arkansans were eager to fight, and Adjutant General Solon Borland issued the call for volunteers and then resigned his state commission in order to become a captain in the new troops. Not to be outdone, Congressman Yell hurried home from Washington to enlist as a humble private. Woodruff harped that Yell had left Arkansas without representation in Washington and that Yell's real purpose was to win the Senate seat. Yell did campaign on another level because on July 4, 1846, the Arkansas regiment elected him colonel. John Selden Roane became the lieutenant colonel and Solon Borland, a major, defeated Whig candidates for these offices in the regiment. The best the Whigs could manage was the election of Albert Pike as a captain.

The politics of military organization upset the state civilian structure. Borland resigned as editor of the *Banner*, but Yell retained his Congressional seat, declaring that the War would be over soon and then he could return to Washington. Interestingly, the legislature disagreed with this view, declaring vacant the office of State Senator J.S. Ficklin, one of Yell's in-laws, because he accepted a captaincy. Eventually Yell resigned as Congressman and in the following special election, Whig Thomas W. Newton won by twenty-three votes over four other candidates. Newton's victory, the only one scored by a Whig in a statewide race, gave him exactly twenty-five days in office before the term expired.

If Yell hoped to be both colonel and senator, he was disappointed. Although his friends nominated him for the Senate, Yell was absent in Mexico and had fallen out political-

Albert Pike *(photographer and date unknown) Despite the levity in Pike's early writing, all portraits show the morose quality that was characteristic of his later years. Here he appears in full Masonic regalia.* **Oklahoma Historical Society.**

ly with Major Borland. With the anti-Ashley faction thus divided, Ashley had little difficulty obtaining the full term.

Meanwhile, the endemic political feuding carried over into the army and became the most prominent feature of Arkansas's participation in the War. Every private was viewed as a potential voter, and each officer took every occasion to publicize any activity for possible future political use. All seem to have delighted in picking on Yell. Albert Pike claimed that discipline was poor and that Yell's neglect of proper camp sanitation led to unnecessary sickness that decimated the ranks. Further, Pike charged that Yell was an incompetent who "has never undertaken to give an order without making a blunder."

American correspondents added to the volume of criticism, calling the men the "Mounted Devils of Arkansas," and charging them with committing atrocities against civilians. It was the fate of an Arkansas detachment commanded by Major Borland to fall captive to the Mexicans at *Hacienda Encarnacion,* "while asleep, with no pickets or sentinels to guard against surprise." The captives, including Borland and Captain Christopher Columbus Danley, were taken to Mexico City, where both managed to escape and participate in the capture of the capital by General Winfield Scott.

The rest of the Arkansas troops remained in northern Mexico under General Zachary Taylor. On February 23, 1847, the Mexicans attacked Taylor at Buena Vista. Not all the Arkansas troops distinguished themselves, and in trying to rally the men, Yell was killed by a Mexican lance that penetrated one of his eyes. Yell's death saddened his friends but did little to quiet the explosive collection of larger-than-life egos still in Mexico. Pike, who saw only limited action during the battle, openly criticized the regiment's participation, blaming the poor showing on the Democratic officers. Although a court of inquiry called the controversy "a misunderstanding," Lt. Colonel John S. Roane, in the last general order, hurled flowery invective at Pike: "The poisoned shafts of defamation from this polluted source have fallen far short of the mark; and he who vilely hurled them is destined to wear the mantle of shame, and be the scorn of all honest and honorable men." In reviewing the regiment's record, Roane completely omitted all references to Pike or his company.

When the principals were back in Arkansas, Pike challenged Roane to a duel. The two men met opposite Fort Smith and fired twice without result before the seconds arranged a settlement that specified no further discussion of the War. The *Encarnacion* captives returned three months later, and after them came Borland and Danley, the only two heroes that Arkansas produced in the War. Danley had suffered a severe knee wound that left him crippled and contributed to his early death. Both men promptly claimed the hero's reward: political office.

Post-War Politics

The "Family" hoped to use the political vacuum caused by Yell's death to advance the interest of Robert Ward Johnson. In early 1848, a carefully chosen state convention nominated Drew for a second term as governor and Johnson for the Congressional seat. The Ashley wing, led locally by Woodruff, gave only token support, while working behind the scenes to promote Solon Borland. Drew and Johnson were easy winners, but the weakness of the Dynasty's position became apparent when President Polk appointed Senator Sevier to conclude the peace negotiations with Mexico. Sevier apparently needed the $20,000 payment that accompanied this work, and he expected his friends in Arkansas to hold his Senate seat for him.

Instead, Governor Drew appointed Borland to fill the senatorial vacancy, and Borland even announced in a circular that he would be a candidate for the full term at the next election. Borland, whom one historian called "as untamed a man as any southern state has ever sent to Congress," had his credentials presented by Ashley. Later in the day, Ashley took to his bed with a fever and five days later was dead. Thus within a short space of time, Arkansas lost Sevier, a senator since statehood, and Ashley, one of the most respected legal minds in the Senate and the man who

Extracts from a Hiram A. Whittington Letter

Hiram Whittington, was a young printer from Boston who came west to Little Rock to earn his fortune. He arrived on Christmas Eve 1826. He worked for William E. Woodruff, publisher of the Arkansas Gazette *until 1832, when poor health forced him to move to Hot Springs. He wrote to the folks back home in Massachusetts from the* Gazette *in the early 1830s:*

Agreeably to promise, I sit down down to write you the news, Arkansas news. Our election for Delegate to Congress and members of the Legislature comes on in August, and the candidates are out electioneering, making stump speeches, etc. We have an entirely different manner of managing our elections from what you have. You do it all by caucus. Here the candidate comes out on his own bottom, tells the people he is a candidate for such an office, and then goes on to tell him how he will serve them with fidelity, energy, etc.; not forgetting to set forth his claims to their support in the most dazzling light, and if he knows of any little sins of his opponent he will not be apt to let them pass unnoticed. They attend all public gatherings, and mount a stump and make speeches two or three hours long. It commonly costs them about twice as much to get an office as the office is worth after they get it. It is expected of a candidate that they are to treat all their friends as often as they see them from now until election, find them in segars, tobacco, etc. . . .

One thing I like to mention, i.e., that I joined a temperance society about a month ago; not because I was in the habit of drinking, but merely to please the ladies, who said they wanted the temperate men to join for the sake of their example. About twenty men, all the ladies in place, old and young, have joined; and I have no doubt Little Rock will soon experience its good effects. I hope you will go and do likewise . . . .

Your affectionate brother,
Hiram

Source: Sarah M. Fountain, Authentic Voices: Arkansas Culture, 1542-1860 *(Conway, 1986) 152-153. The original Hiram A. Whittington letters were copied by Dallas T. Herndon and the copies are in the archives of the Arkansas History Commission.*

---

pronounced Arkansas with the emphasis on the second syllable. Drew immediately appointed Helena lawyer William King Sebastian to the second vacancy.

With two positions now open for the legislature to fill, Dynasty supporter Thompson B. Flournoy suggested that Borland and Sevier each take a seat and so resolve the division within the Party. Borland rejected this practical suggestion as "an insulting proposal" and a "corrupt bargain," whereupon Flournoy challenged Borland to a duel. Borland insisted his quarrel was with "the head of the house" and refused to fight a mere underling. Flournoy exploded in print, calling Borland "a liar, a poltroon, and a coward, and beneath the contempt and unworthy of the notice of an honorable man."

Meanwhile, Borland was scoring political points over Sevier in the first substantive issue ever to divide Arkansas's Washington delegation. At stake was Benjamin Johnson's monopoly as the sole federal judge in Arkansas. Western Arkansans favored dividing the state into two districts, giving the western district jurisdiction over crimes against whites originating in Indian Territory. Johnson, working through his son-in-law Sevier, had resisted any diminution of authority. However, Senator Borland succeeded in winning the creation of a new court, took all the credit, and capped it by getting federal payments for those who had been held prisoners in Mexico.

The 1848 senatorial contest introduced some innovations into Arkansas politics. First, the legislators were chosen by casting paper ballots rather than by the venerable *viva voce* method. This innovation was too much for many Arkansans and subsequently was repealed. A second change, also short-lived, saw legislative candidates pledging to voters that they were for either Borland or Sevier. This presaged the popular election of Senators and gave a new twist to local politics.

When the legislature met, factional lines were drawn sharply. The Whigs stood firmly behind their senatorial candidate, C.F.M. Noland, for behind the scenes, the Sevier forces promised Whigs that David Walker would get a seat on the state Supreme Court. The new system of legislative pledges soon broke down, for state Senator Henry M. Rector, pledged to Borland, switched to Sevier after the first and inconclusive roll call. Voting deadlocked at forty-one for Borland, thirty-seven for Sevier, and eighteen for Noland, until Sevier decided to withdraw and concentrate on getting the second seat. However, this too was denied him as Sebastian won reelection.

Sevier retired to the Johnson plantation, where he died on December 31, 1848, either from the effects of a previous ailment or from a new disease picked up in Mexico. Sevier's death ended the continuity of Arkansas politics between the territorial period and statehood. Only Woodruff, who lived almost to the end of the century, remained, and he lost interest once his friend Ashley was dead. The deaths of these early leaders led to the passing of power to a new generation far less experienced and able than their predecessors.

Besides the appointments of the colorless Sebastian and the too-colorful Borland, a final change came when Governor Drew resigned, protesting that his salary was too low for Little Rock prices. The Democrats in the legislature met in caucus and nominated John S. Roane, who won easily despite being legally ineligible to hold office because of his dueling record. Although Roane had Dynasty support, he utterly failed to influence the legislature. His demand that the state spend its school fund on regional schools was rejected. Instead, the money went to the counties, where it promptly disappeared. His pleas for aid to roads, internal improvements, a state geological survey and banking reform fared no better. Hanging over Arkansas was the unresolved Bank debt. Governor Drew had called for the federal government to aid the state by making a large land grant for levee construction, which, by speeding Arkansas's development, would generate revenues to pay the debt. However, Arkansas first had to come to terms with the state's problem, and Roane did not know what to do:

> What shall be done touching the banks and our state indebtedness? Shall I recommend the legislature to pay the bonds, or repudiate the whole debt? Tell the legislators and the world the truth, the whole truth, and let the bondholders know what they have to rely upon for payment of the obligations? Shall I pursue this or keep up the policy of my predecessors and continue to mystify, promise to pay without to do it, keeping up the bonds without benefiting anyone?

These were hard political questions, and they remained unanswered. The wisdom of hindsight was readily available, for as the Helena *Southern Shield* aptly stated:

> If we had not established banks when we did, our state would now in all probability be in a condition such as

would rank her among the first of this glorious Confederacy. But a false step has burdened her with a debt which she cannot discharge for a quarter of a century. Her destiny must remain darkened for many years to come, notwithstanding she has the elements of greatness scattered in wild profusion around her.

Arkansas was not the only state to experience banking problems, but the benefits had touched only a few in Arkansas while the liabilities had threatened everybody.

To the average voter, modernization had proven to be an expensive curse, consisting of fantasies mixed with fraud. During the late 1840s, the spirit of improvement left Arkansas. Defeated at every turn in trying to get Arkansas moving again, many, like Judge John Brown of Camden, voiced despair: "I feel that I am settled and my means invested and lying comparatively dead in the most hopeless portion of the United States."

Those who felt that way did not have to remain in Arkansas. Many grumbled and moved on to Texas, where Arkansans constituted the largest single source of the Lone Star state's population. Arkansas towns came to present a derelict appearance. Washington was "nearly one fourth tenantless, some having grown tired of the unprofitable monotony, and moved away, and others having caught the Texas fever." In 1844, the state auditor's report showed a decline in state revenue and 538 fewer persons paying a poll tax.

The Decline of the Whigs

Those most likely to stay were the traditionalists. The repeated rejection of every piece of progressive legislation helped demoralize the Whig Party. Divided internally by cleavages between the planters of the Delta and the merchants of the towns, the Whig Party never succeeded in making a coherent state campaign. Whigs were also in trouble nationally as the divisive issue of slavery, reopened by the acquisition of new lands gained in the Mexican War, split Northern "conscience" Whigs from their Southern brethren. By 1850, the state Party was unable to support a newspaper, and William E. Woodruff repurchased the *Arkansas Gazette*, largely for sentimental reasons.

The California Gold Rush

One break in the monotony came when gold was discovered in California. Nothing so stirred the imaginations of all classes of Americans as the thought of getting rich quick. Van Buren and Fort Smith, with access to the southern route to the West, benefited as many state residents, especially from the northern and western counties, hastened to join wagon trains. The first party to leave Fort Smith on April 5, 1849, consisted of 128 persons in fifty wagons. By the fall of 1850, twenty wagons a day were crossing the Bayou Meto toll bridge heading west. According to Senator Borland's estimates, 1,000 persons left the state, each taking an average of $200, and by 1860, it was estimated that 2,000 Arkansans had located permanently in California. Van Buren and Fort Smith might have grown into sizeable towns as gateways to the West, but Senator Borland, fearful of more population loss from Arkansas, opposed any federal spending to improve the route. In time, some Arkansans like Alden Woodruff and William Quesenbury returned home, and Quesenbury noted that many of the gamblers and sportsmen who had given Arkansas a bad reputation during the Flush Times were now found in the California gold fields.

The Mountain Meadow Massacre

A few Arkansans never reached Eureka. On September 10, 1857, an Arkansas party consisting of 120 men, women and children with

900 head of cattle and a prize $2,000 stallion were ambushed in what became known as the Mountain Meadow Massacre. The Arkansans, led by Alexander Fancher, originated mostly from Carroll County. What should have been a routine trip ended in disaster when Utah Mormons, hearing that Mormon missionary Parley P. Pratt had been murdered near Van Buren, decided to take revenge on the closest Arkansans. Although Pratt had been killed by the estranged husband of a New York woman Pratt was attempting to convert, local Mormons led by John D. Lee fell on the Arkansas party, slaughtering all the men and women and sparing only the small children. The Fancher party's possessions were sold at public auction at Cedar City, and the children were distributed among Mormon families.

The crime prompted the federal government into a quasi-war with the Mormons, both on the battlefield and in the courts, for the rest of the century. In 1875, Lee was convicted for his role in the massacre and executed. The surviving children earlier had been returned to Arkansas. The episode did little to enhance the Mormon Church in Arkansas.

CONCLUSION

The economic trends in America from 1836 to 1850 were echoed in Arkansas. The Flush Times mentality embraced all the Southwest, but the hard times that followed were a national phenomenon. Yet in Arkansas, certain local conditions gave special meaning to these events. Arkansas was too underdeveloped to support statehood economically, and the Bank failure demonstrated a weakness in leadership. Because many Arkansans wanted to perpetuate traditional values rather than seek economic gratification, the hard times that arrived in the 1840s vindicated the rejection of modernization. As Arkansas entered the last decade of the antebellum era, frontier conditions still largely prevailed and political paralysis gripped the young state's leaders.

BIBLIOGRAPHIC ESSAY

Most of the memoirs and general accounts from the territorial period carry over into the early statehood period. The most useful guide is Ross, *Arkansas Gazette*. Brian G. Walton has provided a sophisticated analysis in "The Second Party System in Arkansas, 1836-1848," *AHQ*, XXVIII (Summer 1969), 120-155, and "Ambrose Hundley Sevier in the United States Senate, 1836-1848," *AHQ*, XXXII (Spring 1973), 25-60. Additional biographies can be found in Timothy Donovan and Willard D. Gatewood, *Governors of Arkansas: Essays in Political Biography*, (Fayetteville, 1981).

The tangled affairs of the banks occupied Ted R. Worley in four articles: "The Arkansas State Bank: Antebellum Period", *AHQ*, XXIII (Spring 1964), 65-73; "The Batesville Branch of the State Bank, 1836-1839," *AHQ*, VI (Winter 1947), 286-299; "The Control of the Real Estate Bank of the State of Arkansas, 1836-1855," *MVHR*, XXXVII (December 1950), 403-426, and "Arkansas and the Money Crisis of 1836-1837," *JSH*, XV (May 1949), 178-191.

Arkansas's relation to the Mexican War can be found in William Ritchie, "An Episode of the Mexican War," *AHQ*, VI (Winter 1947), 250-255, and Walter L. Brown, "Mexican War Experiences of Albert Pike and the 'Mounted Devils' of Arkansas," *AHQ*, XII (Winter 1953), 301-315. Extensive treatment is given to the California emigration in Francile B. Oakley, "Arkansas' Golden Army of '49," *AHQ*, VI (Spring 1947), 1-85, but Priscilla McArthur, *Arkansas in the Gold Rush*, (Little Rock, 1986) contains significant additional material. The Mountain Meadow massacre became the subject of a popular American folk song and received book-length treatment in Juanita Brooks, *The Mountain Meadow Massacre*, (Stanford, 1950).

A Wattle and Daub Chimney. *(photographer and date unknown) This chimney style was built of a wooden frame covered with mud in the early days of Arkansas. Ozark and Ouachita farmers often replaced these primitive chimneys with stone chimneys made by itinerant stone masons. In regions without stone, locally made sun-dried bricks were used. By the twentieth century, only the very poor used the stick and mud chimney.* **Arkansas History Commission**

Chapter V

Settlements and Society

INTRODUCTION

Arkansas went through all stages of frontier development in just twenty years. For various reasons, the state's development remained behind both regional and national levels. The frontier, although constantly being reduced in size, continued as a factor in Arkansas history into the 1920s. The existence of unsettled areas in the Ozarks and Ouachitas, the Delta swamps and the western border on Indian Territory gave the state an image as a crude, boisterous and violent land. Taming this frontier spirit became a major theme in the state's history.

OCCUPATIONS

Hunters

Although hunters made the earliest economic use of Arkansas, many were heading west by the time of the American occupation of the state. They left behind the myth that Arkansans specialized in hunting bears. Thomas Bangs Thorpe's story, "The Great Bear of Arkansas," was the foremost reason Arkansas was known as the Bear State. Bears figured prominently in the writings of C. F. M. Noland. The White River settlement of Oil Trough is at a site where hunters brought in bear oil. Bears quickly were hunted to near extinction, after which hunters like the real Pete Whetstone, from whom Noland had shaped a fictional character, moved on to Texas.

The Big Bear of Arkansas from Thomas Bangs Thorpe, The Hive of The Bee-Hunter, *(New York, 1854). Although Arkansas produced an extensive hunting literature, only Thorpe of Louisiana seems to have questioned the mentality that viewed animals as game to be hunted for enjoyment and slaughtered with no regard for tomorrow. Friedrich Gerstäcker, although sympathetic enough in discussing people, thought nothing of fighting his way into a mother bear's den and slaughtering the cubs. This was the century's "capital sport."* **Suzanne Kittrell Collection**

Arkansas's abandonment by bear hunters did not mean that all wildlife was gone. Frontiersmen located their cabins more with an eye to hunting prospects than to farming and supplied themselves with meat from wild sources. Venison hams were common, and in the fall, many Arkansans lived on pigeon pie. Throughout the nineteenth century, every town was serviced by hunters who brought in deer and small game, especially the multitudinous passenger pigeons and doves. Though hunters typically were uninterested

in politics, Washington County chose one legislator because of his prowess as the best turkey caller in the region. Another hunter, A. Ray, represented Polk County in the 1861 secession convention. Because of its swamps, eastern Arkansas was especially well supplied with game and remained a hunter's paradise until drainage in the twentieth century altered the landscape.

In addition to those who hunted from necessity, many enjoyed it as a sport. Individuals such as Noland and William Quesenbury took part in the aristocratic sport of fox hunting. Noland celebrated his experiences in nationally published stories, and Quesenbury, one of Arkansas's early artists, drew a portrait of himself in hunting pose and kept journals and diaries of his expeditions. Judge George Conway was "so devoted to the chase, that, while on the bench, he has been known to adjourn court and go bear-hunting." Hunting lured outsiders as well. Friedrich Gerstäcker, a German traveler, hunted all over Arkansas, later using his materials for a popular travel account and a series of German romantic novels.

Although it wasn't as heroic, fishing had adherents who, following the lead of Izaak Walton, celebrated the sport's restful qualities. In 1858, a Batesville editor took great pride in describing how his staff departed on such "a piscatorial expedition."

> Having spent several hours in preparation, and procured wherewith to tempt the finny tribe, they proceeded to the river and with most commendable patience remained until night. They succeeded in capturing a number of fish varying from invisibility to two inches in length.

Others doubtlessly did better, for a species of humor not unique to Arkansas developed about fishing trips.

Herdsmen

The keeping of cattle and pigs in Arkansas dated back to the French occupation. Eastern

Women Smoking in Cabin *(artist unknown) This drawing appeared in* Leslie's *magazine in 1864. Throughout the nineteenth and into the twentieth century, many women either dipped snuff or smoked pipes. Notice the large fireplace, which served most families for cooking as well as heating until late the in the nineteenth century.* **University of Arkansas at Little Rock**

Arkansas was especially favored for the enterprise because the prairies and canebrakes provided food for livestock. In the uplands, the Indian practice of burning the woods in order to retard undergrowth and encourage grasses continued well into the twentieth century even though it came under increasing attack from forest interests and conservationists.

As population increased, cattle yielded in importance to pigs. Pigs, like cattle, were turned loose to fend for themselves in the river bottoms, eating mast and snakes. They were rounded up in the fall, fattened and slaughtered at the onset of winter. This method of raising pigs continued in Prairie County until the 1960s, although at that late date, fencing was required. Pig drives were common, and Pocahontas, Powhatan and Van Buren became active shipping points for marketing surplus pork. Nevertheless, all of the needs of the plantation counties for pork could not be met by the state. Arkansas planters bought pork in Cincinnati, the "Porkopolis" of the West.

The herdsmen were favored legally by the existence of open range. Fencing was a burden on the farmer, not the herdsman. The law did require that both pigs and cattle be marked, and the brands, usually ear notches, were recorded in the county courthouse. The 1827 murder of Isaac Watkins in Little Rock arose from difficulties with a neighbor about the ownership of pigs. The first case in which a woman was convicted of a felony came from the Ozarks and involved the charge of stealing a hog. When traveler G. W. Featherstonhaugh called on Governor Pope, he found only Pope's wife; the governor was out in the woods with an old sow. So central was the hog to the domestic economy that throughout the nineteenth century "meat" meant pork. Occasional outbreaks of hog cholera devastated the countryside and produced serious food shortages.

Farmers

The majority of antebellum inhabitants of Arkansas were farmers. The word "farm" could suggest anything from a neat and tidy frame house to the squatter's leaky cabin. Most herdsmen engaged in some farming, and nearly all farmers engaged in some herding. There was a distinction between farmers and planters, but at what point a farmer became a planter never was resolved.

At the bottom of the frontier economic system rested the subsistence farmer, the poor white of Southern agriculture. Some historians insist their poverty was illusory because the pigs and cattle these people possessed in abundance were not visible to travelers, leading to a distorted picture of their poverty. Others have identified poor whites as victims of plantation agriculture or of diseases such as hook-

worm, malaria, pellagra and tuberculosis.

Many poor farmers were squatters. Squatters arrived ahead of the surveyor, selecting and improving a tract of land. Often this "improving" was only the building of a crude cabin and a small field in which trees were girdled and killed but left standing. Once land was surveyed and placed on the market, many sold their improvements and headed west to find new land. One survey in the 1840s showed that 74 percent of the farmers in the Buffalo River area were squatters. The reality of constant movement, which continued in rural communities into the twentieth century, was remarkably at odds with the romantic myth of Americans settling and putting down roots. In some areas unwritten customs protected squatters, so that many families lived for several generations before finding it necessary to patent their land with the government.

The literary portrait of the squatter came from Colonel Sanford Faulkner in the story, "The Arkansas Traveler," in which a lawyer and a squatter confront each other before resolving their differences in music. The log cabin, which dominated Edward P. Washburn's paintings of the traveler scene, also existed in several forms. The crudest type, with round logs, had only a dirt floor and relied on a wattle and daub chimney. At the other extreme were carefully carpentered log houses like the two-story Wolf House at Norfork that competed with frame homes in comfort and convenience. Most were somewhere in the middle, like the farmers themselves.

More advanced than log cabin folk were families who erected Greek Revival farmsteads. Their neat grounds, fences and outbuildings gave promise of another order. Persons who lived in such houses were likely to engage in commercial agriculture and identify with national rather than traditional frontier values. Despite the political attempt of Whigs in 1840 to associate William Henry Harrison with log cabins, people who lived in them generally voted Democratic and attended, when they did attend, the Baptist church.

Immigrants came with a certain understanding of the kind of lands they wanted. In general people moved due west, violating that rule only in order to keep another rule: that soil types and terrain would remain similar to those in their previous habitat. One diary entry from Madison County summed up pioneer conditions:

> We are in Arkansas and we have found a mighty rough country. This is very good hog country, but as for grass, the hills are too steep to bring grass. It brings plenty of acorns for hogs. Where the land is level enough, in between the hills, it brings good corn. In the bottoms, this is as good land as ever have seen, but it is in small bodies.

Water was one important incentive for location, and in uplands, settlers preferred a site with a spring to one needing a well. Both the quality of the land and the easy availability of water might be sacrificed to other considerations, notably that of kinship. A Madison County study revealed that persons would make a sacrifice of up to, but not beyond, 1.25 miles to locate near kin.

Farmers throughout the Ozarks used furs, pelts and beeswax for currency. Raccoon pelts brought 40 to 50 cents; fox, 25 to 30; and mink, 65 to 75. Frontiersmen followed wild bees in order to garner honey. Local coopers made hogsheads to hold honey after it was separated from wax. Self-sufficient in food, the pioneer family also clothed itself. "You could scarcely visit a house," one man recalled, "but what you would see a loom, big spinning-wheel and little wheel. Sometimes you would see three or four wheels at one house." The dyes, indigo and copperas, had to be purchased, but bark, flowers and onion skins provided home-grown tints. Many even made their own leather shoes, and raccoon or fox-skin caps competed in popularity with felt or wool hats.

The average cabin housed more than five persons, and together with the implements of domestic economy, did not always present a pleasant sight to visitors. Children, clothed in deerskins, were dirty and greasy; the cabin walls were hung with hunting trophies, rifles, dried meat and containers of bear oil and honey. Henry Schoolcraft, who stayed with hunter families in the Ozarks, wrote of the log cabins:

> Nothing could be more remote from the ideas we have attached to domestic comfort, neatness, or conveniency, without allusion to cleanliness, order, and the concomitant train of household attributes which make up the sum of human felicity in refined society.

Pope County was in many ways a microcosm of early Arkansas. Containing both upland and lowland regions, its first settlers had moved from Tennessee, followed by those from North Carolina, Missouri, Alabama, Kentucky, Virginia, Georgia and Illinois. In a more southerly county, Alabama, Georgia and Mississippi would have ranked higher, while farther north Kentucky would have risen on the scale. In 1850, 100 of Pope County's 695 families owned slaves, but only three had as many as twenty. Free blacks were unknown.

Cattle figured prominently, the average being fifteen head a family, with thirty-three hogs and four milk cows. The ratio of only one horse for every three people indicated that oxen still pulled the plows in the fields. Each family raised its own tobacco, the average being seven pounds a family. The county's largest taxpayer reported a mere 680 acres and probably derived his wealth from his store and ten town lots. He paid $33.49 in taxes, compared to the county average of $2.80.

Geography in the Delta modified the economics slightly. There the yearly high water offered a way to market logs. A raft of 150 trees could be floated to Helena or even New Orleans and would net a man $16. Additional income could be produced by cutting wood for the steamboat trade at the rate of $1.50 to $2 per cord. Much of this timber was pirated from unclaimed land. Fishing was especially good, and hogs could be raised without corn "if you give them the run of your pea field." Despite the health problems, some found the region attractive.

Wolf House. *(Harold Phelps, ca. 1950) Although threatened with destruction several times, this log house located at Norfork remains the best state example of a folk architectural form.* **Arkansas History Commission**

As the hunting phase of development diminished in importance, commercial agriculture arose and the production of cash crops such as cotton increased. Southern editors were in the vanguard of popularizing improved farming techniques, and as the sectional crisis grew, the crusade to improve Southern agriculture stressed sectional patriotism.

County agricultural societies promoted improvements by holding county fairs that offered premiums for the best signs of progress. Prairie County, which held its third fair in 1859, raised the prize money from the proceeds of a concert given by the women of Des Arc. The audience, a local paper noted, "properly appreciated the musical talent presented." Much of the emphasis was on cotton, with prizes for the best bale and the best

stalk, but 50 cents went to the best peck of goober peas. To encourage Southerners not to depend on Yankee manufacturers, there were prizes for the best dresses and for homemade cradles and ox yokes.

Doubtless the competition for the best pound cake was heated, but probably most of the people came for the horse race preceded by a cavalcade of riders in comic disguises and a tournament that drew twenty-five horsemen who tilted for rings suspended in the air. The historian of the event concluded:

The record exhibits a remarkably self-reliant and resourceful community that depended on itself in supplying tools, household goods, hardware, and articles of food and clothing. Its arts and entertainment were likewise homemade.

Mammoth Spring (*David Dale Owen, 1858*) *This engraving shows one of the state's early gristmills. Probably no other site in Arkansas has had more uses. After the Civil War, a grand spa hotel arose on the hill above the spring. Then a greatly enlarged flour mill was located on the site of the early mill. A textile mill operated briefly around the turn of the century, and next an electric generating plant harnessed the water power of the spring. Today, Mammoth Spring is a state park.* **University of Arkansas at Little Rock**

The community leaders at least were interested in diversified agriculture and scientific methods.

Despite geographic conditions that divided social classes at both county and state levels, the people in Arkansas had more in common than appearances indicated. The elite, whose wealth was measured by ownership of land and slaves, accounted for only one-tenth of 1 percent of taxpayers in Washington County, but poorer mountain counties such as Van Buren and Montgomery had no elite at all. By contrast, the more one ventured into the lowlands, the more evidence of an elite one could find. Pulaski and Union Counties boasted elites of .7 and .9 percent respectively, while Phillips had 1.4 and Chicot, "the county that symbolized plantation life," contained 11.9 percent. Those who owned no property were at the other end of the scale and made up slightly more than 5 percent in Montgomery and Washington Counties, compared to 22.9 percent in Chicot. Most Arkansans lay in the middle—the middle and upper middle for the lowlands, the middle and lower for the mountains. Statistical evidence suggests that class stability was most pronounced in the uplands.

Pioneer Arkansas was a man's world. The national average of 104 males to 100 females gave way in Arkansas to an upland ratio of 132 males to 100 females. In the lowlands, where many young men came to seek their fortune, the ratio was 145 to 100. Because women represented a civilizing influence in the Victorian age, the surplus of males partially explained the frontier violence for which Arkansas was noted.

Frontier society underwent a transformation in the decade before the Civil War. Gristmills arose at strategic locations. Wheat from northwestern Arkansas went to Elk River Mills, just over the Missouri line. The Mills boasted two pairs of high quality French millstones and ground forty to fifty barrels of flour a day, which was marketed in Van Buren and was reported to be superior to Ohio flour. The first reaping machines arrived in the uplands, where they greatly expanded agricultural output. Even sewing machines began to appear, portending great changes in the lives of women. The movement to grow silk, much agitated for in colonial America, was promoted in Arkansas. One experiment near Batesville failed, but hopes remained. Grapes for wine culture had their adherents, notably in John R. Eakin at Washington, who published an account of his experiments.

URBANIZATION

Only a small percentage of Arkansans lived in towns, yet these centers of civilization served as county seats for government and performed needed economic functions. In contrast to the close kinship pattern that dominated rural settlements, towns boasted persons from all states and many foreign countries.

The beginning of a town often arose as the dream of a speculator. Early Arkansas abounded in schemes for frontier megalopolises. In general, two factors influenced a town's chances for success: politics and trade. It was politics that determined the relocation of the territorial capital from Arkansas Post to Little Rock and that accounted in turn for the failures of Rome and Arkansas near the Post and Crystal Hill across the Arkansas River from Little Rock.

On the county level, locations near the geographic center had priority. When new counties were created, many county seats ceased to be areas of activity and soon lost to a more central town. Carroll County's Carrollton became Old Carrollton after a boundary change, and towns shown on early maps like Elizabeth, Bolivar, Greensboro, Columbia and Kinderhook disappeared. Such failures hurt those who invested in the hopes of gaining great wealth. Crystal Hill, which sold for $9,000 in 1821, went for unpaid taxes of $3.99 1/2 in 1843.

Commercial success depended on river and road transportation. Neither was reliable. Rivers probably presented the greatest threat. Greenock in Crittenden County, Napoleon in Desha and Columbia in Chicot were swallowed by the Mississippi River. Nearly half of both Helena and Pine Bluff and most of Arkansas Post fell victim to bank erosion. Batesville had to move up the hill because its initial location was too prone to White River flooding. Rerouting of roads led to the demise of St. Francisville and the decline of Jackson. The struggle to find a suitable county seat for Lawrence County illustrated the effect of changing roadways on towns. Officials in the second oldest county plotted the town of Davidsonville along the Black River, where they erected a large brick courthouse. The site proved to be poorly chosen and was off the military road. Discontent caused the county seat to be moved to Jackson. When Randolph County was created, Jackson was no longer central so Smithville was chosen. After Sharp County was formed, Smithville gave way to Clover Bend. Because that site was too difficult to reach and most of the population lived north of the Black River, Powhatan gained the honors. However, the railroad and a modern highway missed Powhatan, and Walnut Ridge finally won.

In some instances, the motive for developing a town came after the county had been created. Early maps show a site called "Clark County Courthouse," indicating that the seat of government had been placed before the speculators showed up. Usually it did not

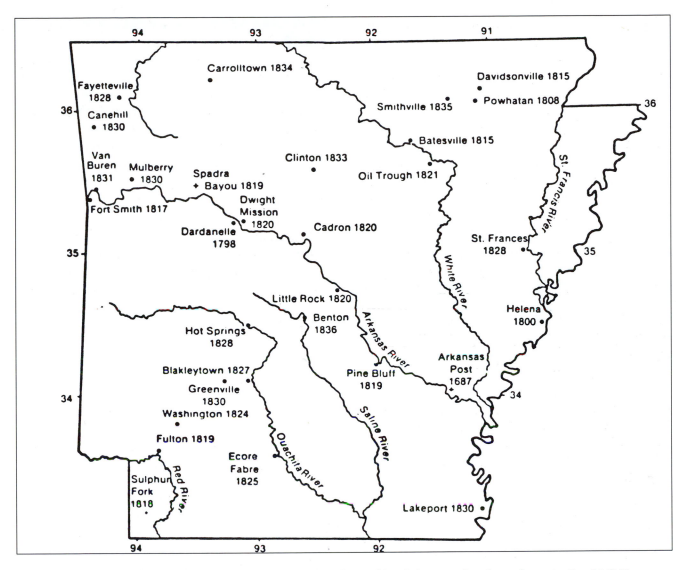

Principal Settlements of Arkansas by 1836. *Note the relationship of rivers and early settlements.* **Gerald T. Hanson**

take very long before a grand name was selected, streets laid out and sales begun. Some town lots were disposed of by auction and others were offered for sale through newspaper advertisements. Mount Maria, a town near Pine Bluff that failed, offered "ten in-lots and ten out-lots of three acres each . . . to actual settlers, regular members of the Methodist Church, and merchants." All were promoted in glowing terms, although one traveler noted that at William Strong's development of St. Francisville, aside from store, house and inn, only little wooden name tags set out in the woods marked the supposed future progress of the city.

Bad health seems to have impeded development of the Red River town of Fulton, despite its location at a point calculated to serve both Arkansas and Texas interests. A large pond behind the town provided enough mosquitoes to keep several doctors busy and the graveyard full. Little Rock, although the capital, was no model of city planning. As early as 1832, the *Gazette* proposed building a canal to drain the town's filth into the river. Town Branch remained a menace for most of the nineteenth century. Public health measures were almost unknown, so that diseases such as cholera, smallpox and yellow fever occasionally struck. Helena suffered a major outbreak of yellow fever in 1855, supposedly from an infected newsboy on a passing steamboat.

Town Government

In England, towns and cities could possess special powers of government derived from a charter of privileges. This custom continued in America with the state legislature making the grants. With special problems of police, fire, sanitation and health, towns needed a wide range of police and taxing powers. Little Rock led the way in 1825 when the territorial legislature incorporated the capital. The first ordinances banned any shooting in the streets on Sunday, prohibited slaves from dancing and ineffectually regulated gambling. Three years later the city even banned shooting in the streets during weekdays.

Towns emerged with a culture different from the countryside, and Arkansas legislators, who were overwhelmingly rural, tended to react negatively to town needs. Municipalities were born half-strangled and led a precarious and starved existence. Often their charters were taken away or greatly modified. Little Rock was rechartered in 1831, and other towns found it necessary to turn again and again to the legislature to get their affairs in order. Because Whigs or in the 1850s, Know-Nothings, generally won city elections, the hostility of the Democratic-controlled legislature often was partisan.

Town services were primitive. A town constable did the policing, and the inefficiency of these elected men was legendary. Little Rock used a town patrol to police slaves but with poor results. Jails, often made of logs, were inadequate, with escapes so common that they were hardly counted. The discovery in 1842 that Little Rock Mayor Samuel G. Trowbridge was head of a gang of burglars and counterfeiters did little to increase public confidence. The most desired town service was fire protection. Most communities had a fire bell to summon all residents to turn out with buckets. By the nineteenth century, the steam engine had been adapted for firefighting and every town worthy of its name acquired an engine. The addition of an engine led to the creation of volunteer fire departments, but in a major fire, such as that which destroyed several blocks of Little Rock's Main and Markham Streets in 1854, machine and men labored side by side. Little Rock's engine, acquired in 1840 and the first in the state, did not save Judge Daniel Ringo's house, for the hose pulled so much Arkansas River mud into the engine that it clogged. Obviously, effective firefighting needed a reliable water source, but aside from the River, Little Rock had only cisterns. A municipal gas system was the one notable improvement Little Rock added in 1860. The nerve center of modern communications, the telegraph, arrived first in northwestern Arkansas in 1860 and in Little Rock in early 1861.

Some confusion existed in the nineteenth century in distinctions between streets and sewers. "We would call the attention of the city authorities to the great nuisance, caused by throwing all sorts of trash, dead cats, rats, & c., in the cross street, near the *Gazette and Democrat* office," one of the papers noted in August 1857, adding that "in this hot weather, the odor from a dead rat, is rather too much for weak nerves." The unpaved streets were often little more than mud holes. Pranksters once planted a dummy in one mud hole, and a coroner's jury was duly summoned to investigate the alleged corpse. A wagon bound for the cemetery in 1863 sank in the mud and remained there all day. "I never saw such mud in any town," a wartime visitor observed.

The Merchant Class

Merchants, the backbone of every town, were economically weak. In eastern Arkansas the old agriculturally biased common law rapidly was being modified to suit the needs of commercial capitalism. One of the few changes to reach Arkansas was abolition of imprisonment for debt. The plantation system often led to wealth and power for planters rather than merchants, with planters owning the towns. Fifty-seven percent of the land in the township containing Helena was owned by only twenty-five persons. Many planters lived in town, their slaves substituting for an urban proletariat. Merchants had problems in other ways, too. "We have no money here and never had," wrote Hiram Whittington from Hot Springs. "Our business is all done in cotton and skins." What money that did appear might be counterfeit, and merchants needed to be aware constantly of the status of banks in order to discount their notes appropriately.

Less significant than in colonial times were auction houses. Little Rock boasted one that dealt in slaves and assorted commodities, but city ordinances prohibited drum-beating and other ancient methods of soliciting business. Although all talked of the advantages of a cash system, merchants bought on credit and extended terms to customers as well. The credit system invariably led to over-extensions followed by bankruptcy. Because it was quicker to liquidate a store than a farm or plantation, merchants suffered the most from these disruptions. Many simply started up again, and little stigma seems to have been attached to the process. As in colonial times, most Main Street buildings were called "stands," and judging by pictures and accounts, customers and owners did a lot of standing. Street names and numbers were used so seldom that in Batesville, W. B. and T. B. Padget, Druggists and Apothecaries, were located at the "Sign of the Big Mortar opposite Uriah Maxfield's old stand."

The range of business was considerable. The first merchants supplied hunters with trading goods and necessities such as salt. Farm wives needed dyes and a few manufactured goods such as cotton cards. Planters bought in large quantities from stores catering to the plantation trade. China, pottery and other kitchen items were imported, but Arkansas attracted a number of artisans who set up shop making hats, boots, silver, watches and a variety of furniture items. Gunsmiths did a flourishing trade, with Little Rock's Jacob F. Trumpler preeminent in the field.

Doctors and lawyers arrived early. William Kilgore Smith, M. D., advertised his services in 1830 as a Surgeon Dentist, indicating he would remain at the Anthony House for a few weeks. John Henry Byrd, the best known of Arkansas's portrait painters, recorded the faces of the elite. The lesser folks had to await the introduction of photography in the 1840s. The Van Buren paper reported in 1847 that C. J. Asbury, "Daguerrean Artist," would visit Fayetteville, Van Buren and Fort Smith. Little Rock generally supported enough trade to keep a man fully employed. Women found honest work as milliners and less honest employment as prostitutes. No married woman, however, had any right to retain her earnings, whatever the source.

Towns offered a variety of service businesses. Gambling dens were ubiquitous in the early days and competed with saloons and billiard parlors. Little Rock's Magnolia House, located on Ashley's Row on Markham Street in 1854, offered the "Choicest liquors ever brought to the State mixed in style not surpassed by any artiste west of New York." The proprietors assured the public that ice would be kept "the entire summer season, or as long as money could produce it." Batesville had at least four ice houses by 1854. Ice was cut from rural ponds during the winter, and if properly stored, would last until July. Its availability made beer, a German introduction, more popular and induced immigrant Charles Heinrich at Batesville to open a bakery and ice cream saloon. In Little Rock, the George family, also from Germany, opened Dutch Garden, an outdoor recreation place with walks decorated with roses and carnations leading to a honeysuckle arbor. Accompanying music came from a grand piano.

Arkansas merchants, artisans and mechanics were of diverse origins. The first blacksmith in Little Rock was a native of Vermont; the Batesville ice cream maker was a German immigrant. Some Irish, brought to Arkansas with the intention of settling in Yell County, chose to stay in Little Rock, where the Hibernian Benevolent

Society was organized in 1851 to aid the poorer members. Other Irish found work along the Mississippi building the first levees. Some stayed on, especially in Helena and Napoleon. A few Jews came to antebellum Arkansas. Isaac Bott settled in Little Rock, and Cyrus Adler, an internationally famous scholar, was born in Van Buren. Aaron Hirsch operated a stage and engaged in various business ventures at Batesville, and pioneer merchant Abraham Block in Washington was the first of a large family bearing that name to become well established. Most were of German origin and located in the principal plantation towns before the Civil War. Even more numerous were the Scotch-Irish, many of whom had roots in North Carolina.

Nineteenth century merchandising relied heavily on individual initiative. At least one Little Rock merchant made annual visits to Philadelphia to place his orders. Others relied on family connections in larger cities for supplies and credit. Although most Arkansas cotton ended up in New Orleans, merchants from Louisville, St. Louis and Cincinnati tried to capture the Arkansas market for food and manufactured items. Ohio, for example, grew most of the apples sold in Arkansas. That one could purchase oysters, champagne, cigars, brandy, Parisian silk hose, cashmere and alpaca in addition to the best furniture, silver, glass and china is a tribute to the versatility of Arkansas merchants in overcoming transportation problems and an underdeveloped economy.

The Laboring Class

Urban areas needed skilled workers, then called mechanics and artisans. Occupations included carpenters, masons, smiths, plasterers, brickmakers, tailors, hatters, shoemakers, bakers and a number of more specialized crafts. The frontier traditionally offered these people higher wages. In the South, however, many found themselves in direct competition with slave labor and at a political and economic disadvantage. The Lit-

tle Rock Mechanics Association was formed in 1839, and the plasterers got together to define rules for their trade and a method of pricing. But when work began on the State House, the Commissioner of Public Buildings placed advertisements in Kentucky newspapers praising the prospects of Arkansas and soliciting workers below the local pay scale.

The state penitentiary's practice in the 1850s of leasing convict labor and training inmates in skilled crafts greatly upset the workers, who feared the cut-rate competition. Town politics always were vigorously contested, and Little Rock newspaper readers frequently encountered frank appeals to class prejudice directed at the laboring man's vote. One issue on which most Arkansas whites could unite was the status of the free Negro. Artisans and mechanics were unable to avoid slave competition because of the economic power of slaveholders, but they could destroy the free blacks, who had few supporters.

Town Architecture

A distinctive feature of towns was their buildings. The transformation of town structures from primitive log cabins to frame and brick buildings depended on the speed of economic development. The first dwelling at Little Rock was a simple hunter's shelter. Cabins made of round logs followed, later replaced by those made of hewn logs. As soon as sawmills arrived, not only could frame houses be erected, but older log structures could be covered with clapboard. The Hinderliter house in Little Rock, today a part of the Arkansas Territorial Restoration, was an example of this, and an unknown number of homes around the state belied their humble origins.

Arkansas had many clay deposits suitable for making bricks, and Little Rock's first brickmaker advertised in 1821. Bricks could be made on the farm or plantation by shaping the wet clay and letting the sun dry it. Fired bricks were more enduring. Little Rock's first mansion, erected by Robert Crittenden, "a home so spacious it was seriously considered for the capitol" required more than 300,000 bricks. Businesses used bricks extensively because they were fire-resistant. By 1827, Little Rock boasted sixty buildings, of which eight were frame and six were brick. Brick was considered lowly compared to stone, so the State House builders covered the brick with masonry painted to simulate the appearance of stone.

Most prominent in the town were the public buildings. In Little Rock, the State House, which faced both Markham Street and the Arkansas River, offered a good example of Greek Revival architecture. Designed by Kentucky's Gideon Shyrock, it was perhaps the first professionally planned building in Arkansas. The architect's designs, however, were too expensive to execute, so Shyrock's assistant, George Weigart, and Governor John Pope modified them. Arkansas's first two ill-fated banks also erected significant buildings, and the federal government began work on the arsenal complex in 1837, erecting a Gothic-towered building in 1841. It still stands as the Museum of Science and History in MacArthur Park. St. John's College also looked like a medieval fortress, and it became Little Rock's education center in 1859.

The town's churches developed slowly. The first church was a log structure erected by Baptists and later sided with clapboard. Presbyterians built a frame building, and the first brick church was erected by Methodists in 1833. When the Christians (Campbellites), who had inherited the old Baptist Church, decided to erect a new building in 1845, the *Gazette* reported that it would be "larger and more imposing in appearance than any church in the city." However, the rival Presbyterians started a new church and in 1852 dedicated their 1,600-pound bell, which had been shipped from Cincinnati. Evidently, none of these buildings, or those of the Catholics and Episcopalians, was designed by professional architects. In one instance, a master carpenter was responsible for the design; in another, the minister.

No other Arkansas community had Little Rock's architectural variety. Fort Smith had a military post, but the federal district court and much of the trade were at nearby Van Buren. The courthouse dominated most county seats from its central location in the square. Little Rock's town planners drew in two squares, neither of which survived.

Business architecture looked remarkably similar to that of colonial times. The shops, or "stands," stood next to each other for the length of the street. Fires invariably engulfed whole blocks even when the buildings were made of brick with slate roofs. Town real estate was a lucrative investment, and few merchants owned their own buildings. Travelers stayed in hotels, the most famous of which in Little Rock was the Anthony House, a brick structure that lasted from early statehood to 1875.

In the beginning, the elite built their homes near their work. The mansion of Chester Ashley, so imposing it served as a hotel into the twentieth century, was just a short distance from the State House on East Markham. As population increased, commercial demands led to the dismantling or conversion of residential property. William E. Woodruff became one of Arkansas's first suburbanites in the 1850s by building a new country house just outside town. Suburban spreads had room for extensive gardens, both ornamental and useful. Absalom Fowler and Albert Pike, both of whom grew rich from the tangled affairs of the banks, led the way in building showcase mansions on what was then the edge of town. Pike's mansion, now known as the Pike-Fletcher-Terry house, is located on East Seventh Street in downtown Little Rock. It now serves as the Arkansas Arts Center Decorative Arts Museum.

Most town residents were not rich enough to afford elaborate homes. Their small frame or brick structures were often in a plain Greek Revival style or were "vernacular," that is, made without a formal plan by practical carpenters. Windows were almost prohibitively expensive. Two stories was the practical limit; canvasses hung and papered might substitute for plaster, and taking in boarders was a matter of course.

An Early View of Hot Springs, Arkansas. *(David Dale Owen, 1858) The natural advantages of the hot springs as the site for a spa were somewhat neutralized because of the failure to settle the question of ownership and poor road conditions.* **Author's Collection**.

Urban Growth

In general, Arkansas towns depended on the development of adjacent agricultural areas. After an initial burst of population from 1819 to 1840, town development languished until the 1850s. Little Rock, which had 1,531 residents in 1840, had only 3,727 in 1860. By comparison, Memphis had gone from almost the same 1840 figure to more than 22,000 by the Civil War. With almost no manufacturing or other source of income except politics and trade, Arkansas towns remained anomalies in a rural world.

Spas

A different sort of urban amenity was provided by the state's spas. Taking the waters

was a popular nineteenth century cure. Certain types of water, notably those that were hot or mineral, were held to have curative values. In the absence of workable medicine, many people believed in the healing powers of taking the waters, and the upper classes used the spas for vacations. Diversions such as gambling and horse races followed; musical entertainments were devised and "visiting" probably dominated.

The acknowledged leader of spa communities in the entire Southwest was Hot Springs. First officially explored in 1804 by William Dunbar and Dr. George Hunter at President Thomas Jefferson's instigation, the springs already gave evidence of use. Within a few years, trapper John Percival had opened a house for visitors and erected some small cabins. His food was described as pork swimming in fat, bad bread and worse coffee, but business was good. By 1818, Major Stephen Long reported finding about fifteen cabins in the vicinity of the springs. What is considered the first hotel opened in 1820, and Ludovicus Belding, whose portrait was painted by John Henry Byrd, provided what the *Gazette* described as "good food, clean linen, silver forks and spoons."

Variously known as Thermopolis and Warm Springs, it did not officially become Hot Springs until 1832. Even more confusing than the town's name was the question of who owned it. Unlike the contest over early Little Rock, this controversy lasted until 1876. Private claimants, one of whom was Governor Henry M. Rector, fought the national government, which created a federal reservation in 1832. The inability to settle the title retarded the town's development because promoters were afraid to erect buildings of any value. Despite its visitors, Hot Springs had only 201 permanent residents by 1860.

A number of antebellum spas competed with Hot Springs, some in the same vicinity. Chalybeate Springs was three miles away and Sulphur Springs eight. Yell County was home to Dardanelle Sulphur Springs; White Sulphur Springs became the town of Searcy. Sulphur appears to have been a lure, for several places used that name. One Sulphur Springs near Pine Bluff attracted a Little Rock crowd, and another of the same name, sixteen miles from Batesville, drew from the northeast.

TRANSPORTATION

Central to the rise of towns was the creation of a transportation network. America used waterways, roads, canals and railroads. No canals ever were constructed in Arkansas, and the state ranked last in miles of railroad track in 1860. Instead, water and roads constituted the basic units of antebellum transportation.

River Transportation

At the beginning of the territorial period, Arkansas still relied on primitive hand-pro-

pelled keelboats, canoes and pirogues for water transportation. Little Rock found itself in 1824 without mail service when the mailman's canoe overturned and he drowned. Paddling or poling against the current was labor intensive and expensive. Yet the first residents received their salt and other necessities by this cumbersome and expensive mode of water transportation. One hunter recalled paying $4 for a set of teacups and saucers, and he complained of Fort Smith merchant John Rogers that, "He sold everything vastly high."

The application of the steam engine to boats revolutionized the use of rivers. On March 31, 1820, the *Comet* was the first boat to venture up the Arkansas to the Post. Two years later, the *Eagle* reached Little Rock. *Intrepid* Captain Phillip Pennywit became the first to reach Fort Smith and Fort Gibson on the Arkansas River and Batesville on the White. Prices fell by half after Pennywit's arrival at Batesville in 1831. The steamboat trip from Little Rock to the White River cutoff took nine days round trip compared to twenty to thirty-five for a flatboat or keelboat. Invariably the first sound of a steamboat whistle caused men and women to quiver with fear and beasts to bolt. In only a few years' time, smaller streams such as the Black and St. Francis were serviced regularly. On the Ouachita, Jacob Barkman, a merchant, speculator and salt springs owner, launched the boat *Dime*, and eventually boats reached Arkadelphia.

Steamboats encountered a number of problems. Snags in the water could sink a boat. The reluctance of the government to spend money to remove navigation obstacles was a touchy political issue in Jacksonian America. The tendency of ship captains to overfire boilers occasionally led to spectacular explosions accompanied by great loss of life. "With almost every issue of our paper," the editor of the Washington *Telegraph* wrote, "we are called upon to record one or more disastrous accidents occurring upon our western rivers. To travel on one of our steamboats is equivalent to gambling ventures upon one's life."

Not surprisingly, the average life of a ship

Two Steamboats on the White River. *(photographer and date unknown) This photograph taken after the Civil War shows the* Randall *stuck on a sand bar and illustrates the problems of early water transportation.* **Arkansas College.**

was only three years. A newspaper correspondent noted in 1861: "The Arkansas is the graveyard of steamboats . . . I noticed the wrecks of the *Frontier City, New Cedar Rapid,* and *Quapaw* standing in the water to their cabin floors at various places, some considerable distance apart." A steamboat wreck ended hope of a Red River commerce with Santa Fe, and on the White River at Forsyth, the *Mary M. Patterson* sat trapped on a sand bar by falling waters from April 1860 to February 1861.

River transportion was subject to other uncertainties. The failure of the Red River to rise in 1855 left 40,000 bales of cotton stranded. One wedding in Little Rock had to be postponed because there was no flour in town to make the wedding cake and low water prevented the arrival of any boats. The River

never rose in 1839, leaving "scarcely water sufficient to float a dug-out." The standing joke was that a catfish wishing to move to another hole had to catch a ride on the back of a turtle.

The boats that plied Arkansas waters were not the large, well-equipped floating palaces that serviced the Mississippi. United States Supreme Court Justice Peter Daniel, who visited Arkansas on his judicial rounds, complained of "very small and unsafe boats . . . crowded with rude, dirty people and scarcely anything eatable." A White River traveler called the *Fox,* "a little, dirty, wheezing, asthmatic sternwheeler."

Steamboats did a good trade, especially during the Indian removals when wealthier tribal members used steamboats to reach their destinations. Steamboats initially were owned by individuals, often by their captains. Some merchants such as Sterling H. Tucker found owning a boat a useful adjunct to their stores, and corporate capitalism began to enter the picture by the 1850s. Steamboats called packets often carried mail and kept regular schedules. Passengers made their Arkansas connections at Montgomery's Point on the White River cutoff or at Napoleon at the mouth of the Arkansas. Many of the hard stories about the state grew out of impressions gained at these two hell holes. Southern-born Judge Peter Daniel, who had written, I "devotedly love the South," and was a more credible witness than Northern or English travelers, could not stomach Napoleon either. He said it was the "most wretched of wretched places."

Access to rivers retarded as well as aided town development. As did Virginia planters on the Tidewater, who traded directly with English ships from their private landings, Arkansas planters often took their cotton to the river bank and arranged for it to be sent to New Orleans. The relative ease with which boats could be loaded often made it unnecessary to use the facilities of a town. The steamer by return trip could bring the planter exactly what he ordered.

Bayous and oxbows extended access along the river. One traveler watched with admiration and horror as his captain left the White River, and maneuvering around cypress knees while the smokestack pushed aside branches, stopped to pick up a cargo from a planter. Steamboats also helped develop a plantation economy that emphasized cotton. It was cheaper to import meat from Cincinnati than buy it locally, a relationship caused in part by the condition of Arkansas's roads.

Road Transportation

Roads were the alternative to water transportation. By Arkansas definition, a road was "a direction marked out, not a surface to travel over." The oldest roads in Arkansas began as Indian trails. The Southwest Trail, which ran from the northeast to the southwest along the edge of the Ozark and Ouachita escarp-

ments, was the first to be improved. By 1818, one could reach Polk Bayou (Batesville) in Independence County by wagon but could continue only with pack horses. On this road and others some work was done by military engineers, hence leading to the designation of "military road."

Government contract specifications called merely for a sixteen-foot-wide lane with brush and saplings leveled to the ground and all trees up to twelve inches in diameter cut to within four inches of the ground. The stumps of trees wider than twelve inches had to be within eight inches of the ground. Little attention seems to have been given to planning, for traveler G. W. Featherstonhaugh observed that although the surveyors had followed the Roman example and made the road straight, they had neglected to remove the hill: "Our horse, therefore, came to a dead standstill."

Rerouting became a common occurrence. Rather than repair the road, any time a tree fell or a washout or mud hole developed, the travelers simply made a new track around the obstacle. This practice remained standard well into the twentieth century.

Although the Southwest Trail facilitated communication and immigration from Missouri, agitation developed early for a road linking Arkansas directly to the east. Here no Indian trail existed as a guide. The first surveyors allegedly crossed over the Mississippi from Memphis to Hopefield, took a look and then went by boat to a point on the White River due west of Memphis. There they stopped, took another look and drew a line connecting the two points. Those parts of this Memphis-Little Rock road traversing the swampy lowlands of the Cache and St. Francis River bottoms were almost always under water. Major rerouting became necessary. "Emigrants continue to flock to this part of the country," the *Gazette* noted in 1837, "but they do it at a risk and cost of passing the most disgraceful bogs, wilderness, and swamps that can be found." C. F. M. Noland in 1854 added: "Life preservers and diving-bells should occupy the coaches." Eventually

Cartoon by William "Cush" Quesenbury (ca. 1855) *In this early drawing, apparently intended only for private circulation, Quesenbury filled a whole sheet of paper with incidents of Arkansas travel. In the detail shown here, passengers, who were charged at the rate of 10 cents a mile, sit with their baggage while the drivers try to get the coach unstuck. The U.S. mail has been tossed out, and nearby lie the remains of a team and wagon. Quesenbury was a staunch Whig who charged that the Democratic Party's policy of road construction was to wait until erosion wore down the mountains.* **Arkansas History Commission**

the military extended the road from Little Rock to Fort Smith, and another important early road linked Van Buren to Fayetteville, Arkansas, Springfield, Missouri, and St. Louis. Federal road funding largely stopped with statehood, and none of the Arkansas roads progressed thereafter.

Because the state had no money for roads, private enterprise was expected to take up the task. Ferries were licensed on major streams, and with the press of traffic, a two-horse ferry went into service at Fort Smith and a steam ferry at Little Rock. The legislature authorized the Little Rock Bridge Company to build a toll bridge over the Ouachita River at Rockport. The $20,000 bridge went into service in 1846, only to be washed away on December 10, 1848, when the River rose eight feet above the highest known mark. The White, Red, Arkansas and Mississippi Rivers all remained unbridged until after the Civil War.

Travel conditions were primitive. The trip from Washington, Arkansas, to Little Rock took fifty hours, and one arrived "more fit for hospital treatment than for business activity."

From Hot Springs to the capital, a distance of fifty-four miles, the mail coach took nineteen and a half hours. "Independence County," complained a Batesville editor, "has no roads sufficiently decent to convey out of her limits a convict to the penitentiary." Wrecks were common, and one left Congressman Thomas C. Hindman partially crippled.

Travelers and editors reached into the depths of printable vocabulary to describe the vehicles that plied the roads. "Miserable, rickety, filthy, slab-sided nuisances, called mail coaches," Batesville editor M. S. Kennard wrote. While in the southwest, William Etter referred to a "rattle-trap sort of non-descript vehicle which has been dubbed a stage." But it took a visiting clergyman, George Foster Pierce, to describe a stage fully:

The stage was a carriage of the sort that is known in different places by different names. By some it is called Jersey wagon; by others, peddler's wagon, dearborn, whimmy-diddle, go cart, but I concluded that the inventive genius of Arkansas had hit the thing exactly, when I learned that it was commonly called a trick. That is the right name, whether we consider its size, its shape, or its business. To put such a thing on the stageline, as a public convenience or conveyance, it is most certainly a trick—and was one of the poorest tricks. Old, shackling, ready to fall to pieces, it looked unsafe to sit in when it was standing still. To cross the mountains with it was daring adventure.

Those who took the trip from Van Buren to Fayetteville—later the route of the California Overland Express—had to cling to one side of the carriage as the driver snaked around the sides of mountains. At times it was necessary to get out and walk, for in places the incline was too steep for man, beast and coach.

Accommodations along the routes were equally primitive. At Rockroe, a major stopping point on the White River, the hotel in 1844 was a half mile off in the woods and contained only three rooms. Four ladies who occupied the loft spent the night "gazing at the stars which shone brightly through the holes in the roof and frightening each other with a coon which was trying to catch the chickens roosting above." Food was also a problem for the fastidious who objected to dirty bread, tough chicken with lard poured over it instead of butter and no sugar for coffee. Finally, travelers were infected with fear. G. W. Featherstonhaugh was shown the site of some murders, and the tales grew in the telling. " My only wonder is that we reached here alive," one traveler to Fort Smith wrote, adding "I expected every night to have been murdered." An Izard County farmer put it differently: "you will have to come with your purse in one hand and your prick in the other and your hat turned strait up before [.] If you will maby you will come through safe."

IMMIGRATION

Despite poor conditions, these routes were used by the Indians during the Trail of Tears removals. The poorer Indians, especially the women, simply walked, and the Creeks left their dead in hollow trees along the route. The pattern for farmers was to arrive during the fall or winter in order to find a site and plant crops in the spring. Most brought their goods in wagons pulled by oxen. Often one family member came first to inspect the land. At Helena in 1858:

> Wagon after wagon, in an almost continuous line, are being put across daily from the Mississippi side of the river by the Messrs. Weather's steam ferry boat at this place. The heavy immigration into Arkansas this season is marked for being composed of people who are well-to-do in the way of wordly goods, woolyheads and large families of intelligent-looking boys and bright-eyed girls.

Yet partly because of what these immigrants saw and experienced on Arkansas roads, "not one out of twenty stops this side of Texas," the *Gazette* lamented. When a modicum of prosperity returned in the 1850s, improving the transportation system was the first item on the agenda.

LAW ENFORCEMENT

Early settlers preceded the arrival of law. In a territory so sparsely settled, the forms of justice made under the common law for a compact agricultural society were too unwieldy to function. Some residents were too remote to even care. While Henry Schoolcraft was a guest at a hunter's cabin, a legal notice arrived from Lawrence County. Because neither the hunter nor Schoolcraft could figure out the notice, the man chose to ignore it.

As counties were created, agencies of law took shape in the form of grand juries, sheriffs, constables, justices of peace, circuit judges and appellate courts. Most Americans had some familiarity with the law, either as defendants or plaintiffs. A man who fell afoul of his neighbors, such as Bazil Boran in Lawrence County, and who spoke harshly of judges, could find himself indicted on a variety of charges. John Irons, who called his neighbor's wife the "damnest [sic] whore that ever was in Lawrence County," was sued for trespass (an early form of tort) by the irate husband and wife. The first change of venue, from Arkansas County to Lawrence, was on a similar suit spurred by Joseph Kuykendall's remark to Mrs. James Currin that "you are a whore and John McElmurry has fucked you a hundred times."

Most criminal violations occurred over drinking and appeared as "A & B," assault and battery, in early court records. There was a code of honor associated with eye-gouging and other affrays that officially the law could not ignore, but which in practice led to cases invariably being dropped unless a man was particularly unpopular. Dueling, which played such a tragic role in territorial politics, also violated the law, but indictments were few and apparently no convictions occurred.

A different problem in early Arkansas grew out of the presence of outlaws and refugees from justice. The Mississippi River Valley attracted criminals because of the considerable trade that went down the River, the absence of a settled population, and the possibility for establishing havens from justice. The first known criminals in Arkansas were the Mason family, headed by Samuel Mason, who were reported to be at the Post in 1802. Their trademark after a crime was a placard bragging "Done by Samuel Mason of the Woods."

Post factor John Treat complained in 1806 about some five families on the White River of whom "it is said they have left to escape justice, several of them have been guilty of atrocious acts." Jacob Wythe Walker, the father of Judge David Walker, and himself the president of a failed bank, was marginally more tolerant:

Men of desperate or ruined fortune are found in new countries in greater proportions than in the old. A change may benefit; he who is already ruined can not be worsted. Besides, new

countries present the greatest theatre for enterprise.

The young men or "bloods" who came to make their fortunes in Arkansas may not have left behind a sordid past, but their hot tempers and addiction to alcohol led to personal violence. On May 20, 1840, *Gazette* editor Edward Cole wrote:

We regret to be obliged to state that frays, fist-fights, and other breaches of the peace are becoming more common in our city, than at anytime since our residence here, and when we first arrived here, the place had a name bad enough.

Nor were things better in Fort Smith, where an editor in 1860 complained, "Murder, vice, and rowdyism stalk our streets by night and by day with brazen effrontery, confident in the feeling that there is no power to restrain them." The rural areas were hardly less violent. In 1857, twenty-five men at Frog Bayou engaged in a "rock fite," and Marion County was disrupted for decades by the battle between the Tutt and Everett families, which at one point became so bloody that the governor called out the militia.

Although personal violence contributed to a negative public image, people were more worried about professional criminal activity. Horse thieves, counterfeiters, Negro runners, robbers and murderers directly threatened the lives and property of at least the respectable element. Log jails were a joke, juries were swayed easily and the law remained full of technicalities. William E. Woodruff, "one of the most indefatigably industrious men of the territory," advocated lynch law, a term that originally meant any extra-legal enforcement such as whippings and tar and feathering, in addition to hangings.

Mississippi River Valley residents were terrified by the publication in 1835 of *A History of the Detection, Conviction, Life and Designs of John A. Murel [sic], the Great Western Land Pirate* by Virgil A. Stewart. Murrell was probably only a small-time Tennessee crook who, in 1834, was sentenced to the Tennessee penitentiary after being convicted of stealing a slave. But according to Stewart, Murrell was the head of a thousand organized followers. At a signal, his followers—the Murellites—were to rise up, free and arm slaves and loot the country. Stewart's book touched off a series of bloody lynchings in Mississippi and the terror spread to Arkansas.

Bandits supposedly kept a Garden of Eden somewhere in eastern Arkansas, and relations between Mississippi County and its Tennessee neighbors were strained. According to Tennessee accounts, flatboats were stopped and robbed on the Arkansas side, especially near Shawnee Village. In retaliation, a Tennessee force crossed the River in 1834, burned cabins and carried back prisoners. A flatboat loaded with tobacco sank under mysterious circumstances in 1835. The Mississippi County sheriff auctioned off for a pittance the damaged property, paying the captain in counterfeit money. Again a Tennessee mob crossed the River and reclaimed some of the tobacco. According to Stewart's book, one of Murrell's confederates was E. Floyd, the first sheriff of Mississippi County.

The common response to perceived outbreaks of crime consisted of organizing "Regulators," a term of colonial origin. During the Murrell hysteria, a group of Regulators in Little Rock, following the example of Natchez, Vicksburg, and other river towns, made war on gamblers and other disreputables. One alleged murderer was divested of his clothes, whipped until bloody, had his head shaved and an ear cut off and was placed in an old canoe without a paddle. Then they "cautioned . . . against ever setting foot in Little Rock again." At Randolph, Tennessee, local vigilantes caught an old Arkansas man and his two sons with burglary tools. After a thorough whipping, the three suspects were tied hand and foot before being cast adrift in the River. The 1839 lynching of four suspected murderers at Cane Hill was probably the most violent outbreak of Regulation in antebellum Arkansas.

The inefficiency of the legal system had diverse causes. In some places the authorities themselves were under suspicion. In addition to the charges against the first sheriff of Mississippi County, questions were asked about the St. Francis County sheriff, William Strong. An early speculator who failed to develop his town on the Memphis-Little Rock road, Strong had sufficient political pull to have his son appointed to West Point. He allegedly had placed stolen goods among travelers' possessions and then arrested and fined the visitors.

A second reason for the inefficiency of the system came from its common law origins. The system had become cumbersome and complicated over the centuries. Although the American tendency was to simplify, codify and reform, these elements failed to make an impression in early Arkansas. The state Supreme Court, under the leadership of Chief Justice Daniel Ringo, usually avoided answering substantive questions by getting involved in small technical points. When the legislature tried to facilitate the criminal justice system by enlarging the duties of justices of the peace, the Court in *Eason* v. *State* (1851) struck down the reform. Thus every criminal charge required a grand jury indictment, the expenses of which were borne by the counties. The criminal justice system cost the counties more than they took in, resulting in the issuing of county scrip to make up the deficit.

Occasional attempts to reform the system failed. James C. Tappan, later a Confederate general, introduced a bill to simplify pleadings in 1850, only to have Governor John S. Roane veto it. Arkansas did adopt the penitentiary system in 1842, but the results were not encouraging. The penitentiary did not reform the prisoners, and Albert Pike's hope that its existence would retard lynching proved illusory, especially for crimes involving blacks. In Saline County in 1854, a lynch mob attacked the jail where a black prisoner had been confined for more than a year, pushed aside the sheriff and hung the prisoner. The alleged abolitionist became another lynching target. He deserved "instant death," a Des Arc editor noted, "and it costs something to keep him a long time in jail or under surveillance."

The one area in which Arkansas did show legal initiative was with respect to the rights of married women. Under common law, women ranked with children and idiots, for a wife's property was completely at her husband's disposal. The territorial legislature passed an act in 1835 to protect women from losing their property to the debts of their husbands. This first attempt was inadequate, and the state legislature returned to the matter in 1840 by passing a statute similar to one that had been enacted by Mississippi, the first such state law in the nation. Governor Archibald Yell vetoed the measure, claiming that giving women rights would break up the happy family. After New York and other states followed Mississippi's lead, Arkansas's legislature passed a bill again and Governor Thomas S. Drew signed it into law in 1846.

In the years following its passage, Arkansas women hastened to take advantage of the law, registering their property in the county deed books. Although the law was largely designed to protect gifts of slaves by planters to their daughters, evidence indicates that a wide variety of women, especially remarrying widows, took advantage of its provisions.

ENTERTAINMENTS

Because frontier life was composed in equal parts of monotony and hard work, all outlets for entertainment were thoroughly explored. Towns provided a geographic locus for many activities, attracting rural people and benefiting local businesses.

Holidays

Antebellum Arkansas had a limited number of holidays. Thanksgiving was a Northern tradition and did not receive general acceptance until the twentieth century. Labor Day and Memorial Day emerged after the Civil War, and little was done to mark the

birthdays of George Washington or Christopher Columbus. That left the Fourth of July and Christmas, with only the former celebrated universally. Typically the Fourth brought displays of patriotic oratory, a lengthy round of toasts at public banquets, and a good deal of disorderly celebration, culminating in the traditional reading of the Declaration of Independence. Even slaves shared in the festivities, for the date coincided fortuitously with "laying by" cotton.

Christmas played a lesser role in Arkansas. Many Protestant denominations openly denounced the holiday as spurious. The Christmas tree, although seen in Fayetteville before the Civil War, was not in common log cabins until the 1890s. Episcopalians led in commemoration, and the celebration of Christmas flourished most in the southern part of the state. The Washington *Telegraph* reported in 1852:

> Christmas made its appearance with its usual escorts—fun, frolic, and crackers, and passed off good-humoredly, without the occurrence of anything disagreeable to mar its hilarity. On Monday night last there was a Ball at Washington House, and the lads and lassies tripped it lightly on the fantastic toe to the music of the violin till day-light did appear.

Because the holiday also marked the ending of the picking season for cotton, slaves were treated to fun and frolic as well.

Close upon Christmas came New Year's, which often generated some revels. Newspaper editors used the first issue of the new year to summarize past events and write predictions, sometimes optimistic and sometimes dire. May Day, an old English spring festival focusing on a May pole and the crowning of a May queen, found a few adherents despite the objections of some denominations.

Dancing

An interest in dancing, popular among the French, was shared by early settlers. Hewes

Gambling Exposed

Gambling was one of the most pernicious vices of early Arkansas. Jonathan Greene, a reformed gambler who "got religion," left this account of one episode. Greene posed as a violent opponent of gambling, but in his book he described all the favorite card games of the era and suggested how to win with them.

I will here give a short account of an occurrence in Columbia [Chicot County], Arkansas, in the year 1835. A man went there and commenced dealing faro. There was no doubt of his being a very desperate man; but still he was encouraged by many in this game, though known to be a very bad man, and brother to the notorious land-pirate of Tennessee, who had been but a short time before taken off for his many misdemeanors in that state. This faro dealer in Arkansas was one night playing as usual, when suddenly the lights were put out by some in the room, and he was then literally cut up; one of his hands was cut entirely off, and he was most horribly mangled. Several stabs penetrated the region of his heart. He, however, escaped out of the house, and ran a short distance and fell dead. Several persons were arrested, but no convictions ensued. The citizens generally approved the act, and thought it a good thing for the community that they were rid of such a man, even by such means.

O! what a lamentable state of society and morals, when gambling is encouraged by one portion, and cold-blooded murder and robbery justified or excused by the other. The town of Columbia has suffered as much from faro as any other place, for the number of its inhabitants. Often, when men lose all on a game, they become reckless and desperate, and are willing to sacrifice any principle, or stoop to any depth, to be equal with those who have swindled them. . . .

Many men will play for amusement only, but they soon find some to flatter them, and tell them that they play well; yea, well enough to venture to play against any of the gamblers. Thus their vanity becomes flattered, and they seek to try their skill against some well-known player, and soon become ranked among the habitual if not confirmed gamblers. And if they are business men, their profits, and frequently more, are spent over gambling tables and in barrooms. And if they be men who have their riches in ready cash, it soon all goes in this abominable way.

Source: Jonathan H. Greene, Gambling Exposed; A Full Exposition of All the Various Arts, Mysteries, and Miseries of Gambling *(Philadelphia, 1843).*

Scull, also the first noted American poet in Arkansas, held a fancy ball at the Post in 1820. Admission to such events was often by ticket. Samuel Evans at Fayetteville was instructed by the managers to pass out tickets in 1839 "to all the Ladies in your vicinity." Lower-class dances on Saturday night attracted large and sometimes rowdy crowds. Little Rock had a dancing school by 1832. Some religious groups, notably the Presbyterians, objected, especially because many started the Sabbath at six p. m. Saturday. "To hop was a sin," one Presbyterian child recalled, "and Father thought a skip must certainly be damnation."

Music

Pioneer music was of the homemade variety. Tunes carried over from England were fitted with new words suitable to the Arkansas frontier and became a part of folk culture. Many of the songs chronicled local events, becoming a kind of folk newspaper.

The various denominations inherited different musical traditions. Composed hymns competed with gospel songs. The first formal concert was held in April 1821 at the Post by a Mr. Fries, but most singing was strictly amateur. Singing clubs and community concerts were popular. Batesville residents had the opportunity to hear Haydn's

Creation. Pianos, although expensive, became increasingly available, and sheet music could be obtained easily. Washington and Van Buren organized brass bands early, and they were much in demand for holidays and political events.

The first professional troupes to visit Arkansas were minstrel companies that mixed music and comedy. River towns were frequented most often, and the level of entertainment was not considered suitable for women. Harry McCarthy, billed as the "Arkansas Comedian," was popular all over the South, and the state itself was the butt of a number of minstrel jokes, the tune and story of "The Arkansas Traveler" being the best known. Some Arkansans had opportunities at Memphis in 1859 to see and hear Adelina Patti, the new Queen of Song, and Jenny Lind's successor. Although Jenny Lind never visited Arkansas, she did inspire one town planner in western Arkansas to name a community after her.

Circuses

The most popular imported event was the circus. The first was that of W. Waterman & Co. in 1838, which came from Missouri and stopped at Pitman's Ferry, Pocahontas, Jackson, Smithville, Batesville and Little Rock. The troupe was led by Mr. Waterman, a two-horse rider, and also contained a single horse rider, a tumbler, plate dancer and balancer, plus a clown and child prodigy. A Batesville paper lamented that alas, there was no monkey. Thereafter, circuses became regular features except for the period 1842-1852 when an anti-entertainment mood dominated. By the 1850s most parts of the state could expect a circus visit at least once a year. Billing notices in the local press were extravagant, as when John Robinson's International Circus and Menagerie in 1857 promised a horned horse. On one occasion the same year, Washburn's Circus, which had stopped at most of the White River towns, drew a poor first night in Little Rock "by report that the Circus was a humbug." As with the theater, newspapers

occasionally ventured criticism, perhaps depending on the size of the circus advertisement.

Horse Racing

Horse racing was preeminent among the amusements of pioneer Arkansas. The first recorded race horse sale was made in 1815 by trader John Luttig at Poke Bayou, and the first jockey club—a group that obtained a track and set forth rules—appeared in Hempstead County in 1820. These early races probably were run by scrub ponies, but with the arrival in 1827 of Thomas Todd Tunstall, the sport emerged from the status of a local entertainment to one warranting the attention of the New York *Spirit of the Times*, the nation's premiere sporting paper.

Thomas Todd Tunstall was a native of Virginia whose family often had owned blooded stock. Tunstall, who started with modest means, moved his growing family from Virginia to Kentucky, Indiana and Illinois before arriving in Chicot County in 1827. Becoming a river pilot on the new steamboats, he worked for Captain Pennywit, piloting some of the first boats in Arkansas waters. Soon he acquired his own boats, usually running them on the White and Arkansas Rivers. He opened a store next at Jacksonport and acquired his first thoroughbred race horse. An 1830 race against Wharton Rector's thoroughbred marked the beginning of his racing career.

The Little Rock Jockey Club with future Governor James S. Conway as president held its first races in 1834 near the site of what is now MacArthur Park, and Tunstall's "celebrated turf horse" and the keystone of his success, "Volcano," reigned supreme. The popularity of the Little Rock contest led Fayetteville, Fort Smith, Batesville, and even Arkansas Post to emulate the capital. In addition to the purses, which ranged into the hundreds of dollars, thousands more changed hands in private bets. Most of the elite participated and betting frequently spilled over into politics. Reputedly the best

Notice of a Three-Day Race Meet at Fort Smith, Arkansas. *Fort Smith* Herald *October 4, 1848. Horse racing appealed to all classes but aroused strong religious opposition, especially after the Depression in 1842.* **Arkansas History Commission**

track in the state was at Fort Smith, where Elias Rector dominated the sport. Arkansas gained a national reputation in turf activities from the active pen of aficionado C.F.M. Noland, whose stories of great races were read nationally.

The Depression of 1839, which reached Arkansas in the 1840s, dealt a death blow to the aristocracy that sustained the sport. A Van Buren city ordinance in 1845 made it illegal to exhibit a stud horse or to put to stud a horse and mare. Racing on a grand scale had ended by 1850. The new settlers of the 1850s, those solid bourgeois religious evangelicals, failed to revive it. Despite a flurry of interest at the turn of the century and at Oaklawn in Hot Springs in the twentieth century, racing never regained its early preeminence.

Theater

Urban areas provided audiences large enough to support even more sophisticated activities. Perhaps the most controversial was theater, for the Puritan objection to the stage remained in the Protestant heritage through the nineteenth century. The first play in Arkansas was put on in 1830 by the soldiers stationed at Fort Gibson. Little Rock followed on November 4, 1834, when the Thalian Club of amateurs did *She Stoops to Conquer* and the farce, *Who's the Dupe?* George C. Watkins, later chief justice, played one of the female roles because polite women could not appear on stage. The first professional season began in 1838 with the arrival of a troupe of ten persons led by Samuel Water. There was no scenery, "not even a curtain," but the saloon attached to the theater, itself a remodeled saloon, presumably did a good business. *The Young Widow* opened a season that also included *Therese* by John Howard Payne, the first American play presented in Little Rock.

Although Water was an active frontier producer and actor, critical reviews were mixed. Newspapers argued that plays were a better and more moral form of entertainment than many of the events happening in the town's streets, but that Water's standards were not high. Women were in such short supply that often one woman played several roles. Shakespeare's *Richard III*, the *Gazette* noted, was "murdered." The first Arkansas play, *Bill Screamer, or, The Man of the West,* by John Field of Hempstead County, surfaced and disappeared in the spring of the 1839. The theater burned on February 27, 1840, and was not rebuilt. With the coming of hard times, the money to support luxuries dried up and the moral tone of repression dominated.

When prosperity returned, Nick Moroney came from Memphis for a season in 1858, and amateur theatricals became common in the smaller communities. Washington, for example, got its first taste of drama in 1860 in a converted barn. A prejudice still remained, however. During the Civil War, Episcopal Bishop Henry Lay disciplined some Pine Bluff women by denying them communion for having appeared in a tableaux to raise money for the Confederacy.

Intellectual Interests

Urban areas also supported intellectual contacts. Little Rock organized a debating society in 1822, broadening it to form the Pulaski County Lyceum in 1835. Batesville's lyceum followed in 1839. William E. Woodruff's circulating library, founded in 1826 and continued for more than a decade, loaned books at 12.5 cents a volume. Helena supported a cultural group called the Atheneum.

The most ambitious program was the Antiquarian and Natural History Society, incorporated by the legislature in 1837 and charged with preserving the state's history and analyzing its natural resources. The Society collected some rare Indian artifacts in the State House but they eventually were lost. Most older states had similar bodies that have endured. In Arkansas, however, the Society failed in 1842, and the state had to wait a hundred years before a permanent body, the Arkansas Historical Association, could be sustained. There were several reasons for the failure: Arkansas failed to develop supporting institutions such as libraries, universities or charitable trusts. Hard times undermined the financial support, and the succeeding generations lacked the broad vision of the founders. The Club of Forty in Little Rock subscribed to a number of magazines during the 1840s, and the lyceum was revived in the 1850s. As the sectional crisis deepened, the South became increasingly intolerant of any book or journal critical of slavery in the slightest way. One by one the great national periodicals disappeared. Many Southerners held fast to their English heritage and continued to read *Blackwood's* and other British periodicals, but a climate of anti-intellectualism increasingly constricted the reading public. The first Arkansas periodical, *Arkansas Magazine,* appeared in 1854. Although it boasted of having articles "from some of the ablest pens in the state," its existence was brief.

Nineteenth century Americans lived in an age of great orators. The spoken rather than the written word dominated in politics, religion and even in education. One of the most popular entertainments consisted of attending public speakings. Lectures were frequent—and often free—as when Reverend Mr. Gilliam at Batesville offered his version of "American Progress" in 1858. Traveling lecturers charged. At Helena in 1850, a Colonel Lehmanowsky offered seven lecturers for $1.50 or thirty cents at the door. His second lecture, on the "Character, disposition, and manners, of Madame Josephine, first wife of Napoleon, the cause of the divorce and dying scenes of Napoleon and Madame Josephine," reflected a popular interest in European history. Transportation problems kept the most famous lecturers away, awaiting completion of the railroad network. In the interval, Arkansas found in local politics and religion no mean diversions.

CONCLUSION

During the antebellum period Arkansas developed less rapidly than Missouri, Florida, Texas or Michigan. Arkansas lagged culturally, displaying not so much the absence of institutions, but rather their presence in an underdeveloped form. The territory and state showed great similarity to the back country in the eighteenth century colonial period of American history.

BIBLIOGRAPHIC ESSAY

Although Arkansas is rich in materials for studying both Western and Southern influences, little systematic use has been made of these records, and the interesting debates of modern social historians figure not at all. Two valuable state studies are Walter Moffatt, "Transportation in Arkansas, 1819-1840," *AHQ,* XV (Fall 1956), 187-201, and broader than its title is Robert B. Walz, "Migration into Arkansas, 1820-1880: Incentives and Means of Travel," *AHQ,* XVII (Winter 1958), 309-324. The only section of Arkansas thoroughly studied is in Dwight Pitcaithley, "Settlement of the Arkansas Ozarks: The Buffalo River Valley," *AHQ,* XXXVII (Autumn 1978), 203-222. Three valuable county studies are S. Charles Bolton, "Inequality on the Southern Frontier: Arkansas County in the Arkansas Territory," *AHQ,* XLI (Spring 1982), 51-66; Carl H. Moneyhon "Economic Democracy in Antebellum Arkansas, Phillips County, 1850-1860," *AHQ,* XL (Spring 1981), 154-172, and Ted R. Worley, "Pope County One Hundred Years Ago," *AHQ,* XIII (Summer 1954), 196-204. Two useful specialized studies by Walter A. Moffatt are "Cultural and Recreational Activities in Pioneer Arkansas," *AHQ,* XIII (Winter 1954), 372-385, and "First Theatrical Activities in Arkansas," *AHQ,* XII (Winter 1953), 327-332.

Of all early Arkansas themes, law enforcement has received the most attention. The first study to go beyond legends was Waddy W. Moore, "Some Aspects of Crime and Punishment on the Arkansas Frontier," *AHQ,* XXIII (Spring 1964), 50-64. The revisionist accounts of Arkansas badmen began with Larry D. Ball, "Murrell in Arkansas: An Outlaw Gang in History and Tradition," *MSF,* VI (Winter 1978), 65-76, and continued in James Penick, Jr., *The Great Western Land Pirate: John A. Murrell in Legend and History,* (Columbia, Mo., 1981).

Useful primary materials appear in most county histories and in local articles and memoirs too numerous to mention. A few of the most helpful are Francis J. Scully, "Across Arkansas in 1844," *AHQ,* XIII (Spring 1954), 31-51, a travel account of unusual incisiveness; Horace Adams, "An Arkansas Alderman, 1857," *AHQ* XI (Summer 1952), 79-101, excerpts from the invaluable John W. Brown diary; Duane Huddleston, "Of Race Horses and Steamboats; The Pride of Captain Thomas Todd Tunstall," *ICC,* XIV (January 1973), 5-144, an extensive biography of the state's premier race horse owner, which must serve at present as a history of early sporting activity; James W. Leslie, *Land of the Cypress and Pine,* (Little Rock, 1976), a treatment of a much neglected part of the state; Clifford D. Whitman, "Private Journal of Mary Ann Owen Sims," *AHQ,* XXXV (Summer 1976), 142-187, and (Fall 1976), 261-291, the best woman's view of the antebellum era, and Samuel H. Chester, *Pioneer Days in Arkansas,* (Richmond, Va., 1927), a fine memoir.

Invaluable is Swannee Bennet and William B. Worthen, *Arkansas Made; A Survey of the Decorate, Mechanical, and Fine Arts Produced in Arkansas, 1819-1970,* 2 vols (Fayetteville, 1991)

A Circuit Rider Preaching a Sermon in the Brush. *From Reverend Hamilton W. Pierson,*
In the Brush *(N. Y., 1881). This preacher seems to be addressing the men at the meeting
although women far outnumbered men as church members. Note that women and children are
seated on one side and men on the other.* **University of Arkansas**

Chapter VI

Religion, Education and Reform

INTRODUCTION

The early years of Arkansas statehood coincided with the beginning of the long reign of Queen Victoria. In time, historians referred to the manners and mores of the age as Victorian, thereby designating the middle-class moral earnestness that found expression in religion and reform movements.

During its frontier stage, Arkansas took on more of the characteristics of the earthy eighteenth century, and many of the elite of Arkansas acted like Regency characters. As conditions grew more settled after 1844, evidence of Victorian morality became easier to find. Victorian sentiments were grafted to the middle-class capitalist economy of the North and reached Arkansas with the spread of commercial farming and merchant capitalism. The conflict between older ways and those of "progress" became a central feature in the state in several arenas as the state began to develop its institutions.

RELIGION

Nineteenth century religion was not just a Sunday morning activity. Churches supplied hope and faith at a time when nearly all human ailments now treated through medicine were considered God's judgment. The churches offered a haven from the terror and uncertainty of disease and social disorder, but on the condition that the believer give total obedience to rigid rules and doctrinaire theology. "The rules," one sinner wrote, "prohibited about everything I could get any fun out of." Thus a great distance separated the saved from the unsaved, and in this heroic age of Protestant Christianity, those who supported churches gave more than casual attendance. In 1800, 6.9 percent of the American population claimed church membership; in early Arkansas the percentage was even smaller.

Roman Catholics

Before Arkansas became part of the United States in 1803, Roman Catholicism was the official religion. Priests had been an irregular feature of life at the Post, but both the Osage and the Quapaw had been converted. The legendary Quapaw Chief Sarasin even became a local saint, depicted on a stained glass window of St. Joseph's Roman Catholic Church in Pine Bluff. The French-Quapaw remained the mainstay of Arkansas Catholicism and even acquired a few new members by conversion. Jefferson County politician Creed Taylor took the religion of his wife, Eulalia Vaugine, the daughter of a former Post commandant. A second was Elias N. Conway, a Methodist, who quietly converted to Roman Catholicism in 1856 at the beginning of his second term as governor.

Missionaries first served the state on an irregular basis by offering baptism, hearing confessions, performing marriages and administering communion. Some remote Roman Catholic families, according to a church historian, went forty years without a chance to receive the sacraments. The first mass was not celebrated in Little Rock until 1838. Roman Catholicism arrived in Fort Smith in 1840, largely because of the presence of Irish soldiers at the Fort.

The appearance of the Irish at Fort Smith portended major changes. American Catholicism, Gallic in outlook and leadership, was liberal before 1840. In Arkansas, French Catholics undertook one last project. At St. Mary's Mission, five miles below Pine Bluff, the Loretto Sisters from Ste. Genevieve established an academy that lasted for a few years. Roman Catholic schools, notably St. Joseph's College at Bardstown, Kentucky, were held in high esteem on the frontier, and despite some prejudice at the popular level, the frontier upper classes were friendly to Catholics.

The Irish, who had immigrated to America largely because of the famine in their native land, gained control of the Roman Catholic Church in Arkansas in 1843. The Reverend Andrew Byrne, from Ireland, became Bishop of the Diocese of Little Rock, which included both the state and the Indian Territory to the west. By the time he arrived, as Father J. M. Lucy, the first Roman Catholic historian, put it, "those of the old regime had departed." Bishop Byrne set to work to recruit more priests and to promote Irish immigration to Arkansas, especially in the Fort Smith vicinity. The Irish, however, were not enthusiastic about the state, lacked both the skills and the money to move readily to the frontier, and were subjected to prejudice. One Arkansan who made contact with the Irish was Fayetteville's David Walker: "I brought up one or two Irish families from the Rock. They learned me a lesson not soon to be forgotten. Lying, thieving wretches, with no pride, being without resentment or shame. I will never have another Irishman about me." During the 1850s, when nativist groups began attacking both the Irish and Catholicism in general, Bishop Byrne engaged in a war of pamphlets with arch-Mason Albert Pike. When Know-Nothingism was at its height, anti-Catholicism exploded in a riot at Little Rock. Nuns were assaulted and wild stories circulated. Catholicism, with only 1.9

percent of the churchgoers, was too remote in the rest of the state to be viewed as a threat.

The Irreligious on the Frontier

With Catholicism too weak to restrain the new American settlers, the forces of moral control were in abeyance. The earliest visitors to Arkansas noted the almost total lack of religion and blamed much of the riotous living on the absence of a suitable number of marriageable girls and the civilizing influence that religion imparted. One new arrival, Hiram A. Whittington, who worked in the *Arkansas Gazette* office before moving to Hot Springs, even defended the idea of an established church. The fear of God, regularly taught, was the only thing that stood between anarchy and civilization:

I have had some experience in this, as you know. When I came here, the people were as completely destitute of any feeling of religion as you or Miss Fanny could possible [sic] wish; the Gospel was not preached, and the people were relieved from the burden of paying a clergy man. But were they happy? Ah, no; far from it. Vice and immorality went hand in hand through our streets; the Sabbath was not kept; peaceable individuals were prevented from enjoying any rest by the midnight revels of your free-thinkers; virtuous females were insulted with impunity; justice had fled from courts; every man carried arms, either for murdering his enemy or for his own defense; murders were of every day occurrence.

Such conditions, true for Little Rock in the period 1820-1830, were paralleled in other towns. Some, like Montgomery's Point or Napoleon, never grew out of that condition. Part of the objection to the Irish was that

their habits so nearly resembled the typical Arkansan of twenty or thirty years earlier. One Irish immigrant, writing from Napoleon, lamented the condition of many of his fellow countrymen:

Many of them are ignorant (unable to read), rude, filthy in their habits, and intemperate. Those of this town particularly so, especially as to filth and intemperance. Drinking is their principal, I might say their only enjoyment. And O! how strong drink degrades a people — turns them from men to imbeciles and demonds [sic], by turns.

Given these social conditions, many influential citizens supported religion in general.

American Protestant denominations were weak and divided in the early nineteenth century. The old theological issue of the eighteenth century over the efficacy of revivals still lingered, and in the early 1800s, debate was touched off again in Kentucky by an evangelical outbreak known as the Second Great Awakening. Westerners tended to support the new emotionalism, and because Arkansas was a frontier area, this influence came to dominate.

No one can be sure who preached the first Protestant sermon in Arkansas, nor can most denominations document their earliest activities. Certainly one candidate for "first" was John Carnahan, a Cumberland Presbyterian who may have preached at Arkansas Post in 1811 and was at Crystal Hill in 1812. Baptists claimed John Clark, who arrived in Arkansas in 1810, and the Methodist Eli Lindsay lived on the Strawberry River in 1815 and kept a regular set of appointments the following year. Reverend Cephas Washbourne (who simplified the spelling to Washburn, although not all his children followed his lead) preached a Fourth of July sermon in Little Rock in 1820 but might have been preceded by John Henry. In any event, all denominations in Arkansas hoped to find souls ripe for harvest. Their different theological messages and approaches gave Arkansans, along with politics and sports, one of the central diversions of the day and became a major molding force in the state's history.

Baptists

Baptists made rapid strides in Arkansas. Fired by the Second Great Awakening, individual Baptists brought their religion with them into Arkansas. Deacon Jacob Wolf, the Indian agent on the upper White River whose double-log house still stands, was one prominent layman. Beginning with the arrival of missionary James Phillip Edwards from Missouri in 1817, John Woodrome from the Home Mission Society of New York and David Orr from Kentucky, the Baptists made a major commitment to Arkansas. Their first church was erected on Fourche a Thomas at what was later Columbia (Randolph County). Orr in particular "possessed almost unlimited influence." More than six feet tall with a commanding presence, "David the High Priest," served in the territorial legislature.

Baptists began denominational disagreement as soon as they gained a little ground. The Spring River Association broke up when some would not accept one Baptist minister because he had been baptized by Cumberland Presbyterians. By 1828, Orr reported little religious activity and turned to medicine, and Woodrome was superintending mail routes. The feuding led some to follow the example of Deacon Wilkerson, who, "being a man of peace, did not unite with any one of these churches." As an example of the disagreements, one church established an "Arm" eighteen miles distant from its regular meeting place in the schoolhouse in which another Baptist church met.

Baptists also were active in urban areas. In 1824, silversmith Silas Toncray arrived in Little Rock and helped organize a congregation. The little group had more than its share of troubles. Member Isaac Watkins was murdered in 1827 by a neighbor who allegedly stole his hogs. Then in 1829, Toncray's departure to Memphis left the group leaderless. In 1832, following a revival led by Campbellite Benjamin F. Hall, the group switched affiliations and Little Rock Baptists had to start over.

Despite setbacks, Baptists by 1860 ranked second to Methodists with 23.9 percent of the churchgoers. Baptists had two sources of strength. First, each congregation was free to license whomever it chose to preach. Throughout the century, most preachers were unpaid farmers with little or no education who felt the call to preach on Sunday. Some, like Elder Henry McElmurry, were illiterate. But as educator Sophia Sawyer observed, "Ignorant preachers are more popular here with the majority of hearers than the learned and talented." One missionary, W. M. Lea, accepted an appointment without pay in return for being permitted to swap horses along the way. Second, Baptist congregations were beholden to no outside authority. This Baptist reliance on individual initiative tapped one of the strongest veins in the Arkansas character.

Religious practices were fundamental, with footwashing common in the early period. Baptist ministers, and ministers from most other denominations on the frontier, seldom were trained in formal public speaking and often affected a style called the "whang-doodle tone." One early minister, it was reported, began in a monotone, slowly heating up, until "at length, in a nasal whine and twang, he would become furious, pacing to and fro . . . he would cease to reason to [sic] talk, but simply rant in the heavenly tone, till mother, good soul, and others would begin to shout." Some early ministers relied on alcoholic spirits as well as those of celestial origin. With their log churches of either dirt or puncheon floor, Baptists accepted the conditions of the frontier and embraced the log-cabin folk culturally and religiously.

The absence of central authority made Baptists especially liable to various divisions of opinion within the denomination. Some could find no scriptural justification for that nineteenth century innovation, Sunday School, and excluded from communion all who accepted them. Others believed that supporting missionaries was sinful. Even before the Civil War, Baptists were dividing into well-defined theological camps, with one group of conservatives calling themselves "Landmark" Baptists.

Methodists

Methodists with 57.3 percent of the churchgoers in 1860 presented a united front. In 1815, Eli Lindsay located on the Strawberry River and by the following year, he had a regular appointment schedule for eighty-eight white and four "colored" Methodists. Because Methodists were under the central authority of a bishop and could send ministers into areas to arouse congregations, their converts on the frontier exceeded those of Baptists. They could obtain the necessary number of men to preach the word because they licensed lay exhorters. The enthusiasm of these men was legendary: "If you heard a disturbance in the canebrake, it was either a bear or a Methodist minister."

What the church did not provide was a good salary. "The White River Circuit," one minister wrote, "is a very poor charge and they make themselves poorer by a persistent determination to receive the Gospel without pay." William Stephenson, an early Methodist, came from the Belle View region of Missouri in the aftermath of the Panic of 1819, bringing with him a band of followers who greatly enriched Arkansas Methodism. This

tendency to gather by clan and denomination for settlement formed an important but often overlooked aspect of immigration.

Methodists had a bias against slavery, and at least one anti-slavery minister was active in the early years. The creation of Southern Methodism in 1845 did much to make the religion acceptable to Southern slaveholders. Although not as likely to be divided by theological issues as Baptists, Methodists did split over the issue of instrumental music, especially the use of organ music.

Methodists, as well as Baptists, effectively exploited protracted meetings or revivals and used campgrounds extensively to reach remote rural populations. Methodists were casual about doctrine and vague about many of their rituals. Their emphasis on recruitment and reform led them to complain early about the problem of intemperance.

Presbyterians

Before 1800, Presbyterians were the pre-eminent denomination; however, they failed to hold their prominence as westward expansion continued. Brought to the South by Scotch-Irish Presbyterians, this church with its Calvinist theology was the most intellectually organized in a land where westward expansion and remoteness from centers of learning meant that most people had little education. During the Second Great Awakening of the early nineteenth century, the western brethren objected that the Presbyterians' rigid educational requirements for clergy and a too strict interpretation of their theology hindered the quest for converts. Cumberland Presbyterians seceded from the main body in 1810 with the result that Arkansas inherited a divided Presbyterian legacy. Both regular and Cumberland Presbyterians appeared in Arkansas, with the Cumberland Presbyterian Church tending to be found in the Ozarks and the other Presbyterians in towns. Statistically, Cumberland Presbyterians claimed 5.4 percent of the state's church members, and 6.4 percent affiliated with the other Presbyterian Church.

Cumberland Presbyterians were the first to arrive in the state. It is doubtful John Carnahan preached at Arkansas Post in 1811 because it was not until 1812 that he was accepted as a candidate for the ministry and ordered to form a circuit. He was ordained in 1816 despite a less than adequate examination and an express charge to improve "himself in high branches of literature, in which he appears to be deficient." Enough ministers were active in 1834 to justify creating the Arkansas Synod.

Although primarily rural, Cumberland Presbyterians displayed a higher stage of modernization than other Protestant groups. An 1838 synod took a stand against ministers or elders making or using ardent spirits, and one minister who led a lynch mob was called to account. Cane Hill College, founded in 1852, reflected the commitment of Cumberland Presbyterians to education. Perhaps their most extraordinary achievement came in 1858 when members of the Washington County Bible Society under the leadership of Reverend John Buchanan sold or gave 2,614 Bibles to local families. As with other denominations, money was a major concern. However, in 1841, they adopted a resolution denouncing the taking of a public collection as profaning the Sabbath. Apparently elders had to pass the plate either before or after services. Regular Presbyterians had the most impact in towns. Reverend John Wilson Moore came to Little Rock in 1828, and by 1835, state leaders organized what in 1856 they also called the Synod of Arkansas. Ironically, the most notable early clergyman began as a Congregationalist. Reverend Cephas Washburn arrived to minister to the Cherokee at Dwight Mission. Washburn taught school, promoted the cause of education and had a distinguished career as a mis-

sionary. In his later years, he served as minister at Dardanelle, Fort Smith and Norristown, and left a memoir of considerable significance.

Perhaps because they had the most learned clergy in Arkansas, early Presbyterian ministers emphasized theology, often at the expense of other denominations. Little Rock's Reverend Joshua F. Green attacked Catholics in what probably were the first two sermons published in Arkansas, *Man of Sin* and *The Confession Unveiled.*

Because education and higher income tended to coincide, Presbyterian churches, even on the frontier, were built more substantially than those of Baptists or Methodists. The Philadelphia Church in Izard County, erected in 1858, was thirty feet wide and fifty feet long, making it about 20 percent larger than the typical log church. The front had separate entrance doors for men and women, a feature common to many groups that usually meant the sexes were seated separately. A row of tall posts down the middle supported lanterns, and a high pulpit that allowed the minister to dominate the congregation physically had a circular bench at its back where visiting preachers waited their turn.

Because Presbyterianism was cultural to the Scotch-Irish rather than evangelical, settlement and church tended to coincide. Presbyterian Samuel H. Chester recalled that at Mt. Holly, in contrast to the lively life on the exuberant frontier, the children were not allowed to dance (although the game of "twistification" was permitted). The sexes were separated at school, "a kind of log cabin college," which kept such high standards that Chester was admitted as a sophomore when he applied to the University of Virginia. Liquor was conspicuously absent, and duels, those personal encounters that formed the habit of high-toned gentlemen, were unknown. The session records of the Wattensas Presbyterian Church, south of Des Arc in

Prairie County, document white and "colored" communicants and note that on August 11, 1872, that "Mssrs. Clarence Wagnon, Wm. Warner, Taren McNeil having been charged with indulging in promiscuous dancing contrary to the word of God, were suspended from communion" until they show signs of penitence and new life. If these conditions can be taken as typical, they show that cultural Presbyterianism was at odds with many of the basic characteristics of Southern life.

Episcopalians

Presbyterians brought from England a bitter hatred of Episcopalians. The Church of England in America had de-Anglicized itself in the post-Revolutionary War period and kept the allegiance of the old seaboard Southern aristocracy. The church followed as the children of the elite moved west. The Episcopal Church first recognized Arkansas in 1838 when the General Convention selected Reverend Leonidas Polk of Tennessee as missionary bishop. Polk, a convert during his West Point days and later an important Confederate military officer, reached the state in 1839. Church officials reported Arkansas had no clergymen at all and "it is not known that one ever officiated." Polk found Arkansas "very destitute of religious privileges" with only "the periodical visits of a Methodist circuit rider, at long intervals, and the occasional services of a minister of the Cumberland Presbyterians, infrequently performed."

Adherents were scattered, some at the Post, others at Pine Bluff, and about twenty-five families at Little Rock. Polk held his first service in a private home at Helena on March 3, 1839, before moving to Little Rock where he preached in the borrowed Presbyterian Church on March 10, 1839, giving a sermon that the *Gazette* called "eloquent and interesting." Because Polk had donned his clerical attire before heading out for the Presbyterian Church, his vestments "may have helped collect the bishop's first audience." From Little Rock he went to Washington and Spring Hill, encountering at the latter at least a dozen persons familiar with the Episcopal liturgy.

Christ Church in Little Rock was organized following Polk's initial visit, its vestrymen including representatives of the business and planting communities. The first minister, Reverend William H.C. Yeager, arrived in 1840 and sustained himself by teaching school. Services were held in "an elegant and large room in the statehouse," and the first missionary activity consisted of the bilingual Reverend Yeager preaching to the town's German community. Polk returned to Arkansas, visiting Fayetteville in 1841, where the chaplain from Fort Gibson, the Reverend William Scull, was holding prayer meetings. After visiting the Indian nations, he returned via Fort Smith, where he baptized the children of Elias Rector. By the time Polk resigned to become Bishop of Louisiana in 1841, Episcopalians had missionary clergy at Little Rock, Fayetteville and Hempstead County, and two organized congregations, one of which — Little Rock's Christ Church — was preparing to erect a building.

After Polk's departure, Arkansas Episcopalians were served by a provisional bishop, Reverend James Hervey Otey of Tennessee. During the hard times that followed the banking collapse, the Fayetteville church was described as "struggling hard to live," and the Pine Bluff region was abandoned. Otey's successor, and the second missionary bishop, Reverend George Washington Freeman, was the first to take up residence in Arkansas, arriving in 1845. The debt of Christ Church threatened to bankrupt the parish at that time. The new bishop traveled some 18,000 miles by horseback, coach and steamboat to minister to communicants

Hirsch & Adler Stagecoach *(photographer and date unknown) This photograph offers a rare early view of an Arkansas stagecoach. The Hirsch & Adler stagecoach line connected Batesville with Jacksonport. Notice the band instruments. Hirsch and Adler were early Jewish settlers.* **Arkansas College**

before his death in 1858. By that year, as Arkansas recovered from hard times, the denomination boasted seven congregations containing about 400 communicants. Bishop Otey of Tennessee assumed supervision until the arrival of Reverend Henry C. Lay in 1859. Lay established his residence at Fort Smith in order to superintend his missionary activities better. His area included Arkansas, the Indian Territory, New Mexico and Arizona.

Bishop Otey observed in 1859 that the whole of Arkansas "seems to be a field for missionary labor, now 'white unto harvest.' From very many places the cry comes earnestly, repeatedly, 'Come over and help us,' and that with the assurance of reasonable support for the helpers. Hitherto few appear to regard the call." Thus unable to fill the need, Episcopalians remained a rarity in Arkansas, with its .8 percent of the church population found only in the planting counties and the more advanced towns. Across the great expanse of the Ozarks and the Ouachitas, where Baptists and Methodists reigned, an Episcopal priest would have been as great a curiosity as a Jewish rabbi or a Roman Catholic priest.

Disciples of Christ

Some individuals in the early nineteenth century became upset by conflicting creeds and sought a simpler and purer form of belief by returning to a New Testament church. Barton W. Stone of Kentucky, under the slogan "Bible things by Bible names," took the name "Christian," thereby greatly upsetting the other denominations. Baptists Thomas Campbell and his son, Alexander, arrived at a similar conclusion at the same time. The two Campbells and Stone merged their followers in 1832, thereby giving birth to a new frontier denomination variously styled Christian, Disciples of Christ or Church of Christ, but which others often called "Campbellite." They rejected the strict Calvinism of Presbyterians and Baptists and instead emphasized every believer's power to discover salvation in scripture. In practice they followed the congregational form of church government and thus lacked the hierarchy of the Methodists. Culturally they were a part of both the frontier and the perfectionism typical of the Age of Romanticism, their unity coming mostly from the circulation of Campbell's newspaper, *The Millenial Harbinger*.

The new denomination got off to a big start in Arkansas in 1832 when visiting minister, B. F. Hall from Kentucky, successfully converted most of Little Rock's Baptists. One convert, William Wilson Stevenson, who had married the widow of Isaac Watkins and had been a Cumberland Presbyterian minister, was chosen to lead the new flock. The Little Rock congregation erected a brick church in 1845 and crowned it with a clock in 1858. It contained a gallery for slaves. Local residents always referred to the first log building as the Baptist Church, and the new one became known as "Town Clock Church."

Disciples also were active in rural areas. Apparently the first preaching of Campbell's doctrine came from Elijah Kelley in 1826 in Pike County. "Parson" Kelley eventually became dissatisfied with the Disciples on some points of doctrine and founded his own Kelleyite denomination, which still exists.

As did many other early Disciples, Kelley thought of himself as a "reform" Baptist, and thus remained on the conservative end of the spectrum. The liberal wing of the Disciples emphasized missionary work, Sunday schools and social reform. One early leader was Robert Graham, an English-born carpenter who had come to Campbell's Bethany College to work on the buildings and stayed to graduate with honors. Graham came to Arkansas in 1847 and settled at Fayetteville, where Judge Jonas Tebbetts and merchant James H. Stirman became prominent members of his congregation.

In order to supplement his income, Graham turned to teaching and in 1852 got the legislature to charter Arkansas College, the first institution of higher education in Arkansas. The school was a success, drawing about 200 students before being closed by the outbreak of the Civil War. Its most famous student was James M. Johnson of Madison County, a prominent figure during Reconstruction. Graham resigned the presidency in 1858, largely because of the growing sectional crisis and his personal hostility to slavery. William Baxter, who succeeded him, shared these views and recorded the troubled history of the region in his wartime book *Pea Ridge and Prairie Grove* (1864).

Claiming 4.3 percent of Arkansas's churchgoers, the Disciples in Arkansas occupied a middle ground between the more intellectual Presbyterians and the more popular Baptists and Methodists. The powerful Johnson clan was converted by prominent evangelist James T. Johnson, the brother of Benjamin Johnson, and Campbell's ideas had a wide circulation through newspapers and travel-

Fayetteville Female Seminary *(Lithograph from a Drawing by William Quesenbury, ca. 1855) Sophie Sawyer's school was but one of the educational institutions near Fayetteville, the "Athens of Arkansas."* **Arkansas History Commission**

ing evangelists. What the denomination lacked were organization and money to translate this success into numbers. In addition, many rural Campbellites rejected modernizers' attempts to bring about a salaried ministry, Sunday schools or instrumental music. These tensions resulted in time in the creation of yet another denomination, the Churches of Christ, which rejected Campbell but not his teachings.

Communes

The perfectionism that marked the Campbellite movement was a prominent feature of religious thinking in the early nineteenth century. Numerous groups across the North attempted to achieve heavenly perfection in a man-made world. Although the Shakers, Mormons and Transcendentalists had little impact in Arkansas, Thomas Nuttall in 1819 recorded encountering the Seekers, a wild vagabond group traveling where their faith took them. Nuttall did not seem to be impressed by their prospects, and no further mention of them has been discovered.

A Mormon missionary accompanied by his six wives visited Helena in 1852, but threatened by a coat of tar and feathers, they left town hurriedly. In the 1850s, a communal group known as the Harmonial Vegetation Society erected a three-story building, grist mill and blacksmith shop on their 520 acres in northwestern Arkansas. Their communal living arrangement included each man reaching into a hopper periodically to draw the name of a new wife. The group was prosecuted, primarily for the crime of working on Sunday and it dissolved. It was not their sexual behavior, but their habit of working on Sunday that infuriated their neighbors and led to legal charges being filed. The group dissolved just prior to the Civil War.

Jews

The lure of the West also attracted Jewish immigrants. Abraham Block, who arrived in

1823, did a thriving business in Washington. Aaron Hirsch, who spoke only French when he started peddling in Louisiana, settled in Batesville. In addition to owning stores in Jacksonport and Batesville, he and partner Simon Adler held a mail contract and ran the stagecoach between those two points.

As early as 1846, I. Ehrman of Helena borrowed a Sefer Torah from Cincinnati for use in religious services. However, because most Arkansas Jews were merchants and made yearly visits to New Orleans or other metropolitan areas where religious services were readily available, the first synagogue was not constructed until 1866 in Pine Bluff. Arkansas also was served by Reverend L. G. Sternheimer of Columbus, Georgia. Known as the Jewish Arkansas Traveler, Reverend Sternheimer served as an itinerant *mohel*, performing ritual circumcisions on young Jewish males.

Religion in Private Life

Some groups existing elsewhere in the nation lacked sufficient numbers to organize in Arkansas. The Universalists did not found a church until 1906, but in the 1840s, Dr. John D. Sims of Dallas County, in the words of his wife, received "coppies of a paper published by the Universalists," and being "very much taken with their teachings," arrived at "idies so intirely difrent from the teachings of any church he knew he did not feel satisfide to join any church." This caused his wife much distress, and when he at last affiliated with the Campbellites, she rejoiced: "How thankful and happy I felt . . . to think that I then had a husban forever[.] I knew if we were seperated for a while we at last could meet in that bright and happy land where we could abide at last forever."

Others never found that satisfaction. Merchant John Brown of Camden, who found "The Jarring discord of the churches has

been in my way about joining either," concluded that denominations "lay down rules, which neither they nor anybody else can comply with in their true spirit." Brown chose to read scripture,

[T]hus bringing myself to a spirit of Charity and forgiveness which I otherwise could not succeed in preserving. On Monday morning I go to work again better prepared to keep my temper and practice forbearance toward my erring fellow mortals.

Many men and women, unable to find in their hearts the certain evidence of salvation required by most denominations, nevertheless attended regularly and often gave financial aid to more than one church.

Religion in Arkansas Life

Despite all the religious activity, only an estimated 17 percent of white Arkansans were church members in 1860. Baptists in particular demanded strong evidence of salvation before admitting one to membership. In addition, moral conduct had to be sustained once admitted. Those trying to get ahead in the world often ran into difficulties. Carney C. Strughan "seemed to be a very zealous, working Christian; but in a short time he became constable and then sheriff, neglected his church and was excluded." The political and social influence of churches often were resented and contested. In Washington County, Cumberland Presbyterians claimed the right to accept or reject the school teachers who shared the church building and on one occasion complained that the closing exercises were "prejudicial to the interests of intelligence and morality." In retaliation, many young men made open war, disrupting revivals and firing guns near churches on Sunday. "Disturbing a Religious

St. John's College *(photographer and date unknown) Designed in castellated Gothic style, the college looked grim and foreboding. Only the east wing was completed.* **Central Arkansas Library System**

Congregation," became one of the most frequent petty offenses before justice of the peace courts.

The "sporting gentry," were best illustrated by the career of C.F.M. Noland, who rejoiced in hunting, tall tales, horse races, dances and frolics—the sins of the world. They were on the defensive once hard times hit in 1844.

Simon Talburt, owner of a Yellville race track, converted to Primitive Baptist and plowed up his popular site. The denominations grew rapidly during the 1850s, but most of the growth came from the newcomers rather than from the conversion of oldtimers. Those who wanted to retain their frontier freedoms moved west.

To a great extent, religion in early Arkansas was a cooperative venture. Methodists and Campbellites often exchanged ministers, and in rural areas, many churches alternated using the school house for meetings. Church-going families frequently attended all services regardless of their nominal affiliation. The same spirit appeared in the use of campgrounds. In Lawrence County, a Reed's Creek campground served the entire community as Baptists, Methodists, Presbyterians and Campbellites were granted two weeks each in the summer. Under this "union" plan, a committee told the ministers to preach only what they all could agree on, although converts could decide which group to join. Ministers chafed at this restriction, for nineteenth century preachers were adroit in criticizing other denominations. Later in the century, as the number of churches grew, these cooperative ventures ended and strict exclusiveness often became a religious hallmark.

Churchgoers in antebellum Arkansas were not exposed to the theological modernization underway in the North or in Europe. The "New Criticism," which studied the Bible as history, made scarcely a ripple in Arkansas, and the publication of Charles Darwin's *Origin of Species by Means of Natural Selection* (1859) passed unnoticed. The closest thing to religious sedition in Arkansas came in Helena in the 1850s when a passing Universalist preached that there was no Hell. Calvinism, so vigorously attacked in Oliver Wendell Holmes's "The Deacon's One-Horse Shay," remained the dominant theological vehicle. Finally by 1860, whatever their private thoughts, no minister dared to hint that slavery was not a God-ordained institution, bestowing profits for whites and blessings for blacks.

EDUCATION

American society made a commitment to public education during the nineteenth century. Underlying that support were two assumptions: that education was necessary for participation in the political life of a democracy and that it was needed for economic reasons. To foster that commitment, the federal government provided territories and states with income from the sale of public lands. That education was needed for political and economic reasons was an idea that was resisted in Arkansas. Arkansas frontier democracy was the politics of personality, requiring no sophisticated understanding of issues, and hunters and self-sufficient farmers needed no book learning. Those who advocated the ideals of education were a minority, and the cause of education languished between 1819 and 1860.

Home Instruction

The aristocracy often chose to educate its children at home. Planter opposition helped retard the public school movement in the South, usually by advancing the argument that public tax money should not be spent for something that only a few used. That argument was heard in Arkansas, but examples of home education were few. One woman recalled that her father taught her to read and for further education, hired a tutor who proved to have a drinking problem and was dismissed. The expense was too great for most, tutors were not in great supply and a safe private school could serve the same purpose.

Private Schools

Individual teachers arrived early in Arkansas. Caleb Lindsey allegedly taught the first school in a Lawrence County cave. Offerings largely depended on a teacher's skills. A typical advertisement in Helena read:

A.G. Underwood will open a school in Helena, on Monday next. For the instruction of Boys and Girls, in the different branches of English education, Geography, Arithmetic, History, and such other branches of education as he thinks himself capable of teaching.

Such teachers rented a room in town or used a log cabin in the rural areas. Some were not qualified. An early Batesville teacher delivered a ringing oration that proved to be taken verbatim from the writings of another man. The discovery ruined his school and he left town. Others left the profession. Harris Flanagin, a future governor, was trained in the eastern United States as a teacher but became a lawyer on arriving in Arkansas. Albert Pike, another early teacher, was discovered by Robert Crittenden, who called him to Little Rock to edit the *Arkansas Advocate*; Pike subsequently entered the legal profession. Not only were the financial rewards of teaching limited but there were other troubles as well. When a Little Rock teacher disciplined one of Governor Rector's children, the irate father came to the school to return the favor, hitting the teacher and cursing, "You God damned son of a bitch, you damned stinking Yankee, you Yankee dog. You strike my son like I would a negro, you God damned miserable Yankee dog." All of this the teacher took: "He had his hand on his pistol & if I had endeavored to make any resistance he would have shot me."

A successful teacher usually opened an academy. These institutions, grandiose in name and design and often endowed by legislative charters, depended for their success on the management and reputation of the teachers. Jesse Brown, who opened Little

Rock's first school in 1823, succeeded. His co-educational school offered eleven months of instruction on a variety of levels for twenty years. Brown even served as city mayor between 1838 and 1840.

One of the earliest schools in Arkansas was Dwight Mission. Founded in 1819 by the missionaries to the Cherokee, it consisted of thirty buildings housing some seventy students. Cephas Washburn, the missionary minister, was the principal founder, and Miss Ellen Stetson was in charge of the females, who ranged in age from five to twenty. One observer noted that she "is very severe with her scholars, many of whom are grown women and as handsome as any woman I ever saw, not withstanding they are squaws." Another teacher there was Nancy Brown, the sister of Jesse Brown of Little Rock. These women encountered some hostility, but as one replied, "I had responsibilities of a man to sustain."

Prejudice against Indians affected the career of Sophia Sawyer's school in Fayetteville. Another female missionary, she was private tutor to the Ridge family and a witness to Major Ridge's murder in 1839. Following the mother and children in flight to Fayetteville, she established her school there, drawing local whites and Indian children from across the line. Miss Sawyer possessed a difficult personality, and she refused to associate her school with any religious denomination. Some local residents objected to the presence of Indian children, and once she received a dirty letter "containing pictures and language of impurity that I had supposed no human being capable of communicating." Her tombstone, erected by her pupils, reads, "She hath done what she could."

Others in the northwest attempted more. The Far West Academy was the most ambitious project. Chartered by the legislature in 1844 and created mostly by Whigs, the Academy met Democratic opposition. Isaac Murphy, a future governor, was one board member, and veteran educator-minister Cephas Washburn was involved prominently. Unfortunately, a disastrous fire and the economic downturn bankrupted the school. Robert M. Mecklin afterwards established the Ozark Institute on the grounds.

In general, Ozark schools were created by Presbyterians, Whigs and merchants. Education emphasized the practical for women, although one Batesville school had a piano and a pair of glass globes for chemistry. Globes for geography were much admired, for the rural folk by no means accepted the roundness of the earth. One Little Rock teacher with a taste for art purchased for his school a plaster copy of Hiram Power's *Greek Slave,* the first American nude. Its arrival created much local excitement.

By contrast, schools in the southwest, where the planting class predominated, emphasized social graces. Spring Hill and Washington were two early centers in Hempstead County. The Spring Hill Female Academy, located near the Red River and erected at a cost of $5,000, went into operation in 1836 with Miss Elizabeth Pratt from New York in charge of thirty girls. Advertisements noted that geography was taught "with the use of Globes," and other offerings included rhetoric, composition, logic, and some sciences. The school drew on the patronage of local planters, including Governor James S. Conway, who sent his daughter there.

The next year the Spring Hill Male Academy arose "some hundreds of yards from the female institution." The school was described as "broken up" when hard times hit in 1843. An attempted reorganization failed, and some patrons transferred their support to nearby Washington Academy, which had been established in 1842. With community and newspaper support, this school endured over the next twenty years, but by 1859, it was reported to be in danger of closing. The

buildings, "old rotten shells, remind you more forcibly of some old, untenanted haunted ruin than Academies of learning."

Tulip was another community that experienced ups and downs. In 1844, Madame d'Estimauville de Beau Mouchel arrived in Little Rock to set up a fashionable finishing school. Although the school did not succeed, she did become overly friendly with editor Solon Borland of the *Arkansas Banner.* She moved to Dallas County the next year and made a good first impression. In addition to taking over a school, she had the honor of having the village named for her. But the romance with Borland went sour, and according to a student, she "spent the night mostly weeping and the day finding fault with her pupils." After Borland married in May 1845, a sad seven-stanza poem in the *Gazette* ended: "Thou heart is cold, or changed, And we can meet no more!"

After the evidence of her "too great intimacy" became visible, she was last seen leaving on a boat with a baby in her arms, and the community of D'Estimauville thereupon became Tulip. The school did not die, and as the Tulip Female Institute, it added a male department. In the 1850s, the Arkansas Military Academy joined in, apparently the only institution in Arkansas ever designated as military.

Colleges

The first elite of early Arkansas often came well educated. George C. Watkins and Chester Ashley studied law in the Litchfield Law School; Solon Borland was a Philadelphia-trained doctor. Those families who wanted the best education for their children sent them to St. Joseph's Academy at Bardstown, Kentucky. Robert Ward Johnson, William Quesenbury and many others attended this Roman Catholic school, although only Benjamin T. DuVal of Fort

Smith is known to have been a Roman Catholic.

Local colleges formed when prosperity returned during the 1850s. Cane Hill College near Fayetteville, supported by the Cumberland Presbyterian Church, began in a two-room log building in 1852, moved into a frame structure two years later, and in 1858, boasted a brick building. It granted Arkansas's first bachelor's degree in 1856.

Robert Graham's Arkansas College, also founded in 1852, was in Fayetteville. The first attempt to found a school with statewide support came from Harvard-trained Albert Pike, who promoted St. John's College, a Masonic institution that opened in Little Rock in 1859. Its failure to thrive was caused in part by state sectionalism: Helena Masons refused to contribute because they felt Little Rock favored Memphis over Helena as the terminus for a railroad.

Public Education

When Arkansas entered the Union, the national government gave the sixteenth section of every township to the state to fund the creation of a seminary of learning. Michigan used its money to create the state university, but in Arkansas the Seminary Fund had a low legislative priority. The first sale in 1840 at $10 an acre was not successful, so the legislature reduced the price to $3. In addition, squatters occupied some of the lands. Rather than remove them, the state simply gave in. Congress obligingly turned the state loose in 1846 to manage the lands without restriction, and as one editor observed, a search for money would be as futile as that for Arctic explorer Sir John Franklin. Plans to establish a university were defeated by arraying the poor against the rich, by the cry of the aristocracy, and by talking of rich men's sons and college education.

In the end, the state used some of the money that was not lost in the bank failure to buy books. "The good people of the state received a heterogeneous mass of obsolete school books — boxes of which are yet laying in the different clerk's offices throughout the state." Then the legislature turned the problem over to the counties, where speculators serving on the school boards got the best land at little cost. By state law, counties were supposed to file reports, but only two bothered to reply in 1860. According to the 1860 census, half the school-age children did not attend school at all; the rest were divided evenly between public and private institutions.

Public schools were run by school boards that usually consisted of patrons. Teachers, invariably men, were hired and paid by the board. A Scott County contract issued by the Pleasant Hill School called for the session to begin on July 7, 1856. The teacher "promises to keep order during school and try & aid the pupils all in his power." The session was to last twenty weeks. No student "under a bad character," was permitted to attend, and "if the teacher gets dissatisfied with the proceedings of the signers, he shall have it as his will to discontinue school and yet [keep] the pay for the time taught." Teachers received very low pay, and there were no performance evaluation standards.

"Education, as a system," wrote one newspaper correspondent, "is too much neglected in Arkansas." And one editor commented: "There is certainly a great amount of ignorance in many portions of the state, and many worthless teachers pretending to instruct the rising generation." Illiteracy was common, for 20,000 persons above the age of twenty — or probably a quarter of the adult population — could neither read nor write. Judging by surviving letters and documents, many more did so very imperfectly. Whigs believed that ignorance contributed to Democratic victories. In the short run, it meant many persons were ignorant of rising sectional tensions; in the long run, it left them even more unable to react meaningfully to the rapid changes that overtook American life in just two decades. Unfortunately for the future, education noticeably lagged in importance behind moral reform and economic development in antebellum Arkansas.

REFORM

One of the religious trends coming out of New England was that churches should concern themselves with the quality of life around them. The church "as social worth," as Emerson put it, soon became active in the various causes of abolition, temperance, women's rights, labor reform, treatment of the insane, education, peace and general betterment. Southern churches did not tend to be a part of this movement. Some considered poverty to be God's judgment on sinners. Denominations of the region's elite found better things to do than attack the economic underpinning of their members. Nevertheless, because Southern religion was a force for moral order, Southern churches did share one social concern with their liberal Northern brethren: temperance.

Temperance

Widespread excessive consumption of alcohol was supported in the South by two traditions. First, planters led lives of conspicuous consumption in which alcohol played a leading role. As late as the 1830s, the Arkansas elite still took many of their values from the eighteenth century enlightenment and rejected the authority of dogmatic religion. Horse races, sports and Saturday night frolics typical of Flush Times featured alcohol prominently. A second sort of conspicuous

consumption existed at the lowest level of society. Many frontier folk had never been reached by religion and drank heavily as a matter of course. Both groups rejected as alien the Yankee notion of "temperance, thrift and frugality."

In between were small farmers isolated in a land without adequate means of transportation who solved their cash problems by turning crops into alcohol. Thus readily supplied, many men and women used spirits daily in their work, at court session, militia musters, elections, and on every public occasion for elaborate toasts. With whisky at a price of between twenty-two and thirty cents a gallon, alcohol was abundant.

Government traditionally attempted to regulate alcohol, mostly for purposes of tax revenue. Arkansas passed taxes on stills and dram shops and turned the difficult task of licensing over to the county courts. No effort was made, however, to go into the woods and find home stills. One reason was that Arkansas had a particular economic interest in alcohol that made regulation difficult. Despite federal laws dating from 1806 that made it illegal to sell alcohol to Indians, many Arkansans profited from these illicit sales. Many sold liquor to Indians passing through Arkansas on the road west, adding to the miseries of the Trail of Tears. A number of Choctaw killed some whites near the Post in 1828 after consuming too much liquor.

Once the Indians were settled in Indian Territory, a lively trade flourished across the border. The Cincinnati *Western Temperance Journal* claimed in 1840 that 3,800,000 gallons of whisky were shipped into Arkansas, where, by "running the mail," it entered Indian Territory. By 1861, maps showed "the Whiskey Road" running west out of Fort Smith. This illegal trade demoralized whites as well and was blamed repeatedly for the numerous murders that marked the border counties.

Temperance was an uphill struggle under such conditions. Whisky dealers followed camp meetings and revivals, horse races and fairs to peddle their wares. The first organized temperance society appeared in 1831 in Little Rock with Reverend William Stevenson as president. Other groups followed in Helena, Batesville and Fayetteville, and anti-gambling messages frequently were included. The purpose of these bodies was to aid individual members in achieving total abstinence. To this end they employed the same disciplinary practices as the churches: censoring and occasionally expelling the recalcitrant from the temperance society. Some who either could not make the grade or changed their minds were, like John J. Stirman at Fayetteville in 1843, honorably discharged. W. S. Oldham, expelled in 1843, refused to defend himself and tore up his summons.

Political men like Oldham had a problem. Voters expected to be treated on election day despite the *Arkansas Gazette's* observation that "the practice of treating for votes is an awful spot on our glorious Republican escutcheon." When all candidates in Helena in 1842 professed membership in the Total Abstinence Society, they collectively agreed not to continue treating. In the heat of an election, however, some forgot their pledges. Thomas W. Newton, a strict Presbyterian and a fiery Whig, fell off the wagon during the 1840 election. Others lacked sincerity from the start. One member of the Little Rock body signed up, "not because I was in a habit of drinking, but merely to please the ladies, who said they wanted the temperate men to join for the sake of their example. About twenty men, all the ladies in the place, old and young, have joined."

By the 1850s, temperance achieved some successes, both in the reformation of individuals and by pressuring for more comprehensive legislation. Town corporations were given expanded powers to regulate the sale of alco-

hol. In the late 1850s, laws permitted liquor to be banned near schools and churches and the first local option law let voters further restrict alcohol sales.

Nevertheless, strong drink was readily available, and many engaged in fierce struggles to control the habit. A. H. Garland, who one year celebrated a "cold water" Fourth of July, appears to have been one conspicuous example. James Woodson Bates, who died in 1847, was "Given to liquor," someone wrote on a copy of his obituary, and drunkenness among the bar was common. That "fine Arkansas gentleman close to the Choctaw line," Elias Rector, was said to get "drunk once a week on whiskey and immediately sobers himself up completely on the very best of wine." To the disgrace of his wife, he was still trying to follow this style of living after the Civil War when his wealth was gone. The legal records of the period give plenty of evidence of families left destitute by the effects of drinking and its first cousin, gambling.

Prisons

The only other reform enacted into law was the creation of the state penitentiary. In the belief that criminals could be reformed and returned to society, penitentiaries were set up in virtually all the states, including one in Arkansas at Little Rock in 1841. Unfortunately, the prisoners rejected the efforts made on their behalf and burned the building in 1846 and 1850. The state began the nefarious practice in 1853 of leasing convicts to private parties called "contractors," in effect giving up the hope of reformation.

The penitentiary contained eighty-nine prisoners in 1858. Most were farmers or laborers. Murder, horse stealing, larceny and Negro stealing were the most common offenses. About a third of the prisoners were labeled intemperate and a fourth were illiterate. Two were "free men of color" and one was an Indian. The sole woman prisoner, Rebecca Wilkins from Newton County, sentenced to a five-year term for murder, had escaped. Even under the prison contractors, the prison offered vocational training, with wagonmaking, tailoring and carpentry work being the most common. The attending physician believed that the inmates' health was far better than those confined in county jails.

Most other early nineteenth century reforms never got past the talking stage in Arkansas. The state failed to establish an insane asylum. Public health measures were grossly inadequate by Eastern standards, and the rural nature of the state limited the role of lyceums, libraries and cultural bodies.

Poverty

One of the most conspicuous institutional failures was Arkansas's response to the problems of poverty. Since the Elizabethan Poor Law of the sixteenth century, it had been the responsibility of local governments to set up programs to deal with those who could not support themselves. Territorial Arkansas, however, enacted a law requiring families to assume that burden.

Such a law was largely irrelevant in helping young males immigrating to the area. Friedrich Gerstäcker recounted the fate of a young German discovered to have smallpox: "and as the man was poor, without a cent in the world, he [the owner] had shut the door, and never been near him again. The poor fellow had been left to himself for three days, without even a drink of water, and at last had died miserably on the floor." Gerstäcker went on to comment, "Littlerock [sic] is a vile, detestable place in this respect, and the boatman on the Mississippi have good reason when they sing:

Littlerock [sic] in Arkansaw, The d—-dest place I ever saw.

In Arkansas the insane, who in other states would have been separately housed, accounted for a quarter of the inmates of the poor house. In 1836, the state assigned the poor to the counties and even ordered them to pay the medical expenses of non-residents. This generosity was short-lived, for in 1846, the non-resident clause was repealed. Little Rock had the greatest transient population and hence the greatest problem, for the aged, who would later constitute the bulk of poverty cases, were conspicuously absent. In 1860, only a thousand persons were age sixty-five and over, and those over forty-five amounted to only 1.8 percent of the state's population.

Little Rock's response to its poverty problem was to build a poor house in 1848, two years ahead of the proper authorizing legislation. By 1854, the *Arkansas Gazette* reported that the house was too small and the poor would be better served on a farm with "pure air and cool shades." Judging by the reports of grand juries and the esteemed Dr. R. B. Jennings, the poor German locked up and forgotten was about as well served as the fifty to seventy inmates: the bedding, "old, ragged and filthy," was never washed or changed, passing from inmate to inmate; corn bread and soup served without utensils was the sole diet; there was "nothing indicating the execution of a single sanitary measure;" and even to hardened nineteenth century nostrils, "the odor in the wards was, in several instances, intolerable."

Fortunately, conditions in the counties were better. Washington County purchased a farmsite in 1852 and eventually erected sixteen log cabins. Independence and Jefferson Counties also erected homes, but most smaller counties put the poor up for auction. William M. Graw, who paid $173 each for the Arkansas County poor in 1859, posted bond and promised to feed, clothe and supply medical attention to his charges, whom doubtlessly he housed on his farm.

In general, the guiding principle was to keep taxes low. Getting public assistance was complicated, public officials who occasionally attempted to be humane were invariably hauled into court by some irate taxpayer, and in every known instance, lost. The embarrassing scandals that later rocked the state prison system, the state hospital and nursing homes were the reflection of well-rooted antebellum ideas of political economy.

Not surprisingly, people turned to each other for support. Children, a valuable labor commodity, always could be placed, albeit at times in conditions closely resembling slavery. Men joined fraternal orders, largely for the primitive insurance protection they provided. The stigma of the poor farm was so well rooted in Arkansas life that newspaperman Tom Shiras in the 1920s could write graphically in "A Pauper's Grave" of the fate which befell a poor old woman bereft of relatives who "went on her county" and in death reposed in "the sequestered paupers lot."

CONCLUSION

Religion, education and reform were not three separate features of Victorian morality. They overlapped, and one way or another, they touched the lives of those who did not want to be saved, taught or improved. Yet all three labored under one disability: nothing could be allowed to threaten the institution of slavery. Because all did, at least indirectly, some men such as Albert Pike switched their perspectives, completely repudiating Northern or Victorian standards. In 1860 planter Napoleon B. Burrow told audiences that Southern whites were the descendants of the sixteenth century English Cavaliers and Northerners came from the Puritan Roundheads. He said the two civilizations were

incompatible, and the Southern version, resting on slavery, was superior. Few Arkansans were interested in working out the philosophical problems inherent in constructing coherent ideologies, but debates on religion, education and reform indicated that the struggle was carried on.

BIBLIOGRAPHIC ESSAY

Generally, religious history of Arkansas has not been set in its cultural perspective. Only the best-established denominations have produced histories, and these are sometimes out of date. Father J. M. Lucey, "The Catholic Church in Arkansas," *PAHA,* II (1908), 424-461 is one early account. For the Baptists, E. Glenn Hinson, *A History of the Baptists in Arkansas, 1818-1978,* is written from the standpoint of the Southern Baptist Convention; other Baptist groups remain largely unsurveyed. Walter N. Vernon, *Methodism in Arkansas, 1816-1976,* (Little Rock, 1976) is a general survey, and Kathryn D. Rice, *A History of the First United Methodist Church in Little Rock, Arkansas, 1831-1891,* (Little Rock, 1980), is the best study of an individual institution. H. L. Paisley, ed., *Centennial History of Presbyterians (U.S.)* , (N. P., 1954), needs improvement. Much better is Thomas H. Campbell, *Arkansas Cumberland Presbyterians, 1812-1984; A People of Faith,* (Memphis, 1985). Margaret S. McDonald, *White Already to Harvest: The Episcopal Church in Arkansas, 1838-1971,* (Sewanee, Tenn., 1975) is one of the longer and better church histories. Lester G. McAllister, *Arkansas Disciples: A History of the Christian Church (Disciples of Christ) in Arkansas,* (N. P., 1984), also is commendable.

Most of the smaller groups and irregular religious bodies have not been studied. E. L. Rudolph, "Another Discordant Harmony,"

AHQ, III (Autumn 1944), 211-216, is a brief account of the most famous commune. Vance Randolph, "A Witch Trial in Carroll County," *AHQ,* XVI (Spring 1957), 89-90 uncovered one episode. References to religion do not abound in the surviving letters and diaries.

T. M. Stinnett and Clara B. Kennan, *All This and Tomorrow Too: The Evolving and Continuing History of the Arkansas Education Association, A Century Beyond,* (Little Rock, 1969), includes a general survey of the public schools. Useful articles include Walter Moffatt, "Arkansas Schools, 1819-1840," *AHQ,* XII (Spring 1953), 91-105; Dean G. Carter, "Some Historical Notes on Far West Seminary," *AHQ,* XXIX (Winter 1970, 345-360, J. D. Reynolds, "Seminary Land Grant," *PAHA,* III (1911), 256-266, and Emily Penton, "Typical Women's Schools in Arkansas Before the War of 1861-1865," *AHQ,* IV (Autumn 1945), 325-339. Reform movements in Arkansas have not attracted much attention, and even temperance lacks a modern study. Austin L. Venable, ed., "Constitution and Proceedings of the Fayetteville Temperance Society, 1841-44," *AHQ,* III (Summer 1944), 164-181, presents an interesting set of documents.

Plantation Bell *(photographer unknown, ca. 1935) The symbol of discipline on the plantation under slavery, the bell, like so many features of plantation life, survived the Civil War and took on altered meanings. It was rung at the noon meal break, primarily because sharecroppers had no watches and could not tell time. Ringing it on other occasions indicated a fire or other emergency.* **Arkansas History Commission**

Chapter VII

Slavery: The Manners and Mores of a Southern Institution in a Frontier Community

INTRODUCTION

The American Revolution created a climate of opinion hostile to slavery. The radical rhetoric of American freedom extolled the rights of man and implied that all humanity was entitled to share in the natural liberty that was reborn in America with independence from the tyranny of the British. The Declaration of Independence declared that all men were created equal and endowed by their creator with certain inalienable rights: life, liberty and the pursuit of happiness. Slavery in the North was of secondary economic importance and rapidly disappeared. In the South at the time of the Revolutionary War, opponents of slavery included some, such as Thomas Jefferson, who had a large economic stake in slavery.

However, the invention of the cotton gin in 1793 created a new cash crop and a new economic order in the South. The Gulf Coastal states grew cotton, and the older Southern states sold surplus slaves west. Instead of withering away gradually as many had hoped, slavery took on renewed economic importance and expanded rapidly into rich, virgin western lands, including Arkansas.

More than half of Arkansas was unsuited to plantation slavery, but the planter class rapidly gained ascendancy in politics and society because the cotton trade meant that planters had money, a scarce commodity on the frontier. Slavery in Arkansas never developed into a mature economic system as it did in states where the plantation economy was better established, and Arkansas slave owners were mostly the rough and ready frontier types discussed previously. Support for slavery cut across class lines, and the determination to keep free blacks out of Arkansas, and later to expel those already in the state, indicated that Arkansas would not have ended slavery without the Civil War.

SLAVERY AS A MORAL QUESTION

The issue of slavery in Arkansas was debated nationally in 1819 and in 1836, but it was not discussed much within the state. Among religious denominations, only early Methodists seem to have been critical. In 1823, Methodists threatened to withhold a license from Joseph Reid as a minister because he owned a slave. Reverend Jesse Haile, presiding elder from 1825 to 1829, was an abolitionist. Anti-slavery agitation largely ended with Thomas Tennant's letters to the *Arkansas Gazette* in 1835. Thereafter, the policy of the *Gazette* was to refuse to print any discussion of the institution, for the reason that Arkansas would become a slave state and that "mischievous consequences" might result if slaves knew their status was questioned.

The debate within Arkansas about statehood in 1836 raised the slavery question obliquely. One opponent asserted that taxes would have to be increased ten times because "my lord is threatened with danger of desertion from his cotton fields" if statehood passed. Just why slavery was more vulnerable under statehood than in territorial status was unclear, but a resentment against Arkansas's ruling class was apparent in the remark. The rejoinder from Albert Pike, an apologist for slavery, was that Arkansas's growth depended on slaveholders, and abolishing slavery would

result in runaways from other states collecting in Arkansas.

The best statement of the public mood in 1836 came from a Jackson County meeting that resolved it was better to bear slavery than to suffer "a still greater evil and incure [sic] an insupportable loss." There was no discussion at all after 1836, and in 1850, the legislature made it illegal to speak or write against slavery. *Gazette* editor C. C. Danley observed nine years later, "We were the first, and we believe, the only newspaper in the state to write a line or speak a word showing that the institution of African slavery was right." Danley, of course, was incorrect, but only marginally so. Some disagreed privately with the practice, but of necessity they were discreet, like teacher Sophie Sawyer, who read the anti-slavery sermons of William Ellery Channing.

THE GROWTH OF SLAVERY

Part of Arkansas embraced slavery avidly. From 1820 to 1850, the number of Arkansas slaves increased more rapidly than in any other state, and from 1850 to 1860, Arkansas ranked second after Texas. The percentages are somewhat misleading in that Arkansas started with such small numbers; in 1820, both New York and New Jersey still had more slaves than Arkansas. In 1820, slaves amounted to only 11 percent of the population. By 1860, the state recorded 111,115 slaves, ranking twelfth in the nation and ahead of Maryland, Florida and Delaware. The white population was 324,143, which meant that a quarter of Arkansas's population was held in bondage.

Distribution and settlement patterns reflected geographic and economic considerations. Slavery in Arkansas was not distributed uniformly, and the pattern of slave ownership shifted from yeomen, who were predominant before 1840, to planters, who achieved supremacy during the 1850s. In the early years of settlement, Arkansans preferred to settle in the uplands and would farm the small amount of good bottomland along upland streams.

Such land was not suited to plantation agriculture but could benefit from extra farm laborers. Thus most slaves in the early period were owned by yeomen farmers in family-sized units. Upland counties were home to 61 percent of all slaves in 1830. Although the total number of upland slaves increased, the percentages fell in each succeeding census so that by 1860, fully 74 percent of the slaves were located in the lowlands. This shift became most apparent in the decade 1850-1860 when levee construction lured more settlers to the eastern lowlands and the Red River Valley prospered.

The first plantation county in Arkansas was Chicot in the extreme southeast corner. Chicot County has rich, deep Mississippi alluvial soils and shared the economic and cultural traits of nearby Louisiana and Mississippi. Chicot County planters were Arkansas's first elite. The creation of the Real Estate Bank was largely their work, and one of the few surviving Arkansas plantation homes is the Lakeport plantation of Lycurgus Johnson. Chicot was a true "black belt" county by 1860, with slaves comprising more than 80 percent of the county's population.

More typical of the lowlands was Arkansas County, which contained flood-prone land, prairie and rich Delta farmland. Arkansas Post remained a local economic hub, dominated by merchant-planter Frederick Notrebe. In 1825, 228 resident taxpayers were recorded. More than half owned cattle and nearly half owned horses, but only 24 percent reported owning land, and a mere 12 percent owned slaves. Probably many "landless" taxpayers were squatters whose primary economic interest was running cattle on the Grand Prairie. Seventy-one individuals had no taxable property at all, a figure that suggests rural poverty.

County conditions changed as Arkansas developed. Arkansas County's distribution of wealth was the same in 1840: the top 10 percent owned 67 percent of the taxable wealth. But the pie was larger, for average per-capita wealth had increased from $114 to $400, a gain of 251 percent. In a typical instance, farmer Achille Godin (Gordan), owner of two horses and six cows in 1825, boasted by 1840 of having three horses, a slave and thirty to forty head of cattle. Obviously, one did not have to be a planter to advance economically, but in the planter counties, those who benefited most commanded land and slaves. Compared with other sections of the nation, the common man had less chance of getting ahead in Arkansas County.

The conclusions reached from examining Arkansas County seem to apply elsewhere. Phillips County bordered on the Mississippi at the terminus of Crowley's Ridge. It contains both alluvial and upland soils. Its upland soils already were showing signs of erosion by 1860, and Phillips County did not compare in wealth to Chicot County. Yet, the County ranked second to Chicot in agricultural wealth and third in cotton production. Although politically dominated by planters, more than half of all farms were smaller than fifty improved acres and a majority of farmers got by without slaves. During the 1850s, the number of slaves increased from 2,591 to 8,940 while the number of whites went up by only 1,590. Not only did plantations get larger, but farm output rose faster than population. Lands that yielded 135 pounds of cotton an acre in 1850 yielded 160 in 1860.

Opportunity beckoned on several levels. Phillips County's largest slaveholder, Thomas B. Johnson, was the son of a Memphis carriage factory owner, and other Memphis residents had substantial investments in the County. Just reaching elite status was no guarantee of survival. Among the large planters, nearly a third could not hold on to that slippery status through the decade. Yet, there was some upward mobility. Of those who had no land in 1850 and remained in the County in 1860, nearly half had acquired real property.

Reality is sometimes less important than perceptions. Arkansans shared the belief that economic growth demanded slave labor. The hope that one could start as an overseer and in time acquire the status of planter motivated many to make their livelihoods in the mosquito-infested, unhealthy lowlands by investing in slaves while Northerners turned to the stock market. By 1860, the counties adjacent to the Mississippi River already had more blacks than whites, and other favored lowland counties were on their way to resembling Mississippi. That the Civil War came in 1861 before Arkansas's slave development was completed meant that frontier characteristics best typified the "peculiar institution."

NONPLANTATION SLAVERY

Despite the attention given to plantations and plantation slavery, about half the slaves in Arkansas did not live on plantations. Some were factory workers, others lived in towns, and a majority were held by small farmers in family-sized units or as individuals.

Factory Workers and Urban Slavery

One of the earliest recorded uses of slave labor for nonagricultural purposes was by Richard and Mark Bean, who used slaves in their salt works and later in a Washington County cotton factory. The Royston Cotton Factory in Pike County also employed blacks, and individual blacks were used in sawmills, tanneries and on steamboats. Many of these diverse occupations involved life in Arkansas towns and villages. Even semi-urban areas provided opportunities for slaves to work as domestic servants and as skilled and unskilled craftsmen. Women were much in demand for domestic work. In Little Rock, women constituted 56 percent of the town's 846 slaves.

Lawyer Chester Ashley's establishment contained stableboys, a blacksmith, gardeners, cooks, maids and nurses. Other urban occupations included butcher, house painter, shoemaker, brick maker, stone mason, and latherer and plasterer. A group of the Ashley slaves made up a band that hired out for dances.

Not only was the work of urban slaves different, but living conditions were less constraining. Many, especially those with skills, "hired their own time." "I have not set eyes on Manuel since last Saturday," wrote the wife of Senator Fulton, who added, "He is indeed his own man." An 1856 Little Rock ordinance prohibited slaves from living "separately and to themselves detached from the immediate and direct supervision of their owners," but the practice remained common. Slaves who hired their own time and paid their masters regularly could expect to be given much free time. The *True Democrat* complained in 1859:

> Negroes traverse the streets at all hours of the night free from hindrance . . . are permitted to carry knives and pistols and in case of a quarrel they draw their weapons with as much bravado as Baltimore or New Orleans rowdies.

Town slaves in Little Rock had another option rarely found in the rural areas: education. Wesley Chapel, the black Methodist church, supported a Sunday School that taught reading, writing and spelling.

Yeoman Slavery

Most nonplantation slaves were owned by small farmers. Small farmers had no need to keep records, and much less is known about slavery conditions on the farm. Post-war accounts suggest that in food, clothing and working conditions, slaves fared just about as well as their owners and certainly no worse than other hired help. Some statistical data support these recollections.

Lycurgus Johnson's Lakeport Plantation House *(photographer and date unknown) Despite a cluster of surviving plantation houses directly across the Mississippi River near Lake Washington, this rather plain, stark and vernacular Greek Revival house in Chicot County is one of the very few Arkansas plantation houses still standing. Built about 1850 by Joel Johnson, an early (1831) settler, it passed to his son, Lycurgus. In contrast to the architectural exuberance present across the Mississippi River, Lakeport has only its size, twelve-foot windows and some molded plaster ceiling medallions to indicate that it was built for the elite planter class.* **Arkansas Historic Preservation**

In Washington County, where the average slaveholder owned 4.6 slaves and the largest owner held 34 slaves, the slave death rate in 1850 was 0.3 percent compared to a statewide average of 1.8 percent and a Chicot County rate of 2.5 percent. Closer personal ties were reflected in the high percentages of mulattoes found in the upland counties and the greater number of free blacks. In Yell County, which contains both upland and bottomlands, the bottoms were home to more than half the slaves who worked most of the cotton by 1860. Slaves in Yell County tended to be younger than the state average, which indicated that many farmers regarded slave

children as a good investment. Some upland farmers owned slaves, and one who owned four set them out to work and gave his occupation to the 1860 census-taker as "Hunting and Fishing."

PLANTATION SLAVERY

Although more than half of Arkansas's 11,481 slaveholders owned fewer than four slaves each in 1860, the public associated slavery with the plantation. Using the ownership of twenty slaves as a definition, only 1,363 persons qualified as planters, and even this number is deceptive in that some plantations were owned by partnerships or were held by estates. Another confusing point was that some planters who owned plantations in more than one county were recorded more than once in the enumeration. However defined, planters constituted one of the most important political, economic and social forces influencing the development of Arkansas.

Planters

There was no strict definition of "planter;" however, planters were at the top of the social order, and during the Civil War, the Confederate Congress set the ownership of twenty slaves as a basis for draft exemption. Many men with far fewer slaves claimed the title, but others owning far in excess preferred to be called farmers.

Confusion came about because "planter" was less an economic term than a social and cultural distinction. In the Southern pro-slavery argument that emerged in the 1830s, the planter became a medieval lord, his slaves happy servants. The Romantic South embraced the Gothic Revival.

During its century-long love affair with the *Waverly* novels of Sir Walter Scott, Southerners became "Southrons," slaves were addressed as "my servants," and the tournament became the favorite community entertainment. The patriarchal world of chivalry justified slavery for the good of blacks and idealized women as fair maidens on a pedestal.

As architectural fashion changed, Greek Revival and Roman styles of building that earlier were believed to be particularly well suited to a republic gave way to Gothic revival architecture. One example conspicuous to many River travelers of that time was the Louisiana state Capitol at Baton Rouge.

This romantic attitude implied a long-established order, as in Tidewater Virginia, Charleston or the Creoles of New Orleans. However, in Arkansas the planter was a frontiersman and often new to the system. Some

were the sons of Eastern planters seeking their fortunes with a small amount of capital and a few family slaves. Typically these men married a woman from the same class, perhaps adding a few more slaves from her dowry. Such young men often found political office or a profession a valuable adjunct to advancement. In addition, young professionals, notably doctors and lawyers, often invested their profits in slaves while those lower on the social scale could begin a successful career by starting as an overseer. Advancement in these ways was within the acceptable limits set by Arkansas society.

Arkansas also became home to some who had failed east of the River and hoped to reverse fortune's fate in a new land. In some instances these men were just a step ahead of a sheriff's execution sale. When traveler G. W. Featherstonhaugh wrote that Arkansas was populated by "bankrupts who were not disposed to be plundered by their creditors," he identified a portion of the planter class. When Flush Times ended abruptly in the 1840s, some of these men, once again over-extended, fled their Arkansas debts by moving to Texas.

Regardless of their point of entry into the planters' world, all persons involved in plantation agriculture found their romantic ideals more useful in the boudoir or parlor than in the plantation business office. Plantation management was hardheaded economic activity based on speculation, extensive use of credit for purchase of land and slaves, and totally dependent on world market conditions for the price of cotton.

With much of Arkansas plantation lands also subject to overflow from the state's numerous rivers, even the weather could make or break a plantation in a year or two. On balance the factors leading to instability and unprofitableness probably outweighed those on the profit side of the ledger. Yet Southern society gave such political and social rewards to planting that a strict balance-sheet approach in no way accounted for the system's

Aunt Letty's Tombstone
(photographer and date unknown) Nearly lost in the woods of Prairie County is the well-kept "Old White Church" cemetery containing this tombstone of Aunt Letty Horne. Born a slave, she stayed with the Horne family after the Civil War, nursing three generations of Hornes. The community was Presbyterian and Letty Horne was admitted to the Wattensas Presbyterian Church on profession of faith on June 9, 1867. Although many blacks left white congregations after the Civil War, Letty stayed and was buried in an integrated cemetery. The portion of the cemetery where Letty is buried is well-maintained, but the forest has encroached on the graves of many other blacks. **Arkansas History Commission**

appeal. More than one man found himself in the position of a Hempstead County resident whose "inability to say 'No' to a neighbor led him into endorsements that handicapped him financially for the last thirty years of his life."

Men who tried to realize Southern aspirations with borrowed capital and frequent recourse to slave markets for additional labor achieved variable results. Not one plantation house on the scale and opulence of those of Natchez or Vicksburg was left behind to com-

memorate devotion to a doomed way of life. Instead, Arkansan Albert Pike produced a poem about Elias Rector of Fort Smith, "a fine Arkansas gentleman close to the Choctaw line," whose visits to New Orleans were notable neither for piety nor sobriety.

The Slave Trade

Although many families brought slaves with them when they moved to Arkansas, most planters acquired additional hands in the market place. Slavery had its defenders, but the slave trade did not initially. In Arkansas, the last gasp of post-Revolutionary War humanitarianism occurred in 1836 when the state constitution authorized the legislature to ban the importation of slaves for purposes of speculation. No efforts were made to implement this power, and opinion became so different by the late 1850s that Arkansas newspaper editors clamored for reopening the African slave trade to fill the needs of Arkansas planters.

No organized slave trade existed within the state, but a few auction services dealt in slaves, as when F. R. Taylor opened his "Auction Mart" in 1836 for "Slaves, Real Estate, Merchandise, Household Furniture, &c., &c." A local market always could be found for humans, and slaves were occasionally included in deals involving horses, cattle and lands. Arkansans and Indians frequently engaged in swaps as well. But most planters relied on established slave marts. Memphis, the closest slave market, was home of slave trader Nathan Bedford Forrest, and New Orleans, where many large planters marketed their cotton, had the largest supply.

Slaves also came into the market when an owner's death made it necessary to sell slaves in order to settle accounts of the estate or divide property among heirs. Economic distress during the early 1840s and after the Panic of 1857 sent the price of cotton down, forcing some marginal or over-extended planters into bankruptcy and their slaves to the auction block.

Slave Prices

A market value for slaves generally was recognized. During the 1820s the average value was $380. Rapid expansion during Flush Times sent the price up to $485, but during hard times of the 1840s the average price fell to $455. Prices climbed again in the 1850s,

and in one 1860 inventory, the average price was $881, which Camden merchant Robert F. Kellam found "enormous." Such averages were a general guide to values, but each type of slave carried a different price. The very young and the old fetched the least; carpenters, brick masons or blacksmiths ranked first, followed by prime field hands and fertile females. In the 1860 inventory, a twenty-five-year-old blacksmith was valued at $2,800. Rising prices were a symptom of slave property becoming increasingly concentrated in the hands of the elite. It is little wonder that those left out agitated to reopen the slave trade.

Slave Work

Plantations were units of production run for profit. In Arkansas, twenty to twenty-five slaves formed the usual work unit. Planters who acquired substantially more slaves set up outlying plantations, usually under the supervision of an overseer. Those who could afford it hired overseers for all of their units and spent their time supervising.

Because slave prices were much higher than land values, good land was the least of the planter's worries. One Mississippian, before moving to Arkansas, purchased more than 10,000 acres at 19 cents an acre and probably used state scrip selling for less than half its face value to make the purchase. Getting virgin land into production was not achieved as easily. Trees had to be deadened and cut, the stumps had to be pulled, and most laborious of all, the "chunks" had to be picked up and burned. Fields had to be fenced to keep out cattle and hogs. Tools for these chores consisted of axes and saws aided by oxen and horses. Clearing was done imperfectly with these crude tools, so uprooting sprouts remained a yearly part of field maintenance. Thus an initial investment in land preparation came before profit could be realized. Established planters seeking future profit also sacrificed current income to clear new fields, usually during the winter months.

Extensive land clearing indicated that Arkansas was still a frontier state during this period, for even with proper management, raising cotton was a full-time occupation. Plowing typically began at the end of January, and planting took place in April and May. After the cotton came up, it had to be weeded. "Chopping cotton," as weeding was called, continued until the Fourth of July, when the crop was "laid by." After a short hiatus, picking began as soon as the first bolls opened. Picking continued until after Christmas. To divert labor by opening new lands meant less picking or plowing time.

Any time not spent on cotton was devoted to corn, for its demands coincided with gaps in the cotton schedule, especially the harvesting in late August and September. Planters gave lip service to diversification and planted some rice in southeastern counties. Only a small amount of land was suitable, for without deep wells and pumps, streams and swamps had to be diverted into rice fields. Rye and other grains, peas, beans, sweet potatoes and orchard products were raised. Planters joined small farmers in raising cattle and hogs.

Despite diversification, the primary emphasis on cotton left plantations short of food. Because of the absence of a state transportation system, the rest of Arkansas's farmers could not make up the deficiency. Arkansas was a food-importing state, dependent on the Ohio River Valley for pork, cornmeal and flour. Planters usually bought in quantity, preferring to maximize labor on cotton production and buy food on the open market.

Not all slaves on the plantation were engaged in agriculture. House servants served both functional and ornamental roles and frequently out-priced ordinary field hands in the market. On a well-run plantation, household slaves supervised cooking and cleaning and helped clothe the labor force. The home sewing machine, first introduced in 1846 and constantly improved, rapidly replaced the traditional seamstress. An advertisement from the Singer Company in 1857 assured planters that one machine could do the work of a dozen women working by hand.

Planters also bought clothes, shoes and hats in quantity from New Orleans factors or in smaller allotments from local merchants. These items were modified on the plantation to fit the slaves. Slave blacksmiths, carpenters, masons and other skilled craftsmen either could be found or hired from those fortunate enough to possess such workers.

Housing

Most Arkansas slaves lived in log cabins similar to those occupied by yeoman whites and even the planters themselves. By 1860, few planters had reached the stage of economic development that found expression farther south in ornate conspicuous consumption. A Clark County resident recalled what was probably the most common housing pattern in Arkansas: for the planter, "a mansion of logs, boards, or brick;" for the slaves, houses "built of the same materials, but laid off in a street eighty feet wide, with a row of houses on each side, the mansion at one end, and the overseer's house at the other end." A large bell was located centrally, "near the house of the foreman, a slave that superintended the farm and other slaves, and did the bidding of the overseer."

By one estimate, each cabin contained 5.74 persons, which compared favorably with the state average for both white and black of 5.72. In the older states, some plantations contained brick quarters, but none has been identified in Arkansas. A slave jail, a log structure with bars and heavy hand-forged iron hardware, survived at the Yellow Bayou Plantation in Chicot County.

Family Life

Life for the slave on a plantation or farm involved endless cycles of work. The whole family shared in labor, and although the male slave was without the authority of his white counterpart, plantation society placed a strong emphasis on the sanctity of the family. Cabin life for blacks was remarkably similar to the life of whites, except that an outside force directed the work schedule.

In American law, the slave family had no legal foundation and rested solely on the owner's good will. On smaller plantations or in town, it often even rested on two owners' consent, for cross-owner marriages were common. In the white man's law, marriage was a solemn contractual arrangement to which Protestant Christianity gave its blessing. There was no marriage contract in slavery because slaves lacked legal standing to contract. Opinion and practice varied on the religious component. "Jumping the broomstick," a ritual that the couple performed in front of the slave community in the presence of the master, was an informal system commonly used. Its advantage was that it could be undone easily if the coupling proved unsuitable.

Many masters, especially those adhering to evangelical religious sects, were more formal in their procedures. Some performed services themselves, entering the names of the couple in a family Bible and admonishing the newlyweds to avoid "fussin'and fightin'." Others permitted or even encouraged church weddings. A Little Rock diarist considered one such ceremony at the Christian Church an important social event. One indication of family strength was the survival of last names. Although white owners often identified slaves only by first names, many slaves created and used last names. The idea that slaves chose last names only after the end of the Civil War is not borne out by examining antebellum records.

Although marriage was important in the black community and stable monogamous relations often resulted, an essentially different set of sexual mores from those of Victorian whites was created and nourished among the

blacks by a number of factors. First, all marriages could be broken up by sale. When husband and wife were owned by different parties, stability in the domestic relationship was uncertain at best. On many plantations, the husband's weekend pass constituted the only time he saw his wife. Second, sexual activity began at an early age, for pre-marital promiscuity was generally acceptable to the slaves themselves. Without legal marriage there could be no legal bastardy, and the production of children without acknowledged fathers carried no stigma.

One well-documented case of slave family relationships surfaced in a modern state Supreme Court case decided in 1950 concerning the heirs of "Old Joe" Edwards. A Union County ex-slave enriched by oil discoveries, Joe had jumped the broomstick first sometime before 1850 with Susan, a slave on an adjacent plantation. From this union came five children. But in 1855, Joe jumped the broomstick with Patsy, who worked on the home plantation. This marriage also produced five children. When slavery ended, Joe took yet another wife, compounding the problem of determining his legal heirs.

Whites often expected blacks to be promiscuous, and owners sometimes contributed to the situation through sexual relations with female slaves. The 1850 census classified 15.61 percent of Arkansas's slaves as mulattoes. Some persons were the products of mulatto parents, but interracial relations were common, especially in Little Rock, where the town's unmarried men frequented black prostitutes. Doubtless as a result of repeated liaisons, one mulatto man sued for freedom, alleging that he was white. The state Supreme Court rejected his appeal, although noting that it must have taken "at least twenty generations from the black blood to be as white as complainant." One Helena slave schedule actually described a child as "white." This heritage of miscegenation is apparent even today when "black" Arkansans are compared in skin color to their Negro counterparts from Africa.

Not all white-black relationships were casual or exploitive. Owners frequently manumitted their slave offspring and made elaborate though not always successful plans for their education and freedom. Such arrangements could lead to family crises, as when the wife of Elisha Worthington discovered her husband's relationship with a slave that predated their marriage. Returning to her native Kentucky, she filed for divorce. In another case, a slave named Viney was given her freedom and $5,000 in her owner's will, but instead of freedom, she was sold in Mississippi and had to be recovered by a writ of habeas corpus from the state Supreme Court. One abolitionist tract, *Inside Views of Slavery on Southern Plantations* (1864) by John Roles, detailed the tribulations of a Fort Smith cook who was exploited sexually by an owner who promised her freedom. When the relationship was discovered by the man's wife, the slave was tortured before being sold. On the other hand, one Washington County white woman conspired with her slave lover to murder her husband. A significant number of Arkansas slaves also possessed some Indian blood, the result of Indian ownership of slaves and the lively cross-border trade.

Food and Clothing

Whites and blacks ate essentially the same food, except that whites had more variety, more liquor and more tobacco. Plantation slaves probably ate better than poor white farmers. Breakfast was at seven a.m., with coffee deemed essential by all classes. Dinner, as rural folk still call the noon meal, came at eleven o'clock a.m., and supper followed at six p.m. Pork was ubiquitous, and slaves and travelers rarely saw the meat for the fatback. Accompanying the meat was cornbread and molasses and the products of gardens and orchards. Alternate sources for fresh meat included game. One plantation retained a full-time hunter. Ducks, geese, bear, squirrels, rabbits, turkey, quail, other birds, and deer commonly were consumed and rivers yielded fish and turtles.

One Arkansas slave "fish story" recalled feasting on a lake turtle that had to be hauled ashore by a mule and whose shell alone weighed 148 pounds. Slaves not only fished during their free time but often were permitted to carry weapons for hunting. Because much work was expected from slaves, planters had a vested interest in keeping them well fed. Evidence indicates that antebellum diet exceeded in both quantity and quality that which nineteenth century and twentieth century sharecroppers endured.

Similarities in diet between races were not matched in attire. Many female slaves continued to wear rolled cloth headgear of African origin. Masters who ordered plantation clothes wholesale caused their hands to have a prisoner-like look. Made of rough cotton cloth often called "osnaburg," slave clothing was exceedingly uncomfortable when new. Sizing was not common, and travelers reported almost as a matter of course that slaves sometimes presented a ludicrous appearance. Because little was wasted, slaves also received presents from whites of cast-off clothing.

One mark of individuality was to modify and personalize apparel. Town slaves and house servants had the most opportunities for sartorial display, and English traveler Ida Pfeiffer wrote of a slave ball in Fort Smith in 1854: "The gentlemen were in black, with white neck-cloths and white waist-coats; the ladies in tulle, and other pretty white dresses; and there was no lack of gold chains and jewelry, or of ribbons and flowers in the hair."

It was not uncommon for children, both white and black, to go around naked, and when first clothed, they wore what one ex-slave recalled was "a long sack-like slip with holes cut for arms and head." Shoes figured only to a limited extent, and, like slave clothing, often were purchased in bulk. Brogans, a rough heavy work shoe, often were worn only in the winter. On some plantations, locally tanned leather was cobbled into shoes by slave artisans. Wool hats were common to both whites and blacks. Clothing was one item that slaves could possess without seriously worrying that whites might take it away. Hence Sundays and holidays were occasions for show.

Medical Treatment

Arkansas had a reputation as a sickly place, with people in the lowlands prone to cholera, yellow fever and typhoid, in addition to the omnipresent malaria. Masters, with a vested interest in healthy slaves, provided medical services. Unfortunately, nineteenth century medicine could offer few cures, and treatment often made bad matters worse.

Much doctoring was done by planters themselves, especially in treating commonly recognized diseases such as malaria. Planters bought quinine in quantity to cope with malaria, and many ailments of a lesser order were treated with folk medicine. The 1850 census, the first to collect mortality statistics, revealed that cholera was the chief killer, followed by various fevers, worms, pneumonia, whooping cough, dropsy, consumption, scarlet fever and convulsions. Of these, cholera and yellow fever came periodically in contagious waves. The census recorded a 1.8 percent death rate for blacks and a 1.32 percent death rate for whites. Better evidence of slavery's exploitation could be found in the birth rate. Perhaps because pregnant black women were worked in the fields, blacks had a lower birth rate, 2.4 percent, compared to the white 3.5 percent.

When medical problems got beyond a planter's capability, an outside physician was brought in. Some plantations kept physicians on retainer, and others paid doctors on a case-by-case basis. Surviving records indicate that in the 1830s, Dr. William C. Howell

of Little Rock charged $1 a mile for daytime calls and $2 at night. Such rates appear to have been usual, for in 1855, Dr. Henry Pernot entered in his daybook, "July 11, 1855, to visit, mileage, examining of black girl for the clap, 5.00."

Venereal disease among slaves often required medical attention, usually consisting of large doses of mercury. For one group brought into southern Arkansas on the eve of the Civil War, the doctor required that the patients, all females, be isolated from black males until after the cure. Dentistry was in its infancy, and the commercial rate for tooth-pulling was $1 a tooth. Midwives were used by both races for help in birthing.

The physical condition of slaves was occasionally an adjudicated matter. Slaves carried a warranty about their condition when they were sold. Controversies about these warranties often ended up in court. In *Plant* v. *Condit* (1861), a slave boy sold as allegedly sound turned out to be a dirt-eater and hence of less value. Although a planter might have legal recourse in some instances, death sometimes left planters holding the bill and crops untended.

Slave Control

How to get the most labor from slaves was a much-debated issue in planter circles. The whip best symbolized the plantation and was used to a greater or lesser degree depending on the personality of the planter. For some it was the first resort, for others the last.

Although whipping represented the ultimate terror, incentives commonly were used to increase slave productivity. These included special favors, extra holidays, cash payments, presents and other rewards. Conversely, masters could deny slaves holidays, withhold favors and inflict such punishments as stocks, chains or slave prisons.

Arkansas society accepted as normal the principle that a slave's life lay in the master's power. Excessive whippings verging on the pathological were not unknown. The state Supreme Court heard in the case of *Pyeatt* v. *Spencer* (1842) that a female slave showing signs of derangement after being separated from her children was staked to the ground by her new master who whipped her at intervals and then rubbed salt into the wounds with a corn cob. No one questioned his right to punish the slave. The question before the court was whether she had been deranged before the sale or if punishment had led to her useless condition. In 1861, a young overseer near Champagnolle witnessed the beating of a female slave whose master believed she had been seeing unwanted males. He whipped her "till she defficated & urinated all over herself & never could make her tell," the boy concluded, "I guess she told the truth when she said she did not no [sic] them."

Death occasionally resulted from such treatment. One overseer who found his slaves "a rough and saucy set of hands to manage," said "he would make the negroes obey him, or he would kill them." Proving to be true to his word, he ultimately killed Nath, "a stout negro, weighing about 200 pounds."

Discipline usually stopped short of sadism or murder, but most slaves were whipped at least once in their adult lives. Overseers were most prone to use whipping, and one that Englishman Henry M. Stanley described as all "vulgarity and coarseness," terrorized slaves as a matter of course. In retaliation, slaves often worked less efficiently for overseers, and in 1860, two or three overseers in Union County were killed by slaves.

At times discipline, even the use of the whip, was in the slave's best interest. Planter James Sheppard's overseer could not get Nora to take her quinine, so Sheppard "gave her about 15 or 20 cutts with my little cowhide & not wanting to whip her, called in Aggy & Patsy & told her I'd gap her if it took the whole plantation. She took then & afterwards . . . ."

Runaways

Despite every effort to instill docility, some individuals rebelled against the system and became runaways. Newspaper advertisements for these persons reveal no clear pattern. Some were trusted body servants who could read and write and some were simple field hands; a majority were males. Some stole money with which to make their escapes; others acted on the spur of the moment. In one 1840 case, Nelson Hacket, a Fayetteville butler and valet, fled Washington County on a stolen race horse, eventually reaching Canada. After being tracked down by slave catchers and taken into custody, he was surrendered by Canadian authorities on the strength of an Arkansas felony indictment. The case attracted international attention. Fortunately for future runaways, it did not prove to be a precedent. After the passage of the Fugitive Slave Law in 1850, only Canada was a safe refuge.

Successful escapes were few, but a temporary desertion could be a form of protest about working conditions. Many notices for runaways admitted as much, as when harsh taskmaster William E. Woodruff advertised for Moses, "a notorious liar and quite boisterous when intoxicated," who was probably "still lurking around Little Rock." Some runaways took to the woods or canebrakes just when work was at its hardest; others were trying to locate family members or even to return home. A few were lured into escaping by criminals who planned to resell the slave to some unsuspecting buyer. Negro-stealing was punishable by law in the territorial period by restitution, fine, whipping, confinement in a pillory and wearing a six-inch red letter "T." A second conviction carried the death penalty.

When an owner became satisfied that a slave had become a runaway, the first recourse was to place newspaper advertisements and offer rewards. Sometimes slaves themselves profited by turning in escapees;

Nathan Warren *(photographer and date unknown) The most successful of Arkansas's free blacks posed for the camera when he was advanced in years.* **Arkansas History Commission**

Slave Uprisings

White Arkansans lived in fear of slave uprisings. Even if they were unfamiliar with events in Santo Domingo and Haiti, most knew about Nat Turner's Rebellion in Virginia and could tell other local stories that frequently never made the newspapers. Such revolts threatened not only the planters but all whites and led to the creation of both formal and informal controls by society over slave lives.

One formal control over slaves was the patrol. In all comings and goings, the slave was supposed to possess a pass from the master. Slaves caught without passes could be given twenty-five lashes on the order of a justice of the peace. In addition, townships were permitted to organize a patrol to scour the countryside at night to detect illicit slave movements. Slaves caught by the patrol could be given twenty lashes immediately, and other punishments were detailed for free Negroes or white men caught fraternizing with slaves.

sometimes professional slave catchers were employed. Some runaways were apprehended by local authorities. Before 1849, the sheriff took runaways into custody and posted an advertisement on the courthouse door. Those not claimed in a year's time were sold at auction. After 1849, unclaimed slaves were delivered to the state penitentiary, and if not claimed, held for life by the state.

The patrol was something of a burden, and the law imposed fines of up to $25 for failing to serve. In the beginning, the patrol system existed largely on paper as a part of the slave code inherited from older slave states. This "slumbering power," as the Arkansas high court called it in 1854, became more important as Arkansas filled up rapidly during the 1850s. New slaves, new owners and new tensions sent rumor after rumor through the white communities of southern Arkansas that led to some hasty actions. In one Ouachita County case, a patrol invaded a neighboring township outside its jurisdiction, found a party of slaves returning from church and whipped the slaves so severely that their cries could be heard for miles. The outraged owner sued for damages, claiming that his slaves were too bruised to work. The state Supreme Court rejected his argument, deferring to the danger of possible slave uprisings.

Slaves accused of crimes were entitled to formal legal proceedings. Yet just as the Ouachita County patrol overstepped its bounds, at times the white community refused to allow the law to run its course. A Benton County slave convicted of murder and confined in jail was taken out and lynched. Three slaves were accused in 1856 of the murder of Dr. James Boone near Fayetteville. Defended by court-appointed lawyers, one defendant was convicted, the state declined to prosecute one and the third, found not guilty, was bludgeoned to death by an irate mob.

Many lynchings came about during times of great racial tension and were intended as warnings to the black community. Arkansas experienced two waves of hysteria, the first in 1835 and a second in the late 1850s. The first outbreak was triggered by the publication of the revelations of Virgil Stewart concerning the criminal activities of John A. Murrell. It was not the robbery or murder charges that spread fear, but rather Stewart's claim that Murrell planned a slave uprising. Lynch mobs took the lives of at least seven white men in Mississippi and perhaps as many as fifty blacks perished. In Arkansas, where slaves did not exist in numbers sufficient to warrant a fear, vengeance was wreaked on gamblers and vagrants.

The second wave of hysteria came just before the Civil War and spread to the state from Texas. One supposed abolitionist, a Northern Methodist missionary, was tracked down in northwestern Arkansas, taken back to Texas, and lynched. Prairie County had a supposed insurrection at Pigeon Roost and Hickory Plains, after which three slaves and a white man were lynched on the basis of testimony extracted through torture. Another Methodist minister was hung at Oil Trough in northeastern Arkansas, and all southern Arkansas was tense.

These outbreaks of hysteria reflected more the fears of the white community than the plans of blacks. Rules of evidence were virtually nonexistent, and in almost every case, whites were convinced in advance of stories that torture extracted: bad white men were trying to lure slaves into revolting, a day had been set, secret signals had been practiced, and Northern abolitionist money stood behind the plot.

Occasionally, as at Hickory Ridge, a planter objected to having his valuable property destroyed by mob action and so made a vigorous public protest, thus insuring some newspaper coverage. The public generally supported the lynchings, for the sacrifice of a few "no-good" whites and blacks in order to achieve a feeling of security was considered worth the price. Although personal relations between individual blacks and whites often were quite close and extended over generations, collective antagonism between the races kept society tense. Institutionally, slavery was degrading, dehumanizing and inherently unstable.

Slave Religion

The spread of evangelical religion across the South in the early nineteenth century heightened the debate about the relationship between religion and slavery. No Southern denomination denied that slaves had eternal souls capable of salvation, but blacks and whites praying together in the same church implied an equality on Sunday that might spark rebellion on Monday. Thus the masters of Arkansas were of contrary opinions about the value of religion. For those who looked to the Bible for literal instruction on the issue, even the Bible was inconsistent, with the Old Testament encouraging slaves to rise up against their masters, whereas in the New Testament, the Apostle Paul told servants to obey their masters. Because one problem with slavery was the inefficiency of slave labor, if Gospel preaching could inspire in the slaves a devotion to work, then many planters felt it worth the risk.

Historian Orville Taylor estimated that perhaps only 20,000 of Arkansas's 111,115 slaves in 1860 belonged to religious denominations. Most were Baptists. One black Baptist minister is alleged to have asserted, "If you see a nigger who ain't a Baptist, you know some white man has been triggerin' with him." If slaves followed the religions of their owners, then black Baptists were most likely to be the property of yeoman farmers or small planters. However, because so many Arkansas slaves had been uprooted, owner and slave affiliations often differed. Episcopal Bishop Henry C. Lay encountered communicants among black hands at the Royston cotton factory. "Although ignorant of the church," wrote the bishop, they "knew the Creed by transmission from their fathers."

Episcopalians were few and scattered, but Methodists were numerous, claiming 15,665 white and 2,897 black members in 1853. Arkansas Methodists had become attuned to plantation slavery only after a bitter internal controversy during which the denomination abandoned its early teaching against slavery. One of the last opponents was Presiding Elder Jesse Haile, who, from 1825 to 1829, created a "hail storm" of trouble for the growing group by agitating against slavery both in and out of the pulpit.

Transferred to Illinois in 1830 after having numerically weakened the sect, Hail had no successors. In 1845, the Arkansas Conference endorsed the split with the Northern Methodists and declared that slavery was not "necessarily evil."

Presbyterians were active among Arkansas blacks but left little record of their efforts. The Wattensas Presbyterian Church in Prairie County listed sixteen colored communicants from 1853-1886. Session records state that on March 28, 1857, "The sacrament of the Lord's Supper was dispensed, and at 4 o' clock p. m. to the Blacks." Five colored communicants were received on profession of faith on June 9, 1867, Letty Horne, Charles Rembert and wife Judy, Bob Moore and Scipio Howard. Ned Given was also baptized.

There were black Catholics, evidence of whom could be found in the baptismal records of the early Catholic churches. Arkansas Christians, the followers of Alexander Campbell, were active and claimed black members. The politically powerful Johnson family was associated closely with the Christians and influenced some of their slaves to join.

Just how blacks were to be converted and preached to was a much-debated point in religious circles. Baptists, Methodists and Presbyterians sent missionaries into the field "white unto harvest." Southwestern Arkansas, with its growing plantation economy, absentee owners and unchurched slaves, was the major area of missionary activity. Churches created specifically for slaves seemed the best answer in plantation counties. But most of Arkansas did not fit the plantation county model in population distribution and hence not in religious practices. Methodists and Presbyterians often set aside the gallery for blacks, thus seating whites and blacks under the same roof. Frequently, as in Little Rock's Mount Holly Cemetery, both races shared the same burial ground.

Sometimes ministers addressed both whites and blacks at the same time but not under one roof. A Benton slave recalled a meeting at which whites sat in a wooden shed while the blacks sat outside by the window:

When de preacher git all warm'up, an'
had de white folks inside de shed
thinkin' on de way ter glory, he sticks his
haid out de window now an' den ter
exhort us servan's; 'you cullud people out
dar — listen at me! De way ter make
good slaves, is ter obey yo' Massa an'
Missis! Obey'em constant,' — 'Den he
sticks his haid back in, and preached till
he had some mo' words fo' us-all.

Black disgust for the "obey your master"
text was noted in the frank comments ex-
slaves recalled in interviews in the 1930s *Federal Writers Project Slave Narratives.* One
Arkansas slave remembered religion to mean
"Serve your masters. Don't steal your master's
turkey. Don't steal you master's hawgs. Don't
steal your master's meat. Do whatever you
master tells you to do. Same old thing all the
time." A young slave resisted religion couched
in such terms: "I don't want to hear that same
old sermon." Boredom set in even for the converted. "We went to church, sat in de back seat
of the white folks' church. It was a Baptist.
Baptized in pool. White preacher said: 'Obey
your master.'"

By contrast black preachers or exhorters
and black gospel hymns offered a fervent hope
of a joyous salvation. With images of freedom
drawn from the Old Testament and Fourth of
July oratory, black religion was sometimes
seen as a dangerous threat to white supremacy. Hence, some masters were indifferent or
hostile toward missionaries. One Union County slave recalled, "We didn't have no church
nor nothing. No Sunday-schools, no nothin.
Work from Monday morning till Saturday
night. On Sunday we didn't do nothin' but set
right down there on that big plantation.
Couldn't go nowhere."

The law recognized the abstract right of
slaves to attend church, and the Sabbath-
breaking statute prohibited masters from
working slaves, but large plantation owners
considered it dangerous for slaves from differ-

ent areas to mix together. On the other hand,
the Sabbath law permitted slaves to labor for
themselves on Sunday, a feature that encouraged slave work habits and indicated that
lawmakers did not consider slaves liable to
eternal harm by desecration of the Sabbath,
even though such labor was in direct violation
of the Third Commandment.

Despite obstacles, black religion did
expand. Baptists, especially, licensed black
preachers. One, "Uncle Tom" Clements of
Greene County, came to Arkansas as the
slave of the Reverend M.E. Clements and
served the Mt. Zion Church. One white Baptist recalled that he "could lead in singing; he
could conduct a prayer service; he could bury
the dead. He could pray with more spirit and
fervor than any one I ever heard, white or
colored." And he officiated at the funerals of
more than 100 area whites. Clements worked
in an area where slavery was marginal, and
his example was seldom duplicated in plantation counties.

Perhaps because Baptists were most active
in recruiting black converts, they also spent
more time than other denominations justifying their work and defending slavery. In 1860,
the Charleston Baptist Church, having
received a batch of abolitionist pamphlets in
the mail, issued a ringing endorsement of
slavery: "We regard slavery as scriptural, and
moral in its tendency, and by far the best situation in which the African can be placed." On
the eve of the Civil War, the abolitionist threat
prompted W.H.B. of Helena to write a serial-
ized story for the *Arkansas Baptist,* setting
forth in simple language suitable for reading
to the slaves a dialogue on the Biblical origins
and justifications for slavery.

One objection by slave owners to conversion
of slaves to Protestant Christianity came from
a conflict with the basic impulse of Protestants toward education. Bibles were readily
available and the repeated injunction of
Protestant ministers that Christians should
read and study them could hardly be preached

to whites and blacks at the same time. Arkansas, unlike some other slave states, did not have any statutes prohibiting blacks from being taught to read and write, but a strong sentiment based on economic self-interest supported keeping slaves ignorant. Advertisements for runaways reveal that many who fled could read and write. A literate runaway might forge a pass or free papers, thus increasing the probability of successful flight to freedom.

It is not known how many slaves in Arkansas were literate. Apparently literacy was not too uncommon. During the Civil War, one Clark County man complained about an exemption from military service granted a quack doctor who can neither read or write as well as many a Negro in this county. Masters were aware of this skill, and one letter directed the slave, Fagans, to read his Bible. Even so, remembering Nat Turner, the Virginia minister whose rebellion was the single most bloody episode in the history of nineteenth century slavery, many whites felt more secure if the slaves remained unlettered, unsaved and docile toward their owners.

FREE BLACKS

Some masters freed their slaves in the aftermath of the American Revolution. Antislavery sentiments diminished in the South after 1830, partly because cotton production had made slavery highly profitable, and also because a rising tide of conservatism repudiated the philosophical assumptions that underlay the American Revolution. Southern planters moved to make it impossible to criticize slavery after the 1840s and insisted instead on the positive good of the peculiar institution. One reflection of these cultural changes could be found in Arkansas's treatment of free blacks.

Because slaves were property and property ranked supreme among the hierarchy of rights recognized by American law in the nineteenth century, it is not surprising that owners had the right to free slaves, subject only — as the 1836 Constitution phrased it — to "the rights of creditors and preventing them from becoming a public charge." The organic law also prohibited the legislature from enacting an emancipation law without the consent of slave owners. When Arkansas framed a new constitution without Congressional scrutiny in 1861, even the right of planters to free their own slaves was denied. The overwhelming public sentiment in Arkansas that slavery should endure forever became a salient feature of the state's Confederate Constitution.

Masters did free their slaves between 1819 and 1860 despite public opinion and the legal difficulties involved. A few seem to have made their philosophical antipathy to slavery public, as when John Latta of Vineyard, Washington County, a bachelor with "Henry Clay notions after slavery," emancipated his slaves in his will. Left a bequest of $2,500, the free blacks returned to Kentucky, where they had been born. Planters often sought to free their children by a slave mother. Elisha Worthington sent his two children, a boy and a girl, to be educated in the North. Gifts of money and property frequently accompanied freedom, and indeed were necessary to some extent because the law forbade the granting of freedom in order to avoid caring for very young or aged slaves.

The hostile climate of opinion in Arkansas toward grants of freedom could be observed readily in court records. In *Phebe* v. *Quillim* (1860), Justice Fairchild observed that "a change from the condition of servitude and protection, to that of being free negroes, is injurious to the community, and more unfortunate to the emancipated negro than to any one else." The courts formerly used to "lean towards the grant of freedom" but had now reversed that policy. As one example of this attitude, in *Jackson* v. *Bob* (1857), the Supreme Court refused to order a master to free his slave despite the master having agreed that the slave could purchase his freedom. And in *Ewell* v. *Tidwell*, (1859) the high court overturned a will under which free Negroes would have inherited slaves: "The ownership of slaves by free negroes is directly opposed to the principles upon which slavery exists among us," wrote Judge Compton, even though the practice previously was legal, not uncommon in older Southern states, and had occurred in Arkansas.

If the state was slow to move against the sacrosanct right of property, it did not hesitate to act against the immigration of free blacks into Arkansas. An early law required any county "damnified by such negro or mulatto" to collect a $500 bond from each person. Free blacks between the ages of seven and twenty-one were to be bound out as apprentices, and freedmen were required to keep papers on them at all times.

Despite hostile legislation, the number of free blacks grew from 141 in 1830 to 465 by 1840. Mountainous Marion County had the largest nonslave black population by 1850, the result of the immigration of two black families from Tennessee, two of whose members held estates worth more than $1,000. Apparently these settlers were tolerated by the notoriously negrophobic mountain men because of the scarcity of population. Most free blacks typically lived in towns. Gad Bradley was town blacksmith in Washington, and Nathan Warren was variously a Little Rock barber, carriage driver, and pastry cook. He was much in demand as a cook for social events and "was always ready to supply them on short notice." Warren eventually bought freedom for members of his family. His wife was cook for the Ashley family, but despite powerful friends, his store mysteriously burned down. Warren's ownership of other family members was not unique. Daniel Earls in Jackson County owned 350 acres and held the franchise for a White River ferry. He was able to buy his wife and children out of slavery over a period of years.

Almost as soon as Arkansas became a state, newspapers began agitating against free blacks. In 1836, a free black named Bunch attempted to vote in Columbia County and was murdered by a mob. The legislature forbade the further immigration of free blacks into Arkansas in 1843 and required those present to post bond. In upholding the law in *Pendleton* v. *State* (1846), the state Supreme Court ruled that Arkansas's constitution "was the work of the white race" and blacks never could be considered citizens. Yet these noncitizens were fully liable at law and were taxed in the same manner as whites. Unable to testify in court against white persons or to bear arms, the entire presumption of the law was against their freedom. As the Court held in 1857, if a person looked African, "he is presumed to be a slave."

What prompted the Court's 1857 exposition on race and slavery was the exceptional case of Abby Guy. The widow Guy, her children, and property were seized by a neighbor. Abby sued for her freedom, claiming that she was a white person. Her case dragged on for years, with two jury trials in two different counties. On one occasion she was paraded down the floor of the courtroom with bare feet on the theory that black blood would be visible in her feet. When the high Court first heard her appeal, they set forth the rule of evidence noted above and added, "the courts should be careful that a person of the white race be not deprived of his liberty," and should "give him the benefit of the doubt." When at last declared a free person, Abby Guy promptly sued for the recovery of her property: some mares, a colt, a yoke of oxen and a cart, which the high Court refused to award to her.

The Guy case demonstrated that not even color provided a clear determination of status. Other records indicated that regardless of law, actual practices were far less technical than statutory requirements. In Washington County, Elizah Williams, "a free man of color," became in one legal document "my true and lawful attorney" of record, or a legal witness.

People convinced of the eternal rightness of slavery had increasing difficulty accepting these contradictions. Beginning in the 1850s, bills to expel free blacks from the state appeared regularly in the legislature, but the state did not act until the U. S. Supreme Court decided in 1856 in the case of *Dred Scott* that blacks were not and could not be American citizens.

In 1858, a "Circular to the People of Arkansas" signed by Little Rock Postmaster and future Governor Thomas J. Churchhill, former Pulaski County Sheriff Benjamin F. Danley, Judge Henry M. Rector and Albert Pike called free Negroes "worthless and depraved" and guilty of "immorality, filth, and laziness." Governor Conway called on the legislature to enact an expulsion law, and at the next session, a new law gave Arkansas's free Negroes until January 1, 1860, to leave the state. The suggestion by the governor that the state provide transportation and a moving allowance was dropped, and those who chose to remain were to be reenslaved. Although Nathan Warren left Little Rock, free blacks in more remote parts of the state seemed to have ignored the law. The 1860 census, taken after the law's deadline, reported 144 free blacks still in Arkansas, mostly in Washington County. In 1861, the legislature extended the date of departure until January 1, 1863, by which time the law, the legislature and slavery itself had become inoperative in some areas.

CONCLUSION

For the yeoman farmer, the largest class of persons in Arkansas, slaves could be simply a form of permanent hired help, an item for trade like horses, or an amenity denoting rising standards of personal comfort. Slaves figured little in the literature of such Arkansas authors as C. F. M. Noland or Thomas Bangs Thorpe. Many traveler accounts, especially those confined to the Ozarks, overlooked the presence of slavery and failed to indicate its significance.

Yet, given the geography of Arkansas, the planting culture quickly established itself around the growth of cotton. The creation of state banks, the erection of levees, and the adoption of a slave code were all the work of planters. Because this class possessed both education and money, it displaced the more numerous yeomen from political office and bought up the best young talent. Men such as Massachusetts native Albert Pike, by close association with the planters, came to voice planter concerns and live in planter opulence. A similar fate overtook *Arkansas Gazette* founder William E. Woodruff, who, although he worked too hard at making a profit ever to be a true Southerner, defended slavery and supported secession.

In Arkansas politics, Archibald Yell, who best articulated yeoman concerns, was also deep into Red River Valley land speculations with Tennessee slaveholder and future President James K. Polk. In 1838, as abolitionists were gearing up their national campaign, Yell told his constituents, "I would rather see the bond that binds us together severed, than the wicked, unholy, and blood-thirsty project of the abolitionist carried into effect." Every Arkansas governor, with the possible exception of Thomas S. Drew (1844-49), readily fit the mold of an apologist for slavery. There were no exceptions among United States senators, and only modest qualifications could be made about the congressmen. County officials and legislators tended to have ties to slavery, even in Ozark counties.

The success of planters was not based simply on money because prestige in the South was not achieved that easily. Instead, Arkansas inherited a social system that elevated the planter for social as well as economic reasons. It was the social prestige of owning slaves that led men to train for slave ownership by becoming overseers. Many plantations of Arkansas were not created overnight by dubious loans or shady deals but rather were the result of years of hard work, buying twenty acres at a time, adding new slaves and taking good care of old ones, serving on school boards and as justices of the peace, and taking part in politics.

For all the rhetoric sometimes heard in Arkansas that Southerners were the descendants of the English Cavaliers and Northerners came from the Puritan Roundheads, most planters, especially in a new land, acted like acquisitive Northern businessmen seeking the main chance. Arkansas did not belong to the "Old South," but to the frontier, and the dominance of planters was so new in Arkansas that, when the great test came in the Civil War, the *Arkansas Gazette* suggested, in all seriousness, that it would help the cause if every white man could be given at least one slave.

BIBLIOGRAPHIC ESSAY

Arkansas is not rich in materials required to write about the history of slavery. Few memoirs made meaningful mention of Arkansas practices, and the slave narratives collected by the Works Progress Administration in George P. Rawick, *The American Slave: A Composite Autobiography,* 19 volumes, (Westport, Conn., 1972) are unsatisfactory because many of those interviewed did not come to Arkansas until after the Civil War. Only minimal use has been made of these testimonies, an exception being William L. Van Deburg, "The Slave Drivers of Arkansas: A New View From the Narratives," *AHQ,* XXXV (Autumn 1976), 231-245.

The standard scholarly account, Taylor's *Negro Slavery in Arkansas,* greatly needs updating. Professor Taylor has begun the process in his "Baptists and Slavery in Arkansas: Relationships and Attitudes," *AHQ,* XXXVIII (Autumn 1979), 199-226, which remains one of the few studies of blacks and religion. The legal aspects of slavery have received only cursory attention.

Florence R. Beatty-Brown, "Legal Status of Arkansas Negroes Before Emancipation," *AHQ,* XXVII (Spring 1969), 6-13, cites only statutes and fails to improve on the pioneering essay by Jacob Trieber, "Legal Status of Negroes in Arkansas Before the Civil War," *PAHA,* III, 175-183. The one case of national significance is discussed in Roman J. Zorn, "An Arkansas Fugitive Slave Incident and Its International Repercussions," *AHQ* XVI (Summer 1957), 139-149.

Two useful county surveys are John S. Otto, "Slavery in the Mountains," Yell County, Arkansas, 1840-1860," *AHQ,* XXXIX (Spring 1980), 35-52, and James Doolin, "Conditions of Slavery in Washington County," *FLASH,* XXX (Fall 1980), 5-8, 30-34. Town slaves dominate Paul D. Loack, "An Urban Slave Community: Little Rock, 1831-1862," *AHQ,* LXI (Autumn 1982), 258-287. Free blacks are discussed in James L. Morgan, "Biography of a Free Negro," *ICC,* V (October 1963), 18-21, and Margaret S. Ross, "Nathan Warren: A Free Negro of the Old South," *AHQ,* XV (Spring 1956), 53-61.

Jefferson County Court House, Pine Bluff *(H. J. Lewis, 1879) Built in 1840 and remodeled after the Civil War, this building survived floods and riverbank erosion until completely destroyed by fire in 1976.* **University of Arkansas at Little Rock**

Chapter VIII

The Making of a Southern State: 1850-1861

INTRODUCTION

The decade of the 1850s was crucial in Arkansas's development. National trends resulted in a renewed interest in the state, primarily for the development of cotton plantations. These trends, which were supported by generous land policies and buttressed by slavery, led to rapid development in the eastern and southern sections of the state. Small farmers continued to settle in the Ozarks and Ouachitas, but this class underwent certain changes. Log cabins remained, but frame houses became more common as did organized religion, respect for law, involvement in commercial agriculture and education.

Both 1850 and 1860 were years of debate on Southern nationalism. Sectionalism destroyed the Whig Party after 1852, and the Know-Nothings failed to make much headway in a state almost totally devoid of foreign immigrants and happy to welcome all newcomers. In the end, the issue of state internal improvements remained to divide the triumphant Democrats. Southern nationalism, which cast hardly a ripple before 1850, became a bitterly divisive issue by 1861.

ECONOMIC TRENDS

Cotton was king in Arkansas during the 1850s. The state produced 20,000,000 pounds of cotton in 1850; ten years later the amount was 150,000,000. This 750 percent increase compared to only a 333 percent increase in the decade between 1840 and 1850. "Ere long," wrote C.F.M. Noland in 1857, "Arkansas will be the cotton state of the Union. If cotton will only hold present prices for five years, Arkansas planters will be as rich as cream a foot thick."

Because of cotton and dependence on slave labor to work it, the years 1850-1860 were crucial in moving the Arkansas economy from a frontier state with a Western character to a Southern state, but the promise of wealth from cotton was never fulfilled.

Land Policy

The rising dominance of cotton was fueled by attractive bargains in Arkansas land. Most important was the federal government's grant of swampland to the state. Although there was a token beginning in 1848, the program really got underway in 1850, when 8.6 million acres of federally owned land, amounting to one-quarter of the state, were turned over to the Board of Swampland Commissioners. With great political acumen but almost total disregard for geography, the Board managed to find swamps in every Arkansas county. Some of these lands were bargains at 50 cents an acre. The income generated was to be managed by the Board for levee and drainage projects, but poor engineering and favoritism meant that the money was spent unwisely.

According to an 1856 report, levees built at a cost of $300 a mile were mere piles of logs and brush with some dirt thrown on top, and often were located too close to rivers to be effective because they did not give flood waters room to expand. The study touched off a hot political debate, but the floods of 1858 and 1859 vindicated its authors. Miles of levee simply rose up and floated away, and

other parts were eaten away by floods. Thus a potentially valuable program for developing Arkansas was sacrificed for the profit of influential individuals.

A second lure to settlement came from selling land owned by the state. Thousands of acres reverted to state ownership for unpaid taxes in the crash of the 1840s. Under the Donation Act of 1840, each family member, including females, could get 160 acres free on the condition that future taxes be paid. By law, these individuals were to reside on the land and make suitable improvements, but these conditions largely were unenforced.

These two sources of cheap land attracted many Southern families. Some bought land thinking they might someday move to the state; others hoped that a general rise in value would justify the risk. One of the most famous speculators was the future president of the Confederacy, Jefferson Davis, who owned land in the White River Valley. By 1859, half the state's swampland had been claimed, but the value of farmland continued to rise. One Pulaski County farm that sold for $600 in 1856 changed hands for $1,300, then for $1,500, and finally in 1861 for $2,500. Because population merely doubled during the decade, this great increase in property value indicated that Arkansas was at last moving out of the frontier stage of development. "Obtain a foothold before 'tis too late," a farmer wrote to friends in the East.

The new settlers of the 1850s differed from the first generation by having a thicker veneer of civilization and by being more economically oriented. From Desha County, one man wrote:

This county has changed more this spring that I ever seen Any place. Good planters are filling up the county. I wish you could see my Milch cows, then walk into our little room, open the old box and look at the butter.

Not all newcomers found Arkansas a Garden of Eden. One Izard County farmer observed:

> The worst I have against tending of it is that I cant hit the ground to with my hoe for there is a rock in the way every time and I cant begin to chaw tobacco and plow.

Even so, he concluded, "I am still well pleased with my move."

One important characteristic of these new settlers was their middle-class orientation. More likely to be literate and church-going, they established new standards of conduct. As one of them wrote home, "Our society here is what I call good — no fighting, but little stealing, we use whiskey in moderation and have a jovial talk every time we meet, and as for revival, we have some here but just below they have it awful bad."

Westward Expansion

Many settlers passed through Arkansas heading for Texas during the 1850s, and Arkansas developed some new western connections just before the Civil War. The California or Butterfield Overland Express linked the West to Fort Smith and Fayetteville. The same route attracted Arkansas cattlemen who took their herds to sell in the California gold fields. Although it took six months to make the trip, a $5 Arkansas steer brought $50 in the fields. James M. Moore, a returned '49er, supposedly made the first such trip in 1853, and others followed. Drover Thomas J. Linton of Dover reported back in 1858 that the market was saturated. By that time, Arkansas herders had found closer markets. St. Louis and Chicago buyers had located in Sedalia, Missouri, which became the first cattle capital of the Southwest.

Industrial Development

Opportunities to exploit Arkansas's untapped natural resources surfaced in the 1850s. Although geologist G. W. Featherstonhaugh reported in 1844 that Arkansas had enough lead for "countless ages," frontiersmen were so short of bullets that in the antebellum pastime of shooting for beef — the predecessor of the turkey shoot — the top four winners divided the meat and the fifth got the lead. Other early travelers had noted possible mineral resources, but because of Governor Yell's veto, the state refused to commission a geological report. Because farmers and planters thought only in terms of agriculture, it was up to the merchant class to promote industry. Unfortunately, their Whig Party was powerless in state affairs and the cause languished.

The industrial age produced the modern corporation. Northern states took the initiative by changing laws to allow companies to form under general incorporation laws. Arkansas resisted this trend, and throughout this period, each company had to waste its energies lobbying the legislature to get its incorporation act passed. However, there was little corporate activity. One of the first goals was the building of railroads, and before the crash, the legislature approved charters for proposed lines to connect Little Rock to Napoleon and Helena. Neither road progressed beyond the planning stage.

Interest revived during the 1850s. One newspaper commented:

> We have frequently directed the attention of the public to the importance of diversifying our agricultural productions, establishing manufactories, opening our mines, and fostering with all care every industrial pursuit.

Economic analysis indicated that Arkansas exported only cotton and imported flour and

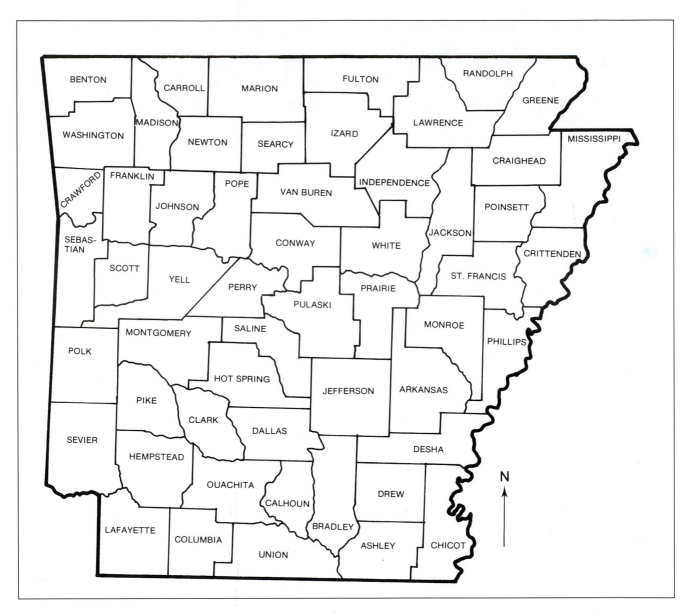

Arkansas Counties, 1860 Gerald T. Hanson

wheat. Rising sectional tension carried over into an editorial demand for diversification. Thus the state hired a geologist, David Dale Owen, a Northerner who was no less than the son of famous Utopian reformer Rosbert Dale Owen. His first two reports, published in 1857 and 1860, provided a general survey of soils and minerals for part of the state.

A variety of mining ventures were underway by 1860. Lead had been mined on the Strawberry River as early as 1818, but production shifted to Newton County, where one shaft near Cave Creek produced some sixty to seventy pounds. In all, more than 20,000 pounds of ore came down from the Buffalo River region before the Civil War. Zinc frequently was found with lead. At Calamine in Lawrence County, the Independence Mining Company opened three small mines and a smelter.

Manganese, discovered near Batesville, was shipped down the White River to market. The first iron works, also in the northeast, shipped 200 blooms in 1858. Coal from Spadra near Clarksville first reached Little

Rock in 1841 but could not be received regularly because the Arkansas River was unreliable. All of these mining operations were undercapitalized and hampered by the absence of adequate transportation systems. Although "firsts," they did not alter the agrarian economy significantly. What they did was show how much Arkansas needed better transportation.

The Internal Improvements Campaign

Between 1850 and 1860, pro-industrial sentiment found a vocal outlet in the creation of industrial associations. Pulaski County merchants in 1852 created the first such body, the predecessor to the Chamber of Commerce of the twentieth century, and other counties followed. Regional conventions, primarily intended to promote railroad construction, were held in Little Rock and Memphis. Communities clashed over the best means to achieve their goals as political and geographic distractions surfaced.

The political position of the Whigs — that the federal government should aid regional development — conflicted with the states' rights theory of the Democrats, which denied the national government an active role. In an 1845 Little Rock convention, Democrats endorsed the goals but not the means that Whigs sought. The Democrats were divided by 1852, for some argued that even in its bankrupt condition, Arkansas should assume a more active role in regional development.

The Beginnings of Railroads

Although the campaign for internal improvements called for greater federal expenditures for river improvements and road construction, the central issue by 1850 had become the need for railroads. "I look upon it as a settled point that without a Railroad

Arkansas is a gone coon," wrote one supporter. In the early 1850s, one editor believed that Arkansas was awakening from its "Rip Van Winkle sleep." "The public mind is engaged in eagerly discussing the various objects that immediately or prospectively affect the interests of the state."

Unfortunately, there was no agreement about what those interests were. One reason was localism, the sectional spirit that selfishly demanded that every project benefit each town, county and section. This spirit, said Albert Pike in a preliminary warning to one convention, "is here, it exists — it governs — it controls everything." The editor of the Washington *Telegraph* warned:

> Once arouse sectional feeling on this subject and nothing will be accomplished. Each geographical division of the state and indeed every neighborhood, will be found advocating its immediate interests, and there is an end to the concentration of our means.

A second problem was that many remained skeptical of progress and unwilling to cooperate. Batesville editor M.S. Kennard, in a lengthy analysis late in the decade, failed to analyze the cause, but he aptly described the symptoms:

> There is a strange and unaccountable disposition in our population which prevents their being united in sentiment upon any subject. In some cases sectarianism and others political partisanship; in still others personal piques and jealousies distract and divide the people so that the accomplishment of any public enterprise in which the cooperation of a number of citizens is necessary is next to impossible.

In the case of railroads, geography already had determined that no road could serve all sections. State Senator W.A. McClain from Johnson County finally concluded: "The north, and south, and east, and west seem wedded to peculiar interests which are impossible to reconcile so as to adopt any system or plan of general improvement."

Nothing illustrated McClain's conclusion better than the 1850 debate about railroads. Internal improvement supporters argued that the state should take the internal improvement funds given to it by the federal government and apply them to one major project. A success, supporters urged, would prove what could be done, and then the state could address sectional concerns. Unfortunately, initial agreement could not be obtained. Little Rock and Memphis merchants wanted a railroad between those points; the U.S. War Department, for military reasons, sought to connect Illinois with Texas; southern Arkansas cried for connections with the Mississippi River and both Napoleon and Helena resented Memphis and wanted rail connections with the capital.

The clash of these competing interests spread into politics. Little Rock merchants forfeited the good will of Helena and Napoleon by voting a $100,000 bond issue in 1855 to aid the Little Rock-Memphis route. In retaliation, Helena Masons, under the leadership of Patrick Cleburne, refused to pay their $1 a head assessment to St. John's College, ultimately helping to kill that promising institution. Meanwhile, Arkansas's Congressional delegation lined up behind the War Department's plan and supported the Cairo and Fulton Railroad. Roswell Beebe, a prominent Democratic speculator, became the first company president and former Congressman Edward Cross succeeded him. As each project pushed ahead, Arkansas's feeble economic resources were over-extended.

The Memphis and Little Rock line made the most progress. Memphis voted $350,000 in bonds to start the work, and more than 400 Irish laborers laid tracks from Hopefield

to the St. Francis River at Madison. The first locomotive in Arkansas, the *Little Rock,* made its maiden run in 1857, but Mississippi River floods that year damaged the line heavily. At the other end, construction started at Huntersville (North Little Rock) but ended during the Panic of 1857. The Civil War spurred new work, and finally, in January 1862, William E. Woodruff drove the last spike on the section linking Little Rock to DeValls Bluff. The middle section between the White River and the St. Francis River through the Cache River bottoms was not completed until 1869.

Even though it was incomplete, the road was the first step in the economic domination of Memphis over eastern Arkansas. More than 3,700 bales of Arkansas cotton headed for the Chickasaw Bluffs in 1860. Local resentment was keen, 'for as one Arkansas editor wrote: "That city has been a huge leech fastened on the side of our state sucking its life blood and never satisfied."

None of the other railroads made as much progress. The lines from Napoleon and Helena and from Little Rock to Fort Smith completed their surveys. The Cairo and Fulton finished its survey and began construction in Missouri but did not reach Arkansas. The Mississippi, Ouachita and Red River Railroad cut a path into the swamps and managed to lay twenty miles of track near Monticello, which were used briefly in 1862. Thus railroads, which figured so prominently in the Civil War, were still not an important part of the Arkansas scene in 1861.

Other Economic Developments

Aside from railroads, the most agitated economic issue concerned building cotton factories. That Southern cotton should have to go abroad or to New England for processing seemed treasonous to Southern nationalists. The South had both the labor and the water power; all that was lacking was capital and expertise. Because Arkansas was blessed with numerous suitable sites, agitation for cotton mills developed early. Probably the first in the state was erected in Washington County by former salt maker Mark Bean. With only eighty-four spindles, its eight workers were the Beans' slaves.

William E. Woodruff led the chorus of industrial promoters in the 1850s. Breaking rank with Jacksonian orthodoxy, he endorsed a protective tariff and called on men to invest in factories rather than land and slaves. Despite the rhetoric, Little Rock investors failed to raise enough money to open a cotton mill at the capital, but one at Van Buren became the state's leading factory. With 1,300 spindles and twenty looms housed in a two-story brick building, the steam-powered operation employed thirty hands when set into operation in 1853.

A second enterprise was the work of industrial promoter Henry Merrill. Merrill dammed the Little Missouri River north of Murfreesboro and powered a saw mill, grist mill, and flour mill, in addition to carding wool and spinning thread. So extensive were these works that the community was called Royston. Pike Countians responded to this New York-born promoter with "cursing and bitterness." Merrill compared his existence to that of Robinson Crusoe. During the Civil War, Merrill, although a loyal Confederate, received so much criticism that he sold out.

Other businesses in Arkansas were craft-oriented like Little Rock's chair factory and hattery. The capital had only fourteen establishments employing seventy-three persons in 1860. The value of the goods produced was a mere $144,125. Aside from a few potteries, the only other industrial activities in the state were rural gristmills, gins and sawmills.

THE REVIVAL OF POLITICS

The arrival of new settlers and the rise of Southern nationalism slowly altered the political system during the 1850s. As more counties were added, new courthouse elites surfaced, straining the politics of personality and patronage. Demagoguery, the art of manipulating people through rhetoric, emerged at the end of the decade in the person of Thomas C. Hindman.

The Fall of the Whigs

The status of slavery in the new lands acquired in the Mexican War touched off a heated sectional debate that culminated in the Compromise of 1850 worked out by the Whig Henry Clay and Democrat Stephen A. Douglas. As a result of the Compromise, the South obtained a new Fugitive Slave Law and the possibility that the new lands might become slave states; the North got California as a free state and ended the slave trade in the District of Columbia. Both Northern abolitionists and Southern fire-eaters opposed the compromise.

In the United States Senate, John C. Calhoun's last speech, written on his deathbed, urged Southerners to reject compromise. Calhoun's most devoted disciple in Arkansas was Democratic Congressman Robert Ward Johnson. In a public letter to voters, Johnson expressed his hostility to compromise and endorsed the secession-minded convention of radicals meeting in Nashville, Tennessee. In Johnson's view, the North had fallen into the hands of fanatics, his proof being an abolitionist letter that Johnson had reprinted in the *Banner.*

Johnson's extremism caught people by surprise in Arkansas. Democratic Senator Solon Borland, who initially had been sympathetic to Calhoun's position, even to exchanging blows with compromiser Henry S. Foote of Mississippi, returned to Arkansas because of family sickness even as the crucial votes were being tallied. This did not keep him from giving several speeches around the state in which he affirmed a strong devotion to the Union but urged delay so that the South could get better terms. Borland's views got vaguer and vaguer in each succeeding speech, and his critics cogently suggested that he ought to be in Washington at this crucial juncture.

Newspaper readers accustomed to considering politics as personality were confused. *Democrat* owner William E. Woodruff hired two successive editors, only to find that their views were substantially different from his own. Those who looked to Woodruff's paper to see where dissident Democrats stood got little enlightenment. In addition, a number of nationally minded Democrats revolted against Johnson's extremist position. "Family" Democrat Thompson B. Flournoy, who had fought hard for Sevier's renomination in 1848, supported compromise, as did Van Buren's dissident Democrat, George W. Clarke. Popular sentiment ran so strongly in their favor that Johnson soon sounded retreat: "No one," he replied to his critics, "would have misconstrued me to be disorganizer per se, except one whose appetite was sharpened by some feeling of prejudice or hostility." Johnson then announced that he would not seek reelection in 1851 and voted only for the new Fugitive Slave Law among the individual compromise measures.

Johnson's decision to withdraw caught his opponents unprepared, and after reconsideration, the wily veteran let it be known he would accept a draft. With Flournoy's support and garbed as a moderate, Johnson defeated George W. Clarke at the Democratic convention. Meanwhile, elsewhere in the South, dissident Democrats joined with Whigs to form Union Party tickets, often successfully unseating anti-compromise Democrats. Arkansas Whigs, however, ran one of their own, Colonel John Preston of Helena, thereby failing to capitalize on potential Democratic discontent. Woodruff gave lukewarm support to Johnson, and without internal division among Democrats, Johnson won with 57.4 percent of the vote. He moved on to the Senate the next year. Johnson kept his sectionalist sentiments throughout the decade, but he practiced studied moderation in controlling the state's patronage.

The Whigs, having failed to divide the Democrats in the House race, applied the tactic to the 1852 gubernatorial contest. The incumbent John S. Roane was retiring, and the Democratic convention chose Elias Conway to carry the Party's banner. "Anti-family" men put forth General Bryan H. Smithson as an independent, and Whigs refrained from making a nomination.

Smithson garnered the support of Woodruff, who called him the "Democratic and Internal Improvements Candidate for Governor," as opposed to "Dirt Road" Conway. Smithson argued cogently that the state had wasted its internal improvement fund and should concentrate on one project. "One work of internal improvements," he said, "will test the advantages and value of the system and will promote the construction of others." He hoped the project would be the Memphis and Little Rock Railroad. Instead, the *Banner* endorsed building three roads, even as Conway appealed to farmers by calling for good dirt roads. Conway's tactic succeeded, and amidst sectional recriminations, the "family" won again.

Conway's victory also buried the Whig Party. Years of failure had left them, as one historian observed, "a political mule [lacking] either the pride of ancestry or hope of posterity." The national alliance with pro-compromise Democrats broke up by 1852, and presidential candidate Winfield Scott went down to defeat, primarily because Northern "conscience" Whigs and their Southern cohorts no longer could associate agreeably. In Arkansas, Whigs from plantation counties had failed to support Smithson, and as usual, the Democratic presidential nominee, Franklin Pierce, carried the state. Opposition to the "family" did not vanish, but it ceased to come from the Whigs.

Constitutional Reform

The failure of the internal improvements campaign led some to view the old 1836 Constitution as an obstacle to progress. *Gazette* editor C.C. Danley observed in early 1854: "Nearly twenty years have elapsed since the adoption of our present constitution and time and experience have developed and clearly marked its defects."

Supporters of reform wanted to simplify the law by abolishing the distinction between common law and equity courts (now circuit and chancery courts), decreasing the number of legislators, expanding the jurisdiction of the justices of the peace, and electing all state officers, including judges.

Although the announced rationale behind constitutional reform was democratic, supporters of reform probably had a hidden purpose. The ban on banking, still in effect as Amendment One, applied even to private banks. Danley called a free banking law necessary for a commercial economy and said they were totally unlike the privileged, state-chartered banks of the past.

Opponents of reform were mostly "family" Democrats and those Whigs who disliked electing judges. The *True Democrat* called the 1836 Constitution "perfect and faultless," and noted that "experience teaches that banks are injurious to the community in which they are established." Attacking a constitutional convention as "a mere scheme to fasten upon us another system of banks," opponents asserted that a convention would cost anywhere from $50,000 to $100,000. In August 1854, voters rejected the convention by a vote of 10,997 for to 15,897 against. As with so many such votes, county totals offered little rationale as to what motivated voters.

The Know-Nothing Party

A new party arose in the aftermath of the Whig debacle of 1852. Its official name was the American Party, but it was universally called Know-Nothing because of the secrecy that at first bound its members to refrain from discussing Party affairs. Xenophobic in ideology, its goal was the elimination of foreigners, particularly the Catholic Irish, from American political life.

Arkansas had only 1,468 foreign-born residents and only seven Catholic churches, making it hard to arouse the voters to these issues. Therefore, it was not surprising that historians have concluded that one of the Party's poorest showings in the South was in Arkansas. To a large extent, local Know-Nothingism was merely Senator Borland's revolt against the "family."

Borland's involvement with the movement began indirectly in Washington, where he smashed in the nose of Joseph C.G. Kennedy, the Superintendent of the Census Bureau, who had annoyed the senator. Shortly thereafter, in 1853, Borland resigned his Senate seat to undertake a diplomatic mission to Central America. He intervened in a dispute about certain Americans accused of crimes in Nicaragua, touching off a riot in which he barely escaped serious injury from a thrown bottle. Returning to the United States, Borland filed a report that prompted the Pierce administration to send a naval detachment to bombard and destroy Greytown, Nicaragua. Meanwhile, Robert Ward Johnson took Borland's vacant seat, and in late 1854, the unemployed ex-ambassador was back in Arkansas editing the *Gazette and Democrat*, which recently had been acquired by his wartime comrade, C.C. Danley.

When Know-Nothingism appeared on the national scene, Borland rushed to embrace it. His main argument was that he was remaining true to principles of the Democratic Party, but that the national Democratic Party leaders had become abolitionist. In short order, an alliance of "anti-family" Democrats under Borland's lead and some Whigs such as Albert Pike organized a state Party. Pike contributed a pamphlet attacking Catholicism, and in 1855, acts of violence against Little Rock Catholics barely stopped short of riot. The Know-Nothings captured the city elections the next year. The most insidious part of the movement was that the secrecy oath made it impossible to know in the beginning who really was involved. Thus, rumor and innuendo took the place of debate until the Party decided to come out into the open.

The state Party nominated James Yell for governor in 1856. The nephew of Archibald Yell, James was a rough and forceful individual with none of his uncle's charisma. At the national level, the Party nominated Millard Fillmore, but Party hopes collapsed when Southerners led by Albert Pike walked out of the convention, claiming that the platform was not sufficiently pro-slavery. Incumbent Governor Conway easily defeated Yell, and James Buchanan won Arkansas's electoral votes.

The Party quickly disappeared in the aftermath of defeat. Solon Borland left Little Rock for Memphis, where he edited the Memphis *Enquirer* for the rest of the decade. Danley took editorial charge of the *Gazette*, dropping *and Democrat* as part of the title because he saw it as inconsistent with his unaffiliated status. Despite Danley's continued hostility toward the "family," the anti-Democratic element in the legislature was reduced by 1859 to calling itself the "Opposition."

The Rise of Southern Nationalism

Southern nationalism began creeping into Arkansas during the late 1850s. When Robert Ward Johnson opposed the Compromise of 1850, Albert Pike penned a poem denouncing disunionism. Six years later, Pike decided that the American Party was unsound on slavery, and by 1860, this Massachusetts native had become a confirmed secessionist. Pike had remained abreast of sectional trends, but most

Arkansans lacked his sophistication. Yet on certain issues, evidence of a growing sectional feeling began to surface.

The *Arkansas Gazette* promoted a "buy Southern" campaign. Editor Danley seemed to have had a fixation on the evils of trading with Cincinnati merchants, which one fellow editor attributed to Danley's overconsumption of Cincinnati rot-gut. At any rate, Danley promoted Southern trade and urged his fellow Arkansans to invest in factories so that Arkansas's money could be kept at home. Another issue was the reopening of the slave trade, closed since 1808. Editor Danley's rationale was that Arkansas's development was being held back by a shortage of slave laborers. Some Democratic papers agreed and added reasons of their own, but others claimed the idea was impractical and disunionist. Danley sat back and enjoyed the fracas.

The language of Southern nationalism remained confined to the upper reaches of society and served mostly as a rhetorical device. When trouble arose in nearby Kansas, and Southern fire-eaters called for positive action, Arkansans, even those of the planter class, sat back and let the free soilers win. Expelling free blacks appealed to widely held racist attitudes and represented the limit Arkansans were prepared to go.

The Revolt Against the "Family"

On the eve of the Civil War, Arkansas was in the midst of a major political uprising, one that greatly influenced the history of the state during the war years. Behind the turmoil lay two factors. First, the rapid increase of population in the late 1850s brought in thousands of voters who were both better educated than the state average and less inclined to follow the old elite. Second, designing men, sensing these realities, planned an elaborate revolt.

The first key figure in the new politics of the late 1850s was Thomas C. Hindman. A Mississippi planter's son and a Mexican

War veteran, Hindman had been a follower of Jefferson Davis and a member of the Mississippi legislature before moving to Helena in 1854. There he married the daughter of prominent land speculator Henry L. Biscoe. Although a lawyer by profession, Hindman's real love was politics, and the young couple spent their honeymoon in Little Rock, where Hindman, a Democrat, surveyed the political scene.

Hindman began his career as a violent critic of Know-Nothings. On one occasion he came to Little Rock, and although not a member of the legislature, boldly entered the floor to manage a bill. His high-handed methods led to a fight before the session adjourned. Back in Helena, he and friend Patrick Cleburne were assaulted on the main street of town at midday in an affray that left one attacker dead and both men seriously wounded. As his reward for this Democratic fealty, Hindman in 1858 replaced Bentonville's A. B. Greenwood as the congressman for the northern district.

In Washington, Hindman fully articulated fire-eater rhetoric in displaying all the characteristics of Southern extremism. "He was perpetually anxious to have a duel," one Northern colleague recalled, and in pursuit of disruption in 1859, fought long and hard to keep the House of Representatives from electing a speaker. He advocated adoption of proposed constitutional amendments to reopen the slave trade, allowing a state to veto federal appointments, denying representation to any state interfering with the recovery of fugitive slaves, and establishing slavery in all territories.

Hindman was not at philosophical odds with the "family" in his quest for power, but he was determined to take control over patronage away from them. After establishing his first newspaper at Helena, Hindman in 1859 set up the *Old Line Democrat* in Little Rock to counter the hostile "family" run *True Democrat*. Thomas C. Peek, a former pro-Douglas editor from Illinois, became its editor and managed to mention Hindman thirty-eight times in the first issue.

The first test of Hindman's power came when Senator William K. Sebastian came up for reelection. This "milk and cider" politician had offended no one. Unfortunately for Hindman's ambitions, Sebastian was also a resident of Helena. Hindman's failure to block Sebastian's renomination cut off one avenue of advancement, for the legislature would never select two senators from the same town.

A second setback came when Hindman was forced by illness to cancel a Little Rock appearance at which he had promised to denounce the "family" to their faces. Senator Johnson took full advantage of the situation, labeling Hindman "a bully and an impostor to the ranks of honor." Stopped in his direct quest for power, Hindman turned underground to overthrow the "family."

A typically hand-picked Democratic state convention nominated Richard H. Johnson to succeed Governor Elias N. Conway in the spring of 1860. Hindman's supporters, although not fielding a candidate, nevertheless protested mightily. Encouraged by the uproar and fairly certain that no "Opposition" candidate planned to enter the race, Henry Massie Rector announced as an independent candidate for governor.

Rector was no newcomer to Arkansas politics. Since his arrival as a youth to defend his father's numerous land claims, including one at Hot Springs, Rector had held a variety of positions: teller at the State Bank, United States Marshal during the Tyler administration, state surveyor-general and state senator and judge on the state Supreme Court. Often financially overextended, Rector once argued in court that he and "H. M. Rector" were not one and the same person, and he had quarreled with his cousin, Elias N. Conway, and his other Rector kin. Hence, although Rector was "fami-

Richard H. Johnson *(William "Cush" Quesenbury, 1860) This woodcut cartoon, first published in the* Fayetteville *Arkansian and then in the* Arkansas Gazette, *showed the* True Democrat *editor as an Indian who scalped rival editors. Subscribers, Cush wrote, "are expected to pay him or vote for him. He is bound to be Governor or get home with an immense sum of money." The money was to go into the barrel pictured in the cartoon.* **Arkansas History Commission**

ly," the ties had been severed by 1860. He could count on the support of his brothers-in-law, Ben T. DuVal of Fort Smith, a prominent legislator, and Edmund Burgevin, a Little Rock merchant of dubious reputation.

Rector posed as a political outsider despite his background. Thomas C. Peek of the *Old Line Democrat*, who during the campaign married Rector's niece, asked: "Who is Henry M. Rector? A poor honest farmer of Saline county, who toils at the plow handles . . . earning his bread by the sweat of his brow." Convinced that governmental inactivity was no longer popular, Rector borrowed from General Bryan Smithson's 1852 rhetoric and campaigned in favor of internal improvements. Wiser than Smithson, he

refused to endorse any particular plan, but instead proposed that state aid be given to railroads, which in turn would then pay off the state debt.

While Rector's plans grew less specific and more ambiguous with each speech, the Johnson platform, inherited from Governor Conway, promised to liquidate the remaining Real Estate Bank assets. An independent auditor's report had shown great abuses and favoritism in the trustees' handling of the debt, and Hindman's father-in-law, Henry L. Biscoe, was one of the trustees. Johnson's plan to force the trustees to settle up and have the state meet its legal obligations threatened those rich men still in debt to the Bank who thus threw their support to Rector.

Rector also tested the support for public education. When planters objected to paying for poor people's children, Rector abandoned this issue, substituting in its stead a call for a tax cut.

Despite the obvious defects in his platform, Rector took the offensive. "He is an orator of the ka-larruping style," one commentator noted, offering in evidence the following sample: "I stand on my pedestal, shorn of the abominations and malpractices where on they relied to cast the nomination upon the present nominee of the Democratic party." Richard H. Johnson, the former *True Democrat* editor, was by contrast "slow, dry, and prosy." A Whig editor, M. Shelby Kennard of Batesville, called Johnson "about the poorest stump speaker we ever listened to," but Johnson did claim sympathy as the first gubernatorial candidate to be born in Arkansas, and "if you don't elect me governor . . . I've no whar to go." Artist William Quesenbury, who contributed a cartoon satirizing the candidates, privately expressed doubts about Rector: "Henry is a violent man and fights people."

The 1860 gubernatorial election resembled some of the territorial contests in its vulgarity and dirty politics. Peek of the *Old Line Democrat* called *True Democrat* editor Elias C. Boudinot, an Eastern-educated lawyer and part Cherokee, a "colored editor" who was not even a citizen. In return, Boudinot refused to deal with a "skulking poltroon" whose words were "well worthy of a man who was purchased in Illinois, shipped to Arkansas, and bid by his owner to heap slander and abuse upon strangers and gentlemen." No more temperate was the southern Arkansas congressional race, where "old swamp doctor" C. B. Mitchel, with "family" support, fought E. W. Gantt, an extremist on the Hindman model.

The "family" suffered its first election defeat in the August state elections. Rector beat Johnson by some 3,000 votes and Gantt defeated Mitchel. Because this election took place during a climactic presidential race, some voters wanted to know where the candidates stood on national issues. Both Johnson and Rector did their best to confuse the issue. A Batesville editor reported that Johnson took "the true Southern ground," but that Rector was "the most ultra," and a Unionist testified that in Bentonville, Rector swore that "though Seward himself were elected to the Presidency of the United States, it were no justifiable grounds for secession and nothing short of an overt act on the part of the North would justify such a step." As for the Johnsons, they "were known to be disunionists."

The most obvious conclusion is that voters wanted a change. Rector's greatest support came from newcomers unfamiliar with Arkansas politics. Knowledgeable ex-Whigs refused to stomach Rector, who carried only eight of the twenty-two traditional Whig counties. No organizer and incapable of working in harmony even with Hindman, Rector was a maverick. The highlight of his term as governor was his inauguration, "one of the grandest explosions of popular enthusiasm ever witnessed in Arkansas," recorded

Hon. Henry M. Rector *(William "Cush" Quesenbury, 1860) Rector, pictured here as a grasshopper, out spat and out jumped Johnson to win the gubernatorial race.* **Arkansas History Commission.**

one diarist. "The long procession of little 'niggers' and noisy boys marched up to the Governor's splendid mansion and 'liquored.'" As for the common people, editor John F. Wheeler of the Fort Smith *Times* observed, "Now as the state election is over with the excitement of the canvass, it may be profitable for our farmers to take a view of the farming interests of the county" and consider improved varieties of corn, buckwheat and turnips. Little did they realize that they had elected the governor who would serve during the coming Civil War.

Arkansas and the Presidential Election of 1860

Even as state affairs turned topsy-turvy, the nation witnessed the death agony of the Democratic Party. Stephen A. Douglas, the author of the Kansas-Nebraska Act, had opposed the Buchanan administration's violation of the doctrine of popular sovereignty in Kansas and survived both an administration-inspired purge and the challenge of Republican Abraham Lincoln to win reelection to the Senate in 1858. He stood as the Northern Democrat's logical choice in 1860 to replace the retiring Buchanan. Although Douglas commanded national support, the fire-eaters remembered his 1858 statement at Freeport that the *Dred Scott* decision of the United States Supreme Court did not guarantee slavery in a territory if the people did not want it. This position was unacceptable to extremists. Whereas they had once held to the theory of John C. Calhoun that Congress had no power over slavery, now they insisted that Congress enact a slave code for every territory.

Lacking an obvious alternative to Douglas, national extremists chose to defeat Douglas by destroying the Democratic Party. Elements of this strife spilled over into Arkansas. Congressman Hindman was on the front line of extremism in his tirades, and Senator Johnson, somewhat tamed by his 1850 experience, predicted the demise of the Union and was unwilling to save it. Only a few other Arkansans even seemed concerned. Ex-governor Thomas S. Drew denounced the fire-eater position as "positive old-fashioned federalism" and "worse than whiggery," but most were apathetic, dismissing the inflammatory rhetoric as the usual political posturing.

When the state convention met in the spring of 1860 and elected delegates to the national convention at Charleston, a compromise slate was chosen. An effort failed to instruct the delegates to walk out if a pro-slavery platform was not adopted. Some of the delegation did join the Southern walkout in Charleston, claiming to be acting on the authority of the convention. A bitter split in the state Party followed, with Albert Rust and Thompson B. Flournoy continuing to support Douglas, the candidate of National Democracy. The Southern bolters held their convention in Richmond at which John C. Breckinridge of Kentucky was nominated. In Arkansas, both the "family" and the Hindman faction united behind Breckinridge, who thus was sanctioned as the regular Democratic nominee.

Southern Whigs responded to the impending Democratic collapse by organizing the Constitutional Union Party. C.C. Danley of the *Arkansas Gazette*, who had never been a Whig, supported the nomination of Texas Governor Sam Houston, but the new group chose Tennessee's John Bell instead. Committed to saving the Union, the Party ran on the platform of "The Constitution, The Union, and The Laws." Republicans, who nominated Abraham Lincoln at their Chicago convention, were not even on the ballot in Arkansas.

The 1860 presidential race was perhaps the hardest fought in Arkansas since the 1840s. The Douglas effort was the weakest, but it did have the editorial support of papers at Van Buren, Pine Bluff, Pocahontas and Little Rock. The other Democratic papers took the line that Breckinridge was the true Party nominee, he stood a good chance to win, and a large Breckinridge vote would give the South a better bargaining position.

While Breckinridge supporters played down the seriousness of the split, the Constitutional Unionists emphasized it. Some of the best-edited papers in the state — the *Arkansas Gazette*, the Helena *Southern Shield*, the Washington *Telegraph* and the Batesville *Independent Balance* warned of the threat of civil war. Funded by the mer-

Letter from a Calhoun County Secessionist, January 5, 1861

Some of the tension generated by the coming of the Civil War appears in a letter written early in 1861. Note the appearance of the first symbol for secession, the blue cockade.

We are getting here quite an excitement about secession. The secession and submission men are very equally divided, but I think the secession men are gaining ground. They had a meeting at the court house about five weeks ago. (I was not there, being sick). On dividing, there was but four or five secession men present, everything appeared to be gloomy at the time for the South. Two weeks later they had another meeting. I was waited on and requested to make a speech. I was very unwell but I would not resist, they sent a carriage for me.

When I got to the church where the people were assembled I found quite a large assemblage. When I approached they unfurled a banner with one Eagle and one star and a blue cockade on one corner. I found about five or six of those present with blue cockades mounted. I was conducted to the stand and made a speech about two hours long which appeared to be well received. At the close of the meeting the submission men and secessionists were drawn out on a resolution urging secession and to me unexpected there were not more than six or seven what voted for the secession resolution and with a tremendous shout of enthusiasm.

Since that meeting it is very common to see persons wearing the blue cockade but it is as I before wrote you very doubtful what Arkansas will do. I am afraid her people are too much under Northern influence, but I hope for the best. . . .

Your Brother,
John W. Moore

Source: Alabama Department of Archives and History

---

chant community, the Bell forces spared no expense. More than a thousand people attended a rally at Washington, and Camden held "the longest, grandest and most imposing meeting ever seen," with "our own and Washington Brass Bands, Barbecue, Dinner, Marches, Procession, Horseback and Carriages at night," and 500 transparencies (lighted pictures and placards).

Despite the effort, some 7,000 fewer voters participated in the November presidential election than in the August state election, and they ignored the alarmist warnings. Breckinridge carried the state with 28,732 votes, followed by Bell with 20,094 and Douglas with 5,277. In the inevitable postmortem, Judge John Brown of Camden found Breckinridge support strongest among "people who did not read." Bearing out this observation, Breckinridge ran best in the Ozark and Ouachita counties far removed from newspapers' civilizing influences. By contrast, the planter counties were pillars of Bell strength, partly because of their Whig tradition, and also because any disruption of the national market would hurt large planters immediately. Breckinridge support was especially strong in the southwest, where the plantation system was expanding, an apparent indication that those on the lower end of the slave ownership scale were more extreme politically than the larger owners.

If voter behavior in this election gives any clue to the degree to which Arkansas voters accepted Southern nationalism, then perhaps less than 20 percent were in sympathy with Hindman's extremism. Significantly, this figure included a disproportionately large number of elected officials and those of the local elite to whom many plain folk turned for political guidance.

CONCLUSION

Arkansas's rich alluvial soils and long growing season made its Delta section suitable for the production of cotton. Thus, geography and economics determined that in parts of Arkansas, slavery and Southern sectionalism would flourish. Despite the overall Southern orientation of the people, Southern nationalism's romantic myth of a medieval social structure basking in moonlight and sweetened by magnolias carried little weight with a frontier people locked in a struggle for survival.

For the average Arkansan, family and local concerns ranked well above national and sectional considerations. The common people accepted their elite, but largely on the condition that the elite mind their own business and leave everyone else alone. It is little wonder that Arkansas played only a minor role in bringing about the great American Civil War.

BIBLIOGRAPHIC ESSAY

The pioneering study of the rapid modern-ization of Arkansas in the 1850s, Elsie M. Lewis, "Economic Conditions in Antebellum Arkansas: 1850-1861," *AHQ,* VI (Autumn 1947), 256-275, has been superseded by James M. Woods, *Rebellion and Realignment: Arkansas's Road to Secession,* (Fayetteville, 1987). One vital theme is discussed in Richard W. Griffin, "Pro-Industrial Sentiment and Cotton Factories in Arkansas, 1820-1836," *AHQ,* XV (Summer 1956), 125-139. A fine local study is Jane S. Joyce, "A Settlement Pattern Study of the War Eagle Creek Region, Madison County, Arkansas, During the Pioneer Period," (M. A. thesis, University of Arkansas, 1981). James H. Atkinson, "Cattle Drives from Arkansas to California Prior to the Civil War," *AHQ,* XXVIII (Autumn 1969), 275-281, first called attention to this interesting phenomenon. Although Clifton E. Hull, *Shortline Railroads of Arkansas,* (Norman, Okla., 1969) offers some background, the political and economic factors behind railroad promotion remain unexplored. Much insight into the mind of a modernizer can be found in James L. Skinner, III, ed., *The Autobiography of Henry Merrill: Industrial Missionary to the South* (Athens, Ga., 1991).

Politics in the early 1850s are treated in Elsie M. Lewis, "From Nationalism to Disunion: A Study of the Secession Movement in Arkansas, 1850-1861," (Ph. D. diss., University of Chicago, 1947), and in Woods, *Rebellion and Realignment.* Brian G. Walton, "Arkansas Politics During the Compromise Crisis, 1848-1852," *AHQ,* XXXVI (Winter 1977), 307-337 is useful, and Harold T. Smith, "The Know-Nothings in Arkansas," *AHQ* XXXIV (Winter 1975), 291-303, chronicled that party's brief career. A short description of one "Family" leader is given in Elsie M. Lewis, "Robert Ward Johnson: Militant Spokesman of the Old South-West," *AHQ,* XIII (Spring 1954), 16-30. One aspect of the theme of Southern sectionalism is pursued by Granville Davis in "Arkansas and the Blood of Kansas," *JSH,* XVI (Winter 1950), 431-456.

The revolt against the "Family" is one theme in Michael B. Dougan, "A Look at the 'Family' in Arkansas Politics, 1858-1865," *AHQ,* XXIX (Summer 1970), 99-111. The 1860 elections are treated extensively in the same author's *Confederate Arkansas: The People and Policies of a Frontier State in Wartime* (University, Ala., 1976) and in Woods, *Rebellion and Realignment.*

The words on the image:

The Arkansaw.

Blown up six miles above Baton Rouge August 1862

The Ram Arkansas *(artist and date unknown) The Confederate sloop-of-war* Arkansas *was christened in Memphis in October 1861. The boat was 180 feet long and equipped with an 1,800-pound cast iron ram on the front. It was considered the most formidable Ironclad on the Mississippi. Before Memphis fell to the Federals in May 1862, the unfinished ram was taken south and hidden on the Yazoo River. In July 1862, Federal gunboats discovered her, but she escaped, passing through the entire Union flotilla, and found safety at Vicksburg, Mississippi. In August 1862, she steamed down the Mississippi River to aid in an assault on Baton Rouge, Louisiana, but engine failure caused her to be abandoned by her crew who set her afire. On August 8, 1862, she blew up and sank.* **Arkansas Territorial Restoration.**

Chapter IX

A Divided State In Wartime

INTRODUCTION

By 1860, Arkansas was not a mature member of the Southern economy. The swamps on the eastern border and the mountain regions on the west isolated Arkansas physically and culturally. The state was home to rugged individualists who were traditional in orientation. Its citizens did not share the devotion to the Union that characterized farmers of the North or the Southern sectional feeling that motivated planters and farmers whose affairs were intertwined with slavery and the cotton economy.

The rhetoric of Southern nationalism carried the day after the firing on Fort Sumter in April 1861, but in the aftermath of the attack, many began to have second thoughts. The War in Arkansas went badly and placed unbearable strain on the state's underdeveloped economy. The Rebel cause languished in spite of heroic efforts by General Thomas C. Hindman to put Arkansas on a war footing. After September 1863, the Confederates controlled only the extreme southwestern corner of the state.

With the breakdown of the Confederacy came an outbreak of guerrilla hostilities that made most of Arkansas a no-man's-land. The War produced some localized destruction, particularly in the Ozarks, where violence became personal. Geography and culture determined that Arkansas would be divided by the Civil War and that the state would suffer from joining the Southern cause.

CONFEDERATE ARKANSAS

The Secession Movement

Abraham Lincoln was elected president of the United States in November 1860, and Henry M. Rector was inaugurated governor of Arkansas. Addressing the legislature on November 15, 1860, Rector formally began secessionism in the state by advancing the novel argument that the Union was dissolved because the North had elected a sectional candidate. He said Arkansas must defend its newly found independence by preparing for war.

Not surprisingly, Rector's position found little support in the press from the self-styled conservatives led by the *Arkansas Gazette*. Even that traditional spokesman of Southern nationalism, the Johnsons' *True Democrat*, opposed "premature agitation or hasty legislation." The legislature was unfriendly to secession, and in a politics-as-usual mood, set about selecting a new United States senator to replace the retiring Robert Ward Johnson. Firmly committed to his quixotic theory, Rector vehemently denied that a Senate even existed, but his influence was minimal.

Five candidates spoke to the legislature in the Senate race. National issues dominated. Their views, which differed in detail, offer some idea about the variety of opinion common in the state. The eminent lawyer George C. Watkins believed that compromise was possible, especially if Southern strength in the Senate could be enhanced by dividing Texas into five states. Samuel H. Hempstead, a long-time "family" associate, also opposed immediate action and proposed that Cuba and Mexico be acquired to balance Northern growth. Dr. C. B. Mitchel, the unsuccessful congressional candidate in August, came out as an "out and out, flat-footed states rights Democrat," but denied that Arkansas had reason to secede at the time. The other two candidates, Napoleon B.

Burrow and Benjamin T. DuVal, both Rector supporters, were the only ones to take a secession stand. Burrow claimed that "a state has the same right to secede from the Union that a citizen has to emigrate—secession and emigration are analogous doctrines." With the conservative vote divided, Mitchel finally won on the ninth ballot, with Burrow and DuVal bringing up the rear.

Even as most Arkansans were following the advice of Fort Smith editor John F. Wheeler and working their turnips, the secessionists in the cotton South, convinced that the time had come, cheered the action of South Carolina in seceding on December 20, 1860, by a unanimous vote in convention. Echoes of that feeling appeared in Arkansas. As Hindman's *Old Line Democrat* put it, "Our destiny is irrevocably linked with that of the other cotton-growing states and we should not falter for one moment to seek that destiny, or pause to deliberate the consequences which may follow."

Secessionists were working out their strategy behind the scenes. Hindman made peace with the Johnsons. Apparently he had given up any hope of controlling Rector and was over-extended financially. The *Old Line Democrat* ceased publication in January, and Rector, with both the *True Democrat* and the *Gazette* in hostile hands, was isolated from the pro-secession leadership.

The first meaningful steps toward secession came on December 21, 1860, one day after South Carolina's proclamation, when Hindman and Johnson issued a joint statement calling on Arkansas to act. At the same time, the secessionists tried to broaden their appeal by having James Yell, the 1856 Know-Nothing gubernatorial candidate, and Albert Pike, perennial Whig and formerly a strong Unionist, make public speeches in Little Rock endorsing the Hindman-Johnson move.

It was obvious that the legislature was hostile, so the secessionists called for summoning a special convention to be elected by the people. The House passed such a bill on December 22, 1860, but it was not until January 16, 1861, at the very end of the session, that the Senate reluctantly followed. February 18 was set as the date for the referendum. If secession were not a constitutional doctrine, as ex-Whigs argued and the *Arkansas Gazette* claimed, then was not a vote for a secession convention actually a violation of the legislators' oath of office?

Momentum clearly favored secession by January 1861. South Carolina had been joined in leaving the Union by Florida, Alabama, Mississippi, Georgia and Louisiana. Texas seceded on February 1, 1861. The pace of secessionism quickened in Arkansas, particularly south of the Arkansas River. Judge Brown in Camden noted in his diary: "A great effort is making to bully the people of this state into revolution." The conservatives had to instruct their voters on the intricacies of the ballot. Voters first would vote for or against holding a convention; then they would vote for delegates in the event summoning a convention was approved. Therefore, many anti-secessionist candidates were telling the voters to vote against the convention and then to vote for them.

The Arsenal Crisis

The federal government had long maintained an arsenal in Little Rock. In early 1861, it was garrisoned by Captain James Totten and sixty-five men of the Second U. S. Artillery. To some secessionists, this post stood as a symbol of Yankee tyranny.

Just as the debate over holding a convention was getting into gear, the forcible seizure of the United States arsenal in Little Rock by an armed mob, supposedly under the direction of the governor, galvanized conservatives and altered the direction of Arkansas politics.

Armed men from southern Arkansas began to arrive by the end of January so that by February 5, 1861, perhaps 5,000 volunteers swarmed the capital. They were not only determined to take the arsenal but believed that the governor had requested their presence. It was not clear if, in fact, the governor did authorize the summoning of the men directly, but his aides, Edmund Burgevin and John Harrell, certainly sent messages south that implied as much. On the other hand, the Little Rock City Council was aghast, and conservatives everywhere were astounded. Even Senator Johnson called it "premature."

The volunteers were not to be gainsaid. In the end, the governor worked out an agreement whereby Totten — who despite repeated requests never received instructions from Washington — evacuated the post. As the federal flag was lowered, the women of Little Rock presented him with a sword amid great ceremony, little dreaming that Totten later would use it successfully against the South as a Union general.

Rector was sadly mistaken if he hoped to reclaim the lead of the secession movement by giving the secessionists a rallying point on the eve of the election. One conservative editor summarized what was soon the popular feeling on the subject: "We deem the whole affair to be one gotten up for political effect in order to bring the state into a rash and exalted secession attitude, because there exists some fears that the moving of Arkansas out of the Union might not be done precipitately enough."

The arsenal crisis galvanized what had been the largely disordered anti-secessionists into a working party. Typical of the spirit of involvement was D. C. Williams, who was described by a friend as "a man of sugar and coffee, cold water, theology and idiosyncrasies." His highest office had been that of Van Buren alderman. Williams wrote his views opposing secession and scattered the broadside all over north Arkansas.

Like Williams, most leaders were ex-Whigs, for even in the mountain counties, the Democratic leadership looked to the south for direction. Hence the anti-secession men sought to avoid being labeled Whigs or "submissionists." Choosing the term "cooperationists," they insisted that Arkansas act only in conjunction with other border states. They endorsed Kentucky Senator John J. Crittenden's proposal to reenact the Missouri Compromise. They also called for Arkansas representation at the Peace Convention then meeting in Washington. One northern Arkansas broadside even attacked the planter-dominated Confederacy: "Do you know that in the Confederacy your rights will be respected? That you will be allowed a vote unless you are the owner of a negro?"

One piece of good news for cooperationists was the result of the Tennessee referendum, in which voters rejected summoning a convention and cast 91,803 votes for anti-secession candidates and only 24,749 for secessionists. Because Tennessee ranked first as the home state for Arkansans, such an example was meaningful.

On February 18, 1861, voters approved summoning a convention but sent a majority of cooperationists to it by what the *Gazette* computed as a 6,000-vote margin. Voter apathy was widespread, and in the upland counties of Perry, Clark and Johnson, no conservative candidates even ran. One refugee later reported being told that the election was conducted in secret, and in southern Arkansas, physical intimidation was practiced on possible cooperationist voters. Although Union men held the majority, events were to test just how far their devotion to the Union extended.

The Secession Convention

On March 4, 1861, the same day Abraham Lincoln was inaugurated, the convention assembled in Little Rock and immediately caucused into two camps: Union and Secession. Most Union leaders were from the "great northwest," with David Walker, a member of the 1836 convention, and Jesse Turner, a Van

Buren merchant greatly interested in railroad promotion, providing the leadership. Other active members, all young men, were editors A. W. Hobson and M. S. Kennard, lawyers Augustus H. Garland and Rufus K. Garland, William Fishback, Jesse Cypert, W. W. Mansfield, Hugh Thomason and Samuel "Parson" Kelley, the pioneer minister. The secessionists were weaker. None of the state leaders served, so the burden of argument was carried by second-rate spokesmen. James Yell, "a very strong man without much cultivation," was the caucus leader, and the most that could be said for men such as Thomas B. Hanly, W. W. Floyd, Josiah Gould, B.C. Totten, James Totten and Charles W. Adams ("Pike the second"), was that they had some judicial and legislative experience. Statistically, they were far more likely to own slaves and possessed greater wealth than Unionists.

The first act of organization, the election of a chairman, predetermined the outcome of the first session of the convention as conservative David Walker won by a forty to thirty-five vote margin over B.C. Totten. The same margin prevailed when, after laborious oratory touching every conceivable and some inconceivable points, the issue of secession at last came up and was voted down.

The northern region rejoiced when news of victory came, but southern Arkansas did not. Southern regional delegates threatened to cause civil war within the state unless concessions were made. One traveler from Napoleon reported: "The disunionists have, I believe, given Arkansas up as a hard case and are going home to secede from northern Arkansas." This threat of force was met by a compromise worked out in conference on March 19, 1861. Under the terms of the agreement, the convention referred secession to the voters in August. Significantly, the voters could choose only "secession" or "cooperation;" there was hardly such a thing in the convention as an unconditional Unionist. The secessionists also agreed that five anti-secession delegates would represent Arkansas at any future interstate meetings. The convention recessed after the passage of a number of anti-secession resolutions.

Both sides organized for a debate on the merits of secession during the next three weeks. The newly popular song, "Dixie," was refitted with lyrics alternately praising or damning secession, and the old favorite, "Wait for the Wagon," became "The Southern Wagon," asking the question:

Missouri, North Carolina, and Arkansas are slow — They must hurry or we'll leave them, Then where would they go?

Opposing politicians took to the stump with Robert Ward Johnson leading the pro-secession cause. Blue Confederate cockades appeared, for while Arkansas was debating and Buchanan hesitated, the cotton South formed a government in Montgomery and adopted the emblems of nationality.

By early April, the nation was long past discussion and the determination of the Lincoln administration to reinforce Fort Sumter in South Carolina led Confederates to open fire there on April 12, 1861, starting the Civil War. The attitude of Arkansans toward the firing on Fort Sumter varied greatly. Some agreed with Conway County convention delegate S.G. Stallings that Lincoln had the right to put down rebellion but did not wish to fight against fellow Southerners; however, they were an unhappy minority. Most ex-anti-secessionists claimed to experience an instant conversion: "We fought manfully for the Union," wrote merchant S. H. Tucker, "let us now fight manfully for the South." One such conversion happened en masse at Bentonville, where Robert Ward Johnson was addressing a hostile audience until news of the firing arrived. Opinion suddenly changed, and all over the state, expressions of support for the Confederacy surfaced.

One reason for the seeming universal secession sentiment was that Arkansas papers got their news from the South and presented the Confederacy's point of view, depicting Lincoln as the man who caused the War. This interpretation convinced most Arkansans, including David Walker, the chairman of the convention. Walker also was misled by information he received from Missouri Governor Claiborne Jackson, who told him that "Missouri will be ready for secession in less than thirty days; and will secede, if Arkansas will only get out of the way and give her a free passage." Walker was also told that if he failed to act, southern Arkansas would not wait.

Thus there was general cheering when Governor Rector refused the War Department's request for 780 troops to put down the rebellion: "The demand is only adding insult to injury. The people of this commonwealth are freemen, not slaves, and will defend to the last extremity their honor, lives, and property against Northern mendacity and usurpation."

Carried along by this enthusiasm, Walker summoned the convention to reconvene on May 6, 1861. Volunteers began assembling to prepare for war, and Governor Rector sent an expedition up the Arkansas River to seize the federal facility at Fort Smith. The Federals withdrew into Indian Territory, and Arkansas was free of enemy troops. These acts were greeted by general jubilation, but some conservatives grumbled privately. A group of Walker's mountain constituents protested resummoning the convention. Rather than joining the deep South, they still demanded a vote of the people before secession, followed by cooperation with the border states.

All doubts and hesitations were suppressed, however, when the convention reassembled and heard the news, somewhat improperly interpreted, that Tennessee had seceded. In short order, the motion to refer secession to the people was voted down fifty-five to fifteen before the actual vote on secession. On secession itself, five delegates, all from the north except Pike County's "Parson" Kelley, cast negative votes. Chairman Walker's request for unanimity led four to agree to change their votes, but Isaac Murphy of Huntsville resisted the appeal. A storm of protest swelled over Murphy, but in a tribute to his Unionism, Mrs. Frederick Trapnall threw him a bouquet from the gallery. At ten minutes past four o'clock on May 6, 1861, the secession convention accomplished its objective of withdrawing Arkansas from the Union.

Many of the conservatives who dominated the convention might have yielded to the pressures put on them, but they were not in a forgiving mood toward those whom they considered responsible. As C. C. Danley wrote in a private letter: "I think the conservative men of the convention should take charge of the affairs of the state and prevent the wild secessionists from sending us to the Devil." In addition, the delegates realized that as a convention they could make whatever organic changes they saw fit in Arkansas's form of government. Thus the convention during the next weeks drew up for Arkansas the Constitution of 1861, effecting a number of old Whig reforms: private banking was legalized, reapportionment of the state Senate was accomplished, and a number of minor changes were made in the judicial system, including removal of the provision requiring that slaves accused of crimes be given impartial jury trials. Emancipation, which previously could be done with the consent of the slave's owners, was now impossible legally.

In carrying out its actions, the convention regarded Rector as totally irresponsible. Just how far delegates talked of going was indicated in a note written in Rector's hand: "Col. Webb says that when the convention meets they will try to declare my office vacant. Oh Hell."

Unable to decide on a replacement, the convention instead followed the course of some other Southern states and created a military board, by which the war power of the governor was invested in a three-man board on which the governor had only one vote. James Yell and Hindman were behind the measure, "to save the state from civil war," as Yell put it. Significantly, the board's original members consisted of one secessionist, B.C. Totten, and one anti-secessionist, C.C. Danley.

The convention did not stop with creating a military board. One small feature quietly written into the new constitution was a schedule for state elections in which the office of governor was to be voted on again in 1862, thus cutting two years from Rector's original term.

Finally, the convention undertook to conduct the war effort in Arkansas. The convention appointed two generals to command Arkansas volunteers: N. Bart Pearce, a West Point graduate, for the northwest, and convention member and former army Major Thomas H. Bradley for the east. Both former anti-secessionists encountered hostility from their troops. Bradley soon resigned. According to the convention's plans, these should have been matters of little moment, for it intended to turn all Arkansas troops over to the Confederacy at the earliest possible moment and spare the state the expense of maintaining them. Rector won a victory in this matter alone.

The Arkansas Army

Much was made of the legendary bravery and natural martial tendencies of Southern boys. "Our citizens," the Van Buren *Press* observed, "have been accustomed to the use of arms from infancy — they possess the love of country — they are emphatically a fighting people."

The problem in the early months of the War was molding this enthusiasm into a fit and disciplined fighting force. This was never accomplished in Arkansas for a number of reasons. First, few men had much military experience, and probably no word was more misspelled than "militia" in the official state records. Their officers were elected more as an honor than for any military knowledge. Books

Arkansas Troops Now Under Beauregard in Virginia. *(artist unknown, Harper's Weekly, 1861) This artist's impression of Arkansas troops incorrectly identified the men as members of the 19th Arkansas infantry, an outfit that saw service primarily within the state at Arkansas Post and Jenkins' Ferry. The "Arkansas Toothpick" image of the state was reinforced by drawings such as this one. One soldier wrote that these knives were useless in battle and that many soldiers either discarded them or sent them home.* **Arkansas History Commission.**

of tactics were in short supply in early 1861 and nearly everything was improvised. The Montgomery Hunters marched off from Mount Ida to a tune from a cane fife and a homemade drum. Its men were armed with flintlocks and shotguns and their baggage was pulled by a team of oxen. Not a man in the company knew the simplest military tactics.

Some enterprising men who wanted to get to "the seat of war," popularly believed to be Virginia, joined regiments recruited directly for Confederate service, but most preferred to stay in Arkansas and defend their homes. Men could join either the contingent of the state army at Bentonville or at Pitman's Ferry on Current River. Uniforms were as varied as the men, ranging from homespun to gray and black trimmed with green flannel worn by the Ouachita Grays. Women set up sewing stations in churches in towns. Almost all clothing was handmade.

The bustle led many — even earlier opponents — to enlist. "It was then Fight or play traitor to my country," wrote one. Henry M.

Stanley, an Englishman, had to be persuaded to join up by the gift of a petticoat, an implied insult to his masculinity. One typical son from the planting class recalled, "So impatient did I become for starting that I felt like ten thousand pins were pricking me in every part of the body, and started off a week in advance of my brothers." Regiments were formed from companies, all with appropriate ceremonies such as flag presentations, departures from home, and marches through new places.

It was very exciting relief from the daily tedium, for as a barely literate Van Buren County private noted:

> [I] wish you could hav bin at garners an seen me shake hands with the girls when we fell in ranks they all come an shuck hand with us their was 200 of them shuck hans with me with their little white hans.

The girls at Clarksville sang "Dixie in its purity." There was cheering everywhere, and, especially to the soldiers' liking, one grocer "threw open his doors & gave away whiskey." Little wonder many summer soldiers reported cases of being "bust scull," "over gayful" and "spun in the head." Troops headed up the Black River to Pocahontas stopped their steamboats to shoot wild turkeys. For some who were heading east, departure from Memphis afforded a first train ride, an event much remembered. As one young man put it, "it out run any thing i ever saw in all my life."

Officers attempted to learn tactics and instill discipline while coping with gamblers, prostitutes and some thievery. All tried to obtain the proper supplies for their soldiers, who were often unarmed and without uniforms.

Meanwhile, Union forces were gaining control of Missouri. Captain Nathaniel Lyon had broken up a pro-Confederate militia encampment near St. Louis and boldly ascended the Missouri River to displace the governor. Many Missourians, more concerned with states' rights than the Confederacy, rallied to the state's defense under the command of General Sterling "Old Pap" Price. By July, Price's forces, often unarmed, had been driven back into southwestern Missouri, and the general called for aid from both Arkansas and the Confederate commander assigned to Indian Territory, General Benjamin McCulloch. However, affairs in Arkansas put the Confederacy at a severe disadvantage.

The policy of transferring the Arkansas Army to the Confederacy hit a snag when B. C. Totten joined with Governor Rector to outvote C. C. Danley, who had gone to Richmond and negotiated the transfer. The reversal of policy left Rector in command, and once General Bradley had resigned, Rector was able to send his ally, James Yell, to command in the northeast. It was almost too late when the Richmond authorities at last saw the need to act. General W. J. Hardee arrived in Arkansas at Pitman's Ferry on July 25, 1861, to assume command, but only if the individual companies voted to accept transfer to Confederate service. Yell and another militia general, Edmund Burgevin, spoke against transfer and convinced a number of the men to return home. Hardee, finding his men poorly outfitted and trained, took no part in saving Missouri but worked on discipline.

Matters were even more complicated in the northwest. General Pearce had established contact with Confederate General McCulloch, and both opposed Rector's policy of a separate Arkansas command. When danger threatened, McCulloch and Pearce called for more volunteers to join them directly, leading Rector to claim that Arkansas's state's rights were being violated. The Military Board issued its own call, but for twelve-month terms instead of three years, and for the men to rally at various regional

Civil War Battles and Troop Movements in Arkansas Gerald T. Hanson

locations instead of reporting to Pearce and McCulloch.

The Battle of Wilson's Creek (Oak Hills) and Its Aftermath

While the authorities were squabbling, Lyon occupied Springfield, virtually completing the conquest of Missouri. McCulloch and Pearce, both exceeding their instructions, crossed the border, joined Price's army and encamped outside Springfield along the banks of Wilson's Creek, preparing to attack the Federals. Lyon, whose 5,400 men were outnumbered almost two to one, divided his force and launched a surprise assault on the Confederate Arkansas-Missouri camp on the morning of August 10, 1861. The attack miscarried, in part because the Union second in command, General Franz Sigel, confused the gray-clad Confederates with his own First Iowa troops. Lyon was killed, and the Union army losses in killed, wounded and missing men amounted to 25 percent. Confederate losses were 1,230 or 12 percent. These extraordinary figures came about partly because of the courage of both sides in this first major battle of the West, and also because so many Confederates were armed with shotguns.

As at the Battle of Bull Run (*Manassas*) in Virginia, the Confederate Army threw away the fruit of victory. Union forces retreated, and as Pearce put it, "we were glad to see him go." Pursuit was left to Price, while McCulloch marched back to Indian Territory and Pearce returned to Arkansas. Back in Arkansas, the army faced transfer to Confederate service. General Hindman, sent by Hardee to oversee the process, used his oratory in vain, for only eighteen men accepted transfer into the Confederacy. The rest went home, wiping out three months of preparation and leaving Arkansas defenseless.

The disbanding of the Arkansas Army came about for several reasons. In the beginning, Southern orators, such as Colonel Decius McCrory of White County, had assured the boys that one Southerner could whip two Yankees. In McCrory's version, it would take two Yankees just to make the first two stand up and fight. Soldiers who had seen the carnage at Wilson's Creek no longer believed this. Common opinion was that the War would be short — and ended by one big battle. Some returning soldiers believed that Wilson's Creek had indeed ended the War and promised to turn out again should another invasion threaten. Finally, some simply wanted a vacation before reenlisting, especially because new clothes were needed as winter approached.

Informed individuals, led by the press, criticized Yell, Burgevin and Governor Rector for backbiting and petty parochialism. Matters grew worse when the legislature assembled in

November. In his address, Rector denounced the creation of the Military Board and accused his critics of "undeveloped treason," singling out editors as "snarling cormorants of newspaper filth." What Rector failed to do in the fall session was address the economic dislocations that war was causing in Arkansas.

Salt prices had risen more than 400 percent. The state had issued $250,000 in state war bonds that now circulated as paper money at a rising discount rate. War widows, the wounded and the disabled needed attention. Little had been done to persuade farmers to grow cereal grains rather than cotton. Little progress had been made to equip and clothe soldiers. Instead of tackling these knotty problems, the legislature repealed a war tax and voted a mere $10,000 for war victims.

The Peace Society Movement

Even as the legislature was sitting, a wave of hysteria broke out over the existence of peace societies, a supposed conspiracy of mountain abolitionists. "I know this county had had a bad name at a distance," wrote militia Colonel Sam Leslie from Wiley's Cove in Searcy County. "We have been called Black Republicans and Abolitionists &c but we have never had aney of thos character amongst us. It is true the citizens of this county war union men as long as there was aney hope of the Union and perhaps a little longer, but Ida of the Union as it onst was is banished . . ." But was it?

The evidence showed that many mountain men had no intention of fighting under "the damned nigger flag," "but if any one would just come along with the stars and stripes that they would arise at midnight and go to it." By late fall, Confederate authorities were in a panic over supposed treason.

The Peace Society movement did not premeditate treason. Its historian concluded that it was neither an abolitionist plot nor the work of Northern spies. Instead, the men were mountaineers "who had no intention of going to war on either side and who wanted to be left alone." One public meeting in Searcy County resolved to take up arms "against any body of robbers, North or South." Such sentiments of neutrality were not new: they had been expressed in all of the border states, especially in Missouri, where neutrality had been the avowed policy of the state government. But what was permitted in peacetime was banned during war. Confederate authorities, led by Governor Rector, were demanding complete support, and the mountaineers refused to give this.

The Societies themselves were shadowy affairs. Organizational names varied from community to community, and borrowing the trappings of Masonry, they were full of secret signs and symbols. Some estimated the membership at 1,700, but such groups hardly kept good records. When word of the movement reached Little Rock, the governor responded by ordering the militia to arrest all suspects and bring them to Little Rock where he planned to have them tried for treason. Some fled, including one legislator. Others, tracked down by bands of militia, were chained and brought to the capital. The seeds of a long and bloody bushwhacker war were sown, for Colonel Leslie reported that he was unable to stop his militia from robbing families of the accused.

Unfortunately for Governor Rector, treason in the Confederate Constitution remained as it was in the American — an overt act provable with two witnesses. Most of the men allowed themselves to be enrolled in the army, but those who stood firm and demanded trials in Confederate district court were acquitted. Many refugees from the persecution ended up in southwestern Missouri where Union regiments were organized. A large number of Confederates deserted to the federal army throughout the War.

Although the Peace Societies were centered in the northern counties, individuals all over the state either dodged military service or were less than enthusiastic. The Confederacy in 1862 adopted a draft to fill the ranks, and the exemption for those owning twenty slaves gave credence to the charge: "rich man's war, poor man's fight." In 1863, a number of draftees mutinied in what authorities guardedly referred to as "the Calhoun County Rebellion." It coincided with a major uprising in Texas that led to the hanging of more than forty men for treason. Albert Pike was even rumored to be involved. The seeds of Southern nationalism needed to promote patriotism were spread unevenly over the state, and as Confederate hopes declined, rank weeds began to appear in the state's garden.

The Battle of Pea Ridge (Elkhorn Tavern)

General Sterling Price attempted ineffectually to regain control of Missouri during the fall of 1861. A rump session of the state legislature met in Neosho, Missouri, in October and voted to join the Confederacy. Many of Price's men rejected transfer, however, and effective control was limited to southwestern Missouri. General Samuel R. Curtis, an 1831 West Point graduate, Mexican War veteran, and former Republican congressman, took control of Federal forces at Rolla, Missouri, and began advancing on Springfield, Missouri, in January. Price called in vain for help, and abandoned Springfield on February 12, retreating on the Telegraph Road south towards Arkansas. The Federals followed, but both armies soon were enveloped by a severe winter storm.

On February 17, the Federal army crossed into Arkansas as the bands played "The Arkansas Traveler." Along the banks of the Little Sugar Creek at Dunagin's Farm, "a right brisk skirmish," as one veteran put it, resulted when retreating Confederates fought back. It was the first Civil War battle in Arkansas.

The Union invasion prompted Governor Rector to call out the militia just as farmers were starting their plowing. Widespread discontent greeted the move, in any case, the state had no weapons left to arm the men. Several new regiments were formed for Confederate service, however, and in Richmond, Virginia, CSA President Jefferson Davis appointed Earl Van Dorn to take command in Arkansas. General Hardee had left the state in the fall, and Ben McCulloch's quarrel with Price had reached the point where it took diplomatic negotiations between their respective staffs before the two generals would even talk to each other. Van Dorn hatched an aggressive plan to capture St. Louis, but instead of liberating Missouri, he found it necessary to dash to northwestern Arkansas to stop Curtis's invasion.

Van Dorn had McCulloch's tested veterans, Price's Missourians, and the new Arkansas regiments. He also ordered Pike to bring his Indian Brigade into Arkansas. What he did not have was adequate food, winter clothing, sufficient ammunition or an adequate staff. Van Dorn also was stricken with a severe fever.

His plan of getting behind Curtis's smaller Federal army and cutting off its retreat ignored all these problems. As one private complained, Van Dorn had forgotten "he was riding and we were walking." In addition, a second winter blizzard hit just as the troops were getting well underway. Curtis, meanwhile, pulled his army into a strong defensive position along Little Sugar Creek and waited.

As Van Dorn approached, he divided his army, with General Ben McCulloch attacking from the west while Van Dorn and Price moved in behind the Union position from the north. Two upside-down and sideways battles resulted.

The first took place at Leetown when McCulloch's exhausted troops ran into Union forces. McCulloch personally went forward to determine the Union position and fell victim to a sharpshooter's bullet. Shortly afterward, General James M. McIntosh, the second in

command, fell in the fighting. No one took command on this side of the field, for General Pike was in the rear. Pike finally ordered most of the remaining troops to retreat and join Van Dorn. The Rebels were soundly whipped, largely because of the deaths of their leaders.

On the other side of the field, Van Dorn and Price were so successful that they believed a Union collapse was imminent. Nevertheless, the Union line held as Curtis managed to turn his army 180 degrees around and save his ammunition and stores. As for the Confederates, it was their fourth day without food, and Van Dorn had misplaced his ammunition wagons. On March 8, the Union army blasted the Confederates with artillery while the infantry drove the Rebels off the field. The Confederate Army of the West became a stream of freezing and hungry fugitives fleeing west and then south.

Van Dorn had lost at least 2,000 in killed and wounded and nearly that many through desertion and exhaustion from his forced march. Union losses were 1,384. The Indians were accused of scalping Union dead, and in the North, General Albert Pike was branded a war criminal, his Masonic reputation notwithstanding. In the aftermath of the battle, Van Dorn took the survivors out of Arkansas but arrived too late to influence the outcome of the Battle of Shiloh.

Called "The Gettysburg of the West," Pea Ridge was an important battle. Curtis's Union army was isolated, with no reinforcements expected. The supply line stretched wagons on dirt roads all the way to the rail head at Rolla, Missouri. A great chance to destroy an entire army was lost. Instead, Van Dorn squandered his opportunities through some of the worst planning found in any Civil War campaign. The one dimensional cavalryman met his doom later in the War, not from a Yankee bullet, but from one fired by an irate husband. Meanwhile, Curtis was allowed without opposition to march into the heartland of Arkansas.

The Battle of Pea Ridge (Elkhorn Tavern) *(artist unknown, 1862) No photographers were present at this or any of the western battles, so only line drawings suggest the fighting. Actually, most of the battlefield was rough hills and woods, and most soldiers saw little of their enemies.* **University of Arkansas at Little Rock**

Curtis found the winter storms had flooded the White River, so he marched across southern Missouri to West Plains and then turned south, reinforced by General Frederick Steele. Union raiding parties went into the hills to destroy the Confederate's saltpeter caves, and Union sympathizers, suppressed months earlier, welcomed the invaders. The recruitment of Arkansas Union regiments followed, and embittered Unionists wasted no opportunity to fall upon the property of their secessionist neighbors. The War in the mountains took another gruesome turn.

Alarm spread as the state of affairs became apparent. On April 15, 1862, the congressional delegation called on President Jefferson Davis to protest the abandonment of Arkansas. While the President temporized, Governor Rector acted by issuing a proclamation reestablishing the Arkansas Army and threatening to "build a new ark and launch it on new waters." The threat of "secession from secession" would have been comical had not the military situation been so serious.

The conservative Washington *Telegraph* even refused to print the governor's message. Meanwhile, Senator Johnson paid a visit across the Mississippi River to General P. G. T. Beauregard and succeed in getting General Hindman detached to Arkansas.

Hindman's Rule

Hindman always had dreamed of independent command, and he found Arkansas — far from the paper forms of the Confederate War Department — an opportunity to implement his total war policy. A general with remarkably modern views of war similar to those of General William T. Sherman, Hindman began by confiscating money, medicine and supplies on his way to Arkansas. Once in the capital, he seized Rector's skeleton state army, proclaimed martial law and began enforcing his version of the conscript law. Because he commanded only a small number of troops, Hindman in Order No. 17 authorized guerrillas to harass the Union army, a move that was well received because of the looting done across northern Arkansas by Union General Curtis's German soldiers. Mountain men who had not been lured into the Peace Society of the Union army responded. Curtis, at Batesville, soon found his communications with St. Louis cut and his army in danger of starvation.

After Memphis fell in May 1862, a Union flotilla headed up the White River with aid. Confederates had fortifications along the River, notably at St. Charles, where they put up a stiff resistance. A lucky Confederate cannon shot entered through the portals of the gunboat *Mound City*, exploded the boiler and scalded to death half the crew. Nevertheless, it was low water on the White River and not the Confederate army that stopped this invasion. Curtis, now desperately in need of food, planned to march south from Batesville and hook up with the fleet.

Curtis's march south along the White River left, in the words of one Illinois soldier, "desolation, horrid to contemplate." Although it was to be five months before the Emancipation Proclamation was issued, Curtis took more than 3,000 slaves with him, and, like Sherman in Georgia later, destroyed both public and private property — an estimated $1.5 million worth in one county alone.

Confederate General Thomas C. Hindman (*photographer and date unknown*) *the diminutive Hindman was more formidable in words than in appearance.* **Arkansas History Commission**

On July 9, Curtis reached Clarendon, Arkansas, only to find the Union navy had departed. Hindman had collected a new army and sent General Albert Rust, who had seen service earlier in the East, to stop Curtis from advancing overland across the Cache River bottoms to Helena, Arkansas. Had Rust been successful, Curtis's force would have been in danger of being cut off and forced to surrender. Instead, Rust mismanaged the Battle of Cotton Plant, and in a portent of things to come, some of his men deserted. Except for poisoned wells, the Union army encountered only mosquitoes, briars and canebreaks before reaching Helena, where it settled in.

Back in control of much of the state, Hindman relentlessly pursued his total war policy as he virtually ignored the law. When some of his draftees mutinied, he had them shot. He ordered cotton to be collected in each county

The Battle of St. Charles *(artist unknown, 1862) After the Confederates put up a stout defense and repulsed the Union fleet, Federal troops disembarked and drove the Confederates away. Hindman received telegraphic reports on the Union navy's progress until, as the telegraph operator reported to him, Union soldiers approached and he felt it expedient to leave.* **University of Arkansas at Little Rock**

where, on the approach of the enemy, it could be burned. When merchants showed a reluctance to take Confederate money and prices rose, Hindman established wage and price controls by military fiat. His ingenuity included digging up and outfitting the old cannons used as hitching posts at the state Capitol. The state's books were turned into cartridges. The people of Arkansas were not prepared for total war, and they objected in particular to economic regulations and the issuance of passes. Some exploded into print, criticizing military tyranny and others pressured the congressional delegation. Senator Johnson, who so often had assured the voters that the War

would be short, remained loyal to Hindman, but pressure was building.

Matters came to a head when Hindman attempted to direct activities in the Indian Territory and intercepted supplies intended for the Indian commander, General Albert Pike. A thorough lawyer, Pike examined the relevant documents concerning Hindman's powers and concluded that General Beauregard had not been authorized to make his appointment. Taking the view that Hindman's was a tyranny worse than Lincoln's, Pike rushed into print to denounce his enemy. Hindman's arrest of Pike did not reduce tensions, and on July 16, 1862, General

Fort Curtis, Helena *(T. W. Banks, ca. 1864) Numerous Helena scenes were photographed by itinerant photographers. The Union army occupied Helena in the spring of 1862, and by the end of the War, fortifications were quite extensive. Remnants can be seen still in Helena.* **Arkansas History Commission**

Theophilus Hunter Holmes was assigned to the Trans-Mississippi under directives from Richmond to undo Hindman's illegal actions.

General Holmes, a personal friend of President Davis, had been in the eastern front but was found wanting, primarily because of advancing senility. Called "old Granny" by his troops, he was sent in opposition to the wishes of most western congressmen, who wanted Sterling Price. After Holmes arrived, he refrained from repudiating Hindman's actions and the fiery general remained in Arkansas as field commander and co-signed most of the major orders. The feud with Pike continued after Pike resigned his command and then attempted to reclaim it. Holmes ordered Pike arrested at one point and sent Pike's inveterate enemy and former governor, General John S. Roane, to carry out the

order. Out of uniform, Pike continued his vendetta, issuing a stinging attack on the Confederate leadership for infringements on civil rights.

The situation stabilized militarily as Curtis remained isolated in Helena and northwestern Arkansas was partially reoccupied. Possession of the region actually counted for little because its mills were destroyed and towns partially burned, while its productive citizens were in the army, terrorized by guerrilla bands, or refugees in Texas.

The Battle of Prairie Grove

All the work Hindman had put into mobilizing Arkansas for war was tested in the fall of 1862 when Union armies again invaded the northwest. Holmes reluctantly consented to having Hindman take his drafted army to counter the threat but only if Hindman promised to return to Little Rock. Hindman agreed but secretly envisioned an invasion of Missouri and a dramatic reversal of Confederate fortunes. Some local urgency was provided by the defection to the Union side by Cherokee Chief John Ross, who took a significant portion of the tribe with him.

Using Van Buren as a staging point, General Hindman gathered his troops, and despite a shortage of shoes and ammunition, led an army up the Boston Mountains in cold and snowy November weather. To inspire the troops, he issued a ringing circular denouncing Federals as "pin-Indians, free Negroes, Southern Tories, Kansas jayhawkers, and hired Dutch cut-throats." With 9,000 infantry, 2,300 cavalry and twenty-two guns, he outnumbered the 7,000-man army of Union General James G. Blunt at Fayetteville.

General Hindman's first plan for catching Blunt failed at an engagement at Cane Hill, when Blunt repulsed General John S. Marmaduke's cavalry. Aware that Hindman's whole army threatened him, Blunt called on General Francis J. Herron at Yellville for aid. By forced marches, Herron traveled the 120 miles to Fayetteville by December 7, 1862, just as Hindman launched his attack.

General Hindman's new plan sought to interpose his army between Blunt's and Herron's to prevent their uniting and then to destroy each. The execution proved defective, for although the Confederates successfully routed Herron's advance, Hindman did not have the infantry ready to follow up the advantage. Instead, Hindman took a defensive position at Prairie Grove and left the next moves up to the Federals.

General Blunt discovered the Confederate strategy and moved quickly to join forces with Herron. Meanwhile, Herron had begun the battle by attacking Hindman's position. Fighting swayed back and forth over hills, a valley, a corn field and a peach orchard. Just as Con-

federates were gaining the upper hand, Blunt's advance arrived on the other side of the field. Fighting continued inconclusively until dark when "a cold battle moon" in frosty December weather illuminated the carnage. Hindman had lost 1,317 killed, wounded or missing; Union losses stood at 1,251. Concerned with reports that more Union reinforcements were due to arrive and aware that his men lacked both food and ammunition, General Hindman decided to retreat, escaping under a flag of truce called to hunt for the wounded.

As at Pea Ridge, a numerically superior Confederate force had attacked and failed to defeat the Union army. In addition, some Arkansas conscripts had deserted to the Federals. After Hindman's retreat, Blunt's cavalry followed, raiding Van Buren and capturing weapons and food. Hindman's career was in ruins, and he returned to the Army of Tennessee at the close of year. The man "determined to make his mark for weal or woe" wrote off Arkansas, calling it "a grave of ambition, energy, and system."

The Fall of Little Rock

Warfare virtually stopped in the winter, and because of the supply problem and guerrilla warfare, the Federals made little effort to extend their control beyond the areas of Fayetteville and Helena. In January 1863, a Union force returning from an unsuccessful assault on Vicksburg, Mississippi, ascended the Arkansas River and attacked the Confederate fort at Arkansas Post, commanded by General Thomas J. Churchill. Although greatly outnumbered, the Rebels put up stiff resistance, inflicting heavy casualties until some of the men, acting without authority, hoisted the white flag of surrender. The fall of the fort opened the way to Little Rock, but because Arkansas played a small role in Union strategic thinking, nothing was done to exploit the opportunity.

Confederate Defenses at Arkansas Post *(artist unknown, 1863) This engraving in an imaginary bird's eye view shows not only the fortifications but also the route that the Arkansas River would take in eroding away the historic Arkansas Post site.* **University of Arkansas at Little Rock**

During the spring and early summer of 1863, Union General U.S. Grant renewed the Vicksburg offensive designed to split the Confederacy in half by controlling the Mississippi River. The defending Confederates suffered from a lack of coordination among various commands. In Arkansas, General Holmes was urged to interfere with Federal control of the Mississippi in hopes of intersecting Grant's supply lines. General Sterling Price took Hindman's place as the district's field commander, and plans were formulated to attack the Union garrison at Helena.

The Confederate advance was no secret to the Helena garrison, and so successfully were trees felled in front of the Union fortifications that, in the attack, the Confederates were virtually unable to bring up their artillery. Gunboats added their fire on the Union side and in a badly bungled attack, Confederates suffered heavy casualties before being repulsed. In defeat, the weeping Holmes ordered the army to retreat to Little Rock, unaware that even had he won, it was too late. The date was July 4, 1863, and Vicksburg had just surrendered, while the Battle of Gettysburg still raged in the East.

The fall of Vicksburg freed Union troops for more peripheral campaigns. General Frederick Steele left Helena in late August with Little Rock as his objective. General Price failed to muster the necessary forces to stop him and was maneuvered out of the capital, which fell on September 10, 1863, without a fight.

The Surrender of Arkansas Post *(artist unknown, 1863) Not all the Confederates were ready to surrender when some Arkansas troops, acting without authority, hoisted the white flag.* **University of Arkansas at Little Rock**

Another Union army operating in Indian Territory had captured Fort Smith ten days earlier. Thus the entire Arkansas River Valley fell into Federal hands. Many deserted during the retreat and for a time, the governor, Harris Flanagin, elected in 1862, went home to Arkadelphia and waited. At last the Confederate state government reorganized with Washington in Hempstead County as the state capital. Flanagin took up residence and carried on with a rump government for the remainder of the War.

The loss of Little Rock was a major psychological blow. Governor Flanagin complained that subsequent desertions probably outnumbered any casualties that might have occurred if Price had fought a battle. In the confusion of retreat, many men from the northern part of the state returned to the vicinity of their homes to "rob union men and strangers in the daytime and secessionists at night." Even those still loyal were disheartened. "I acknowledge that I have never until [now] since the fall of Little Rock felt the real sting of being an exile," wrote one soldier.

With the arrival of the Union army in Little Rock, a number of citizens hastened to give welcome. War weariness had set in. "Dull apathy, sits upon the face of her people," one observer noted, adding "her chivalry has long since gone from her shores." One reason for this was persistent looting by Confederates.

"The general disregard of all law or sanctity of private rights by the officers and men," as Inspector General Jilson P. Johnson put it, had created the feeling that "in many localities the advent of the enemy would be hailed as a relief."

There also was overt treason. Colonel E.W. Gantt, who believed he had been cheated of promotion, went over to the Federals, joining Orville Jennings, the wartime mayor of Washington, and Sam W. Williams, former attorney general and member of the Military Board. Asa Hodges, a pre-war planter of means, came in from the Delta, and merchant Jesse Turner from Van Buren, a reluctant secessionist at the convention, switched sides.

Those who remained loyal to the cause found a scapegoat in General Holmes. That he was "sick or crazy or something else," was the opinion of one private, and a Missouri Confederate wrote: "the opinion among both army and people here [is] that General Holmes is nearly always drunk." His behavior excited much comment. "Just think of a full grown man, a Lieut. General, groaning as a woman in parturition when soldiers bring him news of a little blunder, or his wringing his hands and crying in the streets because an army has fallen back." Most damning was the conclusion of Bishop Henry C. Lay, who privately wrote his wife that the forty-seven-year-old Holmes was mentally "a very old man" with "memory, will, judgment all debilitated to a degree which incapacitates him for any efficient administration." Thus, what Missouri Governor Thomas C. Reynolds called "softening of the brain," and what might have been diagnosed as Alzheimer's Disease in the twentieth century, put Arkansas in a very weak military posture. Despite repeated requests by the congressional delegation to President Davis to replace Holmes, he remained until January 1864.

The Confederate administration did reduce Holmes's responsibilities by appointing General Edmund Kirby Smith to command the Trans-Mississippi region. Smith, a West Point graduate whose wounds in an early battle limited his service, arrived in early 1863, making his headquarters in Louisiana. Remaining in command until the War's end, Smith managed to put the Trans-Mississippi on a war footing by shipping cotton either to the Federals in New Orleans or to numerous buyers in Mexico. He bought supplies for his troops with the money and incidentally stocked the Washington *Telegraph* with otherwise unavailable newsprint.

Convinced that the western situation required extraordinary measures, Senator Johnson, Congressman A.H. Garland, and C.C. Danley called on President Davis to expand the use of guerrilla warfare and invest Smith with added powers. Davis officially refused; in practice, the Richmond authorities, who were cut off from direct contact with this western satrapy, became increasingly irrelevant.

The Politics of a Confederate State

The waxing and waning fortunes of the Confederate armies were reflected in state politics. Conservatives scored the first victory when the 1861 convention selected Arkansas's delegates to the new Confederate Congress in Montgomery, Alabama. Of the five men chosen, only Robert Ward Johnson was an original secessionist.

In the fall elections, the original secessionists scored a comeback by capturing three of the four Arkansas congressional seats. The one conservative victory was in the third district, where Augustus H. Garland, "too bitter a Unionist," was opposed by Jilson P. Johnson, "one of the first to write his name on the roll of those who would run aloft the red flag." Johnson was a cousin of Robert Ward Johnson and Richard H. Johnson and suffered from his "family" association, for Governor Rector certified an early and incomplete set of returns and declared Garland the winner. The Confederate Congress, which in time heard John-

The Removal of the Confederate Government. They Take Their Winding Way Through the Mountains, *(J. W. Woodward, ca. 1862) J. W. Woodward, the friend, confidant and chess partner of Arkansas politicians, made this sketch when Governor Henry M. Rector, fearful of Federal capture of Little Rock, ordered the state archives moved to Hot Springs. Note that the wagons were drawn by oxen and few of them were covered. The papers were damaged badly by rain. Another of Woodward's artistic accomplishments was a facsimile rendering of the Ordinance of Secession, which he presented to the State Historical Society in 1863.* **Arkansas History Commission**

son's complaint, felt compelled to defer to the state sovereignty in spite of ample evidence of Rector's error.

The new legislature also selected two Confederate senators. Rector tried to advance the interests of his friends, James Yell and Napoleon B. Burrow, but Robert Ward Johnson and C.B. Mitchel won easily. Thus the "family" influence dominated at Richmond and was reflected in political appointments and military promotions. Garland, in spite of his earlier Unionism, emerged as one of the most articulate of the delegation, and although the recipient of the governor's favor, remained in the anti-Rector camp.

Rector's difficulties increased apace. An attempt failed to create a newspaper edited by a nephew-in-law, Thomas C. Peek, formerly Hindman's editor at the *Old Line Democrat*, leaving Rector without a political voice. His ill-advised attempt to activate the militia came in January 1862. In March, he called a much-needed special session of the legislature, which passed a number of measures, including laws regulating cotton production, authorizing the counties to aid the poor, and establishing wartime prohibition. The most controversial measure abolished the existing military structure and established a new one. Rector vetoed the bill after the session had

214 / A Divided State in Wartime

adjourned but signed the accompanying appropriations bill, thereby giving himself an additional $75,000 that the increasingly hostile legislature never would have voted him.

When Little Rock was threatened in May and Rector issued his threat to form a new Arkansas, criticism reached the boiling point. Richard H. Johnson at the *True Democrat* attacked the governor for fleeing to Hot Springs: "We would be glad if some patriotic gentleman would relieve the anxiety of the public by informing it of the locality of the State government. The last that was heard of it here, it was aboard the steamer *Little Rock* about two weeks ago, stemming the current of the Arkansas River." Probably deliberately, Rector had forgotten to inform the Supreme Court when he packed off the state government.

Once the danger had passed, Rector attacked Johnson for misrepresenting his actions and promised "to defend the government of this state against its internal and external foes." Johnson asked if this was a charge of treason, and Rector challenged him to a duel. The arrangements of their seconds were never settled satisfactorily, and only newspaper controversy resulted. Rector next came to grief when the state Supreme Court, in response to a mandamus suit by C.C. Danley and Richard H. Johnson, issued an order for an election for governor to take place in October 1862.

Despite his persistence in believing that the convention could not deprive him of two years of his term, Rector announced as a candidate. At first only one paper, the Camden *Herald*, supported him. Late in the campaign, a pro-Rector paper in Little Rock called the *Arkansas Patriot* appeared but listed no editor. Thus Rector relied mainly on a circular that accused his enemies of "Toadyism for everything Confederate" and defended all his controversial acts.

Sensing an opportunity, the friends of James S.H. Rainey of Camden offered him as a candidate. His paper, the Camden *Eagle*,

asked "whether, at public elections, should the votes of faction predominate by internal suggestion, or the bias of Jurisprudence?" There was no confusion as to where Colonel Rainey stood: he has "promptly and unqualifiedly endorsed this cause." A more substantial threat to Rector was the candidacy of Harris Flanagin, an Arkansas lawyer and colonel of the Second Arkansas Mounted Rifles in the Army of Tennessee. His nomination consisted of a public letter signed by everyone from the venerable William E. Woodruff to General Hindman, for both secessionists and conservatives had united on a politically conservative Whig who was also a secessionist.

Only four eastern counties under Federal control failed to participate in the election, and Flanagin, with 18,187 votes, easily swamped Rector at 7,419 and Rainey at 708. Disgusted, Rector issued a blistering address ending in his abrupt resignation. Thomas Fletcher served the remaining eleven days until Flanagin was sworn in.

At the same time the governor's race was being decided, voters elected a new legislature, which became increasingly disillusioned with the War. Senator Robert Ward Johnson sought reelection, but instead of leading the voting, he found himself in hot water, a victim of war weariness blamed on Hindman's excesses. Augustus H. Garland was his opponent, defending civil liberties against military aggression. Johnson won on the twelfth ballot, but the legislature took the public printing away from his brother and gave it to the conservative Washington *Telegraph*. It also condemned various illegal acts in a resolution that Flanagin vetoed as promoting disharmony. The new governor also used his veto power when the legislature, under the powers of the 1861 Constitution, attempted to allow a private bank in Camden.

As the crises of the Confederacy mounted, many war governors took extra powers upon themselves to further state war efforts. Flanagin was not such a leader, preferring instead to follow the letter of the law even as the law fell into disuse elsewhere. Hardships mounted during the winter of 1862-63. Dishonesty and speculation touched government officials, and little effort was made to enforce the ban on distilling liquor. Baptist minister Thomas H. Compere wrote his friend: "I have had it said to me 'your governor loves whiskey too well to get him to stop still houses.'" Most of all, Flanagin did little to cope with the growing problem of law and order. Armed bands of bushwhackers, jayhawkers, deserters, guerrillas and even regular soldiers stole from citizens over much of the state. They often killed as well. An outlaw band, such as that of Captain Martin Hart near Fort Smith, occasionally was hunted down, but civil authority was too weak to maintain order. When the military did act, as during Hindman's early days, citizens complained indignantly about their loss of freedom.

One reason the law broke down in execution was that the elite felt that the rules did not apply to them. In January 1863, Lewisville merchant L. L. Breeden was arrested for selling liquor to troops. According to reports, the soldiers led by their captain were so "very much under the influence of liquor" that they fired off four loaded cannons at midnight to celebrate the New Year. Breeden admitted providing the liquor, not at the $10 a pint or $50 a gallon alleged, but rather "from a disposition of kindness," and wryly observed that on that very evening, Generals Marmaduke and Shelby and Major Smith had "joined me in a social glass."

Officers and Men

The majority of Arkansas troops did not fight at home. They saw service instead in either the Army of Northern Virginia or in the Army of Tennessee. Many volunteers wanted eastern service in the early part of the War, and the First and Third Arkansas Regiments took a prominent part in the Virginia campaigns until decimated. These troops attract-ed the attention of a *Harper's Weekly* artist who drew them as a rather tough looking lot armed with, among other things, the Bowie knife. Stories spread, so that when Arkansas troops entered Lexington, Kentucky, almost the whole population turned out to stare. "I think numbers of them thought they would see men different from what they had ever saw as there was many hard stories told on the troops from Ark."

Those who served east of the Mississippi lost contact with friends and family, for mail service deteriorated when the Federals gained control of the Mississippi. By late in the War, it became difficult to get men to cross the River, and one captain was court-martialed and executed for refusing to leave Arkansas.

Arkansas provided only a few general officers to the Confederate cause. Politician Albert Rust served as a brigadier general early in the East but was found wanting. Defeat at the Battle of Cotton Plant in 1862 ended his career. Helena's Thomas C. Hindman used politics effectively. The first and last parts of his career were spent with the Army of Tennessee and included service at the Battles of Shiloh and Chickamauga, and in the Atlanta campaign. He, too, was no longer in active service by 1864.

Another of Helena's generals, perhaps the finest brigade commander in the Confederacy, was Irish immigrant Patrick Ronayne Cleburne. A Helena lawyer in 1861, Cleburne had served in the British army as a youth and became a druggist on first arriving in America. When local zealots organized the Yell Rifles, Cleburne was elected captain. When the Arkansas Army formed in the spring of 1861, he rose to the rank of colonel and replaced General T. H. Bradley in command of the eastern forces. Cleburne remained a colonel when his men transferred to the Confederate service and crossed the River in late 1861. He became a general in the spring of 1862, participating with distinction at the Battle of Shiloh, and in all subsequent

CONCERT!

The Pine Bluff Amateur band of Minstrels will give an entertainment

AT THE

COURT HOUSE,

ON THURSDAY EVENING, JANUARY 23d, 1862,

For the benefit of a Company in GEN. JEFF. THOMPSON'S
command and commanded by Arkansas Officers.

ENTIRE CHANGE OF

PROGRAMME

Below we publish the following performance by the Amateur
Minstrel Band of Pine Bluff, consisting of these gentlemen—J. R.
Holland, Wm. A. Lee, J. H. Steen, C. Price, Wm. Butler, George
Blaney, Dan. Sullivan, J. Rothschild, J. Baker J. C. Slover and P. A.
Fennerty—to come off the 23d January, 1862. Everybody is expected
to be in attendance.

PROGRAMME:

PART FIRST:

Overture	By the Band.
Opening Chorus,	By the Company.
Song—"Gentle Jennie Gray,"	J. H. Steen.
Song—"See our oars with Feathered Spray,"	Wm. A. Lee.
Song—"Yellow Rose of Texas,"	J. C. Slover.
Song—"Old Folks are Gone,"	Wm. Butler.
Song—"Poor Sister Sue,"	J. R. Holland.
Closing Chorus—Julius' Bride,	By the Company.

INTERMISSION OF TEN MINUTES.

PART SECOND:

Violin Solo,	J. Rothschild.
Characteristic Irish Song	Dan. Sullivan.
Accordeon Solo,	P. A. Fennerty.
Song—	J. Baker.
Fancy Jig,	Geo. Blaney.
Banjo Solo	J. R. Holland.
Ballad	J. H Steen.

INTERMISSION OF TEN MINUTES.

PART THIRD:

Lucy Long Dance.	Holland, Lee, Butler, Steen, and Slover.
McDilldarrall Brothers,	Steen, Lee, Slover and Butler,

ETHIOPIAN STATUES!

HOLLAND, SLOVER AND STEEN.

SHAKING QUAKERS

BY THE COMPANY

The Whole to Conclude with the Representation of

LINCON'S CABINET

AS IT IS.

CHARACTERS BY THE COMPANY.

Tickets 50 cts. to be had at the door.
Doors open at 6½ o'clock.   Performance to commence at 7½.

A Concert Program of the Pine Bluff Amateur Minstrels, January 23, 1862, Jefferson County Court House. The War had its musical side. Minstrel music, amateur talent and parodies of blacks, Quakers and Republicans made up the program for an evening of entertainment by the Pine Bluff Amateur Band of Minstrels at the courthouse. **Arkansas History Commission**

engagements of the Army of Tennessee until his death at the Battle of Franklin, Tennessee, in November 1864.

Cleburne was not only the "Stonewall Jackson of the West," but also an articulate prophet of the Confederacy's manpower problems. He outlined his view in December 1863 that the shortage of soldiers required the army to arm slaves, offering emancipation as a reward. Cleburne read his proposal to an assemblage of officers, some of whom took violent exception to it. The resulting controversy destroyed Cleburne's chances of promotion, even though the Confederacy in the final months of the War reluctantly agreed with his assessment.

Although Cleburne was the best known and most able of Arkansas's generals, the state produced at least sixteen others. Helena claims seven, although documentation is uncertain about two of them. Colonel John Ed Murray of the Fifth Arkansas received his commission on the day of his death in 1864. Had he lived, he would have been at age twenty-one the Confederacy's youngest brigadier general. The mix of politics and patronage probably accounted for the rise of Thomas J. Churchill, a "family" relative who nevertheless served effectively at the Battle of Arkansas Post and in the Red River campaign. A congratulatory letter to General D. H. Reynolds from Senator Johnson illustrated the political connection: "You are appt. at last by dint of your merits, and the devotion, and esteem and perseverance of your friends." Most of the generals fought in the East, and aside from Hindman and Churchill, only General James F. Fagan was active in Arkansas. Those men in state positions disappeared from view early in the War. Rector's brother-in-law, Edmund Burgevin, returned to clerking. N. Bart Pearce, although a West Point graduate, served in the commissary department after 1861.

Those generals most seen in Arkansas usually came from outside the state. Sterling "Old Pap" Price, the very symbol of the cause in Missouri, had a tarnished career after his early successes. He grew so stately that a horse no longer sufficed to carry him about and he rode in a carriage. J.O. Shelby, the iron man of the West, was also a Missourian. J. N. Edwards, a newspaperman on Shelby's staff, later memorialized his leader's finer qualities. John S. Marmaduke, a future Missouri governor, played an active role, and after a raid in Missouri in the spring of 1863, repulsed the Federals successfully at the Battle of Chalk Bluff. Unable to defeat the Federals in the attack on Helena that summer, he did succeed in killing fellow Confederate General Lucius M. Walker in a post-battle duel.

By far the most exotic general was the "Missouri Swamp Fox," M. Jeff Thompson, "a tall, sinewy, weather-beaten man, a queer looking genius, dressed in a suit of snowy white from the plume in his hat to the heel of his boot and with a white sword-belt and white gloves." He was a strange but effective commander for what one observer called "the hardest-looking soldiers I have ever seen." From Texas came General Ben McCulloch, an ex-Texas Ranger, whose black costume made him a conspicuous target at Pea Ridge. In keeping with the times, all exhibited larger than life egos. McCulloch and Price quarreled early. At one point they agreed to confer only at a site equidistant from their respective camps with both men arriving at exactly the same time.

In hundreds of other engagements, major and minor, unsung heroes distinguished themselves gallantly. At Prairie Grove, while carrying the flag forward, Color Sergeant William Gray had his left leg shot off below the knee. Although prostrate he called to the men: "Boys, if you will fight around me, I'll sit up and hold our colors for you." His courage inspired Corporal E.B. Byler to take up the fallen colors and continue the charge. On the other hand, many draftees deserted at the first opportunity, or, like a lieutenant and a sergeant at the St. Charles engagement, "could not be kept at their places."

Although soldiering in the popular imagination involved fighting, most army life revolved around camping, marching and finding enough to eat. The first campaigns in 1861 often generated waves of popular support. "The ladies would come out at every house and crossroad to give us their smiles, and they brought bouquets and flowers of the sweetest fragrance, fruit of the rarest and richest quality to distribute and also buckets of cool fresh water."

But exhilaration soon gave way to boredom. "We walk in mud all day and sleep in mud all night," wrote one soldier stationed in eastern Arkansas. Never adequately equipped or fed, the soldiers "foraged," a polite term for thievery from famished civilians. Captured Union supplies were fair game, with shoes a prized battle trophy and the coats simply turned inside out and worn. "I'm a Yankee within, and a Reb without," one private explained.

About 60,000 Arkansas men served in the Confederate forces, and very incomplete records indicate that 3,080 died from battle-related causes and 3,782 died from disease. Army life was rife with contagious diseases, notably measles, influenza and smallpox. Nineteenth century medicine offered little assistance, and in any case, was in poor supply. Doctors often were drunk and incompetent, and thousands of soldiers died in poorly managed and unsanitary hospitals. "To be sick in the army," wrote Colonel Dandridge McRae, "amounts to a speedy death." The returns for Parson's regiment at the end of 1862 illustrated the extent of illness. From a total of 1,059 enlisted men, only 676 were present and 210 of those were sick. Supplied with few blankets, a half-ration of salt, coarse meal and beef "generally ill suited for debilitated stomacks," the men were "heroically enduring their present privations."

Sustaining the War Effort

Arkansas suffered from several disadvantages at the start of the War. The cotton-growing plantation sections, dependent on Northern flour and corn, experienced food shortages. The army consisted largely of farmers; therefore, as more men swelled the ranks, few remained to grow crops. The authorities called for planters to switch from cotton to corn, but most did so grudgingly if at all. In addition, the 1862 harvest was very scant in western Arkansas, where most of the troops were stationed. A decline in the quality of food was reflected in the poor health of soldiers. "We did well while our flour lasted, but when it came to coarse cornbread with bran in it, it got a great many of us down with diarrhea and fever," one soldier reported. The effects probably were felt for the first time at the Battle of Pea Ridge, where underfed men marched and fought in the cold and rain for five days.

Commissary agents took the brunt of the blame. "The people are clamoring for bread and I have none to give them," wrote A.G. Mayers from Fort Washita in Indian Territory. "What is to be done God only knows. General, this is no overdrawn picture." When local sources ran out, agents scoured the country looking for supplies.

The destruction of the gristmills in northwestern Arkansas in 1861-62 ended hope for supplies from that area, and Texas became the favorite place to buy. Even so, the absence of navigable streams and usable roads meant that supplies could not always be delivered safely. Flour, for instance, often had to be hauled in open wagons because barrels, boxes and sacks were nonexistent. By the end of the War, one soldier wrote from Lewisburg that "I have sene littel chillarn and women having nothing to eat but boild corn and not a nuf of thet." Many were reduced to this because of the depredations committed by the very troops that were supposed to protect them. A Confederate cavalryman justified it: "[W]e had no alternative except to do without them, and that we dont chose to do." Another wrote home, "I was sorry to hear that the troops are camped near Washington and Fulton, for they devastate a vicinity almost as bad as the enemy."

Although food was a general problem, two particular shortages that created consternation early were coffee and salt. The first had to be imported, and in its absence, a variety of recipes using parched grains did not substitute.

Salt was difficult to obtain in wartime and had no substitute for preservation of meat. The Confederate government recognized the problem and encouraged entrepreneurs to redevelop the state's salt springs. General Hindman, on his arrival, perceived that the military defense of Arkansas required putting everybody on a war footing and maximizing salt production by replacing civilian with military control. This policy was too radical for the era's conception of private property rights, and under General Holmes, the salt works were returned to private parties. The government did start its own salt works at Arkadelphia, where production began at eighty-four bushels a day and soon reached 200. The large pans used to boil the saline water were cast in the Camden foundry.

Hindman believed Arkansas would have to become nearly self-sufficient. For the military, that meant making adequate powder and weapons, leather supplies and medicine. The Camden foundry supplied the state with a variety of iron goods but was less than a complete success because of the shortage of coke (carbonized coal) "and a person competent to make it." Arkansas had the coal at already tapped sources near Spadra but no easy way to get it to faraway Camden.

Camden also boasted a tannery that made harnesses and other equipment. Both it and another factory at Arkadelphia, which made 150 pairs of shoes daily, suffered from inadequate leather supplies. Arkadelphia, an industrial center, contained a chemical factory that produced medicines, an armory turning out thirty Enfield rifles a week and a powder mill supplying 1,000 pounds a day. The Little Rock arsenal contained similar equipment, and the powder mill at Fort Smith was used mostly to salvage old powder.

Unfortunately, the District of Arkansas never reached its goal of economic self-sufficiency. Hindman's barefoot soldiers left a trail of blood climbing the Boston Mountains, and more than 1,000 stayed behind because of the absence of supplies.

A shortage of ammunition posed several problems. Missouri contained a number of active lead mines, with Granby, in the southwestern part of the state, the closest to Arkansas. That region soon was lost to the Confederacy, and in Arkansas, only a few small mines were opened. By late 1862, Arkansas was relying on Mexican sources for sulfur, an ingredient in gunpowder. Nitre, which came from bat droppings, could be obtained from saltpeter-rich caves in the Ozarks. These caves, previously identified by geologist David Dale Owen, were developed at first by private enterprise. One cave, four miles west of Cushman, was purchased in 1861 by two speculators for $20,000. Production stopped when Federal forces entered the area. Hindman tried to revive the operation, but guerrilla warfare made it unsafe and desertions among the work force were common. As a result, Confederates lacked sufficient ammunition at Pea Ridge and Prairie Grove.

The home front was hit by similar shortages. Most soldiers relied heavily on clothes supplied from home; in turn, housewives needed cotton cards, a simple wood and iron combing device used to de-seed cotton for making thread. The War, however, cut off the supply even as the demand increased. The state legislature voted money to buy additional cotton cards and private parties began a lucrative trade in these items. In one wartime swindle, a Little Rock bookkeeper offered buyers black market cards at substantial savings. Secrecy was imposed and advance payment was required. The boxes of cotton cards turned out to be empty, and only a suspicious innkeeper's prompt action prevented the fraud from succeeding.

By 1863, soldiers and home folks alike turned to the hated Yankees for supplies, using contraband cotton as the medium of trade but losing some of their Southern patriotism in the bargain. "Some thirty or forty spools of thread, three or four pairs of scissors and a pocket knife have found their way into the great county of Bradley," wrote one observer, "and the result is that the people, even to the women, are demoralized. Confederate money is valueless to them when compared to the life of a chicken or a pound of butter." Under the cover of passes, men of uncertain loyalty roamed the countryside looking for deals.

Wartime at Home

The War was lost at home as well as in the field. On March 10, 1865, a woman living near war-torn Helena recorded in her diary: "This is a fast day by Jeff Davis's appointment. None of us have regarded it though. The prayers and fastings of one or two will avail nothing." Others might have responded that they had fasted enough, especially in 1862 when the wheat rusted, the oats were diseased, the corn "a remarkable failure" and the hogs hit by an outbreak of cholera. Because Arkansas was predominantly rural, most families suffered from a salt shortage. In southern Arkansas, families journeyed to the region's salt springs to boil their own; in northern Arkansas, they even dug up the soil under the smoke houses to reclaim old salt.

The arrival of invading armies or the outbreak of guerrilla warfare made the situation worse. Instead of shortages, the problem became one of survival. Civilian casualties, some of them the victims of impromptu executions, ran in the hundreds if not thousands, and fear led many men to hide in hills and swamps, leaving women to tend fields and harvest crops. Their pleas were futile when soldiers of either side or guerrillas chose to kill livestock and plunder the barn or smokehouse. The Kansas "Red Legs" had the greatest reputation for robbery, and in one well documented instance, a chaplain led a party that tied up and burned the feet of an old man to get him to reveal where his money was hidden. Despite the popular rhetoric, little chivalry on either side was shown in Arkansas.

The region north of the Arkansas River Valley was lost by 1863. During the last year of Confederate control in Little Rock, food supplies had to be sent in by wagon from Texas. After the capital fell, Confederate authorities decided not to seek its recapture because, among other reasons, they lacked the transportation system that military success would demand. When faced with total war, the poorly developed institutions of antebellum Arkansas simply collapsed. Disorganization reached from family farm to Confederate army; it showed up in the politics of the state and made defeat inevitable.

Those who could afford it often decided to depart for safer regions. This practical move often was greeted with some scorn by neighbors and doubtless lowered morale: "Those who ran to get out of danger and have left others to fight in a war which they did much bring upon us, I think ought to have done better."

At least temporarily, the Civil War altered a variety of social relationships. Men assumed in camp what traditionally were women's roles. One private even compared his mess to a family:

> [H]uey Collins is the old man he draws
> the rashen an ike stark is the old
> woman he puts on bread an felix hill he
> is the oledest daughter he fries meat an
> i am the second oldest daughter i make
> coffey and an charles stark and charles
> mack is the sons they get wood and
> make a fire and James bailey he is the
> baby an washes the dishes.

Another private considered the process to be a form of male liberation:

> Pa I am become to be a good cook since I
> have been in the army so if I ever get
> home again I won't ask the woman any
> odds about cooking for I just know I can
> beat any of the women making coffee an
> a baking biscuits . . . I have learned
> more in 1 month since I have been out
> than I would learned in 5 years at home.

The other side of the picture was the alteration of women's roles. For some this began with the loss of servants, especially after the Federals arrived. Others even had to take up men's work. "I warn't full growed then, only jest teenage, but me an' Sis made two craps with a yoke of cowcritters," one Ozark survivor recalled. She and her sister also dug graves to bury their two cousins shot and killed by Yankees in front of their home.

The women of Arkansas were deemed by some to be more patriotic than the men. "The truest patriots that ever trod the soil of the earth," wrote one Confederate minister. Another commented on Arkansas women, "they keep their husbands and sons comfortable clad in the army and themselves and children neatly dressed in homespun and seem afraid of no one." One even took to the bush near Helena, becoming a guerrilla fighter and allegedly killing seven men.

Yet the ravages of the War undermined even women's devotion to the cause. Some became victims. "You can hardly believe that men calling themselves Confederate soldiers would be insulting, beating, shooting at and otherwise putting in fear and dread the noble women who have done so much for us, but 'tis ever so," one disgusted Confederate wrote. Others tried to have fun. Instead of making bandages or helping with the wounded, the belles of Little Rock, "in perfect shoals," went riding, "carrying and thinking as much about the sick soldiers, as if they were so many sheep."

Religion During the War

The War greatly damaged the cause of religion in Arkansas. After invoking God in behalf of the Confederacy, many ministers deserted the pulpit to join the army. One Arkansas regiment contained forty-two "parsons." Services stopped in the absence of ministers, and churches in town often were converted to hospitals. Once the Federals arrived, Northern ministers assumed pulpits. Northern Methodists, in particular, often attempted to claim church property belonging to Southern Methodists as part of the spoils of war.

Personal morality suffered as well. Boys straight and sober enough at home fell into evil ways in the camps. One soldier wrote his mother that, "Last Sunday night I saw some young men playing. Frank and I told them that it was Sunday, but they did not heed. The most of men seem to become reckless by being out in camp." Immorality was widespread and affected both Private "isaac dillion," who "has got in to bad praktis of runing after mean wimen," and Colonel E. W. Gantt, "a second Aaron Burr."

Promiscuity among women increased alarmingly. One Texas soldier observed after arriving in Arkansas that, "there is verry few vertious ones along the road we travailed," and another Texan added, "the boys say that the ladies was very acomadating [,] Got most emnay thing thay wanted."

The counterattack came in 1863 when a strong revival movement surfaced in both the army and the civilian population. The Christian Soldier Association and the Army Church were organized. "I believe the soldier comes before the Christian," commented one cynic, and the movement suffered from a shortage of Bibles, tracts and army hymn books. In an attempt to combat the shortage, the Reverend Samuel Stevenson of Paraclifta issued the *Arkansas Mockingbird*, a collection of hymns and songs.

Because churches had been associated with the pro-slavery argument, their authority diminished as the Confederate cause waned. In the final months of the War, when the slavery question was debated in Arkansas, the argument of the Washington *Telegraph* that "we owe it to God to sustain it" surely rang hollow in the light of the Deity's obvious neglect of the Lost Cause. As for the various denominations, Roman Catholics counted twenty-four priests in 1861; they had only five at the end of the War. Cumberland Presbyterians reported many clergy dead, most of their churches destroyed, and only one small building remaining at Cane Hill College.

Education During the War

Education was another casualty of the War. The few colleges at the beginning were virtually emptied as students and faculty rushed to enlist. Professor William Baxter at Fayetteville, who witnessed the process with mixed feelings, predicted correctly that the War would be a major setback for Southern education. One father, foreseeing these problems, urged his daughter to complete her education because she would have to assume responsibility for the smaller children.

Although teachers could be exempted from the Confederate draft, schools that survived the initial outbreak of hostilities were often in the path of invading armies. The female academy at Arkadelphia was visited by Yankee soldiers, who vandalized it, taking particular pleasure in destroying the school's prized piano and globes. On the other hand, the Paraclifta Seminary flourished in the safety of southwestern Arkansas. Founded by the Reverend Samuel Stevenson, it drew eighty-six students for the first term in the fall of 1861 and 112 students by the third term in the fall of 1862. Perhaps it continued to prosper because of the disruptions elsewhere. St. John's in Little Rock was converted to military use early in the War, and Federals used the grounds to stage the hanging of former student David O. Dodd. Before the War, Arkansas education possessed neither system nor much capital outlay; at the end of the War, both were gone.

UNION ARKANSAS

Some men never endorsed secession. Isaac Murphy, the delegate who voted "no," found his way to Union lines, and William H. Fishback, although pursued by four reliable Confederates, followed. Democrat Jonas Tebbetts unfurled a national flag when Federals first occupied Fayetteville and afterwards went north. Hundreds of mountain men, victims of the Peace Society persecution, fled to Missouri.

President Lincoln, convinced in 1862 that the masses were loyal but misled, appointed Unionist John S. Phelps of Springfield, Missouri, as Arkansas's military governor. A slaveholder, Phelps had been one of the incorporators of the Far West Seminary and was well known throughout the Southwest. The occupation of Helena in the summer of 1862 provided the opportunity to set up a rival government, but Phelps, fearful of Helena's reputation for sickness, refused to leave his St. Louis hotel room and resigned his office. General Frederick Steele became the acting governor until after the occupation of Little Rock, when Isaac Murphy assumed the ceremonial title.

The Arkansas Union Army

During the summer and fall of 1862, the Federal government began enrolling Ozark mountaineer refugees into Arkansas regiments. The process continued after the conquest of parts of the state. In all, 8,829 Arkansas whites enlisted in the Federal service and 1,713 lost their lives. Except for James M. Johnson and Lafayette Gregg, most regimental officers were Northerners, but A.W. Bishop and M. La Rue Harrison (founder of Harrison in Boone County) later played important roles during Reconstruction.

Organizing a Union Government

Arkansas Unionists staged an election in early 1864 designed to show that 10 percent of voters supported the national government. Under Lincoln's plan, a loyal government would receive presidential recognition if it could be reconstituted safely. Supporters framed a new constitution that abolished slavery but did not enfranchise blacks. On March 14, 1864, in a very irregular election that Confederates tried unsuccessfully to prevent, the necessary 10 percent approved the new document, elected Isaac Murphy governor and chose a new legislature. Voting was by voice, and refugees could vote for their counties. Not surprisingly, many legislators were not well known.

Those who hoped for legitimacy for the Union regime looked to William K. Sebastian. The incumbent United States Senator had never taken part in the rebellion but had been expelled from the Senate in the summer of 1861. Many Unionists wanted him to reclaim his seat, but the timid Sebastian refused. Hence, one of the first duties of the newly elected legislature was the selection of two new United States senators.

No political consensus existed, for Union men were divided between those who had been consistently loyal and those who had switched sides only as Confederate defeat became apparent. One nominee, Elisha Baxter, had a modest record of resistance to the Confederacy. A Batesville merchant and lawyer, he had supported Hindman before the War but had refused to aid secession. Baxter became a conspicuous figure when the Union army reached Batesville. Refusing a commission, he fled to Missouri, where Confederates found him teaching school and brought him back to Little Rock for a treason trial. Friends engineered his escape, and Baxter entered the Union army on reaching Missouri. His brother, William, was one of the most notable and consistent Unionists in the divided state of Tennessee.

Arkansas First Light Artillery Battery *(photographer unknown, Fayetteville, 1864) This picture shows the only artillery battery recruited for Federal service in Arkansas.* **Washington County Historical Society and Shiloh Museum**

The other candidate was William Fishback. "Fishy" had been first in the public eye as an articulate opponent of secession before the firing on Fort Sumter. In the May session, however, he had cast his vote with the majority. He had deserted to the Union side in 1862, too late, said many, to qualify as a real patriot. Baxter's selection was uncontroversial, but in Fishback's case, the legislature was in an uproar, and two speakers had to be chosen before he received his certification papers.

When the two men presented their credentials in Washington, radical Republicans, already convinced that Lincoln's presidential Reconstruction program was too lenient, made mincemeat of Fishback. Congress thereafter declined to recognize the legitimacy of Lincoln's new state governments by refusing to seat their senators or congressmen. Although it is possible this course would have proceeded without the Fishback case, the weakness of his credentials embarrassed the administration. Thereafter, the Union state government existed at the sufferance of the military, leading a largely shadowy existence.

Military Rule

Although the tenor of Union policy was toward reconciliation, two events cast a pall over Steele's regime. The first involved the aged William E. Woodruff, who had stayed behind in Little Rock, and as required, took the oath of allegiance. Responding to a pro-

DeValls Bluff *(artist unknown, 1864) DeValls Bluff was the central base for Union operations in Arkansas. Federals seized the western section and terminus of the Memphis and Little Rock Railroad, using it to haul food and supplies to Little Rock.* **University of Arkansas at Little Rock**

testing Confederate in exile, Woodruff wrote that he adopted this course only because of his age and his desire to save his property from confiscation. In accordance with federal regulations, Woodruff took his letter to the provost marshal's office to have it cleared only to be arrested for false swearing and expelled from the city. The Confederate press did its best to make it seem that General Steele was cruel to old people.

The case also could be made that the "monster" Steele did not spare children. David O. Dodd, a strapping seventeen-year-old, was a sometime student at St. John's who, during the War, had followed his father through four states in horse trades and other speculative

dealings before returning to occupied Little Rock in late 1863. After leaving town, he was stopped by a Federal patrol whose examination revealed that Dodd had made Morse code indications of troop strength and armaments. Tried as a spy, he offered to take the oath of allegiance, but the court rejected his offer as irrelevant. Dodd was found guilty and hanged on January 8, 1864, becoming to a succession of panegyrists the "Nathan Hale of Arkansas," albeit one whose record did not bear too close an examination.

Pacifying Arkansas depended largely on establishing law and order and supplying people with food. The military rulers scored only partial success in both. The law and order problem stemmed from Union control being limited to a few established military posts such as Fort Smith, Helena, Batesville and Fayetteville. On occasion, such as during the March 1864 elections, Confederates launched attacks on some of these posts. Perhaps the most serious attack was made against Pine Bluff by General Marmaduke. Union defenders, commanded by Colonel Powell Clayton, repulsed the assault, and during the last two years of the War, Confederates never succeeded in taking any of the major posts.

The countryside, however, belonged to no one. Throughout much of the state, gangs of border ruffians survived by stealing from the civilian population. Those who were said to be of Northern affiliation were called jayhawkers and could be found in both the Ozark and Ouachita Mountains. Some like Captain Martin Hart, a former member of the Texas army who operated near Fort Smith, were ex-Confederates. Others, called "mountain boomers," were native Unionists. In addition, after General Hindman licensed guerrilla activities, numerous Missouri bushwhackers made their winter headquarters in either Arkansas or Texas.

William Quantrill, who boasted of a Confederate commission, was but one of a number of deadly murderers who plagued both sides. In one instance, the Union and Confederate commanders in southern Missouri made a short truce and both hunted this detested enemy. The problem of lawlessness increased as the Confederate cause crumbled and more deserters returned to Arkansas.

Closely connected with the problem of establishing physical safety for Unionists was the need to feed them. The army attempted to relocate loyalists near Fort Smith and Fayetteville and give them protection necessary to raise a crop. This effort largely failed, and one boatload of 487 refugees taken to Cairo, Illinois, and abandoned in the dead of winter got belated national attention after four died.

A different attempt involved the abandoned plantations of eastern Arkansas. Many runaway, abandoned or liberated slaves congregated at posts such as Helena, Pine Bluff and Little Rock. In an attempt to remove them as a charge from government rolls and to enrich Northern speculators, former plantations were resettled with Northern bosses and black freedmen. The Confederates were especially anxious to break up these plantations and scored a few successes. Many of the ex-slaves were not particularly happy to return to plantation ways, and Northern managers tended to be inexperienced and impractical.

Slavery and the War

The debates in the 1864 constitutional convention showed that even the Unionists were divided sharply on the question of slavery. In the aftermath of the War, it became an almost universal assertion that the Civil War was fought over states' rights rather than slavery, but the race issue was ever present for wartime white Arkansans. "Imagine," wrote one Confederate soldier, "your sweet little girls in the school room with a black wooly headed negro and have to treat them as their equal." The belief that the Union could be sustained with slavery died hard in the 1864 convention, and conservatives were not prepared to accept black civil rights.

When Northern armies finally arrived in Arkansas, they found the slavery system already in collapse. Many planters, knowing that slaves would not be loyal, fled with their property to Texas. By one Confederate estimate, more than 100,000 slaves from Arkansas and adjacent states were headed southwest by late 1864. Planters who refused to make the move often received some rude shocks. Mrs. Mary Eskridge from Wapanocca wrote disgustedly that, "those I trusted most have deceived me most and will yet give me trouble on account of their families."

Soldier Families at DeValls Bluff. *(Alfred R. Waud, 1866) Illustrator Alfred R. Waud, the war artist for* Harper's Weekly, *was sent on assignment to Arkansas in 1866. During campaigns, wives and camp followers were sent away, but in garrison towns, soldiers hired servants and family life began to flourish.* **Historic New Orleans Collection**

By hiring or through impressment, numerous slaves worked for the Confederate government. Planters feared that such slaves would not be well taken care of and often made the move to Texas as much to avoid the Confederate authorities as the Federals. "The planters of this region," wrote a Chicot County resident, "have no patriotism. It's get all you can, keep all you get and 'devil take the hindmost' with them." One planter viewed things slightly differently, writing that, I have lost all hope, but at the same time, I deem it my duty to use every effort to save my property."

As the plantation system broke down, large numbers of slaves congregated in towns. Besides being used for such obvious physical activities as building fortifications, blacks were recruited as nurses for the army hospital in Little Rock. Social control disintegrated as slaves from different plantations and areas mixed together. After slaves held a horse race on Sunday in July 1863, blocking one main street, the *True Democrat* reported:

Not withstanding stringent laws and ordinances against negroes hiring their own time, slaves hire houses and have cookshops, beerholes, and other pretended means of support. They are flush of money; buy pistols and horses and get white men to bid for them at auctions. On Markham street, for two or three squares, every third house is a negro brothel, and where it is said, whiskey is sold.

Mrs. Eskridge, some of whose slaves had joined that throng, might instruct her agent to admonish them to be "faithful converted

Christians and good servants" and "hope that Fagans reads the Bible," but the tenor of town life went in other directions.

The arrival of invading Union armies generally led to massive desertions from plantations. Some planters tried to hide slaves in canebrakes, but as one disgusted planter observed, they were "found invariably through bad faith of some of the negroes." By 1864, the Union army had replaced the option of leaving by demanding that all able-bodied men accompany the army while women, children and old people remained behind for the Confederates to feed. The plaintive letters that poured into Confederate headquarters asking for additional exemptions testify to the success of this policy in putting pressure on already underfed Rebels.

Although eager to deprive Confederates of their services, Federals made few provisions for taking care of their new charges. The United States Sanitary Commission, a Northern philanthropic group, provided the first assistance, supplying a model for the Freedman's Bureau after the War. But many Northern soldiers were hostile. By late 1863, a Union officer reported that the slaves "hide from us like the dickins," and a planter noted that "the mania for going to the Yankees subsided," and some returned "better servants from their trial of it."

Although most freedmen were used in physical labor for the North, 5,526 in time joined the Federal army. This experiment caused no little controversy in the North, and black soldiers received inferior weapons, lower pay and were led by white officers. In battle they were not likely to be treated as prisoners of war if captured, as Confederates showed by slaughtering them in the capture of Fort Pillow on the Mississippi River and at the Battle of Poison Springs in Arkansas. It was a sign of the times, however, that black troops escorted the new governor, Isaac Murphy, in his inauguration in 1864. As a symbol of emerging black pride, the troops sang to the tune of "John Brown's Body:"

Oh, we're the bully soldiers of the First of Arkansas, We are fighting for the Union, We're fighting for the law, We can hit a Rebel further than a white man ever saw, As we go marching on.

As the national political consensus moved toward granting civil rights to blacks, President Lincoln began to be seen as a moderate. Those who supported the President and General Steele became known as conservatives, sometimes even opposing the end of slavery and certainly refusing to grant civil rights or the franchise to freedmen. Others argued that the 1864 Constitution, which made no substantive changes in the frame of government except abolishing slavery, was not radical enough for the times. Factionalism broke out among Unionists, foretelling some of the political issues that appeared during Reconstruction.

The Confederate Government in Exile

Although Flanagin's government reassembled at Washington, a period of almost total inactivity followed there. If the Confederate state government was even going to pretend to survive, it had to show some signs of life. Thus the state Supreme Court, bolstered by Albert Pike, ruled that the governor could recall the legislature to Washington and that a quorum consisted of two-thirds of those who arrived. A new session put the government in exile on a legal footing and it voted nonexistent money for such needs as salt for the poor and cotton cards. The selection of a new Confederate senator to replace the recently deceased Dr. C. B. Mitchel saw Augustus H. Garland defeat Albert Pike, thirty-eight to fourteen. This victory was coupled with another Garland success when brother Rufus Garland unseated incumbent Grandison D. Royston in a congressional race in the fall of 1863. Royston was not only an original secessionist but had a son,

The 57th U. S. Colored Infantry, Probably at Little Rock about December 1866. *Aaron Harvey, shown here with the side drum, was a slave from Mississippi brought to Helena with a cotton raiding party. At Helena, he enlisted in Company F, 57th U. S. Colored Infantry. After mustering in on December 2, 1863, the 57th provided protection for supply lines. The 57th also was assigned to guard at the Post of Arkansas, before moving to Little Rock where it helped defend the Memphis and Little Rock Railroad. A small detachment was assigned as engineers and bridge train guard on Steele's expedition into southwestern Arkansas in the spring of 1864.* **University of Arkansas at Little Rock**

Charley, exempted from the draft, who rode around to all the best parties. War weariness was evident even in the as yet untouched Red River Valley.

Arkansas in the Red River Campaign

The Union did not expand the War in Arkansas after taking Little Rock. A few posts at key places and patrols into the interior constituted the Federal presence. Yet, cotton hungry merchants of the North insisted that the military carry out operations designed to enrich them. The result was the Red River Valley campaign in Louisiana of General Nathaniel Banks. Strategy called

for Steele to leave Little Rock heading southwest. General John Thayer from Indian Territory would join him enroute and both would meet General Banks on the Red River. They thought the Confederates would not stand and fight.

Union strategy and tactics were deficient. Although the Confederates nearly denuded Arkansas of defenders, Steele could not take the advantage because he had to wait for Thayer, whose men were so loaded with loot that they fell behind schedule. Eventually Steele's and Thayer's combined forces reached Prairie D'An near modern Prescott, where, one Union soldier observed, it was the only time he ever saw the entire army on the field of battle. The Confederates chose to defend Washington rather than Camden, and Steele obligingly turned his army east and occupied Camden, the last manufacturing center left to the Confederates. There he moved into recently abandoned defenses and looked unsuccessfully for food for his hungry army.

A Union foraging party of some 2,500 men was ambushed by General Marmaduke at Poison Springs. Reinforced by a Confederate Choctaw regiment, the Confederates took their revenge on the black soldiers of the First Kansas. No mercy was shown the living, and those dead on the battlefield had their skulls run over and crushed by Confederate wagoners. The Confederates lost only a few men in capturing the federal wagon train and all the artillery.

Steele had a little better luck in the opposite direction. Just as meat was running out and corn was becoming scarce, a supply train arrived from Pine Bluff and the crisis lessened. But Steele was to cooperate with Banks, who he learned had been defeated and was retreating. In hope of getting more reinforcements, Steele waited and sent his newly arrived wagons back toward Pine Bluff. Confederates ambushed the train at Marks' Mills. The Union force was virtually destroyed, losing 1,300 out of 1,600 men. Confederates again wreaked vengeance on blacks and native Unionist refugees.

The destruction of his train convinced Steele to retreat to Little Rock immediately. His decision to evacuate was timely, for Confederate Commander General Kirby Smith was rushing every available man to Arkansas in hopes of trapping Steele at Camden. Instead, the Confederates engaged in hot pursuit over swampy terrain in the Ouachita and Saline River bottoms. They caught Steele at the Saline crossing of Jenkins' Ferry, where a very poorly planned battle by General Sterling Price led to a Union triumph and a successful escape. Thereafter, war in Arkansas returned to a series of skirmishes.

One Confederate success was a raid on Mississippi River traffic. Colonel Colton Greene seized Gaines Landing in late May 1864, burning a boat loaded with Yankee cotton. Confederates stopped all movement for a time along a section of the River known as the Greenville Bends. The Federals responded by sending General Andrew J. Smith and some 6,000 troops against the marauders. Confederates inflicted heavy casualties at the Battle of Ditch Bayou before withdrawing, their ammunition exhausted. Thereafter, Greene's men were moved, and the Confederates made no new efforts to impede Federal use of the Mississippi despite the ease with which it could have been accomplished.

Instead, General Sterling Price convinced Smith to let him invade Missouri one more time. Price's 1864 raid failed in all of its major objectives. Although he crossed the Arkansas River safely and entered Missouri, Price suffered a major setback attempting to take Pilot Knob. He only could threaten St. Louis and Columbia and nearly lost his entire army at the Battle of Westport near Kansas City. Only a stout defense by General Shelby's Iron Brigade at the second Battle of Newtonia allowed Price to reach safety in Texas.

The War's End

General Ulysses S. Grant finally drove General Robert E. Lee out of Richmond, Virginia, in the spring of 1865. Following the fall of the Confederate capital, Lee, cut off from easy retreat and philosophically opposed to guerrilla warfare, surrendered at Appomattox Courthouse, Virginia, on April 9, 1865. General Joseph E. Johnston surrendered the Army of Tennessee on April 26, 1865, and the course of surrender wove westward. Confederate officers were ready to continue the War in the Trans-Mississippi, but their men were not. Nothing like a formal surrender even took place over much of

Governor Isaac Murphy's Dream of a New Arkansas

Governor Isaac Murphy put forth a vision of a new Arkansas in writing to the nationally famous Reverend Lyman Abbott, the secretary of the American Union Commission (the predecessor to the Freedmen's Bureau). Unfortunately for men of good will, events in the next few years led to results far from what either Abbott or Murphy intended.

Executive Office
Little Rock, AR.
Aug. 7th, 1865

Rev. Lyman Abbott:

Yours of the 29th July is received. The American Union Commission is another evidence that the true spirit of Christianity is spreading Love to our race and kindness to god's creatures — this is true patriotism — it is the principle that will render republican government from unrest. Industry, Education and Christian morality are the pillars of freedom.

Our state is a picture of desolation. The great majority of the people reduced to poverty. The Christian kindness of the benevolent institutions of the Loyal States is producing a like spirit here and softening our hearts hardened by the terrible scenes and sufferings of the war. The farmers are very destitute of stock and tools as well as seeds. However a great exertion has been made to raise something to eat and make something to wear. The people need aid in every way. They need an infusion of Northern example — of energy and industry. Emigrants of the proper character would do themselves and us much good. Teachers are much needed but the people generally are not able to support them. The lands of the State are rich — mineral resources unbounded — the climate as healthy as any other. All the elements of wealth are here, waiting development. Kindness will conquer the most stubborn — and reform if reform is possible. To love our neighbors as ourselves is Christianity — is happiness — and is the foundation of all true freedom. The immense effects of the benevolent institutions of the Loyal States have done more to conquer the Rebellion than our armies.

With high respect,

Isaac Murphy

Source: Historical Society of Pennsylvania

---

the region. Soldiers looted government stores and left for home with weapons, mules and food. It is more apt to say the Trans-Mississippi army dissolved rather than surrendered.

Governor Flanagin sent a delegation to Little Rock to arrange the surrender of Arkansas. The Federals saw no reason to recognize Flanagin's existence. He was permitted only to return the archives to Little Rock and retire to Arkadelphia. Many followed him, witnesses to abandoned and burned homes; uncultivated land overgrown with bushes; half starved women and children; gaunt, ragged men, stumbling along the road, just mustered out of the army, trying to find their families and friends and wondering if they had a home left. Others, fearful of a hostile reception, stayed in Texas. A few, like many of the Missouri officers and General Hindman, headed for Mexico, or in the case of General Thomas P. Dockery, to Brazil. All wondered less about the constitutional and political results of the failure of the Confederacy than about how to get a crop planted this late in the spring. When M. Jeff Thompson surrendered with his veteran swamp fighters at Wittsburg, he denounced his men for lacking courage to the point that "the moss has grown six inches long on your backs," and warned them to expect no rights and to avoid politics.

CONCLUSION

The Civil War left Arkansas's economy in devastation. Although Arkansas lacked the grand plantation houses of the older states, many fine buildings were burned during the guerrilla fighting. Confederates partially burned Fayetteville in 1862, and raids on Union shipping prompted the Federals to cross the River from Memphis and burn Hopefield to the ground. Only the gateposts remained of Henry Rector's Pulaski County estate.

For the most part, however, the double-log cabins of most Arkansans could be replaced easily. Arkansas's factories were another story, for both the Fayetteville and Van Buren cotton plants were war casualties. The Memphis and Little Rock Railroad was a Confederate priority at the beginning of the War. Its track between the capital and the White River was finished by 1862. The fall of Memphis made the line useless, and neglect during the War and occasional raids left it largely in ruins by 1865. Although the War stimulated industries, the only two of significance in Arkansas — salt and saltpeter — were hardly needed in post-war America.

As for the rural economy, the destruction of gristmills threw the farmers back to grinding their own grain. Losses of horses, mules and oxen meant men and women substituted for beasts of burden both during and shortly after the War. Those who had flourished in their rural self-sufficiency by combining the resources of hogs, cattle and farming found their cherished independence gone. Most of all, those who had relied on slave labor to tend their fields were ruined because the loss of slaves meant not only loss of cheap labor but also the loss of their capital investment. The depopulation of Arkansas during the War greatly reduced the state's supply of laborers, and there was no consensus on just how free blacks could be employed.

The greatest ramifications were psychological. Defeat left a bitter taste in the mouths of many, and in the mountains, the War had ignited the classic feud between Union and Confederate sympathizers. The picture one Union soldier recorded in northern Alabama — of refugee Union mothers making their children memorize lists of people on whom to seek revenge — doubtless occurred in Arkansas as well. In the wilder parts of the Ozarks, the animosities were so intense that the Civil War continued for decades.

Some planters never adjusted to defeat, economically or psychologically. Albert Pike, who had come to identify with this class, a decade after the War wrote of being a stranger in the land. Those who refused to accept the outcome of the war often gloried in the "Lost Cause" and used two of its symbols, "Dixie" and the Confederate flag, as signs of protest against dominant American ideals.

BIBLIOGRAPHIC ESSAY

The Civil War is by far the most studied period of Arkansas history. Five pages of the *Arkansas Historical Quarterly Index* list articles on the War, and more than 400 additional entries can be found in Dillard and Dougan Comps., *Arkansas History: A Selected Research Bibliography.*

Most of the basic military correspondence is contained in the *War of the Rebellion: A Compilation of the Official Records of the Union and Confederate Armies,* (Washington, 1880-1901). Unpublished sources are scattered in various archives and libraries. The military records for 1862-1863 turned up in 1976 in the Peter W. Alexander Papers at Columbia University and were used in the preparation of this chapter. The newspapers of the era are useful, including the Washington *Telegraph,* which alone was published continuously.

Only a few Arkansans published memoirs or histories, but John C. Wright, *Memoirs of Colonel John C. Wright* (Pine Bluff, 1982) is incisive. Hundreds of soldiers' letters have survived. Two of the best collections are Mrs. T. J. Gaughan, ed., *Letters of a Confederate Surgeon, 1861-1865,* (Camden, 1960), and Ted R. Worley, ed., *At Home in Confederate Arkansas; Letters to and from Pulaski Countians, 1861-1865,* (Little Rock, 1955).

Histories of individual regiments supplement the survivor accounts: John C. Hammock, *With Honor Untarnished; The Story of the First Arkansas Infantry Regiment, Confederate States Army,* (Little Rock, 1961), and three books by Calvin L. Collier: *First In-Last Out, The Capitol Guards, Arkansas Brigade,* (Little Rock, 1961); *They'll Do To Tie To! The Story of the Third Regiment, Arkansas Infantry, C.S.A.,* (Little Rock, 1959) and *The War Child's Children: The Story of the Third Regiment, Arkansas Cavalry, Confederate States Army,* (Little Rock, 1965).

The leading generals have warranted biographies. Howell and Elizabeth Purdue uncovered new material in *Pat Cleburne, Confederate General: A Definitive Biography,* (Hillsboro, Tex., 1973). A virtual military history of the War can be gleaned from Albert E. Castel, *General Sterling Price and the Civil War in the West,* (Baton Rouge, 1968). Old but still useful is Wiley Britton, *The Civil War on the Border,* (New York, 1890-1899). Arkansas's most controversial leader is treated fairly in Bobby L. Roberts, "Thomas C. Hindman, Jr: Secessionist and Confederate General," (Master's thesis, University of Arkansas, 1972).

Individual campaigns have been a life-long interest of Edwin C. Bearss. His books include *The Battle of Wilson's Creek,* (Diamond, Mo., 1975) and *Steele's Retreat from Camden and the Battle of Jenkins' Ferry,* (1967). Among his nineteen articles are "The Battle of the Post of Arkansas," *AHQ,* XVIII (Autumn 1959), 237-279; "The Battle of Pea Ridge," *AHQ,* XX (Spring 1961), 74-94, and "The Battle of Helena, July 4, 1863," *AHQ,* XX (Autumn 1961), 254-297. Pea Ridge attracted Albert Pike specialist Walter L. Brown in "Pea Ridge: Gettysburg of the West," *AHQ,* XV (Spring 1956), 3-16. Other useful studies include Stephen B. Oates, "The Prairie Grove Campaign, 1862," *AHQ,* XIX (Summer 1960), 119-141; Ira Don Richards, "The Engagement at Marks' Mills," *AHQ,* XIX (Spring 1960), 51-60 and William L. Shea, "Battle at Ditch Bayou," *AHQ,* XXIX (Autumn 1980), 195-207.

The political and social aspects of the War comprise the main theme of Dougan, *Confederate Arkansas.* Biographies of the governors appear in Donovan and Gatewood, *Governors of Arkansas,* and in W. Buck Yearns, ed., *The Confederate Governors,* (Athens, Ga., 1984). Part of the conflict between the civilian and military authorities is traced in Leo E. Huff, *The Martial Law Controversy in Arkansas, 1861-1865, AHQ,* XXXVII (Summer 1978), 147-167. Guerrillas figure in William J. E. Sawyer, "The Martin Hart Conspiracy," *AHQ,* XXIII (Summer 1964), 154-165 and a general study is Leo E.

Huff, "Guerrillas, Jayhawkers and Bush-whackers in Northern Arkansas During the Civil War," *AHQ,* XXIV (Summer 1965), 127-148. Huff also examined "The Memphis and Little Rock Railroad During the Civil War," *AHQ,* XXIII (Autumn 1964), 260-270.

The last stages of the War received scholarly attention in Robert L. Kerby, *Kirby Smith's Confederacy: The Trans-Mississippi South, 1863-1865,* (New York, 1972). Also commendable is LeRoy H. Fischer, "David O. Dodd: A Folk Hero of Confederate Arkansas," *AHQ,* XXXVII (Summer 1978), 130-146. Union Arkansas remains largely ignored save for John I. Smith, *The Courage of a Southern Unionist: A Biography of Isaac Murphy, Governor of Arkansas, 1864-1868,* (Little Rock, 1979).

Officers of the 2nd Wisconsin Cavalry in Helena at the Civil War's End (*photographer unknown, 1865*) *A number of Union veterans chose to stay in Arkansas. Several of the officers pictured here settled in the Missouri Ozarks.* **Author's Collection**

Chapter X

Reconstruction and Modernization

INTRODUCTION

Reconstruction in Arkansas was a period of great social, political and economic change. During a hectic ten-year period, the state began to work out new patterns of race relations, experimented unsuccessfully with two-party politics and made economic mistakes of a magnitude equal to the Real Estate Bank failure.

At the same time the state made one step forward to modernization by encouraging the construction of the railroads, it took two steps backward by developing the sharecropper system. These contradictory features within such a short time explain why veteran politician Jesse Cypert called Reconstruction "a heroic age" in his memoirs. But just who the heroes and villains were has been the subject of varying historical interpretation.

White Southerners and the first historians of the period condemned Reconstruction Republicans as villains without trial. Their main charges were fraud and corruption, but the underlying reason was racism, for Republicans supported civil rights for blacks. In more recent times, the balance in national writing has shifted to a more favorable view of Reconstruction, but the reassessment of Arkansas Republicans has only just begun.

PRESIDENTIAL RECONSTRUCTION: 1864-1867

The first phase of Reconstruction grew out of the military's need to achieve support in conquered areas of the South for restoration of law and order. Convinced that sufficient loyalty existed to allow the reestablishment of self-government, President Lincoln authorized the military to permit the formation of new state governments, one of which was in Arkansas. Because Congress was excluded from this process and did not share the president's conviction about the extent of the South's loyalty, the first Arkansas congressmen and senators were not permitted to take their seats in Congress. After Lincoln's death in April 1865, the new president, Andrew Johnson, continued to recognize the government of the Republican, Isaac Murphy, even though Congress did not.

The Murphy Government

The main concern in early days of the Murphy government was collecting enough tax money to pay salaries. The legislature, although not competent in Congress's eyes to elect United States senators, was permitted to ratify the Thirteenth Amendment to the United States Constitution abolishing slavery. County reorganization remained incomplete. Some counties held elections, but others had officials appointed by Governor Murphy. Municipal charters were suspended pending new elections. Suddenly, when the Civil War was over in late spring 1865, this shadowy embryo was the only government in the state.

The first problem that the Arkansas Union government encountered was the franchise. Believing that ex-Confederates who were not truly repentant might take over the state, the legislature passed a test oath to administer to voters. In *Rison* v. *Farr* (1865), the state Supreme Court struck down the loyalty oath as unconstitutional, thus preparing the way for the return of ex-Confederates to office. In the first post-war election in 1866, antebellum Judges David Walker, F. W. Compton and John J. Clendenin were elected to the state Supreme Court, and ex-Confederates displaced Unionists in the legislature.

Meanwhile, Governor Murphy advocated moderation. In writing his old Whig friend, David Walker, Murphy emphasized Arkansas's dependence on Washington:

> Our position there depends on our behavior here. If we establish justice at home we can demand it with a good face abroad. If we secure to all the good citizens of the state equal rights — the state is sure to obtain her just rights.

Murphy's sentiments were echoed by C.C. Danley in the *Arkansas Gazette*:

> Let us have no more of bowie-knives and revolvers, and Sharp's rifles and other warlike tools. We should be a peaceful community; and our pride should be set upon steam engines and patent corn planters, printing machines and blacksmith's forges.

The Agricultural Problem

The summer of 1865 saw some attempt to follow Murphy's and Danley's advice that the state take a conciliatory attitude and look to future social and industrial progress. Although a reign of lawlessness continued in southwestern Arkansas until federal troops arrived there in July, elsewhere ex-Confederates were paroled and sent home or simply drifted back. All tried to get some kind of crop planted. Black labor was at premium, in part because the forced removal of slaves during the War had reduced the work force. Even five years later, the census

Mustering Out *(Alfred R. Waud, 1866) Sent by* Harper's Weekly *to Arkansas in 1866, Waud made a number of published sketches. This drawing was made in front of the office of army Quartermaster Colonel Page and shows black troops discharged from service. Waud noted that the event created, "a furor among the resident colored females."*
University of Arkansas at Little Rock

showed the black population still below the 1860 figures. Another reason for the labor shortage was that blacks, who had fled to towns during the War, were reluctant to return to the life of field hands. In Little Rock, one editor noted, they "lounge around the streets, half-starved, half clad, and living in miserable hovels rather than work on the most liberal terms." Black women were quitting field work all over the South, believing that they, like white women, should not have to work there.

The federal government entered the farm labor situation through the creation of the Freedmen's Bureau. During the summer of 1865, this agency supervised contracts that often were based on shares divided between workers and landowners, and generally its work was done to the satisfaction of all parties. Some ex-Confederates, among them former secession convention member Jesse Cypert, helped with the work of the Freedmen's Bureau.

The military stood behind the Freedmen's Bureau, but General E.O.C. Ord, head of the military district that included Arkansas,

Scene at Pine Bluff Station *(H. J. Lewis, ca. 1870) The importance of the railroad to cotton farmers is shown in this sketch.* **University of Arkansas at Little Rock**

reported that his small force was inadequate to police the state. In Woodruff County, a band of white terrorists attacked local blacks. In Conway County in early 1867, a gang of local whites aided by supporters from Pope and Perry Counties seized the freedmen just after they had been paid. They took all the freedmen's money and other possessions before driving them away, leaving area planters with no laborers for the next year.

The two great goals for freedmen were to own land and obtain an education. Repeated rumors of forty acres and a mule swept the black community and contributed to a strong desire to leave the old plantation system. At the same time, some planters still believed in the whip as the only way to raise a crop. The Freedmen's Bureau was caught in the middle. Some whites accused Bureau agents of encouraging freedmen not to work. On the other hand, stories circulated that:

[A] planter wishes fifty laborers, he reports to the Freedmen's Bureau, and immediately fifty laborers are soon escorted "under guard" to the aforesaid planter.

Whites justified these measures as necessary to prevent freedmen from starving, but blacks saw it as a betrayal of emancipation.

By 1867, the new *Gazette* editor, William E. Woodruff, Jr., could write:

The question most seriously involving the property of the people in this state at this time is not suffrage, but negro labor. Not whether he shall vote, but whether he will work. [If paid wages] he works lazily and carelessly.

Woodruff believed that black laborers could be made dependable only if they had an interest in the crop and did not get paid until harvest time.

Life returned to normal by slow degrees as the agricultural debate continued. Restoration of mail service began early in 1866 and was completed by October. Church property, often seized by the army or by the Northern faction of divided denominations, was returned as wartime tensions eased. The army band in Little Rock regularly played "Dixie." Trade and commerce revived, and with cotton prices still high and thousands of freedmen converted into consumers, Arkansas's rivers were filled with steamboats. The proposed slogan of the new age came from Woodruff:

Let us trade with the Yankees our asserted love of politics, for energy; our asserted love of ease and leisure, for industry and perseverance.

Ice barges arrived at Little Rock. Hundreds of academies, factories, insurance companies, railroads and turnpike companies applied to the legislature for chartering, and a new law granted tax advantages to cotton factories. After Peter Hanger opened a large planing mill in Little Rock, the *Daily Conservative* observed that lumbering had grown to "considerable importance" and noted that no more log houses were being erected at the capital. Instead, the "Gothic style of building is obtaining largely."

The years 1865-1868 were a false dawn. The issue of Reconstruction was debated violently in the nation at large. President Johnson, after some hesitation, broke with radicals of the Republican Party and began vetoing all legislation designed to aid freedmen. Congressional Republicans in turn became increasingly radical as they encountered this unexpected opposition. The South did not help Johnson at all. Northern newspapers contained long accounts of race riots in New Orleans and Memphis, of Union veterans being persecuted by ex-Confederates, and finally by a lack of contrition in the Johnson-supported state governments.

The End of Presidential Reconstruction

Governor Murphy's hopes for moderation faded when ex-Confederates won control of the legislature. Although justified by compassion, a law making only ex-Confederates eligible for artificial limbs greatly upset Union Army veterans. Only after bitter debate did the legislature consent to bestow even minimal civil rights on persons of African descent. Jury duty, voting, the right to attend public schools and the freedom to marry whites remained denied.

Governor Murphy used his veto power actively, but a number of bills, ranging from one for the relief of the estate of Patrick Cleburne to An Act of Pardon and Amnesty for ex-Confederates were passed just as routinely. Some Southern states enacted rigorous labor laws called black codes that Northern critics claimed were tantamount to reenslavement. Arkansas's version, An Act to Regulate the Labor System in the State, made agricultural contracts enforceable in court. The law authorized certificates of discharge at contract termination and prohibited employers from hiring those already under contract, but there were protections for both parties so that it cannot be considered a black code statute.

Meanwhile, Congress made it plain that the Fourteenth Amendment granting citizenship to blacks had to be accepted before any Southern state could be granted recognition. The legislature refused to do this by a vote of seventy-two to two and instead created a commission to visit Washington and defend the state's lack of action.

Governor Murphy refused to appoint the four delegates he could select, further emphasizing the split between Unionists and ex-Confederates. Unionists held public meetings in several parts of the state to denounce the acts of the legislature and broadcast to the nation the presence of repression in Arkansas against Unionists. The Arkansas delegation heard encouraging words in Washington from the doomed Johnson. Even though the commission's report urged Arkansans to act moderately, the legislature began impeachment proceedings against some incumbent circuit judges — men of marked Unionist sympathies. It also selected Augustus H. Garland for the United States Senate. Of course, Radicals in control of Congress refused to seat Garland, and impeachment was in the air for President Andrew Johnson.

CONGRESSIONAL RECONSTRUCTION, 1867-1874

Congress enacted the First Reconstruction Act on March 2, 1867. Johnson was completely powerless by this time, and Congress, under control of the Radicals, was determined to remake the South in the image of the Republican Party. Arkansas, along with Mississippi, was placed in the Fourth Military District under the command of General E.O.C. Ord. The legislature was barred from meeting, but Murphy was allowed to remain as governor. The Supreme Court was not abolished, but all cases involving whites and blacks were placed under the jurisdiction of military tribunals. An ironclad oath, designed to prohibit ex-Confederates from voting or holding office, was put into effect as military-established registration of voters took place.

The Emergence of the Republicans

Voter registration, completed in the fall, radically altered the political balance of the state. As black males were now eligible to vote, the percentages of voters in the Delta and southwest increased greatly. At the same time, Republicans made little effort to count voters in the mountains correctly. As a result, the percentage of upland seats in the legislature fell from 40 percent to 29.7 percent. These figures then were used to allocate

seats in the Constitutional Convention of 1868 and for the legislature created by that Constitution.

During the summer and fall of 1867, Arkansas debated the question of whether to remain under military rule or to form a new constitution acceptable to Congress. Albert Pike, writing in the *Memphis Appeal,* opposed any involvement: "When our vote is worth no more than an ignorant negroe's [sic], it is not worth picking out of the gutter."

On the other hand, Thomas C. Hindman, home from an unprofitable exile in Mexico, supported involvement:

The exotic weed of radicalism will die out in our midst, its white teachers and preachers will disappear, and its deluded colored converts will be glad to labor quietly with and for their old masters, who are their best friends.

Helena was home to one cooperation meeting at which Hindman, Thomas B. Hanly and other local leaders appealed for white-black friendship. That meeting also marked the first appearance of a newly arrived black, W.H. Gray, who in "well selected language and other respects exhibited the parts of a fine speaker."

However, the majority of whites would not associate with blacks politically, and planters were too weakened by war to take the lead. The Supreme Court, in an able opinion by Chief Justice David Walker in *Hawkins* v. *Filkins* (1866), held that all contracts that did not involve secession were enforceable legally after the War. This decision ruined planters with large outstanding debts who had contracted for the purchase of slaves. Instead of adapting to the new order, many retreated into fantasy that was marked by holding medieval tournaments, modeled after the English revival of chivalry glorified in the novels of Sir Walter Scott. Prominent ex-Confederates, notably General

Thomas Churchill, took the lead in glorifying this new form of escapism at numerous festivals held that summer and fall.

As Confederates debated and fantasized, the embryonic Arkansas Republican Party took form. Those who objected to the actions of the legislature and appealed to Congress to set things right tried first to appropriate the name "Unionists." Ex-Confederates, many of whom called themselves "Conservatives," sarcastically insisted that they were good Unionists, too. In extensive critiques of the wartime activities of men such as Lafayette Gregg and Jonas M. Tebbetts, they charged that most so-called Unionists actually had supported secession at one time. Conservatives angrily rejected the notion that anyone was being persecuted in Arkansas and charged their opponents with wishing to "turn loose the whelps of Hate." Conservatives and Democrats quoted every spiteful remark of Thaddeus Stevens as indicative of Unionist intentions. Meanwhile, meetings at Van Buren and Fort Smith culminated in a Union State Convention in April 1867 at Little Rock. Delegates were a mixed lot who came from all parts of the state. Native Unionists included W.J. Douthet of Lawrence County, a federal registrar who was assassinated a few months later; veteran Democrat Jonas M. Tebbetts, who had played a major role in getting pardons for contrite Confederates, and James M. Johnson, a prominent northwestern Arkansas leader. This conference marked the first political appearance of General Powell Clayton, an ex-Union army officer who was running a plantation near Pine Bluff and was married to a Southern belle. Thus the two characteristic elements of Reconstruction were present: scalawags — the native Unionists — and carpetbaggers — the Northern outsiders. Both terms carried derogatory meanings that in time came to characterize the whole Reconstruction process.

Powell Clayton *(by a black artist, date unknown) The fierce Clayton, made fiercer by his moustache, dominated Reconstruction in Arkansas.* **Arkansas History Commission**

Scalawags and Carpetbaggers

Arkansas scalawags were of at least three different orders. Those from the "great northwest," like Murphy, Tebbetts, Fishback, Baxter and Johnson, were part of the pre-war governing elite, usually with a Whig background. The notable exception was Tebbetts, a prominent Jacksonian Democrat. They spoke for a second group, the thousands of mountain Unionists who, for the most part, were unlettered and apolitical. Murphy, who most nearly resembled his mountain constituents, believed strongly in economy in government, education and the common man. "No State can prosper whose legislation discriminated against labor, and in favor of capital," he told the 1866 legislature. Probably in contrast to most mountain men, he supported a civil rights act.

A third group of scalawags came from the lowlands. Planter Asa Hodges, former Rector supporter A.M. Merrick, and defector E.W. Gantt were the most prominent. Unlike the mountain scalawags, none commanded a home following. Gantt, although eloquent, was morally incapacitated by his desertion from the Confederacy and a subsequent losing battle with alcohol. Hodges was adroit only in advancing his personal fortunes. Mississippi had James Alcorn, but no lowland scalawag leader emerged in Arkansas, and carpetbaggers received the black vote by default.

Two motives that brought Northerners to Arkansas were economic advancement and moral improvement. Many of those in business had arrived during the War to buy cotton and stayed on to develop the plantation trade. Some had military backgrounds, and a few, like General Powell Clayton, had engaged in agriculture on leased plantations. Most had come South seeking riches, although a few like Logan H. Roots arrived with substantial nest eggs. Most important, Northerners came to the South seeking economic rather than political advancement. At the start of Reconstruction, most were located in the Delta, with U.P. Upham in Augusta, John McClure in Arkansas County, Reverend Joseph Brooks at Marianna, Logan Roots at DeValls Bluff and Powell Clayton near Pine Bluff. Only after politics became their primary interest did they gravitate to Little Rock.

Essentially, they were men of the new Northern business mentality, and they looked for investment opportunities, especially in cotton. They established the first federally chartered banks at Fort Smith and Little Rock. Little Rock bankers Alexander McDonald and Logan Roots, who also had interests in DeValls Bluff and Fort Smith, made every effort to involve the local elite in their activities, so it was not surprising that for Christmas in 1867, the Merchants National Bank boasted the best eggnog to be found in Little Rock.

By contrast, the missionaries and Freedmen's Bureau teachers and agents came to Arkansas because of concern about the needs of blacks. In time, a split developed between the pragmatic (critics said corrupt) politics of businessmen and the idealism (critics said misplaced) of missionaries.

The Constitution of 1868

Carpetbaggers and scalawags united in the fall of 1867 to urge the calling of a new Constitutional Convention and the creation of a government acceptable to Congress. Radicals won by an official vote of 27,576 for the convention to 13,558 opposed. This set the stage for the Constitutional Convention that assembled in Little Rock on January 7, 1868.

Dubbed the "menagerie" by the hostile *Arkansas Gazette*, the convention consisted of forty-eight Radicals, seventeen Conservatives and five non-aligned. Radicals divided further into seventeen carpetbaggers, twenty-three scalawags and eight blacks. By controlling blacks, the carpetbaggers dominated the radicals and, therefore, the convention. Carpetbagger Thomas M. Bowen of Van Buren was elected chairman, and carpetbaggers monopolized the key committees. It has been alleged that eight men wrote the Constitution, the debates notwithstanding. In the recollection of Conservative delegate Jesse Cypert, Reverend Joseph Brooks, a former Iowa Methodist minister with a voice like a brindle-tail bull, "was the convention." Those most active in the debates included John McClure, a future chief justice; Miles Langley, a maverick Arkadelphia idealist who startled the convention with his plea for women's suffrage, and black spokesmen W.H. Gray of Phillips County and James W. Mason of Chicot County.

Considering the important task before the convention, much of the discussion was trite, trivial or self-serving. Thus, the convention heard an Ashley County delegate justify his claim of 900 miles for travel and a Mississippi County delegate explain his unusual itinerary by exclaiming: "I am a very timid young man." By contrast, J. M. Bradley of Bradley County, a former Confederate colonel who was elected as a Republican but switched to the Conservatives, came with $1.40 in his pocket and a pair of saddle bags on his shoulder. Money increasingly became a matter of concern, and on the fourteenth day, General Ord managed to obtain some needed funds. In the end, the convention was quite remunerative for those involved and cost about twice the amount expected.

The topic that most occupied the delegates' time was race relations. Conservatives, determined to vote against the new Constitution if it gave any substantive rights to blacks, probed for weakness in the Radical alliance. W. H. Gray, the black spokesman, emphasized the practical necessity of political rights for Negroes, especially jury duty and voting. Phillips County had been the scene of six murders in one month, but where black victims were concerned, white jurors displayed a very casual attitude toward justice. In one case, a guilty conviction was announced summarily because "it doesn't make any difference — it's a nigger — and it's near dinner-time."

Jury duty and voting were political rights, and granting political rights raised the more controversial issue of social relations. "I have promised the black people that I would give them suffrage," said one Union County delegate, "but never that I would give them my daughter." Some delegates supported the view of Miles Langley, "Let society regulate itself on such matters." More popular was the viewpoint expressed by J. M. Bradley, who wanted a high wall of separation between the races so that "a white man shall be a white man, and a black man a black man." But as Gray pointed out, "the purity of blood . . . has already been somewhat interfered with," and proposed amidst laughter and applause that if intermarriage should be made illegal, then if "any white man shall be found cohabiting with a negro woman, the penalty shall be death."

Joseph Brooks (artist unknown, Leslie's, 1874. *By comparison with Clayton, Joseph Brooks possessed a more spiritual mien.* **University of Arkansas at Little Rock**

And so the debate went on over what Bradley called the "irrepressible conflict." The Radical alliance held firm in the end, sidetracking the divisive issue.

On the significant questions of distribution of powers, the Radicals did their work quietly in committee and rammed the results through the convention. A Conservative occasionally would detect an obvious maneuver, such as when one Independence County delegate likened the creation of new judicial positions "to making new teats to the old sow because some men want to suck them." In the end, any hope Conservatives had of influencing the result was lost. The able and independent-minded black delegate, James W. Mason, expressed his dislike for the finished product, but observed that he had to support the document because Conservatives would not extend civil rights to blacks.

As a document of its time, the new Constitution was unexceptionable in its structure of power, and as one historian has observed, was "well within the Arkansas constitutional tradition." Structurally the document continued the four-year term for the governor, added the office of lieutenant governor and gave extensive powers to the executive, including the appointment of all county officials until the legislature regularized county government.

Framed in the Hamiltonian tradition, the Constitution committed the state to modernization, first by promoting railroads and encouraging manufactures; second, by making a formal mandate to protect blacks, women and the poor; and third, with extensive provisions creating mechanisms for public education.

But as one historian noted, partisanship within the new document was "remarkable." The malapportioned voting districts could not be changed until 1876 despite the census to be taken in 1870. The amendment process was difficult, and voter restrictions were the most repressive of any Southern state. Finally, in what D. Y. Thomas called the "crowning iniquity," three Radicals were put in charge of the entire election machinery.

The new Constitution went to the voters in March. The rallying cry of opposition was "a white man's government in a white man's country," but aside from this slogan, they could not even agree on a name. Some called themselves Democrats; others, from Whig backgrounds, preferred the term Conservatives.

Even a central committee set up to coordinate the defeat could not agree on a name and suffered other divisions as well. Meanwhile, carpetbaggers moved to strengthen their position. A reliably loyal newspaper, the Little Rock *Daily Republican*, projected the radical point of view as the word "Unionist" dropped out of use.

The ratification campaign was heated, but very little discussion about the Constitution itself surfaced. The March vote was mostly a referendum on whether to grant blacks civil rights. Republicans had the foresight to revise the voting lists before the election and control the election machinery. The military refused to accept the radical poll and set up separate machinery that recorded only votes for or against the Constitution. The Republican poll prohibited anyone from voting who would not take the oath contained in the 1868 Constitution, so the Democrat-Conservatives usually voted at the military poll. Because the Republican poll also included voting for state and congressional offices, ex-Confederates had little say in these races.

During the two-week long election, the Democrat-Conservatives used intimidation before the voting while Jonas Tebbetts noted that Republicans stuffed ballot boxes and "voted early and voted often, traveling from ballot-box to ballot-box." The state Board of Election Commissioners announced the ratification of the document by a vote of 30,380 to 41, but when General A. C. Gillem produced the military poll figures, the totals were given as 27,913 for to 26,597 against.

Conservative leader Augustus H. Garland estimated that with an honest count, the Constitution would have been defeated by 20,000 votes. Only counties with sizeable Negro populations approved the Constitution, so that allowing for disfranchisement, the new document met the approval of only about a quarter of the state's population. It was on this narrow and divided basis that the burden of Reconstruction rested.

Elected at the state poll was a ticket of officers and judges headed by Powell Clayton as governor and James M. Johnson as lieutenant governor. Congress accepted the election results over President Johnson's veto, and on June 22, 1868, Arkansas returned to the union of states and military rule ceased. Powell Clayton was inaugurated as governor on July 2. He later recalled that when he arrived for the proceedings dressed to the hilt and sporting white gloves, Murphy looked at the gloves and said, "only dudes wear gloves in summer-time." The abashed Clayton yielded to the homespun Murphy.

After the ceremony, the two men returned to the governor's office, which consisted of a long table case of pigeon holes, two homemade split-bottomed chairs, and a picture of George Washington. Murphy fetched a jug from a barrel in the anteroom and poured them both a drink of the real mountain dew.

The contrast between the two men marked the change from Presidential to Congressional Reconstruction. Whereas Murphy, with long-time ties in the state, had been a subtle politician, Clayton, the army commander, retained the characteristics of a general in charge of a threatened post. Treating the members of his own Party as subordinates whose sole duty was to obey his commands, he led his men into battle under the slogan, "men that do the work shall have the rewards."

The inauguration of Clayton was a stunning blow to the Democrat-Conservatives. An estimated 1,500 carpetbaggers and 23,000 voting blacks were, in essence, in control of the state. The new legislature had but one Democrat in each house and the governor appointed county officials, designated state and county printing contracts and controlled the militia.

The Democrat-Conservative alliance fell further apart. Some Conservatives led by David Walker held that this new government might exist de facto but that it was not established legitimately by law. Refusing to participate further, Walker and his friends struck their flags, and like Achilles, retired to their tents. Albert Pike, who shared their views, abandoned the South, moving to Washington to practice law and divine the higher flights of Masonry. He was joined in the fall of 1868 by a discouraged and financially broken Robert Ward Johnson.

A new generation of leaders appeared on the Arkansas scene and kept up the fight. William E. Woodruff, Jr. summarized their view:

In the present political struggle we believe that the end we seek will justify the use of ANY means. We will not "play honest" with utter scoundrelism, but will use any and every weapon with which providence has gifted us to fight it.

These younger men typically were veterans more inured to the violence of war than the give and take of politics. Reconstruction for them was a continuation of the Civil War.

Voters had chosen three congressmen in the March polling. In eastern Arkansas, carpetbag merchant Logan H. Roots and attorney James Hinds were the winners, and in the west, Thomas Boles of Dardanelle, an Arkansas native and Union army veteran, triumphed. They were not seated until June, and their offices were up for election in the fall.

The first counterattack against Republicans came in the fall. The Democratic Central Committee and its mouthpiece, the *Arkansas Gazette*, urged a full registration with the view of winning the seats. However, Conservatives often refused to participate, thus weakening the opposition. Meanwhile, Republicans were at work creating permanent registration boards to register voters. A vote against the 1868 Constitution in March was to be considered grounds for denying the franchise in future elections. Faced with this threat, the Democrats borrowed a tactic from Tennessee: the Ku Klux Klan. What began as a prank was soon discovered to be an acceptable way to intimidate black voters. This first Klan usually dressed in black with white outlines, and their horses were draped in white. Playing on black superstition, a Klansman disguised as the ghost of a dead soldier would appear to consume endless amounts of water that actually went into a concealed rubber bag. More violent means were used when intimidation failed. By one Republican estimate, 385 Republicans were killed in two years.

Faced with mounting Klan violence, Governor Clayton set aside election returns from eleven counties in the fall congressional election when open warfare erupted in several parts of the state. Republicans had to reestablish law and order before they could proceed with their reform agenda.

Law and Order

Klan violence led Governor Clayton to call out the state militia. Because only voters could be militiamen, Clayton's army consisted typically of black soldiers and white officers. Although minor civil wars erupted in Perry, Conway and Columbia Counties, most of the troubled counties were on the edge of the Delta where small white farmers and blacks met. Pre-war and wartime animosities played a major role in keeping feuds going, sometimes for years after Reconstruction officially had ended.

In Governor Clayton's view, all violence could be traced to the Klan and its Imperial Wizard, General R. G. "Fighting Bob" Shaver. His best proof came from White County, where local black leader Ban Humphries and a white man named Albert H. Parker were assassinated. Clayton had tried to place Parker as a spy in the Searcy Klan, but he was killed and his body was found in a well. One participant in the murders confessed and implicated ex-Confederate Colonel Dandridge McRae and editor Jacob Frolich.

Both men fled the state, returning after Reconstruction to a jubilant acquittal in a trial that Clayton called a farce. This case had statewide ramifications. At the time of the initial investigation, *Gazette* editor William E. Woodruff, Jr. charged Circuit Judge John Whytock with corrupt conduct. Whytock retaliated by fining Woodruff and jailing him in a move that attracted wide publicity because it involved freedom of the press.

According to the information Governor Clayton received and Klan sources supported,

some 15,000 armed Klansmen were awaiting a signal from their leaders to march on Little Rock and depose the governor. Clayton tried desperately to strengthen his position. Four thousand stands of arms were ordered, but the steamer *Hesper* carrying the cargo from Memphis to Little Rock was hijacked and the arms dumped into the River.

Clayton then turned to outsiders. After placing a number of eastern counties under martial law, he called on Colonel William Monks from West Plains, Missouri, to move south into Arkansas. First entering Fulton County, Monk's men, hardened veterans of bushwhacking days, fought skirmish after skirmish with the Klan, all the while filling their wagons with loot from any handy farmhouse.

Monk eventually reached Crittenden County, where his arrival saved a black militia unit besieged in the courthouse at Marion. Casualties of this eastern Arkansas warfare included George W. Parker, an English naval captain shot by the militia at Augusta, and Republican Congressman James Hinds, assassinated on October 22, 1868, by the Klan at Indian Bay.

The killing of a congressman attracted national attention. The *Arkansas Gazette* asserted that Republicans had killed Hinds because he was about to switch sides and join the Klan — a Klan the paper also asserted did not exist. Rumors that editor Woodruff himself ranked high in the state hierarchy of the secret organization cannot be proved but were popularly believed. After Hinds's death, James T. "Jim Tom" Elliott of Camden, a former president of the Mississippi, Ouachita and Red River Railroad, a scalawag, and no friend of Governor Clayton, won the congressional seat.

Republicans claimed victims in retaliation. One was former Confederate General Thomas C. Hindman. In the wake of the Republican victory, all talk of cooperation in Phillips County had disappeared, and Hindman, an old fire-eater politician, was soon pursuing the same style that marked his pre-war career. He was assassinated while sitting with his family on September 29, 1868, and expired after making a speech and asking all to forgive him. Controversy about who killed him was prevalent. The Democratic press claimed that local Republicans were responsible and had paid $800 for the deed. Governor Clayton asserted that family marital trouble lay behind Hindman's death. It also was rumored that his death was the result of a grudge left over from his wartime activities in Arkansas. Years later, a black awaiting execution in Georgia confessed to the crime and indicated it was in retaliation for Klan murders in Phillips County.

Southwestern counties also were hit by violence. Desperado Cullen Baker alone seems to have accounted for twenty-seven murders. The militia and the Klan fought a battle at Centre Point in Howard County after the militia robbed citizens of fodder, mules, clothing and guns. A white woman was raped and officers had the accused man hung. A militia officer later called the operation a success, reporting that the Klan was routed and many of its members fled to Indian Territory. Lewisburg in Conway County was also the scene of a disturbance. Here both Governor Clayton and Conservative leader Augustus H. Garland unsuccessfully made personal appearances to quell the disorder. Conway County's troubles, like those of Perry County, involved too many long-standing animosities for outsiders to handle.

The longer the bloodshed continued, the more complaints grew. Finally, even John G. Price, editor of the *Daily Republican*, ventured to criticize the governor's handling of the problem. Clayton's reaction was swift; Price was removed as Speaker of the House and briefly lost the contracts for public printing. Similar forms of retaliation were practiced against other dissidents within the Party.

Klan violence in the South tested President Ulysses S. Grant's will and found it wanting. Although Republican governors were armed with both state and federal laws, Powell Clayton alone launched a successful counterattack on the Klan and won. After nearly two years of violence, Klan-inspired trouble stopped in 1869. General Nathan B. Forrest, the alleged commander of the national Klan, ordered it and its state affiliates dissolved, stranding thousands of secret supporters who were ready to march on Little Rock.

A compromise had been reached in Arkansas, and on April 6, 1869, the legislature passed a general amnesty act covering both the Klan and the militia. In addition, the legislature provided in 1871 that persons who had lost property from militia confiscations could file claims against the state. Almost twice as many losses were claimed as had been originally estimated, and claim adjustment was for a time a lucrative business in Little Rock. The legislature also appropriated money to rebuild the Catholic church at Centre Point in Howard County that had been burned during the troubles.

The militia war had disrupted life, interfering with agricultural recovery and diverting money that Republicans wanted to spend on modernization. Republicans may have won a victory in disbanding the state Klan, but nothing in the settlement prevented local parties from appropriating Klan regalia and secrecy. Klan-like activities remained a feature of Arkansas life throughout the century, and anti-Klan laws, called night-riding statutes, which forbid going in disguise on the highway, continued to be invoked in the twentieth century and were used as a tool in the modern Civil Rights movement.

Railroads and Republicans

With law and order reestablished, Republicans moved forward with their agenda. One of its major features was railroad construction. Arkansas in 1868 had but one active railroad

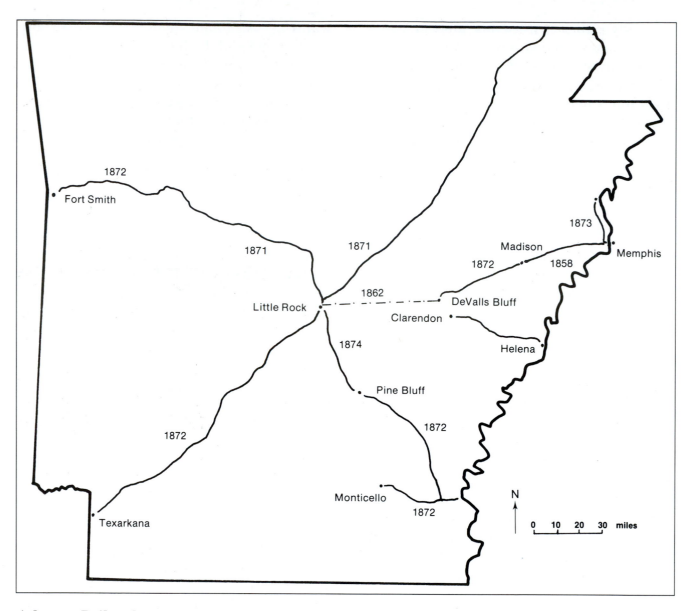

Arkansas Railroads, 1858-1874. **Gerald T. Hanson**

line — the Memphis and Little Rock Railroad, which was still unfinished between the White and St. Francis Rivers. Wartime use without maintenance left the track and the equipment in bad shape. Because economic conditions in Arkansas would not make a railroad profitable for several years, state aid was considered essential to finance the iron horse.

The first railroad aid plan had been passed in 1867 over Governor Murphy's veto. Republicans under Governor Clayton planned to expand on that aid bill. A proposed state bond issue submitted to the voters by the legislature under the title "For Railroads" or "Against Railroads," was approved overwhelmingly. Under the law, a qualifying railroad line could get $10,000 for every mile of track laid and somewhat more if the roadbed doubled as a levee. At the same time, Republicans made plans to pay off the old state debt of $3,363,500, the legacy from the earlier failures of the state banks. Generously (and some said corruptly) included in the funding were the controversial Holford bonds at face value.

In the railroad bonanza that followed, eighty-six companies were formed, proposing to reach every county in the state with their imaginary lines. Leading Republicans usually sat on their boards of directors, making the roads political. From April 1868 to March 1874, $9,000,000 in state bonds financed about 400 miles of track. The most ambitious project, the revived Cairo and Fulton, returned its state aid but still received massive federal assistance.

The Cairo and Fulton Railroad, the darling of the Democrats, got off to a rocky start. One company was chartered in Missouri to build the section from Bird's Point opposite Cairo to the Arkansas line. A second Arkansas-chartered concern would carry the rails to Texas. Roswell Beebe, the first president of the Arkansas section, labored so hard that when he died in New York City in 1856, the words "Cairo and Fulton" were inscribed on his tombstone. Prior to the Civil War, the Arkansas line had completed its survey, and the Missouri branch had twenty-six miles of track in place.

The War ruined the line. After foreclosures and reorganizations, Thomas Allen acquired both the Missouri Branch of the Cairo and Fulton and the St. Louis and Iron Mountain line. Renamed the Cairo, Arkansas and Texas (the "Cat Line"), the road received extensive federal funding, and on February 10, 1873, the section linking Little Rock to Missouri was completed.

Allen's interests were in Missouri, not Illinois, and the Cairo section became less important than the St. Louis connection. The result was that for the next century St. Louis achieved commercial hegemony over much of Arkansas, overpowering Memphis, and yielding only in more recent times to Dallas, Texas.

The first railroad to benefit the state was the Memphis and Little Rock Line completed on April 11, 1871. Even it left something to be desired. Perpetual financial problems plagued the road under a succession of owners, ending with the Chicago and Rock Island and the

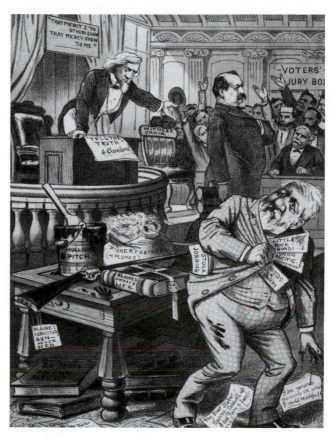

James G. Blaine *(Gillam,* Puck, *1884) Blaine's involvement in Arkansas finance helped cost him the presidency.* **Author's Collection**

twentieth-century bankruptcy of the Rock Island Line. A correspondent for the Cincinnati *Commercial* laid the foundation in 1871 for what became the joke book *Slow Train through Arkansas* thirty years later:

> Some call it the peanut train, others the jerkwater train, and a few refer to the string of slow coffins, as the triweekly train, because they say it goes to Little Rock one week and tries to get back the next.

This run from Memphis to Little Rock crossed the bottoms of the Mississippi, St. Francis, L'Anguille, Cache, and White Rivers before the times of drainage and flood control, so every rain was a potential disaster. In places the track had to be chained to sturdy trees so it would not wash away.

While the Memphis and Little Rock Line opened the middle of the state and the Cairo and Fulton slashed through to the southwest, the Mississippi, Ouachita and Red River Valley Railroad was meeting disaster trying to connect Gaines Landing on the Mississippi to Fulton on the Red River. Begun before the War, this railroad had twenty miles of track in operation by 1862. Refinanced with $600,000 in state aid, the company was defeated by the forces of nature. Workers died or were incapacitated with malaria, and mules suffocated when mosquitoes clogged their nostrils with a welter of blood. The failure of the railroad left southern Arkansas economically isolated and retarded the region's development for years to come.

Nevertheless, Arkansas added 662 miles of railroad track during Republican rule. The cost per mile was not out of proportion with national averages, and one railroad historian concluded that Arkansas was well served by the state program.

Ultimately, the railroads failed to find the traffic necessary to maintain their operations. All companies were in bankruptcy by 1875 and unable to pay the state on bonds that had been issued. The tangled affairs of the Little Rock and Fort Smith, a "little stumptail railroad in a Southern state, which came from nowhere and led no wither," became a national scandal when the "Mulligan letters" revealed that prominent Republican Congressman and presidential hopeful James G. Blaine had engaged in influence peddling in connection with its construction. His subsequent political nickname, "The Continental Liar from the State of Maine," derived from his unsuccessful efforts to clear himself of charges of wrongdoing.

Immigration

A second major Republican objective was to lure immigrants to Arkansas. In addition to the need for more farms and factories, Repub-

licans wanted to use the immigrants to support their Party. While everyone favored immigration in general, just who the immigrants should be became a controversial political question.

Conservatives made a concerted effort to attract Chinese to Arkansas immediately after the War. Spurred by the labor shortage, a group of planters in 1869 organized the Arkansas River Valley Immigration Company and brought 189 Chinese laborers to work in cotton fields. The Chinese had been used successfully in building western railroads, and they were considered to be immune to malaria. Blacks resented the competition, and the company collapsed, but Delta Chinese remained a feature of Arkansas life, most typically as owners of grocery stores.

Republicans sought immigrants primarily from two sources. First, to assuage black sensibilities, Arkansas was promoted as a suitable haven for blacks fleeing worn-out plantation lands to the east. White planters also shared an interest in this endeavor, frequently making trips to Tennessee or Mississippi to recruit new blacks for Arkansas plantations. Second, efforts to lure the foreign-born and Northerners into the state culminated in 1868 with the creation of the Commission of Immigration and State Lands headed by Massachusetts native James M. Lewis. The Commission collected statistics on Arkansas resources and advertised the availability of cheap land. In 1872, James P. Henry's *Resources of the State of Arkansas, With Description of Counties, Railroads, Mines, and the City of Little Rock, the Commercial, Manufacturing, Political and Railroad Center of the State*, promised a bonanza for the prospective settler.

Land was the main incentive. Arkansas had state lands available under a variety of laws. Internal improvement and saline lands sold for $1.25 an acre, seminary lands at $2 an acre and swamp lands at 50 and 75 cents an acre. The passage by Congress of the

Homestead Act of 1862 and its post-war extension to Arkansas even meant that one could acquire land without payment. Finally, large federal grants to the Cairo and Fulton and the Little Rock and Fort Smith Railroads put private companies in the land promotion business.

The immigration boom became noticeable by 1869. The Pine Bluff *Republican* exclaimed:

> Immigrants by the hundreds are daily passing through Pine Bluff. From present appearances Arkansas will receive no less than an additional 10,000 souls to her population this winter and the coming spring. The people in the old states are beginning to find out the vast advantages offered by our State, and are flocking to us by the hundreds.

Even remote counties were affected. Federal veterans settled Union Mountain in Carroll County, and it was reported that "a large immigration is taking place to Montgomery and as a consequence, Mount Ida, Harold and Centreville are all receiving increased prosperity."

Most immigrants came from the traditional supplying states of Missouri, Tennessee, Kentucky, Mississippi, Alabama and Georgia. This was good news for Democrats, for as the *Arkansas Gazette,* in referring to these immigrants from other Southern states commented, "Much is conceded to the enterprise of the people of states farther north; but for true economy and the substantial developments of the material interests of an agricultural country there is [sic] no better citizens in the world." Unfortunately, many were only passing through or stayed but a short time. Texas continued to be the mecca of the Southwest, and as political violence in Arkansas grew in intensity, even established citizens felt the Lone Star State was safer.

Contributing to Arkansas's relatively poor ranking was literature on Southern states from private sources. Journalist Edward King wrote his impressions in a series of articles for *Scribner's*, a popular magazine, and these articles were later collected in book form as *The Great South*. The rough and tumble world described in the river towns evoked negative images of violence.

Foreigners relied extensively on printed matter for information about the state. Germans, a much sought after immigrant group, received more favorable literature printed by the state. The St. Louis and Iron Mountain Railroad, the successor to the Cairo and Fulton, had a land commissioner, G.A.A. Deane, whose *Scenes in Arkansas* tried to popularize railroad land holdings. One critic called it "an extravagant description of the wonders of Arkansas. Not a mosquito nor swamp is in sight." A German translation appeared, and a large proportion of German settlers in Arkansas after the Civil War located along the St. Louis and Iron Mountain's routes. One of the illustrations entitled "Happy Little Arkansas Coons" showed young blacks eating watermelon. Blacks, Deane noted, were "generally happy, contented, well fed and furnish good available laborers." Black sensitivity to this type of promotion was manifested when W.H. Gray, an able black politician from Phillips County, succeeded Lewis as Immigration and State Lands Commissioner.

Immigration failed to fulfill Republican hopes during the Reconstruction years. Only Germans came in any numbers, and settlement initially was limited to Little Rock, where a pre-war enclave already existed. A social club, the *Turn Verein*, was organized in 1867 and remained active throughout the century. A German language newspaper had a brief existence, and the German National Bank became one of Arkansas's leading financial institutions for nearly fifty years. Yet in rural areas, German immigrants, especially Catholics, encountered difficulties. In Franklin

County, Protestants interfered with wine-making, and a large armed group arrived at a Sunday mass because of a rumor that Catholics sacrificed children. It was not until after Reconstruction that Subiaco, a Benedictine monastery located in Logan County, became the leading rural center for the state's German Catholics. Thus in immigration, as in other areas, Republicans planted seeds that others harvested and got the credit.

Education

Education served a twofold purpose in Republican thought. First, it would lead to participation in full citizenship and economic opportunity by blacks. Once blacks were educated, the usual racist objections to their political participation would be eliminated and integration into Arkansas life would follow. Second, Republicans believed that racism and loyalty to the Democratic Party by native whites resulted from ignorance; education was the means whereby white Arkansans would become Americans of Republican persuasion. The Republican education program became a crusade, and these Christian soldiers of the education aroused animosities that added to Reconstruction struggles.

Education in Reconstruction Arkansas was defined by color from the beginning. Northern missionaries connected with the Indiana Friends and the American Missionary Association ministered to the educational needs of freedmen even during the Civil War. The first teachers arrived in 1863. Armed with *McGuffey's First Reader*, they opened their doors to all ages and taught Sabbath schools as well.

Because of the extent of the need, the Indiana Yearly Meeting of Friends assisted Little Rock and Helena schools while the American Missionary Association supported the Pine Bluff effort. Blacks were encouraged to provide financial assistance to make the schools self-supporting. Thousands of students of all ages flocked to these schools as even aged grandmothers labored over letters of the alphabet as if this alone would open wide the doors of opportunity.

Arkansas by 1867 had nineteen day and five night schools taught by twenty-six white and three black teachers. Two industrial schools offered classes in sewing and housework and seven schools were sustained entirely by blacks. Thirteen whites sat beside the 1,296 black pupils, making this the first integrated education in Arkansas.

White public education was not organized until after the Civil War when in 1866, the legislature passed a law providing tax support for schools open only to whites. Radicals demanded a change in this policy at the Constitutional Convention of 1868. W. H. Gray blamed Southern problems on the lack of education and offered the hope that with learning, racial prejudice would "vanish like the hapless fabric of a dream." In an eloquent plea, he urged:

> Give us the right of suffrage; establish a
> school system that will give us
> opportunities to educate our children;
> leave ajar the door that leads to peace
> and power; and if by the next generation
> we do not place ourselves beyond the
> reach of moral man, why, then take
> them away from us if not exercised
> properly.

In order to get broad support for education, black leaders did not make an issue of integration in return for adequate funding of black schools.

The 1868 legislature enacted a modern, centralized system into law. A state superintendent who supervised ten circuit superintendents was responsible for licensing teachers, conducting training institutes, apportioning funds and inspecting schools. Teachers were recruited from the North and from the existing black schools that were taken into the system.

Begun in 1869 as Klan violence was mounting, the system got off to a rocky start. A hostile Arkadelphia paper called the Clark County system poor, the teachers incompetent, the classrooms overcrowded and the school taxes too high. The paper then defended private instruction as the best and safest method of education. Clark County schools remained a battleground featuring a disputed election, troubles over tax collection and reports that officials embezzled funds by reporting incorrectly the number of students.

The high water mark of Reconstruction education was 1870, when 88,585 white and 19,280 black pupils were enrolled from a total school age population of 180,274. State teachers organized their association in 1869, and the next year the *Arkansas Journal of Education* began publication with aid from the Peabody Fund. The great need for education was reflected in the literacy information on the 1869 voter registration lists, which showed that of the 44,832 white voters, 13,365, or almost 30 percent, were illiterate, and among blacks, 18,989 out of 19,142 voters could not write their names.

The school system was in trouble by 1871, hit by over-spending on a limited tax base, the failure of railroads to achieve immediate economic growth, the drop in the international price of cotton and the beginning of a national economic downturn. State, county and city authorities issued scrip to finance schools. When these were made payable for taxes by state Supreme Court action, hard money disappeared from the treasuries, leaving teachers with devalued paper often worth only 39 to 70 cents on the dollar.

Both state superintendents worked hard for the system, but the first, Dr. Thomas Smith, fell afoul of Governor Clayton, and the second, the Ohio-educated black, J.C. Corbin, found the downward spiral impossible to stop. The end of Reconstruction marked the virtual disappearance of public education. In 1876, 15,890 students were enrolled, only 15 percent of those in school six years earlier. Black schools were especially hard hit by what one missionary called the "starvation plan" of financing.

The rapid rise and fall of public education was not paralleled in higher education. Although the state had been given federal lands in 1836 to fund a seminary of learning, Arkansas had refused to act. The 1868 legislature permitted localities to bid for the privilege of having a state-supported university, and Fayetteville outbid Batesville to become the home of "Arkansas Industrial University." The founding was timely; without it, Arkansas would have lost all federal aid. Some delay took place because unsympathetic officials in Washington thought the state's indebtedness to the federal government should have been paid before Arkansas received federal assistance.

The location of the school in the northwest was a mixed blessing. The advantage was that it was far away from the political rings so prevalent in Little Rock and was located in the most educated community in Arkansas. By being far removed from a large concentration of black population, the school did not have to confront the race question. An early black applicant was admitted and taught privately by the college president. One disadvantage of the Fayetteville location was that state sectionalism resulted in only legislators from the northwest voting for the school's funding. In the school's early years, county and city aid was at least as significant as state support. Another problem was that Fayetteville was almost inaccessible for many students in the southern and eastern areas of the state.

The race question in higher education remained unresolved during Reconstruction. Teacher training at normal schools was needed so that blacks could replace missionary teachers. The American Missionary Association began work with black teachers in Pine Bluff in 1870 and continued for six years. Without black high schools, most instruction was preparatory, but this was true of all Arkansas institutions during the nineteenth century. Believing that blacks were entitled to some aid from the state, black politicians during Reconstruction unsuccessfully urged the creation of a normal school convenient to the Delta.

Arkansas Republicans virtually created public education and demonstrated what an educational system ought to be during Reconstruction. White Arkansans of Confederate leaning refused to accept their work and objected to its centralized features. Although local education was revived later in the century, the objectives of state supervision, uniform standards and equality of opportunity have remained missing from the state's educational history until recently.

Other Republican Accomplishments

In addition to encouraging railroads, immigration and education, Republicans also passed a strong civil rights act modeled on similar laws enacted by Congress. It imposed severe penalties on those who tried to discriminate against blacks in public transportation or facilities. Only occasionally enforced even in the Republican heyday, these laws would reappear in American life a century later. Another reform was the establishment of the Code of Practice in Civil and Criminal Cases, which brought Arkansas in line with other states in ending the old common law pleading system with its emphasis on pettifogging technicalities. The establishment of the Arkansas Deaf Mute Institute and the reestablishment in Little Rock of the School for the Blind marked a commitment to help the less fortunate. The state continued its commitment to levee construction and funded drainage and railroads through state bond issues. Finally, a general incorporation law removed the necessity for the legislature to examine each application to form a company.

Reconstruction in the Counties

Republican control of the state rested on a reciprocal relationship between state and county government. Local Republicans were expected to protect blacks, carry all elections at whatever cost to honesty and fill every patronage job from school teacher to the county printer with friends of the government. In return, the ever recurring charges of election fraud would not be investigated by grand juries or would not be prosecuted if indictments were issued. Thus, a new courthouse machine took over with the county judge as its main cog. The 1868 Constitution did not indicate how county government was to be constituted or whether county judges were to be appointed or elected. Some peculiar situations developed as a result. In Arkansas County, Buford C. Hubbard was elected county surveyor but did not receive his commission. He journeyed to Little Rock to look into the matter and came back holding a commission as county judge. A near state of war existed in Chicot County between the followers of James W. Mason and Major B.B. Ragland as both men maneuvered in Little Rock with the legislature and the governor.

Power was cemented in a variety of ways. County printing of legal notices, the costs of which rose substantially, was given to Republican newspapers and so insured their survival. Because the War had destroyed many public buildings, new courthouses and jails were built, sometimes at fraudulently inflated prices. Elections were particularly dishonest. No whites were registered in Clark County if they were known to oppose the 1868 Constitution, and it was estimated that only one white male out of ten was permitted to vote there. Even so, out of 2,011 registered voters, 2,143 votes were cast in the 1870 election. A grand jury called to investigate charges of fraud was dismissed by Circuit Judge Elhanan J. Searle, and the Democratic editor who criticized the judge was promptly jailed four days for contempt of court. A Pope County editor who protested against political conditions suffered a similar fate, and in Camden, federal soldiers led by one of their officers smashed the press of Anson W. Hobson.

Rising taxes caused many protests. Collectively, Reconstruction counties spent more than $1,000,000, almost all of it raised from property taxes. Before the War, the property tax rate was assessed at one half of 1 percent for the state and 1 percent for the counties. The rate continued unchanged immediately after the War on an 1866 total state valuation of $35,723,449. During Reconstruction, however, state government expenses rose from about $100,000 to about $800,000, and county spending kept pace. Taxes on an unimproved half section in Arkansas County went from $2.40 to $29.70.

Such increases were by no means universal, and Democrats often overstated the problem for partisan purposes. One Georgia speculator who acquired a section of Jefferson County land before the War paid $12 in taxes in 1859, $23.52 in 1869, and $15.04 in 1870. The myth that high taxes ruined planters was useful to Democrats but hardly true. By one estimate, the tax rate jumped from six mills to forty, but as the counties issued scrip to cover their rising deficits and the scrip could be redeemed for taxes, landowners could pay their taxes in depreciated paper often worth as little as 10 cents on the dollar. Awash in seas of paper, Republicans failed to provide a stable financial basis for public services.

Republicans used their control of the legislature to create new counties for political purposes. Of the sixteen counties created, most were in the southern and eastern parts of the state. Three — Sarber, Dorsey and Clayton — subsequently were renamed by Democrats as Logan, Cleveland and Clay. Lee County, named for Confederate General Robert E. Lee, was the political creation of black legislator W. H. Gray. Stopping county creation at seventy-five with Cleburne County in 1884 demonstrated remarkable restraint, for Georgia inflicted 169 counties on taxpayers. Although most name changing was done by Democrats after Reconstruction, at least one Republican example exists: Searcy County repudiated its founder, secessionist N. B. Burrow, by changing Burrowville to Marshall, named in honor of Chief Justice John Marshall.

Reconstruction in the Towns

Disfranchisement also altered the power structure in town. Mechanics and laborers as well as merchants had been reluctant Confederates, and many had escaped military service. In addition, federal troops remained or took up positions immediately after the War at prominent points such as Washington, Batesville, Fort Smith, Camden and others. Little Rock was under military rule until the War's end when civilians regained control. All towns had to apply for reincorporation after the adoption of the Constitution of 1868. Republicans took charge, notably in Little Rock, where A.K. Hartman, a heavy-set German known as "Count Bismarck," became the first city boss in Arkansas.

As with Republicans generally, modernization was a main theme in town politics. In their desire to rid Little Rock streets of loose pigs and evil-tempered milk cows, Republicans pushed progressive laws. Efforts were made to control Town Branch, a source of flooding and an open sewer. Street improvements were considered so necessary that Little Rock went into debt largely from financing them.

Town politics pitted the newcomers allied with blacks against "old settlers." The stage at one political rally contained a Democratic rooster united with an old Whig coon, but the Republican elephant proved briefly triumphant. Because towns had acquired larger black populations during the War, black votes were the key to Republican strength. Instead of appealing to blacks, the Democrat-Conservatives made political and physical war on them. One campaign jingle ran:

The radicals love ebony and colors dark or light, For me my tastes are simple; so I'm satisfied with white.

The local paper in DeWitt asserted that white boys spent Sundays "jumping, running and throwing brick bats at little 'niggers.'" Similar episodes occurred in Little Rock, where the authorities tried to prevent such violence.

The schisms that divided Republicans on state issues surfaced in city politics as well. Little Rock Republicans divided into Radicals and Liberals, with the former winning all the elections and causing the Liberals to form a "Citizens" coalition with Democrats in an unsuccessful 1873 campaign. Radicals allotted half the city council seats to blacks, and blacks became members of the city police force. Yet, just as debts overwhelmed state and county officials, so did rising city taxes in Little Rock fail to pay a debt of nearly half a million dollars, hastening the end of the Republican regime.

The Politics of Collapse

The Republican coalition suffered internal divisions from the start. The old Union men of the northwest resented being passed over, and their hostility grew as railroad grants, state and county offices and state contracts went to carpetbaggers. Another aggrieved party was Joseph Brooks, who had been denied major office after manfully marshaling the black vote to adopt the Constitution of 1868. An idealist before, he had a personal pique to sharpen his brindle-tail oratory after 1869.

Brooks and the old Union men generally articulated the same issues: Government had become too expensive because of wasteful laws and practices; the calling out of the militia was not only expensive but had failed to

resolve the law and order problem and there was corruption in the refunding of state debt and railroad construction. Brooks began his rebellion in late 1868, and by the beginning of the new year, the *Daily Republican* demanded that he be purged from the Party.

The second move came from Lieutenant Governor James M. Johnson, who met with a group of supporters in April 1869 to organize resistance to the Clayton regime. Johnson got the chance to do even more when Clayton left the state for New York to arrange financing of the state debt. As lieutenant governor, Johnson should have been notified and left in charge, but Clayton did not publicize his departure, no doubt fearing what Johnson might do in office. When Johnson heard the news of the governor's departure, he set out from Fayetteville for the capital, intent on seizing power. Clayton, forewarned of Johnson's purpose, rushed back from New York and reached Little Rock before Johnson arrived. In retaliation, Clayton had the courts begin quo warranto proceedings to remove Johnson from office.

As open hostilities between Clayton and Johnson divided scalawags from carpetbaggers, some national Republicans became increasingly restive under the corrupt and incompetent administration of President Ulysses S. Grant. Adopting the name Liberal Republicans, they demanded a return to the idealism of the early Party and to the values of honesty and economy that seemed to have vanished in a post-war orgy of fraud. In Arkansas, a group composed mostly of scalawags associated with Johnson met in Little Rock on October 14, 1869, and created a state organization. Its views were articulated by a paper entitled the *Liberal*, edited by veteran newsman Thomas C. Peek.

The popularity of the movement among state Republicans and the danger of a possible alliance with the Democrat-Conservatives was not lost on Powell Clayton. The day after the Liberal meeting, Clayton appropriated their platform wholesale, calling for economy in government, a reduction in taxes and the removal of legal disabilities from ex-Confederates. Clayton's new stance resulted in the Liberals, the Clayton supporters (called Minstrels in derogatory reference to the early career of *Daily Republican* editor J. G. Price) and even Democrat-Conservative orators all saying the same things. The deciding issue became the personality of candidates, and Arkansas politics began to develop on this familiar line.

Liberal Republicanism proved to have little sustaining power. The scalawag Johnson supporters diminished in importance as Joseph Brooks's Brindletails emerged around his magnetic personality. As Republicans were splitting, ex-Confederates remained divided between Democrats and Conservatives, who fought among themselves.

The first major crack in Republican control came in 1870, when elections were held for both the legislature and the three congressional districts. Clayton successfully imposed his discipline on county organizations and insured a safe legislature, but he had less luck with congressional candidates. At one point, Liberals temporarily controlled a meeting of the State Central Committee and used it to endorse a slate of Liberal Republicans hostile to Clayton.

In an election accompanied by much fraud, John M. Hanks, a native of Helena and an early Republican, won as a Democrat. Oliver P. Snyder, a Pine Bluff lawyer, won in the central region, and the western district race ended in a contested election. The incumbent, Thomas Boles, had been opposed by the Liberal, John Edwards. Clayton certified Edwards, but Boles successfully protested the election to Congress and regained his seat. Claiming that Clayton had certified Edwards illegally, United States Marshal R. F. Catterson arrested the governor on September 3, 1871. The court failed to convict him, and Clayton took his revenge by getting

Catterson and a long list of his enemies removed from federal office.

In the aftermath of the 1870 election, the Democrat-Conservatives reemerged as a force in the legislature with eight senators and twenty-nine representatives. Liberals, with nine representatives, had failed to capture the Party from Clayton but were in a position to embarrass him. Meanwhile, the *Daily Republican*, hailing the election as a mandate, promised "to continue its march of progress and prosperity" and move to "fulfill its pledges of retrenchment and reform of all abuse."

Powell Clayton, having learned from the recent election the insecurity of his gubernatorial position, decided to seek a seat in the United States Senate. The first Republican legislature in 1868 had sent banker Alexander McDonald and merchant B. F. Rice to Washington. The two carpetbaggers had successfully promoted their own financial interests; McDonald with his bank and as vice president of the Little Rock and Fort Smith Railroad, and Rice as a member of the syndicate owning the Cairo and Fulton. Neither man evidenced much political skill or commanded a statewide following. When McDonald's term expired, few Republicans opposed Clayton's bid. Ironically, many Democrat-Conservatives welcomed the idea, and on January 10, 1871, they joined Republicans to elect Clayton to the Senate, reasoning that James M. Johnson would succeed Clayton, and in a flash, all the works of the Minstrels would be overthrown. Clayton recognized his error and refused to accept the seat until he could complete a friendly rearrangement of state government.

Virtually the entire state government was reshuffled by early 1871. John McClure succeeded W. W. Wilshire as chief justice and two new associate justices were appointed. The quo warranto proceedings against Johnson were revived, and in retaliation the Liberals and Democrats in the House voted to impeach the governor. A compromise, doubtless involving an exchange of money, resolved the problem in the end. Johnson resigned as lieutenant governor but accepted appointment as secretary of state. Johnson's departure left Ozra A. Hadley, a colorless functionary and president of the Senate, as Clayton's successor when he at last accepted the position of United States Senator on March 17, 1871.

Clayton's removal to Washington had two effects. First, he dictated all federal patronage appointments from his new position of power. So well did he do this work that he remained the state's leading Republican long after his term expired, dispensing federal patronage under Republican presidents almost until his death in 1914, and even while serving as Ambassador to Mexico. Second, the shady way in which Johnson had allowed himself to be bought off destroyed his political career, leaving the northwest with no significant political leaders. Old-timers such as Jonas Tebbetts and William Fishback had begun drifting back to the Conservatives or switching to the Democrats. Internal opposition to the Minstrels did not die, but it concentrated increasingly on Joseph Brooks and his Brindletail faction.

Brooks began his campaign for governor in May 1871 under the appealing slogan of "Universal suffrage, universal amnesty and honest men in office." A passionate exponent of civil rights, Brooks was able to keep black loyalties while at the same time appealing to disfranchised ex-Confederates. Democrats responded, and rather than nominate a ticket of their own, they endorsed Brooks and were given three positions on his slate. The Conservative remnant rejected this policy and again splintered the opposition. Liberal Republicans, unable to gain sufficient concessions from Brooks, nominated Reverend Andrew Hunter, a popular Methodist minister who had been a nominee in 1866 for the United States Senate before declining that honor. After Liberals announced Hunter's candidacy, the Democratic Central Committee advised Party members

to desert Brooks for Hunter, but Hunter broke the bubble by declining to run, greatly embarrassing the Democrats who had quickly switched from Brooks.

Despite the problems in presenting a united front, the insurgents presented such a challenge that when the Minstrels met in convention, they dropped the carpetbagger Hadley and substituted the old scalawag Elisha Baxter, who had been quietly serving as a circuit judge. They promised the same reform, honesty and progress as did Brooks.

The November 1872 election was a masterpiece of confusion. That carpetbagger Brooks ran with Democratic and scalawag support against a scalawag nominated by a Party composed almost exclusively of carpetbaggers was enough to bewilder most voters as well as the modern student. Doctrinaire Conservatives refused to vote at all, and others weighed the advantages and disadvantages both in terms of issues and personalities. Baxter, a rather timid individual, relied heavily on regular Republican control of election machinery; Brooks, the powerful orator, told voters in all parts of the state such tales of woe about state government as to excite a large popular following.

Election day, November 5, 1872, reflected rather poorly on the democratic process. No returns at all came from four counties, and fraud, violence, intimidation, and multiple voting were the order of the day. According to the Minstrels, Baxter won by 2,919 votes, the legislature was safe and Arkansas gave its electoral votes to Ulysses S. Grant, but fanatical Brooks supporters refused to accept the results.

The first legal action came when the Minstrel-certified congressmen attempted to present their credentials in Washington. Lucien C. Gause appeared to challenge Asa Hodges; Marcus L. Bell opposed Oliver P. Snyder and William W. Wilshire drew an attack from Thomas M. Gunter. The House eventually seated Gunter despite Clayton's wire-pulling from the Senate. As for Brooks, his legal remedy under the Constitution of 1868 was to apply to the legislature — the Minstrel-certified legislature.

Promising to be "conservative, honest, just and upright," Baxter took office on January 6, 1873. The legislature refused to give Brooks a hearing while Baxter attempted to undermine his enemy's position by promising new policies and appointing Democrats, Conservatives and Liberals to office. Yet every step Baxter took to conciliate the opposition weakened him within his own faction.

The first break came between Governor Baxter and state Supreme Court Chief Justice John McClure. After the legislature rejected Brooks's appeal, McClure used his influence to have quo warranto proceedings begun against Baxter. However, McClure's move was taken without approval from other Minstrel leaders. The new senator, Stephen F. Dorsey, together with Senator Clayton, rallied behind the governor and the Court rejected McClure's ploy. But neither man approved of Baxter's choice of ex-Confederate Colonel Robert Newton to head the state militia, or the selection of the *Arkansas Gazette* over McClure's *Daily Republican* for the official printing.

Even so, Baxter's position remained secure until March 16, 1874, when Baxter denied a funding request in his official capacity from the Arkansas Central Railroad, a concern whose prime mover was Senator Dorsey. In addition, although Baxter had signed $300,000 in bonds since assuming office, he now questioned whether the approval of any of the bond issues was constitutional. The entire Republican financial scheme for reconstructing Arkansas was threatened with destruction by this announcement.

Reaction was swift and predictable. The Party central committee met three days later as Senators Dorsey and Clayton rushed in from Washington. A plan to replace Baxter with Brooks through the acquiescence of President Grant came out of the meeting.

Elisha Baxter *(artist unknown, Leslie's, 1874) Baxter's portrait fails to convey any of the emotion involved in the Brooks-Baxter War.* **University of Arkansas at Little Rock**

The Brooks-Baxter War

Pulaski County Circuit Judge John Whytock, a minor Clayton functionary, had been sitting on the case of *Brooks* v. *Baxter* since the preceding June. As soon as an agreement between Clayton and Brooks was reached, Whytock gave his decision in favor of Brooks without even informing Baxter's attorney. Chief Justice John McClure, who had sworn the oath of office to Baxter only a year and three months earlier, now swore in Brooks. Thus on April 15, while Baxter sat in his office at the State House, Brooks, supported by what Baxter called "an armed force of a dozen or twenty," gave him the alternative of forcible and unseemly objection, or of such arrest and punishment as he might see fit to inflict." The timid Baxter chose to leave and the Brooks-Baxter War began.

Reinforcements for Brooks *(artist unknown, Leslie's, 1874.) This view shows troops headed across the Arkansas River toward the State House. This building is now a museum known as the Old State House.* **University of Arkansas at Little Rock**

Baxter took up residence at the Anthony House down the street, and Little Rock's Main Street became the front line of a fracas somewhat less serious than a war but more serious and bloody than a farce.

The political maneuvers through which Brooks obtained the governor's office did much to erode Democratic-Conservative support. Accordingly, a number of the old guard hastened to support Baxter. Among them were Augustus H. Garland, who had been out of politics trying to recoup his financial position; U.M. Rose, the acknowledged leader of the Arkansas bar and from Washington, Robert W. Johnson and Albert Pike. But other Democrat-Conservatives, who had claimed all along that Brooks was the legitimate governor, continued their support, including the pro-Brooks members of the congressional delegation.

Meanwhile, Little Rock became a battleground. The Anthony House was the capitol for Baxter men, and Main Street was the dividing line. Both sides formed armed bands of "militia" with ex-Confederate Brigadier General James F. Fagan commanding the Brooks forces and ex-Confederate Colonel Robert C. Newton the Baxter contingent. The Little Rock postmaster dealt with the dual governor problem by delivering Baxter's mail to Baxter, Brooks's mail to Brooks, and simply holding all letters addressed to "The Governor of Arkansas." Violence erupted around the state, and in Little Rock, the mayor asked for federal troops to protect citizens.

Both sides were woefully short of supplies and weapons. The Brooks forces managed to increase their supply by importing arms in cases marked "whiskey" and "Arkansas State

Embarking Troops at Pine Bluff (*artist unknown,* Leslie's, *1874*) *Colonel H. King White raised a force of about 300 blacks, and together with the mayor and other Pine Bluff officials and a brass band, they reinforced Baxter's forces in Little Rock. Note how the Arkansas River had moved perilously close to the business district.* **University of Arkansas at Little Rock**

Reports," but a gathering of Brooks supporters in Jefferson County near New Gascony was routed by Baxter men who arrived on the captured steamer *Hallie*. Overall, some 200 persons were killed in scattered disturbances, including some innocent bystanders in Little Rock caught between the lines when gunfire erupted. Doubtless many echoed the sentiments of black Lee County Sheriff W. H. Forbush, who telegraphed the president:

> We do not care — and I speak the sentiments of the people of Arkansas without egotism — who is governor: all we want is peace. The people will obey. Answer.

But President Grant did not answer.

Each governor advanced logical arguments to support his position. Baxter could point to the president's earlier promise to sustain him in office and to the state Constitution that made the legislature and not the courts the custodian of disputed elections. The state Supreme Court had itself repudiated McClure's earlier attempt to do what, in effect, Whytock had ruled. For Brooks, the appeal to Grant for support rested on the obvious voting fraud that put Baxter in office and denied legislative relief to Brooks. Courts existed to protect persons in their legal rights, and Judge Whytock's decision simply fulfilled the law.

The situation was complicated for President Grant by the obviously unRepublican direction Baxter was taking, the partisan opposition to Baxter from two senators and a portion of the congressional delegation, and by the President's greater involvement in the more important and more complicated affairs in Louisiana where a similar imbroglio existed. Thus Grant hesitated, hoping for compromise but prolonging the agony.

One of Grant's proposals was for both governors to summon the legislature and put the question to it anew. Apparently a compromise along these lines was worked out in Washington, but Brooks rejected it in Little Rock, refusing to recognize the Baxter regime. Baxter went ahead, and on May 13, the old legislature reassembled and set June 30 for the holding of an election to decide whether to adopt a new constitution. Because the main issue was the extension of the franchise to ex-Confederates, this vote was in effect a referendum on the Republican Party. The following day, Grant, convinced of the depth of Baxter's support, telegraphed his support and ordered Brooks to disband his forces. Brooks was rewarded with appointment as Little Rock postmaster as the Democratic-Conservative coalition, with Baxter as its decoy, assumed control of the affairs of state.

The election of June 30, 1874, under the seventh different voter registration system since 1867, was a foregone conclusion: 80,250 votes were cast for summoning a convention to only 8,607 against it. Most Republicans stayed home, and in Washington, the holdover senators were working to get congressional intervention to restore the Republicans to power. The drafting of the new Constitution in the summer and its subsequent adoption, the formation of a new government headed by ex-Confederate Augustus H. Garland and the reorganization of the counties depended on a final vote in Congress on the report of the visiting Poland committee. That group, headed by Congressman Luke P. Poland of Vermont, toured Arkansas in the summer of 1874 and gathered testimony. A majority of the five members accepted the new order while the minority report emphasized that Brooks had been robbed unjustly of his office and should be considered the governor of Arkansas.

Meanwhile, President Grant had second thoughts and urged adoption of the minority report. When former Lieutenant Governor Volney Voltaire Smith made a brief move to establish a government in exile, Arkansas

Governor A.H. Garland proclaimed him a traitor, and President Grant eventually removed Smith to a Caribbean diplomatic post. Congress accepted the majority report on March 2, 1875.

Reconstruction was officially over, and Senator Clayton advised his followers that, "the validity of the new constitution and the government established thereunder ought no longer to be questioned."

CONCLUSION

The opprobrium heaped upon Republicans continued for the next fifty years. Gubernatorial candidate Jeff Davis in 1900 was still villifying Powell Clayton, whose portrait alone among all the governors of Arkansas remained absent from the state capitol until 1978. When state histories were written, Republicans were cast as stage villains in a fifth-rate melodrama: the scalawags as local opportunists who betrayed white solidarity and carpetbaggers as unprincipled outsiders who enriched themselves and moved away. Such stereotypes became so established that although scholars abandoned this point of view in the twentieth century, most Arkansas history textbooks and teachers did not.

Not only were the stereotypes factually inaccurate, but they also misrepresented Republican activity after Reconstruction. A number of scalawags continued to hold office and enjoy the respect of their local communities. One, William Fishback, was even elected governor. Not all carpetbaggers left the state. Powell Clayton was one of the promoters of Eureka Springs, where his name appears on the monument inside the massive Crescent Hotel along with that of Logan H. Roots. A former congressman and federal marshal, Roots bought his way into leading social circles as a Little Rock banker. Joseph Brooks died shortly after the Brooks-Baxter War, but his daughter, Ida, was the first woman president of the state teachers asso-

ciation. She later was one of the first women doctors, the first clinically trained psychiatrist in Arkansas and the first woman to be nominated for statewide office.

Even those who departed did not sink into obscurity. Thomas Bowen, who left Arkansas penniless, served as territorial governor of Idaho and then moved to Colorado, where he was elected to the United States Senate. Stephen F. Dorsey, although indicted for his participation in the Star Route postal frauds, engaged in mining and ranching in Colorado. Benjamin F. Rice and Alexander McDonald pursued important industrial careers.

The Republicans held what the twentieth century came to consider as enlightened views: that all Americans should be equal before the law regardless of race and that the main purpose of government was to promote the general welfare through education, economic development and the maintenance of law and order. The problem with Reconstruction Republicans was that in attempting to achieve these goals, they violated the fundamental principles of American government — due process and equal protection of the law and denied ex-Confederates the privileges and immunities of citizenship.

However worthy their goals, Reconstruction Republicans were sometimes dishonest in their methods. For the sake of Party, leading men tolerated, then embraced and finally practiced graft, fraud, bribery, embezzlement and other dishonesty. Corruption became a national scandal in the case of the federal district court at Fort Smith under Judge William Story. In the end, the lack of moral principle destroyed what small hope they might have had of building a popular Party.

The Republican excuse was that conditions in Arkansas required extraordinary measures. The Democratic-Conservative opposition often acted as if the Civil War had not been lost, that slaves were not free and that the Thirteenth, Fourteenth and Fifteenth Amendments to the

United States Constitution had not been adopted. They utterly failed to head the eloquent plea of W.H. Gray that blacks required the right to vote and education to become full partners in Southern society. Furthermore, their modus operandi — that the ends justified the means — led to the violence of the Ku Klux Klan and the abandonment of morality in politics. To justify the results, one said:

> I freely admit that we were as ready to
> swindle them as they were us, but we
> did it for the good of the people and they
> for themselves.

This proved to be historically inaccurate as the numerous frauds committed by post-1874 officials amply demonstrated.

In all, it was not an age for men of good will either in Arkansas or elsewhere. Newspapers on both sides fabricated stories with regularity, editors blandly denied truths commonly known and violence seemed at the end of every argument. Not surprisingly, one Crittenden County woman remembered Reconstruction as a much harder time than the Civil War. In many ways, it was simply the War's extension.

BIBLIOGRAPHIC ESSAY

The Reconstruction historiography of Arkansas begins with Thomas S. Staples, *Reconstruction in Arkansas, 1862-1874,* (New York, 1923). A student of Professor William A. Dunning at Columbia University, Staples wrote the history of Reconstruction from the Democrat-Conservative point of view, although he made little effort to interpret the material. Another Columbia University product eventually published in book form is Thompson, *Arkansas and Reconstruction: The Influence of Geography, Economics, and Personality,* which focuses primarily on the Conservatives and their reactions to the Reconstruction process. No modern examination of

the material in light of regional and national reinterpretations has been attempted for Arkansas.

Of the participants involved, only Powell Clayton, *The Aftermath of the Civil War in Arkansas,* (New York, 1915) wrote an extensive memoir. Mostly an attack on the Democrats, his book did avail itself of some of the documentary evidence, and he denied killing Jeff Davis's aunt. Even so, the animosities engendered by Reconstruction continue to mar the literature to the present. Representative articles include J. H. Atkinson, ed., "Clayton and Catterson Rob Columbia County," *AHQ,* XXI (Summer 1962), 153-157; Ted R. Worley, ed., "Major Josiah H. Demby's History of Catterson's Militia," *AHQ,* XVI (Summer 1957), 203-211, and Virginia Buxton, "Clayton's Militia in Sevier and Howard Counties," *AHQ,* XX (Winter 1961), 344-350. An overall view is Otis A. Singletary, "Militia Disturbances in Arkansas During Reconstruction," *AHQ,* XV (Summer 1956), 140-150. The 1868 Convention received attention in Joseph M. St. Hilaire, "The Negro Delegates in the Arkansas Constitutional Convention of 1868: A Group Profile," *AHQ,* XXXIII (Spring 1974), 38-69, and Peter Kolchin, "Scalawags, Carpetbaggers and Reconstruction: A Quantitative Look at Southern Congressional Politics, 1868-1872," *JSH,* XLV (February 1979), 63-76. Valuable social commentary on the period can be found in Walter D. Hudson, ed., "Memoirs of James Madison Hudson," *AHQ,* XIX (Autumn 1969), 271-279, and H. M. McIver, "Water Bound in Arkansas," *AHQ,* XIV (Summer 1955), 134-160. The activities of the U. S. military are noted partially in Margaret Ross, "Retaliation Against Arkansas Newspaper Editors During Reconstruction," *AHQ,* XXXI (Summer 1972), 150-165. Railroad issues, so important to the era, are addressed in Thompson, *Arkansas and Reconstruction.*

Educational history during Reconstruction has been examined partially. A good treatment of the freedmen's schools is Larry Wesley Pearce, "The American Missionary Association and the Freedmen in Arkansas, 1863-1878," *AHQ*, XXX (Summer 1971), 123-144; "The American Missionary and the Freedmen's Bureau in Arkansas, 1866-1868," *AHQ*, XXX, (Autumn 1971), 242-259, and "Enoch K. Miller and the Freedmen's Schools," *AHQ*, XXXI (Winter 1972), 305-327. Local studies include Farrar Newberry, "The Yankee Schoolmarm who 'Captured' Post-War Arkadelphia," *AHQ*, XVII (Autumn 1958), 265-271.

The Brooks-Baxter War has been studied frequently. First came John M. Harrell, *The Brooks and Baxter War; A History of the Reconstruction Period in Arkansas,* (St. Louis, 1893), written from the Baxter point of view. A modern summary is Earl F. Woodward, "The Brooks and Baxter War in Arkansas, 1872-1874," *AHQ*, XXX (Winter 1971), 315-336. Useful collections of documents include Frederick T. Wilson, "Federal Aid in Domestic Disturbances, 1787-1903," 57th Congress, Second Session, Senate Document 209 (Washington, 1903), and "Affairs in Arkansas," Report by Mr. Bland, House of Representatives, 43rd Congress, 2d Session, Report No. 2 (Washington, 1874). Other useful studies include James H. Atkinson, "The Arkansas Gubernatorial Campaign and the Election of 1872," *AHQ*, I (Winter 1942), 307-321, and Cortez A. M. Ewing, "Arkansas and Reconstruction Impeachments," *AHQ*, XIII (Summer 1954) 137-153.

Springdale, Arkansas*, (photographer and date unknown) A town created by the arrival of the railroad (seen in the distance), Springdale boasted a wide variety of substantial store buildings on its Main Street.* **Shiloh Museum**

Arkansas as a New South State

INTRODUCTION

The end of Reconstruction marked a sharp break in Arkansas history. The overthrow of Republicans was the keystone of the New South Era, but economic and social forces at work between 1874 and 1886 were equally important.

During this period, the South responded tentatively to the slogans of Atlanta journalist Henry Grady, who called for industrialization and abandonment of old, anti-modern ways. This age of "the great barbecue" in Northern industrial growth led social critics Charles Dudley Warner and Mark Twain to label it *The Gilded Age*.

Robber barons gained control of railroad companies, raising Southern freight and passenger rates to finance their struggles to monopolize the iron horse. Lumbering in the South evolved from a local business into part of a national network. More Arkansas towns came into existence than at any other time, and thousands of acres were cleared and put into agricultural production.

Despite the emerging social and economic complexity of life in Arkansas, its people continually reaffirmed their old values of simplicity and individualism. At the same time, the state and the rest of the New South sought the approval of the nation by attempting to put down agrarian and labor discontent and by suppressing the most obvious signs of racism. The attempt to move in the contradictory directions of tradition and modernism meant that the New South might better be termed the Neurotic South. Events in Arkansas during this period amply reflect this confusion.

POLITICS

The victorious alliance of Conservatives and Democrats dominated the political scene in the aftermath of Reconstruction. Besides framing a new Constitution, the alliance supported New South industrialization, and, although it wrapped itself in the glories of the Lost Cause, was solicitous of blacks. Even as it decried Republican corruption, its members were often less than exemplars of probity in their private affairs. This alliance of old-line Whigs and antebellum Democrats suffered continual strains that would have led eventually to its breakdown even if there had not been the rise of agrarian protest.

Constitution of 1874

The centerpiece of the new regime was the Constitution of 1874. The convention that was called to end the Republican experiment assembled on July 14 and sat until September 8. Although the chairman was Grandison D. Royston, a member of the state's first convention in 1836, the presence of a Washington County Granger delegate who defeated the venerable David Walker was a sign that the new document was not just a return to the antebellum past. Further, about eight black members, led by J. F. White, watched out for minority interests.

This document, still in force today although it has been much amended, is known as the "Thou Shalt Not" Constitution. It was a hostile reaction to everything Republicans had attempted. Sixty-nine of its original 261 provisions deal with financial matters, almost always written in the negative.

Ridiculously low salaries for public officials, beginning with a $4,000 salary for the gover-

nor, were included. Education was hamstrung by a two-mill state property tax limit and a five-mill local property tax limit. Municipalities were prohibited from borrowing money. Hostility toward modernization could be found in the 10 percent maximum rate of interest and in sections dealing with railroads. Among the more obscure clauses was one banning feudal tenures and another prohibiting duelists from holding office. At one point, the Constitution affirmed freedom of religion, but at another, atheists were denied the right to hold office or testify in court. The most progressive feature in the entire document was a clause granting property rights to married women.

The new Constitution was designed to keep the office of governor weak. Almost all offices were elective, and county offices and powers were strongly emphasized. The governor's term was shortened from four years to two, and overriding a veto required only a simple majority vote of both houses of the legislature. The fear of another governor such as Powell Clayton prompted these measures, and the office of governor was largely an honorary position for the next twenty-five years.

Arkansas politics took on a shapeless character, for in guarding against abuses, the authors of the 1874 Constitution thwarted positive leadership. The history of the Arkansas Constitution from 1874 to the present has been the passage of amendment after amendment in attempts to bring the document into line with modern American government. That it would require Constitutional amendments to create kindergartens, use voting machines, establish libraries and hospitals or pass a three-mill county road tax illustrated the deficiencies of the document.

Augustus H. Garland and the New Departure Democrats

Voters adopted the new Constitution by a vote of 77,461 to 24,592 on October 13, 1874.

Republicans largely boycotted the election unless they came just to vote against the Constitution, for there were no Republican candidates on the state level. The new legislature contained only two Republican senators and ten Republican representatives. Thus the victors had full sway. At the helm was Governor Augustus H. Garland, who found the State House a wreck and not enough money in the treasury to buy firewood to heat his office. His departure to the United States Senate in 1877 — to Powell Clayton's former seat — was in part brought on by his statement that the governor's salary was too small to support a family, a refrain heard from all of his successors.

Garland was in many ways a typical "Redeemer." A Redeemer was a man who aligned himself with the Democrats but thought like a Whig. Such men also were called New Departure Democrats. The end of Reconstruction in some states saw the attempted return to power of the old antebellum Democratic elite. Although Garland had dabbled in state politics before the War, his background was Whig rather than Democratic. An early opponent of secession, he first attracted statewide attention by his performance in the aborted attempt to avoid secession. Elected first as a Confederate congressman and then senator over "family" opposition, he built his career on the ruins of the old order. After the War, Garland won the landmark case of *Ex parte Garland* (1866) in the United States Supreme Court, which restored his right to practice law in federal courts.

Garland's main duty was to keep the state quiet in order to show the North that the outcome of the Brooks-Baxter War did not harm essential economic or political interests. As a New Departure Democrat, he encouraged modernization and supported civil rights legislation for blacks, even voting affirmatively on a controversial 1883 federal civil rights bill. What should have been the highlight of his career came when he was attorney general under President Grover Cleveland. However,

Garland had taken 10 percent of the stock in a speculative company that was challenging the Bell company's telephone patents. When the federal government sued the Bell interests, a congressional investigating committee delved into Garland's involvement. Cleveland accepted Garland's account of what historian Allan Nevins called "deplorable indiscretions," but the episode cost Garland the chance to become the first United States Supreme Court justice from Arkansas.

The Debt Issue and the Redeemers

A major goal of the Redeemers was to restore fiscal integrity to state government. Ironically, the Redeemers began this by issuing more state bonds that were known as the Loughborough Bonds after their legislative sponsor, state Senator J.M. Loughborough. These bonds, amounting to $756,000, returned the state to solvency. Arkansas in 1877 carried a debt of $17,752,196, which included some $7,000,000 in railroad bonds, more than $2,000,000 in levee bonds, $1,700,000 due the United States government, and a floating debt of just short of $1,000,000. Pamphlets were written and heated words exchanged about the debt issue. However attractive repudiation of the state's debt seemed, Redeemers respected the sanctity of contract and feared that Arkansas would lose national credibility if its debts were repudiated. This same issue divided people and politicians all over the South.

The debt question was the leading single issue in Arkansas between 1874 and 1884. Governor Garland supported repayment; the agrarian wing of the Democratic Party, which was under the influence first of Grangerism and then of Greenbackism, came out for debt reduction.

Repudiation of the state's debt became the basis for the post-war success of western Arkansas's sometime Republican turned Democrat, William M. Fishback, "The Great

Repudiator," who spoke loud and long on the subject during the period, telling voters that paying the state debts run up by Republicans during Reconstruction was a swindle. Fishback was the director of the Little Rock and Fort Smith Railroad, and he failed to mention that voiding the railroad debts would relieve the company of a major liability.

The first step in debt repudiation was taken by the state Supreme Court. Associate Justice David Walker held in a unanimous decision that the state law authorizing the people to vote for or against railroads had not been ratified properly. The election was a nullity, and the bonds were not binding on the state, even in the hands of innocent parties. In another development, state Land Commissioner J. N. Smithee refused to honor levee bonds brought for payment. The high court again found defects in the law and there was another repudiation. Thanks to judicial interpretation, Arkansas shed more than $9,000,000 in debt.

Debt repudiation remained a controversial issue during the administration of the second Redeemer governor, William R. Miller. Elected in 1876 by a three-to-one margin over Republican A.W. Bishop, Miller was the first chief executive born in Arkansas. An antebellum Democrat, he had been a perennial political fixture as state auditor. He served as state auditor for four years before the Civil War, as auditor in the Confederate state government, again during Reconstruction (1866 to 1868) and finally from 1874 until he was elected governor. A loyal Democrat, Miller encountered his greatest difficulties within his own Party.

The dispute within the Democratic Party focused on the old Holford bonds left over from the antebellum Real Estate Bank. One faction called for compromising the issue in a plan put forth by John D. Adams and Jared E. Redfield, popularly known as the Adams-Redfield Plan, which would have paid bondholders on the basis of what the bank actually had received in specie. On the other side, Fishback

introduced an amendment to the state Constitution to prohibit the state from ever paying either the interest or the principal on the Holford bonds. A. H. Garland and Little Rock lawyer U.M. Rose opposed Fishback on the issue, but voters supported "the Great Repudiator." The Adams-Redfield Plan never passed the legislature, and an amendment to prevent payment, commonly called the Fishback Amendment, was submitted to voters in 1880. Tempers flared, and a physical confrontation between John D. Adams and J.N. Smithee in Little Rock has been called the last duel in Arkansas. Although more voters approved than disapproved the amendment, the measure failed to receive a majority of the total votes cast in the election and was held to have failed.

The 1880 vote also coincided with the election of Thomas J. Churchill as governor. Another antebellum figure, Churchill had a good war record in addition to his "family" connection as the son-in-law of Ambrose H. Sevier. A supporter of refunding like Miller, Churchill and his cause suffered when certain shortages in Churchill's accounts as state treasurer came to light during his term as governor.

The first report showed a deficit of $114,587, and a second raised the amount to $233,616. There were charges that Churchill was involved financially with Zeb Ward, an unsavory character who held the lease on the state penitentiary and reputedly possessed a fortune of more than a half million dollars, most of it gained by advantageous dealings with the state. Governor Churchill denied any wrongdoing on his part and blamed accounting errors. Although Churchill reimbursed the state, his gubernatorial career was limited to one term. The repudiation wing gained the ascendancy in 1882 as James H. Berry succeeded Churchill.

James H. Berry from Carroll County was the quintessential New South Agrarian Democrat. A Confederate veteran whose wound at the Battle of Corinth, Mississippi, had forced the amputation of one leg at the knee, he returned from the War to study law and engage in politics, first in the state legislature and then as a candidate for governor. Berry was not only an active repudiationist but also became the first governor to do more than complain about railroad abuses.

Railroads were the first large corporations active in Arkansas. The state collected taxes of only $24,000 from the lines in 1882 even though Arkansas freight and passenger rates were above the national average. The passenger rate per mile was twice that in Missouri, freight rates were four times those in St. Louis or Chicago and the short-haul rate used by many area shippers was a particular point of contention.

Railroad companies fortified their powerful position by providing legislators with free passes, which meant that the allowance for travel mileage that was paid to legislators by the state became personal profit. Ministers and newspaper editors were given similar treatment in an effort to mute public protest. Two bills to tax railroads and insurance companies mysteriously disappeared during the 1883 legislative session, leaving lawmakers unable to proceed. Governors since Garland had called for taxing the railroad lines, probably as a sop to agrarian radicals, but it was not until 1883 under Governor Berry that state government moved against the companies. The railroads claimed that their charters exempted them from taxation, an assertion that was true only if the companies had not changed hands or been in bankruptcy. The battle between the railroads and the people began when the state Supreme Court upheld Governor Berry in *Memphis and Little Rock Railroad Co. v. Berry,* and *St. Louis, Iron Mountain and Southern Railway Co. v. Berry,* (1883).

The repudiationist wing of the Democratic Party used Governor Berry's victory to stage a successful revival of the Fishback Amend-

ment. With the Refunder wing discredited in the aftermath of the Churchill scandal in 1884, voters overwhelmingly approved a constitutional amendment making it illegal for the state to honor Holford Bonds. This erased a back debt of $14,000,000. The debt due the federal government was not resolved finally until 1897.

The financial system of the New South Era remained chronically backward. No modern budgeting existed, and the state continued to function using scrip "pictorial promises" and warrants instead of federal legal tender. If Churchill's claim of innocence as state treasurer was true, then the state had no idea how much money came in or when, or how old state scrip was canceled. In addition to Churchill's troubles, other shortages were reported in the accounts of Auditor John Crawford and Land Commissioner D.W. Lear. In the biggest scandal in the state's history, Churchill's successor, William E. Woodruff, Jr., state treasurer from 1881 to 1891, was accused by his successor of embezzling some $2,000,000. Woodruff defended himself through four trials, three of which ended in his acquittal. After his conviction in the fourth, he appealed the case to the state Supreme Court, which overturned the verdict on a legal error. As one historian of the times noted: "The Redeemer judicial system dealt gently with officeholders who had influential friends; but it breathed out vengeance upon the vagrant and friendless petty thief." As for Woodruff, the *Arkansas Democrat* called his escape "an outrage upon justice and common honesty."

As the state was escaping from her debts, Arkansas's counties and towns were not so fortunate. Expenses so exceeded Nevada County's ability to pay that county scrip fell in value to 20 cents on the dollar. The debts left from the Republican administration combined with the almost total lack of local taxing power under the restrictive 1874 Constitution so strapped Little Rock for cash that illegal gambling actually was encouraged as a way to bring in additional revenue through a municipal protection system.

A most involved scandal occurred in Clark County, where Republican county officials issued bonds to build the Ouachita Valley Railroad. Instead of beginning construction, they absconded with the money and issued fraudulent bonds. The bondholders found a sympathetic federal judge who ordered the county to honor its obligations. Faced with a huge debt and no railroad, Clark County residents sought repudiation by having the legislature abolish the county, divide its territory among neighbors, and leave the debt unassigned. The necessary legislation passed, but the federal court refused to allow the evasion.

In addition to problems inherited from Reconstruction, Redeemers added some of their own. The Democratic tax collector in Washington County failed to enter tax payments on 38,210 acres of land, which was then sold at public auction. Favoritism in government circles at the county courthouse and corruption in public accounts was a way of life.

The Structure of Redeemer Politics

The Democratic Party ruled Arkansas, but the real question was who ruled the Democratic Party. Battles between refunders and repudiationists tended to pit town lawyers against rural leaders. Given the structure of the Party, the initial advantage lay with the more centrally organized refunders. As in antebellum days, state Democrats claimed to be a reflection of grassroots democracy. In the counties, township meetings preceded the county meeting at which delegates were chosen for the state convention. A tiny minority actually participated. Only six of the thirteen townships of Mississippi County were represented in the 1884 county meeting, and the four delegates sent to Little Rock voted contrary to their instructions. That state politics was merely this system writ large was evident in 1884

when John G. Fletcher, a respected Little Rock banker and businessman, was denied the gubernatorial nomination in favor of Simon Hughes in spite of Fletcher's greater popularity among the rank and file.

Clark County instituted a primary in 1878 to counter the inherent corruption in the old system, but the results were not binding. Fifty-four counties followed Clark County's lead by 1894, resulting in a considerable legal tangle about convention procedure that ended in 1898 when the legislature made primaries binding on the state Party convention.

Corruption was also a factor in the state legislature. The most publicized case involved the attempted return to politics of Robert Ward Johnson. The great antebellum leader had fallen on hard times after the War. His vast wealth in land and slaves was gone, and his name was anathema to Republicans. When Radical control became complete, he left the state for Washington, D.C., where he practiced law with Albert Pike. He and Pike strongly supported Baxter during the Brooks-Baxter War, after which the old warrior returned to Arkansas hoping to regain his seat in the United States Senate and exercise his skill in patronage in the new arena of Gilded Age politics. He was busy working the state by the spring of 1878, endorsing limited repudiation and attacking some of the Northern-imposed impediments on Southern agriculture. Johnson was never a true Jacksonian Democrat, but he tuned his speeches to the emerging agrarian protest movement.

Supported by the *Arkansas Gazette* and many antebellum friends, Johnson was opposed for the Senate by James David Walker, the nephew of the ever-formidable David Walker of the great northwest. The contest had several facets. In some ways it was a battle of sections and in others it was between an antebellum Democrat and the son of a Whig. It also was a struggle between age and youth. Johnson's defeat by sixty-eight votes to forty-seven was a "deep humiliation," but nothing like the embarrassment that followed when it was reported that Logan H. Roots, the carpetbag Republican banker, had offered bribes to two Negro legislators to support Johnson. The *Arkansas Democrat* led the attack on Johnson, while the *Gazette* defended its one-time owner. Broken by defeat and scandal, Arkansas's senior statesman died a few months later.

Antebellum politicians were more successful in recapturing the state's judiciary. E. H. English, chief justice from 1855 to 1864, returned to the state Supreme Court as chief justice in 1874 and served until his death ten years later. His colleagues included David Walker (1875-1878), Jesse Turner (1878), John R. Eakin (1878-1885), and F.W. Compton (1874). The Arkansas congressional delegation tended to include men of Confederate background, but none had been more than a colonel. Only one, T.M. Gunter, who served in the secession convention as an anti-secessionist, had any antebellum experience.

Because the 1874 Constitution deprived the governor of adequate tenure, an effective veto and significant appointive powers, it was not surprising that Arkansas politics became localized in city and county government. State elections frequently turned on county frauds. Moving the date of the state elections separated them from the balloting for federal offices, thus avoiding federal scrutiny. Localism in politics led to ill-advised legislation, much of it of a trivial or even unconstitutional nature. Thus one Pine Bluff editor in 1877 wanted the legislature "stuffed and kept as a curiosity," and the Prescott *Dispatch* said that, "We are willing to have the yellow fever, Digger Indians, drouths, grasshoppers, presidential excursions, or the seven plagues of Egypt, but an extra session of the present legislature, God forbid." The statute books got bigger, but evidence of wisdom declined.

Given these political realities, governors struggled in vain. Only Governor Berry, who opposed public education and supported a tax cut, saw part of his program enacted. Unable

to influence legislation, governors managed to exert some powers over law enforcement. When the Skein family at El Dorado went on a mass murder spree in 1877, Governor Miller responded promptly by offering a $1,200 reward for their capture.

Many instances of executive leadership involved race relations, because the Redeemer governors, fearful of new federal involvement, acted vigorously to protect blacks from unwarranted white aggression. In 1881, Governor Churchill dealt with a crisis at Pine Bluff that occurred when the white militia commander refused to enroll a black company. Churchill personally ordered the men enrolled and court-martialed the offending officer. Both Miller and Churchill used their powers as commander-in-chief to deal with internal civil wars in Pope and Scott Counties, where violence reached Reconstruction proportions, but without Republicans to blame. Ironically, both men lost popularity because of their actions, which reminded too many residents of the acts of Powell Clayton. Although many whites wanted to persecute blacks, the Redeemers stood in the way. Hence in Delta counties, blacks continued to vote and hold office. Some were even welcomed into the Democratic Party.

Education under the Redeemers

Nowhere was the Redeemer attitude toward society more evident than in education. Arkansas farmers still refused to support public education, leaving the family to provide instruction for the children in hunting, farming and domestic labor. Those in isolated areas saw no need for any "book learning;" indeed, many had located in remote places in order to avoid the regimentation of schools. Elsewhere the typical family wanted only the bare elements of literacy needed to buy and sell, defend land titles and partake in politics.

The creation of a statewide system of education begun during Reconstruction far

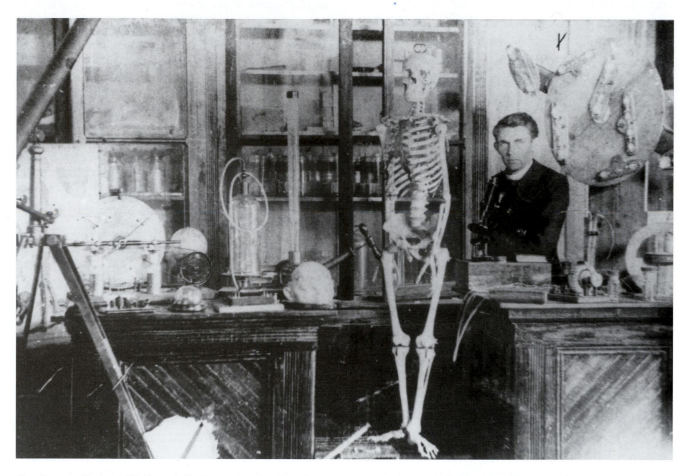

Professor George H. Burr's Laboratory at Hendrix College *must have seemed a modern marvel to nineteenth century students. (photographer unknown, 1895)* **University of Central Arkansas**

exceeded the demands of most Arkansans. There was little public opposition when Redeemers virtually abrogated state responsibility and denied the right of a community to support schools locally through taxation. During the Redeemer years, the legislature robbed the state school fund of its interest-paying federal bonds and replaced them with state bonds on which the interest was never paid. J.L. Denton, the state superintendent of public instruction from 1878 to 1882, was almost powerless but did what he could as an evangelist for education traveling over the state giving pep talks. Only Governor Miller openly championed education, and Berry successfully supported a tax cut at the expense of education.

In the absence of public commitment, private education attempted to fill the void. The 1866 legislature had incorporated no fewer than eleven academies or institutes and one college. Academy towns included Lewisburg, Nashville, Yellville, Camden, Jonesboro and Pine Bluff. The college was to be at Princeton in Dallas County. Interest in academies soared after the collapse of the public schools. Typical institutions were the work of one individual, as when Reverend Isham L. Burrow founded Central Collegiate Institute at Altus. Many founders like Burrow sought religious affiliation less because of church money than for the hope that patronage from church members might result. Burrow eventually transferred his school to the Methodists, who moved it to Conway, where it became Hendrix College. Some academies had high standards, and like Sloan-Hendrix at Imboden, attracted students from a wide area.

Many academies boasted that they offered more than just primary education. Terms such as "institute" and "collegiate" promised more than most schools delivered, but the same forces that created academies also supported colleges. Colleges also tried to find a religious connection. Cane Hill College, a pre-war Cumberland Presbyterian institution, reopened after the War and for a time boasted the art instruction of William M. Quesenbury. Although it closed in 1892, Cumberland Presbyterians also had founded Arkansas Cumberland College in 1891. It has survived as the University of the Ozarks.

Old School Presbyterians had less luck with founding a school at Arkadelphia, but Southern Presbyterians created Arkansas College at Batesville in 1872 after that town failed to win the new state university. Baptists also were active, with Ouachita Baptist College (1886) the largest surviving modern institution. Roman Catholics founded what probably was the most unusual school — St. Benedict's College (1887). Subsequently renamed Subiaco Academy, it was located at the abbey and operated along monastic and European lines. The first students, drawn almost entirely from German Catholic families, had to learn English in addition to their other studies. The study of Latin and Greek dominated the liberal arts curriculm.

Although all schools claimed to teach the liberal arts, most did so through the eyes of religious and political orthodoxy. Science was not emphasized, and in any case, proper instruction required more equipment than most schools could afford. Morality was stressed, both through daily religious instruction and by strict supervision of the students for whom the school stood *in loco parentis*. This system served only a small elite of the population, mostly urban and professional

Southland College and Normal Institute (*artist unknown, ca. 1900*) *A Quaker school near Helena in extreme eastern Arkansas, Southland College failed to survive.* **University of Central Arkansas**

people and the children of well-to-do farmers. A surprising number of memoirs from the period indicate that parents often relocated so their children could attend school. The education given was narrow in focus but deep in intensity. School literary societies debated every issue of the day, and as one Hendrix student recalled, only essay tests were administered. The students might not have been trained for the vocations of the age, but they were taught to reason and lead. Subsequently, Arkansas drew most of its leaders from such students.

Black educational activity largely paralleled that of whites, so that the community had several weak institutions divided by religious differences. The first, Southland College, started as an orphanage in Helena sponsored by the Indiana Society of Friends. In time it grew into a training school for black teachers, adopting the title "college" in 1876. In addition to Quaker financial support, the school owned some 1,700 acres, a brickyard, sawmill, gristmill, cotton gin and grocery. Its education was nondenominational, the Bible and the spelling book, and it survived until 1925.

The Methodist college Philander Smith, the oldest surviving black institution, started as Walden Seminary, changed names in 1882 and became a four-year institution in 1884. The rival African Methodist Episcopal Church started Bethel University in the basement of the Bethel AME Church in Little Rock, moved the school to Arkadelphia and finally returned to the capital under the name Shorter College. Similarly, black Baptists created Baptist Institute in 1884, changing it to Arkansas Baptist College the next year. All these schools were small, and in the absence of black high schools, filled mostly a pre-collegiate function.

Arkansas made a commitment to black education by creating Branch Normal College at Pine Bluff. The impetus for its creation was to reward blacks for their acceptance of the 1874 Constitution. Joseph C. Corbin, the former Arkansas superintendent of public instruction and the holder of a master's degree from Ohio University, became the first principal, holding that position until 1902. The school was designed to train black teachers for segregated schools. Because of the absence of any secondary education for blacks at the high school level, it was largely college preparatory. No student received a college diploma until 1882, and no dormitories existed until 1888. Agricultural and mechanical departments were added after 1890, and the college became eligible for federal education money, most of which was transferred to the University at Fayetteville.

Despite often overt opposition to public education, Arkansas could not escape the national movement toward the little red schoolhouse. Henry Grady's New South rhetoric could hardly be fulfilled by functional illiterates. Some communities continued their commitment to education despite difficulties. Although only 15,890 students were enrolled in the public schools in 1876, the number rose by 1881 to more than 140,000. Terms were irregular, usually split between winter and summer, and teacher pay was low. Professionalism was limited mainly to urban teachers whose high standards were commensurate with Northern educational

ideals. Ida Joe Brooks served as president of the state teachers' association in 1877, and the *Arkansas School Journal* began a brief existence in 1881. Most of the new teachers entering the system were Southerners, and by the end of the period, blacks could not become members and women could not vote. Ida Jo Brooks left teaching to become a doctor, but Charlotte E. Stephens, a black woman who began teaching in 1869, remained in the profession until her retirement in 1939. She was honored in 1910 when an elementary school in Little Rock was named for her.

In contrast to the rigorous standards sometimes present in the private academies, public schools often were poorly taught and supported. "I never got through Roy's arithmetic," Attorney General Hal L. Norwood recalled. "The next teacher would ask how far we got during the last term and then start back towards the first, on the theory that his predecessor was not thorough." History was never brought up to date because the ex-Confederate teachers always stopped before the Civil War.

Under the Redeemers, the state University at Fayetteville was captured from the Republicans. After ex-Confederate General Daniel Harvey Hill became its president, the school existed on the prestige of the Lost Cause with little actual state funding. Arkansas also acquired a medical school, created in Little Rock by local doctors in 1879 and affiliated at least in name with the University. The Deaf Mute Institute, founded before the War in Arkadelphia and moved to Little Rock during Reconstruction, went out of existence in 1875 when state funding stopped. Reorganized the next year, it struggled along. A fire destroyed the main building in 1899. Because of legislative cost-cutting, the structure was uninsured.

Redeemer Law Enforcement

Neglect of education was paralleled by callousness toward the disadvantaged. Arkansas legislators consistently refused to establish a state insane asylum, and some mentally ill people ended up in prison. In one case that attracted much attention, a pregnant, deranged prisoner was put on regular exhibition for the public's amusement by Little Rock jailers.

The state's law enforcement system was even more inhumane. Repressive legislation during the Redeemer years added greatly to the number of crimes, thereby creating more criminals. Redeemers sought to run prisons for profit on both county and state levels, and the result was scandals that attracted national attention.

Part of the cause was in the laws themselves. Any theft above the value of $2 became a penitentiary offense. Because no system of juvenile justice existed, children of nine and older were sent to prison. In 1892, those sixteen and under accounted for 6 percent of the prison population. More adults also were convicted. The black codes were not reenacted literally, but a variety of agriculturally based laws, including selling mortgaged crops, moving during the summer and selling cotton after dark, added to the number of offenses that were particularly applicable to blacks. Vagrancy laws, which made it illegal not to be working, were applied selectively. The state prison contained twice the number of black convicts as white convicts, and whites found it easier to get pardons.

A wave of religious zeal that struck Arkansas in the 1880s added another dimension to the problem. Before 1885, Arkansas had a Sabbath law, which provided that persons observing other than Sunday as their sacred day were free to work on the Christian Sabbath. In Little Rock, however, a move to close the saloons on Sunday collapsed when Jewish saloon owners insisted on their rights. Thereafter, the legislature passed a new Sunday closing law in 1885 with no exemptions. Apparently neither Jews nor

Colonel Robert Crockett (photographer and date unknown) This elegantly hirsute legislator founded Crockett's Bluff in Arkansas County and led the attack on Arkansas's very restrictive Sunday blue law. **Arkansas History Commission**

saloon keepers were the main victims. Instead, law enforcement officials in a number of counties, notably Washington and Hot Spring, began arresting Seventh Day Adventists. Some had been seen gardening, one had mended a wagon brake and another picked peaches. Methodists, Baptists and Presbyterians united in instigating these persecutions, largely from sectarian jealousy.

A storm of protest occurred when the state Supreme Court in *State* v. *Scales* (1886) upheld the law. U.M. Rose, perhaps the most learned member of the bar, wrote an eloquent protest, and in the next legislative session, Colonel Robert H. "Bob" Crockett, a nephew of the famous Davy Crockett, submitted a bill repealing the law. Crockett asserted that in the last two years, there had

Deputy U. S. Marshal Bass Reeves (*photographer and date unknown*) **University of Central Arkansas.**

Bass Reeves

One historian has called him, "a big black man who wore the white hat of the law," for Bass Reeves was the most famous of the black law enforcement officials associated with Judge Isaac Parker's Western District of Arkansas federal District Court.

Born about 1824 into slavery in Texas, Reeves got into a fight with his owner during a card game and bolted to Indian Territory, hiding out until the Civil War ended slavery. After the War, he settled down on a farm near Van Buren, but when Judge Parker came to Fort Smith in 1875, Reeves, who had great familiarity with the Indian languages and the terrain, signed on as deputy marshal, remaining in that position until 1906.

Deputy U. S. Marshals were paid on a fee system, and Reeves averaged about $400 a month during his Indian Territory excursions. Although famous and feared, Reeves's career was marked with controversy. He once shot and killed a man who had thrown hot grease on his pet dog. Allegedly, Reeves allowed the corpse, which had fallen into the campfire, to remain until charred.

One of Reeves's failures was in leading a posse to catch famous outlaw Ned Christie. Although Reeves and his posse trapped Christie in his home and burned it down, the outlaw escaped that time. One of Reeves's successes came when he served a warrant on his own son, who had murdered his unfaithful wife. Reeves, who could not read, memorized the warrants and writs he served. In 1907, he became a member of the Muskogee, Oklahoma, police force. Reeves died of Bright's disease there in 1910.

Reeves's reputation rested almost entirely on oral sources. The white-owned press of Fort Smith ignored his accomplishments, for increasingly after 1875, blacks were considered newsworthy only when lynched.

---

been "three times as many cases of persecution for consciences' sake as there have been in all the other states combined since the adoption of our national constitution." His appeal was successful, and the legislature restored the old law in 1887 with the exception that all saloons must remain closed on Sunday. An examination of the prosecutions indicated that only one was brought against a person who was not a Seventh Day Adventist, and most of those convicted were recent immigrants to the state. In his plea for repeal, Crockett had focused not only on the fundamental question of religious freedom but also on the economic consequences of discouraging immigration.

The Redeemers also operated a repressive local system of justice. Justices of the peace

The Last Words of John Hill, Alias Albert Mansker. (W. D. Ross, 1894) *After George W. Padgett turned state's evidence in the Olyphant train robbery case, three men were sentenced to die by hanging. The executions were held in an enclosure outside Jackson County courthouse at Newport and were preceded by "several ladies and gentlemen who visited them to offer them consolation." Since public executions had been banned and only twenty-five persons were permitted as witnesses, the large crowd had to rely on a local photographer's coverage. Ross published at least four pictures of the execution process, this one showing Hill's speech, in which he forgave the sheriff and asked for forgiveness.* **Jacksonport State Park**

still disposed of most cases, and county prison farms worked their convicts for the profit of private parties. Sheriffs were allowed 75 cents a day to feed prisoners, and by reducing the food to starvation levels, they could make a good profit. More opportunities for enrichment came from charging prisoners room and board. A thirty-day sentence might well result in a term lasting months or years. The county got free labor on the roads or leased convicts to local planters. Arrests always increased around cotton-picking time when extra labor was needed.

The greatest scandal was at the state level. In seeking to make justice a paying proposition, Redeemers leased the prison to private parties, who in turn hired out prisoners. Lessor Zeb Ward acquired one of the largest fortunes in Arkansas during the 1870s. He fed the legislature Thanksgiving dinner in 1871 and performed other acts of calculated munificence, prompting one editor to comment: "If he don't feed his convicts any better than he ought to, he, at least, knows how to entertain his friends."

The coal companies and railroads used

cheap labor and housed convicts in guarded cattle cars even in winter, denying them adequate food and clothing and withholding sufficient medical attention. "A Hell in Arkansas," the *Gazette* called conditions for prisoners at the Quita Coal Company near Coal Hill, where an investigation revealed one prisoner had received 400 lashes before he died. The stench arising from the bunkhouse, where jammed-in prisoners slept on straw and cornshucks, offended even the hardened nostrils of the nineteenth century. The Coal Hill expose attracted national attention, and Arkansas author Octave Thanet (Alice French) wrote a powerful short story about Arkansas justice. Governor Berry had called leasing prisoners "uncivilized, inhuman, and wrong," but the combination of well-placed favors and the state's $25,000 annual profit prevented any real reform.

Federal justice in Arkansas during the Redeemer years was notorious for quite different reasons. The Western District of Arkansas still encompassed Indian Territory and was presided over by Judge Isaac Charles Parker. Before Parker's arrival, the court at Fort Smith had become a national scandal, costing the United States treasury $724,000 in three years. A series of investigations revealed that instead of quieting Indian Territory, the deputy United States marshals actually stirred up unrest, and every kind of fraudulent activity went on in the court.

In 1875, Judge Parker, a former Missouri Republican congressman, arrived to clean up the corruption and remained to become one of the truly formidable judges of the nineteenth century. He was above suspicion of scandal and a hard worker who for twenty-one years and 13,500 cases, kept his docket current. Parker became nationally famous as the judge who "hanged them high," seventy-nine men in all. "The Parker slaughter-house," as critics called it, gave Arkansas a bad name even though the sensational cases originated in Indian Territory. A number of yellow press books reported on Parker's activities as well as those of George Maledon, the nation's most famous hangman, and the tough deputy marshals who tracked desperate criminals through the often hostile lands of Indian Territory.

During fourteen of Parker's twenty-one years on the bench, Congress permitted no appeals from his decisions save for presidential pardons and commutations. This absolute power led to legal abuses grave even by the standards of Parker's time. When his practice of guiding juries to preconceived verdicts came under United States Supreme Court scrutiny after 1889, Parker's decisions were overturned regularly, and the irate old judge accused the court of coddling criminals. In 1896, the Western District was limited to Arkansas, and the notoriety faded. Parker died in November 1896.

If capital punishment has a deterrent effect, then late nineteenth century Arkansas should have been crime free. Hangings in state courts remained public until 1887, and people flocked to these events in record numbers. Some of the era's most notorious executions attracted more than 10,000 persons to watch the condemned being led to the gallows, make his last speech and then swing in the air. The essentially primitive nature of hangings in general was illustrated in the state's execution of Cass Matlock. Matlock's victim's brothers served as executioners, and Matlock protested his innocence to the end, comparing his ordeal with that of Jesus on the cross. Matlock, a black man, was at least given nominal due process of law, for the Redeemers did not condone lynchings. In one well-attended hanging, the spectators got more than they bargained for. The criminal's body fell with such force that the rope severed the victim's head, splashing blood on the front row of the audience.

In spite of conspicuous capital punishment, crime flourished, and individual criminals sometimes received a sympathetic response from common folk. Visitors reported that farmers, oppressed by chattel mortgages, crop liens and falling prices, greatly admired Jesse James, whom local legend placed in almost every community in Arkansas. Many remembered the story of the James gang robbing the Hot Springs stage and returning the watch of a Confederate veteran.

Wartime animosities also figured in the activities of the Bald-knobbers of the Ozarks, Klan-like groups often motivated by fierce parochial hatreds. Women also became outlaws. Belle Starr became a popular character in the literature of the time even though in reality she was a horse thief who consorted with famous criminals. Her daughter, Pearl, was a successful prostitute in Fort Smith.

Criminals who attacked banks and trains might receive some sympathy from the oppressed classes in Arkansas society, but modernizers responded with vigorous law enforcement. On November 3, 1893, an amateurish outlaw gang consisting mostly of small farmers robbed a St. Louis and Iron Mountain passenger train at Olyphant (Jackson County), killing the conductor. Within hours law enforcement officials had organized a posse that soon caught some of the men. Three were hung at Newport. The same year, veteran bank robber Henry Starr, who died in 1921 while trying to rob the Harrison bank, made a successful assault on the People's Bank of Bentonville. Although he got away, one historian noted, "the memory of that fight is a high spot in [Bentonville's] traditions."

GILDED AGE SOCIETY

The Redeemers promised a transformation of Arkansas life, a fulfillment of the dream of modernization that carpetbagger Republicans had trumpeted, but one that supposedly was led by and for Southerners. Nowhere in the South did the reality live up to expectations, but Arkansas probably saw more development than most states when the opening of new lands led to an agricultural boom as well as some industrialization. "Robbers' Roost," the area in Little Rock where Republicans built their splendid homes during Reconstruction, yielded to the new palace of banker Logan H. Roots and the Italianate mansion, Villa Marre, erected by Angelo Marre, a Little Rock saloonkeeper.

Economic Conditions

After the Panic of 1873, some disillusioned Southerners began to doubt that a return to pre-war prosperity was possible and turned on modernization by denouncing vigorously one-crop commercial agriculture and threatening to overturn Redeemer control. Another segment argued for more modernization, increased industrialization and crop diversification. Atlanta journalist Henry Grady was the prophet of this second school, and his followers in Arkansas promoted the state by publicizing a railroad excursion for Northern journalists and capitalists. Their story, published as *The New Arkansas Traveler*, directly repudiated the old values represented by Arkansas's best-known legend.

This promotion of Arkansas as a western and frontier state was valid economically. Older Southern states stagnated during this period, growing at a rate of 1 percent from 1880 to 1900. But Arkansas doubled cotton production between 1870 and 1880, and the state's population increased by 65 percent. Arkansas ranked fifth in production of cotton and sixth in cotton acreage, making it a developing state within a section that was failing to progress. Agriculture continued to dominate, and in 1880, only 6.5 percent of the population was classified as urban. Little Rock with 13,138 residents was the only town above 4,000; Fort Smith claimed a mere 3,000. Yet the agricultural expansion coupled with railroad construction produced numerous small towns, each containing the nucleus for urbanization. The key to such progress was a railroad.

Arkansas in 1870 had 256 miles of track; by 1880 the figure had risen to 859, and it was 2,203 by 1900. Three factors lay behind this explosion. First, the physical resources of Arkansas, now in national demand, could find no other transportation outlet than rail. Second, local interests, as in earlier days, coveted the iron horse as the key to commercial prosperity. Third, the lands offered for sale by the railroads and the government lured settlers and prompted railroad expansion. The construction in 1873 of the Baring Cross Bridge across the Arkansas River at Little Rock facilitated these developments greatly.

The network of rail lines shifted economic patterns. Before 1860, New Orleans virtually monopolized the marketing of Arkansas commodities, although Northern cities, notably Cincinnati, Louisville and St. Louis, sought outlets for their hardwares, clothing, farm implements and liquor. With the completion of the Cairo and Fulton Railroad, soon absorbed into Jay Gould's St. Louis and Iron Mountain system, St. Louis was in a favored position to serve Arkansas retailers. A second St. Louis road, the Cotton Belt, at first a narrow-gauge railway, cut into the Iron Mountain's territory, but both enriched St. Louis. A number of railroad stops along these roads and their satellites grew into towns inhabited largely by Northerners and Europeans. Weiner, McGehee, Prescott, Stuttgart, Hope, Paragould and Texarkana were all born during this period. As a result of rail connections, the St. Louis Cotton Exchange made major efforts to lure Arkansas's chief commodity north. Its leader, J.M. Dowell, was well-connected in Arkansas by marriage to the heiress of the Clover Bend Plantation in Lawrence County.

Town Life

Little Rock was the closest thing Arkansas had to a metropolitan center. In holding to her premiere position among Arkansas municipalities, the capital underwent a transformation from a sleepy governmental center of 3,727 persons in 1860 to a thriving business center of 12,380 by 1870 with blacks accounting for 43 percent of the population. High cotton prices and extensive state and city spending during Reconstruction fueled an economic boom that carried over into residential construction and cultural enrichment. The first opera troupe in Little Rock, led by the famous tenor Pasquilino Brignoli, used the inadequate City Hall as a stage in 1870. A new opera house costing $50,000 opened in 1873 to segregated audiences and played host to a series of visiting opera and stage companies throughout the rest of the century.

For another kind of taste, Little Rock had what was reportedly the most richly furnished billiard saloon in the Southwest. Prostitution flourished, with the Mt. Holly Cemetery being a favorite assignation point. "Fighting Alley" deserved its reputation; for richer customers, Kate Merrick, "the queen of the dell," set the tone for the demimonde. City authorities looked the other way at both gambling and prostitution except when city finances needed a little boost.

However, by the end of Reconstruction, falling cotton prices, a national depression and over-expansion hit the town hard and the party was over. When Democrats gained control of the city, they gerrymandered the black neighborhoods to reduce their voting strength and initiated a program of retrenchment. The city spent $437 in 1876 on street repairs, down from the $38,578 expended in 1871. One legislator finally introduced a bill declaring Main and Markham streets navigable streams.

Extravagant hopes that were based on the arrival of the railroads failed to materialize. Little Rock did not become a cotton center of any importance and most lumber was exported to the North for finishing. Perhaps the town's main accomplishment was avoiding the yellow fever epidemics that hit Memphis, first in 1873, and then with renewed ferocity in

Opera House, Fort Smith *(photographer and date unknown) Every town boasted an opera house with Fort Smith's ranking near the top in size. Most such houses never saw an opera.* **University of Arkansas at Little Rock**

1878. In the second disaster, which in Memphis led to 17,000 reported cases and 5,000 deaths, all Arkansas towns under Little Rock's leadership imposed a ban on travel either by boat or train that was enforced rigorously for seventy-four days and created economic havoc. Little Rock successfully prevented any outbreak, although the river towns, notably Helena, experienced minor panics similar to that in Memphis.

Little Rock appeared to stagnate during the 1870s. The 1880 census actually reported fewer residents than in 1870, but the city limits had not been extended to include new areas of settlement stimulated by the railroads. Towns named De Contillon, Quapaw, Huntersville and Argenta (later named North Little Rock) appeared in succession on the north bank of the Arkansas River. Brick buildings were rising by 1880, when both Republi-

cans and Democrats welcomed ex-President Ulysses S. Grant to Little Rock for a brief visit. Prosperity generated by wholesaling and manufacturing increased the population to 25,874 in 1890 and 38,307 by 1900. The first fruit train from Arkansas arrived in St. Louis in May 1884, and markets developed steadily in spite of freight rates that increased the price of Arkansas coal from $3.25 a ton at Little Rock to $6.75 in St. Louis. Arkansas also exported bois d'arc wood (Osage orange and locally pronounced Bo-dock), which was used in Chicago to pave alleys.

Even during the doldrums of the 1870s, an increasing gulf separated Arkansas rural life from the existence of the city dweller. Jewish synagogues appeared in Pine Bluff and Little Rock after the Civil War, and increasingly nonEnglish names appeared on shop doors, businesses and city directories. Republicans continued to be a force in Little Rock politics, and the presence of blacks on the police force served as a reminder of their still-potent voting strength.

Little Rock's size attracted theatrical talent. Only the barnstorming style of theater flourished during Reconstruction, but with the opening of the new opera house, more companies made Little Rock a stop on their way to Texas. Katie Putnam, who played in 1874, was the first nationally famous star to appear in Little Rock. Entertainment "of the usual blackface variety never failed to please," but occasional visits by opera troupes supplied variety, and those of Emma Abbott's company even offered quality. *Uncle Tom's Cabin,* not necessarily a popular play in the South, trod the boards in Little Rock for the first time in 1874 to the great enjoyment of the community's blacks. Other towns along the railroad lines began erecting opera houses, which often were adequate for a one-night stand.

The key to post-war prosperity was railroad connections. Every town in Arkansas wanted to be on a line, though not all could or would pay the price. The fate of Jacksonport, which loftily rejected the Cairo and Fulton's demand for right of way and died as Newport flourished, loomed over many antebellum villages. Rondo, Lewisville, Norristown, Wittsburg, Grand Glaise, Paraclifta, Rockport, Carrollton and Tulip were among the places that slipped into ghost-town status. A few, such as Washington, constructed their own railroad spurs in a vain effort to stem the decline.

A rail point usually replaced a river port. Rockport on the Ouachita River, which was superseded by Malvern four miles away, was described in 1874 as an "abode of bats and owls." Sometimes the changes came so quickly that entire buildings were disassembled and relocated on the new site. Rail connections were sufficient to overcome seemingly serious obstacles. Hope residents had no water except what was hauled in by wagon; it was easier to find whisky in the town than

safe drinking water.

Typical of the period was the economic activity to be found in Arkadelphia, a high-water point on the Ouachita River that could be reached only part of the year. Roads were poor, and residents had to rely on "mule team wagons, called by courtesy a stage coach," which were operated by partners John T. Chidester, a wartime profiteer and Republican scalawag, and E.H. Searle, a carpetbagger. Yet the very isolation of the town meant that cottage industries thrived. With a population of 1,200 in 1871, Arkadelphia boasted twenty-two dry goods and grocery stores, a hotel, two drug stores, two restaurants, a dozen or more lawyers, six doctors, four churches (Episcopal, Presbyterian, Methodist and Baptist), a tin shop, a steam planing mill, a steam brick machine shop, a cabinet shop, two shoe shops, two jewelers, two gunsmiths, two blacksmiths, one tailor, a wagon shop and a variety of woodworking shops and carpenters. Almost everything was produced locally because transportation was both uncertain and very expensive.

This self-sufficiency was a sign of poverty to the people. "Our very hair stands end," the local paper lamented, "to think of the horrors of our situation — the land of the widow, the orphan and the poor man sold to the bloated speculator for a mere song to pay taxes, every day sinking our people lower and lower, and deeper and deeper, in the depths of poverty, bankruptcy and ruin, and all for the want of a railroad." Little did local editors who dreamed of Arkansas entering the "fast age" of steam and electricity perceive that the cost of that progress might mean the demise of these local industries and even the eventual end of the agrarian world.

Towns were particularly hard hit by fluctuations in the economy. Many of Camden's brick buildings were described as being vacant in the aftermath of the Panic of 1873 and Pine Bluff was reported to be "a bankrupt city" with no fire department. To raise money all towns seemed to have tolerated illegal gambling. With the attitude that "Gambling is all the go, and does not hide its light under a bushel" in Hot Springs, faro and keno were advertised openly, and poker was played even on the Sabbath. A city versus county feud about dividing the revenues ended in the Hot Springs Flynn-Doran War of 1884, marked by a western-style shoot-out. The defeated gamblers merely moved to Pine Bluff, where one disgusted resident ruefully noted: "They landed here and we have the bag to hold."

Saturday was the big day for town merchants, and field hands and lumberjacks reveled on Saturday night. In Harrisburg, a town where saloons were banned legally, the grocery had an inner room "and a Saturday night crowd is especially noticeable." Texarkana had more than forty dram shops, and nearly every town that began during this period opened with liquor flowing.

Not surprisingly, towns faced serious problems keeping law and order. By the 1870s, counties and municipalities could buy iron cages that, when mounted in log cabins, provided some certainty in holding prisoners. A number of towns used these contraptions, and Trumann even mounted its cage on wheels to facilitate carrying the prisoners to Harrisburg, the county seat, for trial. The existence of jails did not prevent disorder. A band of desperadoes shot up Fayetteville on March 29, 1879, and an editor who visited Fulton actually bragged that he was not even robbed.

All towns suffered from a lack of urban services. Little Rock, which had gas lighting before the Civil War, added a street car system in 1877. Fort Smith had both gas and street cars by the early 1880s. Elsewhere conditions were primitive. One editor observed that Prescott needed to incorporate so that dead swine lying in the streets could be removed. Van Buren's porcine problem was slightly different. There the pigs got drunk on the swill from a nearby distillery and charged through the streets, knocking over pedestrians and

disturbing traffic. In nearby Fort Smith, cattle on the main streets were so common in 1881 that the downtown "resembles a stock farm." Public sanitation was unknown, and municipal water, paving and lighting were things of the future in most communities.

The first mark of a real urban community was the purchase of a fire engine. Little Rock led the way before the Civil War and had four volunteer fire companies by the 1880s. Progress was slower elsewhere. A hook-and-ladder company organized in Arkadelphia, and equipment was ordered. But local funds were insufficient to pay the freight on this equipment when it arrived. A number of towns suffered disastrous fires. Because most buildings were constructed of wood, it was hard to contain a blaze once it started. As in the antebellum period, most fires were ascribed to arsonists.

All of the towns were dirty. Walnut Ridge, which had moved off its namesake ridge in order to be on the railroad, was "one long street where only the winds of heaven swept up the papers and light debris of the little general stores." Public accommodations were expensive and inadequate. A visitor at Harrisburg reported paying $1.50 a night for a room at a hotel where the food was prepared badly and the drinking water had insects floating in it.

One significant feature of town life was entertainment based on the self-help principle. The most common activity was the town band. Citizens followed the musical success of their bands with the intense interest later given to sports. County fairs, summertime concerts and the Fourth of July were important celebrations. After the end of the Civil War, only Republicans and blacks celebrated the Fourth until 1875, when the state press made a concerted effort to get ex-Confederates back into the act, especially as the nation's Centennial was at hand. The Pike County celebration of the Fourth in 1877 attracted many who had never heard a band before.

Bradford Silver Band *(photographer unknown, ca. 1895) Dozens of pictures of town bands were made in the late nineteenth century. This is one of the few having female members.* **University of Central Arkansas**

Christmas also became a holiday of growing importance as Protestant prejudices against it faded. Finally, Mardi Gras achieved considerable popularity in the mid-1870s, especially in Little Rock, which had special railroad junket prices to lure visitors there for the celebration.

The Fourth of July marked the end of the cotton chopping season and fall saw the arrival of circuses. Hundreds of circuses toured Arkansas after the War, not always peacefully. Prostitution, pornography, card games and false advertising were companions to circuses. Little Rock even had a city ordinance that required all companies to parade through the town, apparently so residents could form some realistic appreciation of the circus's resources. One traveler reported visiting a circus operating off a riverboat on the

Arkansas. It was of "a miserable variety and low," had gambling tables, dice, roulette, guessing for dollars and passed counterfeit money. One would not guess that these inadequacies existed from the advertisements appearing in the local newspapers heralding a circus company's arrival. It took an entire page of the Arkadelphia *Southern Standard* to detail "The Great International Menagerie, Museum, Aviary, Aquarium, Colossal Hippodrome, Cavaliers Escorting Grecian Beauties." The next issue of the paper reported that burglars following the circus had robbed homes while residents were at the show.

Baseball was another featured entertainment in the post-war era. Ball games had been played before the War, and the Choctaw even came to Little Rock to give an exhibition of

The Harrisburg Modern News Office *(photographer unknown, ca. 1910) L. D. Freeman, center, established the paper in 1888 and made extensive use of his family. His son, Orange, sits at the typecase. The twins, Era and Vera, are on the left, and Mrs. Freeman stands behind the two younger sons, Ewell and L. D., Jr. In the 1920s, the family acquired a Linotype machine. According to legend, L. D. got fed up with the Linotype machine and unable to move it out of the office, dug a hole in the floor and buried it. A computer took over typesetting in 1988, the centennial of family ownership.* **Arkansas State University Museum**

Indian ball, albeit with the players clothed. But the standardized rules of baseball made it the first community sport in Arkansas. Any field would do, and the sporting equipment was primitive and frequently homemade. Teams also got into unexpected trouble. One Fort Smith team that called itself the Klan was arrested by an unamused Republican sheriff. Little Rock children were arrested when they tried to play ball on Sunday. Play on Sunday was only one Sabbath issue during the era. Others included attempting to prohibit trains from running on Sunday in Georgia, persecution of Seventh Day Adventists and a controversy about Sunday theater. When the Brignoli troupe came to Arkansas in 1870, it gave a Sunday afternoon sacred concert without recorded opposition, but in Memphis, where the company had played previously, some ministers were wildly indignant and attempted to prevent the performance. Arkansas began to catch sacred Sunday fever in the 1880s. In addition to jailing more than 200 Seventh Day Adventists, Arkansas banned Sunday hunting and fishing. The story of a man petrified while fishing on Sunday in Pike County led hundreds of people to flock to the spot to see this sign of God's wrath.

The movement to legislate and enforce morality on an independent people generally had the support of local newspapers. Community betterment became a central newspaper theme during the 1880s in contrast to the almost complete emphasis on politics that marked the antebellum period. Reconstruction editors perhaps had been the most overtly political of any in the state's history, but as political tempers cooled during the era of the New South, editors began to emerge as spokesmen for their communities.

Papers often experienced both financial insecurity and less than perfect freedom. Opie Read once ran a paper from a boxcar on a siding, and hard times forced many editors to sell their outside pages to a patent medicine "ready print" supplier who forced the editors to sign a "red clause" prohibiting any editorial discussion of the well-known evils of patent medicine. Times got so hard that one Searcy editor took in fifty pounds of flour, four chickens, five dozen eggs, four large beets and three bushels of wheat in lieu of cash for subscriptions. Others even solicited barter.

It was in the press that the first signs of liberated women began to appear. The Helena *True Issue* had the first woman compositor, the daughter of editor W. W. Lewis. There was another by 1871 in Little Rock, "with all the appliances of curls, crinoline, chignon and calico." The honor of being the first woman editor went to Mrs. George L. Brown of the Ozark *Banner*, who took over the editorship "with signal ability" after the death of her husband, and was admitted to the Arkansas Press Association.

Editors assumed a protective attitude toward their communities. The Arkadelphia *Southern Standard* reported farmers' complaints about dishonest scales at gins but assured readers that town ginners were fair. Less forthright was the Helena press's handling of the 1878 yellow fever epidemic. The local outbreak began with the arrival and death of a Memphis woman. Because local doctors would not state positively that yellow fever was the cause of death, the press reported business as usual even as scores of cases began to be reported. Fear of the disease led to nineteen volunteer nurses being expelled from their boarding houses, and even two women from the red-light district were allowed to help. However, the local press avoided the topic like the plague.

On a more positive note, editors campaigned for agricultural improvements, especially economic diversification and local self-development. They boosted local industries, particularly railroads, and although they received free passes from the railroad to attend the state press convention, not all editors were silent on railroad abuses. In reporting on circuses, they acted as reviewers in rating the attractions for the public. Even so, political coverage was most important, and election times usually found Arkansas editors at their metier.

The Farmers' World

The New South was a farmers' world from beginning to end. Yet that world was changing from the self-sufficient agriculture of the past into an increased concentration on raising cotton as a cash crop. Editors reminded people that the War had destroyed the easy, idle life of the plantation, and that "economy, industry,

enterprise and carefulness" were now the order of the day. Yet few could resist a backward glance:

> That old spinning wheel is sweeter
> music to our ears than the most
> scientific touch on organ or piano as it
> takes us back to brighter and happier
> days before sin had entered the soul,
> and men and women were what they
> seemed and always paid their
> subscriptions to newspapers in advance.

Arkansas fortunes rose and fell with the price of cotton. Arkansas cotton took prizes at the Atlanta Exposition of 1881, at Louisville in 1883 and at New Orleans in 1885. Only three counties had fewer than a thousand acres in cotton production in 1889. From the "shoe-top" cotton in the uplands to the prize-winning bolls of Chicot County, Arkansas was enslaved increasingly to the market price of cotton. Lee County devoted 86 percent of its farm land to the white crop, while at the opposite end, Benton and Madison counties stood at .02 percent. Quality as well as acreage varied. Although upland cotton presented a spindly appearance, it actually received better cultivation on family-owned farms than from tenant farmers in the lowlands. The rapidly depleting soils of the Gulf Coastal Plain produced the lowest yields. Union and Ouachita Counties grew only .37 bales an acre compared to Chicot County, the state leader, with .94 bales an acre.

Next to cotton in importance came corn and wheat, grown mostly for local consumption. Only 6 percent of the corn and 23 percent of the wheat were shipped outside the counties in which they were grown. Both were ground at local mills that usually were powered by water in the uplands. Millers were paid in kind, receiving eight out of every fifty-six pounds of corn. Steam-powered engines ran combination grist and sawmills in the lowlands, and a few animal-

Weighing Cotton at Sundown *(photographer and date unknown) Weighing cotton sometimes resulted in violence. Pickers charged scales were inaccurate, and planters claimed pickers stuffed their sacks with sticks and rocks. In order to guarantee that sharecroppers did not sell the landlord's cotton on the side, sales after sundown were illegal. Notice the formal coat and white shirt on the white man at the scales, an indication of his social class.* **Arkansas History Commission**

powered mills were still used in isolated areas or for making sorghum molasses. Mills played a significant social role because farmers talked politics while waiting for their grain to be ground.

Arkansas's entry into the world of commercial agriculture meant that success or failure rested on variables outside the farmers' control. The immediate post-war period saw high prices but also a labor shortage and the continuation of a discriminatory national tax on cotton. When cotton prices began falling in the early 1870s, some farmers were unable to pay their property taxes and lost their land. One county editor concluded by 1873 that, "Few

men in the South since the war have made anything more than a bare living, while many are worse off than they were the day the war closed." The wife of one-time rich planter Elias Rector wrote, "It is hard to come down to poverty," and those who could not adjust to altered conditions soon found themselves in genteel poverty, respected for their family and kinship, but without the economic or political clout they once possessed.

Farming practices were a combination of old and new. The few issues of the *Arkansas Agricultural and Mechanical Journal* promoted modernization of farming, and a few old ways passed into oblivion. Oxen were half as

Team of Oxen *(photographer unknown, 1915) The claim that this was Batesville's last team is doubtful, but the use of oxen declined greatly after 1880.*
Arkansas History Commission

efficient as horses and virtually disappeared from the state's farm life except to haul logs from the swamps. Those who encountered them remembered the experience:

> I would hear the heavy wheels squeaking and knocking in their hubs. Then, I would see the huge steer between the shaves, pulling a large heavy cart along. The horns stood high and curved towards each other with large Brass balls screwed on the point of each horn, plus a bell around the steer's neck that had a high pitch sound.

The Berryville paper reported in 1914 that:

> a crowd of citizens stood in the rain yesterday morning to see something of a curiosity for Berryville in the way of two wagons of movers pulled by oxen. One wagon had four yokes of oxen hitched to it and the other three. The movers were from Heber Springs and were going to Garfield in Benton County. They were the first ox teams that have passed through Berryville in a good many years.

Although the cotton mule displaced oxen in the lowlands, tools remained limited and consisted only of plows, pitchforks, shovels, hoes and rakes. Most were homemade. Plowing consisted of scratching the ground to a depth of three to five inches, and always in a straight line regardless of drainage patterns. Lighter soils, particularly on Crowley's Ridge and in southern Arkansas, eroded so badly that many antebellum fields became thicket-filled gullies.

Very little crop rotation occurred, and land that occasionally was let to "rest" was often burned over, a practice long continued in the Ozarks, where setting the woods on fire later facilitated grazing scrub cattle. After plowing came seeding, done by hand. Cotton was grown in rows, but corn often was planted in groups of hills. The entire family participated in farming. Children weeded the fields until around the Fourth of July, after which time they were sent to schools, if any existed, while adults had their revivals and politics.

Harvesting began in the fall, and many families earned their year's income by helping harvest crops, moving by covered wagon from community to community. New land was cleared in the winter, although many stumps were left in the field and covered with soil. A few signs of progress appeared. Wheat reapers were the first major machines introduced in Arkansas, arriving before the Civil War. Used primarily in the northwest by progressive farmers, reapers rarely were seen on the steep hills and hollows, where hand-harvesting remained common. Deep plowing was introduced by William M. Fishback, who used a steel plow. He reported greatly increased crop yields, which were avidly publicized by county editors anxious to prod the ultra-conservative farmers into experimenting. Fishback also began raising apples for export, shipping them down the Arkansas River.

In addition to raising crops, most farmers ran hogs, turning them loose in the woods to forage for mast and snakes until caught and

Funeral Notice.

The friends and acquaintance of W. C. and MATTIE BOOTH are requested to attend the funeral of their son WILLIE IVER BOOTH, from their residence this evening at 3 o'clock p. m.

Des Arc, Sunday June 20th, 1880.

Funeral Notice for Willie Iver Booth, Des Arc, June 20, 1880. *Funeral notices spread the word of death before the telephone was widely used.* **Publisher's Collection**

fattened in the fall and slaughtered in the winter. Each owner marked his pigs by cuts on the ear or by branding. December and January were hog-killing months and every part of the animal was used, including feet, blood pudding, sausage, lard, cracklings, well-cured hams, mincemeat and brains, which were scrambled with eggs. No attempts at controlled breeding existed, and pig hunts in the fall were capital sport.

A major stereotype of Arkansas emerged in the image of one particularly wild type of porcine: the Arkansas razorback. Introduced in 1904 by humorous writer Marion Hughes, the label was at first much resented. The lack of control over hogs meant that no protection existed against hog cholera, a disease that could kill up to three-fourths of the hogs in a neighborhood and leave communities meatless for an entire year. Although hogs were raised throughout the state, only Ozark farmers marketed a surplus. This was achieved by means of a hogdrive in which one man led, two men guarded the sides and a fourth man with a wagon in the rear picked up the fallen. Once slaughtered and pickled, the pork was sold to the Delta counties where, as before the War, food production was not emphasized.

Cattle raising recovered slowly from wartime losses of breeding stock. As farmers

began to fence more land, the area available for open stock decreased. Sometimes quite violent local controversies erupted about open versus closed range. The herders increasingly found their way of life threatened. Wire fencing, available by the 1880s, put additional pressure on space. Some modern historians hold that these former herders, unable to survive in the post-war world, became the first white sharecroppers under the new economic system.

Arkansas farm families also kept some poultry. Flocks were small, and "chicken-eater" was a name for Yankees. Eggs were marketed locally, sometimes by peddlers who worked the rural areas on foot or by wagon. Although cattle were common, milk cows were not, and cows usually were milked only in the spring. The Arkansas antebellum diet of pork, corn and molasses remained universal, and, although remembered nostalgically by subsequent generations, was both bad nutritionally and often was prepared poorly. Game, which supplemented this diet, became scarce in Arkansas, with the passenger pigeon hunted to extinction. Two proposed game laws were defeated, the first because legislators thought that killing all game would encourage industry in Arkansans, and the second because of lobbying by hostile city sportsmen. One rural editor blamed the rising number of crop pests on Negroes having guns and killing all the birds.

Perhaps the most controversial bill proposed during this era was one to put a tax on dogs; it was designed primarily to aid the emerging Arkansas sheep-raising industry. Had such a law been adopted and enforced, it would have raised a substantial sum; the editor of the DeWitt *Gleaner* in 1883 estimated the town's population at 500 persons and an equal number of dogs.

In spite of heroic sacrifices and the new roles women had played in the Civil War, the Arkansas farmers' world remained a patriarchal society. A few women continued to make

The Tennis Club at Newport (*photographer unknown, ca. 1896*) *Recreational exercise for women grew in popularity in the late nineteenth century. Although croquette could be played at home, the socially popular sports of golf and tennis inspired the creation of private clubs.* **Jacksonport State Park**

use of married women's property laws, and farm wives who could read newspapers learned of the national debate on women's suffrage. For most, however, the man made the decisions and the woman bore a succession of children.

A large family obviated the need for outside farm labor, but it also was at the heart of the land problem, because as Arkansas became settled, it became harder for a young man to get a start. The older farmer was left without cheap labor once his children left home. At a father's death, a family farm might have to be divided from among three to a dozen children. Thus a marked turnover in

land was compounded by the typical American's quest for something better. The same family often might stay in one county but move many times.

Another labor question was foremost in the thought of many farmers. On what terms could blacks, now free from slavery, work? The first answers came during Reconstruction when black women withdrew from the fields and men demanded weekly wages. The Freedmen's Bureau supervised these contracts immediately after the War, although whether it was to the benefit of blacks or whites depended on local politics.

Falling cotton prices during the 1870s forced black women to reenter the labor force. An 1870 contract from Arkansas County defined women's legal position: "It is understood that a woman is 3/4 of a man." Squad labor continued to be the norm, with each squad leader responsible for tools and for drawing rations to feed his members. Working hours were sometimes contractually defined, and the hands on one plantation got two hours at noon during July and August but only one hour and a quarter the rest of the year. Each squad was required "to keep its portion of the plantation in good order." Rations usually consisted of four pounds of meat and one peck of corn a week, and on one plantation, workers were prohibited from owning any stock of their own.

Planters soon concluded that squad labor was inefficient. In particular, fences caused no end of trouble, because workers were strongly tempted to convert them to firewood in the winter. Increasingly elaborate contracts, variously called articles of agreement, chattel mortgages or crop liens, spelled out in detail just how much food was to be provided, what was to be done about fencing, how crops were to be divided and how disputes were to be settled. One 1871 contract in Arkansas County by T.C. Flournoy provided that delinquencies and forfeitures be determined by the selection of two disinterested parties chosen by both sides. If these two could not agree, a third person would be chosen similarly to cast the deciding vote. The landlord in one Calhoun County contract let the tenant use the cistern in return for chimney and fence repair.

Squad labor was replaced between 1870 and 1880 by subdivision of the plantation into twenty-acre to forty-acre units farmed by tenants working for shares. Standardized forms for chattel mortgages and crop liens replaced individually negotiated contracts. In the most intensely cultivated county in Arkansas — Chicot — "the crop is made entirely on a credit system." In the 1880 agricultural census, a Crittenden County planter explained the transformation:

It is better for both owner and laborer when the contract is faithfully carried out. The negro has his home, garden patch, and fuel free of charge; has the loan of a cow, if he does not own one. He generally raises pigs (all his own), and his house is situated "away" from the "quarter." These conditions engender feelings of respectability and pride at home, a laudable ambition to excel in farming, and to a great extent obviate the necessity of overseeing on the part of the owner. The best class of colored citizens work this way, and prefer it. Only a portion of the land is able to be worked in this manner. When hired labor is employed, the hands are irresponsible, lazy and vicious and require wages every Saturday. When paid they leave for the city; when "broke" they return and work another week; are inveterate gamblers, and are called "roustabouts."

Tenancy, which ran from 10 to 20 percent in the Ozarks to more than 50 percent in the Delta, encompassed 82 percent of blacks. Ironically, it was the Granger legislature of 1875,

a body so rural that there hardly were enough lawyers to make up the Judiciary Committee, that put the final legal seal of approval on debt peonage by making the removal of mortgaged crops a felony.

As tenants became sharecroppers, landlords struggled with mortgages on their lands. Hard times forced many farmers to mortgage first their lands and then future crops. Not so jokingly called *anaconda* mortgages after the South American snake that slowly choked its victims to death, these feared legal instruments became one method by which lands changed hands. Because federally chartered banks did not exist outside of Little Rock and Fort Smith and could not lend money on land, the local merchant was often the source of credit. Although the 1874 Constitution set the interest rate maximum at 10 percent, little enforcement effort followed because almost no competition existed for loans. Prevailing rates in many rural areas ranged from "10 percent to grand larceny."

The rural store was one major feature of the new economic order. Those stores on plantations that generally served only local tenants were called commissaries. Most operated without money. Some issued their own scrip and others kept records in "doodle'em" books. The independent merchants often enjoyed a territorial monopoly that they used with credit to ensnare their customers. A number of large farming operations of the next century owed their origins to the country store in the late nineteenth century.

Such stores could be immensely profitable. Not only were prices high, but interest charges ran from 25 to 300 percent. In addition, it was doubtful that an honest set of scales could be found in a country store anywhere in the South. A "pound" of bacon usually weighed honestly at three-fourths of a pound. Farmers were in a poor position to fight the system, for over the South as a whole, 79.5 percent of them were illiterate.

Farmers were aware of their helpless condition. The Granger legislature in the 1870s debated laws regulating merchants' profits without solving the problem.

Blacks and the Agricultural System

Built into the system of sharecropping was implicit racism. Blacks would be tolerated if they worked hard and surrendered the fruits of their labor willingly to white landlords. One Arkansas ex-slave interviewed by the WPA in the 1930s was bitter about this new kind of freedom:

> After freedom, we worked on shares a while. Then we rented. When we worked on shares, we couldn't make nothing — just overalls and something to eat. Half went to the other man and you would destroy your half if you weren't careful. A man that didn't know how to count would always lose. He might lose anyhow. They didn't give no itemized statement. No, you just had to take their word. They never give you no details. They just say you owe so much. No matter how good account you kept, you had to go by their account and now, Brother, I'm tellin' you the truth about this.

A chant sometimes heard outside the plantation commissary ran:

> Naught's a naught,
> Figger's a figger;
> All for the white man —
> Nothin' for the nigger.

The total subjugation of blacks in Arkansas did not come until after 1900, but all its essential elements existed during the era of the New South. Even under sharecropping, as long as black labor was needed, a man with luck might start without tools or animals, and

Black Family at Rosboro, Clark County. *(photographer and date unknown) An itinerant photographer caught this family in a pose that suggests the dangerous nature of rural Arkansas for blacks.* **University of Arkansas**

by diligent application, make increasingly advantageous arrangements until he could in time lease or rent land. But the last step, and the one to which blacks overwhelmingly aspired, to own land, was the hardest. It was at this point that whites wanted to draw the color line.

Most blacks lived in the lowland counties where the best farm land was taken already. When blacks tried to move into the areas best suited for small farming, violence erupted. The Forrest City *Times* on January 24, 1913, printed an obituary on Anderson Frierson, a "well-known, industrious and thrifty colored farmer." When Frierson had settled in L'Anguille township, "the few white people who then lived there looked on the coming of the negro as an encroachment on their rights." Because Arkansas remained underpopulated, resistance to black advancement was localized during the New South Era.

Some fortunate blacks prospered during these years. One was Scott Bond of Madison, whose 1917 autobiography, *From Slavery to Wealth: The Life of Scott Bond, The Reward of Honesty, Industry, Economy and Perseverance*, remains one of the most significant memoirs of black achievement in the Mississippi River Delta. Born in 1853 in Mississippi, this son of a white plantation manager was reared in Cross County. He was so fair-skinned that when he traveled on trains in the era of segregated coaches, conductors often tried to put him in the wrong cars. Bond began as a common laborer and saved his money, married wisely and reared a large number of sons. He began leasing land from whites and then acquiring land outright. He was not only supported by his antebellum connection within the white community but also had close financial ties to local Jewish merchants and lawyers. Bucking the trend toward one-crop concentration, Bond never grew only cotton but raised potatoes and Jerusalem artichokes during times of depressed prices. His main hobby was raising prize cattle.

Although Bond was the most spectacularly successful black farmer, there were others. Pickens Black moved to Arkansas in 1878 at age fourteen and settled in Jackson County. Like Bond, he started at the bottom but rose to own the all-black town of Blackville, home to more than 300 families. Like Scott Bond, Pickens Black was aided by influential whites, the antebellum owners of his wife, and by the firm of Wolff and Goldman of Newport. In Crittenden County, George Berry Washington managed to acquire five plantations and leave behind a marble tombstone later painted by Carroll Cloar, a prominent Arkansas-born twentieth century painter, as *Angel in a Thorn Patch*.

Blacks who rose from poverty plainly were exceptions. To a large extent they owed their prosperity to the exploitation of other blacks. A folk story among Scott Bond's tenants that he really was a Jew illustrated the vast gulf that separated this small elite from the illiterate masses of freedmen and women.

There also were black communities of landholding families. Menifee in Conway County was one example. Founded after the Civil War on land purchased from the railroad, Menifee attracted blacks from Tennessee who came as small farmers and held on to their farms well into the twentieth century. Some engaged in trade, and a correspondent to the Indianapolis *Freeman* noted that, "They own most or all business houses in this place, [and] there are a great many wealthy families here."

Despite the arrival of a large number of black settlers in Arkansas in the late nineteenth century, Arkansas proved to be less than the "Land of Opportunity" that state literature and black promoters promised. Because blacks in America suffered first and worst in times of economic distress, the downturn of cotton prices in the 1870s and 1880s resulted in two departure movements among Arkansas blacks. The first of these was the Exoduster movement of the 1870s that was spurred by reports coming from Kansas that blacks could obtain land there and prosper. The entire black community in the Mississippi River Valley was divided in the debate about the Kansas opportunity. Supporters in Arkansas held a state convention in 1879 and a number of families left. White newspapers reported every difficulty, reflecting the unease whites felt over a possible loss of the labor supply. Perhaps only a few hundred people were involved directly in the movement in Arkansas, fewer than in Mississippi or Louisiana, but it vocalized the resentment blacks felt about the new economic order and led to vivid accounts of what eventually would be called the "Southern agrarian question."

Populism repeated the same process for white farmers and sharecroppers five years later.

Hard times in the 1880s led to a second loss of faith in Arkansas. This produced a revival of interest in Liberia, reflecting a belief that black people would never be truly free in America. A number of small farmers sold their lands in order to finance the trip, and Scott Bond, who disapproved of the idea, used the occasion to enlarge his holdings. The small sum raised proved inadequate to the task. One group from Phillips County became stranded in New York, where their plight attracted national attention. Found destitute, the thirty-four men, thirty-two women, and thirty children told a tale of woe that led influential Northern clergyman Dr. Henry Highland Garnet to conclude: "They left Arkansas to avoid oppression. Except that they were not held in bondage, their condition was worse than when slavery existed."

The state's white press denied that blacks were abused in Arkansas and continually asserted that immigration was impractical and unrealistic.

The agitation led to bloodshed in Jackson County. Dr. G. P. E. Lightfoot had organized blacks in Woodruff and Jackson Counties apparently without making his plans clear. Lightfoot was murdered by a hostile group in a rural black church on December 10, 1892. Fifty bullets were removed from his body, and the corpse had been slashed by razors. Other blacks still believed in him, however, and ill feeling continued to divide the community.

CONCLUSION

As America celebrated her Centennial in 1876, Republican President Rutherford B. Hayes succeeded President U. S. Grant in an election that marked the end of Reconstruction. Thereafter the South receded from the nation's attention. A select group of Democrats was allowed to control, provided they adhered to the Civil War settlement by respecting

Northern economic interests and not reenslaving blacks. In the face of rising agrarian discontent, Arkansas Redeemers did their part, losing only on the debt repudiation issue.

At the same time, the dramatic arrival of the railroad fundamentally altered economic relationships and patterns of settlement. Arkansas was pulled further from her Southern orbit by the geographical implications of railroad lines that connected the state to the North rather than to the South. To some extent, settlement patterns followed the rails. Rapid economic development, even in the face of regional decline or stagnation, kept Arkansas from experiencing many of the deepest animosities generated in older regions. The characteristics of a frontier society continued to dominate throughout much of the state.

The process of repudiation of the state's debt left Arkansas embarrassed financially for years to come as lenders felt that the state's word and credit were not to be trusted. However, the biggest and most long lasting failure of the period was that of the Democratic Party to continue the embryonic system of statewide education that was begun during Republican Reconstruction. Without a comprehensive system of public education for whites and blacks, it was impossible for the state to correct the educational deficiencies that were to lie at the heart of racism and the failure of economic development for the next 100 years.

BIBLIOGRAPHIC ESSAY

The Redeemers in Arkansas have escaped close scrutiny. Joe T. Segraves, "Arkansas Politics, 1874-1918," (Ph. D. Diss., University of Kentucky, 1973) is a useful survey. Waddy W. Moore collected a number of relevant articles into *Arkansas in the Gilded Age, 1874-1900* (Little Rock, 1976). Walter Nunn, "The Constitutional Convention of 1874," *AHQ*, XXVII (Autumn 1968), 177-204, supersedes previous literature on the subject. Judith Barjenbruch, "The Greenback Political Movement: An

Arkansas View," *AHQ,* XXVI (Summer, 1977), 107-122, is a short treatment on the opposition. The pros and cons of state finance are debated in Garland E. Bayliss, "Post Reconstruction Repudiation: Evil Blot or Financial Necessity?" *AHQ,* XXIII (Autumn 1964), 243-259. The sordid history of law enforcement can be studied at the state level in Garland E. Bayliss, "The Arkansas State Penitentiary Under Democratic Control, 1874-1896," *AHQ,* XXIV (Autumn 1975), 195-213. Judge Parker has attracted extensive attention. A modern summary is John E. Miller, "Isaac Charles Parker," *AHQ,* XXXI (Spring 1972), 57-74.

Economic and social conditions in Arkansas differed substantially from those in the older Southern states. For blacks, a good beginning is Dan A. Rudd and Theo Bond, *From Slavery to Wealth: The Life of Scott Bond,* (Madison, Ark., 1917). Useful articles include James L. Morgan, "Dr. Lightfoot, 1892," *SH,* XVI (April 1978), 3-12 and Phil James, "Pickens Black, Planter," *SH,* XVI (October 1978), 11-19. A surprisingly useful source, considering that the main emphasis was on slavery, is George R. Rawick, ed., *The American Slave: A Composite Autobiography,* (Westport, Conn., 1972).

Jeff Davis *(photographer and date unknown) This hunting picture from the 1880s captures the spirit of Governor Jeff Davis better than his studio portraits. Note the handsome dogs and the cigar.* **Old State House**

Chapter XII

The Populist Era

INTRODUCTION

The Civil War signaled the triumph of industrial capitalism in the nation's political life, but few common people realized this at the time. The majority of Americans remained farmers, but voted without a clear political sense of their economic condition. The Grange and the Greenback Party provided the yeast to raise the farmers' level of consciousness, and hard times in the 1880s bred discontent that took form as the Populist revolt.

Populism was both a cultural phenomenon and a political party. The Party failed, but in 1896, the Populist movement in the person of William Jennings Bryan captured the national Democratic Party. In its economic critique of capitalism, Populism emphasized the agrarian roots of early America by identifying as evil the monopolies, trusts and robber barons who rose to power after 1865. Politically, Populism propelled new men to power who were less concerned with the tarnished Lost Cause, and at least initially, with negrophobia. Just as the Age of Andrew Jackson produced Arkansas's Archibald Yell, Populism produced Arkansas's Jeff Davis, even though Davis was never a Populist Party member.

The failure of Populism to ameliorate agrarian economic hardships was followed immediately by a marked increase in racism. White farmers were encouraged by

Democratic politicians to vent their frustrations on blacks. *De jure* segregation became the legal policy for oppressing blacks, but white hatred also led to an increasing number of burnings, beatings and lynchings. In the end, Populism left a divided legacy, hostile to many of the processes of modernization, but with a willingness to experiment with radical social ideas, many of which appeared later in Progressivism and in the New Deal.

THE FARMERS' REVOLT

Cotton acreage increased after the Civil War, but cotton brought less money. Ironically, the more prices fell, the more farmers depended on cotton. The result was a generation in debt, with land, crops in the field and even their unplanted crops mortgaged. Auctions, sales, foreclosures and tax sales became common as the crisis worsened in the early 1880s. In Columbia County, 1,430 separate parcels of land were advertised as tax delinquent; some 70,000 acres in Woodruff County were sold for taxes. The Waldron *Reporter* in Scott County observed:

From all directions we hear of attachments for debt, many for rent, closing out under mortgages for supplies, suits on notes, filing schedules for exempt property, etc. All the direct result of the ruinous credit system, and raising cotton to sell below the cost of production.

Troubled farmers blamed everyone but themselves. When they turned to politics, they asked that the state suspend tax collection. Failing that, they began to question the authority of the Redeemers, whose only claim to office was a ragged Confederate uniform and the ability to conjure up the wraith of Powell Clayton. Top officials in both county and state government had major short-

ages of funds in their account books, and little could be done to correct the problem. The Redeemers stood together solidly as a class so that malfeasance invariably was acquitted through "quibbles and technicalities, and the ingenuity of skillful attorneys."

Farmers touched a raw nerve in political circles when they called for honest men regardless of the "bloody shirt, secession, war and reconstruction nonsense some are still preaching." It was one thing for farmers to gather and discuss their problems; it was quite another for them to suggest new policies and new politicians.

Prelude to Protest: The Farmers' Entry into Politics

From the end of the Civil War to the present, Arkansas farmers have organized and reorganized in attempts to reverse the course of history that has taken the nation from the Jeffersonian dream of "a nation of farmers" to a commercial and industrial society. Farmers nationally began to realize in the 1880s that overproduction and free enterprise led to lower prices even as the capitalists who handled their produce — shippers, warehouses, factors, merchants and middlemen — formed organizations that took an ever larger share of farm income. The first organized protest movement, the Grange, was strongest in the Midwest, but it also caught the attention of interested persons in Arkansas, notably John Thompson Jones and Simon P. Hughes, both planter-lawyers from Phillips County. By 1872, the Grange claimed 20,471 Arkansas members in 631 locals. Grangers opened cooperative stores, and a number of Grange-supported candidates reached the Arkansas legislature. Grangerism in Arkansas faced two problems. First, farmers were isolated and not informed sufficiently on farm policy to recognize the need for organization. Such indifference kept farmers from forming a united front. Legislation that would benefit landlords at the expense of tenants further divided the farm community. Second, the Grangers' cooperative ventures and their friends in the state legislature could do little to reverse national economic trends. The Grange movement, therefore, aroused hopes that were dashed quickly. The organization lost half its members within four years and merged with the Farmer's Alliance in the 1890s.

The Grange movement provided a forum for a national idea sweeping the farm states: Greenbackism. The federal government had financed the Civil War partially by inflation caused by issuing paper money. Inflation resulted in prosperity for farmers and in turn led to unwise investments in land and machinery. After the War, the money supply shrank even as the economy expanded. Farmers across the nation suffered as it became more and more difficult with each passing year to pay debts contracted in more affluent times. Greenbackers reasoned that because paper money had created their prosperity, a return to it would solve their problems. On the other hand, orthodox economists insisted that only gold was money and denounced any human attempt to tamper with the God-ordained money supply as wildly revolutionary. The issue divided Redeemers. The ex-Whig element led by Augustus H. Garland was wedded to orthodox economics, and a bitter internal feud divided the Party during the 1870s.

Greenback clubs first appeared in Arkansas in 1876 and existed for seven years. Organized first as a pressure group, the Greenbackers initially were able to get support in the legislature. By 1879, however, state Democrats had come to regard Greenbackism as dangerous heresy. Giving the excuse that Negroes and Republicans sometimes were involved in the cause, state leaders charged that support for a Greenbacker was actually a vote for the hated

Powell Clayton and all the evils of Reconstruction. So warned, a number of early supporters, including N.B. Burrow, Poindexter Dunn, W.P. Grace and F.W. Compton, left the movement, and Henry M. Rector declined the Greenbackers' gubernatorial nomination in 1880.

The outcast Greenbackers resorted to an alliance with Republicans in a vain attack on Democratic hegemony. Although logical on a local level, this 1880 fusion was the weirdest of alliances when viewed from the national stances of both parties. W. P. "Buck" Parks ran against Democrat Thomas J. Churchill, but polled only 31,284 votes, some 4,000 fewer than Republican A. W. Bishop's total in 1876.

Greenbackism drew some black support, for Green Thompson and Isaac Gillam served as Little Rock aldermen and state legislators. Such black activity led to reduced white support, and Greenbackism was killed by the racial prejudice that the Redeemers mustered against it. In a last feeble effort, Rufus K. Garland, the perennial supporter of lost causes and the personal and political antithesis of his educated brother Augustus, carried the Greenback banner for the last time in 1882 when he came in a poor third behind regular Republican W.D. Slack and Democrat James H. Berry.

Greenbackism and the Grange were national movements that found few opportunities to grow in Arkansas. However, they gave expression to discontent and articulated a philosophy counter to that of the Redeemers. They also warned farmers of the impending agricultural crisis and sowed the seeds for Populism in what proved to be the farm battle of the century.

The Agricultural Wheel and the Brothers of Freedom

All these considerations were in the minds of seven life-long Democrats, six of whom owned their own farms, when they met in a

***The* Wheel (1889)** *Newspapers established by the Agricultural Wheel gave full play to symbolic implications, putting every possible worker-related motif on their mastheads. This Batesville newspaper was run by two deaf-mutes.*
Independence County Historical Society

log schoolhouse near Des Arc in Prairie County in 1882 and organized the Wattensas Farmers' Club. These men articulated the fears of farmers so well that the club became the nucleus for the Agricultural Wheel, the first indigenous farm organization in the state. The symbol of the Wheel invoked the rings that encircled the embattled farmers. The group was composed at first of farmers only, who made every effort to keep to themselves. "Senile editors" and "proto lawyers" could not join, and chapters could not be organized in towns. As with the Grange, self-improvement was a major theme. The Wheelers in time established newspapers to promote the virtues of the cash system of buying farm supplies, and to renew the cry for farmers to diversify and support cooperative marketing and purchasing plans. Arkansas was home to 114 subordinate Wheels by 1888, and the movement spread into Tennessee and Texas. After merging with the Brothers of Freedom from northwestern Arkansas, the Wheel swelled to 50,000 members and had the support of the black Sons of the Agricultural Star.

The Brothers of Freedom, founded in Johnson County in 1882, was a more radical group that told farmers to avoid the capitalist world entirely through self-help. This ideology appealed to Ozark farmers who were new to commercial agriculture and skeptical of all "progress." The Brothers of Freedom did not hesitate to enter politics and demanded immediate reform on the local level. The Brothers had no qualms about splitting Party ranks, for Redeemers could make little use of their standard charge that farmers were betraying white solidarity in a region that was almost without black citizens. Emboldened by their early success, the Brothers merged with the larger Wheel and gave up their name, but not their determination to use the Wheel for daring purposes.

The Election of 1884

The first opportunity for these movements to try political action on a wide scale came in the election of 1884. The national Democratic Party nominated Grover Cleveland for president. Because the Party condemned the high protective tariff that was largely paid by farmers, Cleveland became the first Democratic president since the Civil War. Farmers in Arkansas supported Simon P. Hughes for governor. He was an antebellum Whig, Confederate veteran, Grange organizer and farmer-lawyer. A long-time politician, Hughes had been a member of the Constitutional Convention of 1874 and served as attorney general from 1874 to 1876. Hughes won handily over Republican Thomas Boles, a western Arkansas congressman from 1868 to 1873. Hughes's call for regulating railroads and banning mortgages on unplanted crops echoed part of the agrarian protest. However, the feeling that years of feeding at the public trough had made him too remote from farmer concerns was supported when it was discovered that Hughes condemned the railroads' free pass system even as he participated in it.

Farmer tickets in the 1884 election were successful in seven of the eleven counties in which they appeared, greatly increasing the group's sense of accomplishment. When agrarian legislation failed, more plans were made. Isaac McCracken, the former head of the Brothers who became the Wheel president, pushed for the adoption of a slate of candidates for state office. By a vote of forty-seven to thirty, the Wheel board decided to enter the big arena and oppose Hughes for a second term in 1886. John G. Fletcher, an agrarian Democrat from Pulaski County often denied high office by his Party, was offered the nomination but refused it. Charles E. Cunningham, a little-known Wheeler, accepted but came in a poor third. Undaunted, the group made more extensive plans for the 1888 election.

The Election of 1888

Farmers were not the only ones aggrieved. Arkansas also was home to members of America's first national labor union, the Knights of Labor, which considered every working man or woman a suitable prospect for membership. In 1888, the Wheel and the Knights created the Union Labor Party, an organization affiliated with the National Union Labor Party and composed primarily of Western farmers. The leadership of the Party and the Wheel were virtually identical in Arkansas.

C. M. Norwood, a one-legged Confederate veteran and state senator, won the gubernatorial nomination at the Party's first convention. The voice of orthodox Democrats, the *Arkansas Gazette*, labeled him "the most ignorant man who ever aspired to high position in Arkansas," and was equally hostile to a platform that called for regulated railroad rates, a 6 percent limit on utility profits, a prohibition on land ownership by noncitizens, the ending of forced labor on roads, reform in school taxes, abolition of convict labor and laws to prohibit corporations from hiring private armies.

The emergence of the Union Labor Party put political pressure on Democrats. The Democratic convention took 126 ballots before it rejected Hughes's third-term bid and chose James P. Eagle as its gubernatorial nominee. Eagle, a Lonoke planter, was put forth as a farmer even though his tenants farmed and he minded the farm store. A prominent Baptist, he had been converted in the army during the Civil War and later served as president of the state convention (1880-1904) and of the Southern Baptist Convention in 1902. He denied ever extracting a crop lien and made much of his religious background. Essentially a political innocent, Eagle was nominated to cover the political robbery of the century with his mantle of respectability.

That the election of 1888 would be something special became apparent when the state's Republican Party declined to nominate a slate and endorsed Norwood. Because Republicans usually mustered about 50,000 votes, or half the Democratic total, the Union Labor Party needed only one-fourth of the Democratic vote to win.

The Democratic response set the tone for Arkansas politics for the next fifty years. "The mask has been torn off," cried the *Arkansas Gazette*, "and the authors of the crimes of the Reconstruction era stand forth in bold relief." Democratic strategy was overtly racist and tried to convince Arkansas farmers that Norwood had betrayed the white race.

Election day in Arkansas was marred by violence, particularly in the racially divided Delta. In Crittenden County, where blacks outnumbered whites four to one, power had been shared through a "fusion" system in which members of both races held office. Whites ended that arrangement in 1888 when they rode into Marion on election day, seized the election machinery and drove elected black officials out of the county. One white commented, "this county's getting too small for you edicated [sic] niggers and we white folks."

The inspiration for this type of electioneering came from Louisiana, where it was called bulldozer tactics. Elsewhere, a system of terrorism called the "Mississippi plan" kept blacks from going to the polls. To further their plans, white voting officials imported ballot boxes manufactured in Memphis that contained false bottoms.

The official results showed Eagle had won with 99,650 votes to Norwood's 84,273. The Union Labor Party protested that Eagle's margin had been achieved fraudulently and demanded a recount. The Democratic controlled legislature agreed on the condition that the Party deposit $40,000 to pay for the recount. The price of justice was too high for a Party comprised of poor farmers and workers, and Eagle became the new governor. However, even the legislature could not stomach the fraud in Pulaski County where the Democratic victory came from counting 6,000 bogus ballots in six boxes and then tossing them into the Arkansas River. Although the legislature refused to investigate fraud in the governor's race, it did unseat the Pulaski

County Democrats and replace them with their Republican opponents.

While Norwood was opposing Eagle, other Union Labor candidates were running for Congress. Two races were suspiciously close. Congress was the ultimate judge of federal elections so the two losers appealed to the House Elections Committee. Testimony in the resulting hearing shed considerable light on how elections were stolen in Arkansas.

The first contested seat was in west central Arkansas, where Republican John M. Clayton, popular brother of Powell Clayton, made a determined race with Union Labor support. The best example of fraud came from Plumerville. There Republican election judges were ejected and only Democratic votes were counted. Then the sheriff's posse stole the box containing the ballots. Prominent Little Rock Republican lawyer M.W. Benjamin went to investigate and was beaten to death when he got off the train. The next victim was John Clayton himself, murdered in Plumerville by an unknown assassin. During the investigation that followed, a federal election supervisor narrowly escaped assassination and then was indicted for playing cards. Plumerville Democrats became heroes, and a local history written in 1970 praised Clayton's assassin (no longer anonymous) as a patriot.

The congressional committee took a different view and unseated Democrat Clifton R. Breckinridge. The murders served their purpose, however, for Breckinridge won the special election to fill the seat.

The second contested seat came in the Delta's first district. Wheel candidate L.P. Featherston of Forrest City forged an alliance of white and black farmers against lawyer W.H. Cate of Jonesboro, who represented planters. Cate was the announced winner, but testimony revealed his victory came about by coercing black voters. After reexamining the totals, the House declared Featherston the winner.

The Aftermath of the Election of 1888

The 1888 struggle represented a high-water mark emotionally for political insurgency. In 1890, the Union Labor Party ran Methodist minister Napoleon B. Fizer for governor, who garnered fewer votes than Norwood, and in eastern Arkansas, Cate regained his congressional seat from Featherston. Yet the possibility that future discontent again might threaten the Redeemer status quo led to the adoption of a new voting law as the first in a series of repressive moves.

One element of the new law was positive, for last-minute transfers of polling places were prohibited. Another reform was the introduction of the "Australian" ballot that eliminated party symbols and required the voter to mark the name of his choice at the polling place. Illiterates, especially blacks, effectively were denied the franchise:

> The Australian ballot works like a
> charm It makes them think and scratch,
> And when a negro gets a ballot He has
> certainly got his match.

The law allowed an illiterate to ask an election judge to mark his ballot, but few would do it because illiteracy was a badge of shame. In addition, the law created a centralized system of control vested in a state board of election commissioners that appointed all election officials in the state. Although Republicans or Populists sometimes were chosen, loyal Democrats always maintained control.

Hard on the heels of this change, Redeemers proposed a poll tax. Put on the ballot in 1892 as a constitutional amendment, the proposal imposed residency requirements for voting and each voter had to show a poll tax receipt. This also was promoted as a reform because the $1 poll tax went mostly to education. A majority of those voting on the issue favored it, but not a majority of the total vote cast in the election. In open violation of the language of the state Constitution (Art. 19, Sec. 22), the Speaker of the House declared the amendment had received a legal majority and had been adopted. The legislature quickly enacted discriminatory enforcement legislation, setting the payment schedule at the time when tenant farmers usually moved and requiring racial designation on the receipt.

U.S. District Judge Jacob Trieber observed in 1905 that the alleged amendment had never been adopted constitutionally. The following year, the state Supreme Court noted the explicit language of the Constitution in *Rice* v. *Palmer* (1906) and declared that the judiciary rather than the Speaker of the House would make a final determination. Faced with a certain court test, the legislature resubmitted the poll tax amendment to the voters, but the attorney general ruled that every person voting still had to possess a poll tax receipt. The amendment finally received the required majority in this coercive atmosphere.

A third development was the adoption of the white primary. Primary elections to determine party candidates had become common by 1898, but because blacks participated in the Democratic Party, white control was uncertain. Then local Democrats began to exclude blacks, and in 1906, Governor Jeff Davis ordered the rule adopted statewide. All three moves sought to insure the perpetuation of white Democratic control. Blacks were the primary victims, in part because they voted Republican and also for no other reason than the color of their skin.

The adoption of restrictive voting mechanisms stopped at this point. Arkansas never went as far as Mississippi, Texas or even Oklahoma. A proposed constitutional amendment requiring a literacy test combined with a grandfather clause to exempt whites failed in 1912. Total disfranchise-

Aunt Caroline Dye

In the late nineteenth century most women toiled anonymously at home. A lady's name appeared in the newspaper only three times: at birth, at marriage and at death. Delta women were famed for their quilts and Ozark women for their canning. But Caroline Dye of Newport had a national reputation, albeit of the sort not common to history books.

Born a slave in South Carolina in 1843, she was brought by William and Nancy Tracy to Rosie in Independence County. Freed by the Civil War, she married Martin Dye, whose previous owner was Henry C. Dye, a merchant of Sulphur Rock. The young couple settled at Elgin and moved to Newport about 1900.

Although she signed her name with an "X," Caroline Dye had "the gift." She once told a reporter that even as a small child, adults had tied her to the bed to make her tell fortunes. This clairvoyant and faith healer in time developed a large clientele of both blacks and whites. By the time of her death in 1918, she owned eight farms and had thousands of dollars hidden around the house. Her estate was worth more than $100,000. She had built a substantial home and kept a skilled cook. Her reputation was nationwide. Some small Newport children made good money meeting the trains and guiding visitors to her home. Others sent requests, accompanied by money, in the mail.

W. C. Handy, the Memphis songwriter, advertised her and Newport in the song "Sundown Blues:" "I'm going there to see Aunt Caroline Dye." During her heyday, Aunt Caroline was the best known black, male or female, from Arkansas. Believers still tell of how she told one man where his missing mule had gone or where one Newport woman had lost her diamond ring.

Aunt Caroline Dye (photographer and date unknown) In the early 1900s, this former slave had a national reputation as a clairvoyant and faith healer, amassed a sizable fortune, was the most famous Arkansan of her era and was honored by W. C. Handy in his song "Sundown Blues." **Jackson County Historical Society**

ment of blacks was unnecessary to white control because only a quarter of the state's population was black. A proposal by Reverend Wallace Carnahan, rector of Christ Church (Episcopal) in Little Rock, to have a poll tax of $10 a year and a property qualification of $1,000 got nowhere. If adopted, it would have disfranchised over 75 percent of the voters.

The Populist Party in Arkansas

The death of the Union Labor Party hastened the collapse of the Agricultural Wheel. As a result, the new farmer movement of the 1890s, "Populism" did not play as great a role in Arkansas as it did in some other Southern states. The old agricultural issues remained, but Populists added the demand for free and unlimited coinage of silver. Free silver dwarfed all other issues as the hottest debate topic in Arkansas between 1890 and 1896.

A complex debate on economic policy lay behind the silver issue. Populist theory held that farm prosperity could be restored if the government would increase the supply of money by coining silver. W. H. "Coin" Harvey, who lived after 1896 at Monte Ne in Benton County, was perhaps America's foremost popularizer of the Silver Crusade. Fired by the simple lessons in Harvey's book, farmers joined with representatives from silver producing states to carry the Populist crusade to the country.

The issue of "funny money" was strong within the agrarian wing of the Democratic Party. William Fishback captured the Democratic gubernatorial nomination in 1892 primarily because of his fame as "The Great Repudiator" of Holford Bonds. Republicans and Populists fielded candidates, but Fishback won by 60,000 votes. All the Democratic congressmen were reelected, but only Breckinridge was a Gold Democrat. By making hard times worse, the Panic of 1893 led voters to seek scapegoats. Violence against blacks increased, although Fishback abstained personally from overt racism.

In 1892, Southern Populists made a determined effort to elect their presidential candidate, James B. Weaver. Weaver campaigned in Arkansas and he encountered some dirty political tricks. As Weaver got up to speak at Prescott, an overheated steam engine sent up a roar that drowned out his remarks. In the end, Arkansas remained loyal to Cleveland and Populism faded.

Historians have debated whether Populism was forward-or backward-looking. The state Populist Party progressively supported federal supervision of state elections in order to limit fraud. Democrats then accused Populists of being Republicans who wanted to restore black supremacy. At the same time,

the Party did little to appeal to blacks, and Populists who returned to the Democratic fold carried with them increased rancor toward blacks. Religious bigotry also appeared in the Populist movement. Populist candidate and Methodist minister T.M.C. Birmingham unsuccessfully made W.C. Terry's Roman Catholicism an issue in one congressional race. Populists supported a railroad commission and a law against monopolies and trusts, but they also tended to oppose education, especially funding of the state university.

The depression that followed the 1893 panic pushed Arkansas Democrats closer to Populism. Cotton fell to 7 cents a pound and suffering of farmers intensified. Wage cuts led to strikes in coal mines and a walkout by union men on the Gould-owned St. Louis and Iron Mountain Railroad, producing $35,000,000 in business losses in Arkansas. The legislature responded to the crisis by rejecting funding for Arkansas's participation in the Columbian Exposition in Chicago, leaving it up to private parties to see that the state was represented. Democrats repudiated the leadership of Gold Democrat Cleveland at their 1894 state convention and nominated James P. "Old Cotton-Top" Clarke, a Phillips County planter, for governor.

Fishback, who had been trying to get a Senate seat since 1864, failed to displace James H. Berry and was forced into retirement. Republicans and Populists fielded gubernatorial candidates, but despite the hard times, 25,000 fewer voters participated than two years before and the total vote was down by 70,000 from 1890. The 1894 election was for some time the last in which blacks actively participated. For the first time since Reconstruction, the legislature was all white, and in city government, Little Rock had abolished wards, replacing them with at-large elections in which no black candidate stood a chance. Newly elected Governor Clarke spoke openly of the need for reform and while in office, freshman legislator Joseph T. Robinson of Lonoke County, who later became a powerful United States Senator, introduced a bill to create a railroad commission and regulate rates. Iron Mountain railroad lobbyist T. L. Cox marshaled "Cox's Army" against the bill. Clarke, whose cotton-top belied a hot temper, encountered one railroad supporter in a Little Rock hotel and demanded a private interview. When the man declined, Clarke seized him by the ear, spat in his face and pulled a pistol on him. Yet Clarke sat on the board of the Springfield, Little Rock and Gulf Railroad and lobbied hard for the line's interests. Not surprisingly, the bill failed.

Leading the fight for reform was that staid old matron of Arkansas Democracy, the *Arkansas Gazette*. J. N. Smithee, who began his newspaper career before the War and had been an active politician in the 1870s, returned from the West to edit the *Gazette* in 1896. He used union labor and editorially urged readers to buy and study Henry D. Lloyd's Populist gospel, *Wealth against Commonwealth*. Smithee pointed out that because of the cottonseed trust, the price paid Arkansas farmers had fallen by two thirds, from $18 a ton to $6. The *Gazette* proclaimed after the initial defeat of Robinson's railroad bill: "Arkansas belongs to the Goulds."

Creeping Populism reached national proportions at the Democratic convention in Chicago in 1896 when William Jennings Bryan, the silver-tongued orator of the plains, captured the presidential nomination by proclaiming that mankind should not be crucified on a cross of gold. The silver wing of the Party replaced Clarke with another silver devotee, Daniel Webster Jones. In addition to being an ex-Confederate, Jones was a sometime attorney for the Goulds. Enthusiasm for Bryan actually led more persons to vote in the federal election than in the state — the only such occurrence during the period when state elections were held on a separate day.

The Jones administration also continued the politically popular practice of appropriating Populist issues. After twenty-five years of struggle, the legislature passed a constitutional amendment creating a railroad commission, and the voters approved it in 1899. According to Jeff Davis, the bill passed only after the chief railroad lobbyist was locked in a house of ill repute for ten days. In addition, Elias W. Rector of Hot Springs, a genteel reformer, sponsored the Rector Anti-Trust Act. Populist issues now were a part of the Democratic platform, and the Populist Party died, leaving the state securely in Democratic control.

The Spanish-American War

The reform movement was blunted in 1898 by the outbreak of the Spanish-American War. Arkansas volunteers served with Teddy Roosevelt in the Rough Riders and in two state regiments. The first Arkansas regiment was commanded by Colonel Elias Chandler, a former military instructor at the University of Arkansas, and the second was led by Colonel Virgil Y. Cook of Batesville. Many men volunteered for the "splendid little war," and they were needed, because 25 percent failed the physical. Neither regiment saw action, but fifty-four men died in camp, largely from malaria or from sanitation problems. It did not help that the chief medical officer was a veterinarian. The chief consequence of the War for many Arkansans was the return of veterans with a new strain of smallpox. The disease soon reached epidemic proportions in part of the state and revealed the almost total lack of public health protection available. The War was popular in Arkansas, but in 1902, Governor Jones failed to oust Berry from the United States Senate by riding the coattails of imperialism.

The Career of Jeff Davis

Democrats had made overtures to Populists by adopting old Populist causes, but no one had adopted the Populist style. That distinction went to Jeff Davis. Born Jefferson Davis in Sevier County in 1862, he grew up at Dover and Russellville, where his father was a successful attorney. Jeff Davis had witnessed the Reconstruction-era militia wars as a child. Glorifying the Lost Cause of the Confederacy, he made political capital of his name. One rustic voter, supposing him to be the ex-president of the Confederacy, called him "the greatest and longest-lived man that ever was." A sometime student at the state University and the Vanderbilt Law School, Davis was licensed to practice law at nineteen.

Discovering the mood of the people, this regular Democrat of the 1880s changed from a respectable small-town lawyer into agrarian avenger. He was slow to get started politically. Although serving as a state presidential elector in 1888 and as district attorney, he failed to win a bid for Congress and considered moving to Oklahoma before he decided to run for attorney general in 1898.

Davis won the 1898 nomination largely because his principal opponent, university law professor F.M. Goar, died during the primary. Davis took office along with a legislature composed largely of Democrats with no previous experience and a strong Populist orientation born of their admiration for William Jennings Bryan. Various bills proposed that lobbyists wear badges, that railroads fence their rights of way and that railroad taxes fund the railroad commission. Most of the hostile legislation was sidetracked, but the Rector Anti-Trust Law emerged from the session. In sweeping language, this law banned any firm that engaged in any price-fixing from doing business in Arkansas.

Davis interpreted the law broadly as attorney general and filed suit against every fire insurance company in Arkansas. He swore: "My God, if there ever was a cold-blooded, arrogant, high handed, obstreperous, hard-to-down trust it is the insurance business."

He broadened the attack for good measure, saying: "I sued Standard Oil, I sued the American Tobacco Company, the cotton trust, I sued the express companies, I sued everything that looked like a trust, I sued them all."

Fire insurance companies reacted by canceling most of their Arkansas policies, which left the state's business community with no protection. At that time, fire insurance doubled as a credit rating, so that all foundations for commercial credit were destroyed as well. Frightened businessmen who descended on Little Rock heard Davis refer to them as the "high-collared crowd," and they "hissed, hooted, and howled down" the attorney general.

With reform-minded editor J. T. Smithee gone, the *Arkansas Gazette* called for the law's repeal: "The businessmen of Arkansas will not tolerate any interference with the progress of their state." Conservative Chancellor Thomas W. Martin quickly ruled against Davis in court, and the state Supreme Court in *State* v. *Lancashire Fire Insurance Co.* (1899) sustained Martin's decision. But in losing the battle, Davis won the war.

Davis was a wild man — totally at odds with reality. The elite assumed the storm was over once his lawsuits were thrown out of court. But Davis sensed that common people hated the aggregations of great wealth that had been erected at their expense and would support him as he continued the attack. Proclaiming the Rector Act was "the entering wedge . . . the first stroke in the great battle of the masses against the classes," Davis became a "Karl Marx for Hillbillies." Whether Davis actually possessed any ideological orientation is doubtful, but the politics of catharsis was reborn for the first time since the days of Thomas C. Hindman.

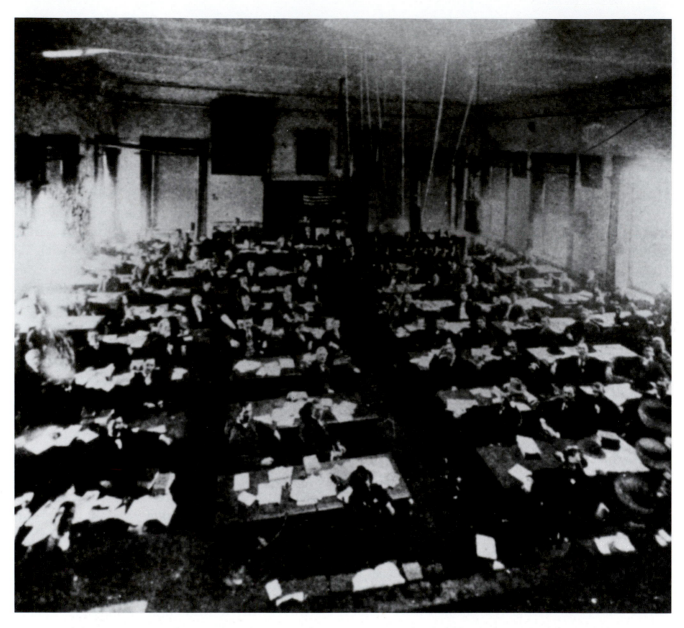

Interior of the Old State House *(photographer and date unknown) This photograph shows the House of Representatives in session about 1880. The state's medical doctors complained constantly about the building's unsanitary conditions.* **Old State House**

Even as the trust controversy was raging, Davis took on another issue by opposing the erection of a new state Capitol. The State House, despite remodeling, was plainly too small for state government. Better times had come after 1898, and a new industrial prosperity was crowding Little Rock with buildings that dwarfed the little Greek Revival temple on the River. "Building a million-dollar state house," the *Arkansas Gazette* promised,

"is one of the best evidences of a state's progress." After part of the Senate chamber collapsed, injuring a number of persons, the legislature created the Board of Capitol Commissioners to get the work started. Davis denounced the law as a swindle and tried to block it. Failing that, he began political warfare on supporters of the new Capitol.

Certainly there was much to criticize. The Capitol, as Davis predicted, eventually would cost two and half times the original estimate, and its construction was marked by an eclectic mixture of stupidity and corruption. Supporters located the new Capitol on the site of the old penitentiary; in their haste to get the project started, work began before plans were completed. Then it was discovered that the first foundation had not reached bedrock and would not support the building's weight, so work had to start over.

With an issue like that to work with, Davis ran for governor in 1900. Benefiting from the new primary system under which a candidate could appeal directly to voters without having to ingratiate himself with the self-serving courthouse rings, Davis took to the hustings with a performance that has remained unmatched, although often emulated, in Arkansas history.

Davis was the first major candidate to appeal openly to racial prejudice. He never claimed to be the blacks' "best friend" as he sought the "wool hat" vote. In his early race for prosecuting attorney:

> I told the boys around Morrilton, Russellville and Plumerville, that if they elected me, I would fill the penitentiary so full of niggers their feet would be sticking out of the windows.

Then Davis appealed for sympathy, claiming that because of his fight for the people in the anti-trust struggle, his hotel had raised the rent, the long-distance telephone manager refused him service and the German National Bank declined to cash his checks.

Davis took to the stump along with candidates J.E. Wood, A.F. Vandeventer, John G. Fletcher and Judge Edgar E. Bryant. He relished the criticisms heaped on him and never failed to quote the Helena *World*, which had called him a:

> Carrot-headed, red-faced, loud-mouthed, strong-limbed, ox-driving mountaineer lawyer and a friend to the fellow who

brews 40-rod bug-juice back in the mountains.

Newspapers — a conspicuous force for modernization — were his enemies, and Davis made it a point to denounce "squirrel-headed editors." In one speech he told the crowd that:

> I have a little boy, God bless him, a little pale-faced, white-haired fellow. . . . If I find that boy is a smart boy, I am going to make a lawyer out of him, and if I find that he has not a bit of sense on earth I am going to make an editor out of him and send him to Little Rock to edit the *Arkansas Democrat*.

By replying in kind, newspapers made a martyr of Davis. One editor warned, "if the *Arkansas Democrat* and several other papers don't let up abusing Jeff Davis, they will elect him Governor."

On the stump, Davis used a combination of Populist economics, homely anecdotes, Southern sectionalism and bitter personal attacks on his opponents. He denounced Judge Bryant, "the Silver-tongued Orator of Arkansas," for admitting to a Chicago audience that the Confederacy's defeat had been a blessing. According to Davis, John G. Fletcher had hounded his Populist brother to an early grave. On the issues, J.N. Heiskell of the *Arkansas Gazette* accurately observed:

> He labors to divide the people against themselves in order that he may become the champion of the bigger class, those whom he invidiously calls "the common people."

Thus Davis made generalized agrarian and working-class appeals without addressing the issues that divided tenant farmers from planters. The authentic old-line Populists never supported him and few of their substantive proposals figured in his rhetoric. The other candidates began dropping out as gubernatorial hopefuls went from county to county and Davis moved from victory to victory. He was triumphant in the end, carrying all but one of the state's counties. Davis also had called on voters to oust the state Supreme Court judges, "the five jackasses," and to elect incumbent Senator Berry over ex-Governor Jones.

Republicans, hoping to capitalize on Davis's extremist stands, nominated Harmon L. Remmel, the state's ranking Republican, who had the political misfortune to be an insurance agent and a capitalist. Davis did not treat the Remmel threat lightly, and he made especially effective use of a purloined telegram from the head of the New York Mutual Life Insurance Company, which gave Remmel permission to enter the race. By a two-to-one margin, Davis was again successful and became the first Arkansas governor of the twentieth century on January 18, 1901.

Davis called for a new anti-trust law, the passage of a fellow servant law to aid injured workers and changes in the building plans for the new state Capitol. He won on a few minor issues such as a Confederate pension law, but he failed to reach most of his goals. That suited Davis just fine, because it gave him issues to take back to the voters two years later.

Davis announced in 1902 as a candidate for the traditional second term, and he also told voters to support James P. Clarke against incumbent Senator James K. Jones, who Davis accused of being allied with the trusts. Davis's enemies united behind Elias W. Rector in a gubernatorial race that revolved around a new penitentiary scandal and Davis's excessive drinking habits. Rector gave Davis little trouble, and Clarke's victory over Jones gave him loyal support in the Delta counties, where he had less opportunity to use his oratorical talents because of planter dominance and machine control. Although he easily defeated regular Republican Harry H. Myers, a native of Iowa, and insurgent Republican Charles D. Greaves, Davis had some weakness that was

revealed in the general election because he ran nearly 8,000 votes behind the rest of the Democratic ticket.

A particularly acrimonious episode occurred in the aftermath of the campaign when Davis told ex-Governor Eagle to resign from the Capitol Commission. Eagle refused and forced Davis to fire him. The legislature supported Eagle by denying the governor's right to fire Eagle and insisting that it alone could fill vacancies.

Davis took on the state prisons in addition to the continuing Capitol controversy. Prison affairs lay in the hands of the State Penitentiary Board, which consisted of the governor and four other state elected officials. In order to terminate the vicious convict-lease system, reformers proposed to acquire a prison farm and work the convicts for the profit of the state. The Board voted to purchase the Cummins Plantation, which Davis said was a malaria-infested bog covered with Johnson grass. The Board, led by Attorney General George W. Murphy, defended the purchase during a legislative investigation of the governor. Charges of financial improprieties surfaced and led to a demand for Davis's impeachment, but the final committee report vindicated the governor.

One of the most colorful episodes in Davis's career came during this struggle. Believing that Davis intended to veto a number of its pet bills, the Senate waited until the end of the session to send its legislation to the governor for him to sign. Davis responded by vetoing the whole lot, which he then had loaded in a wheelbarrow and dumped on the Senate floor. A protest and a court challenge followed, but the governor was upheld.

Tradition alone limited a governor to two terms. Davis not only broke this tradition but told voters that he would run against Senator James H. Berry after his third term as governor. By that time, however, anti-Davis forces were stronger. Davis's success in getting a new state law that banned insurance companies was followed by a forty-block fire in Hot Springs that destroyed property worth more than $1,000,000. The Second Baptist Church expelled him for public drunkenness and gambling; prohibitionists were offended by his wholesale pardoning of bootleggers, and in a highly publicized maneuver, he pardoned a black prisoner on condition that the man move to Massachusetts.

Associate Judge Carrol D. Wood of the state Supreme Court opposed Davis for a third term. The race became something of a monument in Arkansas politics for its mixture of verbal and physical abuse. Davis's remarks at Hope so infuriated Wood that he hurled the governor from the platform. A fight followed, and both men were arrested for breach of the peace. Davis's enemies tried to turn the race issue on him by pointing out that the governor had pardoned a convicted black rapist. Davis retaliated by charging that Wood had appointed blacks to juries in the 1880s. Wood's effort to exploit Davis's church troubles led Davis to remark that he admitted to being a "Pint" Baptist but those who expelled him were actually "Quart" Baptists. Davis said of Wood's singing in the choir:

> When Judge Wood gets up to speak I want you farmers to call on him for a little song. I can't sing. I ruined my voice calling for gravy when I was little. Judge Wood makes more racket singing in the choir in Little Rock than one of you farmers calling your hogs home.

The *Arkansas Gazette* supported Wood, and Davis replied by saying, "that old red harlot. I had rather be caught with a dead buzzard under my arm or a dead polecat." Davis claimed repeatedly that all troubles came from his firm determination to protect the state treasury and never abandon the people. His private secretary later wrote:

No man ever lived who intuitively knew the psychology of the average Arkansas audience as he did. He spoke to them in a language which they knew and which they understood. So complete was his domination over his followers he could have organized a gigantic army and swept the capitol off the map.

Even those who disagreed came away impressed. One child remembered his speech at Cotton Plant this way:

> He waved his arms; he pounded; he stomped the floor; he mopped his brow and he drank a pitcher of ice water. I thought he put on a great performance.

And Jeff Davis defeated Judge Wood.

Racism dominated all issues during Davis's third term. In arguing for segregating school tax money by race, he adopted the slogan that "Every time you educate a 'nigger' you spoil a good field hand." In one speech he announced:

> We may have a lot of dead niggers in Arkansas, but we shall never have negro equality, and I want to say that I would rather tear, screaming from her mother's arms, my little daughter and bury her alive than to see her arm in arm with the best nigger on earth.

Davis failed, however, to get his law enacted. His racism achieved national attention when President Theodore Roosevelt visited Little Rock in 1905. Although personally popular with Republicans and ex-Rough Riders, Roosevelt had undercut his Southern support by dining with the great black educator, Booker T. Washington, in 1901 and occasionally appointing blacks to minor offices.

When Roosevelt arrived at Glenwood Park to address a crowd estimated at 40,000, Davis welcomed him in a speech that praised lynching as sound public policy. Roosevelt was so incensed that he departed from his prepared text to lecture Davis:

> You and I, Governor, and all other
> exponents of the law owe it to the causes
> of civilization to do everything in our
> power . . . to drive the menace and
> reproach of lynch law out of the United
> States.

Davis declined to attend a lunch after the
program because it would mean sitting at the
same table with Powell Clayton, who he
claimed was responsible for the death of an
aunt in the militia wars. Roosevelt allegedly
commented to Clayton that the militia had
killed the wrong woman, and Davis turned
the incident to his advantage by claiming
that Senator Berry, who was present, frater-
nized with murdering Republicans. Unlike
the 1880 Arkansas banquet tendered ex-
President U.S. Grant, no blacks had been
invited to the lunch.

Davis already had announced that he
intended to oppose Berry for the United States
Senate. In order to insure success, Davis had
the Democratic convention agree to make the
primaries binding on the legislature. Then he
announced a speaking schedule that the aged
Berry could not hope to meet. The *Arkansas
Democrat* called the contest "the vilest and
meanest state campaign ever witnessed in
Arkansas." Actually, Davis was rather
restrained. He abstained from personal
attacks, claiming only that Berry had
betrayed the people by supporting a railroad-
supported assessment bill, by voting for
Arkansas's settlement of its debts with the
federal government and by failing to vote for a
law regulating trade in agricultural futures.
Berry, who made only a few speeches, stood on
his record and relied on his friends.

The heat in the campaign came from elsewhere. Davis and ex-Congressman Hugh A.
Dinsmore clashed in Fayetteville when Dinsmore asserted that Davis had stolen a letter
from Berry. Davis broke the cane previously
used on Judge Wood at Hope over Dinsmore's
shoulder, and Dinsmore pistol-whipped Davis.
In spite of repeated charges that Davis was a
drunk and sold pardons for $500, he covered
Arkansas like the dew, delivering 225 speeches, and he swamped Berry by more than
10,000 votes.

Davis had hoped to remain a power in state
politics by installing John S. Little of
Sebastion County in the governor's chair.
Although Little won the election, he quietly
had gone insane and could not serve. X.O.
Pindall, who filled out the term, was a bitter
enemy who moved Davis's portrait from the
reception room to the bathroom.

Davis was a fish out of water in the United
States Senate. Promising to "knock down the
cobwebs before I am there two weeks," he
broke precedent by giving his "cobweb speech"
a mere eleven days after he was sworn in. A
large crowd gathered, and it was to them
rather than to his senatorial colleagues that
Davis vented his agrarian spleen. The national press was critical and the Senate scornful;
thereafter, he mostly answered correspondence and mailed free seed. He was challenged
six years later by Congressman Stephen Brundidge. In desperate political trouble, Davis
summoned all of his physical and political
reserves in attempting to show voters that he
had made a good senator. Although he polled in
excess of 10,000 more votes than his opponent,
a shift of 1,200 votes in twenty-three counties
would have deprived him of renomination in
the convention. He died at his Little Rock
home on January 2, 1913, before being sworn
in for his second term.

Jeff Davis represented the triumph of a
bastard strain of Populism. Always a regular
Democrat, he used Populist issues and oratory effectively, but actually accomplished
very little in office. The new schools for the
deaf and blind would have been created
under any governor. The state Capitol
remained unfinished, and its great expense
was caused at least in part by Davis, who

fought it so tenaciously. Davis made a difference on only three issues. First, he vigorously supported the Railroad Commission in lowering the passenger rate from 5 cents a mile to 3 cents and in reassessing railroad property. Second, Davis obtained a reform school for young offenders by threatening to pardon everyone under the age of eighteen until the legislature voted the money. Finally, he obtained the enactment of an insurance law that forced insurance companies to operate underground for some years. As senator, he was one of the least effective men Arkansas ever sent to Washington. Davis came to be classed, not without reason, as a Southern demagogue.

Davis looked like a nineteenth-century Populist. He almost always wore Confederate gray, never owned evening clothes or attended social functions of any kind and openly despised the refinements of Victorian society. Fishing and hunting were his two nonpolitical passions, and his ideal of a woman was "one that knows how to tune a hot stove and bake big hot biscuits with pimples on them." He made a fetish of rural values:

If you red-necks or hill-billies ever come to Little Rock, be sure and come to see me — come to my house. Don't go to the hotels or wagon yards, but come to my house and make it your home. If I am not there tell my wife who you are, that you are my friend and belong to the sunburned sons of toil. Tell her to give you some hog jowl and turnip greens. She may be busy making soap, but that will be all right; you will be properly cared for, and it will save you a hotel bill. The word "welcome" is written on the outside of the door for my friends.

Every visit to a crossroads community saw Davis trying to buy a pair of homemade socks, promptly discarded after he left. Davis, who never farmed and always lived in town,

manipulated agrarianism. His rednecks or hillbillies would have been astounded to see the mansion, the Villa Marre, that he rented. He was a consummate politician with all of his appointments, actions, friendships and hates revolving around the office. He criticized railroads and generously used railroad passes. Always quick to tag an opponent for questionable dealing, Davis's own financial affairs reeked of bribes and kickbacks. His legacy to Arkansas, a political machine called the Old Guard, was splintered badly even before Davis's death and failed to endure. The "backbone of demagoguery" went half a century after his death before it found a new leader. Many lamented the loss, however, and Davis's career inspired a play, a novel, and this poetic tribute from Orto Finley:

If Jeff could only come back now for one
   small day
And see the petty politicians' peevish
   play —
Behold the dazzling "intellects" that
   dare aspire
To seats of fame that only statesmen
   should acquire
In fancy I can see the "Old Guard" fall in
   line,
With guns unlimbered, waiting for the
   first faint sign
To forward march — God, what a change
   would mark the day,
If Jeff could only come back now to lead
   the way.

In American history the opening years of the twentieth century were called the Progressive Era. But Jeff Davis put Arkansas right in step with the Mississippi of James K. Vardaman and the South Carolina of "Pitchfork Ben" Tillman. Arkansas shed the vestiges of the old gentility in politics with its good manners, scholarship and integrity. It was the triumph of one-gallus Democracy and racism — at a heavy price.

BLACKS IN THE POPULIST ERA

A system of accommodation between the races had been reached during the Redeemer years. Redeemer leaders did not repudiate the Thirteenth, Fourteenth and Fifteenth Amendments to the United States Constitution openly, leaving blacks with some personal freedom and the right to participate in politics. Segregation existed, but the degree and scope of it varied considerably around the state.

Race relations took a turn for the worst during the 1890s. White racism nationally led the Republican Party to abandon Southern blacks, and the end of the frontier signified an end to opportunity locally. Blacks were singled out for the failure of Populism, and repression and even genocide found favor in the eyes of the law in the age of Jeff Davis.

Race Relations Before the Coming of Segregation

Blacks continued to be active in politics during the 1880s. Potential racial tensions were resolved partially before elections in counties with large black populations by forming "fusion" tickets that awarded offices to leaders from both races. As in the Reconstruction period, most leaders were immigrants; only one of the 1891 black legislators (nine representatives and one senator) is known to have been born in Arkansas.

The reason for the immigration was that at least some Arkansas blacks prospered, for in addition to farmers, there were black physicians, lawyers, businessmen and eight black newspapers. Pine Bluff's Wiley Jones was probably the wealthiest black in the state. This ex-slave opened a saloon after the War and plowed the profits back into real estate, including the local race track and fairgrounds. He controlled the city streetcar line and acquired property in Oklahoma, Texas, Chicago, St. Louis and San Francisco. Book-

Three Black Men (*photographer and date unknown*) *This picture, taken at Cotton Plant or Brinkley, reflects an optimism and sence of accomplishment at the turn of the century that proved unjustified.*
Author's Collection

er T. Washington, a Victorian purist, noted that Jones was neither educated nor completely moral, "but he won the respect of the community by his business integrity." Washington, who surveyed the black elite in Arkansas, also cited Mifflin W. Gibbs, the registrar of the federal land office and United States Consul to Madagascar; John E. Bush, the founder of the Mosaic Templars of America and J.E. Henderson, a black Little Rock jeweler.

Blacks were most likely to prosper in the urban settings of Pine Bluff and Little Rock. Three of the eight city councilmen in Pine Bluff were black, as well as half the policemen and some justices of the peace. Little Rock had black aldermen, policemen and members of the board of trade and professional organizations. Mifflin W. Gibbs wrote in 1902 that, "It can be truly said of Little Rock that the press and leading citizens have been more just and liberal to her colored citizens than any other Southern city."

Evidence of equality could be found in a state law that remained on the books until 1907 requiring all public carriers, hotels, saloons, restaurants and other public facilities to provide equal service regardless of race. There was some attempt at enforcement, for Gibbs and another black attorney won a discrimination suit against a Little Rock saloonkeeper. The city's West End Park was used by blacks for Emancipation Day celebrations as well as by ex-Confederates for picnics. In 1890, the state actually spent more per student on schooling black children than it did on white children. At the federal government's free bath house at Hot Springs, each day more than 500 persons, "Negroes and whites altogether, no distinction," bathed.

On the other hand, the theaters of Little Rock were segregated partially and only a token number of blacks were admitted to the School for the Deaf. Visiting dignitary Frederick Douglass was refused service in a Little Rock restaurant in 1889. The school system was segregated, although one visitor found the buildings to be alike.

Rural practices were far more restrictive. Edward Palmer, who searched in 1881-1883 for Indian remains on both the highways and byways, was accompanied by a black photographer and left a number of contradictory examples in his diary. In Osceola, the county seat of Mississippi County, blacks served on juries despite some criticism. Yet in the northern part of the county, Palmer visited one hunter living amidst fowl and fleas who said he "did not want any of the trash on his place" or anywhere near him. This attitude came to dominate west-

ern Mississippi County, where a "red line" — originally a road surveyor's mark — defined where blacks might live. The same practice existed elsewhere. Blacks might farm in the White River Valley but could not cross the Cache River to the east. Palmer also reported one instance of discrimination when a black teacher was refused a cabin on a steamboat. Her threat to sue was countered by the captain's assertion that he could assign passengers to any part of the boat he chose. Surprisingly, some blacks did continue to sue and in the Eastern District of Arkansas, they found a sympathetic federal judge in Jacob W. Trieber.

Racist ideology was growing in magazines, newspapers and wherever white men gathered. Palmer conversed with a rough specimen of the old planter, who complained that the young blacks did not know their place. When the old slave generation had passed, "the new race must move or be killed." Governor Jeff Davis echoed this theme, claiming as his favorite song:

Naught is a naught.
Figure is a figure.
Multiply the white man
And subtract the nigger.

Rural Arkansas blacks suffered their greatest discrimination under the local legal system. Vagrancy and petty thievery laws commonly were applied under processes that were hardly color-blind, and blacks suspected of major crimes were sometimes lynched without trial. Judge Gibbs told a Little Rock audience:

In no instance is the penalty of law enforced against the white man for the murder of a negro . . . whilst in most cases the bare accusation of a negro committing homicide upon a white man is sufficient warrant for law with all its form, to be ruthlessly set aside and the doctrine of lynch swift and certain to be enforced.

The law, he added, "always failed to mete out justice to the colored man." Hardly a month went by without an example of Gibbs's assertion occurring somewhere in the state. A black father who rescued his daughter from a white rapist in Morrilton was fined $14 for assault while the rapist received a $50 fine and three months in jail. The attitude of many whites that black women existed to be raped appeared in Howard County in 1883. The editor of the black *Arkansas Mansion* commented:

> I say to colored men that are left behind to stand firm and if our women are beaten and outraged [to] riddle the perpetrator of it with bullets, let the consequences be as it may.

Blacks in Howard County apparently acted on this theory and killed an alleged rapist, which led to a local civil war of such proportions that Governor Berry sent in the militia. Some members of the black lynching party were convicted of murder; most were pardoned, but one was hung.

Violence increased with the passing of the frontier, and racial resentments rose as competition for farms increased. Whites who formerly had tolerated blacks at a distance opposed them when they lived in close proximity. The attitude in the hills was expressed by the Waldron *Reporter* in 1906: "There are fourteen negroes in Scott County. They are prosperous and happy, but we are not needing any more."

When more arrived, as in the sawmill town of Leslie, the result was a race riot. A dozen "white-caps" ordered a planter and his black hands in Lincoln County to leave the area within ten days. Some said it was because a few pigs had disappeared, but others simply did not want blacks around.

By the 1890s, whites carried the race war to areas where blacks had long been established. Poor whites attacked all white families employing black servants at Marked Tree, and Paragould's forty black families were ordered to leave in 1908. Arkansas opinion makers increasingly defended or apologized for lynching. Episcopal Bishop William M. Brown defended lynching because the South had "no remedy adequate to suppress the crime for which this has been made a punishment." The lynching of rapists drew the support of Governor Dan Jones, the *Arkansas Gazette* and Congressman Bass Little. It was in this atmosphere that whites undertook a legal offensive against blacks, erecting laws of segregation that resulted in the systematic long-term degradation of blacks that left to modern society a legacy of poverty and racial hatred.

The Separate Coach Law

The legal attack on blacks began with demands that public transportation be segregated. As the Fort Smith *Times* noted:

> The people of Arkansas have borne with this negro nuisance on railroads a long time, hoping that the negroes would learn how to be decent, while a great many do behave themselves, others are intolerable. A Saturday night train out from Little Rock to Pine Bluff is hardly safe, to say nothing of the fact that not one in eighty uses Pear's soap or any other kind.

State Senator J. N. Tillman of Washington County introduced the Arkansas Separate Coach Bill in 1891. Tillman justified his proposal by pointing to a similar law that had been upheld by the courts in Mississippi and by denying that the move was discriminatory. Few in the black community were convinced. President J.A. Booker of Arkansas Baptist College claimed at a protest meeting in Little Rock that the bill was an attempt to turn back "the wheels of progress" and warned that blacks might leave Arkansas for Oklahoma or Africa. Other black speakers agreed that separate service never could be equal.

The small black contingent in the legislature fought a losing battle. The only black state senator, George W. Bell of Desha County, countered Tillman in debate, arguing that if the law was passed:

> The dirtiest peasants from Europe, the Nihilists, and cut throats of every government can come here . . . [and] receive better protection before the law, and in their civil rights, than we, who have helped to make this country what it is.

Bell ended with a moving appeal for "a common cause, a common humanity, and a common interest" that "would make us one people in a truly Solid South."

John G. Lucas of Jefferson County led the opposition in the lower house. Lucas eloquently summarized the black experience in Arkansas and warned that to abandon the ideal of an open society would be to transport Arkansas:

> [A]cross the Mississippi River, where yoked to the crimson soil of Mississippi, [Arkansas] shall be as incapable of advancement as is a fixed star to alter its course.

The bill would prevent "free men from the right to choose their own company," thereby creating "an unlawful imprisonment." With some acute social perception, Lucas suggested that many whites opposed riding with blacks not because "we use less of soap and God's pure water than other people," but because whites most resented those blacks who "more nearly approximate . . . our white friends' habits and plane of life." Finally, he jokingly anticipated Justice John Marshall Harlan's dissent in *Plessy* v. *Ferguson* (1896), which suggested that if railroad coaches could be

segregated, why not housing, sidewalks, streets and all public facilities? The bill passed easily in the end, although an amendment to extend its provisions to streetcars was rejected. Ironically, Lucas's sarcastic humor proved to be the direction Southern states were about to take.

Exclusion from Politics

Coinciding with the Separate Coach Law was a renewed complaint about black participation in politics. Race-baiting had been a favorite theme in the 1880s as Democrats struggled to defeat the agrarian revolt. "The Caucasian race must govern America," proclaimed Craighead County Representative Dr. J. A. Meek in 1888 as he urged repeal of the Fourteenth and Fifteenth Amendments. A second argument was that white men could differ freely if blacks were removed. Ideology and practical politics merged in the 1890s.

Racism was manifest even among Republicans. Some local leaders proposed a lily-white Party that could better win white support. National Republicans began to ignore the needs of blacks by the turn of the century. Ferdinand Havis of Pine Bluff was unable to achieve appointment as a postmaster in spite of some white support because both Arkansas senators refused to endorse or approve appointing blacks to office. In 1909, President William Howard Taft threw his support to the lily-whites. The Pulaski County Republican Committee held its meetings at the segregated Marion Hotel so blacks could not attend; and the all-white primary, the poll tax and the "Australian" ballot eliminated blacks from Arkansas political life.

The Effects of Segregation

At the turn of the century, many Arkansas blacks listened to the accommodationist philosophy espoused by Booker T. Washington. In addition to urging acquiescence to segregation, Washington challenged blacks to create through self-help and self-improvement their own self-sufficient world. The emergence of black-owned services began in Arkansas before 1890, and patrons even included some whites. An 1898 Little Rock directory reported thirty black barbers, thirteen blacksmiths, fifteen shoemakers, fifty-five educators and teachers, fifteen dressmakers, twenty-eight grocers, thirty-eight ministers, five physicians, six lawyers and a variety of other trades. Two black banks fell victim to the Bankers' Panic of 1907, but the fraternal orders, the Knights of Tabor and the Mosaic Templars, sold insurance, and the Knights erected an impressive brick building in Little Rock.

Once whites united to deprive blacks of every vestige of self-respect, individual or group progress became impossible. Blacks who wished to live in Arkansas had to learn a dehumanizing servility or face the threat of extinction. Those who chose freedom left the state, beginning with leaders such as J. Gray Lucas, who moved to Chicago and eventually became an assistant United States attorney. The July 18, 1912, *White River Journal* reported that the exodus of Negroes from Prairie County had grown to such proportions that it concerned local plantation owners. The *Journal* reported that about "2,000 Negroes left Arkansas for points in the industrial centers of the North and East in a week," and crowed that "many of those migrating to the North are walking the streets in Chicago 'broke and hungry, and wanting to return South.'" By the 1970s, Little Rock's black business district was reduced to nothing but a row of empty buildings to be destroyed when city fathers planned the Wilbur Mills Freeway.

Segregation denied management the right to make the most effective use of a worker's talents. The manager of a factory that attempted to employ blacks in Jonesboro was "warned out." A few businessmen fought the system. The town of Crossett was created in 1898 after Hamburg property owners refused to sell land to a company that employed blacks. Blacks were cast permanently into the role of agricultural menials and found it increasingly difficult to buy land or maintain the farms they already owned.

One conspicuous example of the new order came at Branch Normal College in Pine Bluff, where James C. Corbin was president. Democratic politicians such as Jeff Davis wanted to close the school, while its white supporters demanded that it be converted into a trade school. Corbin insisted the school remain a liberal arts institution, so a white treasurer was appointed who assumed de facto control. Corbin was fired in 1902 as whites attempted to make the institution into a copy of Tuskegee Institute, where manual training rather than education was emphasized. The abandonment of even a feeble commitment to the higher education of blacks reflected the segregationist mentality. Because blacks were considered inferior, it was not deemed necessary to provide them with a quality education or superfluous luxuries such as libraries. After a few decades spent denying blacks economic and educational opportunity, whites then logically could conclude segregation was justified because blacks had not progressed.

INDUSTRY AND LABOR

Northern industry invaded the South during the late nineteenth century, usually after it had exhausted readily available natural resources elsewhere. It was dig out and get out in mining, cut out and get out in lumber, and in all instances, it was buy out the legislature. Severance taxes were virtually nonexistent or were avoided by various subterfuges. Wages were low, and workers were unorganized. Most profits flowed to out-of-state owners, making Arkansas an underdeveloped region in the Age of Imperialism.

Lumbering

Arkansans had been harvesting timber since territorial days. Most of the wood was used locally until the arrival of railroads tied Arkansas to Northern markets. Beginning in 1880, large companies entered the state, bought land intended for settlers, cut the wood and abandoned the land before paying taxes. To reach the timber, companies built shortline railroads connected to the major sawmills. Tram lines snaked their way into the swamp or up the hills and hollows to reach lumber camps. Fallen trees were stacked on railroad cars and hauled to sawmills that became larger with each passing year. The pattern varied in eastern Arkansas, where logs often were floated downstream to mills to be caught by booms laid across the river. In the Buffalo River area, where red cedar was cut to make pencils, 175,000 logs were recorded in one float on the stream.

Lumbering brought many families into a commercial economy. Two men working half a day cutting crossties could earn enough (50 cents) to buy a can of peaches at a country store. The red-cedar trade netted some families as much as $125 a year, and the lumbering towns created markets for produce and meat. By 1909, the peak year for Arkansas lumbering, 36,662 workers were employed in the lumber industry. With growth came consolidation and regimentation. Instead of the casual local labor first employed, some large firms brought in their own gangs of workers. Technological improvements led to specialization, so that lumbering communities came to reflect a hierarchical social system. Company control in towns such as Mauldin, Graysonia and Crossett was virtually complete.

The lumbering frontier was not without

Logging in Ashley County *(photographer and date unknown) Rails provided the means to reach into the forest and then remove logs for processing. These tram lines were temporary and were pulled up after the timber had been harvested.* **Arkansas History Commission**

violence. Some lumber companies ran roughshod over the rights of small farmers who got in their way. They tried to control their own workers by paying them in scrip redeemable only at the company store. The accident rate was very high, for lumbering is dangerous work in all of its phases. Company oppression invited unionization, but when the radical International Workers of the World (IWW) tried to organize the workers in 1910, companies used violence against the organizers and stirred up racial hatred to defeat the effort.

The lumbering industry never achieved its full potential in Arkansas. Discriminatory railroad rates dictated by Eastern interests made it cheaper to process most wood out of state. A few factories turned out barrels, wagon spokes, golf clubs, staves and cheap furniture in Fort Smith and Little Rock, but Arkansas was important mostly as a source

Rogers Planing Mill *(photographer and date unknown) Most Arkansas industries were timber related. Planing mills were common over much of the state.* **University of Arkansas**

of wood. The early methods of extraction led to about 65 percent of the wood being wasted. As late as 1900, an acre containing 40,000 to 70,000 board feet of lumber was valued at only $40.

The lumber industry went into rapid decline after 1909. Many companies moved on once the best trees had been cut. Abandoned railroad lines, huge piles of sawdust and rusting boilers were frequently the only visible reminders of a flurry of activity. Towns such as Graysonia and Mauldin even disappeared from the map. Production in 1926 was half that of 1909.

Mining

Mining was also important in Arkansas. Coal was the greatest resource, for the thick veins of the Hartshorne seam ran under much of western Arkansas and eastern Oklahoma. This high-quality semi-bituminous coal was used by public utilities and steam locomotives. The state was producing two million tons of coal a year by 1900, largely from Sebastian, Johnson and Franklin Counties. New towns sprang up, and as with lumbering, the settlers were culturally different from

farmers. Hartford had a section of town known as "Little Italy," and other immigrants came from Germany, Hungary, Poland, Lithuania, Bohemia and Russia. Arkansas boasted one Italian mine owner, Galio Magnani. A number of blacks worked in the mines near Fort Smith, but were not permitted to labor around Russellville.

Coal mining mixed with politics when state prisoners were leased to mining companies. Not surprisingly, unions entered the fields, beginning with the Knights of Labor in the 1880s. Most companies were owned by outsiders, but one exception was the Arkansas Anthracite Coal Company, founded by Harmon L. Remmel and George B. Rose, which developed the town of Scranton.

The miners' union won recognition early in the century, established the "closed shop" by 1903, and engaged in regional collective bargaining. In 1914, one owner decided to challenge the union and create an "open shop." The result was a major battle pitting the United Mine Workers against the Coronado Coal Company and eight associated concerns. The company brought in strike-breakers and hired guards from the W.J. Burns Detective Agency. The union struck back by having some of the guards arrested for violating the state's anti-profanity ordinance. When lawful means failed, workers attacked the guards and posted a sign reading "This is Union Man's Country." The company refused arbitration, and after getting federal marshals to help guard the mines, had miners jailed for violating federal court injunctions. In another effective use of the court system, the coal company took bankruptcy but had its owner, Franklin Bache, appointed as receiver. Finally, the company took the union to court. The long trial consumed more than 1,000 pages of testimony but ended in a company victory. The United States Supreme Court in *United Mine Workers v. Coronado Coal Co.* (1922) held the union could be sued and was liable for damages under the Sherman Anti-trust Act. Despite

Coronado Company Coal Mine, *South Sebastian County Industrial violence was not unknown in Arkansas. The photograph above is the Prairie Creek Coal Mine No. 4 on November 19, 1913. The photograph below was taken on July 20, 1914, after the mine was destroyed. Two men were killed here when over 200 miners battled company guards.* **University of Arkansas**

another round of strikes in 1919 and 1920, Arkansas mines were "open shops" by 1927, when coal began to decline.

The same pattern — rise in the nineteenth century, maturity early in the twentieth century, and decline in the 1920s — appeared with other minerals as well. Manganese was discovered in 1849 and briefly mined before the Civil War near Cushman in Independence County. Production revived with the coming of the railroad and reached a peak in 1917, when 10,140 tons were produced. In contrast to culturally isolated coal miners, Cushman miners tended to be part-time farmers. The town did share western mining-town characteristics with transients in the population and hot times on Saturday night.

Lead and zinc mining also had antebellum origins. The largest concentrations were in the Ozarks, but most mines were small and remote. The White River branch of the St. Louis and Iron Mountain Railroad stimulated zinc production around Yellville but did not reach Rush near the Buffalo River, where most of the mines were located. Miners there had to rely on oxen or a good rain on the Buffalo River to get their zinc to market. Part of the roadbed was laid for a railroad, but the mines already were declining by early in the twentieth century and the railroad never was completed. Other small mines benefited from the Missouri and North Arkansas Railroad, which extended diagonally across northern Arkansas and stimulated both lumber and zinc production.

In the late nineteenth century, bauxite ore suddenly became valuable as a source for aluminum. First identified in 1882 by State Geologist John L. Branner, it was found mostly in Saline and Pulaski Counties. Commercial production started shortly thereafter, but ownership was almost entirely in the hands of out-of-state companies. The town of Bauxite was a model of company control, with all of its homes and municipal services company-owned. No processing was done in Arkansas until World War II, and the mining left large areas of land ruined by bauxite pits.

Boom towns for silver sprang up in the Ouachita Mountains during the late nineteenth century. Promoters engaged in extensive stock sales and lured some 1,500 persons to the town of Bear. State Geologist Branner broke the bubble in 1888 by denying that Arkansas's silver resources warranted development. Enraged that a state employee should disparage Arkansas, the legislature cut off funding for his agency, and at Bear — today a ghost town — Branner was hung in effigy. Diamond mining was another commercial failure. Farmer John Wesley Huddleston discovered diamonds near Murfreesboro, but repeated attempts to mine the site for profit failed.

The Factory System

By 1880, the creation of a national railroad system led to a wave of industrialization that adversely affected local industries. Arkansas had only 4,557 wage earners in 1879; the number stood at 14,143 a decade later, and by 1909, 44,982 persons were at work in factories, nearly three-fourths of them in lumbering. Factories grew larger during these same years, averaging three workers per factory in 1879 and ten per factory by 1909. The increasing use of machinery was even more striking. The average horsepower utilized by workers increased from six to fifty-nine. The small local factory lost out in this process. By 1914, even though three-fourths of all Arkansas factories were owned by single individuals or partnerships, more than three-fourths of the state's output came from factories owned by corporations.

Textiles were one area where promoters expected Arkansas to excel. With cotton grown in every county, a history of antebellum cotton factories and plenty of good streams for power, the state seemed ripe to join North Carolina and Georgia in taking away New England's monopoly of the textile industry. A few textile mills went into operation during the late nine-

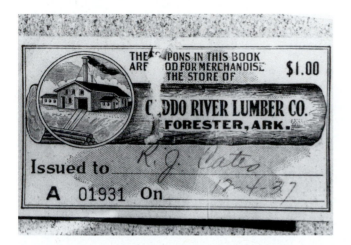

Coupon, Caddo River Lumber Company (1937)
*Company control in towns like the now vanished
Forester rested in part on trade monopolies. Generally,
prices were higher at the company store than at
independent merchants. Planters in the Delta often
used a similar system called "doodle 'em books."*
University of Central Arkansas

teenth century. Mammoth Spring, previously
dammed to support a flour mill, powered a mill
making handkerchiefs. Monticello was home
to a mill with 8,000 spindles, and the Delta
Cotton Mill at Helena boasted 1,300 spindles.

Despite the advantages, Arkansas mills
failed to survive. Only two mills were left by
1919, and Arkansas, with only 14,656 spindles, ranked behind both Oklahoma and Missouri in textile production. Presumably discriminatory railroad rates doomed these
enterprises.

Labor Unions

Industrialization brought labor unions in
its wake as working men tried to protect
themselves from abuse. The first wave of
activity came with the arrival of the Knights
of Labor, which was founded in 1869. The
Knights of Labor wanted to organize all working people and had 203 locals in Arkansas,
including female domestics in Hot Springs,
Crittenden County sharecroppers, railroad
workers and coal miners. Unions invariably
led to strikes, and in the first phase of organized labor activity between 1881 and 1886,

there were three by coal miners, two by railroad brakemen and one by black sharecroppers at Tate's Plantation nine miles south of
Little Rock.

The railroad strike gave Arkansas its first
taste of industrial relations in the era of robber barons. The Knights of Labor recorded
some successes in the Southwest in 1884,
spurring the organization of a state assembly
in Arkansas. The firing of a Knight member in
1886 led to a general walkout against the
Gould-owned railroads, including the Iron
Mountain in Arkansas. The strike began
peacefully enough in Little Rock, but violence
flared when management and nonstriking
workers tried to keep the trains running. The
local press was sympathetic to the strike at
first because the railroad refused arbitration.
But sentiments changed after the destruction
of property led Governor Hughes to deploy the
state militia at Texarkana. The trains came
through guarded by troops. Hughes claimed
this saved the Arkansas economy, but it
destroyed the union. The defeated workers
were not rehired and were black-listed for life.
By 1892, there were only thirteen Knights
assemblies (locals) in the state, down from 139
in 1887. Most were in the coal mining region
where Knights leader W. B. W. Heartsill
served two terms in the state legislature. By
1895, miners had abandoned the Knights but
joined the United Mine Workers.

The initial sympathy for railroad workers
was not extended to farm laborers. Thirty men
on the Tate Plantation near Little Rock quit
their jobs demanding $1 a day paid in real
money instead of plantation store charge tickets. The strikers gave in after their leader was
arrested for attempting to draw a gun on the
Pulaski County sheriff. The same fate befell
the Cotton Pickers League in 1891 when it
demanded payment of $1 per 100 pounds. A
few walkouts took place, notably in strife-torn
Lee County, but the action cost at least fifteen
black lives as the union was "ruthlessly and
totally suppressed."

*A Parade Float made in the Form of a Boxcar, Argenta Lodge 423, BRCA, (Brotherhood of Railway Carmen of America) (photographer unknown, c.a. 1915) These Carmen were union workers who built, repaired, maintained and inspected freight and passenger railway cars at the Chicago, Rock Island and Pacific (CRI & P) Biddle Shop in Little Rock. Railroads were part of the national economy and union contracts were negotiated nationally and provided some of the highest paying jobs in Arkansas. These workers probably made between 30 cents and 40 cents an hour at a time when other men in Arkansas made $1 a day. They are well fed, well dressed and smiling. All apear to be white. **University of Arkansas***

In general, Arkansas agrarians were receptive to the demands of labor even though many workers were foreign and Roman Catholic. They saw the close connection between their difficulties with railroads, stores, and grain elevators and those of the working man. But the Arkansas elite placed the right of private property above that of free association. In addition, state government easily was corrupted. Railroad lobbyists dominated every legislative session and defeated efforts to pass any kind of worker protection already common in industrialized states. As Governor Jeff Davis said, "Human life with them is too cheap." In addition to defeating labor legislation, the companies kept taxes low and defeated conservation measures. The lumber industry could not stop President Theodore Roosevelt from creating the Ouachita and Ozark National Forests, but it did get the legislature to ask Congress to abolish them. Perhaps the best example of labor's weakness was its inability to abolish the convict lease system through which prisoners competed with paid workers.

Abuses of corporate power could be found in the histories of company towns. Free speech, the right to join a union and other personal liberties were sacrificed for steady employment, housing and sanitation that were above the Arkansas average.

The defeat of the agrarians was thus mirrored in a small way by the defeat of the unions. In the twentieth century, the quest for social justice led former Wheel leader W. Scott Morgan to turn to socialism, as did many workers.

CONCLUSION

Rising farm prices muted agrarian discontent during the early years of the twentieth century. Some reforms were passed, and others seemed less urgent. Arkansans found their voice in Jeff Davis, even if his actions failed to match his rhetoric. Middle-class reformers, often from the Republican Party, nationally supported the style and substance of Theodore Roosevelt in demanding a new national policy balancing labor with capital, preserving national resources and restoring honesty in government. Little of this progressivism appeared in state politics during the Jeff Davis era. Yet the forces of modernization were working underground, taking over once Davis departed for Washington. Populism in the Jeff Davis style still lingered, however, for as long as the state remained predominantly rural, voters continued to respond to a politician who introduced not only his wife but his hunting dogs, too. After 1900, blacks disappeared from the state's political life. The overt and vicious racism exemplified by Jeff Davis declined and was succeeded by a more "genteel" white racism that became the state's accepted ideology. Blacks who stayed perforce adopted the Booker T. Washington policy of non-involvement, but got little to reward them for their quiescence.

BIBLIOGRAPHIC ESSAY

The Populist era has not been studied exhaustively. The Agricultural Wheel attracted scholarly attention in F. Clark Elkins,

"Arkansas Farmers Organize for Action: 1882-1884," *AHQ*, XIII (Autumn 1954), 231-248, and "The Agricultural Wheel: County Politics and Consolidation, 1884-1885," *AHQ*, XXIX (Summer 1970), 152-175. Berton E. Henningson, Jr., "Northwest Arkansas and the Brothers of Freedom: "The Roots of a Farmer Movement," *AHQ*, XXXIV (Winter 1975), 304-324 provides some data on a contemporary body. Its entry into politics is the theme of Clifton Paisley, "The Political Wheelers and Arkansas's Election of 1888," *AHQ*, XXV (Spring 1966), 3-21. Participant W. S. Morgan, *History of the Wheel and Alliance, and the Impending Revolution,* (Fort Scott, Kan., 1889) provides much biographical and personal detail, and *The Red Light—A Story of Southern Politics and Election Methods,* (Moravian Falls, N. C., 1906) is disguised as fiction. Also useful are the Congressional hearings on the contested seats: *Clayton* v. *Breckinridge,* 51st Congress, 1st Session, House Report 2912, Washington, (1889), and *Featherston* v. *Cate,* 51st Congress, 1st Session, *House Report 306* (1889).

The politics of the era are surveyed in two dissertations. In addition to Segraves, "Arkansas Politics, 1874-1918," see John McD. Wheeler, "The People's Party in Arkansas," (Ph. d. diss., Tulane University, 1975). Biographies of the governors can be found in Donovan and Gatewood,*The Governors of Arkansas.* Legislative addresses provide some insights. Biographical studies include Paige E. Mulhollan, "The Public Career of James H. Berry," (M. A. thesis, University of Arkansas, 1962), and the same author's "The Issues of the David-Berry Senatorial Campaign in 1906," *AHQ*, XX (Summer 1961), 118-125. For obvious reasons, Jeff Davis attracted the most attention, beginning with L. D. Dunaway, *Jeff Davis, Governor and United States Senator; His Life and Speeches,* (Little Rock 1913), and continuing with a surprisingly objective biography by his private secretary, Charles Jacobson, *The Life Story of*

Jeff Davis, (Little Rock, 1925). One critical modern assessment is Cal Ledbetter, Jr., "Jeff Davis and the Politics of Combat," *AHQ,* XXXIII (Spring 1974), 16-37. Another is Raymond Arsenault, *The Wild Ass of the Ozarks: Jeff Davis and the Social Bases of Southern Politics.* (Philadelphia, 1984). Davis's role in the state capitol controversy is reviewed sympathetically in John A. Treon, "Politics and Concrete: The Building of the Arkansas State Capitol, 1899-1917," *AHQ,* XXXI (Summer 1972), 99-133. The small role Arkansas and Arkansans played in that "splendid little war," is discussed in Bertha Davidson, "Arkansas in the Spanish-American War," *AHQ,* V (Autumn 1946), 208-219.

It was Arkansan C. Vann Woodward, *The Strange Career of Jim Crow,* (New York, 1966), who first challenged the prevailing notion that segregation began immediately after Reconstruction. A useful overview is John W. Graves, *Town and Country: Race Relations and Urban Development in Arkansas 1865-1900,* (Fayetteville, 1990). Contemporary evidence is assembled in Willard B. Gatewood, Jr., "Arkansas Negroes in the 1890's: Documents," *AHQ* XXXIII (Winter 1974), 293-325, and useful comments can be found at random in Edward Palmer, "Arkansas Mounds," *PAHA,* IV (1917), 390-448.

Additional insights can be gained from autobiographies and biographies of individual blacks. Mifflin W. Gibbs, *Shadow and Light: An Auto-biography with Reminiscences of the Last and Present Century,* (1902) is valuable in the former category. A contemporary promotional tract is D. B. Gains, *Racial Possibilities as Indicated by the Negroes of Arkansas,* (Little Rock, 1898), and there are Arkansas portions of Booker T. Washington, *The Negro in Business,* (Boston and Chicago, 1907). A scholarly perspective that includes Arkansas examples is Herbert G. Gutman, *The Black Family in Slavery and Freedom, 1750-1925,* (New York, 1976). Recent biographical studies include Tom Dillard, "Scipio A. Jones," *AHQ,*

XXXI (Autumn 1972), 201-219, and "Golden Prospects and Fraternal Amenities: Mifflin W. Gibbs Arkansas Years," *AHQ,* XXXV (Winter 1976), 307-334; James W. Leslie, "Ferd A. Havis: Jefferson County's Black Republican Leader," *AHQ,* XXXVII (Autumn 1978), 240-251, and Thomas Rothrock, "Joseph Carter Corbin and Negro Education in the University of Arkansas," *AHQ,* XXX (Winter 1971), 277-314. Further information on the role of Branch Normal can be found in Fredrick Chambers, "Historical Study of Arkansas Agricultural, Mechanical and Normal College, 1873-1943," (Ed.D. diss., Ball State University, 1970). Statistical data on Arkansas blacks can be found in Henry Gannett, *Statistics of the Negroes in the United States,* (Baltimore 1894).

Segregation's legal origins have attracted John W. Graves, "Negro Disfranchisement in Arkansas," *AHQ,* XXVI (Autumn 1967), 199-225, and "The Arkansas Separate Coach Law of 1891," *AHQ,* XXXII (Summer 1973), 148-165. Tom Dillard, "To the Back of the Elephant: Racial Conflict in the Arkansas Republican Party," *AHQ,* XXXIII (Spring 1974), 3-15, shows how even the Republicans abandoned blacks.

The lumber industry across the state awaits treatment, but Kenneth L. Smith, *Sawmill: The Story of Cutting the Last Great Virgin Forest East of the Rockies,* (Fayetteville, 1986) is an exciting account of activity in the Ouachita Mountains. A short survey is James W. Leslie, "The Arkansas Lumber Industry," (M. S. thesis, University of Arkansas, 1938). Fred H. Lang, "Two Decades of State Forestry in Arkansas," *AHQ,* XXIV (Autumn 1965), 208-219, is also useful. On the local level is Corliss C. Curry, "A History of the Timber Industry in Ashley, Bradley, and Drew Counties, Arkansas," (M. A. thesis, University of Arkansas, 1953) and his "Early Timber Operations in Southeast Arkansas," *AHQ,* XIX (Summer 1960), 111-118. Two memoirs are Walter L. Brown, ed., "Life of an Arkansas Logger in 1901," *AHQ,* XXI (Spring 1962), 44-

74, and Daniel B. Lackey, "Cutting and Floating Red Cedar Logs in North Arkansas," *AHQ,* XIX (Winter 1960), 361-370.

Coal mining remains largely untapped. Jerry H. Moore and Lonnie C. Roach, *No Smoke, No Soot, No Clinkers; A History of the Coal Industry in South Sebastian County, Arkansas,* (N. P. 1974) contains memoirs, photographs, and interviews. Samuel A. Sizer, "This is Union Man's Country," Sebastian County, 1914," *AHQ,* XXVII (Winter 1968), 306-329, tells the story of the 1914 strike and the breaking of the union. Also of interest is Robert D. Besom, "Little Rock Businesses Invest in Coal: Harmon L. Remmel and the Arkansas Anthracite Coal Company, 1905-1923," (N. P. UALR, 1970). One excellent study is Dwight Pithaithley, "Zinc and Lead Mining Along the Buffalo River," *AHQ,* XXXVII (Winter 1978), 293-305.

Transportation is the theme of Lawrence R. Handley, "Settlement Across North Arkansas as Influenced by the Missouri and North Arkansas Railroad," *AHQ,* XXXIII (Winter 1974), 273-292. William Spier, "A Social History of Manganese Mining in the Batesville District of Independence County," *AHQ,* XXXVI (Summer 1977), 130-157, is thorough and complete. Aluminum is treated in Gordon Bachus, "Background and Early History of a Company Town: Bauxite, Arkansas," *AHQ,* XXVII (Winter 1968), 330-357.

A general summary on manufacturing with useful statistics is T. C. Bigham, "Later Developments of Manufacturing," in D. Y. Thomas, ed., *Arkansas and Its People, II,* (1930), and there is material on individual factories in J. E. P. Griner, "The Growth of Manufactures in Arkansas, 1900-1950," (Ph.D. diss., George Peabody College for Teachers, 1950).

Arkansas's labor history remains largely unwritten. There is, however, Ralph V. Turner and William W. Rogers, "Arkansas Labor in Revolt: Little Rock and the Great Southwestern Strike," *AHQ,* XXIV (Spring 1965) 29-46, and by Rogers alone, "Negro Knights of Labor in Arkansas," *LH* X (Summer 1969), 498-505. The cotton pickers' strike is the theme of William F. Holmes, "The Arkansas Cotton Pickers Strike of 1891 and the Demise of the Colored Farmers'Alliance," *AHQ,* XXXII (Summer 1973), 107-119.

Fourth of July Parade at Mountain Home *(Arthur Keller, ca. 1915) Seven girls, not all wearing shoes, pose with a decorated horse and buggy prior to taking part in a Fourth of July Parade. Note the long-sleeves and drop-waist style of the girls' summer dresses. The girl on the right is wearing long white stockings and "Sunday" shoes.*
University of Central Arkansas

Chapter XIII

The Progressive Era

INTRODUCTION

The Progressive movement in America dated from the swearing in of Theodore Roosevelt as president in 1901 to the end of World War I in 1918. A new wave of reform overtook America in that period. Some issues, such as the trusts and equitable economic policies, were not new, but the reformers themselves, young men and women of the post-Civil War generation, were. National profiles indicated that Progressives were middle-class businessmen and women who were traditionally Republican in party affiliation. Their orientation was primarily urban, their outlook consciously modern and their background professional. Progressivism had captured both Democrats and Republicans by 1912.

Progressive sentiment was present in Arkansas but made little headway until the death of Jeff Davis marked the return to more rational and less emotional politics. The Progressive ascendancy came later in Arkansas than in the rest of the nation, but it lasted longer, for the 1920s showed a strong continuity with the previous decade.

Progressivism was less than a complete success, but the word itself so entered the political vocabulary that virtually every politician for the next fifty years appropriated it for every conceivable purpose.

PROGRESSIVE POLITICS

The Republicans as Progressives

Republicans lost every statewide race during the late nineteenth century. It mattered little whether the candidate was an old-line Southern Unionist like Thomas Boles or the Party was in alliance with revolting farmers. Perhaps because the Party was such a hopeless minority, especially after the disfranchisement of blacks, Republican leaders led in articulating some progressive issues. For obvious reasons, they were also the first to run men of the post-Civil War era for political office. Harmon L. Remmel, second in power to Powell Clayton, was a Northern investor who came South after Reconstruction. A gubernatorial candidate in 1894, 1896 and 1900, he ran his strongest race in 1900 when he opposed Jeff Davis, offering Arkansas voters a real alternative.

H.F. Auten, the Republican gubernatorial candidate in 1898, was from Michigan. As an early real estate developer, Auten had created Arkansas's first streetcar suburb, the segregated Pulaski Heights. Wallace Townsend, candidate in 1916 and 1920, strongly endorsed woman's suffrage, tax reform and good roads. More enigmatic was James A. Comer, a strong Roosevelt supporter and Progressive, who became state grand dragon of the Ku Klux Klan in the 1920s. After Progressivism captured the Democratic Party in 1908, not even the attempted expulsion of blacks from the Republican Party could make Republicans popular again in Arkansas.

The Socialist Challenge

The first call for reform in the early twentieth century came from the Socialist Party. Socialism was a nineteenth-century political doctrine devised from diverse economic and religious sources. Karl Marx, the father of "scientific" socialism, organized the ideology by articulating a view of the world, *Weltanschuuang*, which forecast that capitalism would collapse from within and ultimately be replaced by a higher economic order based on community values rather than the profit motive. The cooperative aspects of socialism appealed to agrarian radicals who had inherited the tradition of Populism and to workers who saw first-hand the exploitation that resulted from the factory system. Because many workers were drawn from the farm, agrarian issues figured prominently in Arkansas Socialism.

The state Socialist Party was organized on May 23, 1903, in Little Rock. Prominent in the early structure were Ernest W.M. Perrin, the "blacksmith orator" of Little Rock; Father Thomas Hagerty of Van Buren, a suspended Catholic priest; Dan Hogan, an Arkansas-born son of an Irish immigrant and editor of the first state Socialist newspaper, the Huntington *Southern Worker*; George E. Mikel, the Socialist mayor of Hartford and president of the State Federation of Labor, and teacher Ida Callery. The first platform called for collective ownership of industry; reduced working hours; a national insurance and pension program; full employment; free, compulsory, and nonsectarian education; equal rights for women; initiative, referendum and proportional representation, and recall of elected officials. The Party also opposed the incipient "militarism" of the Boy Scout movement then getting underway in Arkansas.

Eugene Debs, the nationally famous leader of the Party, came to Arkansas in 1903 for the first of several appearances, and the Party claimed twenty-eight locals by the end of the year. Testing their political strength, Socialists nominated William O. Penrose, a Woodruff County sawmill owner, for governor and polled 1,364 votes in 1904, trailing the Prohibition candidate with less than 1 percent of the vote. Determined to gain more rural support, the Party in 1908 entered farmer J.

Sam Jones of Harrison, who polled 6,284 votes. Debs, who spoke at Pine Bluff and Fort Smith, got 5,842 votes in Arkansas in the presidential election.

The Party claimed 121 locals by 1910 and the support of a number of newspapers. Most Socialist newspapers, like the one at Jonesboro, were short-lived, but Clarendon, Green Forest, Hot Springs, Judsonia, Maddock, Piggott, Pine Bluff and Van Buren readers got the Socialist message for a brief period. *The People's Friend* at Rogers survived for about nine years. Its editor, A.M. Merrill, "a lone crusader against all the evils of the day," served as secretary of the local school board. J.S. Faubus of Combs, father of future Governor Orval E. Faubus, was an important hill-country organizer.

The Party continued to persevere. Hogan gathered 9,196 votes for governor in 1910; Mikel garnered 13,384 in 1912, one-third of the Republican total in the peak year for Socialist political influence and 8 percent of the total votes cast in the election. Some Socialists, unhappy with the conservative policies of established labor unions, supported the new International Workers of the World (IWW), a radical group that claimed Father Hagerty's allegiance. Splits in the Party followed, and hopeful William Davis polled 4,000 fewer votes in the 1916 gubernatorial contest than Mikel had in 1912. Wartime persecution led to fewer votes in 1918 when school teacher Clay Fulks of McRae opposed Governor Brough. The Socialist Party was dead in Arkansas after 1920.

Socialists won few victories, but they did provide a focus for radical rhetoric. Parts of their platform even became law during the life of the Party. Because Arkansas Socialism owed much to immediate conditions and little to theoretical Marxism, it may be considered as a continuation of agrarian radicalism. New sprouts appeared on the old socialist twig in the 1930s and 1960s.

Progressive Triumph

State affairs were in considerable disarray at the end of Governor Jeff Davis's third term. By counting the property of the schools as income, Davis had told the legislators that the state had a surplus and should give voters a tax break. The legislature complied and increasing deficits in the state treasury resulted.

The unfortunate mental illness of Governor John S. Little left X. O. Pindall, an enemy of United States Senator Jeff Davis, as governor. In the next gubernatorial election, Davis resolved to regain his influence by supporting William F. Kirby. Kirby's major opponent was George W. Donaghey, a self-made man who had begun as a carpenter and furniture maker and then entered the construction business. A member of the Capitol Commission, Donaghey claimed to be the best informed individual about the state Capitol construction, a leading embarrassment and expense, even though a modern critic called him "the man who set the Capitol crooked on its lot and mislaid the foundation." Substantial work on the state Capitol had been done during the Davis years, but it was accompanied by charges of fraud and corruption in the construction and substandard workmanship in the building. An angry and weary legislature finally cut off all funding and left the partially finished capitol to decay. Donaghey, exploiting public discontent, claimed that as a practical businessman he could get the job done, and he did.

After defeating Kirby in the primary and winning the general election, Donaghey set about achieving his goal, using convict labor, making unauthorized expenditures and working around costly strikes. The General Assembly moved into the unfinished building in 1911, even though several more years passed before the entire project was completed.

In addition to this building project, Donaghey oversaw the adoption of a number of progressive causes. A firm believer in education, he brought in the Southern Regional Educational Board to help raise the state's educational standards and add new programs. His administration sponsored the creation of a tuberculosis sanitarium at Booneville and the state compulsory smallpox vaccination law. He endorsed the initiative and referendum constitutional amendment whereby voters themselves could pass laws and constitutional amendments or repeal those found objectionable. Initiative and referendum were supported strongly by prohibitionists who believed a bone-dry law was more likely to come from voters than from the legislature. Initiative and referendum were opposed by the *Arkansas Gazette*, which questioned the wisdom of so much democracy.

The adoption of initiative and referendum in 1910 added to the already considerable confusion about what constitutional amendments were in force in Arkansas. It and many subsequent amendments were in and out of the courts as a result, and a new version of initiative and referendum was approved in 1920. Finally, in *Brickhouse* v. *Hill* (1925), the state Supreme Court held that the initiative and referendum amendment now required only that an amendment have a majority of the votes cast on it. A number of amendments previously thought lost were declared adopted retroactively, but the legal confusion was such that even today the current "official" list of amendments issued by the Secretary of State is misleading.

The passage of initiative and referendum in Arkansas was the first such move by any Southern state, and it was put to use immediately. In 1912, by referendum, voters repealed the 1912 tax reassessment law that had been passed to straighten out the state's finances. The initiative was used to pass a child labor law, although this law was promptly weakened by the next session of the legislature. A rather different sort of reform was found in the passage of Amendment 15 in 1913 that

limited the legislature to a sixty-day session. Voters had become convinced, not without reason, that legislative sessions were prolonged in order to increase legislators' per diem pay. Significantly, the last session before the amendment took effect cost $200,000, the first one after it cost a mere $80,000. The amendment did not stop the flow of trivial legislation, another progressive objective. Laws were passed in one session regulating the length of fish caught from Cabin Creek, fixing the size of train cabooses and legalizing a four-wire fence in portions of Saline County. The initiative was used to introduce Amendment 14 banning local and special legislation, but subterfuges have been used to this day to get around the amendment's intent.

Donaghey also took up the perennial issue of prison reform. On discovering that some prisoners were being held by contract lessees after their prison terms had expired, Donaghey used his pardoning power to release 360 carefully screened prisoners. The loss of half the prison inmates deprived prison labor contractors of their work force and led to the return of prisoners to state control. Donaghey had less influence on county conditions, but he called attention to the practice of releasing prisoners to labor to whomever would pay their fines. Even though Donaghey was consistently anti-Negro, he cited an example from Phillips County where two black men convicted of forging an order for a quart of whisky had received eighteen-year and thirty-six-year sentences. A convict in Chicot County had worn shackles until his legs rotted off.

As a result of Donaghey's efforts, the state again assumed responsibility for prisoners and opened the Tucker farm as a prison in Jefferson County in 1916. Convicts also were put to work building roads under state supervision. Even so, the evils of the old system were only mitigated, not abolished. With a legislative mandate for prisons to be self-sufficient, prisoners themselves were used as guards and living conditions were primitive. A 1915 inves-

Governor George Donaghey and Williams Jennings Bryan on a Special Train Near Leslie (Barnes, 1910)
Three-time presidential nominee William Jennings Bryan long remained a hero to Arkansans, speaking in many towns across the state in 1910 in behalf of the Initiative and Referendum Amendment. In company with Governor Donaghey, he is shown here on the back of a train. **Arkansas History Commission**

tigating committee found a prison chief cook with syphilis, boys twelve to sixteen incarcerated, sexual abuse of inmates, and books, notably donated Bibles, being put to unintended ends in the absence of toilet paper. A minister on the committee was incensed greatly by stories of the warden's swearing, for by Arkansas law, the warden could whip prisoners but not curse them. The committee took down much testimony and made many recommendations, but legislators continued to ignore them.

By Donaghey's second administration, Arkansas had another problem: money. In a special session called in 1913, Donaghey pointed out that the state could not pay its debts. The financial crisis was caused by more than the recent tax cut. Arkansas, like all agricultural states, relied heavily on the property tax for income. But assessing the value of property was done by county officials who were notorious for favoritism. Under what critics called the "old dilapidated system of assessment" full of "confusing and incoherent details," taxes were assessed irregularly and unevenly with large landowners often paying less than small farmers. Therefore, when Donaghey stood for a third term in 1912, it was as a supporter of reassessment.

Opposing the governor was Joseph T. Robinson, a sometime student at the University of Arkansas and a graduate of the University of Virginia Law School. Robinson had served a term in the legislature that was notable primarily for his controversial bill to regulate railroads. He had been elected to Congress in 1902, and it was as an incumbent congressman that he announced for governor. Robinson supported reducing expenses rather than raising taxes and called for putting the state on a cash basis. His progressive ideas included the establishment of a state banking commission and the passage of a corrupt practices act. He courted the support of the wets by favoring local option on liquor sales rather than the statewide prohibition that Donaghey advocated.

Robinson won the 1912 primary and defeated token Republican opposition but did not remain governor long. The death of Jeff Davis on January 3, 1913, created a vacancy in the United States Senate. *Arkansas Gazette* owner J. N. Heiskell filled the position until the legislature elected Congressman Joe T. Robinson in March, the last such election before the implementation of the Seventeenth Amendment to the United States Constitution that made the office of United States Senator popularly elected. Because Robinson's congressional term had not expired when the governor was elected to the Senate, Robinson held three offices in a two-week period. A Memphis paper noted that Robinson had better be careful or he might pick up another vacancy on his way to Washington.

It was clear that Robinson was now a sen-

ator, but there was great uncertainty about who was governor. W. K. Oldham and J. M. Futrell fought in court about whether the past or future president of the Senate was Robinson's successor. The confusion, which ended in a victory for Futrell, prompted an amendment to restore the office of lieutenant governor. A special election was held July 23 to fill Robinson's vacancy. Stephen Brundidge, an enemy of Jeff Davis and former congressman, opposed George W. Hays, who had been a farmer, clerk and teacher before practicing law.

George W. Hays, who was less progressive than Brundidge, was elected governor because Phillips County, represented by the enormously powerful St. Francis River Levee Board, threw its support to him. Phillips County's returns arrived late, just in time to give Hays a margin of victory. Brundidge was outraged and took his evidence of fraud to the Democratic State Committee. After conducting "a feigned and pretended hearing," the Committee rejected his plea. A chancery court intervened for Brundidge, but a divided state Supreme Court, in a decision written by Judge William F. Kirby, declared that political rights could not be enforced by the courts, effectively leaving Brundidge without a remedy at law.

Governor Hays's administration retreated from progressivism. His biographer noted that his critics viewed his record as one of "inactivity, irresolution and vacillation." Hays simultaneously signed and vetoed a bill to legalize pari-mutuel betting at Hot Springs, much to the confusion of the courts and the legislature. The new initiative amendment bore fruit in 1914 when Stephen Brundidge, mindful of the ways of Arkansas elections, fathered a new election law to correct some of the obvious faults. His bill failed in the legislature but was passed by the voters in 1916. In addition, state elections were made to coincide with the federal election day, a move of little consequence because the Democratic primary settled all significant questions by 1915. In the first election in which voters could select United States senators, incumbent James P. Clarke was opposed by Judge Kirby. Kirby was the apparent winner until Poinsett County returns were resubmitted, giving Clarke a 200-vote victory. In fitting irony, Kirby's previous decision in the Brundidge case stood as a bar to any questioning in the courts, even though Poinsett County listed 1,537 paid poll taxes and recorded 1,971 votes. Kirby gained the seat after Clarke died on October 1, 1916.

As progressives were trying to clean up Arkansas elections, Hays was working hard to build a political machine based on control of state boards. Beginning with Jefferson Davis, who would appoint only his white male Democratic supporters, governors sought to extend their influence over every person even remotely connected with state government. By 1916, the gubernatorially appointed St. Francis River Levee Board had become synonymous for political control over eastern Arkansas. The legislature passed a law to make the board elective, but Hays vetoed it.

After serving two terms, Governor Hays did not run for re-election in 1916. Four Democrats announced for the race: Thomas McRae, a former congressman, banker, lawyer and hybrid progressive-conservative from southern Arkansas; Earle W. Hodges, the incumbent secretary of state; L.C. "Shotgun" Smith, who appealed to the agrarian vote by asking for "a cake of cornbread and a pint of potlicker," and Charles H. Brough.

Charles H. Brough

The most active progressive other than Donaghey was Charles H. Brough. A native of Mississippi, Brough graduated from Mississippi College in Clinton before attending Johns Hopkins, where he studied under the noted historian Herbert Baxter Adams, wrote a dissertation on Utah irrigation and heard lectures by visiting Princeton Professor (later President) Woodrow Wilson. Returning to

Mississippi, he obtained a law degree in 1902 and was active in the organization of the Mississippi Historical Society. After failing to get the position he wanted as head of the new Mississippi state archives in 1903, he moved west to teach at the University of Arkansas.

Brough supported the newly created Arkansas Historical Association and soon became a popular lecturer and speaker, averaging some thirty commencement speeches a year. He was elected president of the Arkansas State Teachers' Association in 1913 and lectured on the Chautauqua circuits. His most memorable observation, not original with him but much repeated thereafter until it became a joke, was that a wall could be built around Arkansas, and the state could survive and prosper because of the diversity of its resources. That Brough harbored political ambitions first became apparent in 1913, when he made an aborted effort to gain Robinson's vacated gubernatorial seat.

Brough had built a statewide network of former University students by 1916. In taking his message to the people, he reached seventy of Arkansas's counties and called for more aid to education, the election of the St. Francis River Levee Board and support for labor. He promised not to oppose woman's suffrage. McRae soon dropped out, leaving Hodges and Smith to battle Brough. Despite the substantive issues raised in the race, considerable mudslinging took place. The Hodges forces charged that Brough was pro-Negro and a Mormon. Brough turned his attendance at Woodrow Wilson's lectures into a regular disciple relationship, promising to be the honest scholar in politics. The other two candidates replied by attacking the University for fostering aristocracy and played on the anti-intellectual sentiments of many voters. Brough, with 48,892 votes, out-polled Smith with 34,918 and Hodges with 32,292. Runoff races had not been adopted yet.

Brough's first term saw the accomplishment of progressive reforms: adoption of statewide prohibition, creation of a girls reformatory, an expanded commitment to public health, a compulsory school attendance law, more aid to education and the mother's pension law to aid distressed women and children in some counties. Members of the St. Francis Levee Board were elected, and inspection of cotton gins and agricultural extension services were begun for farmers. The tick eradication program, begun to counter the threat of Texas Fever, was one of the first government programs to reach farmers directly.

What should have been the high-water mark of progressivism was the Constitutional Convention of 1917-18. Called to remedy the many defects of the 1874 document, the Convention voted to give women the right to vote, raise the low salary levels of constitutional officers, establish juvenile courts, provide for state regulation of insurance rates and prohibit sales of alcoholic beverages. As a favor to labor, blacklisting was prohibited. Despite its progressive orientation, the new constitution continued a number of needless or dubious features, including the ban on duelists holding office and legal discrimination against atheists. Although the constitution banned local legislation, the Convention proposed creating two new counties by dividing Clay and Logan Counties.

The proposed Constitution of 1918 aroused little enthusiasm when put to vote. J. O. A. Bush, a black leader, called it a rich man's document, although the *Arkansas Gazette* endorsed its adoption as part of the "fight for democracy." A rumor that it would raise taxes, a low turnout caused by the influenza epidemic and the failure of soldiers to vote combined to defeat it. Many of its progressive features were subsequently enacted into law over a long period.

PROGRESSIVE CAUSES

The United States became involved in World War I shortly after Governor Brough took office. Progressives viewed the struggle as an opportunity to achieve many of their social objectives in shaping the modern American character. Several of the most important progressive achievements owed their success to the War.

The Women's Rights Movement

One successful progressive movement was the granting of legal rights to married women and the adoption of woman's suffrage. Both items had long been discussed. Arkansas had passed its first Married Woman's Property Law in 1835, but Miles Langley's suffrage clause had been laughed down in the 1868 Constitutional Convention. He wrote Susan B. Anthony:

> The Democrats, are my enemies because I assisted in emancipating the slaves. The Republicans have now become my opponents because I have made an effort to confer on women their rights. And even the women themselves fail to sympathize with me.

More progress was made on the issue of legal rights for women. Judge James W. Butler urged the cause of women in the 1874 Constitutional Convention. Because of his insistence, a clause in the Constitution gave a married woman the right to own property that "may be devised, bequeathed, or conveyed by her the same as if she were a femme sole." At the next session, the state legislature passed an Act for the Protection of Married Women, under which a woman could insure a man's life; was not liable for his debts "except such as may have been contracted for the support of herself;" was granted the right to bargain, sell, assign or transfer property; could carry on a trade or business; sue and be sued; and her husband was not made liable for her separately contracted debts.

The state Supreme Court took a dim view of the liberation of women and emasculated the law in a number of late nineteenth-century decisions. An 1881 case, *Chrisman* v. *Partee*, held that a woman's contract was not binding on her. This had the practical legal effect of prohibiting women from making contracts, thus excluding them from the business world and all business transactions. In *Felkner* v. *Tighe* (1882),the court set aside both the Constitution and the law, ruling: "It is the settled doctrine of this court, that the disabilities which the common law has thrown around married women for her protection remain. . . ."

This last case was marked by a vehement dissent by Judge John R. Eakin, who observed that under common law, women had the "same capacity as an idiot," which was why the "all embracing provisions of the Constitution of 1874" were adopted.

The women's rights movement was reborn in Arkansas in the aftermath of these decisions. The way had been prepared during the 1870s when Phoebe Cousins and other visiting lecturers brought news of the national movement. Even county editors began to carry stories about women's rights. Mary W. Loughborough started the publication of the *Arkansas Ladies Journal* in 1884. The paper was not overtly pro-suffrage, but it did score men on a number of issues. For example, when it was suggested that politics was too dirty for women, the editor responded, "Why wouldn't it be a good idea to change politics so that it shall be fit for women?"

Complementing Mrs. Loughborough was Lizzie D. Fyler, a Massachusetts native who settled at Eureka Springs and organized a local suffrage society at the resort town. In 1884, she became the first Arkansan to attend the National American Women Suffrage Association meeting in Washington, D.C., but interest in suffrage declined with her death in 1885.

The next leader was Clara A. McDiarmid, the wife of a carpetbagger Republican. Mrs. McDiarmid had been a lawyer in Kansas City. Although legally barred from practicing

law in Arkansas, she opened an office to give free legal advice to women. She organized the second suffrage movement in Little Rock in 1888 and began the publication of the *Woman's Chronicle*. In addition to the franchise, the paper supported equal pay, temperance, and "true womanhood, both in the home and before the world." The *Chronicle* became the official organ of the Arkansas chapter of the Women's Christian Temperance Union (WCTU) during the next five years and a free copy was provided to each legislator when the Assembly was in session. But there was little widespread support. The membership, "few in numbers, weak in influence, poor in purse, but valiant in spirit," remained essentially a Republican women's club with few Southern-born members.

Repeated efforts to spread the suffrage gospel outside Little Rock proved unsuccessful. The group did bring Susan B. Anthony to give addresses at Helena, Fort Smith and Little Rock. Anthony was introduced at the Capitol by Governor James P. Eagle, whose wife was active in Baptist women's circles. According to newspaper reports, Anthony was received warmly.

Usually, suffrage leaders barely were tolerated. "Go home and attend to [your] house and babies," *Chronicle* editor Catherine Cunningham once was told. The paper asserted that Arkansas thinks "it unwomanly" for women "to think and act for themselves as rational beings, and they are not yet fully awake to the vital importance of the movement." There was also more religious opposition than support. The Arkansas Women Suffrage Association made a pointed call for ministerial support in 1894 "in as much as the churches are largely made up of and supported by women."

The movement languished politically. The Prohibition Party in 1890 adopted the first resolution in the state supporting women's rights, but the WCTU was divided on the question. A bill to give the vote to white women failed in 1891. Several bills to give women the vote in school elections failed to pass. After Mrs. McDiarmid's death in 1899, the *Chronicle* ceased publication and organized activity disappeared.

Although all women were not ready for civil rights, many were ready to join women's clubs. The Arkansas Federation of Women's Clubs organized in 1897 and contained 126 clubs with 15,047 members by 1914. These early clubs were not limited to cultural and artistic ideas. The 1900-1901 yearbook claimed:

> Woman has not only discovered herself but she has discovered her sisters, and they together are working out, among other problems, woman's economic independence without the strike of the sex that the pessimist has foretold.

Kindergartens, the Mothers' Pension Law and pure food were among their causes, in addition to a 1914 stand "against the prevailing mode of dress."

The state Supreme Court continued to render decisions restrictive of the rights of women. Women's lobbying resulted in some minor legal victories in the 1890s. An 1893 act gave women the power to make legal conveyances of property. An 1895 law gave married women the power to make contracts and execute powers of attorney. Federal Judge Isaac C. Parker, more famous for hanging men than adjudicating for women, ruled a woman could not escape the legal consequences of her actions, a conclusion the state courts had not reached yet.

The women's rights movement rapidly came back to life in the Progressive era. In 1913, a few years after the United States Supreme Court upheld protective legislation for women, Arkansas enacted a law requiring that female workers be provided seats and not be worked more than nine hours a day, six days a week. The Political Equality League was established in 1911 by a new generation of militant

women whom the *Arkansas Democrat* characterized as "tired of theatre parties and poodles." Reorganized in 1915 as the Arkansas Women's Suffrage Association, its members were not pleased by a frivolous debate in the legislature about women, and some radicals even formed a chapter of the militant National Women's Party.

Charles H. Brough was the first governor to support women's suffrage. The proposed 1918 constitution gave women the vote, but when it failed, other expedients were adopted. One was giving women the right to vote in party primaries. This was done without a constitutional amendment in 1917, and 40,000 women's votes were recorded in May 1918 for incumbent Governor Brough. In addition, Stella Brizzolara was elected to the Democratic Central Committee. One result was apparent. Every Arkansas congressman in 1915 had opposed a national constitutional amendment granting woman's suffrage; in 1918, after women were given suffrage in the state primary, every congressman supported it. Women were at last admitted to the bar, and other statutory disabilities and common law restraints were removed in 1919. Even so, when Republicans put Dr. Ida Jo Brooks on their ticket in 1920 for the office of Superintendent of Public Instruction, the attorney general ruled that women could not hold office in Arkansas.

The Arkansas General Assembly was one of the first Southern legislative bodies to approve the Nineteenth Amendment to the United States Constitution granting suffrage to women. But when Arkansas voters were given the chance to extend the franchise to women by a state constitutional amendment, they gave it a two-to-one margin, but it initially failed to receive a majority of the total vote in the election. Eventually, as an aftermath of the *Brickhouse* case, it too was declared adopted belatedly.

The success of the progressives in institutionalizing the equality of women was more apparent than real. Annie L. Stuckey, elected Jackson County treasurer over five male opponents in 1923, recalled:

> Most of the older men up there did not believe in a woman holding office. It was all right for them to work in the office and do the work of the office, but they didn't want a woman to have the honor of serving in a public office.

The most conspicuous example of female officeholders was in the small town of Winslow, which had a woman mayor and an all-female city council from 1925 to 1929. Efforts of the "petticoat government" to clean up the town and improve roads attracted out-of-state press attention. Winslow was not unique, for women also ruled the antebellum village of Washington. The subsequent elections of Pearl Peden Oldfield and Effiegene Wingo to fill congressional seats left vacant by the deaths of their respective husbands in 1929 and 1930 provided a precedent for widow Hattie W. Caraway's elevation to the United States Senate in 1931. In each of the three instances, however, the women insisted to the voters that they were just wives and not professional, troublemaking women. Despite getting the vote, women did not attack other areas of law and custom where sexual discrimination prevailed and the true emancipation of women did not begin until modern birth control devices gave most women the option of limiting family size. Women did not begin to serve on juries until the late 1940s.

The Foundation of Modern Education

A commitment to education was another hallmark of progressivism. Progressives tended to believe that education was the solution to everything "un-American," from the ways of immigrants to the "behavior" of blacks. Immigrants were not a major concern in Arkansas,

but primary education was. Progressives believed it was a crime against humanity and America that "The Great White Race," as represented by some of the purest Anglo-Saxon blood, should grow up uneducated and unable to claim a leading role in the new America.

The rebirth of the Arkansas school system began in the 1880s. As in roads and a number of other reforms, localism dominated. The 1903-1904 Report of the Superintendent of Public Instruction summarized what was wrong with the Arkansas "system." The state spent only $4.33 per pupil per year, and that money was not put to the best use:

> Much of our money is being practically wasted because of small schools, poorly paid and incompetent teachers, short terms, nepotism, favoritism, and other influences.

Funding was so inadequate that if a building had to be erected, it usually was necessary to suspend classes until the cost of construction was paid off. Washington County had 161 separate school districts, Madison 123 and Craighead 77. One Craighead district was formed from lands no other districts wanted and was called "Chicken Gristle" because of its appearance on the map. Churches often shared community facilities, which meant classes were suspended for funerals. Floors often would be covered with tobacco stains after such meetings. School officials were prohibited from having an organ or piano at Surrounded Hill in Jackson County, where the schoolhouse doubled as the Church of Christ.

Conditions were primitive. Children had begun to substitute gum for tobacco, putting it behind their ears when not in use. Licorice was also popular. Dental hygiene was little practiced, and to ward off sickness, students wore an asafetida bag on a string, which emitted a smell that would "stink a buzzard off a gut wagon." One veteran scholar recalled that, "no rural school ever smelled exactly like a rose

Public School in Fayetteville *(Burch Brabill, ca. 1910) These Fayetteville children enjoyed better than average classrooms and better paid teachers. Note the modern desks and blackboards. The students are well dressed.*
Shiloh Museum

garden." Teachers were paid an average of $34.46 a month, compared to $59.80 in Western states. There was little incentive to remain in the teaching profession and much turnover. One student recalled that in his thirty months of school, he had ten different teachers, all men and none a college graduate. Arkansas also was the only state in the Louisiana Purchase without a normal school to educate white teachers. Teachers either were trained in summertime institutes or not at all.

These summer institutes were instructional

sessions that usually lasted a week. First begun during Reconstruction, they received aid from the Peabody Fund until 1898 and state assistance on rare occasions. Teachers were required by law to attend or have their licenses revoked. Although most counties held sessions by 1900, the academic results were hardly encouraging, and educational reformers kept demanding a normal school. The legislature finally authorized the creation of a teacher's college located at Conway in 1907; it became a four-year institution by 1920 and is now the University of Central Arkansas.

A constitutional limit on property taxes was one reason Arkansas schools were underfunded. The McFerrin Amendment in 1906 allowed voters to raise the millage rate, but voter resistance remained strong. Northerner Charles B. Spahr, observing the Arkansas system at the turn of the century, found that the rich and their dependent clients always voted against the schools, and small farmers with many children generally supported them.

In 1909, the Farmers' Union was active in the creation of four district agricultural high schools at Jonesboro, Russellville, Magnolia and Monticello, each of which became a four-year college in time. In addition, the Farmers' Union supported the creation of an agriculture department at the University of Arkansas in 1905. These improvements gradually doomed the old institutes, and only one-third of the counties still held them by 1919.

Another feature of the early twentieth century was the passage of a compulsory school attendance law in 1909. Localism was so strong, however, that each county could decide whether to participate in enforcement, and most chose not to. By 1911, high schools had become common in towns, and the newly created state Board of Education provided financial assistance for them. The state accepted federal assistance for vocational education in 1917 and passed a uniform elementary textbook law. Efforts to get free textbooks were defeated by voters.

One articulate exponent of educational progress was Governor Brough. "The touch of the teacher is the wand of the modern Orpheus," he told teachers. However, for him the progressive goal of efficiency was incompatible with local control of the thousands of small Arkansas school districts.

After passage of a voluntary consolidation law, Palestine (St. Francis County) held the first consolidated graduation with Governor Brough giving the address in 1915. Brough reported with dismay in 1917 that twenty-six counties had failed to establish compulsory attendance so that only 446,525 of Arkansas's 649,083 school-aged children were enrolled. Worse yet, only 292,413, a mere 45 percent of school-aged children, attended class regularly. The result of the governor's labors was a new compulsory attendance law.

Teachers emerged as a growing lobby for education during the Progressive era. The state teachers association claimed only 150 members in 1900; by 1915, the number stood at 1,500, making teachers "by far the largest, the most compact and coherent organization in the state." State education policy became a major issue after the turn of the century.

The Struggle for Prohibition

The temperance movement, which began in antebellum Arkansas, encouraged individuals not to use alcohol. By the Progressive era, temperance had been superseded by prohibition — the determination to eliminate through laws the manufacture, sale and consumption of alcoholic beverages.

Organized prohibition activity was led by Methodists and supported by Presbyterians. By contrast, the denomination most representative of the pioneer log cabin folk, the "Hardshell" Baptists, resisted prohibition. Evidence of the evils of excessive alcohol consumption was not hard to find, especially where railroad construction workers or lumber workers were. Newspapers repeatedly recorded scenes such as that at Argenta in June 1879 when a large group of discharged railroad workers celebrated to such excess that the *Gazette* sent a reporter across the River to find out what was going on. He reported men passed out on the railroad tracks, lying in ditches and gullies, and "vomit, blood, and slime covered earth and floor" in the bars.

State laws on liquor grew apace after Reconstruction. The legislature passed a law in 1875 banning the sale of alcohol within three miles of a college, university or academy,

Arkansas WCTU Cross (ca. 1902) Constructed by
students at the Arkansas School for the Deaf for the
state chapter of the Women's Christian Temperance
Union, this cross was inscribed with the motto
"Excelsior" from Tennyson's poem. **Old State House**

except in incorporated areas. For this law to
become operative, a majority of the adult residents in the township had to petition for its
implementation. Naturally, the statute books
grew full of exemptions and local qualifications. Agitation for tightening the law came
from a variety of groups. The Grand Councils
of Temperance Reform was formed in 1872,
the United Friends of Temperance dedicated
Temperance Hall in 1875, the Arkansas State
Christian Temperance Union was organized in
1879, and most importantly, the Women's
Christian Temperance Union (WCTU) took
form in 1879. Persistent agitation led to more
legislation.

In 1879, qualified voters rather than the
county court were allowed to decide on local

liquor licensing, and in 1881, the legislature
allowed inhabitants rather than voters to
decide. Presumably inhabitants included
women, and the state Supreme Court sustained the law in *Trammel* v. *Bradley* (1881).
Judge Eakin chivalrously observed that
women:

> [A]re not being wholly ignored by the
> constitution and the law, and there is
> much reason to believe that their
> womanly instincts and keen foresight of
> demoralization influences are truer than
> the often careless judgments of electors.
> [It is] undoubted everywhere that men
> and children are safest under the moral
> influences and social surrounding which
> are approved by women.

A Sunday closing law was applied to saloons
in 1885, and after 1893, children under eighteen needed a written order to buy liquor. In
1895, licensing was required of private clubs
and the first law designed to regulate unlicensed sales was passed. License fees were
raised several times, and it became illegal to
buy liquor for another person in 1899. All this
legislation was mostly attributable to the
WCTU, whose members applied the zeal of
religion to the prohibition cause, adding new
words to old songs and agitating the public
ceaselessly.

The WCTU's campaign ran into repeated
obstacles. Often unwilling to compromise, its
members voted in 1884 to support only temperance candidates for office. Republicans
promptly put temperance in their Party platforms, and Democratic prohibitionists were
stranded politically. A national Prohibition
Party formed and ran state candidates, but
drew small votes.

Many temperance supporters in earlier
years had looked on wine as a much lesser evil
than hard liquor. Difficulties developed when
Judge John R. Eakin published his treatise on
the possibilities of growing grapes commercial-

ly in Arkansas, and German and Italian farmers began wine production on a modest scale. The State Horticulture Society approved a resolution supporting the production of wine by a one-vote margin, and the legislature granted various exemptions from the licensing laws to wine producers. Another problem came in the 1890s when the Free Silver Prohibitionist Party seceded from the main unit.

The male equivalent of the WCTU, the Anti-Saloon League, organized in the state in 1889. George Thornburgh, a prominent Methodist layman and long-time legislator from Lawrence County, proved a masterly leader in the final drive to dry up the state. Another tactic was employed by Carry A. Nation, a hatchet-wielding fanatic noted for smashing bars. "Hatchet Hall" at Eureka Springs was the center of her activities; it was there she published *The Hatchet*, a magazine for temperance extremists.

The battle for local option on the sale of liquor ebbed and flowed. Thirty of the state's counties were dry in 1900, and in 1904, for the first time, "drys" recorded more votes statewide in local option races than "wets." An Inter-Church Temperance Federation under George Thornburgh united Methodists and Presbyterians in 1905 for the final struggle, which even included taking advantage of the postcard craze to flood the state with cards reading "The Real Issue, The Saloon or the Boy and the Girl." Thornburgh proclaimed, "We have passed the local stage," when only twelve wet counties were left in 1912.

In summarizing the controversial subject early in the century, one author held that state laws showed "a true Anglo-Saxon conservatism, unmixed with bigotry and intolerance." Ironically, racism became a major feature in prohibition after 1910, largely because the remaining wet counties contained substantial black populations. Thus in 1914, the Going Law required that a majority of white inhabitants must approve every grant of a liquor license. Blacks were denied the right to

vote on the issue and went to court. The state Supreme Court ruled in *McClure* v. *Toph & Wright* (1914) that local option votes were not elections. The law would have been discriminatory, the court said, only if black persons were not permitted to sell liquor when white men could. The legislature, it continued, knows "what class of citizen could best give proper information as to evil that might result from the liquor traffic."

One problem with local option was that it relied on local enforcement. Considerable consumption of liquor continued despite alleged dryness. Hard drinking was one of the rites of manhood, and homemade liquor was plentiful in both hills and swamps. Moonshiners and bootleggers always voted "dry" in order to eliminate legal competition. Most of all, abuses abounded in the form of "blind tigers," which were retail establishments that sold liquor privately and illegally. In 1907, after considerable debate, a new blind tiger law made the property owner responsible for any illegality committed on the property.

Federal revenue officers on the trail of untaxed liquor were more important to regulation than feeble state efforts. Serious efforts at enforcement started after the Civil War but labored under great difficulties. Federal Judge Henry Caldwell observed that moonshiners not only "overawe and coerce" all people living in the vicinity of their still, but they even go so far as to put life itself in jeopardy. He added:

> It is well understood that many good citizens have lost both their property and their lives either because they would not cooperate with these pestiferous violators of the law, or because it was feared they would give information to the government officers.

The tide turned as Arkansas became settled. In 1909, federal agents captured "Old Tige," a 104-gallon still that had been used for decades in Newton, Madison and Carroll Counties. State officials also became increasingly active. In 1915, the Mississippi County sheriff, accompanied by a detachment of militia, raided Island Number 37 on the Mississippi River. The bootleggers battled the lawmen and killed the sheriff. The murderer died in jail from wounds received in the struggle, and the head bootlegger, who was not even on the island, was lynched in his Crittenden County jail cell.

Politicians sought out the dry vote as prohibition increased in popularity. The issue was featured prominently in 1912 when Governor George W. Donaghey, seeking an elusive third term, endorsed the statewide prohibition amendment. Liquor interests lured blacks into voting against the law, promising to oppose an initiated law to restrict black voting by establishing a "grandfather clause." Donaghey's opponent, Joseph T. Robinson, opted for local option and won the election as both prohibition and the "grandfather clause" went down to defeat.

The Bone-Dry Law finally passed four years later. One limitation on the victory was that nothing in the law prevented persons from bringing their own liquor into the state. A 1919 law remedied that defect and mere possession became unlawful in 1925. Prohibition became the law nationwide with the passage of the Eighteenth Amendment in 1918.

Prohibition during the 1920s created a national market for bootleg liquor that Arkansas producers rushed to fill. The quality of home brew declined, and the repeal of prohibition in 1933 was a hard blow to the state's economy. The moral assumptions behind prohibition proved unworkable in practice. Enforcement became selective and often was marked by naive hypocrisy. The immoderate zeal of prohibitionists led to a variety of infringements on civil liberties. An 1899 law authorized searches for illegal liquor on mere suspicion of possession. The state high court struck down the statute in *Ferguson* v. *Josey*

(1902) but let stand the confiscation.

One proposed law would have banned from the state all publications with liquor advertisements, and although it failed to pass, communities often censored plays, books and movies that contained references to alcohol. More positive was a state law mandating teachers to instruct students about the evils of alcohol.

Although enacted during the Progressive era, prohibition sprang from other roots. Victorian morality, which made the wife the defender of the home, explains why so many participants in prohibition were middle-class church women. However, in rural areas remote from cheap transportation, stills continued to flourish. The coming of the railroad gave small farmers other outlets for their grains, thus removing the economic necessity for liquor production. By the early twentieth century, Missionary Baptists, a conservative group, joined the prohibition movement. Yet in those areas still outside the tentacles of civilization, liquor use continued to flourish.

Prohibition played an inadvertent role in liberating women in the late nineteenth century. Church women active in temperance societies often concluded that female suffrage was needed, and with their political consciousness raised, some went on to other issues such as child labor, education reform and community betterment.

Pugilists and Coffin-Nails

Prohibition was but the most conspicuous example of the imposition of middle-class values on Arkansas society. The 1879 legislature passed a law against cruelty to animals that gave extensive powers to Arkansas groups interested in animal welfare. Bear-baiting and other time-honored sports officially disappeared. Even the sale of toy guns became illegal early in the twentieth century.

The most conspicuous attack on violence concerned boxing, which the legislature banned and made a felony but subsequently reduced to a misdemeanor. The law did not stop Hot Springs officials from planning a national boxing championship match between "Gentleman" James J. Corbett and Bob Fitzsimmons. Governor Clarke threatened to call out the militia unless the fight was canceled. Meanwhile, Chancellor Leland Leatherman declared the law void, finding that boxing was not assault and battery and that the statute had been enacted improperly. Leatherman was reversed by the state Supreme Court, and the two fighters were placed under a peace bond when they arrived in Little Rock. The great fight never took place.

Anti-pugilism remained vigorous well into the twentieth century. Football rules had to be modified greatly before public acceptance grew, because many objected that the sport was too violent. Governor Donaghey personally invaded a Little Rock movie theater in 1911 and chastised the audience for watching a boxing film. When the theater owner protested that the sport on the screen was wrestling, Donaghey unabashedly asserted that both were "immoral and against the peace and dignity and laws of the state."

Although no state law banned boxing films, the Little Rock City Council promptly enacted an ordinance prohibiting all future displays of boxing and of bullfights as well. Boxing did not return legally to Arkansas until 1927. An irony of the times was that sentiment should be so strong against boxing and so feeble against lynching.

Another Progressive era morality law was the passage in 1907 of the McKenzie Bill, which banned the sale, manufacture and possession of cigarettes. The law had been urged for some time. Though it unanimously passed the state Senate, considerable effort was expended in the House to exempt certain counties. When the bill passed the House at last, the *Arkansas Gazette* observed that, "in all probability the habit will not become extinct in the state as long as cigarettes are sold in other portions of the world."

Interestingly, local tobacconists were not especially disturbed because cigarettes constituted such a small part of their sales. Opposition to this new form of tobacco consumption lay in a general anti-tobacco sentiment typical of the middle-class Victorians and the association of cigarettes with pool halls and other forms of dissipation. The law remained on the books for more than a decade, and some effort was made to enforce it. Boy Scout leaders appeared at a Jonesboro City Council meeting in December 1920 to demand that the law be enforced.

Eventually the ban on sales of cigarettes gave way to a tax on them that became a regular source of state revenue. In an ironic twist on the women's rights movement, young women in the 1920s turned to cigarettes in increasing numbers to show that they were modern and independent. Scientifically founded objections to cigarettes did not arise until later, and it was well into the second half of the twentieth century before these women learned that the freedom conferred by cigarettes was the freedom to die young of lung cancer and heart disease just like men.

Roads

Road policies were controversial in Arkansas before the advent of the automobile and in time became the central issue in state politics. Like schools, roads were under local control. The county court could establish a road, but any twelve landowners could protest the route. These roads were little more than wagon trails because there was no money to make improvements. The road from Guion to Melbourne crossed the same creek thirty-two times, and a Lawrence County resident wrote:

Roads in this country are so rocky and hilly, that in traveling a mile on a straight line, you are compelled to go about three; and if you are not used to traveling in a God Forsaken country,

Car Wreck *(photographer and date unknown) Automobiles were subject to accidents, with drivers at fault at least as often as road conditions.* **Arkansas Endowment for the Humanities**

over rocks and hills, by crooked roads, you will imagine at the end of your short journey, that you have traveled ten, and will be sore accordingly.

Meandering streams and lack of money for bridges in the Delta caused roads to make long detours to outflank water. Upkeep was minimal and done only when agricultural needs were not critical.

A few turnpike and bridge companies made improvements to some of the more densely traveled routes, but the Arkansas public was averse to paying tolls, and profits generally were disappointing. The agrarians loudly complained during the Populist years about the old medieval system under which all men between eighteen and forty-five had to give five days labor each year to the public roads supervised by the county judge. Northern journalist Charles B. Spahr observed, "infinitely less work from men who understood the business would give far better roads." But all efforts at reform failed "because the financial interests of the leading citizens were opposed to it."

The presence of the automobile rapidly

altered the attitude of the rich in the early twentieth century. The first cars were reported in Little Rock in 1902, and by 1903, Arkansas boasted fifty vehicles. Owners formed the Arkansas Good Roads Association in 1903 and began lobbying for more modern legislation. In 1909, the state legislature allowed local voters to form special road districts so that a group inside a county could tax itself to improve roads. The Dollarway Road from Pine Bluff to Little Rock was the first improved automobile road in the state. In 1911, counties were authorized to hire county engineers.

The State Department of Lands, Highways and Improvements was created two years later and funded by a $10 motor vehicle tax. The number of cars increased dramatically and reached 4,800 by 1914. Road districts were allowed to borrow money, and in localism gone wild, the 1919 legislature chartered 689 separate road districts.

Behind these changes stood the labors of a number of modernizers. The Arkansas pathfinder was the monetary theorist W. H. "Coin" Harvey of Monte Ne, who organized the Ozark Trails Association to mark roads in 1913. More than 6,000 miles were delineated by white rings painted on trees and posts. Armed with a guide book, the prospective traveler would read his speedometer at "4m. cross RR, at 4.58 turn right, at 5.12 jog right to corner and turn left. . . ."

The state began designating highways in 1917, and a system of numbering began. The Trails Association held its annual meeting in Jonesboro the same year. Large delegations arrived, and Governor Brough was the major speaker. State Senator John Carter of Eudora explained how Pine Bluff merchants had cut into Little Rock's trade by aggressive road building. In what must have been a very popular speech, E. B. Guthrey of Tulsa, Oklahoma, expounded on how to build roads without taxation. Three percent of the state's roads were improved by 1918, and 190 miles had a hard surface. The movement for better roads could be stopped no longer.

The increase of cars and trucks during World War I and the seizure and operation of the railroads by the federal government during the War triggered the long decline of the rail system. One of the Arkansas Railroad Commission's first regulations led to a reduction in intrastate rates and passenger fares. Falling profits followed. Many railroad lines were speculative at best, with poor grading, sharp curves, light rails and many wrecks. Freight hauling dropped as the lumber industry declined. In addition, a complex 1910 federal decision led many lumber companies to close unprofitable rail lines. Some Arkansas shortlines merged with major companies.

Public Health

Few changes had more impact in Arkansas than the emergence of modern medicine. The death rate began dropping dramatically in the early twentieth century because the discoveries of Louis Pasteur and Robert Koch in bacteriology led to public health measures that forced changes on an often unwilling public. In time, these changes pushed the fear of childhood death into the background, thereby undermining the morbid mentality of many nineteenth-century families. Better health also increased agricultural and industrial efficiency.

One of the first improvements was to establish uniform licensing requirements for doctors. In 1880, one physician estimated that more than 600 persons died annually because of improper treatment. The legislature passed a registration law the next year that was dubbed the "Quack Law" because virtually anyone could obtain the medical license it required. Of the state's 2,000 doctors, only slightly more than 700 were graduates of medical schools. Under the law, candidates could go from county to county until finally they were admitted to practice. Saline County, which had only eleven physicians, certified

149 physicians in ten years (1881-1891). Repeated attempts to strengthen the law were rebuffed, and the legislature resolved in 1883 that, "Surgery and medicine are Humbug."

Reform came slowly. A law on false advertising in 1891 provided the means to prosecute some of the notorious Hot Springs "drummers" who flourished among the spa's sick by promoting blatantly false cures. An 1895 licensing law created county boards and required that two members had to be medical school graduates.

The existence of different philosophies of medicine made implementation of the law difficult. Dentists were licensed in 1881, and a state examining board modernized the requirements in 1915. Osteopaths won the right to separate licensure in 1903, and chiropractors followed in 1915. Registration of nurses began in 1913, optometrists in 1915 and midwives in 1923. New laws gradually required college degrees rather than apprenticeship. The Turner Act of 1909 ended the days of apprenticeship for doctors and established another progressive feature: reciprocal licensing with other states. A 1923 regulation required that midwives, who often were illiterate "Granny Women," carry proper obstetrical tools.

A new view of death became institutionalized when the Arkansas Funeral Directors' Association was founded. Before then, funerals followed immediately after death and usually were held at home. Caskets were homemade, the hardware being obtainable at any country store. It became possible to keep a corpse indefinitely with the invention of embalming during the Civil War. The process meant that distant family members could attend the final rites, and this increased the popularity of undertakers and led to the professionalization of funerals. In 1909, the State Board of Embalmers was established to regulate the practice.

Not all the changes were improvements. Doctors used opium and its derivatives extensively during the Civil War. Popular patent medicines, sold heavily in the South after the War, were laced generously with narcotics, and addiction became a major problem. Doctors proposed a modest labeling law, but pharmacists, supported by patent medicine concerns, defeated it. The opposition of patent medicine concerns was expected, but pharmacists opposed the law because many of them made their own secret concoctions.

Finally, after protracted debate, the legislature passed a law in 1907 requiring labels to indicate the presence of opium and alcohol. Little enforcement came at the state level. Federal authorities filed a few suits against Arkansas concerns after the creation of the Food and Drug Administration. The Mountain Valley Spring Water Company in Hot Springs was enjoined from promoting its "radioactive" water as a cure for Bright's Disease, diabetes, rheumatism and a dozen other ailments. A few small concerns went out of business as a result of federal prosecutions.

The emergence of modern medicine, especially the development of the germ theory of disease, doomed the spas. Drinking spa water had little scientific value. Persons bathing with victims of venereal diseases, who accounted for three-fourths of Hot Springs bathers in the 1880s, could contract the disease. Many of the smaller spas were dying by the beginning of the century. Hot Springs survived by promoting physical therapy and offering horse racing and gambling.

The largest public health problem remained the spread of communicable diseases. Yellow fever was still a feared disease during the late nineteenth century, although it abated after major outbreaks in the 1870s. The last recorded American occurrence was in 1905, when the towns of Newport, Pine Bluff, Arkansas City, Helena and Texarkana were under quarantine. As yellow fever declined, the mechanisms used to fight it — information, inspection and isolation — gradually were abandoned, and Arkansas was left with no public health policy. Despite pleas from the medical

***Butcher Shop,
Eureka Springs***
*(photographer and
date unknown) This
remarkably clean
butcher shop is devoid
of the wild game that
appears frequently in
earlier pictures. Note
the bare light bulbs
and sides of beef,
bacon and ham
hanging from hooks
in the open.* **Shiloh
Museum**

society, no law required public officials to keep vital statistics. Complete mortality records existed for many states and cities, but the absence of such records in Arkansas left the public poorly informed about health problems. Malaria was by far the most prevalent disease in Arkansas. It was estimated that the work output in eastern Arkansas was cut in half by the debilitating effects of the "chills." A typical Delta doctor's practice consisted of from one-third to one-half malaria victims; 300 of the first 450 patients at St. Bernard's Hospital in Jonesboro had the illness.

A cure existed in the form of quinine, commonly sold as "bitters." Most Arkansans took their bitters in some form of patent medicine, but a few companies put only enough quinine in the brew to curb the symptoms without eradicating the disease, an unethical technique that promoted extra sales. A leading study of the disease was written in 1909 by Dr. William H. Deadrick, who had practiced at Marianna. Malaria even became a source of humor:

The little frogs in the swamps pipe in their shrill voices, "Quinine, Quinine, Quinine," while the big bullfrog with his deep bass voice chimes in "Double the dose! Double the dose!"

Wire screening of windows, doors and porches, introduced in the late nineteenth century, was one new method of protecting against malaria. Common in towns by World War I, wire screening rarely was seen in the country and almost never among sharecroppers. The cropper's method of coping with mosquitoes and flies consisted of burning green leaves both inside and outside the house to smoke the pests out. Screens also helped protect against flies, which were everywhere in the late nineteenth century.

The Little Rock city market "never closed and never cleaned up." City streets were littered with dung; garbage was thrown out the back door, down ravines or left for pigs, and flies abounded in open sewage, known as "typhoid temples." Homeowners who cared to fight could buy flypaper or use a popular homemade device consisting of a fruit jar with molasses placed under the lid. When enough flies collected inside, a good shake would knock them off into a lye water solution in the bottom of the jar. The 1913 "Swat the Fly" campaign, which used a cartoon to demonstrate how flies carried feces from the outhouse to the dining table, was one of the first efforts to get the public involved in public health.

Arkansas was home to one important federal experiment in public health during the Progressive era. In 1916, the government funded a program at Crossett that eradicated mosquitoes by drainage, cleaning up and poisoning. The number of reported cases of malaria fell by more than 80 percent, and the cost — $1.26 per person — was probably less than the amount spent locally for bitters and medical treatment. The public greatly resisted this type of governmental activity, however. Dr. W. H. Abington of Beebe, a prominent politician and physician, asserted that blacks were never bitten by mosquitoes, and a move to fund the Crossett program statewide collapsed. Malaria remained a problem until the discovery of the pesticide DDT during the 1940s, and it was not eradicated until the 1950s.

A state Board of Health study found in 1913 that 53 percent of rural residents had no toilet facilities and only one out of ten churches, schools or factories had outhouses or toilets. There was progress, however, because corncobs were yielding to pages from mail-order catalogues as wipers. Customers ordered two catalogues, one as a wish book and the other for outhouse use.

One of the first urban services was the establishment of a city scavenger wagon. Scavengers, who usually worked at night, went down alleys with wagons, emptying outhouses and hauling sewage out of town for dumping. Quicklime then was used to disinfect outhouses. In areas without this service, residents were forced to move their outhouses

to new locations when the holes filled up.

Contamination of wells by outhouses contributed to typhoid fever — about 10,000 cases and 1,000 deaths annually. Three-fourths of the families at Melbourne were affected in 1897. One cause was the "utter disregard of the people for its contagious nature. Most of the patients expectorate on the floor, never using a spittoon cup." Many who recovered became carriers and infected others.

One way to limit the disease was to create safe municipal water and sewer systems. Some were formed in the early twentieth century as improvement districts, and others were capitalist ventures. With them came local controversies about individual rights and the common good.

Progress was not free of mishap. Ben Hardee reports that Monticello had public water service early in the twentieth century. When residents began to notice a strong deterioration in the quality of their water, an investigation revealed that "a cow had wandered onto the wooden roof of the reservoir on Rough & Ready Hill and had accidently fallen in and been unable to negotiate her return." For several days Hardee's only water supply "consisted of the water my sister and I carried in lard buckets from one of the good wells in the neighborhood."

The introduction of paved streets, telephones, electricity, city water, gas and ice marked the beginning of modern urban society in Arkansas, but only a small percentage of the population was affected. "Outside of the cities," the editor of the *Journal of the Arkansas Medical Society* noted, "the world has advanced little since the days of Moses."

Many unhealthy practices continued well into the twentieth century. Little Rock did not begin meat and dairy inspection or garbage pickup until 1912. Fresh game hung in store windows in various stages of decomposition throughout most of the state. Milk was guarded laxly. Brucellosis (Bang's Disease) and tuberculosis were milk-transmitted; efforts were not made to promulgate and enforce sanitary testing regulations and pasteurization until the 1940s. Shady practices abounded in the absence of food regulation. One Augusta tamale seller undercut his competition by converting the town's stray dogs into cheap tamales.

Arkansas was totally unprepared for the Spanish influenza epidemic, which hit in the fall of 1918. The great killer virus, which claimed 22,000,000 lives worldwide, arrived in the state in September. By early October, the state Board of Health put all Arkansas under a quarantine after 1,800 cases were reported statewide. At Camp Pike, temporary home to 52,000 soldiers, men were falling sick at the rate of a thousand a day, and the post soon ceased publishing obituary notices. Armistice Day, November 11, 1918, came and went, but the plague continued into the winter. In parts of the state, so many were ill at the time of the November election that some polls never opened, and elsewhere people feared to venture out, thus greatly reducing the vote and dooming the proposed new constitution. In central Arkansas, at least one out of every four persons reported sick. Five doctors at Fort Smith and Fayetteville died, and many of the approximately 7,000 casualties were young men and women.

Smallpox was probably the most feared disease of the age. The Fort Smith *New Era* in 1881 noted that, "In regulated communities smallpox epidemics are unknown, because the authorities very properly made vaccination compulsory. This should be done here."

Despite repeated localized outbreaks, it took a major disaster to prompt Arkansas to take action. That event came in 1899 when a soldier returning from the Spanish-American War brought the disease to Salem in Fulton County. Local doctors denied that the outbreak was smallpox, and nothing was done to contain its spread. By the time Dr. H. C. Dunavent, president of the powerless state Board of Health, reached Salem, he found "people walking about the streets of the town broken out with the disease, pockmarked and pitted, and others falling every day." Some 400 cases were reported, and the disease was spreading.

Half the counties in the state reported cases by 1900. More than 100 persons died in Mississippi County, eight deaths were recorded at Little Rock, and an outbreak at Galloway Female Boarding School in Conway nearly drove the school out of business. The raging disease claimed the lives of forty students at Beavoir College at Wilmar in 1905. Some 10,000 cases probably occurred yearly. When an outbreak was reported, the sick person was isolated and made to sleep between sheets greased with lard. All the patient's possessions were destroyed and towns often paid for the burned property.

Panic led many people to get vaccinated, although some rural physicians, such as White County's powerful Dr. W. H. Abington, asserted that the treatment was useless. A 1916 state law required the vaccination of all school children. The Supreme Court upheld the law in *State* v. *Martin and Lipe* (1918) and *Brazil* v. *State* (1918). It was the first law of its kind in the nation, and smallpox rapidly declined, although cases continued to be reported into the 1920s.

There were other serious contagious diseases. Consumption, as tuberculosis was called in the nineteenth century, afflicted an estimated one out of every sixty Arkansans and accounted for one of every seven deaths. It worked a special hardship on women and became a reason for having an abortion because a tubercular mother usually died within two years after the birth of a child.

Cerebrospinal spinal meningitis broke out in 1898 and Little Rock recorded fifty-seven deaths; it, too, remained a constant threat.

Like the rest of the South, Arkansas was home to hookworms. Not identified in America until 1893, hookworms produced the same anemia symptoms as malaria and were ignored usually despite the half-inch size of

St. Vincent Infirmary (*photographer and date unknown*) *This medical facility was established on July 19, 1888 in the former Alexander George residence on East Second Street in Little Rock. The open windows appear to be unscreened.* **St. Vincent Infirmary**

the worms. A 1902 study indicated that a large portion of the Southern population had hookworms, and a new theory for Southern distinctiveness was born: the South was sick.

Arkansas was the land of the barefoot, and because hookworms entered the body through

the combination of feces and bare feet and the absence of sanitary outhouses, the state became a matter of concern to the Rockefeller Sanitary Commission, which started aiding states on hookworm eradication in 1909. School children were found to have an infection rate of 5 to 65 percent with 25 percent being the state average. Dr. Morgan Smith organized the first program, in which some 12,000 persons received free treatment. Worm medicine took its place next to quinine bitters on the family medicine shelf.

Pellagra, a disabling disease caused by malnutrition among those who ate beans, cornbread and fatback exclusively, appeared in lumber camps and textile factory towns and frequently was misdiagnosed. At Mauldin, a lumber town in Montgomery County, doctors first used various heroic means, including arsenic, to no avail until correct diagnosis put the patients on Brewer's Yeast, which provided the necessary niacin. Pellagra was less prevalent than in North Carolina or Georgia because textiles were not important in Arkansas. However, long-term victims of the disease did constitute a significant portion of the patients at the State Hospital (insane asylum). Ironically, some inmates developed the disease after they were committed, which surely reflected on the institution's diet.

The identification of diseases and the adoption of new cures led to progressive reforms in law and custom. The most significant was the establishment of hospitals. Antebellum Arkansas had only the federally created Marine Hospital at Napoleon. Temporary hospitals existed during the Civil War, but most treatment afterward was at home. Many towns isolated those with contagious diseases in shacks outside of town called pesthouses.

St. Vincent Infirmary, a Roman Catholic hospital in Little Rock, appears to have been established in 1888 in the old Alexander George home. St. John's Hospital in Fort Smith was founded by the local Episcopal priest in 1884. Thereafter, the movement to create a centralized and modern place for medical care grew. Fort Logan Roots Hospital in North Little Rock, assisted by a $20,000 donation from Mrs. Roots, opened in 1894, Fort Smith Charity Hospital in 1897 and St. Bernard's in Jonesboro in 1900. Hospitals almost immediately began nursing programs, and Fort Logan Roots Hospital graduated its first class in 1900.

Early hospitals encountered numerous problems. Those founded by Roman Catholics were the subject of Protestant prejudices. Rumor had it that the nuns at St. Bernard's at Jonesboro kept their husbands and children in the basement. St. Bernard's encountered another problem when a quarry accident maimed dozens of black workers. When they were taken to the hospital, all but one of the white doctors left, and a general public boycott followed. Eventually, St. Bernard's built little frame houses adjacent to the main building to house blacks. The exclusion of blacks from hospital facilities throughout the state contributed significantly to their higher mortality rates.

New regulatory laws made up another aspect of progressive reform. Dr. Morgan Smith's hookworm eradication campaign began in 1910, funded largely by the Rockefeller Sanitary Commission. A more powerful state Board of Health was created in 1913 with a state health officer charged with supervising county health officials. The Bureau of Vital Statistics was established in 1914 to record births and deaths; marriages had to be reported to the state beginning in 1917 and divorces in 1921. Arkansas adopted a law requiring inspection of hotels and restaurants.

A state tuberculosis sanitarium was established at Booneville. When the sanitarium became overcrowded in a few years, the state bought small portable wood cabins called "Burrough Cottages" so that the sick could be isolated and cared for at home. With the spread of information about good hygiene, the communal water glass at school was replaced by individual cups, and many religious bodies retired the community communion chalice. The study of hygiene had arrived, and in progressive fashion, schools were the chosen instruments for correcting the problems of society. The Arkansas Federation of Women's Clubs took the lead, sponsoring baby health contests and lobbying for the Sheppard-Towner Maternity Act passed by Congress in 1921 under which the states received direct federal assistance.

The Beginnings of Welfare

Private suffering increasingly became a public problem in the twentieth century. In the nineteenth century, family breakups led to thousands of children being raised in foster homes. This often was done informally by kin or neighbors, but if this failed, the hapless child was turned over to the county. One distressed woman in 1922 repeated the common fear that "my children will have to be given out to people in the country, to be slaves, without any schooling." In light of numerous hardship stories, such fears were not without basis.

Many men joined fraternal organizations to help prevent such a fate. The International Order of Odd Fellows had 32,000 members in 589 lodges in 1910 and was but one of scores of such bodies, black and white."We command you to visit the sick, relieve the distressed, bury the dead and educate the orphan," the IOOF seal stated, almost summarizing the social needs of the age. Many associations, particularly the black Mosaic Templars, sold insurance on the side.

The movement for state welfare assistance began in the 1890s when the Ex-Confederate Association bought land southeast of Little Rock on the Sweet Home Pike and opened a rest home for veterans. The state took over the home in 1892; by 1920, it housed 165 veterans and wives. A subsequent law even permitted daughters to move in. The state reenacted an artificial limb law for Confederate veterans in 1907 similar to the one that Governor Issac Murphy had vetoed in 1867. The state later even offered burial assistance. The glowing rhetoric of the Lost Cause justified this

favored treatment for veterans; aid in other areas followed slowly.

The state insane asylum, built in 1881, was filled to capacity in six months. More than a third of its patients died in 1894 from an epidemic of dysentery caused by a polluted well. Nutrition was so poor that outbreaks of pellagra were common at the institution. Inadequate state support led to minimal staffing, and patients were forced to do much of the work. Some county judges solved their own welfare needs by declaring their elderly insane and sending them to what in the early twentieth century became known as the State Hospital for Nervous Diseases.

Overcrowding led to extensive use of physical restraints instead of treatment, and the public and the legislature showed little understanding, either of causes or cures. Governor Hays made politics the main qualification for employment and was denounced for it by the medical profession. The same stigma that attached to the poor farm soon was applied to the State Hospital.

The modernization movement found its champion in 1912 at the first session of the Arkansas Conference on Charities and Correction. This assemblage of social workers and supporters debated a wide range of issues, including delinquency, better treatment for the feeble-minded, prison reform and public health. One early success came in 1917, when the Mothers' Pension Law provided aid to those with dependent children in the amounts of $10 for the first child and $5 for each additional infant. Eligibility was determined by the county or juvenile court and was limited to "proper persons."

The monthly payment rate for the second child was equal to that for tobacco allowed veterans at the Confederate Home. In addition, the legislature exempted twenty-eight counties from the law, including populous Washington County and Mississippi County. The favored status of veterans was enhanced again in 1927 when the state voted a comprehensive pension law costing millions of dollars. The objective expressed by Dr. Morgan Smith in 1912, that "from the first cry of the new-born baby is heard until old age closes the scene, government should always be in intimate touch with the daily lives of its citizens" was fulfilled only partially.

PROGRESSIVE SOCIETY

The Progressive era involved much more than politics and social causes. The infrastructure of railroads, substantially complete by 1910, integrated the state into the national economy. With these ties came some maturity, and towns developed standard urban characteristics. The frontier had become a memory, and the Civil War was represented by fewer and fewer graying veterans.

The Emergence of Specialization

One major aspect in the modernization of American life was the formation of associations to promote business, professional or special interests. Only a few groups existed before the turn of the century in Arkansas, but hundreds more were formed within a few years. The first to coalesce were the professions: teachers, doctors, lawyers, pharmacists, newspapermen and a few skilled craftsmen such as typographers and railroad workers. They generally sought restrictive licensing regulations aimed at raising group standards. Single-issue lobbying bodies appeared after 1875. Some, like the prohibitionists, were highly visible; others, like the Arkansas State Horticultural Society (1879), rarely made the newspapers. The Society for the Prevention of Cruelty to Animals organized in the 1870s and achieved the enactment of a landmark piece of legislation in 1879 that not only prohibited cruelty but gave the Society the right to enforce the law and collect the fines from it.

The attempt to organize a permanent historical society was among the casualties of the age. Efforts had failed in 1842, 1875, 1887 and 1897, although the 1887 group decided officially on the pronunciation of Arkansas (Arkan-saw) that the legislature subsequently enacted into law. The Arkansas Historical Association appeared in 1903 and managed to produce four volumes of history and got the legislature to establish the Arkansas History Commission in 1909. State funding subsequently was cut off, and the Association died in 1917.

Many organizations were created at the turn of the century: the State Federation of Women's Clubs (1897), Arkansas Music Teachers' Association (1896), Arkansas Hardware Dealers (1902), Arkansas Good Roads Association (1903), Arkansas Association of Retail Lumber Dealers (1904), Arkansas Underwriters Association (1907), Arkansas Association of Photographers (1910), Political Equality League (1911), Arkansas Motor Club (1912) and many more.

The creation of these specialized bodies indicated the increasing complexity of a society in which individuals congregated according to their special interests rather than as general participants in a common culture. Such groups dramatically changed the nature of the legislative process, because they usually decided what bills they wanted, wrote them and found a legislator to shepherd them into law. If the bill was controversial, it was necessary to raise "corn;" the going price for greasing the wheels of the Arkansas legislature was $10,000. The term "common man" became a figure of speech, and the general welfare became increasingly hard to identify.

The state Supreme Court heard the case of *Columbian Woodmen* v. *Howle* in 1918. The decision involved no great points of law and doubtlessly is forgotten today. Yet the facts are worthy of note as an indication of things to come in Arkansas society. John W. Howle had been shot and killed by the Searcy town marshal. According to his widow, Howle had been driven insane by the marshal's enforce-

Interior of the Bank of Melbourne.
(photographer unknown, ca. 1905) Although private financing remained the common source for most agricultural loans, more and more people were drawn into a commercial economy. Most Arkansas banks were as small and simple as this one at Melbourne. Note the spittoon. **Arkansas History Commission**

ment of Searcy's ordinance that prohibited cows from running loose in town. John W. Howle was modern enough to take out an insurance policy, but he proved unable to cope with the regimentation encountered as society grew more complex. Large numbers of individuals increasingly acted out their own particular versions of insanity in the twentieth century. Farmers dynamited tick-dipping vats; some retreated into religious cults and others refused to pay their taxes. Yet most, like Howle and his widow, wanted some of the benefits but not all of the obligations of the new order.

The Progress of Urbanization

Sue Harper wrote to a friend in 1887 that DeValls Bluff, where she had taken a job as a governess, had "real good society." She added: "I am somewhat surprised at that. I had expected to find people rough, but instead they are truly refined and elegant people."

Miss Harper's discovery, although tempered by her subsequent observation that the elite consisted of newcomers to the state, typified the end of the frontier in Arkansas, a process that was completed long before the rest of the nation recognized it.

Rapid economic development brought to the state new men and women who expected to achieve standard American goals. They translated their beliefs into action, erecting schools, building solid Victorian houses and modernizing society at every point. Yet Arkansas native Cyrus Adler, a famous twentieth-century educator, returned to Van Buren and recorded a different interpretation: "They did not want any Jews, they did not want any Italians, they did not want anybody except themselves." A man newly arrived from Iowa was a foreigner. Cheek by jowl, progress and reaction marked the process of urbanization.

Many communities were still in a transitional stage in 1910, and those connected with lumbering generally remained that way. Businessmen erected wooden stores, often with a false-front second story. Wooden sidewalks that flanked the mud streets ran between the buildings. In frequently flooded eastern Arkansas, buildings were built on piers, those in Arkansas City rising ten feet off the ground. Brick buildings arose when permanence became assured. Instead of the handful of banks that existed in 1880, every town and crossroads community boasted one or more of these often unsound institutions by 1920, and it was hard to find a bank doing business in a wooden structure.

Town politics matched the mud in the streets. Gamblers, saloon keepers and prostitutes were common and were institutionalized to a large extent by 1900. Fort Smith had its "row," a series of elaborately decorated houses where the ladies of the night, led by Belle Starr's daughter, Pearl, entertained. Gambling continued to flourish, especially at Hot Springs, and horse racing staged a modest revival. Sports fans also could watch major league baseball teams hold spring training at Hot Springs.

Was regulation of vice better than ineffectual attempts to ban it? Gubernatorial candidate William Fishback called the red light districts in the 1890s a necessary evil, and more towns than just Little Rock relied on income derived from tolerating vice to fill city coffers.

Those who opposed these vices frequently found the election processes too corrupt to use effectively and resorted to extra-legal steps to fight sin. One such attempt was the reorganization of the Ku Klux Klan. Klan activity officially had ended during Reconstruction, but nightriding, whitecapping and other terms synonymous with the Klan were applied to groups that went beyond the law all during the late nineteenth and early twentieth centuries. The Klan ruled Corning between 1872 and 1882. Despite its power and a successful local option election late in the century, Corning's mayor in 1903 warned "bad characters" to leave town immediately.

The battle for control waxed and waned. Forrest City, though legally dry, had "blind tigers:" "[D]rug stores have holes in which the money and bottle are placed, the money is displayed, the bottle is filled, returned and no one is seen." Early Arkansas City was "noted for saloons and a hard crowd." Fort Smith, full of hunters, cowboys and lumberjacks who "lose control of themselves," had a continuing bad reputation. Local communities that defeated vice took extraordinary steps to stay clean. "Notice to Hoboes, Tramps, Thieves, Thugs, and Weary Willies. Don't Let the Sun Set on You in Hoxie, Arkansas," read one posted notice. Many Ozark towns would have added blacks to the list by 1910.

Despite the move toward homogeneity, towns were illustrative of the melting pot. Chinese made bricks in Osceola and owned laundries and grocery stores all over eastern Arkansas. Brinkley attracted a Russian watchmaker named Meyer; no one could talk to him until the school teacher bought a grammar book and opened communication. Meyer learned English in time, albeit a strongly accented version, and "belonged" despite initial difficulties. Another Russian turned up in Washington County.

The most conspicuous minority were Jews, who opened an expanding number of dry goods stores in eastern Arkansas during the 1880s. Most were Germans from St. Louis. Flourishing on a combination of low prices and calling black customers "Mister," stores owned by Jewish merchants were common in Little Rock and in the Delta. Gus Blass was successful in Little Rock. Jews encountered rising prejudice in the early twentieth century, but it never became a political issue. Jacob Trieber, a Republican lawyer and a Jew, became United States District Judge, and Jeff Davis, seemingly a likely anti-Semite, had Charles Jacobson, a prominent Little Rock Jew, as his personal secretary.

Arkansas attracted other diverse elements. Syrian peddlers could be found in eastern

Arkansas, and in Helena, Habib Etoch opened a cafe in 1888 that eventually featured a large ballroom. He manufactured and sold fruitcake for years.

Transportation improvements began to affect towns by the turn of the century. Little Rock's streetcar line extended to Highland Park, a residential suburb, by 1888. The system was electrified in 1891, and the ease of travel stimulated urban growth. Little Rock's population rose from 13,000 in 1880 to 28,000 in 1900 and 45,000 by 1910. A streetcar line connected Hoxie and Walnut Ridge, and one even serviced Sulphur Rock near Batesville. The streetcar system made the emergence of women's clubs possible, for a middle-class woman could now leave and return to her home without a carriage. Women's clubs developed into important social and political vehicles for reform.

Because many towns grew up around factories, the morning usually began with noise. Brinkley had three railroad yards and numerous sawmills, each with its own whistle. At the turn of the century, most town dwellers cultivated a small garden, raised chickens and kept a cow, although pigs were banished to the country.

The fireplace vanished from the kitchen and was replaced by wood or coal stoves. Coal oil was used for lighting. Coal oil stoves had been introduced, and the newspapers often reported terrible disasters, usually begun by children playing with hot stoves. Housewives relied on home deliveries from the butcher and the grocer because only the largest towns supported an ice plant for iceboxes. Fayetteville in the mountainous northwest was something of an exception, because many families cut ice in the winter from their ponds and stored it in icehouses for the summer. If no supply of ice existed, perishables were lowered into the well or simply not kept at all. Telephones had been introduced in Arkansas as early as 1879 but were used primarily by businessmen. It was not until the twentieth century that home phones became common and it was possible to call from one town to another.

Children were raised largely by their parents, particularly their mother. Middle-class children were taught to avoid those dens of iniquity — the pool hall and the livery stable. Swimming was popular but was segregated by sex because bathing suits were a Northern innovation. One man recalled, "The fear of pregnancy hung like the sword of Damocles over the head of every girl that let her dress fly above her knees or stayed out after dark."

An exposed knee was sinful, but public breast feeding was universal. One old man remembered, "I knew the size and shape of every mother's nipple in the whole community." Children traded Barlow knives, read dime novels, played marbles and flew kites.

Church was important to the middle class. A Hamburg girl remembered that her Presbyterian minister had a war wound that made it impossible for him to be understood, and the children simply were expected to keep quiet during the service. Failure to maintain silence in church was a crime — disturbing a religious congregation — and one laughing child from Lawrence County was hauled before the local justice of the peace court to answer for his misconduct. Theology was still taken seriously, and religious debates drew large crowds. One in Jonesboro between a Baptist and a Presbyterian on the proper method of baptism drew more than 10,000 people.

Singing was popular, and one Little Rock resident remembered popular hymns such as "That Awful Day Will Surely Come," "One More Day's Work for Jesus, One Less of Life for Me," and "When This Poor, Lisping, Stammering Tongue Lies Silent in the Grave." Emma Jean Booth of Des Arc recalled the strong impression made by the singing of "Shall We Gather at the River" at the funeral for a child who died by drowning. On a brighter note, "Jesus Loves Me for a Sunbeam" was a perennial favorite for children. Churches also afforded a certain amount of unintentional humor as when the

Tennis at the Little Rock Country Club *(photographer and date unknown, ca. 1910) By 1920, urban and small town elites often centered their social lives around the country club. All clubs excluded blacks from membership, and it varied from club to club whether Catholics and Jews were eligible. Change came at a snail's pace. Although membership records are private, the* Arkansas Democrat-Gazette *reported that the Little Rock Country Club, which first admitted Jews in the early 1970s, approved its first black member in 1992. Note in this photograph the feeling of newness conveyed by the stripped hillside in the background.* **Arkansas History Commission**

soloist sang "Tell Mother I'll Be There" after a hell-fire-and-damnation sermon.

Saturday was a time for weekly baths, and in preparation for Sunday, most men were shaved at the barber shop. Only the bank president was shaved three times a week in many small towns.

Circuses continued to be popular for entertainment. Famous lecturers came to Arkansas, and perennial Democratic presidential candidate William Jennings Bryan always

drew large crowds. Frank James spoke of Jesse and the outlaws to excited audiences at Brinkley and other towns. Sheet music made the nation's newest songs readily available, and "She's in the Baggage Car Ahead" was a sentimental favorite. Folk music declined, and one Northern visitor found "plenty of people who could repeat the jokes, but it was not so easy to discover a fiddler." He finally found a Negro who could play "The Arkansas Traveler" and pronounced it "a quick reel tune, lively and attractive." The introduction of the phonograph added a new musical dimension, and rural folks enjoyed the country humor of "Uncle Josh" or the genial racism of "Three Black Crows."

The first free library was erected at Fort Smith in 1908 through the generosity of Andrew Carnegie. Little Rock, Eureka Springs, Hot Springs and a few other towns soon followed Fort Smith's example. The public library in Jonesboro grew out of the work of a number of progressive women who stocked a resting area for farm wives with donated books.

Towns possessed a sense of community that marked them off from the ruggedly individualistic countryside. The sense of community found expression in humor, an important ameliorating aspect of nineteenth-century life. Appalling practical jokes were common and frequently trapped the elite. Little Rock folk took special delight in telling stories about rural legislators. In one story, two representatives were unable to sleep because the street light outside kept them awake. One man went down and tried to put it out but failed. "They had shut the derned thing up in a bottle," he explained. Another source of amusement was the elevator. Many rural folks were afraid to ride one; in Hot Springs, a hardened moonshiner brought in for trial fainted on his first trip.

Passions for reform during the Progressive era invariably reached into municipal affairs. Little Rock's last fling coincided with the 1911 Confederate Veterans Reunion, when it was reported that lines of men ran down the sidewalks and out into the street at some popular houses of prostitution. Charles E. Taylor won election as mayor of Little Rock on a reform ticket the same year. "I am not a politician, I am a businessman," he said, and claimed that the capital's reputation as "a wide-open town" hurt economic and cultural development. It took two elections to get Taylor in office because the first was deadlocked

hopelessly in disputed returns. Once in power, Taylor made relentless war on vice. Under Taylor's regime, white and black commissions were appointed to study urban social problems. Vice was driven underground, but suggestions for youth programs from the black committee were ignored. Under Taylor, Little Rock also at last began to inspect milk and meat in a campaign to improve public health.

Throughout the period, municipalities had to contend with financially restrictive clauses in the state's constitution and a generally hostile attitude from legislators. Municipal progress was difficult to achieve, and Arkansas towns were generally far behind those in Midwestern states in achieving adequate municipal services. The movement toward larger and more efficient units of government received a setback when the state legislature passed the Hoxie-Walnut Ridge bill that allowed two adjacent towns to be incorporated.

William and James Faucette, who quietly had incorporated the town of North Little Rock outside the Little Rock city limits, then proceeded to annex Little Rock's eighth ward on the north side of the Arkansas River. The Supreme Court sustained the move, and dual Little Rocks came into being, creating useless duplication.

Agriculture in the Progressive Era

Agriculture was traditionally slow to change, but a number of subtle innovations were made. Although separate farmer political movements were a thing of the past, deep ideological divisions split the farm community. One side consisted of the Farmers Union. Founded in Texas and active in Arkansas in the early years of the century, it claimed 75,000 members in 1908. Eschewing partisan politics, the Union built warehouses and cooperative stores. The Farmers Union benefited from good times and better management than past farmer business ventures and remained

Farm Extension Agents and Farmers Near Mountain Home *(Arthur Keller, ca. 1920) Demonstrations of new techniques and crops attract a group of area residents. Compare the size of the tractor and plow to modern farm machinery.* **University of Central Arkansas**

an enduring if increasingly less significant organization throughout the century.

The Union began fading in part because of a rival group: the Arkansas Farm Bureau. The Union represented small family farms, and the Bureau came to represent corporate agriculture. The beginnings of the Bureau could be traced to the Arkansas Profitable Farming Bureau established in 1914 by the Little Rock Board of Commerce. The Smith-Lever Act of 1914 offered federal funding for county extension agents. Little Rock's progressive businessmen, notably banker E. J. Bodman, believed the family farm was inefficient and enlisted the help of county extension agents to promote a greater emphasis on cash crops. In 1919, bankers even challenged the University of Arkansas, claiming that the school had been slow to promote the new efficiency. In what was really a campaign directed against school President John C. Futrall, the banks urged farmers to grow velvet beans and sweet potatoes. The beans failed to produce as promised, and sweet potatoes would not grow successfully in all Arkansas soils. Despite the campaign's failure, the alliance between extension agents and the Farm Bureau proved enduring and embittered Farmers Union members.

The introduction of rice into Arkansas was one Progressive era development. Rice was

Commercial Fishing *(photographer and date unknown) Arkansas's rivers and streams, particularly in the Delta, were rich in fish. Thousands of "river rats," as they called themselves, earned their livelihood from commercial fishing such as that pictured here. the making of fishing nets by hand was a local art form. It was the "law of the river" that stealing fish from another man's lines was a capital offense. Many people relied on sport fishing for food. Dams on the upper White River and its tributaries had a serious adverse effect on sport and commercial fishing on the lower White River. Other streams in the Delta were degraded by twentieth-century drainage projects, land clearing and agricultural run-off.* **Arkansas History Commission**

grown to a very limited extent during the colonial period. The perfection of upland irrigation systems in 1894 allowed manual control over the water supply, and W. H. Fuller, an Ohio farmer who studied rice production in Louisiana, began experimenting with rice cultivation near Hazen. His successes prompted the establishment of an agriculture experiment station in Lonoke County in 1904 and the first rice mill in Stuttgart shortly thereafter. The crop proved to be par-

ticularly suited to the Grand Prairie where little but hay previously had been grown. It also attracted newcomers. Few Southern farmers cared to grow rice, so 60 percent of rice farmers came from Illinois, Indiana and Ohio. Surrounded by the plantation system, they created an entirely different society, which was more similar to that of their native Midwest than to the Arkansas Delta.

Drainage was another innovation in Delta agriculture. Indiana had developed drainage systems in the late nineteenth century, causing engineer Otto Kochtitzky to promote the idea in Missouri and Arkansas in 1891. In *Cribbs* v. *Benedict* (1897), the state high court upheld the constitutionality of the first drainage law against the charge that ditching taxes, which were not uniform, violated the Constitution. The Court held that "Local assessments are not taxation," thus paving the way for a variety of quasi-governmental bodies to develop.

Ditching districts were created amid great local controversy. Streams provided employment to fishermen, who shipped 2,000 pounds of fresh fish a day from the St. Francis River alone in 1899. Fishermen, hunters and small farmers feared the high taxes that the districts threatened to impose. Lumber interests often joined the opposition, and an angry mob of opponents in Mississippi County so terrified the judge that he adjourned court and fled. Mississippi County supporters eventually triumphed with the assistance of Governor George W. Donaghey, and within a decade, Mississippi County became America's fastest-growing county. Robert E. Lee Wilson, a local farmer and businessman, owned banks, railroads, sawmills and more than 37,000 acres of land. He employed some 1,500 persons, mostly black sharecroppers. Wilson differed from other planters by experimenting with various crops, practicing crop rotation and establishing almost total control over his domain. He owned everything but the electric plant in the model village of Wilson.

Proponents of drainage ditches claimed that each mile of ditch reclaimed one section of land, and drainage districts sprang up overnight without fear or planning. In Mississippi County, where District 9 built 302 miles of ditches, thousands of acres formerly under water became dry land. Title questions kept the courts busy for years. New land appealed to planters like Wilson and to farmers from Indiana and Illinois. The northernmost part of

Mississippi County became theirs with the "Red Line," originally a surveyor's road markers, being used to keep out blacks. In towns such as Jonesboro, Corning, Piggott, Paragould and Blytheville, the Northern element frequently became socially and politically dominant. High cotton prices during World War I spurred more ditching, and Arkansas had $37,500,000 invested in 4,974 miles of ditches and by 1930 ranked second to Florida in area drained.

Ditching failed to fulfill all the hopes of its supporters. Farmers labored under an ever-growing weight of taxes throughout the Delta. Taxes ran to more than $1 acre in the Farrell Lake Levee and Drainage District. When some farmers became unable to pay, the District raised the rate to make up the difference. The 1927 flood sent the District into bankruptcy. In Beaver Dam Drainage District in Greene and Randolph Counties, taxes ran to $25 per forty acre parcel on land worth only from $15 to $35 an acre that was covered with second-growth timber. One landowner tried to market his land, but apparently the ditch was not working. As the lawyer reported, the deal "fell through on account of the fact that the prospects refused to buy after seeing so much water thereon."

High taxes, especially burdensome after the collapse of cotton prices in 1920, hurt the small farmer the most. In Crittenden County, where two-thirds of the land lay in drainage districts and $1,714,000 had been spent on their construction, 90 percent of the inhabitants were tenants, mostly blacks. Small farmers lost their land, and large planters survived by squeezing their tenants. One planter confessed that, "Chiselling croppers out of their cotton money was embedded deeply into the tradition of cotton growing." The great Mississippi River floods of 1912 and 1913 forced many into bankruptcy, and often several sets of owners went broke, overwhelmed by drainage ditch taxes. The land boom was virtually over by 1920;

Cotton Picking Time

This romantic and idealized description of cotton picking in Texas in 1923 could just as easily have been in Arkansas. It is interesting not only for its description of King Cotton in the South, but for its expression of the racial attitudes of the day.

It was cotton picking time in Texas. After the lethargic heat of summer, the land and the people were bestirring themselves to care for the great crop into which had gone so much of the labor and which held so much of the hope of the state. Tingling energy thrilled along every wire, in every pulse, in every clod. Texas, her siesta ended, was alive and awake, and rose laughing to her mighty task. Texas, or that part which is farm land, was almost a one-crop state, and cotton is a jealous crop that demands all seasons for its own, and claims the rounded cycle of the year.

In winter, the land lying passive and chill must be cleared of its weedy growth, must be ploughed in preparation for the planting. The leafless stalks, with bolls hanging frayed and weather-stained, left standing like an army of old men on some forgotten battle-field, must be cut down. The steel cuts deep graves to bury these old soldiers out of sight, while blackbirds flock down the rows as noisy mourners.

In spring, the sower plants the seed, little secret seed so inert yet potent, soft cocoons filled with magic life, tiny creatures asleep in their silky grey fur, dreaming what bright-colored dreams — dreams so vivid that they wake the sleepers and send them climbing toward the light, to see what may be this world they visioned in their slumbers — to find a world all full of sunshine and bird-song, with breezes gypsying over it, with perfume and gay colors like a carnival.

Through the long summer the cotton must be "chopped." The tireless hoe must cut out upstart weeds and loosen the soil about the striving roots so that the young plants may grow more greenly and more lustily. Through flood and drought, through golden days of pitiless heat, the cotton struggles sturdily. Through march and counter-march of serried enemies [boll weevils and army worms] the cotton battles for its kingdom and its life. Insects, fragile and tiny yet terrible in their might, slip across the border from Mexico to attack the fields. But while the thousand thousand hoes flash simultaneously through the summer days, men slave in laboratories to check the foe. And daily the blossoms open in the sun, lovely as mallow or hibiscus [cotton is a member of the mallow family] against the graceful scalloped leaves of green on the erect, upstanding plants. At dawn they are pearly white, but as the sun burns through the blue they turn a delicate pink, and as twilight nears, the petals are pale lavender before they close and die. Daily they bloom and fade, while daily "squares" of green form as the bolls begin to grow, a ceaseless cycle of renewing life.

In autumn the fields are like other flower-gardens, opened boll a great white chrysanthemum upheld on a five-pointed star. Level the fields stretch, vast, illimitable against the sky where rides the golden sun across his field of blue, where clouds hand fleecy as the cotton-wool. This

---

frontier days ended, and an uncertain future lay ahead. Blacks suffered the most in this process. Helena physician C.E. Nash predicted at the turn of the century:

> When the rich bottom lands become ditched and drained, and the water utilized, and the country freed of its

malarial poison, then and not till then, will these lands become habitable for even the southern white man. There must and will be a survival of the fittest.

One reason for the boom in lands in the upper Delta was the widespread destruction caused by the boll weevil across the lower *is the time toward which the whole year turns, toward which the ardors of the wind, the cool assuagement of the dew and rain, the burgeoning beams of sun have gone. The cotton now is ready to be picked, for nature has done her part and perfect stands the yield. Man must do the rest. The air is mild and yet vast fields of snow stretch out and away. The year has passed with its wheeling changes, the elements have all been servitors for this. In such a white field one may trans-substantiate the furrowed winter, bare and gaunt, the mystic seed-time, the golden spears of light, the silver rain, the cruel heat, the drought of summer, the hopes and dreams and toil of myriad men. The heart of the south is visioned here.*

Cotton-picking time is the negroes' carnival. On every country road you may see vehicles carrying black workers to "the patch," wagons spilling over with darkeys of every shade from soot through ginger-cake and polished tan to what is scarcely distinguishable from white; antique buggies and surreys with fringed tops, buckboards, dilapidated carts go past, drawn by as varied steeds, horses, donkeys and mules. With laughter and song the colored folk are going to the field. To work hard? Yes, but in the open air, with bright sun as overseer, with birds calling from every thicket, with the companionship of their own kind and color to lighten labor.

Into the "cotton patch" with shout and song and wild, barbaric mirth, troop the gay negroes, children of the sun, lovers of light and heat. With ebon, flying fingers they pick out the cotton from the bolls, swinging their supple bodies to and fro with rhythmic grace, dragging their sacks behind them. The women with their bright bandanaed heads work beside their mates, the children along with them, the pickaninnies playing on the ground. All join in the joy of harvest with a state of mind peculiar to cotton-picking time. In lazy languor they work on, with many a stop to gaze across the field, with many a pause to bandy words and jests or to incite some fellow-laborer to comic competition.

The colored people go to the cotton-field as others of a different class visit mountain or sea, for a change of scene and for social gaiety. Incidentally, they can make more money in a few weeks at picking cotton than at any other task, and hence they change the everyday-ness of their steady jobs for the out-of-doors when autumn comes. Like mice to the Piper's tune they go. They all go! And for a few weeks the whites must struggle on without them, doing tasks that ordinarily black hands perform. With a half-laughing apology or none at all, the negroes slide from under proffered work. Fortune's wheel turns annually in Texas, and its inevitable revolving brings the blacks on top in cotton-picking time.

Yet cotton is the master of them all, in spring as as autumn, in winter as in summer. Yellow or white or black, all men in the south are slaves of cotton, subject to its power, prospering as those white fields flourish, and failing as they fail. King Cotton may be cruel or benignant, but he wields his mighty sceptre over the whole south.

Source: In the Land of Cotton *by Dorothy Scarborough (Macmillan, New York, 1923)*

South. The worm entered the United States from Mexico early in the twentieth century and moved relentlessly east, sometimes destroying 90 percent of the cotton. No records were kept on outbreaks before 1911, but between then and 1935, the state experienced nine significant outbreaks, with the most severe in 1925. The weevil was believed to be susceptible to cold weather, so as infestations appeared in the southernmost areas, planters responded by pushing the cotton frontier northward. Chemical pesticides such as arsenic were applied, first by hand and then by airplane, and Arkansas suffered far less damage from the weevil than many other Southern states.

Harvesting Apples *(photographer and date unknown) Children and migrant farm workers aided at harvest time.* **Shiloh Museum.**

The farm story was different for areas not involved in drainage. Farmers benefited from better times and escaped the toils of the credit system. Cash purchases became more important, and the rise of towns provided a market for surplus chickens and eggs. Most tried to practice self-sufficiency. As an example, of 87,623,651 gallons of milk in Arkansas in 1920, only 4,332,116 (less than 5 percent) were sold.

Southern herdsmen went into decline as the production of crops increased. The long-established custom of burning the woods to stimulate the growth of grass became illegal because of the power of forestry interests. Open range disappeared as each session of the legislature passed more four-wire fence laws. Over much of the state, the burden by 1920 was on the stockman to keep his hogs and cattle confined rather than on the farmer to protect his crops. Herdsmen profited in only one

respect. Suing railroads for hitting cattle and hogs became a favorite rural pastime.

Alternative crops to corn and cotton was one theme reiterated in the press and at farmer meetings. Tobacco seemed promising in northwestern Arkansas for a time. Arkansas produced more than 500,000 pounds a year in the late 1880s and early 1890s. Grown for home consumption all over the state, tobacco became an industry for a brief period in the Bentonville area. But the founding of tobacco trusts in the Carolinas and a marked decline in prices led the federal government to drop Arkansas from the list of tobacco producing states in 1898.

In its wake came apples, carried by railroad to Northern markets. Apples had been a commercial item since the end of the Civil War, and some 7,000,000 bushels were harvested by 1919. Vinegar and other by-products were produced at local factories. The "Arkansas Black" was one local apple variety that became much prized and is still cultivated. However, disease had begun to strike the crop by 1910 and grew worse with each passing year. Arkansas had 11.2 million apple trees in 1910, but only 125,000 by 1980.

Peaches also were grown on Crowley's Ridge, around Leslie in the Ozarks, in the Arkansas River Valley and near Nashville. Sweet potatoes, cantaloupe and watermelons became locally important, particularly on Buffalo Island in eastern Arkansas. Strawberries, first grown commercially at Judsonia in 1873, soon spread to neighboring Bald Knob, and 345 freight-car loads headed north to market by 1916. Ozark towns along the Missouri and North Arkansas Railroad entered the market in the early twentieth century, with Harrison, Berryville and Marshall dominating. Strawberries were a good cash crop that could be grown on rocky hillsides and picked with child labor.

Canning factories were connected closely with these new crops. Canneries needed only a modest investment, used farm women and children for work and could can almost anything that farmers grew. Tomatoes, a relatively new crop to Southern farmers, became paramount, but beans, spinach, blackberries, squash, okra and other fruits and vegetables were canned as time permitted. Many canneries were small rural operations that paid little attention to sanitation. One Ozark canner used water that ran through a pig lot, and most made catsup from rotten tomatoes. These practices later provided a fertile field of investigation for the new federal Food and Drug Administration.

The progressive years increased the cleavage between different sectors of the farm population. Some kept to their fireplaces, made home brew and home chew, dynamited dipping vats when federal agents tried to treat their cattle for ticks and admired Jeff Davis. Others modernized, replacing the fireplace with a kitchen stove, swore off drinking, chewed their tobacco only outside, subscribed

to a newspaper and painted the house. The beginning of Rural Free Delivery (RFD) in 1896 broke the monopoly of the country store and gave the farm family the mail-order catalogue that spread the wonders of the industrial age on every page. The draft in World War I took thousands of boys from their homes into the great world beyond. For those who were not drafted, the help-wanted posters put up in every post office lured many to Northern cities. Highways and automobiles arrived just in time to make escape easier.

Many Arkansans came to idealize their rural past. Although few survivors of the early pioneer period went into ecstasy, in time hundreds of memoirs would celebrate the last days of pre-modern life, usually from the vantage point of one who left and made money elsewhere. In reality, the predominance of farming in Arkansas life was over. A modest population decline was already evident in some Ozark counties, and ruinous tillage practices were depleting the soil. Only World War I, by calling Europe's farmers on to the battlefield and sending farm prices rising, delayed the decline.

Blacks in the Progressive Era

The progressive spirit was oblivious to the plight of blacks. Progressive leaders, whatever their personal feelings, realized that in the aftermath of the violent racism of the 1890s, any cause, whatever its merits, could be defeated if someone could find it was beneficial to Negroes. Major reforms, therefore, were devoid of racial connotation or were designed specifically for whites only.

As a growing number of institutions became segregated, or new facilities such as libraries and parks were denied to blacks, black resentment began to show. One unconscious example that attracted considerable local attention came in the spring of 1903 when a young black woman prophesied that Pine Bluff, once a model for black progress, would be destroyed in a cloudburst on May 29. When dark clouds

Three Black Soldiers *(photographer and date unknown) Many Southern whites opposed World War I, fearing the effects of arming black soldiers. Although the U. S. Army limited the role of black soldiers, wartime experiences revolutionized the lives of many blacks. Some suggestion of new pride can be seen in this photograph of black soldiers, probably from Brinkley.* **Author's Collection**

engulfed the city on that day, many, both black and white, fled the town as businesses suspended operation and factories closed. Ironically, the storm that soaked the area largely missed Pine Bluff but hit those who had taken safety in flight. The woman was arrested and briefly confined in prison. In the absence of any statutes banning prophesies, she had to be released.

A resurgence of interest in the "Back to Africa" movement was a conscious reaction to the climate of racial persecution. Isaac B. Atkinson, born a slave in Dallas County and a member of the 1888 state legislature, moved to St. Louis and was an organizer of the "On to Africa Congress" in 1912. Instead of leaving

for Africa, more black Arkansans headed north. Job advertisements appeared in Arkansas post offices during World War I. Blacks disproportionately took advantage of the opportunity to leave, beginning a migration that lasted for fifty years. Some of those who remained repudiated the subservience of Booker T. Washington and joined the National Association for the Advancement of Colored People (NAACP).

The sagging hopes of Arkansas blacks were reflected in the problems that beset Isaac Fisher, president of Branch Normal College at Pine Bluff. Brought in from Tuskegee Institute in Alabama to implement the philosophy of Booker T. Washington, Fisher found that his title was merely nominal because whites had taken financial control of the school. His tenure was stormy from the start and included a barely aborted attempt by the legislature to allocate school money by race, vetoes of the school's funding by Governor Jeff Davis, and persistent harassment by white officials bent on discrediting Fisher and the school. Frustrated by his inability to function, Fisher resigned in 1911. Fisher left Arkansas to become a leading black educator, leaving Branch Normal as an example without peer among Southern black schools of the true meaning of "Separate but Equal." Students staged a general strike four years later to protest a white administrator's sexual abuse of black female students.

The Elaine Race Riot

Blacks were subjected to a rising tide of extra-judicial murders known as lynchings throughout the early years of the twentieth century. Racial tensions in numerous Midwestern and Northern cities overflowed during World War I into full-scale wars commonly called race riots. Tulsa, St. Louis and Chicago became scenes of violent unrest and much destruction of property. In Arkansas, the small farming town of Elaine in Phillips County was the scene in 1919 of one of the bloodiest racial encounters in American history.

The origins of the Elaine Race Riot are obscure. Blacks and whites told different stories and have held to their respective versions over the years. Rural Phillips County was a hotbed of racial unrest. Landowners, often Northern immigrants busy opening new land, were squeezing sharecroppers. R. L. Hill, who claimed to be a "United States and Foreign Detective," arrived in Winchester (Drew County) during World War I and began organizing the Progressive Farmers and Household Union. The threat that even black household "help" might be unionized galvanized whites into action. Black detectives from Chicago were imported to mole into the organization, and whites prepared for a showdown. The Union, replete with oaths, rituals and regalia, promised sharecroppers a better price for their cotton, and Hill left the impression he had U. S. government sponsorship. To further its goals, the union retained the well-known Little Rock law firm of Bratton, Bratton & Casey to file individual law suits against leading planters. One member of the firm was in the field completing the research when the violence destroyed all hopes for a peaceful adjustment.

According to the authorities, two lawmen and a Negro trusty were chasing a bootlegger when they came on a black meeting at the Hoop Spur Church near Elaine. Shots were fired, although by whom and at whom has never been answered satisfactorily. When lawmen returned to the scene with a large posse, blacks resisted and widespread fighting broke out. The authorities claimed that an insurrection was underway and scores of bloodthirsty whites from Mississippi to crossed the River by train and car, killing all blacks they encountered. Lawmen early took into custody Helena dentist D. A. Johnson and his four brothers. According to official accounts, they tried to resist and all were killed in police custody.

Convinced that the great, long-feared black rebellion was real, Governor Brough sent troops from Camp Pike. All area blacks were rounded up and put in stockades. Identifiable Union members were charged with murder in a process that, according to black attorney, Scipio A. Jones, consisted of a white committee of seven using torture, electric charges and drugs to coerce confessions. Area blacks were released in time on the issuance of a pass if a white person would vouch for them. Five whites and eleven blacks officially were reported killed, but estimates of the number of black dead have been placed conservatively at more than a hundred.

The aftermath of the riot proved to be as controversial as its beginnings. In a mob atmosphere, sixty-five blacks were indicted in nearby Helena for murder and others for lesser offenses. The accused were tried in groups of six rather than individually. The defense attorney barely got to see his clients, and the jury reached a guilty verdict in about five minutes. Twelve death sentences eventually were handed down and fifty-four persons were sent to the penitentiary.

The first group of six appealed. It was discovered that the indictments were defective, and they were retried and convicted again. The cases had attracted national attention by this time. The NAACP adopted the legal defense of the accused as part of its 1921 program and spent more than $11,000 in attorneys' fees. After the state Supreme Court overturned the convictions because blacks were excluded systematically from Phillips County juries, the cases were transferred to adjacent Lee County where the state failed to prosecute in time and the high court ordered the charges dismissed.

The local circuit judge defied the court and ordered the Lee County sheriff to take the prisoners to the state penitentiary. The sheriff complied, but the warden refused to accept the men, and they simply wandered off.

The second group of six had a somewhat different fate. Their convictions were upheld in state court. After the United States District Court denied them a writ of habeas corpus, the NAACP appealed to the United States Supreme Court, enlisting the nationally famous lawyer, Moorfield Storey, to present their case. In arguing *Moore* v. *Dempsey* (1923), Storey observed, "The public demanded victims, and the public demand overawed the courts with the result that these helpless and ignorant Negroes were convicted with a view to their prompt execution." Claiming that "the evidence on which they were convicted was manufactured, the witnesses were beaten and terrorized," Storey cited the demands of the Helena Rotary Club, the American Legion post and Governor Brough for quick executions.

The Court agreed, and in an opinion written by Justice Oliver Wendell Holmes, found that the mob atmosphere had so tainted the proceedings that even though the forms of justice were followed, the accused still had been denied due process of law. The *Arkansas Gazette* denounced the decision, but it became a milestone in civil rights litigation, laying the foundation for the NAACP's work over the next four decades.

Meanwhile, Union leader R. L. Hill had been apprehended in Kansas. The governor of Kansas refused to honor extradition papers from Arkansas, claiming that the prisoner could not receive a fair trial in Arkansas. Thus Hill never was prosecuted.

The Elaine race riot (sometimes called the Phillips County War) was in stark contrast to the urban race riots taking place in Northern cities. It was a classic confrontation with roots deep in the psyches of both races. On the white side, the *Arkansas Gazette* took the position that it was "not a race riot but an insurrection in which ignorant negroes, led by vicious and designing members of their own race, organized an insurrection the purpose of which was to murder the white planters and confiscate their property." The *Gazette* placed the ultimate blame on Republicans and Northern manufacturers. In the aftermath of the riot, Governor Brough appointed a committee that reached essentially the same conclusions.

Not all Arkansans were satisfied. University of Arkansas political scientist David Y. Thomas disagreed, as did ex-Confederate George W. Murphy, a former attorney general and counsel for the first group of defendants. White attorney U.S. Bratton, who agreed to undertake legal work for the Union, called the riot "a pre-conceived plan to put a stop to the negro ever asking for a settlement." Not surprisingly, Bratton's son spent a month in jail in Helena, and the family relocated in the North following the trials.

The Jonesboro *Enterprise*, boasting of the town's race relations, noted in 1903:

> The negro is fast working out his salvation in this country, where he enjoys "life, liberty and the pursuit of happiness." He is not admitted to social equality here and never will be, but no avenue in which his feet are fit to travel is closed to him.

The *Arkansas Democrat* reassured readers some years later that the Arkansas black was a happy field hand and "just a little less happy than when he was a slave." A Northern observer concluded, however, that employers of blacks were:

> [T]hose who wanted servility, and particularly those who wished to underpay their help, to drive them contemptuously to menial or excessive work, to feed them scraps and lodge them in disreputable shanties.

The Elaine race riot marked the end of black hope for a better life in Arkansas. Taking advantage of opportunities in the North, they let their feet do their protesting and fled Arkansas in earnest throughout the century.

Singing Convention at the Beedeville Church of Christ, October 3, 1915. *Beedeville is on a ridge between Cache River and Bayou DeView in Jackson County. It was founded as a lumber and farming community with a stave mill and saw mill. Most land nearby has been clearcut and drained for farming and there is little evidence of the original swamp that surrounded the ridge. W. W. Beede was the son of the founder of the town and is first man wearing a hat on the left.* **Mary Etta Madden**

Modernization and the Churches

Arkansas religious life flourished amid a variety of controversies during the Progressive years. Splits widened nationally between groups willing to accept the new science of evolution proposed by Charles Darwin and those fanatically opposed. The rise of the Social Gospel challenged churches to consider social conditions. The responsibility of the church to redress conditions in this world was a hotly contested area of religious debate. Attempts to legislate religious beliefs appeared in every legislative session.

Baptists actively debated the appropriate role of the Church in twentieth century life.

The Baptists' great strength, the belief that each individual church may govern its own affairs, occasionally led to violent disagreements within the denomination. Schism generally developed from two sources. Some rural Arkansas Baptists expressed opposition to Sunday schools, printed bulletins, choirs, hymnals without "shaped notes" and a paid clergy. Only 8.4 percent of the state's Baptist clergy had college or seminary training, and these men usually filled urban pulpits. Meanwhile, urban Baptists began to erect increasingly imposing church buildings. Urban Baptists also responded to Walter Rausenbush's Baptist version of the Social Gospel.

Brother Benjamin Marcus Bogard

From the time of his arrival in Searcy, Arkansas, in 1899, until his death in 1951, Brother Benjamin Marcus Bogard dominated Arkansas religious life, particularly among the state's Baptists. He was pastor of eighteen churches during his career, preached 279 revivals, fought in 193 religious debates and delivered 14,741 sermons and lectures.

Brother Bogard was born in a small log cabin in Kentucky in 1868, the son of a Confederate veteran. Beginning his career as a boy preacher, he came to Searcy in 1899. State Baptists at the time were split. Most supported the Southern Baptist Convention; their conservative brethren organized the Missionary Baptists. Bogard allied himself with the conservatives and became the state's most articulate opponent of modernism, especially after 1920 when he took over the pastorate of Little Rock's Antioch Baptist Church.

Brother Bogard opposed most of the changes then underway in American life. He was a leading anti-Catholic and political critic of Al Smith in 1928. He allowed himself to be called only "elder" or "brother" explaining: "Romanism is behind the 'reverend' every time you see it or hear it." An opponent of "mingling of races," Bogard was a zealous worker for the Ku Klux Klan.

On January 22, 1928, Brother Bogard became one of the first Arkansas ministers to use
radio. His sermon, "Man or Monkey, Which?" reflected his strong opposition to Darwin's Theory of Evolution, which he linked to communism. He found communism in the Federal Council of Churches during the 1930s and 1940s, opposed the New Deal, and observed that: "The great majority of colleges and universities, supported by taxes, are at this very minute teaching what Atheistic Communists want taught."

Brother Bogard was combative and happiest in old-fashioned debates, holding his last one — a four-day affair — in Monette in 1948. In the early years of the century, many Protestant ministers were prepared to defend their denomination's stands on infant damnation or the proper method of baptism, but most of Bogard's debates in his later years were against Church of Christ ministers, whom he always called the "Campbellites," a term they did not appreciate.

Possibly the most interesting debate never took place. During the evolution law controversy in 1927, self-proclaimed atheist Charles Smith set up signs in downtown Little Rock reading, "Evolution is true. The Bible is false. God's a ghost." City police had to rescue Smith from a mob that already had a rope around his neck. After Smith was jailed for blasphemy, Bogard offered to debate him, but nothing came of the challenge.

A second division arose over theology. Conservatives, or Landmark Baptists, had been active in Arkansas before the Civil War. They had become so unhappy with the state convention by 1900 that they seceded and formed the Baptist Missionary Association. Missionary Baptists not only insisted on different theological beliefs but also rejected many of the physical improvements to church facilities planned by urban Baptists. This schism confused many congregations and individuals,
and it took more than twenty years to complete the reorganization.

The Christian or Campbellite movement splintered into the more conservative Church of Christ and the more liberal Disciples of Christ or Christian Church. Other denominations had disagreements, too. Texarkana Presbyterian Minister F.E. Maddox, "the chaplain of progress," taught that old doctrines that hindered social progress ought to be dropped. He argued that modernists were "more useful

Baptizing *(Arthur Keller, date unknown) A majority of Arkansas Christians believed in baptism by immersion. Arkansas religion had become increasingly feminized, a fact in evidence by the number of women in this photograph from Mountain Home.* **University of Central Arkansas**

in life" than fundamentalists. When this pragmatism led to his trial for heresy by Presbyterians, he became a Congregationalist and took most of his followers into a liberal denomination little represented in Arkansas.

Nowhere was the Social Gospel stronger than in the Episcopal Church — a denomination not known for social activism. Under

Bishop William Brown, who eventually became known as the "Red Bishop" for some of his social teachings, Episcopalians attempted to reach out to blacks at a time when other denominations shunned them.

One gradual change underway in Arkansas was the greater participation of women in church affairs. Women accounted for three-quarters of church members by the late nineteenth century but were severely restricted in their participation because of admonitions of the Apostle Paul in his letter to early Christians that women should keep silent in religious assembly. The Universalists had repudiated sexism in the North by ordaining the Reverend Olympia Brown in 1863; they established a beachhead in Little Rock in 1906 with Reverend Athalia L.J. Irwin in charge.

The issue of the participation of women surfaced in other denominations as well. Some Methodist churches seem to have let women serve as deacons in an unofficial way, and Cumberland Presbyterians formally considered women ministers in 1891 and 1892 before finally affirming female participation in 1921. One Arkansas Presbytery ordained Mrs. R. A. Dunlap in 1897, only to have the action declared illegal.

When women began to take part in urban church affairs, prohibition became a leading social issue, and attacks were made on tobacco, movies and sex. The war on sex in Pine Bluff even extended to married couples. Junius Jordan, the state superintendent of education, wrote a friend:

> A man must get permission of his pastor and church friends before he can sleep with his wife. One fool is actually going around and trying to organize an order known as the anti-sleeping watch of husbands and wives.

At the same time, organized prostitution existed in probably every town in Arkansas.

As urban churches grew more ecumenical and emotionally restrained, many people — longing for the old emotionalism — joined new denominations. The Assemblies of God were organized in Hot Springs in 1914, and rural Methodists often found the Church of the Nazarene more compatible with their childhood backgrounds when they moved to town. Most of these new groups appealed to working-class people new to the urban environment.

The conflicts of earlier ages remained vigorous in the twentieth century. Women who lobbied the legislature for protective legislation on child labor cited scripture. Prohibition had elements of secular reform, but had become a theological issue in Arkansas by 1900. Many of these issues could not be settled, and continuing debate marked the rest of the twentieth century.

WORLD WAR I: THE TRIUMPH OF PROGRESSIVISM

In August 1914, the European powers finally blundered into the War that destroyed European hegemony. The Great War, as it was called until 1939, had a major impact in Arkansas. It sent food prices up in a trend that lasted until 1920, benefiting farmers and enriching middle men. The War was significant only as a news item during its early years when American involvement seemed unlikely. With few German immigrants, Arkansas was not the scene of divided loyalties. Arkansas voters were not internationally minded either.

Senator James P. Clarke was an anti-imperialist with no close ties to the Wilson administration, and Clarke's successor, William F. Kirby, was an agrarian radical who filibustered the administration's Armed Neutrality Law as one of the "little group of willful men." Although he voted for war, he stated: "[I]f there was the slightest chance on God's earth that my vote against it would defeat it, I would stand here and vote a thousand years if it might be that we do not go to war."

Kirby's defeat in his bid for reelection in 1920 by Thaddeus Caraway, another agrarian radical, was perhaps largely a result of the unpopularity of Kirby's anti-war stand. Otis Wingo was another war opponent in the House, although he escaped without political retribution and held his seat until his death in 1930.

Arkansas was officially patriotic and scared once the War broke out. The Waldron *Advance Reporter* warned that "all sections of Waldron and suburbs must be guarded on short notice against possible night raids by alien enemies." Arkansas also became alarmed about supposed enemies in its midst. Poor black and Indian tenant farmers in neighboring Oklahoma, urged on by Socialists and IWW organizers, staged the Green Corn rebellion to resist the draft. Arkansas draft officials encountered armed resistance in Searcy, Polk and Cleburne Counties. The Cleburne County outbreak, subsequently styled a "war," was the most important. In it, a number of Russellites — called Jehovah's Witnesses after 1931 — refused induction and had an armed encounter with a sheriff's posse. Reinforcements, including a company of National Guardsmen wielding machine guns, failed to find the men, who eventually were starved into surrendering. In all, 8,732 Arkansas boys deserted or evaded the draft, which equaled 15.5 percent of those eventually inducted from the state.

The War brought triumph on the homefront for the progressive impulse toward social conformity. The state's high court upheld the compulsory vaccination of school children, partially justifying the intrusion into private and local affairs by citing the disruptive effects that lack of vaccination might have on the draft. The federal government set up the National Council of Defense in May 1917, and it helped organize the Arkansas Council of Defense that consisted of thirty-three citizens appointed by Governor Brough. Mostly middle-class businessmen, a few of whom were Republicans, the Council interested itself in everything from how a man's cow endangered the war effort through an unfortunate encounter with a train to the enactment of new vagrancy laws. In denouncing "loafers and idlers" and closing pool halls as "a menace to the morals of young men and productive of habits of idleness," the Council sought to suppress that part of the Arkansas character that held "in the summer we make love and fish, but of course in the winter it is too cold to fish." The Council helped mobilize social pressure against "slackers" and set up a system to reward those who helped catch deserters.

The location of Camp Pike as a major training ground near Little Rock gave the Council ample opportunity to use its morality campaign to safeguard soldiers. A controversy about the local venereal disease rate spurred better efforts at identification and treatment, including a drive to get pharmacists not to sell cures without a prescription. Physicians were required to record the number of cases treated. The Council, which had one female member, also organized a woman's auxiliary that promoted home efficiency through cooperative laundries and community canning. As a part of National Children's Year, the woman's committee helped get infants weighed, measured and treated by health officials. The committee also helped with the sale of Liberty Bonds on the county level. Arkansas over-subscribed to all four bond drives and two Red Cross appeals with contributions totaling $11,783,000.

Arkansas provided raw materials and manpower to the remote War. Some 72,000 Arkansans served, 1,400 of whom were women. A number of Arkansans became heroes. Oscar Franklin Miller, killed in action, was on General Pershing's list of the top 100 heroes and was the posthumous recipient of the Medal of Honor, the *Croix de Guerre* and the Bronze Star. A Franklin County native, Miller enlisted in the army and died leading his men in an assault. Arkansas also produced Herman Davis of Manila, a hunter and trapper before the War who was also on Pershing's list. He returned to his swamps after the War and refused to make patriotic speeches or discuss his War experiences.

Three Arkansans were prominent fighter pilots. Captain Field E. Kindley of Gravette in Benton County survived the War but died in a post-war plane crash. Another survivor was Wendel A. Robertson of Fort Smith. John McGavock Grider, who grew up in eastern Arkansas, served with the British and died in combat in 1918. His anonymously published and much-edited diary, *War Birds: Diary of an Unknown Aviator*, related a significant account of the War in the air.

The state war effort largely ignored blacks. The Council for Defense was all-white, and a black auxiliary was formed only two months before the War's end, largely on the insistence of federal officials. Its goal was to prevent racial troubles. P. L. Dorman, field agent for the Council, made a number of speeches warning all returning Negro soldiers to "conduct themselves in the proper manner, under all conditions, to avoid anything that would provoke outbreaks. . . ."

Toleration vanished during the War. Anything German was alien, so the town of Germania in Saline County became Vimy Ridge, the German National Bank in Little Rock changed its name and the Little Rock German-language newspaper, the *Staats Zeitung*, stopped publication. Farmers who resisted tick eradication were branded as enemy agents. And it was asserted that spies burned the Second Baptist Church in Little Rock because Governor Brough made four patriotic speeches there. A man who said "to hell with the Red Cross" was taken out by a mob and spanked. Socialists and various anti-war religious groups were persecuted.

The hysteria went on after the War in the form of the Red Scare that gripped the nation in the first post-war winter. Wild rumors spread that a Communist revolution was imminent. The Arkansas public believed that the IWW was responsible for the Elaine Race Riot and that the group had been "feeding their sort of stuff to all the negroes of the South for the past year, and a lot of harm has been done." Without much background on European radicalism, the *Arkansas Gazette* mirrored the popular misunderstanding by

defining Bolshevism as "barbarous murder, gross immorality, unbridled looting and chaos generally," all the result of a German plot. The answer to these fears for Governor Brough could be found in a progressive program of better roads to help farmers get their crops to market, women's suffrage and improved education.

CONCLUSION

The great industrial age created a national market and national social problems. Progressives are best remembered for their success at the national level: The Federal Reserve System that created modern banking, the Food and Drug Administration that began a program of food safety, the establishment of national forests and the beginning of concern for the environment and labor legislation that took the government directly into the economy. Yet most government functions that did not cross interstate lines remained under the jurisdiction of states. In Arkansas, where rural isolation was common, few saw much need for state action. Some reforms enacted into law were then crippled by county option clauses that often undermined their effectiveness. A significant segment of the population opposed many progressive programs but was submerged by the buoyancy of rising prices and general farm prosperity. Thus the legacy of progressivism endured into the 1920s.

BIBLIOGRAPHIC ESSAY

The politics of progressivism have been surveyed by Segraves, *Arkansas Politics, 1874-1918*. Local Socialists were investigated in James R. Green, *Grassroots Socialism: Radical Movements in the Southwest, 1895-1943*, (Baton Rouge, 1978). G. Gregory Kiser, "The Socialist Party in Arkansas, 1900-1912," *AHQ*, XL (Summer 1981), 119-153, unfortunately fails to carry the story on to 1920.

Thomas S. Baskett, Jr., "Miners Stay Away, W. B. W. Heartsill and the Last Years of the Arkansas Knights of Labor, 1892-1896," *AHQ,* XLII (Summer 1983), 107-133, shows the connection between the radicalism of the nineteenth and twentieth centuries. Erwin Funk, "Rogers Has Seen Many Newspapers Come and Go," *BCP,* III (July 1958), 10-12, contains a brief account of "The People's Friend," and Claude Johnson, "Who Remembers Clay Fulks?" *WHC,* XVI (October 1978, 86-86, provides a short sketch of a one-time gubernatorial candidate.

The Autobiography of George W. Donaghey, (Benton, 1939), is naturally laudatory, and different aspects of his stewardship are treated in Thomas L. Baxley, "Prison Reforms During the Donaghey Administration," *AHQ,* XXII (Spring 1963), 76-84 and Treon, *Politics and Concrete: The Building of the Arkansas State Capitol, 1899-1917.* The 1915 prison investigation is entitled, "Investigations of a Report Upon Conditions at the Arkansas Penitentiary . . ." (typescript at the Arkansas History Commission.)

Joseph T. Robinson, one of the major figures in national politics, largely has disappeared from the pages of national and regional history because his papers have been inaccessible until recently. The only general study is Nevin E. Neal, "A Biography of Joseph T. Robinson," (Ph. D. diss., University of Oklahoma, 1958). A useful article is Stuart Towns, "Joseph T. Robinson and Arkansas Politics, 1912-1913," *AHQ,* XXIV (Winter 1965), 291-307. Little attention has been given to George W. Hays, though there is a good biography of him in Donovan and Gatewood, *The Governors of Arkansas.* By contrast much has been written on Brough. Charles W. Crawford, "From Classroom to State Capitol: Charles H. Brough and the Campaign of 1916," *AHQ,* XXI (Autumn 1962), 213-230, traces his early career, and a short survey is Foy Lisenby, "Charles Hillman Brough," *AHQ,* XXXV (Summer 1976), 115-126. Another useful

study is Larry Cook, "Charles Hillman Brough and the Good Roads Movement in Arkansas," *OHR,* VI (Spring 1977), 26-35. Marvin F. Russell, "The Rise of a Republican Leader: Harmon L. Remmel," *AHQ,* XXXVI (Autumn 1977), 234-257, sheds light on the inner history of Republicans during this era.

Progressive accomplishments are studied in Samuel W. Moore, "State Supervision of Railroad Transportation in Arkansas," *PAHA,* III (1911), 265-309, and David Y. Thomas, "Direct Legislation in Arkansas," *PSQ,* XXIX (March 1914), 84-110 and "The Initiative and Referendum in Arkansas Come of Age," *APSR,* XXVII (February 1933), 66-75. Abe Collins provided "Reminiscences of the Constitutional Convention of 1917-18," *AHQ,* I (June 1942), 117-123. The document itself is in the *Address to the People of the State of Arkansas,* (n.p., n.d.)

Women in Arkansas generally have begun to receive more attention. Elizabeth A. Taylor, "The Woman Suffrage Movement in Arkansas," *AHQ,* XV (Spring 1956), 17-52, is better on nineteenth than twentieth-century developments. A good survey is Janie S. Evins, "Arkansas Women: Their Contribution to Society, Politics, and Business, 1865-1900," *AHQ,* XLIV (Summer 1985), 118-133. One short biography by Dorsey D. Jones is "Catherine Campbell Cunningham: Advocate of Equal Rights for Women," *AHQ,* XII (Spring 1953), 85-90. Michael B. Dougan, "The Arkansas Married Woman's Property Law," *AHQ,* XLVI (Spring 1987), 3-26, addresses legal issues.

Education is explored in Balys H. Kennedy, "Half a Century of School Consolidation in Arkansas," *AHQ,* XXVII (Spring 1968, 59-67, and John W. Payne, "Poor-Man's Pedagogy: Teachers' Institutes in Arkansas," *AHQ,* XIV (Autumn 1955), 195-206. The various biennial reports of the Commissioner of Education provide valuable statistics and insights.

Arkansas is dry on recent scholarly treatments of temperance. Old but still useful is George M. Hunt, "A History of the Prohibition

Movement in Arkansas," (M. A. Thesis, University of Arkansas, 1933). Mary D. Hudgins, "Carry Nation Brings Her Famous Crusade to Arkansas," *CCHQ,* IX (March 1963), 15-18, treats a well-known personality. Otto E. Rayburn, "Moonshiners in Arkansas," *AHQ,* XVI (Summer 1957), 169-173, provides an overview. Isaac Stapleton, *Moonshiners in Arkansas,* (Independence, Mo., 1948), has color. Richard S. Daniels, "Blind Tigers and Blind Justice: The Arkansas Raid on Island 37, Tennessee," *AHQ,* XXXVIII (Autumn 1979), 259-270, is a colorful account of one episode.

Evidence remains buried in statute books and newspapers about Arkansas's quixotic crusade against the cigarette, but Larry D. Ball, "Redeemed, Regenerated and Disenthralled: Arkansas Resists the Pugilists," *REC,* XVIII (1977), 15-26, recounts the controversy about boxing.

Public health is another neglected field. A study of licensing is David M. Moyers, "From Quackery to Qualification: Arkansas Medical and Drug Legislation, 1881-1909," *AHQ,* XXXV (Spring 1976), 3-26. Problems with diseases are discussed in John H. Erwin, "History of Public Health Measures in Malvern, Arkansas," *HERHS,* V (1978), 53-67, and Creo A. Jones, *Public Health in Montgomery County, Arkansas,* (N. P., 1980). One old survey of state laws is G. W. Garrison, "The Development of Medicine and Public Health," in Thomas, ed., *Arkansas and Its People,* II, 549-562. Most of the data come from newspapers and the reports of the Surgeon General of the United States. A rural doctor's perspective is that of E. H. Abington, *Back Roads and Bicarbonate: The Autobiography of an Arkansas Country Doctor,* (New York, 1955).

Early road development is a theme in Clara B. Kennan, "The Ozark Trails and Arkansas's Pathfinder, Coin Harvey," *AHQ,* VII (Winter 1948), 299-316. The effect on railroads is followed in part in Clara B. Kennan, "A Railroad Empire Rose and Fell in Benton, County," *AHQ,* XIII (Summer 1954), 154-159, and Lee

A. Dew,"The Arkansas Tap Line Cases: A Study in Commerce Regulation," *AHQ,* XXIX (Winter 1970), 327-344.

Other progressive developments are discussed in Fred O. Henker, "The Evolution of Mental Health Care in Arkansas," *AHQ,* XXXVII (Autumn 1978), 223-239; Foy Lisenby, "The First Meeting of the Arkansas Conference of Charities and Correction," *AHQ,* XXVI (Summer 1967), 155-161, and by the same author, "The Arkansas Conference of Charities and Correction, 1912-1937," *AHQ,* XXIX (Spring 1970), 39-47; Svend Petersen, "Arkansas State Tuberculosis Sanitarium: The Nation's Largest," *AHQ,* V (Winter 1946), 311-329, and Jim Moshinskie, *Early Arkansas Undertakers,* (N. P., 1978).

The social history of the progressive years has been derived from a variety of sources. Interesting memoirs include T. Alexander, *Experiences of a Trapper and Hunter from Youth to Old Age,* (Linnton, Or., 1924); De Emmett Bradshaw, *My Story,* (Omaha, Neb., 1941), and three articles by Boyce House, "A Small Arkansas Town 50 Years Ago," *AHQ,* XVIII (Winter 1959), 291-307; "In a Little Town Long Ago," *AHQ,* XIX (Summer 1960), 151-168 and "Arkansas Boyhood Long Ago," *AHQ,* XX (Summer 1961), 172-181. One of the most candid memoirs is Claud E. Johnson,*The Humorous History of White County, Arkansas,* (N. P., 1975). Two female views are given in Pearl E. Young, "Memories of an Ashley County Childhood," *AHQ,* XVI (Winter 1959), 342-357, and *AHQ,* XVIII (Winter 1961), 375-400, Mrs. Hay W. Smith, "Life in Little Rock in the Gay Nineties," *PCHR,* V (December 1957), 69-74. Two outsider views are given in Clifton Johnson, *Highways and Byways of the Mississippi Valley,* (New York, 1925), and J. Russell Smith, *North America,* (New York, 1925). One of the best examinations of rural conditions is by Charles B. Spahr, "America's Working People, III. A Typical Primitive Community," *O,* LXI (April 1, 1899), 749-755, reprinted with an introduction by Michael B. Dougan, "Uncle

Bill Ishmael and Butch Dickson Receive a Northern Visitor," *CrCHQ,* XIX (Winter 1981), 3-13. Other valuable studies include Nancy Zilbergeld and Nancy Britton, "The Jewish Community in Batesville, Arkansas, 1853-1977," *ICC,* XXI (April 1980), 2-32, and Martha W. Rimmer, "Progressivism Comes to Little Rock: The Election of 1911," *PCHR,* XXV (September 1977), 49-60, which is continued in her "Progressivism in Little Rock: The War Against Vice," *PCHR,* XXV (December 1977), 65-72.

Progressive area agriculture has not been studied systematically. One memoir is S. E. Simonson, "Origin of Drainage Projects in Mississippi County," *AHQ,* V (Winter 1946), 263-273. Additional information can be found in Ophelia R. Wade, *The Heritage of Blytheville,* (Bragg City, Mo., 1973). W. H. Fuller, the first rice grower, contributed "Early Rice Farming on Grand Prairie," *AHQ,* XIV (Spring 1955), 72-74, and other information can be found in Florence L. Rosencrantz, "The Rice Industry in Arkansas," *AHQ,* V (Summer 1946), 123-137, and Henry C. Dethloff, "Rice Revolution in the Southwest, 1880-1910," *AHQ,* XXIX (Spring 1970), 66-75. W. H. Plant, "When Tobacco Was King in Benton County," *BCP,* IV (March 1959), 13-15, is followed chronologically by Thomas Rothrock, "A King That Was," *AHQ,* XXXIII (Winter 1974), 326-333, which discusses apples. Both the Farmers' Union and the Farm Bureau are discussed in Robert A. Leflar, "The Bankers' Agricultural Revolt of 1919," *AHQ,* XXVII (Winter 1968), 273-305.

Surprisingly, little has been written about blacks. Elizabeth L. Wheeler, "Isaac Fisher: the Frustrations of a Negro Educator at Branch Normal College, 1902-1911," *AHQ,* XLI (Spring 1982), 3-50, catches the dominant theme of the era. Historians have long recognized the importance of the Elaine Race Riot, but scholarly attention has been fragmented until the publication of Richard C. Cortner, *A Mob Intent on Death: The NAACP and the Arkansas Riot Cases* (Middletown, Conn., 1988). Arkansan Isaac B. Atkinson appears in I. K. Sundiata, "The On To Africa Congress," *JNH,* LXI (October 1976), 393-400.

The only study of progressivism in religion is Larry R. Hayward, "F.E. Maddox: Chaplain of Progress, 1908," *AHQ,* XXXVIII (Summer 1979), 146-166.

Arkansas's role in World War I is the theme of David O. Demuth, "An Arkansas County Mobilizes: Saline County, Arkansas, 1917-1918," *AHQ,* XXXVI (Autumn 1977), 211-233, and Gerald Senn, "Molders of Thought, Directors of Action: The Arkansas Council of Defense, 1917-1918," *AHQ,* XXXVI (Autumn 1977), 280-290. Draft resistance is discussed in James F. Willis, "The Cleburne County Draft War," *AHQ,* XXVI (Spring 1967), 24-39. A contemporary memoir is Frank M. Wells, *War With Germany and Why We Won,* (N.P.,N.D.). Politics is the theme of Richard L. Niswonger, "William F. Kirby, Arkansas's Maverick Senator," *AHQ,* XXXVII (Autumn 1973), 252-263. Wartime heroes are studied in John A. Johnson, "Oscar Franklin Miller: Arkansas's Forgotten Hero," *AHQ,* XXXI (Autumn 1972), 262-275; Margaret S. Ross, "Herman Davis: Forgotten Hero," *AHQ,* XIV (Spring 1955), 51-61 and James J. Hudson, "Captain Field E. Kindley: Arkansas' Air Ace of the First World War," *AHQ,* XVIII (Spring 1959), 3-31. On the Red Scare, see Joey McCarty, "The Red Scare in Arkansas: A Southern State and National Hysteria," *AHQ,* XXXVII (Autumn 1978), 264-277.

Batesville Bridge Dedication *(photographer unknown, 1928) Local politicians posed at this bridge on July 4, 1928, as the first car crossed the White River. The bridge cost $330,084 and was dedicated by U. S. Senator T. H. Caraway.*
Independence County Historical Society

Chapter XIV

Confronting the Twentieth Century: Arkansas in the 1920s

INTRODUCTION

In the popular imagination, the "Roaring Twenties" are associated with fast cars, bootleg alcohol, the decline of Puritanism and a booming stock market. However, only the bootleg liquor among these was common in rural Arkansas during this period. President Calvin Coolidge set the national tone with his pronouncement that the business of America was business. In Arkansas, still a largely rural state tied to its agrarian past, the attitudes of modern businessmen and promoters were controversial, especially if they threatened higher taxes. Promoters of modernization focused on better roads and schools because the progressive impulse remained surprisingly strong during this period. The discovery of oil altered life in southern Arkansas, and Hot Springs was in its heyday with illegal gambling, sports heroes and mobster visitors from the North who came to enjoy its "healing" waters. Running battles between modernism and religion continued in what was now called "The Wonder State."

ECONOMIC DEVELOPMENT

The Wonder State

The 1920s was the era of the booster. In *Main Street* and *Babbitt*, Sinclair Lewis characterized the booster as always emphasizing the good, ignoring the bad and promoting the future. In place of the old unofficial nickname, "The Bear State," the Arkansas legislature in 1923 adopted as the official motto "The Wonder State," largely because of the fervent agitation of Governor Charles H. Brough. Brough toured the nation on the Chautauqua circuit during the 1920s, presenting audiences with encouraging statistics on the number of Arkansas children attending Sunday school and boasting that the state possessed "as pure a stream of Anglo-Saxon blood as flows in the veins of the people of any American State."

Some people were impressed. In a 1921 article in *Outlook* magazine, journalist Sherman Rogers was thrilled because he never heard a foreign tongue spoken during his stay and said, "I never heard so much real loyal, one hundred percent American talk as I did during my fourteen day stay in Arkansas." For the most part, however, the claims of Governor Brough and other boosters of the state did not gain national acceptance. Arkansas's *bete noire* during the decade was the formidable H.L. Mencken of the Baltimore *Evening Sun* and *American Mercury*.

Although one survey ranked Arkansas as the forty-fourth worst state and another placed it forty-sixth, it was Mencken's words that angered Arkansans: "The most shiftless and backward State in the whole galaxy. Only Mississippi offers it serious rivalry for last place in all American tables of statistics."

According to Mencken, Arkansans "are too stupid to see what is the matter with them, and even if they were intelligent they would lack the capital to make a change." Mencken believed Arkansas was dominated by professional politicians and crossroads evangelists, and he urged flight:

Naturally enough every youngster of any human value who grows up in such a wallow clears out as soon as possible.

Arkansas thus grows progressively poorer intellectually, and large areas of it are already sunk to the level of Haiti or Albania.

A heated correspondence between Brough and Mencken further amused the American public. Brough listed the names of dozens of Arkansas poets, and Mencken replied by noting that Arkansas ranked sixth in lynchings. Despite the furor, few people in Arkansas cared or even knew of the debate or the fact that Arkansas ranked forty-seventh in newspaper circulation and forty-eighth in libraries.

Industrialization

Despite all the booster talk, real progress was lacking. During the "Wonder State" debate, Herbert Thomas, the dynamic president of Pyramid Life Insurance Company in Little Rock, caustically observed that the real wonder was that God gave Arkansas so much and yet the people owned so little of it. Arkansas was the most rural state after Mississippi; its urban areas contained only 16.6 percent of the population in 1920, and 20.6 percent by 1930. Although it was a cotton-growing state, Arkansas had a mere sixteen textile mills in 1929, despite constitutional Amendment 12 that exempted them from all taxes for seven years. Only Florida among cotton-growing states had fewer mills.

Arkansas also failed to attract the fledgling automobile industry. One company opened in Little Rock in 1919 and during the ensuing five years produced some 200 trucks and cars appropriately named Climbers. Inadequate financing, lack of experience in production and management and Northern competition led to the company's demise in 1924. Arkansas's coal production decreased annually, and a sharp drop in lumber output closed many processing plants and factories Arkansas remained a nineteenth-century state in the twentieth century. With little manufacturing, her small towns continued as centers of farm trade, and her farmers led a doomed way of life.

The Arkansas Oil Boom

All generalizations about economics fail to apply to the part of southern Arkansas affected by the discovery of oil. What the Gold Rush was to California, the oil boom was to El Dorado. The presence of petroleum under Arkansas soils was reported first in 1887 at a seepage in Scott County. The first well was drilled to a depth of 1,600 feet at Mansfield in 1889 by Harry E. Kelley. The gas discovered first was used to supply Fort Smith and Van Buren. By 1907, Arkansas ranked third in gas production with forty-three producing wells. Thirty-one towns used the new energy source.

The oil boom arrived with a bang near El Dorado on June 13, 1920, when the explosion of a test well killed five persons. Then oil came in on January 10, 1921. Trains full of people swarmed to the town, and the population rapidly went from 4,000 to 15,000 and on to 35,000 within a year. Smackover, a mere flag station in 1920, soon had more than 20,000 residents. A contemporary description caught the oil fever that infected the area:

> Thousands of men moved in excitement. Unnumbered teams under cries of the charioteers wheeled through the torn muddy fields and stretches of woodland. Everywhere there was the ring of hammers, excitement, animated conversation and strangers. Through the gloom beyond the brilliantly lighted streets there arose from the tree tops thousands of derricks, lit with a string of bright lights, like unto Christmas trees. The babel of voices was punctured with occasional revolver shots. Every man wore dirty khaki and every woman seemed hard of visage and likewise wore dirty shirts and men's trousers. They

A Gusher *(photographer and date unknown) This early photograph shows the primitive conditions prevailing when the first oil wells were drilled near El Dorado.* **Arkansas History Commission**

> chewed tobacco, put their feet in the windows and on the backs of seats before them. In vile language they cursed their men friends and women who had "double-crossed" them.

The chaos broke down the fabric of law and order and other social services. Mules dying in the streets were run over where they lay. New Year's Day 1922 in El Dorado was celebrated by the firing of pistols in the streets instead of the traditional firecrackers. Church bells were a favorite target, and fourteen persons were killed. Venereal disease and race riots thrived in the violent oily ooze, so that the strength of the Ku Klux Klan in the area was hardly surprising. Hundreds of other wells were drilled around the state in hopeful imitation.

Environmental problems abounded. Oil production was largely unregulated by state or federal authorities until after the Great Depression. With operators free to work as they wished, oil was stored in earthen ponds that sometimes flooded nearby land after rains, killing all vegetation and poisoning the water supply. Lightning occasionally ignited the ponds and evaporation was a problem. In the haste to find oil, natural gas was vented into the atmosphere and irretrievably lost. Primitive and not always honest drilling practices brought less than complete recovery from wells.

The first oil-boom was short-lived. Arkansas rose to fourth in the United States in oil production in 1924, but output fell by one-fourth in 1926, and prices were less than the cost of production in the Depression. A second boom came in 1937. Drilling to 5,500 feet, twice as deep as in the first wells, led to the opening of the Shuler field. Arkansas's production recovered and remained stable for a number of years.

State control over the oil industry was greatly needed, but not until 1939 was a regulatory body established. Its policing powers and efficiency were greatly limited, probably harming the industry in the long run. State governors, beginning with Thomas C. McRae, urged the legislature to enact an adequate severance tax so the state could obtain some revenue from the rapidly depleting resource, but oil men found the legislature as pliable as the railroads had, with the result that the tax was long deferred and then ridiculously low.

One Arkansas oil man, Thomas Harry Barton of Lion Oil, became a conspicuous figure in Arkansas political and social life, a lesser rival of Arkansas Power and Light's Harvey Couch. One of America's most colorful oil millionaires, H.L. Hunt, got his start farming, gambling and raising a stake in Lake Village and then in the Arkansas oil fields before moving to Texas.

The oil discovered in Arkansas, although of no more than passing importance in the nation's oil history, was highly significant to the poor state. The value of oil at the height of the boom was twenty-four times greater than the capital of all the banks in Arkansas or the total assessed valuation of the state. Opera and concert stars such as Amelita Galli-Curci, John McCormack and Jascha Heifetz performed in El Dorado at a time when such events were virtually unknown elsewhere in the state.

The Rise of Utilities

Although the impact of the oil industry was limited mostly to the southern section of the state, the utility kingdom of Harvey Couch reached beyond state boundaries. Nationally, the 1920s saw the consolidation of small power companies into national holding companies. Samuel Insull of Chicago, whose empire collapsed in the Depression, was the most famous national figure, but the person to reckon with in Arkansas was Harvey Couch.

Couch was a south Arkansas boy born in Calhoun (Columbia County) who began his career marketing eggs on the side while working for the railroad. His success story, straight from Horatio Alger, began when he set up small telephone companies in areas not served by the Bell system. He learned the value of friends in the state legislature early. When the Bell companies tried to crush his infant concerns by denying long-distance hookups, Couch had the Arkansas legislature pass a law compelling such service. He owned fifty exchanges with more than 1,500 miles of line in four states by 1910. Then he sold the concern to the Bell system for more than $1,000,000, making him a millionaire at age thirty-four. His next move was into electric power, and in 1913, he formed the corporation that eventually became Arkansas Power and Light (AP&L). Because Arkansas was capital poor, Couch went to Eastern bankers to raise the funds needed to erect his statewide system. He had to sell the public on the uses of electricity at the same time in order to create a market for his product. Couch played the role of industrial promoter, particularly in trying to get cotton factories to locate in Arkansas. The owner of an early radio station, Couch promoted consumer use of electricity as well. Increased demand led to the building of Remmel Dam on the Ouachita River, named for Republican Harmon Remmel, who helped obtain federal approval for damming a navigable stream.

Couch worked equally well with Republicans in Washington and Democrats at the state level. His greatest success came when he lured an International Shoe Company plant to Malvern. City lighting created "great white ways," electric water pumps appeared in rice fields and reliable electricity became available in the home. Like the "New Arkansas Traveler" promotion of the 1870s, Couch brought Northern capitalists to Arkansas for tours. Some industrial development resulted, but Arkansas came too late to catch North Carolina and Georgia in textiles and suffered from the discriminatory railroad rates that protected Northern factories from Southern competition.

At a time when the promoter-capitalist was considered the greatest American, Harvey Couch ranked as the greatest Arkansan. But there was another side to the utility story. AP&L's attorney, C. Hamilton Moses, wrote the legislation creating the state's first public utility commission in order to free the company from some long-term contracts that became disadvantageous after World War I inflation. Thereafter the company remained in politics. Moses became one of the state's leading kingmakers, controlling public opinion and giving money to all politicians so that the Company never lost regardless of who won elections.

During the 1930s, AP&L used its influence with United States Senator Joseph T. Robinson to veto a planned federal hydroelectric project on the Arkansas River. Frustrated fed-

eral planners moved the project to the Tennessee River, creating the Tennessee Valley Authority (TVA) and pulling that region out of poverty. Although AP&L was founded and run by Arkansans, the bulk of its stock was held by Eastern interests, reinforcing the colonial nature of the Arkansas economy. Public power advocate Clyde T. Ellis later wrote: "I could have been born in no better place than Arkansas to see first-hand what an electric power monopoly could do to the people."

FARM LIFE

Forty-cent cotton in 1919 spurred Arkansas farmers to go further into debt to buy more land and expand output. Optimism collapsed when cotton fell to under 10 cents by 1920, and a long decade of financial difficulties began. Tenancy was increasing: half of Arkansas's farmers were tenants in 1910; nearly two-thirds fell into that category in 1930. Tenancy was what Howard W. Odum, one of the era's leading scholars, called the "pathology of submarginal folk." By his definition, one-third of the state's counties were submarginal. Arkansas farmers ranked forty-sixth in the use of farm machinery, forty-fifth in the value of farm property and used less fertilizer than farmers in any other Southern state.

The average farm in 1925 was 70.4 acres, and plots of ten and twenty acres were common in the Delta. Agricultural experts cited small farms as one reason for low incomes; the Southern farmer earned less than half as much as his Northern counterpart. The high birth rate, the low standard of living and inadequate agencies for cultural development created a vicious cycle of rural poverty. Less than 10 percent of Arkansas farm families owned a radio by 1930, and less than 20 percent had a telephone. An inequitable property tax system forced those least able to pay to finance the state's extravagant road building program. Delta farmers labored under the added weight of drainage taxes.

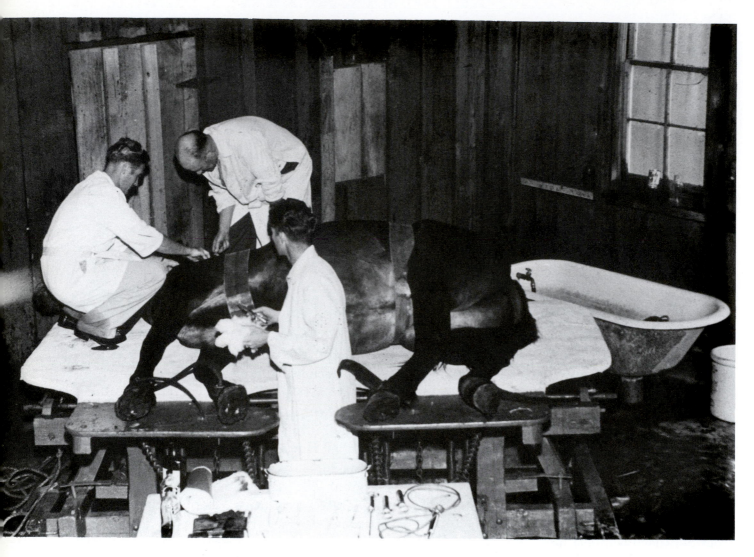

Mule Hospital, Robert E. Lee Wilson Plantation *(photographer unknown, ca. 1930) Wilson kept three veterinarians on full-time duty. The medical care given to mules far exceeded that available to sharecroppers in the Mississippi Delta.* **University of Arkansas**

The changes in cultural character were most visible in the Delta, where drainage had destroyed wildlife that had provided food and employment for many. In the first 100 years of Arkansas history, the character of Delta people differed little from their Ozark brethren, but small farmers could not prosper under the burden of drainage taxes. In heavily drained Crittenden County, the tenancy rate increased from 88.88 percent in 1920 to 94.83 percent in 1930, a condition an FBI report in the 1930s blamed on drainage taxes.

High taxes and low cotton prices hurt Delta farmers and planters alike. Buffalo Island farmers marketed squash, melons and other truck crops. Planter E. Ritter of Marked Tree sold his own brand of radishes nationally. Robert E. Lee Wilson consolidated his holdings and sold one of his railroads. Nearly all the large planters were in debt to Northern insurance companies.

Agricultural decline in the 1920s was particularly painful in the Ozarks, where mixed farming had achieved substantial success early in the century. Orchards in the northwest suffered from devastating winters, the onset of the San Jose scale disease, and worst of all, competition from new orchards in Ore-

Mules

Mules, though their number has declined since tractors took over much of the level land, are still preferred to horses in cottonfields. The mule is tough, stubborn, and wiry. He drinks water so muddy that a self-respecting horse would snort at it. He humps his back to a wintry wind and nibbles forage a mustang would scorn. It would seem that a mule has a governor to control his speed, just as a steam engine has. Most horses show an eagerness in their work and, if careless hands are on the lines, will sometimes kill themselves on the gumbo soil under a blazing sun. But if a teamster peppered his mules with a shotgun, they would go just so fast, and no faster. Unfortunately, a mule generally becomes most evil-eyed and active when you try to hem him up so you can slip the bridle on. In such a situation, planters agree, the average Negro farm hand is supreme, artfully supplementing his barrage of threats with enough coaxing to leave the mule uncertain whether to bolt or submit. And if the mule kicks, it is not with the intensity of hate that a high-strung horse directs at an enemy. The mule's cussedness is merely genial and rough, as impartial as the cockleburs in his tail.

Source: Arkansas: A Guide to the State, Compiled by Workers of the Writers' Program of the Work Projects Administration in the State of Arkansas *(Hastings House, New York, 1941)*

---

gon and Washington. Little could be done about the weather, but fruit farmers failed to unite to fight diseases or form cooperatives like the Western fruitmen did to develop marketing strategies and win concessions on freight rates from railroads. Arkansas fruit sent to Northern markets sometimes brought less than the shipping and handling charges, leaving farmers with debt. The collapse of the orchards ruined fruit dryers, vinegar makers, other subsidiary firms and a number of small railroad lines dependent on the trade.

The same stubborn independence that led farmers to dynamite tick-dipping vats also led them to reject improved farming techniques suggested by farm agents. Charles Morrow Wilson, a sympathetic observer, noted in 1935 that many families had not had their heads above water in more than a quarter of a century. Some, determined to hold on to their land, began experimenting with mass-produced poultry, which would take advantage of the new highway system and reach market by truck.

Rural overpopulation became noticeable and led to emigration during the 1920s. Steady population loss occurred in the Ozarks and Ouachitas, and black emigration increased dramatically, with 1.2 percent of the state's blacks leaving. Much of this loss came not from the predominantly black counties of the Delta, but from along the periphery where race relations traditionally were strained.

Lynching of blacks did not stop despite the active opposition of Governor Thomas C. McRae and the persistent work of Methodist church women. Indeed, the decade opened with one of the most blatant and sadistic examples of lynching to be found in American history, when Henry Lowry was lynched on January 26, 1921, at Nodena (Mississippi County). Lowry had fled the state after killing a white plantation owner at settlement time. Caught in Texas, he was extradited to Arkansas. Deputies took a return route through Mississippi, where a mob from Arkansas stopped the train just outside of Memphis, removed the prisoner and took him by car to Nodena. The widely reported execution was described by the Memphis *Press*:

With the negro chained to a log,
members of the mob placed a small pile
of leaves around his feet. Gasoline was

Flour Milling at the Wilson Plantation *(photographer and date unknown) Planter Robert E. Lee Wilson specialized in cotton, but he was more adventurous than most in trying to diversify. Shown here is his flour operation.*
University of Arkansas

then poured on the leaves, and the carrying out of the death sentence was under way. Inch by inch the negro was fairly cooked to death. Every few minutes fresh leaves were tossed on the funeral pyre until the blaze had passed the negro's waist. As the flames were eating away his abdomen, a member of the mob stepped forward and saturated his body with gasoline. It was then only a few minutes until the negro had been reduced to ashes.

Governor McRae called the lynching "the worst outrage in the world" and blamed Sheriff Dwight Blackwood, who was in Memphis at the Peabody Hotel. Blackwood responded that "nearly every man, woman, and child in our county wanted the negro lynched. When public sentiment is that way, there isn't much chance left for the officers."

The best option for Arkansas blacks in the 1920s was to move to Northern industrial cities, and perhaps because of the existence of this outlet, the number of lynchings declined during the decade. Although lynchings influenced blacks to leave the state, whites were leaving, too. A total of 230,000 persons moved west to Oklahoma and Texas in search of opportunity during the decade. Ironically, their places often were taken by farmers from the worn-out lands of Tennessee and Mississippi, and Arkansas recorded a modest population gain in the 1930 census.

From planter to farmer to tenant, the 1920s fulfilled little of the promise touted by incum-

Coming Into Town With a Load of Watermelons, *Tupelo (1908) Edd Taylor and Homer Patrick hauled a load of prime watermelons raised by Ed Wallace to the Rock Island railroad tracks.* **Jacksonport Museum**

bent Republican presidents, who successfully vetoed every measure of farm relief but gladly raised tariffs and lowered taxes to benefit Northern industry. The feeling of being left out of the good life partially explained such features as the lynchings and the militant rural opposition to many of the ideas and programs of modernization.

TOWN LIFE

Arkansas towns during the 1920s reflected rural problems. Only the main streets were paved in most places. Sidewalks became more common but were not universal. The progressive impulse toward town improvement did not die out completely. Pine Bluff in 1922 sup-

ported a drive by the Chamber of Commerce that raised $4,000 for mosquito control. The weakness of urban resources was shown by a 1926 fire at Newport that destroyed 365 homes and left 1,500 persons homeless. The building boom of the early years of the century tapered off, and towns dependent on the lumbering industry often declined rapidly with the cutting over of the timber lands and the closing of wood processing factories. One positive economic indicator was that in southern Arkansas, the Crossett Lumber Company began replanting, a practice that became common by the 1940s.

Despite Arkansas's remoteness from style-setting New York, the "Flapper" was very much in evidence. One critical observer noted that the extremely short skirts led to results

Laying Pipe in Conway
(photographer and date unknown)
Sidewalks, paved streets, sewers,
water mains, gas lines, electric
and telephone lines were among
the disruptive improvements in the
first three decades of the century.
Arkansas History Commission

"painful to the eye of the trained observer and anatomist:"

> Some limbs are bowed, some look at if they might be edematous and others appear as though they were about ready to break down and endanger the life of the owner. At this point we hear some prude say, "Why observe so closely?" One might as well say, "Why notice automobiles? when the streets are full of them."

Another critic, applauding the movement away from Victorian prudery, asked, "Why be ashamed of the human body? It seems quite probable that we are going to see more of it."

The battle for law and order continued. In many little hamlets such as Kelso in Desha County, "a fairly lawless little town," quick tempers, abetted by moonshine, produced Saturday night violence. Inquests were held in the back of Uncle Charlie's store, presided over by the justice of the peace, and they usually ended in acquittals. Many town fathers became increasingly conservative and supported the Ku Klux Klan as a way to cope with criminal behavior that the law could not reach.

Small town banks were still the target of robbers, who now came and left by car. The impact of the automobile led to a test of wills between urban progressives and rural reactionaries. At stake in courthouse towns was the traditional hitching rail around the court square. Enterprising modernists carried the rails off, often at night, and irate farmers set them back by day. The hitching post was gone from the main streets by the end of the decade, and farmers arriving by horse and wagon were forced to park away from the square. Gone too were the early city ordinances that limited automobile speeds to under ten miles an hour and required drivers to honk at every intersection.

Some found it difficult to adjust to change and became the butt of jokes about how slowly they drove. Sheriff Jim Grady of Prairie County was one such local folk hero who was quoted as telling his son, Socrates, that he "ought not to be speeding them cars around. Ten miles an hour will get you anywhere." Sheriff Grady is reported also to have driven so slowly between Hazen and DeValls Bluff that a thief was able to jump on the running board of his car and demand, "Your money or your life!" Not to be hurried even then, Sheriff Grady is reported to have replied, "I don't have any money with me boy, but if you hang on 'til I get to the Bluff, I'll write you a check."

Town life became less self-sufficient during the 1920s, primarily because national culture via the movie house and radio displaced local entertainment. The 1921-22 season of Broadway road shows proved to be the last in Little Rock for many years. Only amateur theatricals were performed thereafter. The Malone Theater in Jonesboro, which had opened to Walter Whiteside in *Hamlet* and had been used by notable concert artists Sophie Braslau and Albert Spaulding became home to a car dealership. Others theaters were converted to movie houses. Almost all town bands had long been disbanded by 1930, although high school groups took their place to some extent.

What did flourish in the 1920s was the radio. Harvey Couch arranged a demonstration for the Pine Bluff Rotary Club on November 15, 1921, and Arkansas's first station, WOK, went on the air February 18, 1922. The Pine Bluff *Commercial* called the craze "Radioitis" as listeners to primitive, battery-powered sets tried to tune in an increasing number of stations. Radio in Arkansas began as a local amateur endeavor. Businesses were slow to realize the advertising potential, and early stations were limited greatly in programming options. All local talent had a chance to perform, and time was given to speakers on every conceivable topic. Stations often stopped operations in the summer.

Commercials began to dominate by 1930, however. The first network linking the separate stations, the National Broadcasting Company (NBC), was formed in 1926, and Columbia Broadcasting Company (CBS) and Mutual Broadcasting Company (MBS) followed. Station KTHS in Hot Springs became the state's first NBC radio station in 1929. Before nation-

al shows completely displaced local efforts, Mena businessmen Chester Lauck and Norris Goff went on the air with a "homefolks" routine. They went on to national fame from Hot Springs as Lum 'n Abner, whose folksy stories of a mythical Pine Ridge entertained millions on radio and in the movies.

A different audience responded to radio evangelism. Starting with the pioneering efforts of John Brown at Siloam Springs and Benjamin Bogard in Little Rock, several ministers took to the airwaves to preach the Gospel. Radio diluted community togetherness by keeping people at home, although its supporters said it strengthened the family. It also fueled the sports craze. Not only could local games be given coverage, but an enterprising announcer using the Western Union telegraph ticket could reproduce a baseball game from St. Louis, complete with simulated applause and a pencil on the microphone for the crack of a bat. Direct broadcasting from St. Louis by the late 1930s reinforced the Missouri connection in the Arkansas culture and made pitcher "Dizzy" Dean a folk hero.

The Decline of Newspapers

The 1920s marked the emergence of the consumer. The Gospel of Business emphasized buying and selling in the age of the advertiser. A diminished role for newspapers was one indirect result. Arkansas papers peaked in popularity about 1910. With the economic decline in the 1920s, many small town and weekly county papers either consolidated or disappeared. Those that survived were not necessarily stronger. Many troubled papers had sold their outside pages to the patent medicine companies in the nineteenth century. That practice declined with the coming of federal regulation early in the century. Local advertising increased instead and became in time a paper's major source of revenue. A loss of independence came with this change. The patent medicine companies had imposed only the requirement that nothing hostile to their wares be printed. An editor otherwise was free to embark on whatever causes or personalities might be of interest.

When advertisers became a paper's mainstay, this freedom gradually was curtailed. C. Hamilton Moses of AP&L always made it a point to drop in on newspaper offices in his trips around the state. The political orientation of papers declined, family and social news increased, outside news came from national news agencies and sports became of paramount interest. Weeklies almost gave up reporting national news and concentrated on homely accounts of family comings and goings. As argument and controversy declined, a dull conformity emerged, and many papers were on the road to becoming little more than advertising supplements.

Spas and Resort Towns

The modest statistical increase in urbanization during the 1920s coincided with the decline of some towns. The erroneous ballyhoo about the purported medicinal properties of certain kinds of spring water in the late nineteenth century fed the rise of Eureka Springs, Ravenden Springs, Siloam Springs and others. All declined during the decade. Eureka Springs, the most important tourist site aside from Hot Springs, had passed its peak and was on the way to becoming a quaint home for curious tourists, artists and Ozark writers. The monumental Crescent Hotel first became a girls' school and then a quack's cancer clinic.

Hot Springs, however, prospered despite a serious fire and its reputation as a den of iniquity. Some major league baseball teams trained there, but horse racing at Oaklawn and illegal gambling were central to its prosperity. With local officials readily for sale and state authorities willing to look the other way, Hot Springs was a neutral ground where the nation's top criminals, including Al Capone, visited peacefully.

Presiding over this venal world from 1927 to 1947 was Mayor Leo P. McLaughlin. With his carriage and four white horses, McLaughlin matched such contemporary urban bosses as Ed Crump of Memphis and Tom Pendergast of Kansas City. Hot Springs had such a tolerant attitude toward criminals that the FBI kept secret its raid there that captured Frank Nash, a Paragould badman who once denied committing a murder because he said he was busy robbing the Black Rock bank at the time.

Hot Springs also continued to draw people with medical problems. The publicity about Franklin D. Roosevelt's water therapy at Warm Springs, Georgia, for paralysis resulting from polio led Hot Springs to become home for many victims of the disease, later including opera singer Marjorie Lawrence.

One new community that arose during this period was Bella Vista in Benton County. Created as a model vacation site in 1927, it appealed to Oklahoma oil millionaires as a retreat from the summer heat. The resort held elaborate dances in a cave and had its own radio station. The glitter of Hot Springs or Bella Vista — flashy cars, dances, bands, radio, concerts and illegal liquor — clashed sharply with the rural poverty and stern morals of the surrounding countryside.

POLITICS

Arkansas in the 1920s remained a one-party state with all major races decided in the Democratic primary. Issues were of little importance compared to personality, and fraudulent elections continued to be a way of life. Most campaigning was done in the summer, providing relief from chopping cotton and attending revivals.

Thomas C. McRae

Thomas C. McRae was the first governor of the decade. A relic from the past, McRae claimed to have served in the Confederacy and had been the youngest member of the state legislature in 1871. Elected to Congress in 1884, he remained there for eighteen years, a nineteenth-century record for Arkansas congressmen. He embarked successfully on a banking career on retirement and became president of the Arkansas Bankers Association and later head of the Arkansas Bar Association. Despite being sixty-nine years old at the time of his election, he probably was the most progressive governor during the decade and certainly the most able.

McRae's experiences showed that unless a governor possessed the audacity of a Jeff Davis, he was at the legislature's mercy in trying to enact a program and at the people's mercy when he tried to assert moral authority. Strongly opposed to lynching, which he said "should not be tolerated," McRae supported the anti-lynching movement by proclaiming Law and Order Day. The Lowry lynching at Nodena came seventy-two hours later.

Governor McRae urged the legislature to substitute a tax on incomes for the unfair property tax, establish a severance tax on oil, fight discriminatory railroad rates and aid education. Results were disappointing. Free schools, the governor noted, would never exist until the state supplied free textbooks. McRae also tried to establish a meaningful state highway program, but federal mandates rather than gubernatorial leadership eventually accomplished that objective. McRae was the first governor elected after passage of the Nineteenth Amendment (woman's suffrage), and he appointed some women to state jobs. No major women's voting block emerged, however, and McRae's successors removed the women he appointed from office because they felt that women in positions of authority degraded men. During McRae's first term, a group of club women attempted to get a comprehensive morals bill enacted, but legislative opposition defeated it.

The Ku Klux Klan

A new wind was blowing in Arkansas by the time McRae left office in 1924. World War I ushered out the Victorian age and the moral verities that white middle-class Southerners took for granted. In the new age of relativism, psychoanalysis, cubism, flappers and gangsters, a revived Ku Klux Klan offered the safety of moral conformity for upset businessmen. This second Klan bore little relationship to the first except in name and was developed with hate as a profit-making scheme to collect dues and sell regalia. Largely concentrated in towns, it expressed repugnance for blacks, Jews, Catholics, wife-beaters, bootleggers, prostitutes and labor union organizers.

Arkansas was a relatively weak area for the Klan because it was a rural state, and the social evils the Klan agitated against were far less evident than in neighboring Texas or Oklahoma. Even so, the Klan became a major factor in Arkansas politics over a four-year period. One woman legislator later wrote that, "Everybody who was anybody and everybody who wanted to be somebody joined the Klan. My boss joined, my friends joined, I joined." Some who joined the Klan did not stay with it. John W. Booth of Des Arc, owner of a general mercantile store, resigned when his children found his costume in a window box in the attic and his wife objected that the Klan did not set an appropriate moral standard for his children.

The Klan's first public rally was in Little Rock in 1922 and it attracted more than 1,000 state members. Leaders claimed 25,000 Klansmen by the summer of that year. Local Klans found plenty to do. The first recorded act of Klan violence occurred in Texarkana on January 8, 1922, when a black male was whipped for "fooling about a white woman." Threats were more common than actual violence, and warnings against wife-beaters probably constituted a majority of the actions undertaken by local klaverns.

H. L. Mencken and the Arkansas Ku Klux Klan

H. L. (Henry Louis) Mencken, (1880-1956) the early twentieth newspaperman, editor of the Baltimore Sun *and founder of* The American Mercury *attacked Puritanism, the Ku Klux Klan, conservatism and religion. He excelled at satire and was known for framing insults that elicited violent retorts from what he labeled the "Booboisie."*

One such retort came from the state meeting of the Knights and Women of the Ku Klux Klan at Little Rock, Arkansas, September 7, 1925. It must have given Mencken, who loved to be hated, great satisfaction. The Klan resolution, which was unanimously adopted at the state meeting stated:

WHEREAS, one H. L. Mencken is the author of a scurrilous article recently published in the Baltimore *Sun*, describing the Klan parade in Washington, D. C., August 3, [1925] in which he viciously slurs and insults the good women and patriotic men who marched in that parade to the number of more than 100,000, declaring that there was not an intelligent or comely face among them, that they looked like a gang of meat cutters and curve greasers on a holiday and many other slanders and insults too vile and indecent to be repeated, therefore be it:

RESOLVED, By the Knights of the Ku Klux Klan of Arkansas, a State which the said Mencken has in times past slandered as "a land of morons," that we condemn in the strongest possible language the vile mouthings of this prince of blackguards among the writers of America, to whom virtue, patriotism and democracy are only a subject upon which to expend the venom of a poisonous pen; that we further condemn the Baltimore *Sun* for heaping insults upon the good men and women of America, and that we commend the course of the Baltimore Chamber of Commerce in protesting against the calumny too degrading and false to come from the heart of one who is not himself a moral pervert.

RESOLVED FURTHER, that copies of this resolution be sent to the *Baltimore Sun, National Courier*, Baltimore Chamber of Commerce and H. L. Mencken.

Source: Arkansas Gazette, September 8, 1925

The oil fields of south Arkansas were fertile with sin, and the Klan claimed to have driven out 2,000 "undesirables," mostly gamblers, prostitutes and bootleggers. Several instances of anti-labor activity by the Klan were recorded as well.

A group as large as the Klan inevitably became involved in politics. Clarence P. Newton, the secretary to Governor McRae, was a Klansman, and the Fort Smith Klan ousted Mayor Fagan Bourland, a Catholic. The Klan conducted a city-wide purge in Little Rock and successfully elected a Klan-sponsored ticket led by Homer Adkins for sheriff and Heartsill Ragon as congressman. The two most prominent Klan leaders were ex-Republican James A. Comer and the one-time progressive Democrat Lee Cazort, a former speaker of the House.

Klan support became a major issue when Klan candidate Cazort opposed Tom Terral in the 1924 Democratic gubernatorial primary. Terral felt he could not win without neutralizing the Klan's aid to Cazort. On Cazort's orders, no Arkansas local would admit Terral to membership, so he returned to his native Louisiana, where he was admitted, and came back to Arkansas as a "Klansman without a home." The move confused voters because Terral emerged from the primary and won the runoff. Discontented Democrats led by Fred H. Isrig started a reaction against Klan interference. Factionalism and charges of financial irregularity surfaced, and the Klan rapidly faded from view in Arkansas, as in the nation at large. But as Brooks Hays remembered, "It did considerable damage, however, in the estrangement of neighbors and the sowing of seeds of religious and racial distrust and prejudice."

Even without Klan leadership, the kind of hatred it nourished continued to flourish. A young white girl was murdered in the bell tower of the First Presbyterian Church in Little Rock in the spring of 1927. Unable to get at the seventeen-year-old black boy accused of the crime, the mob turned its attention to a suspect in another attack. The crowd hung the man and then fired more than 200 bullets into the corpse before setting it ablaze. The mob ruled Little Rock for two days, terrorizing blacks and refusing to disperse. Both the mayor and the chief of police were out of town, so the city council finally prevailed on Governor Martineau to send in the National Guard. When the troops arrived, one mob member was found at the corner of Tenth and Broadway, directing traffic with the lynching victim's badly charred arm.

The Election of 1928

The presidential election year of 1928 found the Klan greatly reduced in power and influence. The national Democratic Party nominated a "wet" Catholic, New York Governor Al Smith, for president and honored Arkansas by selecting Senator Joseph T. Robinson as Smith's vice-presidential running mate. This forced many voters to choose between the Democratic Party or the Pope. Some Baptist ministers in Arkansas denounced Smith as the agent of the Anti-Christ and urged from the pulpit that church members vote for Republican Herbert Hoover. The Democratic response was to accuse these ministers of turning the state over to "nigger-loving Republicans." Robinson, placed on the ticket to keep the South loyal, covered more than 25,000 miles and made more than 200 speeches in Smith's behalf. A Democratic Victory Legion was formed to combat the ministers in what became a dirty campaign.

One Smith supporter who came under much fire was former Governor Charles H. Brough, a prominent Baptist layman who recently had served as president of Central College in Conway. Dr. J.S. Compere, editor of the *Baptist Advance*, claimed that the opposition to Smith included "the awakened motherhood of America, the National WCTU, the Anti-Saloon League" plus every responsible organized moral force in the United States." Invoking the name of the Baptist State Convention, Dr. Compere and Dr. J. S. Rogers sent Brough a telegram ordering him not to address a scheduled Democratic rally in El Dorado: "We solemnly warn you that we believe our people and the Convention will not stand for it." Brough went ahead with his speech, and read the telegram aloud, denouncing it as "one of the most flagrant cases of attempted coercion." The El Dorado paper covered the speech under the headline "Brough Defies the Church," and a lively debate on the issue of separation of church and state followed.

Isaac McClellan, a Sheridan lawyer and Baptist, wrote Brough of his support against "so-called ministers trying to run every worldly interest and business they see proper," and a Brinkley resident observed that, "The fact that you are President of a Baptist College does not argue that you cannot think for yourself." In an attempt to discredit Brough, some

Mrs. Cora Bodenhamer's Millinery and Hardware Store, Mountain Home *(Arthur Keller, 1928) Women increasingly entered business, and in this photograph, a placard of the presidential and vice-presidential Democratic nominees, Al Smith and Joe T. Robinson, is displayed in the store window.* **University of Central Arkansas**

enemies insisted he favored open communion and that he was unsound on the evolution question. Arkansas voters stayed loyal to the Party at the polls, although there were cracks elsewhere in the solid South as the Republican Hoover won the election.

Politics and Highways

The automobile in Arkansas was at first a rich man's toy, but Henry Ford's inexpensive machines put Arkansans and the nation on wheels by the 1920s. Arkansans owned 113,102 vehicles in 1923, more than half of which were Fords, and the number was growing by about 15,000 a year. Observers found that cars became a family's most cherished possession, one that took financial precedence over nearly every other obligation. Highway construction therefore assumed the same role in state politics.

Road construction began in earnest after 1910, but it was localism gone wild. Arkansas had 527 road districts by 1920, each maintaining an average of 30.2 miles and all without coordination or adequate financing. One typical eastern Arkansas road consisted of large concrete slabs that ran to the county line and stopped abruptly, pitching unwary drivers into a mudhole. Governor McRae called for the elimination of such districts, but powerful local interests dominating the legislature thwarted the move. The lack of system had become such a national scandal by 1922 that the federal government, which had given Arkansas almost $5,000,000 between 1915

Safety Sam, the Road Sign Man, Near Helena (*photographer unknown, ca. 1920) The road is identified as the Gateway Hiway. Note the absence of any highway numbering system.* **Author's Collection**

and 1919, threatened to cut off funding.

Continued pleas from Governor McRae availed nothing, until federal money actually stopped in 1923, forcing a special session of the legislature. The legislature passed the Harrelson Road Law that gave the state control over the districts. Many agrarian groups, notably the Farmers Union, opposed this or any other centralizing measure, but federal pressure left no alternatives. The law's primary result was that local questions came to dominate state politics.

Road affairs figured largely in the one term that Tom Terral served as governor. The homeless Klansman was, in Brooks Hays's memory, "a big, bumbling likable person, young and vigorous," but whose "education

lagged far behind his aspirations." He never really had a chance to learn. Elected on a contradictory platform promising better roads, improved schools, and more law enforcement, all with lower taxes, he angered many by announcing that he would grant absolutely no pardons during his term. Given the unfairness and severity of Arkansas law, such a move was uncharitable and politically damaging. But road politics was the main cause of his downfall. Because the state now had taken over responsibility for road management, road districts demanded that the state assume their debts. Governor Terral saw no reason why all the people should pay the debts of some districts and opposed the scheme. The districts ran John E. Martineau for governor as their pliant tool in 1926, using the slogan, "Better Roads to Better Schools," a motto that historian George B. Tindall used to describe all Southern politics in the decade. In eastern Arkansas, where road districts were plagued with problems, Martineau piled up huge majorities and swept into office, denying Terral the traditional second term.

As governor, Martineau gave his name to the Martineau Road Plan under which the state assumed the debts of the local districts, provided direct financial assistance to the counties, began buying the private toll bridge companies and inaugurated a plan of state road construction financed by a new issue of state bonds. The role of the state was explained by the man most responsible for the program, Little Rock promoter and highway commissioner Justin Matthews:

> Under our system we allot the road funds available to each county, 50% on population basis and 50% on road revenue basis based on car license. Then we charge up to each county the turn back that the State Highway Department makes to the county court and charge up the bonds that the state assumes, and these two items deducted from the total allotment leaves the money that a particular county is entitled to for construction work.

In addition, money was diverted from large population centers and given to smaller counties. Matthews himself was a direct beneficiary in that his Metropolitan Trust Company received $365,000 from the state for suburban streets that were not built. The operations of the Highway Department were so secretive in various ways that the obvious political motives escaped easy detection.

Martineau did not stay long at the helm, resigning as governor to accept an appointment as federal district judge arranged by Senator Joseph T. Robinson, his cousin. The first

Arkansas lieutenant governor to become governor, Harvey Parnell, took over in March 1928.

Parnell fit in well with the road contractors, the cement and asphalt men, and they supported him in 1928 for a full term. His opponents in that race included former Governor Tom Terral, who was out for revenge; Carrol Cone, the state auditor, who promised rigid economy; and a new figure, former Assistant Attorney General Brooks Hays. Hays favored a broad range of progressive proposals, including better support for schools, the adoption of a state income tax, new hospitals and an audit of highway expenditures. Parnell won in a squeaker although he lacked a majority of the votes cast. The voters liked roads. Parnell won again in 1930, this time with a majority of the votes cast.

The Martineau-Parnell road program was a financial disaster for the state comparable to the failure of the Real Estate Bank or the debts of Reconstruction. The state assumed $70,556,000 in road district debt, some without being audited; put $13,000,000 more into new highway construction and added $14,000,000 more for increased pensions for Confederate veterans. The state debt by 1935 stood at $166,410,350. Arkansas ranked forty-sixth in income per capita but first in per capita indebtedness. More than half the state's revenue was pledged to pay the bonds, an amount that was nine times the state's average gross revenue earlier in the decade. The Wall Street firm of Halsey, Stuart, and Company, which marketed the bonds, overstated the property valuation of Arkansas by two times, leading unwary investors to believe the state had much better resources than actually existed.

The new program did provide some uniformity and added needed bridges and other linkage. But the 1927 flood washed out 511 bridges and ruined hundreds of miles of roads so that money had to be diverted for repairs rather than new construction. The worst result was the great temptation for ill-gotten gain that road con-

R. M. Ruthven Bridge, Cotter *(Michael Swanda, 1988) The "Trout Capital of the World" got its patented Marsh Rainbow Arch Bridge in 1930. More than 100 local men worked on the project, and two died in accidents. Although the original electric lighting and toll booths are gone, the bridge became Arkansas's first National Historic Civil Engineering Landmark in 1956.* **Arkansas Historic Preservation**

struction presented. Dwight M. Blackwood, the chairman of the Highway Commission, deposited $105,000 in various banks from a salary of $5,000 a year. Charged with misfeasance, his response was that the money came from the fees he previously had collected while sheriff of Mississippi County. Investigations eventually turned up considerable instances of fraud, favoritism and kickbacks between contractors and highway personnel. A 1933 legislative resolution stated that the Parnell administration was "the most corrupt since the days of Reconstruction and the most extravagant and wasteful in the history of the state."

The Highway Department gave governors a vast patronage power they had not enjoyed previously. Parnell used it effectively, setting the example that each of his successors denounced on the stump and practiced once in office. As something of a Southern progressive, Parnell supported shifting taxes from property to income, got new buildings for the tuberculosis sanitarium and the School for the Deaf, and acquired the campus of Henderson-Brown in Arkadelphia from the Methodist Church to form Henderson State Teachers College. A supporter of school consolidation, Parnell brought in a New York management firm to make recommendations on increasing administrative efficiency. The legislature, however, refused to implement the resulting proposals.

Had the prosperity of the 1920s continued, feeble though it was for Arkansas, the state might have been able to extricate itself from its road debt. Instead, the Great Flood of 1927, the Great Drought of 1930 and the Great Depression turned Arkansas into a financial disaster — the only American state to default on its debt. In the words of a student of state finance, the Arkansas experience "illustrates the danger of borrowing in a poor state with inadequate financial administration and a relatively low level of political morality." Finally, because of all the money and attention given to roads, other public needs had to take — to use a transportation metaphor — a back seat.

EDUCATION

Public Schools

The 1920s opened with strong words for education from Governor McRae but little aid from the legislature. Like roads before the Harrelson Act, education was a local responsibility. As a result, eighteen counties had no high schools in 1922 and a high school education was accessible to all students in no county. By comparison with other states and the District of Columbia, Arkansas ranked forty-sixth in educational expenditures and forty-eighth in length of the school term in 1923. The typical high school in 1929 consisted of three teachers and sixty pupils. Some efforts were made to improve the situation, and by the end of the decade, Arkansas ranked forty-ninth in high school enrollment, forty-seventh in school attendance, and because of the fertility of the population, tenth in the number of school-age children. The average school term was 150 days for whites and 132 days for blacks.

Teachers and their allies continually called attention to Arkansas's neglect. The main objective, in addition to the perennial issue of improving teacher salaries, was state assistance to provide equality of opportunity — for white students. The failure to defeat the forces of localism doomed the effort. Because the road issue touched more people and generated more opportunities for enrichment, only the first part of Governor Martineau's successful slogan, "Better Roads to Better Schools," was implemented.

Two types of education dominated during the 1920s. First — and most common — were rural schools that still practiced the split term, opening in July, breaking for the fall harvest, starting again in the winter and stopping for spring plowing. Rural teachers were hardly more educated than their charges but now were increasingly unmarried young women. Both professionalism and pay were very low. Rural teachers still were paid in county warrants, which merchants took only with a considerable discount. Many had obtained their teaching license through correspondence courses rather than by actual attendance at a college. Cheating on teacher tests was not uncommon and was sometimes encouraged by school administrators eager to get cheap teachers.

Local patrons determined school policy. When future Congressman James W. Trimble interviewed for a Washington County district post and said the world was round, the board refused to hire him. Physical conditions matched intellectual ones, because screen wire, sanitary toilets and safe water were rare. The only outhouse at Pine Ridge was reserved for girls; the boys retreated into a nearby woods. Heating schools was such a serious problem that black school patrons often were required to send coal with their children.

Towns generally developed adequate school systems. Many teachers, particularly women, made permanent careers in education, sometimes teaching three generations of the same family. Professionalism was greater, and the schools became sources of local pride. Children of middle-class families were most likely to stay in school through graduation, and some went on to college.

Black education, segregated and unequal, languished. Only nine counties had black high schools. Thirty-six percent of the teachers in black high schools worked in one-room schools, teaching an average of sixty-nine pupils. Only 1.8 percent of the state's student-age blacks attended high school in 1928. White hostility toward black education remained high. Robert E. Lee Wilson erected a splendid new school for his Mississippi County black tenants, but a mysterious fire consumed the building before it opened. Local officials diverted state aid intended for black schools in fifteen counties and distributed it to the white system. Outside money from the Rosenwald, Jeanes and Slater Funds and aid from the General Education Board kept black schools operating. The Julius Rosenwald fund alone contributed $1,952,441 from 1917 to 1948, helping build 389 schools in thirty-five counties, many of them for whites.

The only positive note in education occurred outside the system. The state created the Arkansas Illiteracy Commission in 1917 and Governor McRae won a $23,000 appropriation to fund "Opportunity Schools." The governor proclaimed "Illiteracy Week," and volunteers enrolled 8,689 pupils in 449 schools by 1922. Although Arkansas ranked thirty-seventh in literacy, it stood tenth in decreasing illiteracy by the end of the decade.

Higher Education in the Twenties

Some progress was recorded in higher education during the decade. The state's agricultural high schools became junior colleges first and then four-year institutions. In 1929, the state acquired Henderson-Brown College at Arkadelphia after the state's Methodists decided amid bitter controversy to concentrate their energies on strengthening Hendrix College at Conway. Ex-governor Donaghey, a former Hendrix board president who favored creating a

new school in Little Rock, showed his displeasure by donating two Little Rock buildings worth more than $1,500,000 to the newly created Little Rock Junior College. This endowment presumably would have gone to the Methodists had they relocated their college in Little Rock.

College enrollment rose toward the end of the decade, but Arkansas ranked forty-sixth in college attendance. A scholarly community protected by emerging tenure policies at Fayetteville began to speak out on issues of public importance. Political scientist and historian David Y. Thomas, who earlier had criticized the accepted version of the Elaine Race Riot, became a vocal critic of utilities. AP&L unsuccessfully pressured school officials to get Thomas dismissed. Less enduring was Hendrix professor Edwin L. Shaver, who in 1922 commented at a Chicago meeting that evolution had made a monkey out of William Jennings Bryan. Shaver was forced to resign for this and the additional statement that, "I refuse to take an old-fashioned literal interpretation of many thinkings in [the Bible]."

Baptist professors during this period were required to sign loyalty oaths to prevent hiring anyone with modern leanings. Outside the University of Arkansas, free speech hardly existed for college professors, and the limits on a "liberal" education were enforced strictly.

Black higher education was far below the standard for whites. The only positive note was that both the University of Arkansas and State Teachers College at Conway allowed black teachers in 1927 to take extension and correspondence courses, and more than 2,000 teachers were enrolled by the second year of operation. Otherwise, a 1928 study revealed that Arkansas had the lowest proportion of blacks in college of any Southern state. Branch Normal College at Pine Bluff became Agricultural, Mechanical, and Normal (AM&N) in 1922 but remained basically a junior college whose faculty was overworked, underpaid and bereft of freedom to criticize these conditions or lead the black community. The school enforced daily devotionals, Wednesday night prayer meetings and Sunday services. Dancing was discouraged, and smoking and drinking were banned.

Black private colleges were starved for money. Shorter College in North Little Rock went five years without printing a catalogue because of the absence of funds. Arkansas Baptist College in Little Rock received some aid from white Baptists, but all the colleges were limited greatly because so few blacks were able to attend high school.

Sports and Schools

Sports flourished during the decade. Arkansas's road program came to mean "Better Roads to Bigger Games," a reality both on the high school and college levels. The national popularity of football and basketball reached Arkansas and found a happy home. With no regulating bodies, ambitious schools recruited athletes regardless of grades, age or locality. The high school coach became the most important school official and could look forward to becoming principal or superintendent or going into business.

Colleges were equally sports conscious. Modern football began in 1904 after eighteen deaths the previous season spurred an outcry that led to stricter new rules. Intercollegiate football in Arkansas was born in the aftermath of that change. Hendrix College fielded its first team in 1906 and followed with basketball in 1908. The University of Arkansas began its sports career in the "bad old days," losing its first intercollegiate football game 54-0 to the University of Texas in 1894. At first called the Cardinals, the football team became the Razorbacks after 1916. The school was a founding member of the Southwest Conference in 1914, but other Southwest teams refrained from coming to Arkansas because of Fayetteville's remote location.

The historian of the Razorbacks observed, "Football fulfillment came late to Arkansas — twenty to fifty years behind other powers in the region." That Hendrix College almost beat the University of Arkansas in 1926 indicated how far football had to go. Some winning teams emerged under Coach Francis Schmidt, and one hero was halfback Bill Fulbright, later a Rhodes scholar and internationally famous United States Senator J. William Fulbright. The black community mirrored the white as AM&N began intercollegiate play in 1929.

Football fever prompted the building of what at the time seemed large stadiums. Hendrix College's Young Memorial Stadium, named for World War I casualty Robert W. Young of Okolona, cost more than $75,000 and seated 5,000 persons. Team heroes became campus celebrities, and the old literary, honor and debating societies quietly died. Fraternities and sororities, which tended to be actively anti-intellectual, took their place along with football booster clubs and cheerleaders.

Sports produced heroes during the 1920s. The first Arkansas sports star was James A. "Indian" Rector, the grandson of the Confederate governor, who came in second in the 100-meter dash at the 1908 Olympics. Arkansas had its first gold medalist at the 1928 Olympics in Eddie Hamm of Lonoke, who overcame repeated bouts of malaria to win the long jump. The only Arkansan to win two Olympic gold medals was Pine Bluff's Bill Carr, whose 1932 record in the 400-meter competition lasted until 1960. Significantly, all three Olympic stars attended out-of-state colleges. College attendance was uncommon for baseball players, most of whom came off the farm. Dizzy and Paul Dean, "Arkie" Vaughn, Bill Dickey, George Kell and others made their ways from cow pastures to the big time.

Sports did much to popularize education. The automobile and new roads made increased attendance at sporting events possible, thereby offering the public a new diversion. As sports moved to the center of school

Arkansas College Football Team (photographer and date unknown) Equipment became increasingly complex as football became a major spectator sport in Arkansas in the 1920s. **Arkansas College**

life and communities judged their schools by the success of their teams, important educational values often were lost. As the Razorbacks started to gain the limelight, success in football hid all other shortcomings. The University got an appropriation in 1925 to erect agriculture and engineering buildings. During the rest of the decade, however, the legislature's concern with higher education consisted of discussing the consolidation of all engineering courses in the state at Arkansas Polytechnic College in Russellville.

RELIGION

The challenge of modernization in the 1920s transformed existing churches and led to a reaction against modernism that further fragmented the religious community.

The Protestant Triumph

One result of progressivism in Arkansas during the 1920s was that protestant Christianity became the unofficial state religion. Denominational growth continued during the decade, producing the erection of new churches and special facilities ranging from orphanages to hospitals. Church colleges were consolidated and strengthened. Standards for church membership and church discipline were relaxed so that more people participated. A 1926 survey showed that more than 75 percent of Arkansas churchgoers were Baptist or Methodist. The Arkansas legislature was more than half Methodist and Baptist and had one Unitarian and one Jew. Both Jews and Catholics were objects of Klan hatred, but neither group was well represented in Arkansas, which had 4,900 Jews and 17,027 Catholics.

Statistics do not reveal the growing cleavage between traditionalists and modernists that marked the decade. The gripping emotionalism of frontier religion declined as the major denominations established schools and became supplied with clergy of higher educational attainments. Many older Arkansans, especially from the rural areas, came to believe that their churches had grown cold. During the 1920s, painter Thomas Hart Benton walked through parts of the White River Valley, where he observed the splintering that

Revival Truck *(photographer and date unknown) The automobile cut into church attendance, but churches fought back. In this picture, a truck has been converted into a miniature church to advertise a revival preached by Dr. Broughton at the First Baptist Church of Fort Smith.* **University of Arkansas**

developed into new sects, then loosely called "holy-rollers." Benton believed that these groups fragmented the unity of Protestantism.

At times, internal religious strife spilled over into the public forum during the decade. Baptists were divided badly about Al Smith's Catholicism. However, they managed to stay united in opposing evolution, supporting Sunday closing (blue) laws and denouncing dancing and drinking. Methodists, led by moderate Bishop Edwin D. Mouzon, refused to make denunciation of Darwin a test of church membership despite efforts by Georgia's arch-conservative Bishop Warren A. Chandler to influence them. Hendrix College was criticized for allow-

ing some very restricted dancing and for relaxing the ban on smoking cigarettes. Caught up in the confusion of the age, Methodists repeated demands for thorough blue laws, strict prohibition and banning from the state of all magazines showing couples dancing. On the other hand, Methodist women called for the establishment and enforcement of child labor laws, better treatment for blacks and improved jail conditions — all typical of the Social Gospel.

The Evolution Debate

The evolution issue that divided Methodists became the most important statewide morality issue of the decade in 1925 when Tennessee, prodded by William Jennings Bryan, enacted a law prohibiting the teaching of evolution in the public schools. The law was challenged in July by biology teacher John T. Scopes in what became known as the Dayton "monkey trial." Clarence Darrow, America's foremost trial lawyer, unsuccessfully led a cadre of Eastern lawyers and scientific experts against the aged Bryan. The stage was set for a similar battle in Arkansas after Scopes was convicted.

Science and religion had skirmished before in Arkansas, but Bryan's crusade galvanized rural opposition to modernism. In 1922, Arkansas doctors heard Ozark physician Thomas Douglass denounce Bryan. "The real menace to Christianity is not Darwinism but orthodoxy," he observed, and Dr. J. T. Clegg added, "the fact of evolution is accepted by all observing and thinking men and women." Douglass called for giving evolution "a square deal" in the schools, but conservatives saw the matter differently. "Shall the Devil Have Our Schools?" the *Baptist Advance* asked as a coalition of fundamentalists organized. Conservative Lutheran Reverend Earl Kretzschmar tied evolution to liberalism, which "wrecked Eden's happiness and perfections; it condemned Jesus to death on the cross . . . [and] it is the source of present day crime waves." A.L. Rotenberry, a Pulaski County legislator, introduced an anti-evolution bill and battle lines were drawn.

The state's moderates led the opposition to the bill. Reverend Hay Watson Smith, pastor of Little Rock's Second Presbyterian Church and the author of *Evolution and Presbyterianism* (1923), found no conflict between science and religion. Some of his parishioners disagreed, and Smith spent ten years in church courts before being acquitted of heresy. Hendrix College President John Hugh Reynolds also joined in the attack, insisting that fundamentalism was "the dead hand of past generations trying to control the bursting life of today." Most other college presidents and

many newspapers also voiced opposition to the proposed law. When the legislature finally rejected it, the *Arkansas Democrat* noted approvingly that, "the province of the legislature is not to settle debates over theology."

But the bill's supporters were not dissuaded. They circulated petitions, and the bill appeared as Initiated Act No. 1 on the ballot in the 1928 general election. Opposition came from educators, including Charles H. Brough, recently a Baptist college president; University of Arkansas President John C. Futrall; medical school Dean D. Frank Vinsonhaler, and *Arkansas Gazette* owner J.N. Heiskell. However, the act passed easily with 63 percent of the vote. The new law was worded vaguely, making it unclear whether just teaching evolution was banned or whether any printed reference to Darwin was legal. J. P. Womack, the state superintendent of public instruction, cautioned that schools might have to remove all dictionaries and encyclopedias, but fundamentalists refused to create a test case. Hostility to science remained, and Missionary Baptist minister Ben N. Bogard charged in 1930 that Hendrix College's erection of a science building was a "premeditated and concerted movement to destroy confidence in the Bible." A second religious victory came in 1930 when state law mandated daily Bible readings in the public schools.

Blue Laws

If fundamentalists won on the evolution issue, they were less successful in saving the sanctity of Sunday. During the 1920s, an informal alliance of Methodists and Baptists railed against Sunday golf, fishing, baseball, tennis, motion pictures, gasoline sales and mixed swimming on any day. It generally was accepted that the man in the moon went to hell for burning brush on Sunday, and no decent housewife would hang her washing on the line on this Holy Day. The children of John W. Booth of Des Arc were not permitted to play card games on Sunday, however, "Author" cards were excepted from the ban as being educational. The Booth children's Sunday was not as strict as that of their first cousins, the Reinhardts, who were not permitted to read the newspaper comic sections on Sunday.

Baptist editor J. S. Compere likened Sunday work and entertainment to an evil spirit destroying civilization. Defending the "Anglo-Saxon type of Sabbath" was largely in the hands of local officials. Arrests for Sunday hunting remained common in many communities, and one Jew was arrested in Jonesboro for cutting his grass on the Christian Sabbath. Governors Terral and Martineau vetoed legislation to permit Sunday baseball in Little Rock. In 1929, however, Governor Parnell signed permissive legislation, and a Little Rock Travelers minor league Sunday game followed.

Fundamentalists and Sects

The overwhelming majority of religiously conservative Arkansans remained in mainline Protestant churches, but some chose to follow inspiring evangelists. Following in the footsteps of Dwight Moody and Billy Sunday, John Brown, a Methodist laymen and Salvation Army veteran, boldly created his own following in Arkansas and California and founded John Brown College in 1920 at Siloam Springs. Brown was one of the first evangelists to use radio, and politically he courted the support of Jesse Jones in Texas and future Governor Carl Bailey in Arkansas. His work-oriented school was created in the manual labor tradition and differed significantly from the liberal arts aspirations of Hendrix College or Ouachita Baptist College.

The unordained Brown had another Arkansas compatriot in Brother A. A. Allen, a native of Sulphur Rock. Born in extreme poverty, Allen moved westward in quest of followers, settling at Miracle Valley, Arizona. Known for his flamboyant style and emphasis on miracles and the apocalypse, Allen attract-

ed a large rural following that grew with the popularization of radio. In contrast to Brown, who sometimes was called the "laughing evangelist," Allen drew on a darker and more somber aspect of the Christian fundamentalist tradition.

The 1920s also gave rise to what many mainline church members saw simply as cults. One that flourished briefly at Gilbert was the Incoming Kingdom Missionary Unit, founded by John A. Battenfield. Dedicated to the defeat of liberalism through the building of self-sufficient rural colonies and cooperative stores, Battenfield prophesied that Roman Catholicism would be destroyed in 1926 and the millenium would begin in 1973, at which time it would be necessary to speak Hebrew. The group published a newspaper and enjoyed some success until 1925, when Battenfield failed to restore a dead man to life after repeated attempts on the decaying corpse. Battenfield suffered a nervous breakdown as a result. The leaderless group scattered, leaving behind a still-standing concrete and creek-stone store in Gilbert.

MEDICINE

The first great steps in public health had been taken during the Progressive era. Little was done during the 1920s to further the movement. The state even attempted to suppress unfavorable statistics about pellagra because the presence of this dietary disease undercut promotional efforts. At Governor McRae's urging, the state finally built a tuberculosis sanitarium for blacks. The justifying argument had nothing to do with blacks' higher incidence of the disease but was based instead on the fear that tubercular black servants might infect whites. When the state received federal assistance in 1920 under the Maternity Act, a state health truck and trained professionals went into the field to educate pregnant women and raise the level of midwife assistance. One of the women so employed, Dr. Frances Sage Bradley,

Midwifery Class *(Frances Sage Bradley, ca. 1922) Assisted by federal funding, Arkansas attempted to reduce infant mortality. A state health truck went into service and professionals conducted training classes for the state's midwives. Midwifery became illegal in Arkansas in 1957, but was recognized by the legislature in 1983 when it said midwifery could be practiced under regulations adopted by the state health department in certain counties where the income of at least 31 1/2 percent of the population is under the government established poverty level. In other areas of the state, including Pulaski County, midwives continue to deliver babies illegally in 1993 and receive no training or official recognition.* **Emory University**

enjoyed a national reputation in the field but encountered such difficulty as both a woman and an "outsider" that she soon left the state.

One thing Arkansas did not lack during the decade was an adequate number of doctors. The *Journal of the American Medical Association* contained an article in February 1920 entitled, "What is the Matter with Arkansas?" The problem, as the *Journal* saw it, was that Arkansas had an abundance of quacks and charlatans. In a national campaign to reduce the number of doctors, the American Medical Association (AMA) used its powers to close weak medical schools and raise standards at surviving ones. The medical school in Arkansas, associated in name but little else with the University, entered the decade with a substandard designation. It survived through the work of its two deans, Morgan Smith and Frank Vinsonhaler, but at one point was accredited for only a two-year course. Heavy lobbying produced increased appropriations from the 1923 and 1925 legislatures.

Rural legislators saw the AMA plan as a threat to the traditional country doctor. Led by doctor-legislator W. H. Abington of Beebe, the rural bloc fought the medical school at almost every turn. Hence the 1928 legislature reluctantly voted $60,000 for the school and approved $30,000 for a Confederate reunion. Only governors' vetoes kept the legislature from granting medical licenses by statute to individuals who failed to meet certification standards. Despite the rural hostility toward the medical school, medicine was still an avenue to success open to poorer students. It was also one requiring some fortitude: in the absence of modern clinical facilities, cadavers were floated in a cement tank and beginning students were required to fish out bodies with

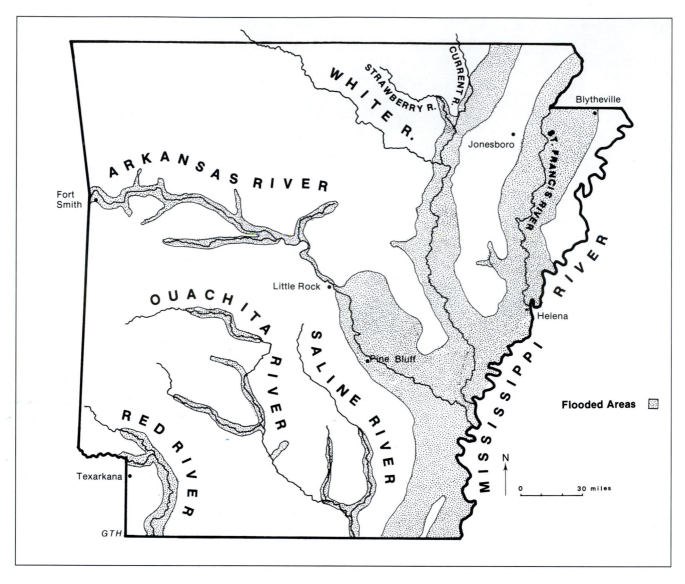

The Flood of 1927. **Gerald T. Hanson**

a hook when needed for classroom work.

The AMA could control the activities of those professing to be regular M.D.s, but it had no power over those from other "schools," of which five were recognized legally in Arkansas. In asking what was wrong in Arkansas, the AMA was demanding a monopoly in delivering medical services. Its main arguments came to focus on the Arkansas careers of John R. Brinkley and Norman Baker.

John R. Brinkley settled in Judsonia in 1914 and soon acquired a degree from a Kansas City diploma mill. He became famous in time for his

goat gland operation on "that troublesome old cocklebur," the prostate gland. His famous sex-restoring operation led him to other careers in several states, and for a time before returning to Arkansas, he operated a high-powered Mexican radio station that mixed medicine and religious fundamentalism. Federal authorities in 1941 finally had him arrested for using the mails for fraud. Part of the embarrassment to Arkansas was that state authorities had done nothing about him over the years.

Norman Baker operated out of Eureka Springs, where he converted the Crescent

The Flood of 1927, Arkansas City
(photographer unknown, 1927) Like
Arkansas City, most of eastern
Arkansas was under water. Other low
lying towns along the rivers were also
hard hit. **Arkansas History**
Commission

Hotel into a cancer clinic offering to cure malignancy with carbonic acid, watermelon seed, corn silk and clover seed. Again federal authorities stepped in to rescue the profession. The Arkansas legislature looked the other way during the 1920s, leaving the issue for later periods.

No class embraced the automobile more eagerly than doctors because it meant they could make more house calls and treat many more patients. Hospitals and clinics became more common as the car also allowed the patient to come to the doctor. Standards slowly improved despite quacks. "Horse and buggy medicine" passed, although some doctors failed to realize the changes in time. Specialists emerged in urban areas, hospitals became increasingly sophisticated, and levels of care for whites improved. Very little of this progress aided blacks, because segregated care was a virtual death warrant for blacks with complex medical needs.

PRECURSOR OF DEPRESSION: THE FLOOD OF 1927

The 1920s began with one natural disaster — the dramatic drop in cotton prices; it ended in another — the Flood of 1927. There

had been no major floods for more than ten years when the 1927 disaster left Arkansas the hardest-hit state in the Mississippi River Valley. More than 6,000 square miles or 13 percent of the state was under water in early 1927. Property losses were placed at $14,936,000 and 127 lives were lost. Miles of railroad track and highway washed away, acres of land were ruined by quantities of sand "boiled up" on it by flood waters; many persons found safety only on the levees or in flight.

In the town of Des Arc, on the high west bank of the White River, farm families from the White and Cache River bottoms refuged for weeks, staying in the homes of town people. Local residents had worked feverishly to sand-bag the levee before it broke, and Nathan Nunley, a black man, was shot dead by local road crew foreman Pearl Drowns, who was directing the crew filling sandbags using Prairie County road equipment. Nunley protested when ordered to work by Drowns, saying that he could not work because he had been sitting up all night with a critically ill wife and was on his way to get the doctor. Delta children, like Emma Jean Booth, a girl of eight during the flood, had life-long nightmares about the tremendous roar of the floodwaters when the levee broke on the east bank of White River and the mildewed stench of the few personal belongings refugees were able to salvage.

The national Red Cross offered some assistance in Arkansas. Officials who saw the depth of Delta poverty left the state greatly alarmed. Commerce Secretary Herbert Hoover, ever-active in crises of this kind, produced an interesting memorandum suggesting that tenant farming should be replaced by small family farms acquired through a resettlement program. That memorandum and the national attention that the flood unwittingly brought contrasted sharply with the "Wonder State" image that the state's leaders sought to promote. The flood's cleanup helped bankrupt many drainage and levee districts and further sabotaged the state's road program.

CONCLUSION

The decade of the 1920s was a time of prosperity and hope for Americans. The "American Way of Life" was defined rigidly and tenaciously sought. Arkansans shared in the go-getter dream but lacked the resources to accomplish it. The hope expressed in 1927 by Governor Martineau that Arkansas was on the verge of "a long deferred industrial awakening" echoed prophecies that had been voiced in vain for fifty years. The reality was the devastation of the 1927 flood, the corruption of the highway program, the divisive issues of modernization and the usual scandal of politics.

It was the prelude to the Great Depression.

BIBLIOGRAPHIC ESSAY

There are no comprehensive secondary studies of the 1920s. Relevant statistics on the period may be found in Howard W. Odum, *Southern Regions of the United States*, (Chapel Hill, 1936); William H. Metzler, *Population Pressures in Upland Areas of Arkansas*,

(Agricultural Experiment Station, 1940); Rupert B. Vance, *Human Geography of the South*, (Chapel Hill, 1935) and Samuel Tilden Bratton, "The Geography of the St. Francis Basin," *UMS*, I (July 1926). Town life has been much neglected for this era, but there is a history of one resort community by Ellen Compton Shipley, "The Pleasures of Prosperity; Bella Vista, Arkansas, 1917-1929," *AHQ*, XXXVII (Summer 1978), 99-129. Oil is treated in a recent account by A. R. and R. B. Buckalew, "The Discovery of Oil in South Arkansas," *AHQ*, XXXIII (Autumn 1974), 195-238, and earlier in Gerald Forbes, "Brief History of the Petroleum Industry in Arkansas," *AHQ*, I (March 1942), 28-40. An interesting memoir is T. O. Rorie, Jr., "Beyond the Oily Gates of the Arkansas Oil Fields," (Prescott, n.d.).

The image problem of Arkansas in the 1920s has received considerable attention, notably in Charles Orson Cook, "Boosterism and Babbittry: Charles Hillman Brough and the Selling of Arkansas," *AHQ*, XXXVII (Spring 1978) 74-83. Contemporary accounts may be found in a file of H. L. Mencken clippings in the University of Arkansas Library; Sherman Rogers, "A Defense of Arkansas," *O*, CXXIX (October 26, 1921), 294-298; William H. Skaggs, *The Southern Oligarchy*, (New York, 1924) and Charles Hillman Brough, *Arkansas, The Commonwealth of Opportunity and Achievement*, (Little Rock, 1930).

Little useful literature is available on the utilities in Arkansas. Aside from a laudatory and undocumented biography of Harvey Couch, Winston P. Wilson, *Harvey Couch: the Master Builder*, (Nashville, 1947), there exists only an unpublished paper, Richard D. Roblee and Mark Schlesinger, " The Changing Influence of AP&L on Arkansas Politics," (UALR Library, 1978), and two articles by Leland DuVall in *Arkansas: Colony and State* (Little Rock, 1973).

Political affairs during the decade can be examined through the addresses delivered by the governors and assembled in one volume at the University of Arkansas. Biographies of these men can be found in Donovan and Gatewood, *The Governors of Arkansas.* Three successive articles by Charles C. Alexander treat the Klan: "White Robed Reformers: The Ku Klux Klan Comes To Arkansas, 1921-1922," *AHQ,* XXII (Spring 1963), 8-23; "White Robes In Politics: The Ku Klux Klan in Arkansas, 1922-1924," *AHQ,* XXII (Autumn 1963), 195-214 and "Defeat, Decline, Disintegration; The Ku Klux Klan in Arkansas, 1924 and After," *AHQ,* XXII (Winter 1963), 311-331. Other political issues are treated in William Foy Lisenby, "Brough, Baptists, and Bombast: The Election of 1928," *AHQ,* XXXII (Summer 1973), 120-131; Nevin E. Neal, "The Smith-Robinson Arkansas Campaign of 1928," *AHQ,* XIX (Spring 1960), 3-11, and in two memoirs, Harry Lee Williams, *Forty Years Behind the Scenes in Arkansas Politics,* (Little Rock, 1949), and Brooks Hays, *Politics Is My Parish,* (Baton Rouge, 1981).

The evolution controversy is discussed in R. Halliburton, Jr., "The Adoption of Arkansas's Anti-Evolution Law," *AHQ,* XXIII (autumn 1964), 271-283, and Cal Ledbetter, Jr., "The Anti-Evolution Law: Church and State in Arkansas," *AHQ,* XXXVIII (Winter 1979), 299-327. Blue laws are the subject of Lee Miller, "Foul Ball: The Religious Response to the Blue Law Controversy in Arkansas in the 1920s," *OHR,* VII (Spring 1979), 31-40.

A scholarly study of Arkansas highways is needed. Part of the story is told in David Rison, "Arkansas During the Great Depression," (Ph.D. diss., University of California, 1974), and financial angles are covered in Lee Reaves, "Highway Bond Refunding in Arkansas," *AHQ,* II (Winter 1943), 316-330.

Education history is covered lightly in Stinnett and Kennan, *All This and Tomorrow Too* and other sources include U. S. Department of Interior, Bureau of Education, *Survey of Negro Colleges and Universities,* (Washington, 1928); *Report of the Arkansas Illiteracy Commission,* (Little Rock, 1920 and 1923), *Pertinent Facts About the Public Schools of Arkansas,"* (N.P., 1932) and Roy Vergil Simpson, "Reminiscences of a Hill Country School Teacher," AHQ, *XXVII (Summer 1968), 146-174.* The role of football is celebrated in Orville Henry and Jim Bailey, *The Razorbacks—A Story of Arkansas Football,* (Huntsville, Ala., 1973). The story of the University was discussed most recently in Robert A. Leflar, *The First 100 Years,* (Fayetteville, 1972).

W. David Baird, *Medical Education in Arkansas, 1879-1978,* (Memphis, 1979), is useful for far more than just the history of the medical school. The story of one quack is found in Albert J. Schneider, "That Troublesome Old Cocklebur: John R. Brinkley and the Medical Profession of Arkansas, 1937-1942," *AHQ,* XXXV (Spring 1976), 27-46.

Some light on religious developments during the era is given in the standard denominational histories. An unusual memoir is A. A. Allen, *Born to Lose, Bound to Live,* (Garden City, 1970). Thomas Hart Benton's reflections are found in *An Artist in America,* (Kansas City, 1951), and the story of the Incoming Kingdom is told in Doris Thompson, "History of an Ozark Utopia," *AHQ,* XIV (Winter 1955), 359-373.

The Flood is studied in Pete Daniels, *Deep-'n As It come,* (New York 1977). Other useful sources include Bruce A. Lohaf, "Herbert Hoover's Mississippi Valley Land Reform Memorandum: A Document," *AHQ,* XXIX (Summer 1970), 112-118; Edythe Simpson Hobson, "Twenty-seven Days on the Levee— 1927," *AHQ,* XXXIX (Autumn 1980), 210-229, and T. H. "Buck" Pryor, "The Flood of 1927," *CrCHQ,* XVII (Winter 1979) 3-11.

Abandoned House Near Russellville (*J. B. Priddy, ca., 1937*) *The ups and downs of farming are told in this picture. On the right, in front of the frame house, stands a log cabin. Doubtless once a family dwelling, it probably became a detached kitchen after the big house was built. The owners fell on hard times and the place was abandoned by the late 1930s.* **University of Central Arkansas**

The Great Depression

INTRODUCTION

The American stock market collapsed on October 29, 1929, "Black Tuesday." The crash that supposedly could never happen if businessmen ran the economy became the greatest economic disaster in American history. A ripple effect went throughout the land from the nation's nerve center on Wall Street. Banks and insurance companies too intimately involved in speculative finance were the first to suffer. From there the effects reached the corporations whose over-priced stocks had been objects of investment. When the catastrophe eventually reached the plants, workers lost their jobs. Some layoffs produced others, and the ripple became a tidal wave, engulfing the country and finally reaching down into the hamlets of Arkansas.

The absence of rain in 1930 was of far more immediate significance for the average Arkansan than the rumblings from Wall Street. After the terrible flood of 1927, nature prepared the people for the Depression by inflicting on them the state's worst drought to that time. Only when the price of cotton fell below the cost of production in 1931 did the reality of the Depression sink in for Arkansans.

State government proved to be next to useless in the crisis. Federal assistance, which alone saved Arkansas, brought the average person into daily contact with the national government for the first time. The results of these encounters profoundly altered the scope and function of government, changed farming patterns and set forces in motion that dealt fatal blows to many cherished traditional values.

The decade also saw the American discovery of Arkansas, both in regard to the cultural uniqueness of the Ozark mountaineer and the poverty of the Delta. The ease of communication and the simplicity of reaching Memphis from Washington or New York and then crossing the Harahan toll bridge (shared with trains) into the Arkansas Delta allowed outsiders access to the sharecropper's world that lay only minutes from downtown Memphis. The Eastern press covered Socialist Norman Thomas's visits to Arkansas in the 1930s and exposed the anatomy of the more grisly parts of the state's agriculture to the nation.

If outsiders could look in, insiders could look out. The goal of every youth during the 1920s was to own a car. Detroit's ability to turn out inexpensive cars and the local mechanic's ability to keep them running propelled Arkansas into the Automobile Age. Radio also began to tie Arkansas lives into the national mold. Rural radios were still expensive and battery-operated, but even the presence of one or two in a community was enough to make an impact, because neighbors gathered from miles around to hear their favorite programs, the World Series, or President Franklin Delano Roosevelt's fireside chats telling how their government was on the side of the common people.

More than any decade before or since, the 1930s was recorded on film by government photographers. Words alone do little justice to the faces of the people, whose hopeless, defeated, gaunt and pathetic expressions stared out from a bleak landscape of ramshackle cabins and crossroad stores. Along with the defeated, however, were the faces of the angry, the rebellious and the determined. The old order began to crumble in Arkansas during the Depression, and after the War that followed, things would never be the same.

THE DROUGHT OF 1930

Before Arkansans could feel the worst effects of a man-made disaster, they had to survive a punishment inflicted by nature. The Drought of 1930 was part of a long-term problem that produced the dust bowl conditions farther west that John Steinbeck made famous in *The Grapes of Wrath* published in 1939. During June and July, when cotton desperately needed water, Arkansas recorded its lowest rainfall on record, and in August, temperatures regularly soared over 100 degrees. Already faced with bank closings, falling markets and a psychology of depression, Arkansas farmers could do nothing but watch as their cotton and their home gardens burned up. Arkansas in 1930 produced only 60 percent as much cotton as it had in 1929, and farm income fell by 62 percent. The result of these conditions was a nationwide focus on hunger in Arkansas and the active intervention of the Red Cross. During the winter of 1930-1931, a third of the people subsisted on wild game, particularly "Hoover Hogs" (rabbit) and squirrel, herbs, roots, nuts and the ever-popular turnip sandwich: "three slices of turnips and put one in the middle." A 70 percent decline in corn yields meant that farm animals were in no better shape than humans.

The fight against hunger began locally. Will Rogers, the cowboy humorist, took in contributions of $39,000 for relief, but private charity was stretched to the limit by January 1931. The suffering was intense in some counties. Ninety-six percent of the population in Chicot County, or virtually all the sharecropper families, was dependent on free food.

The breaking point came in the small Lonoke County town of England during January 1931 when Red Cross officials ran out of forms. A group of irate farmers marched on the town, their organizer saying: "Now then, when we gets to town, we'll ask for food quiet-like, and if they don't give it to us, we'll take it, also quiet-like."

Rather than face a riot, local merchants gave in to the mob, hoping to be reimbursed later. Perhaps because England was close to Little Rock, the "riot" attracted national press attention, but the scene was enacted throughout eastern Arkansas in dozens of communities.

Starvation in Arkansas touched off an angry national debate about disaster relief. Red Cross aid hardly met standards of nutrition. Half the population of St. Francis County was fed (after a fashion) for $1 a person a month. The Red Cross fed Arkansans only meal, flour and beans, and even that was delivered inefficiently or sporadically. When the Red Cross became unable to continue feeding so many people, the question of federal assistance was debated seriously in Congress. President Herbert Hoover, the great humanitarian noted for his relief work during World War I, did not approve of feeding people with government money, although he agreed to provide federal funds to feed the farmers' livestock. Hardly a radical, Arkansas's senior Senator Joe T. Robinson found this policy ridiculous, and summed it up this way: "It is alright to put a mule on the dole but it is condemned, I see, to put a man on parity with a mule."

Hoover's insensitivity to human need as dramatized in the food crisis foreshadowed his reaction to unemployment and convinced millions of Americans that their president was concerned only with corporate suffering and not about people, so that the Depression became the "Hoover Depression," forever identified with his name.

The rains returned and crops grew the next year, but the drought had left a searing experience on many lives, demonstrating that Arkansas had to look beyond its own borders for help in an emergency.

THE DEPRESSION COMES TO ARKANSAS

The rhetoric of progress was louder than its results in Arkansas during the 1920s. In fact, the decade was one of decline because the most accessible raw materials already had been removed from the state. Diversification was retarded because Arkansas lacked the capital necessary to finance industry. Banks, the usual agent for such developments, were abundant, but they were local, lacked significant assets and were tied largely to the rural economy. As the 1920s were not a time of boundless prosperity in Arkansas, it was not surprising that bank failures were common before 1929.

The pace accelerated greatly when the drought of 1930 undermined local agriculture. 204 banks closed their doors before the Bank Holiday of 1933. The largest was the American Exchange Trust Company in Little Rock, part of a holding company put together by financier and highway bond profiteer A.B. Banks. After Banks became involved in a failing interstate bankers's syndicate, depositors withdrew more than $5,500,000 in a run on his main bank office in Little Rock before it closed on November 17, 1930. Its fall brought down sixty-six other banks around the state that Banks had acquired and drained of their assets.

The collapse of a local bank was preceded in many communities by favored individuals quietly withdrawing their money. W. H. Stewart of Des Arc frequently retold the story of how he withdrew his money from a Hazen bank one morning after observing the light on in the bank late one night. He reasoned that no one would be working that late if the books were in balance. Not wanting to start a run on the bank, he wrote checks to his employees for the balance in his account and the checks were honored before the bank closed.

Not everyone was so fortunate. A robbery closed the bank in one community, although local residents were unsure just who the robbers were. In one typical instance, a man who went duck hunting returned home to find all his savings and checking accounts lost and the $41 in his wallet the only ready money he had left.

Schools were the hardest hit by these closings. Unpaid school warrants amounted to $5,000,000 by May 1931, and by February 1932, school debt had risen to $32,000,000. Many communities closed or sharply curtailed their school year. A 40 percent drop in financing occurred between 1929 and 1933; 92 percent of the school districts failed to hold full terms, and more than a third of the teachers were not paid in cash. Teachers' salaries, which even before the crash were the lowest in the nation, fell from an average of $595 a year to $489 by 1934.

As credit and money disappeared, the entire land-owning class was threatened with bankruptcy. "I have made every effort to save my 80-acre farm which will be certified to the state (for failure to pay real estate taxes)," a small farmer explained, "unless I can raise $28.34 for taxes." But big money like that simply could not be had. Taxes were delinquent or forfeited by 1933 on 10,151,147 acres, a third of the state's total land. Small and large farmers alike were threatened because the price of cotton showed no signs of stopping its fall. The perils of a one-crop economy, a theme reiterated in county newspapers, became a haunting reality in the first years of the Depression and spurred a revival of political radicalism.

The Revival of the Radical Tradition

Radical political thought had never been without adherents in Arkansas during the nineteenth century. Jacksonian Democrats, Greenbackers, Populists and Socialists had appeared in the years before World War I. This tradition of protest virtually had disappeared during the boosterism of the 1920s.

The Depression changed that, making the 1930s a time for the expression of unconventional thoughts.

One revolt against the standard orthodoxy of "business progressivism" came from a Nashville, Tennessee, group called the Southern Agrarians. Their 1930 symposium, *I'll Take My Stand,* denounced the kind of modernizing activities typified in Arkansas by the Parnell administration. One contributor to the book was Arkansas imagist poet John Gould Fletcher. The Agrarians helped fuel a new pride in Southern distinctiveness by looking backward to a largely imaginary, golden, romantic past of paternalism, fundamentalism and self-sufficient agriculture. Little of what they wrote was relevant to Arkansans in acute economic distress.

An entirely different point of view came to Arkansas through the activities of Commonwealth College. Begun as the Llano Cooperative in California, it moved to Louisiana before locating near Mena in 1924 and founding a labor school calling itself Commonwealth College. Offering no degrees, the school was supported by the student workers, usually about forty-five in number. The group was torn from the start by dissension about both means and ends and relied heavily on outside contributions to stay alive.

Commonwealth's reputation in Mena was not favorable. Residents objected to students wearing knickers and reported mixed swimming parties. But the Depression gave the school a statewide forum. Commonwealth people were active in reorganizing a state Socialist Party in 1931; they labored in 1932 for the National Farmer's Holiday Association, one of the more radical Midwestern farm groups. As Mena was not far from the western Arkansas coal fields, long an area of violent labor unrest, Commonwealth reached out to workers with a proletarian play, *What Price Coal?* and presented *Can You Hear Their Voices?,* a play based on a pamphlet by Whittaker Chambers (later a famous anti-Communist) subtitled *The Arkansas Farmers Fight for Food*. Commonwealth President Lucien Koch declared the sharecropper to be "unequivocally the most exploited worker in America," a pronouncement that led to his arrest in Lepanto and a legislative investigation of the school.

The Agrarians and Commonwealth College demonstrated that radicalism still could attract attention in Arkansas, but neither group had the power to do anything about the worsening conditions. For the first two years of the Depression, the people had little choice but to watch the death throes of the administration of Governor Parnell and his bankrupting road plan.

The Politics of Collapse

As Socialist agitation was reappearing in Arkansas, Governor Harvey Parnell espoused self-help and hard work as cures for the Depression. "This," said the governor in his second inaugural speech, "is not the time to try out fantastic schemes nor visionary panaceas for all our ills."

With every available cent committed to ballooning bond issues, state government had no funds to carry out any idea Parnell might have had. Even so, a few measures were passed. A mortgage foreclosure law provided landowners an extra three months to make payment, and the Agricultural Credit Board made emergency loans secured by crop liens. The legislature also enacted cotton acreage reduction legislation to reduce the land planted in cotton by 30 percent. The product of a special session in which legislators served without pay, this bill was similar to those of several other states but failed to go into effect because all cotton states would not agree.

What aid the state gave in the drought crisis came from additional borrowing, as did the money that went into the sagging public school system. When Harvey Parnell left office, his "business progressivism" stood condemned in

the public eye. His controversial handling of state banking liquidations and his pardoning of convicted defrauder A.B. Banks left his formerly all-powerful machine in ruins.

There was little doubt Arkansans would support the Democratic presidential nominee, Franklin D. Roosevelt, against the hated Republican President Herbert Hoover in the election of 1932. On the state level, two races offered voters significant choices. Because the tarnished Parnell machine left no successor, twelve candidates initially announced for governor. By the end, the race was between former Governor Tom Terral, former State Comptroller Howard Reed, former Highway Commissioner Dwight Blackwood and Chancery Judge Julius Marion Futrell. Of the four, Futrell was the most conservative, promising to cut state expenses by 50 percent. His election to office was a clear victory in Arkansas for the same kind of fiscal conservative that voters had repudiated when they rejected Hoover for Roosevelt.

That the people of Arkansas could be of more than one mind on these matters was demonstrated by the result of the 1932 Senate race. Junior United States Senator Thaddeus H. Caraway died unexpectedly on November 6, 1931. Every politician in the state hungered for the office, but Governor Parnell appointed the late senator's widow, Hattie, to fill the office until a special election could be held in January. At the January election, Mrs. Caraway ran as a candidate for the eleven months remaining in the term. She received only token opposition in an election that was notable because the state had no money to pay election expenses, and the officials, mostly women, were volunteers. This marked the first appearance of women in significant numbers in the political process and was followed within the year by the Arkansas Women's Democratic Club demanding equal patronage and representation on county committees.

Once in office, Mrs. Caraway showed a marked reluctance to retire. She entered her

Hattie Caraway with Huey Long's Sound Truck (*photographer unknown, 1932*) *This was apparently the first sound truck in the state and it became a major attention getter for Huey Long and Mrs. Caraway.* **World Wide Photo**

name as a candidate for the full term on the last day before the filing deadline. Arrayed against her were some impressive figures: O.L. Bodenhamer, an El Dorado businessman and former National Commander of the American Legion; Charles H. Brough, ex-governor and publicist; William Hutton, Pulaski County sheriff and football star; William F. Kirby, an associate justice on the state Supreme Court and a former United States senator; Vincent Miles, for seventeen years the state Democratic national committeeman and Melbourne Martin, a well-financed lawyer.

Mrs. Caraway was given only an outside chance to win until Senator Huey Long, who sat next to her in the Senate, announced he was coming from Louisiana to aid her campaign. The whirlwind Long, full of his share-the-wealth schemes, head of the most powerful state political machine in the nation and a magnetic campaigner in the Jeff Davis style, expressed a chivalric desire "to pull a lot of potbellied politicians off a little woman's neck." Roaring into Arkansas with the first sound trucks the state had ever heard, Long and Caraway attracted huge crowds to hear a message that differed markedly from the message of fiscal restraint and budget cutting that Governor Futrell was delivering. Hattie Caraway was victorious with 44.7 percent of the vote and became the first woman in America elected to a full Senate term. She carried not only the counties where Huey helped but many others as well.

The 1932 presidential campaign was the last race for William H. "Coin" Harvey, the octogenarian candidate of the Liberty Party, who still believed that the answer to everything was free and unrestricted coinage of silver. Harvey, who lived at Monte Ne in Benton County, had constructed a partially completed pyramid to save a few relics of civilization from the collapse he believed inevitable. His pyramid is now beneath the waters of Beaver Lake.

Hattie Caraway returned to Washington, Franklin D. Roosevelt moved into the White House and J.M. Futrell became governor in Little Rock. Of the three, Futrell had the hardest time. The sixty-two-year-old conservative said in his inaugural address that discounting state warrants was no longer a problem—no one would even take them. Highways were in bad repair, drainage districts bonds were in default, and between the unpaid warrants and the arrears on the highway bonds, the state was short by more than $2,000,000. Futrell was the most avowed enemy of education among all Arkansas governors. Attacking a lack of thoroughness in the schools, he complained that many students "do not spell well, and know little about punctuation." It was his view that state aid to high schools should be stopped completely.

Although pledged to reduce state expenses and trim the number of state employees, the governor found himself besieged by job seekers. An estimated 30,000 persons applied for state positions, hounding Futrell day and night in his office, at his meals, by telephone and even in his automobile. After three months and no letup, Futrell was ready to resign. Critics charged that Futrell favored Greene County residents for jobs and questioned whether the state's interest was served when the professional administrator at the State Hospital was replaced by an "inexperienced country doctor" after the entire hospital board was fired. Another victim was Dr. C. W. Garrison, the active and efficient state health officer since 1913. The conservative Futrell replaced him with Dr. W. E. Grayson, a former railroad surgeon, who was philosophically opposed to public immunization programs. Thus while Roosevelt began the New Deal with the One Hundred Days of new ideas, programs and legislation, Futrell was engaged only in petty patronage programs.

If unable and unwilling to fight the Depression, the governor and the legislature were serious about reducing state expenses. Appropriations were actually cut by 51.6 percent, and various measures were instituted to prevent deficit financing in the future, including the establishment of a new sinking fund, the abolition of deficiency proclamations, and Constitutional Amendments 19 and 20 to make over-spending more difficult in the future. None of these addressed the real problems of unemployment, deflation, foreclosure and unrest.

The Federal Government Fights the Depression

Federal intervention in the nation's economic problems began immediately during the first One Hundred Days after Franklin Roosevelt's inaugural. His assurance that "the only thing we have to fear is fear itself" and his message of hope in his fireside chats earned him an immediate place in the nation's heart.

President Roosevelt's first positive action was the closing of the nation's banks in order to avert a total banking collapse in New York City. The move really was not needed in Arkansas, where most of the banks already had failed, and those that had not had little to lose. One remote Ozark bank at Franklin actually missed the beginning of the Bank Holiday because of its geographic isolation.

The first New Deal legislation was the National Recovery Administration (NRA) for American industry and commerce. It was designed to establish codes for labor and management in order to increase the number of workers and end the deflationary spiral of wage and price cuts. Participating stores displayed a blue eagle with the slogan "We Do Our Part." Some 15,000 to 25,000 persons marched in Little Rock as bands played,

"Happy Days Are Here Again" on NRA Day, September 28, 1933. The NRA turned into such an administrative nightmare that even the Roosevelt administration was happy when the United States Supreme Court finally declared the act unconstitutional.

The NRA provided some initial hope in manufacturing, but jobs and food were more important to most Arkansans. The plan from Washington called for each state to set up an administrative system for relief and for Washington to supply the money. Aubrey Williams, a social worker from Alabama responsible for setting up federal relief programs in the South, found Arkansas intractable. Governor Futrell and the legislature opposed the introduction into Arkansas of "foreigners," a term that meant anyone from outside the state. They even tried to purge the faculty at the University of all such persons.

In addition, Futrell was determined to control all federal patronage appointments in Arkansas. As Arkansas had few trained social workers, virtually no one could be found to meet both Futrell's and Williams's standards. After bitter controversy, William R. Dyess, a Mississippi County planter and contractor and a political friend of Futrell's, became the first head of the Federal Emergency Relief Administration (FERA) and continued with its successor, the Works Progress Administration (WPA). In addition to these agencies, others active in Arkansas included the Public Works Administration (PWA), which employed skilled workers on major construction projects, notably streets and post offices; the Civilian Conservation Corps (CCC), which used unemployed youth, largely in forest conservation work, and the Civil Works Administration (CWA), which did "make work" jobs.

Confusing terminology and overlapping areas of interest undermined the main goal of feeding and funding work for needy people. One agency, the Federal Surplus Relief Corporation (FSRC), was set up to distribute the huge farm surpluses to those in need. The idea of feeding people with no strings attached threatened the entire economy of plantation agriculture. However, some planters were able to dictate the terms of relief because a large degree of local control existed over food distribution and hiring for public works. Relief of $1.50 a month was "a travesty on the term" in the words of one federal investigator.

Despite ineffective administration, the government did unload surpluses on Arkansas families and helped change the Arkansas diet in the process. One notable example was citrus fruit. One Ozark woman complained that she never wanted to see another grapefruit; she had boiled them, baked them and fried them, but still could not get her children to eat them. Some Izard County families used them for softballs.

The FSRC also was responsible for starting the hot lunch program in the schools in 1936 and introduced the first use of food stamps in 1939. Many people were highly critical of the waste that often accompanied these programs. One example was the distribution of top-of-the-line suits to hill farmers who needed overalls. Jokes about the inefficiency of government projects were legion.

Food and make-work were only short term in their effects. The better-funded and more ambitious programs sought to achieve the rebuilding of the American economy by stimulating jobs in the private sector. It took time for these programs to take effect in a poor state like Arkansas with a largely unskilled labor force. William Dyess, the virtual czar of federal programs, had some 15 percent of the families in the state on relief rolls by September 1933. One social betterment project connected with relief was the dissemination of canning instructions for farm women. A majority of women in Arkansas probably canned food for the first time during the Depression.

As the federal government was pouring in millions of dollars in relief, state government was cutting back. Futrell insisted on patron-

Governor Futrell with the Arkansas State Rangers *(photographer unknown, 1935) Governor Futrell, front left, poses here with three board members and the entire Arkansas Ranger force, eleven uniformed patrolmen; J. E. Scroggin, immediately above Governor Futrell, who set up the state's fingerprint files; and one civilian employee, Leon Gershner, on the extreme left, who joined the force in 1948. The name "Rangers" was changed to Arkansas State Police Department in 1937.* **University of Central Arkansas**

age control but offered nothing in the way of state aid. One reason for the policy was that Arkansas had defaulted on its debt. In passing the highway bonds, the state promised to keep revenues at $7,500,000 a year — enough to cover the legal obligations. But the legislature let the bonds default in its 1933 orgy of reaction. The Ellis Refunding Act, which converted the direct obligation bonds into unguaranteed bonds, was challenged immediately in the courts. A three-man federal court, which included the not exactly disinterested Judge Martineau, a former governor, eventually ruled against the state. The

legislature and bondholders agreed in 1934 to extend the maturity date of the bonds, but with no change in the rate of interest. Thus the matter was passed for the moment.

The legislature found little time and no money for anything else. It seemed to officials in Washington, notably to Dyess's boss Harry Hopkins, that Arkansas was turning over legitimate state responsibilities to the federal government. Nowhere was this more apparent than in the area of education.

Education historically was a state and local matter. It became a federal concern in Arkansas during the Depression. With school

***President Franklin Delano Roosevelt at the
Arkansas Centennial*** *(photographer unknown, 1936)
The presidential party arrived by rail at Hot Springs.
Roosevelt is second from the left.* **Shiloh Museum**

district debt in February 1932 standing at
$32,000,000, Arkansas education almost
stopped. The FERA put teachers on the relief
rolls, thus saving the school districts from the
necessity of paying salaries. The FERA had
spent $696,077 to subsidize education by the
end of the 1933-1934 school year.

The reaction of state officials to this federal
aid was to cut state support of education even
more. A law passed in the spring of 1934
allowed property owners to redeem tax-forfeit-
ed land with three years delinquency by paying just one year's taxes. Federal displeasure
took the form of an order from Harry Hopkins
to stop aid to education the following year.
Senator Caraway protested that innocent children would be the victims of this move. As conditions in Arkansas worsened in the 1935
school year, the FERA spent more than
$1,000,000 on 4,000 teachers and added jani-
tors and bus drivers to the payrolls. Again,
Arkansas was perfectly willing to let the federal government carry these expenses, and no
move to resume state aid took place.

The state also failed to make any provision
for the aged, the sick and the blind. The 1931
legislature had passed the first pension law,

but the courts found it was financed unconstitutionally. After a proposed initiated act was
taken off the ballot by a divided court for
defective wording, Harry Hopkins renewed
his demand that the state assume at least
some of its lawful duties. In token compliance,
the 1935 legislature created a Department of
Public Welfare and established old-age pen-
sions without voting any funds. Hopkins considered the state's fair share to be $1,500,000
but almost nothing was forthcoming.

Enraged, Hopkins stopped all federal relief
in March, pulling the plug on 400,000 persons. Futrell called the legislature back into
session, warning that "unless hungry mouths
are fed, angry mobs will be running loose in
this state. We are sitting on a powder keg
right now." In response, the state legalized
and taxed hard liquor. Sale of wine and beer
had been allowed previously. Churches rallied
to oppose the move, and Governor Futrell
supported a convict corn-plan under which
the prison system would become a distillery.
Conventional legalization of hard liquor prevailed in the end. Dog races became legal at
West Memphis, and horse races returned to
Hot Springs. The state taxed betting proceeds
on both. Finally, the legislature passed a
"temporary" 2 percent sales tax. The sales tax
law apparently was poorly written and
brought several lawsuits. The Pulaski County
chancellor declared it unconstitutional, but
the state Supreme Court sustained it in June.
A continuing controversy over the law's interpretation occupied Arkansas throughout the
rest of 1935, but federal funds returned and
the crisis passed.

New ideas about relief in Washington
brought changes in Arkansas. The FERA was
replaced with the WPA, which tied the giving
of aid to work programs. Those not eligible to
work were to be supported by the state.
Because of the delay in establishing a state
public welfare system and then in financing it
adequately, the Arkansas levels of aid to the
blind, aged, handicapped and other unemploy-

ables were the lowest in the nation. Meanwhile, Arkansas's poverty prompted more federal aid to help school districts get through the 1935-1936 school year. This time the amount was $411,589, or less than half of the previous year's aid.

WPA projects in Arkansas helped build courthouses, post offices and other civic improvements. Most of these projects would not have been built without federal money. As workers helped build a new tomorrow, the young labored in CCC camps planting trees, artists painted murals and women learned canning. Family life stabilized, crop prices edged upwards and a new spirit could be found. The worst was over by the time Arkansas celebrated the centennial of statehood in 1936 with a visit from President Roosevelt. But the antagonisms that had been buried by the magnitude of the crisis could now blossom. The last half of the 1930s saw a renewed bitterness in politics and a major debate about the nature of the agricultural system.

Politics and the New Deal

The crisis of economic collapse had various political ramifications. Because Arkansas always voted Democratic, New Deal programs were not used for the partisan purposes sometimes employed in two-party states. Battles were fought instead over control of the patronage system. When the New Deal came into existence, federal patronage was dictated largely by Governor Futrell and Senator Joe T. Robinson, neither of whom had much sympathy for reformers.

One man who came to symbolize the simmering reform movement in Arkansas was Brooks Hays, the state's Cassandra on the highway construction fiasco. The Fifth Congressional seat, which included Little Rock, became vacant in 1933 through the elevation of former Klansman Heartsill Ragon to the federal bench. Governor Futrell tried to get

★ Read The Facts! ★   ★ Know The Truth! ★

Carl Bailey and the People— United In Their Stand Against the Statehouse Gang and Their Midget Mussolinis!

Elect CARL BAILEY Your Governor

Carl Bailey Political Advertisement (ca., 1936) *Fascism was becoming increasingly unpopular in the United States, and Carl Bailey tried to capitalize on it in his gubernatorial campaign.* **Author's Collection**

the Democratic State Committee to appoint his friend, Sam Rorex, to fill the vacancy, but Hays and other reformers forced a primary election. Rorex was opposed by Hays and David D. Terry in a race that was perhaps the most dishonest congressional contest of the century in Arkansas.

As Hays began to take a commanding lead on election day, machine bosses decided that Rorex could not be elected and so began shifting votes to Terry. One veteran courthouse warrior exclaimed, "I've been stealing votes from Brooks all night and giving them to Sam, and now I've got to take them from Sam and give them to Dave." As a result of these manipulations, Hays failed to poll a majority and had to face Terry in a runoff. Machine politicians spared nothing, so the official vote showed 9,776 for Terry to 9,151 for Hays. Yell County was an example of how these figures were obtained: With 1,651 registered voters there, 2,454 "persons" voted, and Terry "carried" the county. In Mountain Township, with fifteen voters, Terry got 122 votes. Hays had recourse to the state courts, but machine control made his pleas futile. As was usually the case in Arkansas politics, personality and alliances were more important than issues. Loyalty to the New Deal was not the issue, because as one historian observed, "If Hays had been elected, he could not have given the President more support."

The entrenched order succeeded in defeating Hays, but it had less luck with another maverick Democrat, Carl Bailey. Born in poverty in Missouri, young Bailey read law and then practiced in Trumann and Augusta before settling in Little Rock. Elected prosecuting attorney, he rose to statewide prominence with his prosecution of the bankrupt Arkansas banking king, A.B. Banks, the kingpin of the Parnell administration, who was defended by no less than Senator Joe T. Robinson himself. Bailey supported Brooks Hays in 1933 and defeated incumbent Attorney General Hal Norwood in 1934.

Bailey proved in office to be a thorn in the side of the Futrell administration. His fame was enhanced in 1936 when he turned down a $50,000 bribe to frustrate the extradition of racketeer Lucky Luciano from Hot Springs to New York. Meanwhile, the Futrell administration worked to change the Arkansas Constitution in 1936 by having Arkansas adopt a four-year term for state officials. Most political observers felt the idea was good in principle, but its timing plainly revealed a desire to perpetuate the power of political incumbents. The *Arkansas Gazette* labeled it the "Grab Amendment" and pronounced Arkansas politics a disgrace, a "reversion to those flagrant practices

of the darkest days of the state's life." Calling for "rehabilitation and redemption," the *Gazette* triumphed when voters rejected the amendment by a two-to-one margin.

The Futrell machine collapsed in the 1936 Democratic primary. Carl Bailey was the announced anti-administration candidate for governor, but the machine was unable to agree on a candidate in time to be effective. By the time it decided on Secretary of State Ed McDonald and armed him with a slush fund skimmed from the salaries of state employees, it was too late. Bailey not only made the expected attacks on machine malpractices but even promised aid for the largely disfranchised sharecroppers. As Bailey explained later to visiting North Carolina journalist Jonathan Daniels:

> A few years — even a few months ago — it would have been politically suicidal for a state official to talk out loud about the tenant problem. State officials were supposed to be devoted to proving that everything was beautiful and everybody was happy. We were supposed to meet every effort to identify bad conditions and to inaugurate plans to correct them with a blast of demagoguery.

At least some voters responded to his realism, and Bailey won with 31.9 percent of the votes because the law requiring runoffs had been repealed.

Bailey promised an active administration. Futrell's retiring remarks consisted of warnings about spending too much, but Bailey called for action on farm tenancy, rural electrification, prison reform, free textbooks for students and the establishment of a civil service program for state employees. Bailey also saw that the Depression crisis had forced the state into an unfavorable settlement on highway debts. Refunding the debt and beginning new construction were administration priorities.

Bailey also was interested in advancing his own political fortunes. The moment for doing so came unexpectedly in July 1937 when Senator Robinson, triumphantly reelected only the year before, died in Washington. As Senate majority leader, Robinson had been responsible since 1933 for guiding the passage of New Deal legislation. Unquestionably the most powerful man in the Senate, he managed patronage in Arkansas as well. His last service for President Roosevelt had been as quarterback for the "court-packing" scheme to reverse the pronounced tendency of the Old Guard Republican majority on the United States Supreme Court to declare major pieces of New Deal legislation unconstitutional. Robinson's supposed reward for this was to have been his appointment to the bench. His death instead changed the whole Arkansas political situation. New alliances were forming even as Robinson was being buried. One historian noted that, "Arkansas had seen nothing like it since Jeff Davis's death in 1913 enabled Robinson to gain election to the Senate."

Bailey wanted to do what Robinson had done in 1913 — go directly to the Senate. Perhaps doubtful of his popularity, he chose to try to gain the seat by manipulation. First, he refused to make an interim appointment. When Mrs. Robinson was suggested, he replied that one widow in the Senate from Arkansas was enough. Therefore, Arkansas had only one senator from July until November. Then Bailey persuaded the State Democratic Committee not to hold a primary but to certify him as the Democratic nominee in the November election. The governor's position was less than consistent because he had opposed the same tactic by the Futrell machine.

Much of Robinson's political power fell into the hands of one of his trusted local lieutenants, Homer Adkins. The former Klan-supported sheriff of Pulaski County had become the Collector of Internal Revenue in 1933, and

he worked closely with both Robinson and Futrell as the head of the "federal faction." But with Futrell's retirement and Robinson's death, Adkins now came into his own. Above all, Adkins abhorred the Hays-Bailey wing of the Party. Having masterminded the defeat of Brooks Hays in 1933, Adkins proposed to thwart Bailey in 1937.

Several prominent Democrats were canvassed, including Congressman John McClellan, but John E. Miller of Searcy eventually agreed to make the race against Bailey in the general election as an Independent, allegedly for a promised $20,000. Miller got the endorsement of Mrs. Robinson, all but one of the incumbent congressmen, and Senator Caraway. Appealing to the voters to save Arkansas's unborn generations from dictatorship, Miller ran as if he were a Democrat. Bailey pictured himself as the friend of the New Deal, kept the support of Brooks Hays, and attacked the motives of his opponent. With Adkins using his immense patronage network, Bailey was defeated easily. Miller, a mere cipher as United States senator, resigned in 1941 to take a federal judgeship and had a long career as an able jurist. Adkins continued as the most powerful man in Arkansas by working through Senator Caraway. When Congressman John McClellan challenged Caraway in 1938 with the claim that "Arkansas needs another man in the Senate," Adkins rallied his forces again and returned Caraway to Washington. She had been Huey Long's "little widder" six years before; now she became President Roosevelt's "my old friend."

Bailey had not given up the governorship to make the Senate race, and a chastened Bailey returned to state problems after his defeat. One important victory was obtaining money to buy the remaining toll bridges in Arkansas, thus making the state eligible for federal highway funds. This objective was not accomplished easily. The case of the toll bridge over Black River at Powhatan involved extensive legal maneuvering and the establishment of a competing free ferry to force the bridge company to surrender its franchise. Bailey sought a second term in 1938. While Adkins was occupied with electing Caraway, Bailey was able to defeat former Pulaski County Judge R. A. Cook in the Democratic primary with more than 51 percent of the vote.

Bailey's second term was marked by continued sparring between state and federal factions. Bailey tried to make things uncomfortable for Adkins, and Adkins was maneuvering behind the scenes to do Bailey in. The governor's attempt to refinance the state highway debt lay at the center of state affairs. Two different refunding measures were thwarted by court action, so the victory Bailey wanted to carry him to a third term was illusory.

The kingmaker decided to become king when Bailey announced for a third term in 1940. Adkins resigned his federal position and ran against Bailey. In a campaign fought primarily over the evils of third terms and who best could refund the state debt, Adkins won by 30,000 votes. As an example of how federal officials could be helpful, two top state officials were indicted during the heat of the campaign for conspiring to evade state and federal liquor laws. Their subsequent acquittals probably came too late to help Bailey. Thus the New Deal in Washington helped overthrow a candidate in Arkansas who stood the closest to it ideologically during the Depression. Arkansas ended the decade as it began — in the hands of conservatives.

Arkansas and the Farm Crisis

Industrial workers in America expected unemployment. The Depression was unusual only in the depth and length of the layoffs. On the other hand, farming was a way of life, whether for family farmer, plantation landlord or tenant. The impact of the Depression on farming in Arkansas was to bring about changes that destroyed a way of life that had been the center of the American dream. These changes brought farmers out all over the country with their pitchforks, dumping milk in Wisconsin and vegetables in New Jersey and abandoning eroded or drought-ruined land everywhere.

The nature of the response to the Depression for Arkansas farmers varied with the kind of farming they did. Seventy-four percent of the state's farms were classified as cotton farms, averaging twenty-eight to thirty-seven acres a farm and producing an income of $134 to $260 a year. Only 10 percent were general or mixed, averaging eighty-six to 144 acres with an income of $834 to $973. The "self-sufficing" farmers now accounted for only 7.5 percent. Fruit farms (1.4 percent) and dairy-cattle farms (1.1 percent) were negligible.

Ozark farmers began the decade raising cotton as a minor cash crop. Their practice of plowing in straight lines up one hill and down the next was ruinous to the soil, but expert advice on contour plowing given by county extension agents rarely was followed by these opinionated, independent yeomen.

An estimated 16,000,000 acres of land was farmed in 1940, but 20,000,000 acres had been ruined. Fortunately, few persons wanted to acquire Ozark farms, so when cotton temporarily ceased to pay the taxes, the Ozark farmer still had wheat, corn, tomatoes, turnips and other garden crops in addition to hogs, cattle, sheep and chickens. Only a catastrophe of the sweeping proportions of the drought of 1930 could make much of a dent in their self-sufficient way of life.

Rice, a new crop in Arkansas, flourished on the Grand Prairie and other "hard pan" soil areas. Relying more on technology than on hand labor, Arkansas rice farming was largely in the hands of Midwestern immigrants, often of German background. Rice prices also fell during the Depression, but these farmers held on until government assistance in the form of price supports and acreage restrictions stabilized the market.

Thomas Hart Benton in the Ozarks

Missouri painter Thomas Hart Benton believed that America's art should reflect the lives of real people. Accordingly, he spent considerable amounts of time in Arkansas in his quest to understand the folk spirit of the country. After one such trip, Benton wrote this impression of the hill country on the edge of modernization:

The towns around the hill country vary considerably in their character, but even those on the main arteries of travel, where the garage, the filling station and the soda fountain have found their place are yet full of the rustic and frequently dilapidated spirit of America's yesterday. At the county seats, the court house, nearly always of brick, sits in the middle of the square with the false-front frame stores, usually painted white, set round about. The sidewalks, when there are any, are of boards that are sometimes not even nailed down but just laid out for rainy weather. The hitching post is still a factor of importance for the mule is not only the most important piece of agricultural machinery round about, but the commonest means of transportation. Automobiles of every variety and description crowd up against wagons, buggies, mules and even sledges which are still used in the roughest part of the hills.

The hotels, like the towns, vary immensely, and while there are places where steam heat and modern plumbing are to be found, the great majority of hotels in the back hills depend on the old-fashioned pot-bellied stove set in the big front room which serves for the desk and for lounging. The heat gets upstairs as it may. Usually the food in these rustic hotels is all placed on the table at once and you reach for what you want. Late comers are likely to be out of luck. . . .Another feature of the past still surviving in the

county seats of this region is the medicine show. With a tent and rough stage and a couple of blackface minstrels, these shows, providing a rough and ready music and a run of broad and simple jokes into which the element of sex enters only where the old maid is concerned, can draw every farmer and family for miles around. The doctor puts on his big performances always on Saturday afternoons and evenings when the towns are sure to be full of people. He mixes his entertainment judiciously with the exposition of the qualities of his medicines, and while he is talking, his entertainers work the audience standing in a packed mass before his tent. Fifty cents for relief, a dollar for a sure cure.

The mail order houses and the big manufacturing firms have not altogether knocked out the old methods here and the loquacious, slick-tongued salesman with his bags and stories yet finds a field where the personal touch is worth more than the quality or desirability of goods. I knew and traveled with one, who, in a rickety car to the rear of which a great box-like cupboard was bolted, made the rounds of all the little settlements and isolated stores of the back country and traded a cheap grade of coffee, and three for-a-penny candies, for ginseng root and picked walnuts. Wherever a car could go, he worked his trade, dickering for long hours, telling stories and making himself at home and a part of the life of the people.

Source: Travel, *July 1934*

What readers of national circulation magazines came to regard as the Arkansas agricultural crisis was manifested mostly in the plantation counties of eastern Arkansas. By 1935, 60 percent of the state's farmers were tenants, and a vast majority of these (more than 90 percent in some counties) were concentrated in the Delta. Sharecropping stood on the brink of revolution there in 1932.

The ideology of sharecropping taught that

economic success, universally regarded as landowning, could be achieved through hard work, luck, a productive wife and numerous children. In theory a man began with nothing but the labor of himself and his family and then acquired mules, equipment and more land, eventually working his way up to renting, leasing and finally buying his own farm land. But statistics showed that instead of men rising to become landowners, landowners were losing their land and becoming tenants. This retrogression during the 1920s and 1930s hurt blacks the most. Cut off from the political system, isolated by ignorance and dependent on whites for money, blacks lost the gains they had made in the early years of the century.

"Everywhere in the South," Jonathan Daniels commented, "the poorest men are on the richest land." Visitors were hard pressed for examples to compare to what they saw in Arkansas. Frazier Hunt found a fanciful resemblance to Chinese coolies; Herbert Agar thought Russian labor camps in Siberia might compare but most found nothing like it. Fred Kelly, a free-lance writer said, "I have never seen worse living conditions or lower standards, even in backward sections of Europe."

English novelist Naomi Mitchinson conceded that: "I have traveled over most of Europe and part of Africa, but I have never seen such terrible sights as I saw yesterday among the sharecroppers of Arkansas."

Sharecroppers lived in box houses, thrown together from rough lumber without studding. Screen wire and electricity were nonexistent. Houses rarely were painted and had newspapers or colorful pictures tacked to the walls to keep out the cold. The family lived around the cook stove, ate from an oil cloth covered table, and slept as many to an iron frame bed as family size dictated.

Diet was monotonous and was not nutritious, sickness was common and education was minimal. Whole families worked in the fields from "can to can't" in what had become by 1934 a deepening cycle of defeat and despair.

White and black, all people suffered, but blacks disproportionately so. Reported infant mortality for blacks was twice that of whites, and informed observers suggested that the figures were actually much higher because many deaths were unrecorded. Midwives, not always well trained, delivered more than half the Delta's babies. Blacks customarily were cheated in economic dealings, "settlement by forty-five revolver" being common. Covert pressure saw to it that all blacks learned their place early in life, so that they were "amazingly submissive" by the time of the Depression.

Whites were in competition with black sharecroppers. Subtle racial settlement patterns limited the kind of tenants a planter selected and how he could treat them. Whites generally had a better chance of emerging from sharecropping into renting or owning land. Even during the Depression, many whites continued to pour into Arkansas from the washed-out land of western Tennessee and northern Mississippi, and others filtered down from the Ozarks. Many were prone to violence and had criminal records; some had engaged in the cottage industry of making and marketing bootleg whisky, which had declined with the repeal of Prohibition in 1933.

Life in the Delta was a hardscrabble, hand-to-mouth existence. The Southern myth of the well-to-do planter aristocracy that sent its sons and daughters East to school was just that—a myth. Eastern Arkansas lacked almost entirely an upper-class with vision, sophistication, education and a sense of social responsibility. Much land was owned instead by large outside lumber companies that had the land cleared after cutting its timber. These investors hired riding bosses, whose large, neater homes stood in marked contrast to the sharecroppers's hovels. The riding bosses usually were deputy sheriffs, so that the rules of the plantation had the force of law. The wealth of Arkansas did not find itself displayed in elaborate plantation homes or in local good works. Instead, Memphis, the capital of the Delta, was the center of eastern Arkansas cultural and commercial life as well as the home of many of its landlords.

Local men occasionally rose to success through the system. The farm operation of Robert E. Lee Wilson in Mississippi County was one of the largest, best run and most paternalistic in Arkansas. Wilson experimented with various kinds of crops and different methods of cultivation. The Ritter Company in Marked Tree arose from the classic Southern story of the merchant who extended credit until he owned the farms.

A policy of force prevailed on many farms. Every planter availed himself at the minimum of the laws that required a tenant to work until the crop was harvested. Those needing extra labor needed to look no further than hobos riding trains or "vagrants" as defined by the law.

In eastern Arkansas, land-owning interests were not in the best financial condition. Owners were "land-poor." The more a man owned of the newly cleared, cultivated and drained land, the more trouble he was in financially. The knots of tired men who gathered around the west door of the courthouse for forced sales were visible reminders of over-enthusiastic local improvement districts and the resultant taxes. Because 40 percent of the farms run by tenants were mortgaged, the landlord felt as hard-pressed as the tenants he worked. Land passed from hand to hand, frequently ending up in the possession of absentee owners and insurance companies.

When landlords changed, tenants sometimes had to move. The prospect of a better chance and sometimes just plain restlessness led tenants to move on. Moving was legal only when crops were harvested, but difficulties arose even then. At least one planter kept barbed wire stockades and used force to keep tenants. As America entered the fourth decade of the twentieth century, some of the rural poor lived in peonage. Most remained ignorant of the living standards Americans generally had come to regard as normal. One innovative businessman in Tyronza (Poinsett County) installed a flush-toilet complete with toilet paper, but sharecroppers continued to use their traditional corn cobs, stopping up the toilet every time.

Bad as conditions normally were, the drought of 1930 brought life to a standstill and forced the Red Cross and other charities to bail out the system. Falling cotton prices precluded recovery. Only 42 percent of the taxes assessed were paid in Arkansas in 1932. The sharecropper had an estimated family income, including the value of home gardens, of $284 by 1934. When cotton could not be sold for an amount equal to the cost of production, there was nothing to finance the next year's crop. Local banks were sucked into universal ruin. Farmers faced with falling prices redoubled their efforts to enlarge their crops. Disaster was looming in 1933 when the new administration of President Roosevelt took over in Washington.

Relief money from the New Deal was the first program to reach Arkansas, but given the politics of the Delta, the funds did not necessarily go where they were needed most. H.L. Mitchell, a dry cleaner merchant turned Socialist, recalled that the planters at Tyronza controlled which sharecroppers worked on CWA jobs, and the work often consisted of cleaning ditches or repairing roads on private property. Those not favored got no aid. Some 200 unemployed men attended a protest meeting at Tyronza, and a state official demanded that all present recite the pledge of allegiance to the flag. One irate voice came from the back of the room:

> That boy scout oath is all right, I guess, but this is not the time or place. We came about one of those relief jobs. If you have anything to tell us about the jobs, let's hear it. If not, you sit down, and let somebody talk who does have something to tell us that we want to hear.

Temporary relief could not solve the problem of over-production. Thus the Agricultural Adjustment Act (AAA) was instituted to reduce production acreage. The 1933 cotton carry-over was 12.5 million bales, virtually enough to see the country through the next year's needs. As a result, farmers in 1934 were paid to plow up their crops. The goal was to destroy one-third of the cotton, giving rise to an inaccurate assumption that every third row was plowed under. Farmers actually destroyed crops on their least productive land. Their mules, trained to avoid the tender plants, initially balked at the chore, but the work was done, and slightly more than 1,000,000 acres of cotton in Arkansas went under plow. Farmers received some $12,000,000 in federal payments.

Seventy-nine percent of Arkansas cotton was covered by the first AAA contracts, and the percentage grew to 92 percent in 1934 and 97 percent in 1935. Probably no New Deal program was more popular, at least with landlords.

All the payments for crop reduction went to landlords under the AAA. They were supposed to pay their tenants a share, but the AAA lacked both the power and the will to enforce equitable treatment. In addition to withholding payments, landlords used crop reduction to evict unneeded tenants. By one estimate, more than half of the croppers were denied some or all of their money; conditions typically were the most oppressive on the large plantations with absentee landlords and black clientele sharecroppers.

The magnitude of the problem led local Arkansas radicals to invite Norman Thomas, the famed national leader of the Socialist Party, to visit Arkansas. Thomas spoke at Tyronza in his first trip in February 1934 and criticized the way government agricultural programs were favoring large planters over tenants. The seed that Thomas planted came up that summer when eleven whites and seven blacks met at the Sunnyside School-

house on the Hiram Norcross plantation to organize the Southern Tenant Farmers Union (STFU). One black member was a survivor of the ill-starred Elaine union.

The STFU never became a union in the Northern, industrialized sense of the word. But in focusing attention on the plight of the nation's poorest people, it attracted the enthusiastic support of a number of educated Eastern reformers. One of those, Howard Kester, wrote the first history of the Union in his 1936 book, *Revolt among the Sharecroppers*. Because poor sharecroppers could not support the movement through dues, Northern money was tapped to send organizers into the field.

Planters reacted angrily to the threat of unionization. Ward Rodgers, a Methodist minister and Vanderbilt graduate, warned in Marked Tree that if threats of violence against him continued, he could "lead the sharecroppers to lynch every planter in Poinsett County." Rodgers was arrested for this hypothetical statement and charged with "anarchy, attempting to overthrow and usurp the government of Arkansas and blasphemy." His trial was covered nationally and took place in a circus atmosphere.

Rodgers's was only the first in a long list of organizers arrested for tampering with labor, collecting union dues and other illegal acts. Marked Tree adopted a city ordinance that prohibited public speeches without permission. "Of course the law don't mean that church people can't hold speakin'," the mayor commented, "Just the radicals, that's all." The Union's leaders found it personally unsafe to remain in Arkansas, and they set up headquarters in Memphis.

The national press also covered the return of Norman Thomas to Arkansas in March 1935. After visiting Governor Futrell and pleading in vain for state intervention, Thomas made a number of speaking stops in eastern Arkansas. Howard Kester rose to introduce Thomas at Birdsong in Mississippi County but got no further than "ladies and gentlemen" when a rough voice shouted: "There ain't no ladies in the audience and there ain't no gentlemen on the platform."

Then a mob of armed men, all wearing deputy sheriff's badges and accompanied by the Mississippi County sheriff, surged forward and jerked Kester from the platform. Norman Thomas in vain waved a copy of the Arkansas Constitution and demanded the right to speak. He was told, "There ain't goin' to be no speakin' here. We are citizens of this county and we run it to suit ourselves. We don't need no Gawd-damn Yankee Bastard to tell us what to do with our niggers and we want you to know that this is the best Gawd-damn county on earth." Howard Kester did not share the planter's opinion: "No section of Arkansas is more slave-ridden or barren of anything that remotely resembles what we ordinarily think of as being culture than Mississippi County."

When Thomas insisted on his constitutional right to speak, riding bosses, all wearing deputy sheriff badges, surged forward and dragged him from the platform.

When Thomas reached safety, he labeled conditions in Arkansas "the vilest exploitation in America" and urged President Roosevelt to intervene to avert tragic bloodshed. A spokesman for the planting interests claimed, however, that Arkansas had "suffered too meekly the influx of labor agitators, social reformers and investigators ignorant of farming conditions."

One result of the STFU publicity was that the Agriculture Department sent a lawyer, Mary Connor Myers, to Arkansas to investigate. Her report, "one long story of human greed," was suppressed by Department officials despite repeated pleas from the American Civil Liberties Union, the Methodist Federation for Social Service and other groups. Individuals sympathetic to the rights of tenant farmers were fired from the Agriculture Department in Washington. The crisis in Arkansas took on national dimensions, including articles in virtually every influential magazine and a film reenactment shot at Colt (St. Francis County) entitled *March of Time.*

Because the success of the STFU depended more on publicity and outside pressure than on direct Union activity, it was with one eye on the press that it conducted a cottonpickers' strike in the fall of 1935. The Union hoped to achieve a payment of $1 per 100 pounds but compromised in October for 75 cents. As a partial result of this alleged victory, the American Federation of Labor recognized the STFU at its next convention. Within Arkansas, however, strike leaders passing out leaflets urging workers to avoid "trouble" by quitting the fields were arrested under Arkansas's night-riding laws that had been passed to curb the first Ku Klux Klan.

Union activity continued during the winter of 1935. Parkin planter C. H. Dribble evicted nearly 100 former tenants for alleged STFU activity. To dramatize their plight, the Union set up a tent village along the highway and summoned reporters. Washington and Little Rock responded reluctantly. Governor Futrell visited the area in early 1936. After hearing complaints from croppers against landlords, Futrell repeated the advice given over and over to blacks since Reconstruction: "You had better listen to the white folks who have always been your friends . . . There are people who will get you into trouble if you listen to them."

In correspondence with Senator Robinson, Futrell enunciated his belief that tenant farmers were sub-human, and the Senator, also a plantation owner, indicated that he had managed to avoid a congressional investigation of the Arkansas problem. Some federal officials were concerned, notably Aubrey Williams and Harry Hopkins. Hopkins told Eleanor Roosevelt in the end, however, that, "Because of the fact that relief in Arkansas is now a state and local matter, largely controlled by boards of local citizens, we were completely unsuccessful in our efforts."

Evicted (John Vachon, 1936) Driven off the Dribble Plantation for alleged union activity, these sharecropper families camped along the highway. **Library of Congress**

Following publicity over the tent colonies, the STFU organized a cotton choppers' strike in the spring of 1936. Reports of terror tactics circulated, the state police were assigned to investigate and the Union got national coverage again. Governor Futrell, responding to Union calls for an impartial investigation, sent Chattanooga lawyer Sam W. Whitaker into the troubled Delta. Whitaker's report, labeled a whitewash by the Union, conceded that the legal system was being abused by planters. Particular reference was made to Crittenden County Deputy Sheriff Paul D. Preacher, who worked prisoners on his own farm.

The dramatic issue the Union needed came shortly after Whitaker filed his report. Two Union supporters, the Reverend Claude Williams from Little Rock and Miss Willie Sue Blagden, a prominent socialite from Memphis, were kidnapped near Earle and whipped.

Williams was kept for a day before finally being released. Their stories made national headlines and led to additional Arkansas articles in the national press. "Slavery in Arkansas" was the headline in *Time* magazine.

Although no prosecution resulted from this violence, a federal grand jury in August indicted Paul D. Preacher for "aiding and abetting in holding in slavery." Preacher's trial was held in Jonesboro and featured the testimony of thirty Negro witnesses who had been forced to work on the deputy sheriff's farm. United States District Judge Martineau told the jury that "every circumstance in this case points to the guilt of this man," and Preacher was convicted. The victory offset the defeat of the choppers' strike and buoyed Union morale. It also led to the abandonment of some of the worst abuses of local law enforcement. A new state law in 1938 banned the hiring out of

Refugees from the 1937 Flood *(photographer unknown) The flood of 1937 hit in mid-January and was followed by an intense cold snap. Human suffering was severe, but this flood failed to capture as much national attention as the 1927 flood. Some refugees were housed in tent cities. Others were transported to shelters miles away from their homes.*
Library of Congress

county prisoners, but the practice of loaning seems to have continued.

One result of the new Union's success was that its political efforts began to be taken seriously. There were always persons in the New Deal who were sympathetic to the tenant family's plight. With Senator Huey Long proclaiming that his "share the wealth" program had elevated Hattie Caraway to the United States Senate, it would not do in Washington to get the reputation for callousness that ultimately had undone Herbert Hoover.

One mark of the changing attitude could be found in the actions of that embodiment of Party regularity, Senator Joe T. Robinson. With a whispered United States Supreme Court appointment in the offing, Robinson became more receptive to the tenant problem.

Governor Futrell formed a Tenancy Commission on the state level to study Arkansas conditions and even appointed two STFU members to it. The Commission produced a study that was truly radical. Denouncing tenancy, the Commission advocated home ownership through federal financing. True to its Socialist origins, the STFU argued for cooperative farms, but most farmers wanted private ownership rather than group regimentation. State action was followed by the creation of a federal Committee on Farm Tenancy. In contrast to Futrell's intransigent opposition, Governor Carl E. Bailey began to discuss farm problems publicly.

The Union, which claimed 200,000 members at its peak, began following the pattern of most farm organizations and went into a rapid decline in 1937. Written contracts between tenants and landowners, new pilot programs, increased income, a decreased need for sharecroppers and the friendly ear of Governor Bailey took the edge off the tenant's urgency. When the Union joined the Congress of Industrial Organizations (CIO), it had to make a systematic effort to collect dues, and its membership declined rapidly from the 30,000 supposedly on the rolls.

There also was an internal problem. A burgeoning Communist Party made a strong effort to penetrate the Southern protest movement during the 1930s. Communists were active in the legal defense of the black boys accused of rape at Scottsboro, Alabama, and in the Alabama Sharecroppers Union. STFU President J. R. Butler discovered documents in 1938 signed by the Reverend Claude Williams that indicated a planned Communist takeover. This scandal tarnished the Union and helped lead to a new state law that incidentally closed the Union's former supporter, Commonwealth College.

Finally, the end of the old agricultural order could be anticipated in the mechanical cotton-picker that Memphis inventors John and Mack Rust were perfecting. Ironically, the Rusts were Socialists and supporters of the STFU. In time their machine displaced sharecroppers. Their view that machines would spare people contrasted sharply with that of Governor Futrell, who insisted, like the Southern Agrarians, that machines were the enemy, putting people out of work and threatening to end the farmer's world.

The most immediate result of STFU agitation was to spur agricultural reform by replacing farm tenancy with farm ownership. Direct assistance to farmers beyond the AAA payments began in 1934 with an agricultural rehabilitation program that was designed to make small family farms self-sufficient through home repairs and loans for machinery, seed and food.

But assistance to selected individuals paled before the plans of William Dyess to make an entire model community out of retooled farmers. Dyess formed a nonprofit corporation and with federal money bought 15,144 acres along the Tyronza River in Mississippi County. At a time when farmers were being paid for not growing crops, workers at the colony cleared and drained cutover land to make it suitable for farming.

Simple houses were designed, all with electricity, although only the five-room models had indoor plumbing. In all, 500 farmsteads were established, and the focal point of the community was a meeting center and a business district with paved streets. Dedicated on May 22, 1936, four months after its founder's death in an airplane crash, the Dyess community consisted of selected farm families owning twenty acres each who were saddled with repaying the costs of the experiment. Farm ownership and labor was individual, but a part of the operation was collective. All farm crops were marketed through a cooperative, and a staff of home demonstration agents, farm advisors and 4-H clubs provided direction.

The Dyess community preceded the report of the President's Committee on Farm Tenancy and the subsequent federal Bankhead-

Jones Farm Tenancy Act, which took Dyess's example and made it federal policy. Resettlement projects were developed in different parts of the nation, but those in Arkansas were given special federal attention because of the severity of its farm crisis. Sixteen resettlement projects were located in Arkansas, the largest number of any state in the region. One of the earliest was Plum Bayou near England, where 180 families were relocated. Lakeview, the first of several black settlements, was near Elaine. Lake Dick, near Altheimer, was closer to the European collective model in that a village cluster pattern was used instead of farmsteads. Project families collectively owned the land, gin, barns, store and community center. Working as day laborers for wages, the men joked that they owned "only children and chickens." There also were what some called "infiltration" units, which were smaller purchases for individual resettlement that did not have the community features associated with larger projects. The resettlement program attracted much attention from visitors, the local press and interested farmers. With its neat homes, flowers and gardens, Dyess was to Chicagoan Phillip Kinsley "like banners of dignity and freedom" when compared to the regimented company housing of the nearby Robert E. Lee Wilson plantation. Strife, controversy and politics lurked under these banners, however. Trouble first surfaced at Dyess. Colonists who had not been told their actual costs became unhappy with what they considered mismanagement by community officials and were badly hurt economically by the flood of 1937. Politically, and most actions taken by office holders in Arkansas were political, the selection of the Dyess site in the southern part of Mississippi County favored certain interests over others. That William R. Dyess had supported J. M. Futrell over Blytheville's Dwight Blackwood in 1932 added a local complication.

Futrell's enemy, Governor Carl Bailey, used discontent at Dyess as a means to embarrass federal officials he could not control. Bailey had the Arkansas Corporation Commission declare the Dyess Colony legally dissolved because of technicalities. After a series of maneuvers, the colony reorganized under the auspices of the Farm Security Administration (FSA). Controversy continued and surfaced at other resettlement projects until their liquidation during World War II.

The FSA tried to help tenants but failed to make much of a dent in the problem. A 1935 study showed that 40,200 persons should be resettled, but only 1,400 actually were. Resettlement bypassed the established political and economic elites, threatening their version of the American way of life. The agency and its administrators and policies were under constant attack as being subversive or Communistic from the beginning to the bitter end. "Uncle Sam's farmers" also found themselves out of step with the growing mechanization of agriculture, a reality reflected at Dyess when the upper limit for a man's holdings was changed from twenty acres to sixty. In reality, the small American farmer was a man whose time had passed as new farm machinery and the mechanization of agriculture changed farming from a labor intensive to a capital intensive business.

Planters were the biggest beneficiaries of New Deal agricultural policies. Those planters with the most land had the most financial troubles before 1935. Those who survived until the New Deal came to their assistance began to make money after 1935 by expanding and reorganizing their operations. By eliminating sharecroppers and substituting day laborers, planters were able to manage their own plantations as they saw fit, invest in machines and keep all federal payments. Thus economies of scale came to be applied to Arkansas agriculture, as the myth of the sharecropper's becoming a landowner passed into history. Far less land changed hands annually, and when it did, large farmers usually acquired it from their less efficient or productive neighbors.

Tenants operated 152,691 Arkansas farms in 1930; by 1940, the number was 115,442. As opportunities diminished in rural areas, many people had to move. A few went to nearby towns, and the percentage of urban population in Arkansas increased from 20.6 percent in 1930 to 22.2 percent in 1940. Others left: 179,135 Arkansans moved out of state between 1935 and 1940, 31,432 of them to far-away California. Yet Arkansas still represented hope to many east of the Mississippi. Therefore, despite a loss of 10 percent of the native population, Arkansas managed to attract 103,672 new residents, who, when combined with the high birth rate, gave the state a net population gain of 5.1 percent. Only 26,048 blacks emigrated, probably because of extraordinarily high black unemployment rates in the North. The problem of too many people on the land remained, and only federal subsidies prevented massive starvation and violence.

Arkansas Blacks Face the Depression

The Depression meant little if anything at first for the black people of Arkansas. One remembered: "I think that everyone thought that the Depression, like everything else, was for white folks, so it had nothing to do with them." One historian summarized it this way: "They were provided with the minimum of subsistence living, exploited to the maximum for productivity, and discarded when their labor was no longer needed." By all apparent signs, the iron laws of segregation were accepted by blacks "with little outward evidence of resentment."

Given the realities of Southern life, blacks suffered first and longest when hard times hit. Blacks accounted for 20 percent of the population in Little Rock but 54 percent of the unemployed. Among the aged, 23 percent of blacks over age sixty-five were on relief rolls, compared to only 13 percent of aged

whites. Blacks were over-represented on the rolls, but they were under-represented in benefits. A welfare payment for a white family was $12 a month; for blacks it was $6. When WPA projects were established, few blacks were allowed to work on them because the prevailing wage scale was so far above what blacks normally were paid that it was feared racial unrest would result. When WPA wages were reduced in the fall of 1935 from 35 cents to 20 cents an hour in response to the protests of planters, blacks protesting at the Little Rock WPA office were clubbed and arrested by the police.

Discrimination prevailed in other New Deal agencies as well. The Civilian Conservation Corps (CCC), one of the most politicized of New Deal programs, virtually excluded blacks, in part because whites feared that black CCC camps would be socially disruptive. The AAA's crop reduction plan actually made matters worse for blacks, because so many were concentrated in the sharecropper category that was considered expendable under government policy. The exclusion of maids and farm workers from the new Social Security program left most blacks with no social insurance. Finally, the entire relief system reflected the politics of Governor Futrell, whose attitude toward the poor was that many "were not worth the powder and lead it would take to blow out their brains."

Rural blacks were mostly sharecroppers, renters or owners of very small farms. The most enterprising already were in flight to town. The 1930 census showed 12,165 Arkansans in Chicago and 10,450 in Missouri. Some found work in the lumber industry of southern Arkansas, others as porters and servants in the resort of Hot Springs, and a select few in the railroad yards of the Rock Island Railroad and the Missouri Pacific Railroad in Little Rock. In all instances, what they could do and how much they could get paid for it reflected the social policies of segregation rather than economic realities of the marketplace. More than half of all black females also were employed, 86 percent of them as maids for $2 to $5 a week. The only positive statistic was that Little Rock had the largest percentage of black homeowners among similarly sized Southern towns.

Arkansas remained unhealthy for blacks. Little Rock was first among twenty Southern cities in infant mortality and was one of ten American cities where tuberculosis was a leading cause of death. There was only one black doctor for every 3,300 Negroes. Dentistry was virtually unknown. Some white doctors found time for Negro patients, but others would not. "I'd rather stick my hand in a dog's mouth than in a nigger's," a Stamps dentist commented.

Poor education matched poor health. The white community, believing that black education was useless, kept it that way. The school superintendent of heavily black Jefferson County declared:

> I started out on the theory that the county superintendent is superintendent of Negro schools as well as white, but that being a white man, I should first take care of the white schools. This is the only policy with which a county superintendent may work in the South.

The practice of diverting state funds intended for black schools to the white system continued. Crawfordsville in Crittenden County displayed perhaps the greatest disparity in the state, spending $1 per capita on blacks and $57 on whites. Only 32 percent of black children statewide attended school, and only 4 percent went to high school. The average class size was fifty-two. The eldest child of sharecroppers almost never attended school because his or her services as a laborer or babysitter could not be spared. Disparities existed even in Little Rock, which historically had provided the best education in the state for blacks. Dunbar High School for blacks opened in 1930, but the city spent twice as much on white children as on blacks. The rate was three times as much in rural Pulaski County.

AM&N at Pine Bluff, Shorter College, Arkansas Baptist College and Philander Smith College continued their precarious existences during the Depression. No graduate work was offered for blacks anywhere in the state, and no professional training was available.

The decade of the 1930s did bring some improvement in race relations. The Little Rock race riot of 1927 proved to be the last episode of that magnitude in the state. Blytheville and Pine Bluff had potentially violent situations but no lynchings in 1938 and 1939. In fact, the state Supreme Court ruled in *Bone* v. *State* (1940) that exclusion of blacks from state juries was cause to overturn a conviction. That case, in many ways a microcosm of Arkansas law, began when a fight broke out between a planter and some cotton pickers about payment and quality of the pick. The planter's wife was shot and killed in the melee. Two black suspects called the sheriff's office and surrendered. At the trial, Little Rock lawyer Scipio A. Jones claimed that blacks had been excluded systematically from jury duty for some forty years. Seeking to head off the issue, the state displaced three whites from the panel without warning and added three blacks before proceeding with the trial. Jones appealed the conviction of his clients to the state Supreme Court, which, somewhat surprisingly considering the racial climate in the state in 1940, found the jury selection unconstitutional.

A second trial was held, and the prosecution again obtained guilty verdicts. On a second appeal, the Supreme Court reduced the crime to manslaughter, sparing the men's lives. The state Supreme Court's ruling on jury selection was the first victory that blacks had scored in recent years and portended black strategy for the years to come. The practical results of the decision were limited because the jurymen were drawn from the voting lists, and only 1,500 blacks held poll tax receipts in Pulaski County.

The career of Joe Louis, the Brown Bomber, was the most important symbol for blacks during the Depression. Louis took the heavyweight boxing crown from the former circus stuntman, Primo Carnera, in 1935, lost it in 1936 to an embodiment of Aryanism, Max Schmeling, and regained it in a memorable first-round knockout in 1938. Radio carried these events directly to the people, and even black church-going elders crowded around radios to follow their hero's victory over the incredible odds of a white-dominated society. Many who traveled long miles to hear the fight stayed overnight. The night after Louis had beaten a white man was not a good time for Arkansas blacks to be on the road after dark.

Arkansas Industries in the Depression

The amount of news coverage given to the agricultural crisis led to the relative neglect of the state's industrial sector. Such an omission was unjustified because in 1929, the value of manufactured products stood at $172,106,050, or 33.4 percent of the value of the state's farm products, mines and timber harvest. The Depression hit Arkansas industry even harder than it did agriculture. The value of manufactured products had fallen by 1933 to a mere $33,678,907 or 20.6 percent of Arkansas's 1929 production. Losses were felt in Little Rock freight yards, where a 70.7 percent decline was registered over those years. The furniture industry fell by only 34.9 percent and was the least hurt. The number of wage-earners overall fell from 44,000 to fewer than 20,000, and wages, which amounted to almost $40,000,000 in 1929, plummeted to less than

$15,000,000. Many factories closed their doors. Of 1,731 establishments in 1929, only 819 remained in 1933. The New Deal provided relief for unemployed workers, but Arkansas's industries were not among those most likely to benefit from government policies. Only the stave business received a big boost when the repeal of Prohibition increased the demand for whisky barrels. Arkansas forests were still in an era of declining production, and tree replanting was still too new to have much impact. Trees had not been replanted in the Delta at all, and cutover land still was being converted into farms. Although timber and timber-related businesses accounted for the greatest number of Arkansas's industrial jobs (17,322 in 1937, compared to 2,315 workers in canning factories), the lumber industry was becoming concentrated in the southern third of the state, where the rapid growth of softwood lumber brought quick returns.

Democratic policy makers were convinced that corporations had too much power and the workers too little, and that this was one of America's problems. A variety of legislation sought to alter this situation. The NRA had tried to make workers equal with management in setting wage and price codes. After the NRA was declared unconstitutional, Congress tried to strengthen union bargaining powers by establishing the National Labor Relations Board (NLRB) and limiting the ability of management to prohibit the dissemination of union materials. All of this made the late 1930s a time of intense industrial strife in the Northern states, especially in those industries that previously had barred unions. Because of its limited industrial base, the contest between labor and capital in Arkansas was much more muted. Labor scored positive gains in reclaiming coal mines and took the struggle into the lumbering towns. The Sawmill and Timber Workers Union struck lumber companies at Warren and Crossett in 1935. The strike failed at first. The Bradley Lumber Company closed its mills for more than a month in a successful lockout. The NLRB ruled against the company three years later and ordered it to rehire forty-four factory workers. The Union had more than 2,500 members in the leading southern Arkansas timber towns by 1940.

Even with the beginnings of a modern labor movement in Arkansas and a modest industrial boom after 1936, Arkansas wages remained near the bottom nationally and below the regional average. With few exceptions, Arkansas workers in 1940 were unskilled or semi-skilled and were engaged in extractive industries, the model of a colonial economy.

Promoting Arkansas

After the New Deal began to inspire hope and confidence, state promoters again got busy. Problems remained basically as they had been since the 1880s. There was an inadequate capital base to support local industry. Little could be done to import industry, and factories remained small and capital-starved. Studies also showed that railroad rates favored the eastern areas of the nation. Transportation costs literally priced Arkansas goods out of the national market, perpetuating the colonial status of the state's economy. Finally, AP&L's defeat of proposed hydroelectric plants on Arkansas's rivers contributed to high energy costs.

The Arkansas State Planning Board advocated a wide range of measures in 1934 to lure new industry. This board was replaced in the political merry-go-round by the Arkansas Agricultural and Industrial Commission, which convened a major conference of state leaders in 1937 to analyze the problem. The renewed attention led to two new constitutional amendments. The first, Amendment 26, created workmen's compensation, a form of social insurance that was well established in the Northern industrial states for a generation before it reached Arkansas. The amendment's biggest opponents were personal injury attorneys who specialized in sensational job injury lawsuits. Supporters claimed that major industry would avoid a state without such laws. The second, Amendment 27, granted tax exemption of up to ten years for building new factories or expanding old ones. Arkansas again was trying to create a more favorable business climate.

The promotion of Arkansas, a theme familiar from earlier days, returned again with the celebration of the state's Centennial in 1936. Both the *Gazette* and *Democrat* published extensive accounts of state progress. President and Mrs. Roosevelt were the guests of honor at the celebration. Houses along the road on the presidential drive to Hot Springs were whitewashed, at least on the side the visiting party would see, in order to present a more prosperous and well-kept appearance, and STFU malcontents were kept away.

The legislature created the Publicity Advisory Commission in 1937 but failed to fund it. The following year, Director M. C. Blackman addressed the image problem in a newspaper article entitled "Is it true what they say about Arkansas?" His answer predictably was no, but he apologized for the "pitiful and shameful" exhibit at the 1933 Chicago World's Fair, before stating what he considered to be the main problem: "One audience thinks we are funny. Another thinks we are tragic." The STFU publicity supported the tragic view. For many Americans, however, Arkansas was home to Van Buren-born comedian Bob Burns, and his famous homemade musical instrument, the "bazooka" (a term that took on a different meaning in World War II), and Lum 'n' Abner of the "Jot'em Down Store" of radio and films.

Arkansas leaders actually were trying to prove that the state was truly American. The Arkansas Territorial Restoration in Little Rock, the first serious effort to save the state's architectural heritage, was modeled after Colonial Williamsburg. The world it sought to recreate existed more in the imagination of prominent club woman Louise Loughborough than in the more complex reality that subsequent historians have revealed. Even so, the restoration spawned other attempts to save old landmarks, most notably the Old State House, which Little Rock planners wanted to turn into a parking lot in the 1940s. The Arkansas Historical Association was reestablished in 1942, and its *Quarterly* provided a forum for an emerging scholarly literature about the state.

Religion During the Depression

Arkansas religious developments paralleled the political and economic crises in many ways. The debate about modernism was still raging at the start of the decade. The leading event was the appearance in Little Rock of famed lawyer and agnostic Clarence Darrow on November 3, 1930. Invited for a debate with Temple B'nai Israel's Rabbi Ira E. Sanders, Darrow found himself caught up in a local controversy when minister Ben Bogard was refused equal time. Taking to the radio for an attack on agnostics and Jews, the minister predicted that the rabbi would "burn in hell for a thousand years." What did happen was that 2,000 persons came to hear the debate and others read the complete text printed in the *Arkansas Gazette*.

Hard times hit Arkansas churches in several ways. One problem was metaphysical. Fundamentalist Christianity always assumed a close relationship between this world and God's. The economic disaster overtaking the nation was viewed by some as a punishment for sin. Such preaching was common, especially when only the collapse of Wall Street or the closing of banks was involved. It became a different matter when the double whammy of the drought of 1930 and falling farm prices hit churchgoers. Some responded with extreme

apocalyptic visions of the end of the world, and others, feeling no more sinful than they had when prices were higher, became disenchanted with theology and turned to the government for aid.

One of the most bizarre episodes of the period overtook Jonesboro's First Baptist Church in 1930-1933 in what became known as the church war. The event began innocently enough in the spring of 1930 when Jonesboro Baptist College and the First Baptist Church invited Joe Jeffers, an actor-comedian turned revival preacher, to hold services in Jonesboro. Fresh from fighting the devil in Oklahoma City, Jeffers was a stunning success. His tent attracted more than 25,000 persons and 400 conversions. Jeffers also acted as temporary minister to the First Baptist Church. Some local Baptists espoused his fiery fundamentalism, and when Jeffers returned to town in August 1931, a disaffected minority at First Baptist welcomed him with open arms. Preaching the imminent second coming and at times claiming to be a prophet, Jeffers denounced the First Baptist minister as immoral and attacked the Jonesboro mayor, asking, "How many children in Jonesboro call Mayor Bosler 'Daddy?'"

This caused violence that escalated from words to action. A fist fight erupted after a 1931 church service. When a Jeffers supporter was jailed, a mob of 600 marched on the jail and obtained his release. At the trial the next day, while Jeffers prayed for God to strike the mayor dead, one of his followers knocked both the mayor and the police chief to the ground. Unable to control the mob, city officials called for outside help. Governor Parnell sent in state militia units armed with machine guns, tear gas and fixed bayonets. The immediate result was larger crowds for Jeffers, who expanded his attack to include bootleggers, prostitutes and other lawbreakers, whom he identified by name.

After a few weeks of peace, the troops were withdrawn, and violence returned. A tear gas bomb thrown into Jeffers's tent one night choked the audience. The tent later became the target of an arsonist, leading Jeffers and his followers to erect a wooden tabernacle with a dirt floor.

When Jeffers left town, his church appointed a new pastor. Almost a year later, Jeffers returned to Jonesboro and demanded to have "his" church back. Just as the First Baptist Church had divided, so did the new tabernacle. Both factions held services simultaneously, until chancery court ruled against Jeffers. An attempt to gain possession from the night watchman appointed by the Jeffers faction led to an exchange of gunfire that killed the watchman. The opposing pastor was jailed on murder charges. An attempt to assassinate the minister in jail failed, and he was acquitted in early 1934. Jeffers left Arkansas, founded the Pyramid Power Yahweh group in Missouri, and continued his brushes with the law.

The episode left great personal bitterness in Jonesboro. Coming during the heart of drought and Depression, it demonstrated the enormous pull of religion. To critics, Joe Jeffers was the "Elmer Gantry of the Southwest." To his admirers, he was a true man of the Gospel.

Arkansas religion could not afford to respond to the economic crisis with an extensive program of individual assistance. To some, such work smacked of the Social Gospel, a dreaded Northern heresy. But more important than theology, the churches simply had no money to spare. Many ministers also held down another job, and with no budgets worthy of the name, many churches in Arkansas fought just to stay open.

The state's Southern Baptists were in deep financial trouble because of a large debt from an expensive expansion program during the 1920s. Other denominations also labored under difficulties. The abbey and school at Subiaco had just been rebuilt after a disastrous fire when the Depression hit.

Battling creditors was the monks' major activity during the decade. The First Methodist Church of Little Rock opened the decade by installing a fine new organ, but the church mortgage was in default by 1937. State Episcopalians were unable to pay even the bishop's salary.

The financial crisis led to a debate about the values of capitalism. Southern Baptists denounced Communism, blaming it for Arkansas's repeal of Prohibition and the state's lax divorce law, but they also indicted the free enterprise system in 1933 and asserted the primacy of Christian over business ethics. The farm crisis particularly upset Delta Christians. Some established churches supported planters and denounced the STFU as atheistic. One of Marked Tree's religious leaders was reported to have said:

> I don't know, though, but what it would have been better to have a few no-account shiftless people killed at the start than to have all this fuss raised up. We have had a pretty serious situation here, what with the "mistering" of the niggers and stirring them up to think the Government was going to give them forty acres.

On the other hand, STFU locals frequently organized and met in rural churches where sharecroppers congregated. Many of the Union's leaders were lay ministers, and a strong religious overtone was present both in the message of the organization and in its songs and rituals. Controversial "outside agitators," such as Ward Rodgers and Howard Kester, came from ministerial backgrounds. The Presbyterian Reverend Claude Williams, denounced as a Communist infiltrator by the STFU, and later head of Commonwealth College before the state closed the school, was an example of how radical politics and Christian theology could be combined.

Appealing for Aid (*photographer unknown, 1939*) *The New Deal agricultural policies involved some local control. Socioeconomic differences in the farming community are highlighted in this picture from Harrison as a debt adjustment committee considers the appeal of a farmer threatened with the loss of his land.* **Library of Congress**

Home Canning (*photographer unknown, ca. 1935*) *This Independence County woman proudly displays her jars of peas and other vegetables. Home canning greatly improved the standard rural diet and remained an important aspect of rural life long after the Depression.* **Library of Congress**

Loading Cotton at the Lehi Gin *(Russell Lee, 1938) A classic photograph suggestive of the Delta environment and the world of cotton.* **Library of Congress**

Split Log Fence and Barn *(Dorothea Lange, 1938) The Ozarks still projected the image of the rural American farming world in 1938. Photographer Dorothea Lange specialized in portraits of people, and this Ozark still life is a rare exception.* **Library of Congress**

Joe Bogey *(Russell Lee, 1938) Though "down and out" at the knees and lean in the belly, this Lake Dick farmer still had a car. The commitment of Arkansans to the automobile already had become a notable feature of the state's life before this photograph was made.* **Library of Congress**

Josie and Albert Terpening *(Ben Shahn, 1935) The effects of hard work are plainly shown on the faces of this Boone County couple and seem to have influenced the boy.* **Library of Congress**

Farm Family at Dyess *(Arthur Rothstein, 1935) The success of relocation is emphasized in this picture of a Dyess farm family.* **Library of Congress**

The Rolling Store *(Russell Lee, 1938) In the 1930s, some enterprising merchants in the Mississippi Delta began putting stores on wheels. These rolling stores could carry canned foods and dry goods in addition to the items peddlers once supplied. Much resented by established stores, they vanished with the passing of the sharecropper families after 1950.* **Library of Congress**

Day Labor, Memphis, Tennessee *(Dorothea Lange, 1937) Arkansas planters recruited day labor directly off the streets of Memphis and other large towns. Residents gathered early at the curbs to be picked up and transported to the cotton fields. Day laborers were the bottom of the social order and fathers would warn their daughters to avoid boys, "who were never going to be anything but day labor."* **Library of Congress**

A Housewife at the Chicot Farms Rural Rehabilitation Project *(Russell Lee, 1939) Rural amenities before the coming of Rural Electrification Administration power lines dominate this photograph: a battery-powered radio, kerosene lights and a wind-up clock.* **Library of Congress**

Cultivating Cotton *(Dorothea Lange, 1938) These mule teams are photographed in the fields of the Lake Dick Cooperative Farm. This picture must be just for show because the farmers could not be lined up to plow as there is no "turn-around" room. In reality, each farmer would set off what he could plow in one day.* **Library of Congress**

Moving Day *(Dorothea Lange, 1936) A ritual as old as sharecropping was recorded in this photograph. Traditionally, croppers could only move during the winter; however, this picture was taken in August.* **Library of Congress**

Although the major denominations were recovering their financial footing by the end of the decade, the differences between rural and urban religion, even within the same denomination, became more and more marked. Talk of ecumenical union blossomed in town churches, especially in 1938 when the Northern and Southern branches of the Methodist Church reunited. Southern Baptists remained opposed to union with their Northern brethren: "Our answer to the periodical appeal of unionizers should be a fervent campaign of indoctrination." Except for closing a few denominational colleges, most religious activities returned to normal after being suspended during the crisis. Arkansas religion was ready by 1940 to face a new challenge in World War II.

THE WANING OF THE DEPRESSION

The New Deal tried to operate on three levels. First, temporary relief measures would take care of immediate human needs. Then recovery policies would get the economy rolling again, obviating the need for relief. Finally, economic reforms would prevent such collapses from happening again. The theory proved defective in practice because relief assistance proved necessary for the entire decade. Federal funds accounted for 95.6 percent of all public money spent in Arkansas during the Depression. Arkansas was given special consideration because of its poverty: it received $279,143,021, or more federal dollars than Alabama and nearly as much as Georgia, both more populous than Arkansas. By 1937, the state's Public Welfare Commission was giving direct assistance (commonly called welfare) of $6.25 a month to some 6,000 persons who were not eligible for WPA or similar federal programs. This system replaced the old county poor farms. Only twenty-seven counties

still maintained poor farms by 1939. WPA projects alone accounted for 11,417 miles of road, 467 new schools and forty-four new parks.

As the nation's economy began to recover in 1937, the administration thought the time had come to discontinue relief. The PWA was terminated in June and cutbacks in the WPA followed, reducing the number of employees in Arkansas from 32,480 to 18,521. The hope that the private sector could find work for these people failed to materialize. In addition, the flood of 1937, which hit in January, inundated low-lying areas of eastern Arkansas and caused considerable damage. When the full national effects of the cutback were felt in 1938, another wave of unemployment gripped the land. Arkansas per capita income, which had reached $247 in 1937, fell to $226 in 1938 and failed to recover to the 1937 level until 1940. The administration had no choice but to restore programs and rehire people. The decade ended with Arkansas as a federal dependent in all but name.

CONCLUSION

It is hard to over-estimate the importance of the New Deal to Arkansas. Government assistance programs prevented complete agricultural collapse and the possibility of armed violence. Relief programs became an important source of income to many families, the CCC looked after youth, and communities received public works they otherwise never could have afforded. Towns benefited from the rescue of the banking system and the creation of the Federal Deposit Insurance Corporation (FDIC). The aid extended to persons threatened with foreclosure on their homes helped save many family dwellings from the auction block. Finally, government projects put people back to work. Many still existing school buildings, bridges, courthouses, sidewalks, parks and roads are reminders of how public works in a time of unemployment could benefit society. It was the WPA funding provided to zoologist Sam

Dillinger at the University of Arkansas that began modern archeological studies in Arkansas.

None of this could have been accomplished if Arkansas had been forced to rely on the efforts of state government. Arkansas became the only state government during the Depression to default on its debts, but the attitude that government exists to aid the people remained essentially foreign to Arkansas's politicians. Thus the people discovered the federal government for the first time. Families related to their young during the next fifty years how they made it through hard times. Franklin Delano Roosevelt became a folk hero, the president who cared, and Hoover became the bogey man who caused the Great Depression. As the Civil War faded with each passing veteran, the Depression replaced it as a gripping event that reached ordinary people's lives. The greater social and political implication of reform escaped the average person's awareness, but the world of simple ways and simple people, in decline since the Civil War, had suffered a blow from which it could never recover. Modernization was in the wings and needed only a national crisis for its siren song to sound in Arkansas.

BIBLIOGRAPHIC ESSAY

The Great Depression is by far the most investigated aspect of Arkansas history in the twentieth century. One adequate dissertation, David E. Rison, "Arkansas During the Great Depression," covers the period as a whole. A useful essay is Donald Holley, "Arkansas is the Great Depression," in *Historical Report of the Secretary of State* III (Little Rock, 1978), and a highly personal account can be found in John Gould Fletcher, *Arkansas* (Chapel Hill, 1947).

Political affairs are recalled vividly in Brooks Hays, *Politics Is My Parish,* and additional light is shed by the biographies of Governors Parnell, Futrell, Bailey and Adkins, in Donovan and Gatewood, *The Governors of Arkansas.* The collected inaugural addresses, located at the University of Arkansas, help reveal plans and policy. The last hurrah of "Coin" Harvey is the subject of William Heischel Hughes, "Octogenarian Nominee of a Newborn Party," *AHQ,* XXII (Winter 1963), 291-300.

Valuable articles on the early stages of the Depression include Gail S. Murray, "Forty Years Ago: The Great Depression Comes to Arkansas," *AHQ,* XXIX (Winter 1970) 291-312; Pamela Webb, "Business as Usual: The Bank Holiday in Arkansas," *AHQ,* XXIX (Autumn 1980 247-261, and C. Roger Lambert, "Hoover and the Red Cross in the Arkansas in the Arkansas Drought of 1930, *AHQ* XXIX (Spring 1970), 3-19. A revisionist view relevant for Arkansas is David E. Ham, "The Causes of the Banking Panic of 1930: Another View" *JSH,* LI (November 1985).

The writings of the Agrarians can be studied from their collection of essays, *I'll Take My Stand,* (New York, 1930). The history of Commonwealth College is contained in a series of articles by William H. Cobb: "Commonwealth College Comes to Arkansas, 1923-1925," *AHQ* XXIII (Summer 1964), 99-122; "From Utopian Isolation to Radical Activism: Commonwealth College 1925-1935,"*AHQ,* XXXII (Summer 1973), 132-147, and Donald H. Grubbs, "Arkansas Commonwealth College and the Southern Tenant Farmers' Union," *AHQ,* XXV (Winter 1966), 293-311.

America's first elected woman senator has attracted some scholarly attention in recent years. A good introduction to her career can be found in Diane D. Kincaid, ed., *Silent Hattie Speaks: The Personal Journal of Senator Hattie Caraway,* (Westport, Conn., 1979).

One area in which a superabundance of material can be found is the farm crisis in Arkansas, particularly the rise and fall of the Southern Tenant Farmers Union. Howard Kester, a participant from the early stages, led the way with his *Revolt Among the Share-*

croppers, (New York, 1936) and the founder, H. L. Mitchell, settles old grudges in his perceptive *Mean Things Happening in this Land,* (Montclair, N. J., 1979), valuable also because it contains sharecropper poems and songs. Secondary books include David Eugene Conrad, *The Forgotten Farmers: The Story of Sharecroppers in the New Deal,* (Urbana, 1965), and Donald H. Grubbs' pro-union *Cry from the Cotton: The Southern Tenant Farmers' Union and the New Deal,* (Chapel Hill, 1971). The resettlement administration received attention in Michael H. Mehlman, "The Resettlement Administration and the Problems of Tenant Farmers in Arkansas, 1935-1936," (Ph. D. diss., New York University, 1970) and a fuller treatment is Donald Holley, *Uncle Sam's Farmers: The New Deal Communities in the Lower Mississippi Valley,* (Urbana, 1975). One view from the planter's side, albeit atypical, is Thad Snow, *From Missouri,* (Boston, 1954); another is Donald C. Alexander, *The Arkansas Plantation, 1920-1941* (New Haven, 1943).

In addition to these books, numerous magazine accounts appeared at the time. Professor Holley, *Uncle Sam's Farmers,* contains a bibliographic essay on this category as well as the scholarly articles. Particularly useful is Floyd W. Hicks and C. Roger Lambert, "Food for the Hungry: Federal Food Programs in Arkansas, 1933-1942," *AHQ,* XXXVII (Spring 1978), 3-28.

Passing references to Arkansas blacks can be found in most secondary sources. A poignant memoir of a Depression childhood is Maya Angelou, *I Know Why the Caged Bird Sings,* (New York, 1969). Statistical data can be found in Mehlman, *The Resettlement Administration,* and in C. Calvin Smith, *War and Wartime Changes: The Transformation of Arkansas, 1940-1945,* (Fayetteville, 1986).

Religious history during the Depression is mentioned in most of the standard church histories. Darrow's visit is discussed in Elizabeth C. Perry and F. Hampton Roy, "The Rabbi and Clarence Darrow," PCHR XXVIII (Summer 1980), 2-3. A good account of the Jonesboro "church war" is Dusty Jordan, "Baptists Bring War to Jonesboro," *CrCHQ,* XXI (Winter, 1983-1984), 1-9.

Despite the human suffering it caused, the 1937 flood has been much neglected in study to date. The best brief treatment is Don Hamilton, "Jonesboro and Arkansas During the Flood of 1937," *CrCHQ,* IX (Winter 1971), 2-11. Arkansas industrial history can be studied in James E. Griner, *The Growth of Manufactures in Arkansas, 1900-1950.*

Broadway Bridge, Viewed from North Little Rock (photographer unknown, January 31, 1956) *This photograph documents the impact of the automobile age in Arkansas with cars and trucks everywhere, not to mention gas and tire stations. Note that even in this urban setting, pickup trucks are numerous.* **University of Central Arkansas**

Chapter XVI

World War II and Post-War Dilemmas

INTRODUCTION

The Great Depression placed immense stress on all classes in Arkansas, and the collapse of the nation's industrial economy actually encouraged people to return to or stay with their rural ways. Only sharecroppers, displaced by new federal agricultural policies, did not benefit from the New Deal. Except for them, Arkansas life generally had returned to normal by 1940. A strong national conservative resurgence found local expression in the political career of Homer Adkins, the wartime governor of Arkansas.

World War II, which arrived unexpectedly for most Arkansans, induced more economic and social change in four years than any other event in the state's history since the Civil War. Between the draft and wartime jobs, more Arkansans than ever before came face to face with the modern world. Modernizers, led by Sid McMath, regained control of Arkansas in the War's aftermath and attempted once again to bring the state into the modernist mode. Governor McMath's partial failure prepared the way for Orval Faubus, who as governor confronted another aspect of modernization that until that time had been zealously avoided by white Arkansans: integration.

THE IMPACT OF WORLD WAR II

The Coming of World War II

The events preceding the German invasion of Poland in September 1939 were long in the making. The American public began to receive subtle intimations in the middle of the 1930s that the United States policy of isolation practiced since 1919 was coming to an end. Because Arkansans were not internationally minded, few of these hints had much impact. Walnut Ridge editor J. L. Bland, a prominent Democrat, spoke for many as late as May 1939 when he stated he would never support another war. When the extent of Hitler's aggressive plans became apparent, however, newspapers rallied to the Allied cause and led their readers into internationalism.

Despite America's early neutrality, the War caused uneasiness in the state. When a Cabot businessman hired an airplane to drop miniature advertising parachutes over the town, the residents became hysterical and one old man armed with a shotgun pumped seventeen blasts into the air at the "Nazi" invaders. On a less comic note, in June 1940, a Danville blacksmith was beaten to death because he tried to distinguish between the German people and the Nazis. His attacker, a World War I veteran, was not even indicted by a grand jury. Such intolerance for anything German was echoed statewide by *The Arkansas Legionnaire*, which called for concentration camps and firing squads for anyone who was pro-German.

As the crisis in Europe deepened with the fall of France and President Roosevelt actively began to help Great Britain, Arkansas congressmen responded by supporting key pieces of legislation, including the highly controversial Lend-Lease Law. Tensions finally were resolved — not by the Germans — but by the Japanese surprise attack on Pearl Harbor on December 7, 1941. All pretense of neutrality disappeared as unanimity of purpose dominated the state.

Wartime Sentiment

Arkansas was remote from the field of battle and unlikely to see a submarine, but this did not keep the people from expressing strong feelings about the War. Much of this translated into hatred of the Japanese. The selling of war bonds in Jonesboro was done by "Slap a Jap" clubs, and the farmers' slogan to increase production ran "Slap a Jap with a Pig." Chamber pots were sold with Adolph Hitler's face in the bottom. Because war fever ran high, the techniques needed to foster unity in World War I were less in evidence.

Bond sales constituted the most visible feature of wartime patriotism, and Crossett workers won a United States Treasury Department "T" award for having 90 percent participation in payroll deduction bond sales. Bond buyers in Piggott were honored by having an airplane named *City of Piggott*. Despite overwhelming support for the War, a few Arkansans did not share the spirit. The most conspicuous conscientious objectors were a new religious group called Jehovah's Witnesses. Renouncing the world and all its wars except the last one marking the coming of the Anti-Christ, members of the group quoted scripture in refusing to participate in displays of national solidarity.

One case that reached the state Supreme Court, *Johnson* v. *State* (1942), concerned a farmer who came into Marshall to procure federal commodities for his wife and eight children. The clerk at the welfare office said she had heard that the man had been seen with the Jehovah's Witnesses and demanded that he salute the flag before getting his benefits. He refused to do this, saying that he supported the ideals behind the flag, but that the thing itself was a mere "rag." He was not only denied benefits but was arrested under a 1919 law that made it a misdemeanor to insult the flag. The Supreme Court confirmed his conviction despite the impassioned dissent of Chief Justice Griffin Smith.

Instances of persecution multiplied after Pearl Harbor. A Texarkana Jehovah's Witness and World War I veteran was jailed for thirty days and fined $100 for distributing religious literature. His attorney produced a letter at the trial from J. Edgar Hoover, the head of the FBI, stating that the sect posed no threat to national security. Rejecting this evidence, the judge snorted, "neither Mr. Hoover nor any United States attorney is enforcing the law in Arkansas."

Jehovah's Witnesses encountered great hostility from local draft boards who repeatedly ignored instructions from Washington on how Witnesses and conscientious objectors were to be classified. Albert H. Blakely, an ordained Witness minister, was first fired from his job with the Arkansas Highway Department and then had his ministerial status revoked by his draft board. Despite overwhelming evidence supporting his deferred status, the state Selective Service director, General E. L. Compere, supported the local board, noting that Witnesses "were lower down than a snake." It took an appeal to President Roosevelt before Blakely regained his status.

In addition to loss of jobs and private persecution, at least one anti-Witness riot took place. In the fall of 1942, a planned Witness meeting on Little Rock's Asher Avenue was broken up when laborers from a government camp assaulted Witnesses, shooting seven and beating others with pipes while a mob cheered. Police responded by arresting the Witnesses for disturbing the peace. Oscar Winn, a one-armed, sixty-five-year-old attorney for the Witnesses, was severely beaten while trying to collect information on the incident. Being a Jehovah's Witness was not one of the Four Freedoms most people wanted to protect from Adolph Hitler.

Wartime Recruitment

Arkansas's main contribution to the War effort was manpower. In all, 55,748 men enlisted and 138,897 were drafted. The draft began before the War when on September 16, 1940, Congress passed the first peacetime draft law in the nation's history. In short order local boards were established and eventually all men aged 18 to 64 were registered. At first a lottery determined who would be called up, but in June 1942 the date of birth was substituted. The draft was administered locally by ninety-four boards under a state director.

Many middle-class boys did not wait for the draft. The author's brother, then a trouble-making student at the University, volunteered for the Army Air Corps and with other students was sent to Little Rock to take the required tests. The entire high school football team at Lepanto volunteered, and one boy who flunked the physical was so distraught that he tried to commit suicide by swallowing carbolic acid.

The major problem encountered by the military in Arkansas was not public opposition to the War, draft dodging or slackers, but the physical condition of Arkansas's citizens. At the beginning of the War, the state had a ratio of one doctor for every 1,500 persons and only 653 nurses, the least per population of any state. Lack of access to doctors and few public health programs retarded Arkansas's contribution to the War effort. In the spring of 1940, Dr. W. B. Grayson of the State Health Department, reported that a survey of school children found 90 percent displayed some physical ailment. Problems such as pellagra, rickets, obesity and undernourishment were the results of ignorance and poverty.

Arkansas's Selective Service officials inherited these problems. The rejection rate for inductees for Arkansas was 43 percent; only South Carolina with a 46 percent rate sent a smaller percentage into the military. The main causes of rejection for Arkansans were educa-

WACS at Conway (*photographer unknown, 1944*) *World War II was especially revolutionary in its impact on women, who served in large numbers in a variety of roles.* **University of Central Arkansas**

tion levels and health. Thirty-five percent of those rejected by the military had either serious dental or eye problems. In 1943, when manpower needs mounted, Selective Service officials began taking men with venereal disease. New sulfa drugs made effective treatment possible, something the men were very unlikely to have received back home. The military also lowered education standards. Intelligence tests were substituted for the requirement that men have completed four years of education. Educationally unprepared men were put in thirteen week crash courses in what the military styled a salvage operation.

Those who fought in the War participated in both the Pacific and European theaters. One important hero was Clarksville's Major Pierce McKennon, a "boogie woogie" piano-playing pilot credited with more than twenty kills in

the air. Nathan Gordon and Maurice "Footsie" Britt were Medal of Honor winners who had post-war political careers, and the wartime experiences of Huntsville's Orval Faubus filled a book, *In This Faraway Land* (1971). Other ordinary Arkansans distinguished themselves, too. Roy C. Brown of Gurdon received the Bronze Star for bravery in assisting wounded fellow soldiers. Colonel William O. Darby of Fort Smith, who had organized an elite command unit known as the Ranger Battalions, was killed only two days before the Axis forces in Italy surrendered.

Wartime Changes in Business and Industry

The War not only solved American's unemployment problem but also created a demand

World War II Comes to Chester and Jeff

Jeff Shope was a sharecropper eking out a precarious living near Okolona in Hempstead County. His vision of the abundant life —a fine mule and a house full of boys— had only partially been fulfilled. Chester was a fine mule, and while there were seven children, six were daughters. The only son had early heard the siren song of modernization, brought by a school bus that took him to high school in Hope. He carried the message home to his father: "Daddy, I need some shoes for gym."

The father, who had a lot of modernizing to do, replied: "Who in the hell is Jim?"

Although the Southwest Proving Grounds was some miles distant, it was War-time and planes filled the skies. Chester, the mule, preferred watching the planes to plowing, and when a plane went by Chester turned his head to follow its flight. "It was one of the few times you could

see both ends of a plow mule at the same time," Jeff recalled. Finally, the mule spoke, not in words, for mules are too intelligent to talk, but with his eyes: "Look, dummy, planes are flying overhead and trucks are roaring up and down the road. And look at us. Me pulling this plow and you walking behind the handles looking at my backside from sunup to sundown."

Jeff Shope got the message. He unhitched the plow and then the harness. Chester retired to a pasture, and Jeff walked away from his agricultural career into the brave new world of industry.

It was a story repeated endlessly with many variations by farmers in all parts of the state. It was a story sometimes told with sadness, sometimes with humor and sometimes with a sense of excitement.

Source: Charles Allbright, "Arkansas Traveler," Arkansas Gazette, February 28, 1991

---

for factory workers to replace those being drafted into the army. Federal laws regulating prices and raising taxes redistributed income so that more persons had purchasing power. Bank deposits in Arkansas went up as Wartime shortages and price controls limited purchasing power. The rapid mobilization of American society for war brought more modernization to Arkansas in four years than had occurred in the previous twenty.

The nation's crisis was a ray of hope for poor Arkansans. Some 10.9 percent of Arkansas's population left the state between April 1, 1940, and November 1, 1943, usually for higher-paying jobs elsewhere. The federal government did not select Arkansas for major war production facilities. Economic factors, such as a lack of electric power, played a role, but politics was the major cause. Arkansas had no political clout in the Senate after Joe T. Robinson's death, and five of the state's six congressmen were serving their first terms in the House of Representatives in 1940. Without a powerful lobby in Washington, Arkansas received only 1.16 percent of federal defense spending. Other Southern states, traditionally almost as poor, used large federal expenditures to begin moving into the American economic mainstream, but Arkansas was left behind.

What federal facilities did appear in Arkansas, however, had a profound impact on local economies. The prime example was bauxite ore, used to make aluminum. Output increased twelve-fold during the War years, mostly because of demand for the light metal to build aircraft. Processing began for the first time with the erection of plants at Jones Mill and Hurricane Creek, even though 70 percent of the electricity used in the manufacturing process had to be imported from out of state.

Eight defense construction projects were funded during the War years. One, the Norfolk Dam on the White River, had begun before the War. Others included the Blue

Mountain Dam on the Petit Jean River, Camp Chaffee at Fort Smith, the Incendiary Munitions Plant at Pine Bluff, the Maumelle Ordnance Plant and the Jacksonville Ordnance Plant. The Jacksonville plant employed some 13,000 persons and turned Jacksonville from a sleepy village to a bustling town overnight. The largest expenditures were for the aluminum plant at Magnet Cove, which was built together with the Lake Catherine Steam Generating Plant, at a cost of $33,000,000.

The impact of these federal facilities was immediate and powerful in all affected communities. The government first took away farmers' land, often at pre-war prices, and forced many from farms held for generations. The Southwest Proving Grounds, an air base near Hope, caused the population of that town to rise from 7,475 in 1940 to 15,475 two years later. Overcrowding affected all the towns, perhaps most notably Pine Bluff, where people paid rent to sleep in car chassis, cardboard boxes and closets. Prostitutes, gamblers and bootleggers sought to profit from the new markets. The need for workers was so intense that it pulled many women into factories. Never before a major part of the labor force except as servants or in canning factories, the 80,000 women working by the summer of 1943 accounted for 20 percent of the labor force. The legislature passed a law limiting women to fifty-four hours a week in an expression of social concern. Another concern arose as black women left domestic service, creating a major social crisis for white middle-class women. Rumor had it that Eleanor Roosevelt was somehow behind maids quitting their jobs, demanding higher wages and taking Saturdays off.

Wartime Changes in Agriculture

The labor shortage had its deepest impact on Arkansas farming, where it made the family farm an endangered species by 1940. Many people had remained on the farm only because

A Mechanical Cotton Picker (photographer and date unknown) Delta agriculture was revolutionized by the cotton picker during the 1960s and 1970s. This two-row John Deere cotton picker could pick ten bales of cotton in one day with each bale weighing 500 pounds. Such a machine cost about $15,000 and displaced about 60 agricultural laborers. The four-row model, common in the 1980s, cost more than $100,000.
Arkansas History Commission

there were few outside opportunities. The War generated new jobs and accelerated rural flight, which lasted into the 1980s. Some 19,700 families abandoned their farms in 1943, leaving 420,538 acres untended. The untenanted shack in the Delta and sagging house and tumbledown barn in the Ozarks remained visible reminders of collapsed dreams. Even these eventually vanished, and often only daffodils marked the spot where generations had lived and died.

With mechanical cotton pickers still in their infancy, Delta planters who had been anxious to expel labor only a few years before now were frantic to keep it. Vagrancy laws were used in Marked Tree and Harrisburg to force blacks into the fields to pick cotton. More questionable means were adopted by some planters who apparently believed that the old ways still could be applied. Two major prosecutions by the federal government for peonage were made during the War. One was of a Mississippi County planter, James Buchanan, who fled the country, and the second was of Cross County planter Albert Sidney Johnson, who was convicted and sentenced to two-and-a-half years in prison for holding two families in captivity.

Social Problems in Wartime

The urbanization that accompanied the War and the arrival of thousands of Northerners at military bases created a variety of challenges to old ways. The War had a major impact on the Arkansas family. Thousands of new families were created as couples rushed to get married before the man left for the service. Women, traditionally "barefoot and pregnant" in the lower classes, often got high-paying wartime jobs. Having babies was popular. New family relationships manifested during the War produced a rising divorce rate, sometimes because women literally took to wearing pants in defiance of their husbands. War brides did not always display fidelity to their departed mates. Others became war widows. These dislocations, both physical and psychological, led Arkansas to record more divorces than marriages during the war years.

Drinking and cigarette smoking by both sexes increased. Child abandonment became a statewide concern, and venereal disease, which was especially associated with "Victory Girls," was a major problem around military bases and was discussed openly in the press for the first time in the state's history.

The state legislature looked at some of these matters. Critics claimed that Arkansas marriage and divorce laws were farces

Wartime Couples in Batesville *(photographer and date unknown) World War II resulted in a flood of marriages, a loosening of family ties and a rising divorce rate. Some of the liberation is suggested by this snapshot of two couples.* **Author's Collection**

designed to enrich county justices of the peace and that they gave the state a bad name. One 1941 bill proposed a blood test for venereal disease before issuance of a marriage license. As with many other progressive ideas, this one ran afoul of Arkansas's racial sensibilities. "Only Negroes had syphilis," proclaimed Mississippi County Senator Ivy Crawford, who stated that the bill was an insult to white women. The 1945 legislature finally passed a law sponsored by Sebastian County Representative Russell Turnipseed requiring a three-day waiting period that a judge could waive for cause. "Cause" was usually $50 in the border towns of Arkansas where the quickie marriage market continued to thrive. Residents of these towns remembered seeing couples marrying who were too drunk to stand up.

The resurgent conservatism that marked the era found one manifestation in wartime liquor legislation. The passage of Initiated Act 1 in 1942 allowed 15 percent of a county's voters to place local option liquor laws on the ballot. A spate of counties, mostly in the hill country, reacted to wartime dislocations and especially the absence of servicemen by voting "dry." In Craighead County, where it was estimated that 5,000 voters were absent, the "wets" campaigned under the slogan "Leave It Alone Until the Boys Come Home." The "dries" won, but the absentee vote was heavily "wet."

The law banned sale but not possession, so a new type of bootlegging became common in Arkansas, with adjacent wet counties benefiting from the trade. This determination to continue a social experiment that most of the nation had abandoned marked Arkansas as a "Bible Belt" state.

Most communities did not have a military base or munitions factory, but World War II touched the lives of all Arkansans. The home folks of Arkansas felt the effects of the War in various ways. Nationwide rationing of food was greeted with a good deal of scorn in many rural areas. Enforcement was most effective in urban areas. An active black market flourished, especially for meat. Farm families with cattle were able to send their meat coupons to relatives in the North or West. Gasoline rationing and lower speed limits interfered with Arkansas males' favorite romance, their cars. Newspapers reported some wines were selling more of their best brands than ever before. Farmers were granted special rights, including access to scarce rubber tires. Many converted anything with axles into farm wagons so they could acquire extra sets of tires. Some were sold on the black market, but others were hoarded throughout the War. Anoth-

er prominent feature was the home victory garden designed to increase agricultural production of vegetables. The recycling of metal, home canning, knitting sweaters and support for patriotic activities involved most families.

Blacks in Wartime

World War II propaganda emphasized American freedom and democracy in contrast to Nazi persecution and dictatorship. Black Arkansans, who shared unequally in freedom and democracy, responded with a patriotism probably equal to that of a majority of whites and emerged from the quiescent state that had prevailed so long. Wartime labor shortages even brought blacks into Arkansas factories. Nondiscriminatory federal hiring came when black union leader A. Phillip Randolph's threatened wartime march on Washington forced President Roosevelt to make nondiscrimination a legal requirement for government contracts. The armed services remained segregated, but army supplies were produced by integrated factories.

Arkansas politicians responded negatively to these developments. Eli Collins, state director of the Division of Unemployment Compensation, claimed that "Negroes need training not in fields of competition but in those areas in which he [sic] is traditionally accepted — domestic, custodial and agriculture work." Even so, a federally sponsored national defense training program in construction opened in Little Rock for blacks with experience and a tenth grade education. One obstacle remained on the local level. Unions continued to deny membership to blacks.

Arkansas blacks were influenced greatly by the presence in the state of drafted Northern blacks, many of whom had been raised in integrated environments and were not intimidated as easily as those from Arkansas.

The first recorded wartime racial episode in the state happened near Gurdon. A state highway patrolman spotted the all-black 94th

Engineers Battalion singing as it marched and ordered the white officer to keep his men quiet in the presence of whites. This the officer not only refused to do, but he had the temerity to reply that his men were "as good as if not better than white people." This remark so enraged the patrolman that he assaulted the officer. Local whites believed that the great and long feared race war had indeed erupted and armed themselves to fight the blacks, but further violence was avoided. The slaying of black Sergeant Thomas B. Foster by a Little Rock policeman proved to be internationally significant when German propaganda used it to encourage disaffection among black soldiers. "Why should we go over there and fight; these are the sons-of-bitches we should be fighting," one black soldier commented.

In contrast, the *Arkansas Democrat* blamed the National Association for the Advancement of Colored People for the slaying. The incident prompted Little Rock to hire some black policemen for the first time since the end of the nineteenth century. Assigned only to the black West 9th Street corridor, they were not permitted to touch whites, and were not included in the policemen's pension fund.

As Northern blacks were pushing for the removal of segregation, Arkansas blacks went to court during the war years just to implement the "equal" part of the *Plessy* v. *Ferguson* (1896) "separate but equal" doctrine. One galling subject for Arkansas blacks was inequality in education. The United States Supreme Court had held in *Missouri ex rel Gaines* v. *Canada* (1938) that if Missouri provided a law school for whites, it had to offer one of equal quality for blacks. There were no facilities at all in Arkansas for graduate education for blacks: no law school, no medical school and no graduate degree programs. Instead of seeking compliance with the decision, Arkansas decided to offer blacks what had been declared unconstitutional in Missouri — namely a personal grant of funds

John Debrao, Sailor *(photographer and date unknown) Even though the Armed Forces remained segregated, World War II provided many opportunities for black men.* **Author's Collection**

for out-of-state study. Funded at first by $2,000 and increased to $5,000 by Act 345 of 1943, the funds came from AM&N's already pitiful budget. The War delayed a test case on this evasive action, but the hollowness of the sacred racial doctrine became increasingly apparent, even to some whites.

Of more immediate concern to the Arkansas Teachers Association, the professional group of black educators, was the issue of pay differentials between equally qualified black and white instructors. The United States Supreme Court upheld without comment an appeals court ruling in *Alston* v. *School Board of Norfolk* (1941) that discriminatory pay was unconstitutional, and Susie Morris, a black English teacher at Little Rock's Dunbar High

School, filed suit in federal court challenging the Little Rock School District's policy. United States District Judge T. C. Trimble heard testimony from Annie Griffey, the white supervisor of primary teachers, that although the plaintiff had top grades from the University of Chicago, "no white primary teacher in Little Rock is inferior to the best Negro teacher."

Impressed, Judge Trimble ruled in favor of the school district but was reversed in 1945 by the Eighth Circuit Court of Appeals. However, the reversal did Susie Morris little good because she was fired immediately and not rehired until 1952. The moral was that individual blacks might win theoretical victories in faraway courts, but because equalization of pay scales would cost the state more than $1,000,000, it would be opposed on a case-by-case basis.

Education was not a basic constitutional right, but voting was. The United States Supreme Court also began examining Southern voting regulations against blacks in a series of cases and rendering decisions that threatened the white establishment. Two versions of Oklahoma's "grandfather clause" fell before the court as did the Texas White Primary Law.

Restrictions on black voting in Arkansas were not as blatant as those in Oklahoma's Constitution or Texas state law. After the United States Supreme Court gave blacks the right to vote in the Democratic primary in *Nixon* v. *Herndon*, (1927) Arkansas blacks made an effort to exercise their voting rights. The state Supreme Court reasoned in *Robinson* v. *Holman* (1930) that although party primaries were legal elections under state law, the state had no control over private bodies such as the Democratic Party if it refused to allow blacks to vote. The United States Supreme Court agreed with this logic in *Grovey* v. *Townsend* (1935).

Despite their inability to participate in the Democratic primary, Arkansas blacks organized the Arkansas Negro Democratic Association (ANDA) as blacks moved nationwide

from being Republicans to strong supporters of the New Deal. Northern Democrats increasingly made overtures to black voters in ways that alarmed Southern segregationists. South Carolina's United States Senator "Cotton Ed" Smith walked out of the 1936 Democratic National Convention, appalled that Negroes were seated on the platform. A reflection of this sentiment came in Arkansas in the 1940 gubernatorial race when Homer Adkins distributed a picture of Governor Bailey talking with a black woman.

Racism was featured even more prominently in 1942 when Brooks Hays announced for David D. Terry's vacated Congressional seat and was opposed by Lieutenant Governor Bob Bailey. Bailey claimed Hays favored racial equality and asked his audiences rhetorically, "Well, we don't want any nigger votes, do we?" Hays was quick to deny the charge and countered by distributing a resolution from the Women's Society of the Methodist Church, South, strongly denouncing the use of racism in politics. In a wartime atmosphere that was hostile to racism, Hays, a Baptist, was able to defeat Bailey and finally obtain office. Even so, the average white Arkansan was alarmed by the new political assertiveness of blacks. In Congress, E. C. "Took" Gathings opposed a bill giving soldiers the right to vote absentee because it might have led to more blacks voting. The United States Supreme Court returned to the question of primary voting during the height of the War. *Smith* v. *Allwright* (1944) reversed the earlier decision that political parties were private and held that when the selection of candidates for public office was given to political parties by state law, primaries became state action from which blacks could not be excluded. Exultant, some Arkansas blacks who had been rejected from the polls in 1942 went to vote in July 1944 and this time were successful.

The opening of the Democratic primary to black voters terrified some whites. Governor Homer Adkins proclaimed that, "The Democratic Party in Arkansas is a white man's party" and supported two methods to limit black participation. The first was a test oath for Party membership that required all persons to swear to support the permanent separation of the races. A similar requirement was enacted in South Carolina in 1949 and was overturned by the United States Supreme Court; apparently no attempt was made to enforce the oath in Arkansas before the Court's invalidating decision.

Governor Adkins also tried to create a double primary system, once again separating state and federal elections. At a time when all state functions were strapped for cash, Arkansas assumed the additional expense for two years of holding two primaries for the sole purpose of minimizing black voting. In reality, the possibility of black participation in primary elections was not worth the cost. As long as payment of the $1 poll tax was required to vote — it had survived a major repeal effort in 1937 — poverty and ignorance were the most effective deterrents to black political participation.

The 1940s produced a voice for Arkansas blacks. Mississippi-born salesman L. C. Bates always wanted to own his own business, so he saved his money, bought a press, and began publishing the weekly *State Press*. Although he was dependent on white business advertising, Bates voiced support for further black participation in politics and for economic advances ending racial discrimination. Bates tried to cover all black activities within the state and had agents selling the paper in Helena, Forrest City and other Delta towns. This first statewide voice, although carefully muted, gave Arkansas blacks a focus that proved important in the years ahead.

Education in Wartime

Arkansas's educational system was just recovering from the Depression when War came. The state still had some 3,000 separate school districts, and teacher salaries averaged $750 a year. Only 70,000 of the 170,000 youths of high school age actually were enrolled. Many teachers could not resist the combination of the draft and the lure of high-paying jobs in defense factories. Forty schools failed to open in the 1941-1942 school year, and an additional seventy-seven subsequently closed as teachers either could not be found or walked out on their contracts. By 1942, the turnover amounted to 46 percent of the teaching force. With neighboring states paying salaries more than twice that of Arkansas, teachers with experience and qualifications found new opportunities elsewhere. About 900 teaching vacancies were reported in 1943. One man reported having nine different teachers in just one year. Many of the replacements had fewer than 12 hours of college credits.

School officials across the nation called for federal assistance. Little was heard from hard-pressed Arkansas districts because it was unlikely the federal government would allow whites to keep most of this money from blacks. Arkansas congressmen voted against wartime federal assistance. Schools in Arkansas survived with makeshift teachers and depleted classes.

Colleges also experienced interruptions. Enrollment dropped by 20 percent in 1942 at Arkansas State College in Jonesboro. The 114 civilian students enrolled by 1943 were mostly females. Similar problems hit other schools, but the military's need for training solved the problem of empty classrooms. Cadet airmen trained at Jonesboro, and AM&N at Pine Bluff finally obtained a black ROTC program over white opposition.

Japanese Relocation and German Prisoners

As a defense measure during World War II, the United States government undertook the removal of all persons of Japanese birth or ancestry from the West Coast. This unselective group punishment was based more on anti-Japanese racial sentiment than on any military threat. Of the more than 112,000 persons affected, two-thirds were American citizens, and many of them had volunteered for military service. Yet these people were forced to sell their possessions and report to prison camps, two of which were in Arkansas. One near Rohwer in Desha County housed largely middle-class internees and the second smaller camp at Jerome in Chicot County housed farmers.

Besides the mixture of businessmen and farmers, the relocation camps contained skilled professional people. Henry Y. Sugimoto was already a professional artist at the beginning of the war. Most of his pre-war paintings, subsequently worth thousands of dollars, were lost when he evacuated to Arkansas. At Jerome, he taught art and soon attracted the attention of Hendrix College art professors who arranged for a show at the college. This, and a strong encouraging letter from John Gould Fletcher, encouraged Sugimoto to paint numerous scenes of camp life. These were subsequently published after the war in Japan. Another artist, George Akimoto, was confined at Rohwer where he became the cartoonist for the camp newspaper. Akimoto invented a camp mascot, "L'il Dan'l," who wore a coonskin cap and affected Arkansas ways. Akimoto subsequently became a successful commercial artist.

Neither state officials nor private citizens were happy about the Japanese in Arkansas. Governor Adkins violently opposed the move, not only because of hatred for the Japanese but also because of the fear that Japanese school children might try to attend public schools, thereby threatening the segregated system. The sentiments of the governor were echoed in the legislature by Senator Richard K. Mason of Camden, who proposed that all those of Asian ancestry be excluded from the white school system. The measure died, but Attorney General Jack Holt told state officials not to issue birth certificates to children born in the camps. Act 47 of 1943 prohibited Japanese or anyone with Japanese ancestry from owning land in Arkansas. Subsequently, the attorney general declared the act constitutionally defective.

Both camps were located on swampy, forested lands that had been forfeited for failure to pay taxes. The internees were put to work clearing the land as their contribution to the War effort. Afterwards, the land was sold at from seven to fifteen times its original value, although none of the proceeds went to internees.

Other examples of hostility were common. The University of California had compiled a list of colleges where former students could continue their work. Arkansas A&M at Monticello initially agreed to admit student internees, but school president Marvin Bankston quickly changed his mind: "My school does not want any Japs." The Arkansas Medical Society was equally hostile. Its contribution to the persecution mania was first to keep any Arkansas doctors from treating the internees and then trying to prosecute under its monopoly licensing statutes a Tennessee doctor brought in to care for the Japanese by the federal government.

Civilians continued to complain to the Arkansas congressional delegation that the evacuees were getting special favors, especially too much food, and were not working hard enough. Governor Adkins continued his opposition and saw to it that no internees were allowed to work in defense plants. One irate World War I veteran finally told the governor, "Your empire from every conceivable angle is one of the poorest—culturally, economically, socially and politically. And if it is your fear that we might get involved in your messy social systems, then banish that fear, for we are too intelligent, too well educated, and too 'Americanized' to have any part of it." The *Arkansas Methodist* urged church members to extend a "hand of Christian greeting" to the "victims of the folly and madness of war."

Sketch of the Japanese Concentration Camp at Rohwer (artist unknown, 1944) Although a number of photographs of the Camp exist, none conveys the sense of a concentration camp better than this drawing. Given to what is now the University of Central Arkansas, the drawing was filed away for years under the title, "Oriental Art." **University of Central Arkansas**

What the Methodists had in mind was a massive conversion campaign. Most Arkansans seemed unaware that a majority of the internees were American citizens and probably shared the sentiments of one Arkansan who "tried to imagine a swarm of Japanese hoodlums swarming that [American Legion] hut telling our servicemen to bow to Allah."

The internees were confined to the camps and had little contact with local people. Those who did interact with the public found the results were not particularly encouraging. Two men working in the fields were fired on and wounded by a local farmer who thought they were trying to escape. Others were shot at during deer season. A private in uniform was shot in a Dermott cafe after he admitted his Japanese ancestry, and no charges were filed in the case. Hostility extended to whites working in the camps, and one school teacher was told she would never get a job in Arkansas again. After it was discovered that the internees were mostly loyal Americans, the camps were reduced in size and eventually closed. Probably no more than six families decided to stay in Arkansas.

Many Arkansans who were employed in the camps were impressed by the Japanese culture. Mary Reinhardt of Des Arc remembered that when she first began to teach at Rohwer there were no proper seats for her students, but only boards placed on top of tree stumps. One day she fell from one of these and her dress flew up. She noted that an American class would have hooted with laughter, but not the Japanese. Her students averted their eyes so that they and she could "save face."

German prisoners of war were almost welcomed in Arkansas. A total of 23,000 German prisoners, most from the Afrika Korps, arrived in Arkansas with some Italians after 1944. The main facilities were Fort Chaffee, Camp Robinson, and at Dermott, but thirty branch camps were established, mostly in the Delta, where some 7,000 prisoners were used as farm laborers. These camps formed a

Internees at Rohwer (*photographer unknown, 1944*) *This photograph of a class pageant at the Japanese Concentration Camp at Rohwer is full of irony. One boy is costumed as Uncle Sam, a girl as the Statue of Liberty, and in the rear, one child is in blackface.* **University of Central Arkansas**

strange contrast to Arkansas life. With camp orchestras, libraries and pianos, they displayed a higher cultural standard than that among the captors.

Prisoners in the fields helped sustain agriculture during the wartime labor shortage. They made poor cotton pickers, but German-American rice farmers in the Stuttgart region reported success from prisoner labor. Mickey McGahhey, a Stuttgart farmer who brought prisoners to the Letchworth Farm near Des Arc to work in the rice fields, reported that the Germans were good workers and that he had no discipline problems, except with one prisoner. That was quickly remedied, however, by McGahhey's refusal to buy beer for any of the workers on the way back to camp in Stuttgart on the days when this one recalcitrant prisoner misbehaved.

Politics and the Conservative Reaction

The crisis of the Great Depression had forced panic-stricken planters, merchants and corporate leaders into accepting new modes of thinking, new federal programs and new economic theory. Old patterns reappeared when the crisis passed. The conservative reaction against the New Deal was nationwide, and it had full play in Arkansas at both state and local levels.

No politician in Arkansas had benefited more from the New Deal than Governor Homer Adkins, but no man personally had less in common with the ideological directions that New Deal programs frequently took. Adkins's victory in the 1940 gubernatorial race over Carl Bailey had come about in part because Adkins controlled the votes of more than 20,000 federal employees. Yet Adkins had accused Bailey of making political use of state employees and promised to take the University of Arkansas out of politics. Once in office, he replaced Bailey men with his own supporters and launched an attack on the University that led to the ousting of its president, J. William Fulbright, largely because his mother, the publisher of the Fayetteville newspaper, the predecessor of the *Northwest Arkansas Times*, was a strong Bailey supporter. Adkins was unsuccessful two years later in keeping Fulbright from winning a congressional seat, and he also failed to stop archenemy Brooks Hays.

Adkins's troubles continued when he proved either unwilling or unable to fulfill his promise to end horse racing at Hot Springs and dog racing at West Memphis. Many counties were reacting positively to a new morality campaign by voting dry and moving against vice, but Adkins, who claimed to be a moral leader, failed to score any major victories.

Despite increased industrialization and a high demand for workers, the war years witnessed major setbacks for organized labor. The chief wartime troublemaker was United Mine Workers chief, John L. Lewis. In 1941, as war was threatening, Lewis called an industry-wide strike. Businessmen used patriotism to undermine support for Lewis and then extended the attack to all unions. The next year the Arkansas legislature was bombarded with anti-union bills aimed mostly at the Congress of Industrial Organizations (CIO), which had announced plans to sign up sharecroppers and domestic workers. There were grave dangers to the established racial order, one planter observed, "when agitators get among the Negroes and begin to preach social equality."

State Senator W. H. Abington of Beebe led off by offering his Anti-Violence Bill, which he claimed was intended only against the "Communist" CIO. The bill's main features made violence or threats of violence in labor disputes a state felony but only if done by labor. The bill received critical support from eastern Arkansas planters, and Governor Adkins, all the while protesting his support for working people, let it become law without his signature.

In 1943, John L. Lewis and the miners struck again, and public hostility to unions surged. The United States Army Mothers Club of Arkansas telegraphed the president demanding that Lewis be interned; a Sheri-

LET'S KEEP POLITICS

OUT OF THE UNIVERSITY ADMINISTRATION

The University should not be branded as a political football. The qualifications of the high office of president should be retained on merit, and NOT because of politics. It is for us, as students and future alumni, to assert our opposition to this atrocious maneuver of our state politicos, and to protect the good name of our institution.

• • •

Attend Student Rally
FRIDAY, 5:00 P. M.
MAIN AUDITORIUM

—— *Hear* ——

A. J. YATES, CORNELIA WILMANS, LAWSON CLONINGER, EDGAR BETHEL
AND OTHERS

Music ! —— Music !

Student Protest, May 16, 1941. Despite being warned not to mix in politics, University of Arkansas students rallied to the defense of President J. William Fulbright by a vote of 200 to 35 when he was fired by Governor Homer Adkins' newly appointed board. Roberta Fulbright, the owner of the Northwest Arkansas Times *and Fulbright's mother, compared Adkins unfavorably to Adolph Hitler. Fulbright later had his revenge by defeating Governor Adkins in the United States Senate race.* **University of Arkansas**

dan draft board refused to induct any more men until the government suppressed strikers. Congress responded by adopting the Smith-Connally Act giving the president additional authority to stop strikes. In Arkansas, a coalition of businessmen and eastern Arkansas planters gave to the voters a proposed constitutional amendment to destroy the unions' most potent weapon, the closed (i.e., all-union) shop.

The center of anti-union activity was in the southern Arkansas lumber industry, especially the Crossett Lumber Company and the Dierks Lumber and Coal Company. One AFL organizer observed, "they have always operated along the old feudal system and can't get the idea in their heads that the worker has any right to question what they are or are not given by the big industrial concerns." Both companies had running battles with unions for some time. In 1942, when the Office of Price Administration (OPA) had granted timber workers a 50 cents an hour increase, the Crossett Lumber Company had refused to honor the raise. When workers protested, the company threatened them with jail. The company also attempted to get German POWs as an alternate labor supply to keep the men docile. Both companies hoped to use the War to defeat the AFL.

There can be little doubt that most voters in 1944 did not understand the full meaning of Amendment 35. The tactics used to sell "right to work" stressed the freedom of each individual to decide independently whether to join a union. Editorially, the *Arkansas Gazette* opposed the amendment, but it passed easily. A weakened organized labor was unable to get the state to pass minimum wage laws, and other worker protections were inadequate. Thus World War II inaugurated a labor climate that formed the basis for future industrial promotion and cemented business political hegemony. It was not a climate very friendly to labor.

The conservative reaction also managed to eliminate the Farm Security Administration. The New Deal's agricultural policies had saved the large plants from bankruptcy and thrown a few crumbs to the small farmers. The FSA had loaned money to 23,981 farmers to improve their operations, and farmers had increased their per capita incomes from $396 in 1940 to $596 in 1941. The prospect of further aid antagonized the Arkansas Farm Bureau, which represented the planter interest. "There is no place in history for a decent standard of living except on the basis of com-

mercial agriculture," its president, Robert E. Short, proclaimed, and went on to denounce the agency for "perpetuating insidious and indefensible ideologies and socialistic experiments." FSA supporters, poor and unorganized, responded differently, claiming that the Farm Bureau "wants small farmers and farm laborers for legalized slaves."

In Crittenden County, Congressman E. C. "Took" Gathings took alarm when with FSA money a group of black farmers formed a homestead association and had white and black women working in the same office. Nationally, a combination of Republican and conservative Southern Democrats emasculated the agency in 1943 and succeeded in abolishing it in 1946. Not only did the small farmers lose a source of loans, but the agency's experimental farming projects were closed out after 1946. The land was sold, usually in such large chunks that small farmers had little chance to buy. The victory of the Arkansas Farm Bueau was complete, and the Farmers' Union, the small farmer organization, began a sustained decline. The dominance of the Farm Bureau added a major organized conservative voice to Arkansas politics.

Conservatism was also evident in the area of public health. At the start of the War, the Office of Defense Health and Welfare Services was set up under the Farm Security Administration. Organized by county health associations, families paid $12 for a membership and $1 for each family member. The program covered doctors' expenses but not medicine. Another federal program reached out to the wives of enlisted men and offered maternal and infant care.

Both programs came under attack from the Arkansas Medical Association. Although in the early years of the century the association had been in the vanguard in advocating public health measures, once the AMA had achieved a virtual monopoly on health services through its control of medical licensing, a rigid conservatism set in. Denouncing any federal involvement as socialized medicine, AMA president Dr. W. R. Brooksher claimed federal assistance "establishes the base for a much larger federal controlled program to cover all classes of citizens." The AMA forced the state Board of Health to drop its sponsorship, but the program was revived under the Children's Bureau of the Department of Labor. Despite all the wartime dislocations and social problems, the infant death rate in Arkansas fell in half, from 7.3 deaths per 1,000 births in 1936 to 3.8 deaths in 1943.

Some progressive measures were adopted despite the prevailing conservatism. The road debt adjustment plan that Governor Bailey was unable to enact was accomplished easily by Governor Adkins, and five new constitutional amendments added progressive features to state and local government. Amendment 30 provided for maintaining a city library through a local one-mill tax. Amendment 31 allowed cities to set up municipal police and firemen retirement funds with a two-mill tax, and Amendment 32 allowed a one-mill tax for county or city hospitals.

Amendment 33 aroused the most controversy. Prompted in part by Governor Adkins' firing of University of Arkansas President J. William Fulbright, the amendment sought to take the boards and commissions for various state institutions out of the governor's control. Terms were set from five to ten years, members could not be fired, and appointments were to be staggered. The amendment did have the effect of locking in Adkins' current appointees and was passed by the voters in 1942 by only 1,589 votes. At the same time, voters approved Amendment 35, a similar amendment applicable to the Game and Fish Commission, by a 40,000 vote margin. Finally, the voters in Amendment 36 allowed armed forces personnel absent from the state to vote without having paid the poll tax.

Overshadowing these accomplishments were the big political battles that developed around Homer Adkins. This long-time kingpin

of Arkansas politics had his eye on the United States Senate. Senator John E. Miller resigned in 1941 to take a federal judgeship, and his term was completed by Lloyd Spencer. The 1942 Democratic senatorial primary was an important event. Adkins chose not to run but reportedly encouraged Congressman David D. Terry, whom he earlier had supported against Brooks Hays. By another account, however, Adkins wanted Attorney General Jack Holt to win. In a three-way race between Terry, Holt and Congressman John D. McClellan, Holt came in first but lost the runoff to McClellan. Holt blamed his defeat on the failure of Adkins to deliver the necessary support. Embittered, Holt joined Bailey, Fulbright, Terry and others in the anti-Adkins camp.

Senator Hattie Caraway's term expired in 1944. Adkins had been her campaign manager against John McClellan six years before, but now he was the chief contender for her seat. Mrs. Caraway announced as a candidate for reelection, but she was almost forgotten in what was called "the million-dollar race." The chief contenders were Governor Adkins, oilman T. H. Barton of El Dorado and Congressman Fulbright. Barton spent large sums to import Grand Ole Opry stars for his campaign, but he and Senator Caraway were eliminated, leaving Adkins and Fulbright to fight it out.

All politicians in the state now ganged up against Adkins, and he went down to defeat. The elevation of J. William Fulbright to the United States Senate, joining John McClellan, reintroduced stability into federal politics in Arkansas. Fulbright, despite creating a wide variety of enemies, survived until defeated by Dale Bumpers in 1974.

Senator McClellan, although challenged by others more nearly in the Democratic mainstream, held his office until he died in 1977. Wilbur D. Mills of Kensett arrived in the House in 1939 and became the titular head of the Arkansas delegation as well as one of the most powerful men in Congress through his

The Arkansas Congressional Delegation *(photographer unknown, ca. 1945-1949), left to right, John L. McClellan (1896-1977), U. S. House of Representatives, 1935-1939, U. S. Senate 1943-1977; Wilbur D. Mills (1909-1992), U.S. House of Representatives 1939-1977; William F. Norrell (1896-1961), U. S. House of Representatives 1939-1961; Oren Harris (1903-), U. S. House of Representatives 1941-1966, U. S. District Judge, Eastern and Western Districts of Arkansas from 1966 until retirement in 1992; James W. Trimble (1894-1972), U. S. House of Representatives 1945-1967; J. William Fulbright (1905-), U. S. House of Representatives 1943-1945, U. S. Senate 1945-1975; Fadjo Cravens (1899-1974), U. S. House of Representatives 1939-1949; Brooks Hays (1898-1981), U. S. House of Representatives 1943-1959. E. C. "Took" Gathings (1903-1979), U. S. House of Representatives 1939-1969, is not pictured. Arkansas's delegation to the U. S. House of Representatives had seven members in 1940 and four in 1950 as a result of decrease in the state's population.* **Wilbur D. Mills Papers, Hendrix College**

mastery of the Internal Revenue code and as a member and then chairman of the powerful Ways and Means Committee. Other enduring figures were E. C. "Took" Gathings (1939-1969) from West Memphis; Fadjo Cravens (1939-1949) from Fort Smith; W. F. Norrell from Monticello (1939-1961) and Brooks Hays (1943-1959). A generation that had seen the federal government help solve local problems took over and stayed in power long enough to make their mark.

POST-WAR DILEMMAS

The Post-war Challenge of Modernization

Paul McNutt, the War Manpower Commissioner, proclaimed in 1945 that "This is a New Arkansas, an industrial as well as an agricultural state, a state matured by war." It was true that wartime federal expenditures had pushed many toward the threshhold of the new world. AP&L serviced 10,000 customers in 1940; the number stood at 74,000 by 1943. Eighty-one percent of the new jobs during the period had been created by federal money.

Arkansas faced a crisis when the War stopped. Regardless of the optimistic words of the commissioner, a 1945 poll of Little Rock high school seniors revealed that 63 percent of the boys and 57 percent of the girls planned to leave the state after graduation. Arkansans had tasted cream during wartime and showed no desire to go back to blue milk after the War.

Farming in Transition

One Lawrence County farmer wrote Congressman E. C. "Took" Gathings about the new atomic bomb that had been dropped on Japan. Could the Congressman get him one of these, the farmer asked, to use in his fields to get out the stumps? Almost as the farmer was writing his request, technology was producing the machines that replaced teams of mules, and modern land clearing was about to begin. Farming was about to undergo a revolution in this and in a variety of other ways.

Returning veterans often found that farming was not a desirable occupation. The ideal of the family farm had died in the poverty of the Depression, and the federal government's wartime and post-war policy of selling off the holdings of experimental farms produced a land market that only the well-heeled could enter. Federal farm price supports, especially for rice, encouraged eastern Arkansas farmers to clear land in the Delta at an accelerated pace. Almost 400,000 acres were added to production between 1945 and 1948, mostly to existing farms, and another 200,000 acres of cropland went into production between 1948 and 1955.

The southwestern Gulf Coastal Plain counties reverted to timber. Timber companies bought land from small farmers and planted trees with increasingly scientific precision in many southern counties. Farmers occasional-

ly discovered a new crop to replace cotton, as in Bradley County where the pink tomato became a major business after 1945 following its introduction in 1938.

While agriculture was being redirected, the lure of Northern jobs spurred the introduction of more and more machinery into the fields to replace lost laborers. Planters experimented in the early 1950s with Mexican *bracero* labor before it proved too expensive. Mechanical cotton pickers had been tested in the late 1930s and became a reality as the minimum wage paid to handpickers climbed. Larger tractors meant larger plows and cultivators, and output per farm laborer increased even as the number of laborers declined.

Post-war mechanization occurred in milk production. The typical 1940 farmer kept a few cows who gave an average of a gallon of milk a day. Most local communities were supplied from farmers' surplus, but Little Rock imported milk from out of state. With the introduction of electricity into rural areas, usually through the Rural Electrification Administration (REA), the enterprising farmer could buy an electric milker capable of servicing forty cows. Milk producers associations were formed, planned breeding produced a steady stream of milk, and the typical family farm no longer kept a cow by the early 1950s.

The same mechanization occurred in another cottage industry: chicken farming. Nearly all farm families in the 1940s kept chickens, mostly for eggs, and sold the surplus in town. Egg measurers created standard sizing by the 1940s. The first attempts to mass-produce eggs in the 1930s failed, but egg farms had become a specialized agricultural activity by 1950 and the brown egg was seen no more.

Broiler production was another local industry developed extensively in the Ozarks, often amid the ruins of early apple orchards. As with milk cows, selective breeding meant that the proverbial "spring chicken" became a year-round commodity. Chicken processing plants provided jobs but produced some of the foulest

"Me and Paul"

One way to escape rural poverty was through sports. The first team sport in Arkansas was baseball, which was played in every small town in the early twentieth century. When the sport grew in popularity in the cities during the 1920s, scouts actively recruited the very best small-town players for the big leagues. One of the first from Arkansas to become a national celebrity was Jay Hanna "Dizzy" Dean.

Born in Lucas (Logan County) in 1911, Dizzy grew up picking cotton. A desire to play ball, a natural skill in promoting himself and a disinclination to pick cotton led him into baseball. He began his professional career in the Texas League and went to the St. Louis Cardinals in 1930. Dizzy Dean, the strike-out artist, became a national celebrity during the height of the Depression when jobs were hard to find. A line drive broke his toe during the 1937 All-Star game, and his career as a pitcher was over within a few years.

He began a second career as a baseball announcer for the St. Louis Cardinals in 1941. His fractured English, with expressions such as "He slud into home," led the English Teachers Association of Missouri in 1946 to complain to the Federal Communications Commission. Dizzy replied

that, "All I got to say is that when me and my brother Paul were picking cotton in Arkansas, we didn't have no chance to go to school much." Dizzy moved from radio to television, becoming a permanent and well-loved fixture for more than a decade. Fortunately for persons worried about the fragile Arkansas image, he made his home in Mississippi, and few were aware of his Arkansas origins.

Dizzy's brother, Paul, joined the St. Louis Cardinals in the 1930s. A quiet, unassuming man quite the opposite of his flamboyant brother, Paul attracted far less media attention. He also kept his ties to Arkansas, retiring in the Springdale area.

Unlike Paul, Dizzy traded on his rural background in the same way as Lum 'n Abner and Bob Burns. His homey stories and erratic English took many listeners back to a simpler past. Something of a moralist, he refused to do cigarette advertisements or plug beer on Mother's Day.

In time, dozens of other Arkansans headed north to sports fame. George Kell, Arkie Vaughn, Brooks Robinson, Bill Dickey, Lou Brock and many others had important careers. Some chose to remember with affection their Arkansas origins; others did not.

---

odors ever encountered in Arkansas. The Springdale-based Tyson Food Company became one of the giants in the poultry industry by the 1980s.

Thanks to low-cost loans from Production Credit Associations (PCAs), hard work, new land-clearing methods and specialization, families who bought the land of those leaving and expanded their operations became agri-businessmen, even if some refused to admit it. For every farm family that remained, from five to twenty left. Of the 254,000 farms in 1933, only 74,000 remained by 1970. The farmer who failed to think and act as a businessman found survival difficult in the new world.

The most conspicuous feature of the new agriculture was the population loss that cost Arkansas one congressional seat in 1950 and two in 1962. Alexander Township in Chicot County had 1,283 persons in 1930; forty-two remained in 1950. Between 1940 and 1950, 17.7 percent of the state's whites and 32.5 percent of its blacks left Arkansas. The loss was even greater in the next decade: 19.1 percent of whites and 34.9 percent of blacks. So many people from Lawrence County relocated in Rockford, Illinois, that the Walnut Ridge *Times-Dispatch* added a weekly correspondent from the Illinois city.

The losses were greatest for the most productive members of the population. More than half the college graduates left immediately after graduation, and three-fourths of those remaining followed later. The very old and the very young stayed behind. In 1920, 3.5 percent of the state's population was sixty-five and over; that figure rose to 5.4 percent by 1940. By 1950, 7.8 percent were seniors, and the percentage was 14.1 percent by 1983, although by the 1980s retirees moving to Arkansas were inflating the percentage.

One lingering effect of World War II was in showing young men the military as a possible career. The manpower needs of the Cold War meant the reinstitution of the draft, but for the children of farm families, graduation from high school often meant enlistment in one of the services. Some made careers in the military, but most served their terms, learned a trade and settled outside the state, perhaps coming back to retire. The old folks back home continued farming until retirement and then sold out.

One-third of the elderly were on welfare by 1950, and the percentage increased despite the fact that benefits were extended grudgingly and the 1950 benefit rate of $33.16 a month was $20 less than the national average. Even less was done for children, perhaps because unemployed black mothers were often welfare recipients. The payment per child was 51 cents a month compared to the national average of $2.17. Rural poverty remained even as population declined.

Towns in Transition

Small towns and hamlets that served as trading centers were the hardest hit by rural flight. Some enjoyed a modest prosperity immediately after the War. The 1950 census revealed that all towns with more than 10,000 population had grown since 1940. North Little Rock even doubled in size from 21,137 to 44,097. In the Delta, the figures

Main Street, Jonesboro *(photographer unknown, ca. 1956) The sheer number of automobiles overwhelmed the traditional downtown shopping areas. By the 1960s the suburban shopping center rapidly was replacing the traditional downtowns.* **Author's Collection**

were misleading as an indicator of real gains. Some older farmers sold out and retired to town, increasing the percentage of nonproductive persons.

Higher wages for farm laborers had meant more money to spend in town stores, but as mechanization became increasingly common after 1950, dry goods and grocery stores that had formed the heart of the small-town economy rapidly closed. A symbol for Arkansas in the 1950s was the abandoned rural store, perhaps formerly a commissary, constructed usually of wood but sometimes of brick, its windows barred with iron to deter the rural poor and surrounded by a weed patch. Perhaps nearby would be the old railway cut because another death blow to many small communities was the end of railway service as in the folding of the Missouri and North Arkansas line in 1946, and the abandonment of nearly half the trackage in the Delta.

Industrialization and Promotion

One way for a small town to survive was to change from a farm trading area to a factory town. Unionization drives in the North motivated industrialists to examine Southern opportunities after the War. The equalization of railroad rates in 1946, which was the result of intensive legal work to which Arkansas contributed, removed one major barrier keeping Southern goods from the national market. Wartime industries had created a labor force and accustomed people to a national standard of living. Therefore, the goal of state industrial leaders was to perpetuate wartime prosperity after the War.

The "Arkansas Plan" began as a promotion of AP&L in 1943 and led to the establishment of the Arkansas Economic Council (AEC), which promoted industrialization with the slogan, "There Will Be No Apple Selling in Arkansas." The Arkansas Resources and Development Commission (ARDC), created in 1945, put state government behind the effort. The "Right to Work" amendment kept Arkansas labor unions weak, and other anti-labor legislation was directed against the threat of union violence.

The Arkansas Plan failed to solve all the problems. As a capital-poor state, Arkansas lacked investment money to aid new industries. Local bond issues occasionally helped new concerns but rarely those that already were established. Arkansas also had few facilities to train skilled workers. Finally, Northern white-collar managerial personnel voiced a marked reluctance to come to Arkansas, in part because of its image, but also because of its obvious education and health care deficiencies.

Arkansas leaders would do little about these substantive problems but did tackle the image issue. The post-war years saw an outpouring of books and articles designed to rescue the name of Arkansas. When *Look* magazine pictured an Arkansas hillbilly and linked that image to Nashville country music stars such as the Weaver Brothers, Elvira and comedian Bob Burns, it was said to "cheapen the ideals of the state." One Arkansas coun-

terattack came from Marguerite Lyon, an Ozark writer, who toured the state immediately after the War. At a time when Americans increasingly were accepting and cherishing cultural diversity, her book, *Hurrah for Arkansas*, was a throwback to the racist propaganda from earlier in the century. She noted that Texarkana's Confederate Memorial was the town's main attraction and De Queen's only Jew attended the Baptist Church. She avoided mentioning the ever-present mosquitoes when visiting Stuttgart and the Delta.

Karr Shannon, a newspaper columnist who had written affectionately about how woodpeckers once destroyed the Izard County courthouse, wrote a searing attack entitled *On a Fast Train through Arkansas*. Shannon castigated Henry Rowe Schoolcraft, Opie Read, Thomas Jackson and a dozen more obscure writers. He said that all the trains in Arkansas were fast, modern and efficient, which was a statement he perhaps could make in good faith because the Missouri and North Arkansas known as the MN&A, (Might Never Arrive), was now defunct. He asserted that the only thing wrong with Arkansas was a bad national image based on falsehood. Shannon was followed by the prolific Avantus "Bud" Green. Ozark writer Vance Randolph observed that Green "exaggerates the boasting of the Chamber of Commerce crowd to a degree that reduces the whole thing to absurdity."

A somewhat different picture of Arkansas life could be found in the 1948 publication of ten prize-winning essays by state high school students and published by the Arkansas Economic Council. Students were aware by exposure through radio, magazines and newspapers that Arkansas roads were bad, schools were underfinanced and civic pride often lacking. Their essays revealed a frustration with a number of these deficiencies: Mena had no natural gas, Clinton had no sewers, drainage was a problem in Tillar, city streets were unpaved in Sheridan, there were no parks in

Forrest City and libraries everywhere were inferior, if they existed at all.

Apologists claimed that industrialization would solve these problems. From advertising put forth at the state level, one could get the impression that all little towns were so anxious to welcome industry that they would do almost anything to accommodate themselves to changing ways. Actually, some rural trading centers were so entrenched in their habits that they preferred to perish rather than modernize. Many small town bankers, as well as those in Little Rock, were hesitant to make industrial loans. Thus, the conservative temper of the elite sometimes clashed with the progressive modernism of the age.

Some towns died as a result. One example was the small Mississippi County town of Joiner. Its merchants, foreseeing the decline of the farm trade, wanted to set up an industrial park. No landlord would sell land for it, however, and Joiner was empty and abandoned by 1989.

Arkansas attracted industries that paid wages below the national average. Little effort could be made to alter this pattern once it was established because that would mean stealing workers from going concerns.

Shoe manufacturing was the first post-war industry to invade Arkansas. Reaching south from St. Louis, shoe plants hired unskilled women who formerly might have picked cotton or worked as maids or waitresses. Landowners in the cotton-growing areas sometimes opposed shoe factories because they threatened their supply of pickers. When the federal minimum wage was 75 cents an hour in 1951, most Arkansas women worked in uncovered occupations for $1.25 a day.

During World War II the University of Arkansas received some federal money for research on war-related projects. These federally funded projects, Ordark and Arno, suggested to some that the University might have major research potential. In 1946, Wladimir W. Grigorieff arrived on campus with an engi-

neering degree from a Swiss institution and a Ph.D. from the University of Chicago and took over the management of the programs. In hopes of continuing this lucrative work in the post-war world, the University created the Institute of Science and Technology in 1948 with Grigorieff in charge. In only three years the Institute employed 36 scientists and utilized 23 graduate assistants. The budget was $532,000 of which less than a fourth came from University funds.

Both inside and outside the University, the Institute aroused fears. Older faculty, unfamiliar with research and resentful of the dynamic Grigorieff, insisted that research was not part of the University's purpose. State politicians, notably Congressman Boyd Tackett, claimed that outsiders, foreigners and subversives were on the University payroll. In 1953, bowing to pressure, Grigorieff left the University, joining the faculty of the highly secretive Oak Ridge Institute in Tennessee where the federal government did its major nuclear research. After his departure, the Institute was dismantled.

A quite different story took place in North Carolina, where under somewhat similar circumstances, a research triangle emerged that helped propel that state aggressively toward the national average in income per capita. Arkansas had its opportunity but chose another road. The state has always ranked at or near the bottom of federal research grant money received.

Politics in the Post-War Era

Continuity between wartime conservatism and the post-war era was provided by Governor Benjamin Travis "Business Ben" Laney's administration. A former mayor of Camden who was enriched when oil was discovered on the family farm, Laney was elected governor in 1944 after a three-way race eliminated former Congressman David D. Terry. State Comptroller J. Bryan Sims, who was to meet

Laney in the runoff, withdrew amid charges of a payoff, leaving Laney with only the usual token Republican opposition. Reelected without serious opposition in 1946, Laney claimed to be "conservative yet progressive" and a supporter of "old-fashioned Americanism." As a conservative, he endorsed the right-to-work constitutional amendment, called for greater efficiency in government and supported lower taxes on property offset by higher taxes on liquor and cigarettes. As a progressive, Laney masterminded the Revenue Stabilization Act under which state expenditures could not be made until funds were actually available, thus ending the old headache of deficit spending and laying the groundwork for a stable, modern state government.

The first indication of a change in the wind came when returning veterans entered politics. The federal government had engaged in extensive propaganda campaigns during the War to teach the American soldier the difference between Hitler's Germany and Roosevelt's America. Thus educated, returning veterans quickly became aware of the contrast between American ideals and Arkansas realities. Only one out of five possible voters participated in elections. The poll tax was one reason, but there was also indifference caused by widespread corruption. Poll tax receipts could be purchased in bulk for $1 each and sometimes were assigned to the names of the dead and to mules. The secret ballot was a joke because ballots had to be signed in the presence of election judges. Ballot boxes in some counties consisted of oil drums or Prince Albert tobacco boxes and results often were altered before being submitted to the secretary of state.

As bad as practices were in the state as a whole, they paled before those in Hot Springs. This resort and gambling center was experiencing its heyday in 1946. Part German spa town and part frontier gambling inferno, Hot Springs life was wild and luxurious amid casinos and brothels. The presiding political boss,

Leo McLaughlin, based his power on manipulating poll tax receipts and financed his position through a regular licensing system under which gamblers and prostitutes paid for protection from the law. Previous governors, responding to moral attitudes of the Arkansas voters, occasionally engaged in off-season raids but otherwise left Hot Springs alone.

The first wave of resurgent progressivism in Arkansas began in Hot Springs with the formation of the Government Improvement League, soon shortened to GI and identified with veterans. It was in Hot Springs that the movement found its leader in the person of Marine hero Sidney McMath.

Challenging the McLaughlin machine, McMath asked about the veteran:

> When he returns to his own community from the War and finds his own people deprived of their right to vote, when he discovers that their lives and liberties are not secure, when it is threatened that if he exercises the right of citizenship and runs for public office without the consent of the political boss . . . what is his reaction?

After being counted out at the polls, McMath and his allies managed to get the case into federal court, where McLaughlin had little power. Judge John E. Miller overturned the election and McMath swept to victory as prosecuting attorney. Veterans movements experienced varying results in other counties, winning in the Pine Bluff city elections and capturing the county judge's seat in Pope County but losing narrowly in machine-ridden Crittenden County, where Judge C. H. "Sly Cy" Bond ruled.

The race made McMath a statewide political figure and a candidate in 1948 for the governor's seat being relinquished by Ben Laney. The 1948 gubernatorial race was a reflection of the travail of modernization in many ways. McMath's opponents were Horace E. Thomp-

Uncle Mac MacKrell *(photographer unknown, 1948) This radio evangelist turned politician added to public interest in a hotly contested gubernatorial race in 1948. A few years later, MacKrell moved to Texas where he mixed insurance, politics and fundamentalism. He returned to Arkansas and made another unsuccessful race in 1970.* **University of Central Arkansas**

son, an eastern Arkansas politician; Frank Holt, the former attorney general and James "Uncle Mac" MacKrell, a popular radio evangelist. All previous political campaigners since Jeff Davis paled in comparison to MacKrell. Political scientist V. O. Key, Jr. summarized him as having:

> an appeal based mainly on irrelevances, a fantastic ignorance of governmental problems, a spectacular platform manner, and a capacity to stir the rustic.

McMath not only revived progressive rhetoric but got support from both AP&L and the rural electric cooperatives, and from Homer Adkins and Carl Bailey. He also called

for voters to approve a new state bond issue for major highway construction. The other candidates soon offered similar programs, and the battle became one of personalities. McMath led the field in the primary with 27,000 more votes than Holt and 30,000 more than MacKrell but failed to win a majority. For the runoff with Holt, MacKrell offered to sell McMath his support for $25,000 and the right to name some key officials in the new administration. Thinking they would win handily, the McMath forces rejected the deal.

Accepting the offer might have saved some trouble, because Holt claimed in the runoff that McMath was unsound on segregation. President Harry S Truman had so agitated

President Harry S Truman in Little Rock, Arkansas. (photographer and date unknown) *Arkansas supported Truman in 1948, and he returned the compliment.* **Arkansas History Commission**

Southern Democrats by moving against segregation that ex-Governor Ben Laney was trying to split the Democratic Party and obtain a following for Dixiecrat Strom Thurmond. Little use had been made of racism in Arkansas, however, until Frank Holt demanded in a full-page advertisement in the *Arkansas Gazette*: "SID, ANSWER THESE QUESTIONS." Eight of the twelve queries were racial in origin, and were, in the language of rhetoricians, "loaded." McMath's strategy of not replying put him on the defensive, and his victory margin over Holt was a close 10,257 votes.

Pollsters said the 1948 presidential contest was supposed to be won by New York Republican Thomas Dewey. One faction of the Democratic Party bolted to support Henry A. Wallace, and the Truman civil rights package boosted the candidacy of Strom Thurmond in the South. But incumbent President Truman refused to concede defeat. He found a strong ally in Governor-elect McMath in Arkansas. Supporting Thurmond were the Dixiecrats led by Ben Laney and the Arkansas Free Enterprise Association. Fresh from its victory over

labor in the 1944 right-to-work amendment, the association claimed that civil rights proposals were "communist-sponsored proposals to destroy states' rights."

McMath managed to control the Democratic State Convention in September and prevented the Dixiecrats from putting Thurmond's name on the ballot as the Democratic nominee rather than Truman's. Thurmond outpolled Truman only in those states (Alabama, South Carolina, Louisiana, and Mississippi) where he was listed as the Democratic nominee. Arkansas stayed true to Truman in November, and the civil rights issue moved to the back burner for the next few years.

Because neither United States Senators J. William Fulbright nor John McClellan worked actively for Truman, it was McMath to whom the victorious president turned for patronage advice in Arkansas. Conservative resentment against McMath surfaced two years later when Ben Laney emerged from retirement to challenge McMath's bid for a second term. Laney's slogan, "Re-elect Ben Laney a Second Time" was designed to convince voters that he was not running for the ill-charmed third term. The McMath people countered with The Complete Record of Ben Laney's Four Years as Governor of Arkansas, 1944-1948, a pamphlet of four blank pages. They also issued a comic-book life of their hero that would have made Horatio Alger blush. The Korean War was underway, incidentally boosting the president's popularity, and McMath offered a more aggressive approach to providing needed services. The voters responded to McMath's red, white and blue campaign by giving him a two-to-one margin over Laney.

Governor McMath's national stature exceeded that of any Arkansas chief executive up to that time. In addition to McMath's close ties to the president, Arkansas had two other natives serving in Washington: John Snyder as Secretary of the Treasury and Frank Pace as Secretary of the Army. Although individual Arkansans excelled, often after leaving the state, the McMath administration's challenge was to bring state services up to a level with the rest of the country. The issues that would dominate Arkansas domestic politics for the next half century were debated hotly during the McMath years. Roads, schools, industrialization and utilities were hardly new subjects, however, and the post-war years began with a remarkable similarity to the unlamented 1920s in both rhetoric and politics.

A New Era of Highway Construction

"We are not all spending our time on white-columned verandas sipping mint juleps, and plotting to keep our people in economic slavery," the governor told a Northern audience in 1949. In fact, the administration was trying to figure out how to deliver all the various paved roads that had been promised in order to win the election. Roads were the primary issue because they had been neglected for twenty years. Construction stopped with the onset of the Depression, and most maintenance was

deferred. The Adkins administration's refunding act gave the state the option of renewing work for the first time, but the War made labor and materials unavailable. The ancient highway system was deteriorating at the rate of $6,000,000 a year by 1947. The Chrysler Corporation advertised the durability of its products nationally by saying they had passed the "Arkansas mud test."

The McMath plan required voter approval of a new state bond issue. Some opposition developed, but voters gave four-to-one approval to the new indebtedness. During the next four years, the state spent more than $72,000,000, half on the primary system and the rest on secondary roads. Seven county seats saw their first paved connections, and Newton County got its first paved road. Twelve weight stations were built, roadside parks and picnic tables were set up and efforts were made to mark roads with proper lines and route markings. One administration bill made it illegal to run cattle, horses, mules, hogs, sheep or goats on the rights of way, and other laws raised the driving age from fourteen to sixteen, required examination of drivers and established motor vehicle inspection. The highway program also provided opportunities for corruption and partisan politics, ultimately helping end McMath's political career.

The Reform of Education

Long-suffering public education remained a perennial political topic. From the 900 teaching vacancies reported at the height of the War, Arkansas was still 800 teachers short in 1946, and 100 schools closed because of it. The number of school districts had declined from 5,112 in 1921 to 1,598 by 1948, but even that was too many in the eyes of educators. Local patrons, however, often wanted low taxes, minimal services and opposed innovative programs. The modernizers won a major victory in 1948 by gaining the passage of Initiated Act No. 1, which established procedures for consolidation and reduced the number of districts to 424. Another victory was Amendment 40, which removed the old nineteen-mill taxing limit on school districts. The closing of the one-room school helped bring the end for many communities. It meant damaged friendships and hard feelings for those actively involved. When the Board of Education in Carroll County reduced the seventy-four districts to three, two sticks of dynamite were found in one board member's car. The abandoned school joined the boarded-up store as a symbol of the fading away of the values of the agrarian age.

The GI Bill gave thousands of men the opportunity to attend college, greatly swelling enrollments and democratizing the schools in the process. This was tantamount to education for departure from Arkansas. With the smallest white collar class of any state, Arkansas had few jobs for college graduates. Their leaving for better jobs hurt education politically because college graduates generally supported education. A 1951 report examined colleges and concluded that they were underfunded, too numerous, and too subject to local politics. The statute books also groaned with obsolete laws: all students at Arkansas State Teachers College at Conway were required to teach for two years; Jonesboro, Russellville, Magnolia and Monticello were supposed to teach textile manufacturing, and paid leaves at Fayetteville were illegal.

The most vivid example of the legislature's attitude came with the passage of the Peebles Act, which required the medical school to accept applicants by county of origin rather than by qualification. Accreditation of the medical school became a controversial problem. Governor McMath proposed a major overhaul by building a new medical center and a state hospital. The Buchanan Estate of Texarkana donated a $500,000 for the medical facility, but legislative inaction delayed the project for several years.

Arkansas teachers faced a challenge from the Ford Foundation. The "Arkansas Experiment in Teacher Education," sometimes called the "bold experiment" or the "Arkansas Purchase," was an attempt to modify teacher training by requiring that the first four college years be spent in content courses and a fifth be devoted to pedagogical concerns. The college departments of education, believing that knowing how to teach took precedence over knowing what to teach, resisted the Ford Plan bitterly and it was abandoned by 1959.

One aspect of education that received increased public attention was the nature of the dual system of education for whites and blacks. To avoid providing graduate schools for blacks, the state had begun paying the costs during the War for those who left the state to study. There were more than 100 applicants and the cost had risen to $20,000 by the end of the War. Governor Laney favored regional segregated graduate schools and tried with little success to interest black leaders in the idea at a 1948 conference at Pine Bluff. The first chinks in the "separate but equal" wall began to appear inevitable.

McMath's administration publicly admitted some of Arkansas's problems. At the Arkansas Conference of Social Work on April 5, 1949, Education Commissioner A. B. Bonds charged that state funds destined for black schools were being diverted at the local level to white education. Ed McCuiston, State Director of Negro Education, showed that $4,250,000 had been diverted in the previous year, and Governor McMath threatened lawsuits if the diversions continued. The governor also supported funding for AM&N, a notable difference from the hostile attitude that Governor Laney had displayed toward the institution. The state appropriation for AM&N more than doubled in 1949, and new construction got underway. The school finally achieved full accreditation from the North Central Association of Colleges and Secondary Schools, and McMath named J. R. Booker, a black Little Rock attorney, to the AM&N board.

With new voting rights, more funds for education and an end to lynching, Arkansas blacks could be more confident of the future even though their numbers were declining rapidly. Few persons, white or blacks, foresaw how soon the cornerstone of the old segregated system, the public school, would be swept into litigation before the Supreme Court. Instead, the most commonly expressed desire, echoed by the state's black newspaper, the *State Press*, was to make separate but equal a reality.

McMath and Industrial Promotion

All Arkansas governors were committed rhetorically to industrialization. However, McMath placed less emphasis on the pool of unskilled labor and the negative attitude toward labor unions and tried instead to obtain higher grade industry. The state obtained 509 new or expanded factories valued at more than $209,000,000 during his administration. The outbreak of the Korean War also helped move industry forward in Arkansas because the state received federal facilities and war plants as a reward for supporting Truman in 1948.

McMath also made a major effort to alter the state's image. The first governor since Brough to appear before national audiences, McMath spoke at conventions of such diverse groups as the American Legion, the Veterans of Foreign Wars, the American Federation of Labor and the Urban League. In addition, he observed on the Arthur Godfrey radio program that, "We not only wear shoes but we manufacture shoes in Arkansas."

McMath's modernization program was not completely successful. State government projected a $10,000,000 shortfall between expenditures and income by 1951. McMath called on the legislature to tax soft drinks, and increase the income, cigarette and liquor taxes. The legislature balked, rejecting the income tax and soft drink proposal and raising the cigarette and liquor taxes only slightly. A legislative scheme to raise the sales tax met opposition from a governor hostile to regressive taxation. A special session failed to resolve the differences and led to early school closings in 1951.

The End of the McMath Era

The conservative resurgence — temporarily thwarted in 1948 by Truman's victory — emerged triumphant with Dwight D. Eisenhower's Republican victory in 1952 that coincided with the end of the McMath administration. After winning a second term handily in 1950, McMath began to take stands on issues that angered C. Hamilton Moses of AP&L, who had presided over the destiny of the most powerful business in Arkansas since the death of Harvey Couch.

A lawyer with immense political experience, Moses enjoyed the role of kingmaker. His quarrel with McMath began in 1949 when the Arkansas Electric Co-operative Corporation applied to the REA for a $10,000,000 loan to construct a steam generating and transmission plant at Ozark. AP&L, noted for its hostility to the co-op movement in general, was especially threatened if the co-ops could generate their own electricity. Co-op leader and former congressman Clyde Ellis had been active among the McMath supporters and found the governor receptive to his contention that AP&L was sacrificing the state's economic development in order to perpetuate its monopoly on generating power. The die was cast when McMath supported the co-ops before the state Public Service Commission.

The Ozark battle was protracted, with maneuvering in Little Rock and Washington before administrative bodies and in the courts. In supporting the co-ops, McMath found himself at odds with former schoolmate and incumbent Congressman Boyd Tackett of Nashville. Tackett labeled co-ops socialism, a charge that McMath denied by asking why it was socialism for co-ops to borrow the money but not socialism for AP&L to get Reconstruction Finance Corporation loans. As the Governor observed, "when it's all summed up, it's just a matter of who is borrowing the money."

The charge of socialism was related closely to the most emotionally disturbing issue of the 1950s: Communism. Anti-communism was housed institutionally in a business publication called the *Free Enterpriser*, which equated Socialism with Communism and both with labor unions. The magazine joined the crusade to get Magruder's *American Government* textbook banned in Little Rock, denounced the income tax continually, warned against something called Sunday School socialism and noted that a horticultural program entitled "One World of Flowers" furthered the Communist conspiracy. The magazine mysteriously noted that Arkansas contained forty-nine Communist Party members and 441 fellow travelers, none of whom was identified.

Harding College at Searcy, whose president, George Benson, was the Arkansas Man of the Year in 1954, responded to the threat of Communism by sponsoring the Freedom Forum, to focus attention on the threat of Communism to free enterprise and the American way of life.

Charges of corruption in the Arkansas Highway Commission created a second issue during the McMath years. Anti-McMath legislators forced the creation of the Highway Audit Commission (HAC) and placed a number of the governor's enemies on it. Little incriminating evidence was unearthed at first, but Attorney General Ike Murry joined the fray and the charges were broadened from inefficient, fraudulent and politically motivated purchasing to the claim that embezzlement reached the highest levels. One issue was the Indian Bay Road in Monroe County. Local residents had raised about $3,000 for its construction and signed the money over to Henry Woods, the McMath campaign manager, (later United States District Judge) rather than to the Highway Department. Woods deposited the funds into the campaign account. The Commission was refused access to McMath's campaign records, and the governor declined to appear in person to testify before the Commission.

McMath insisted that politics and not fraud was really the issue. He subsequently testified before a United States Senate subcommittee investigating monopolies that AP&L was behind the HAC and had harassed him in the legislature, all because of his support for the Ozark power plant. Even so, the audit revealed a seamy side to highway affairs that was obviously illegal even if it was the way state contracting had been done since statehood. The GI leaders were supposed to be above such things, and the red, white and blue governor went into his third term bid with his halo tarnished.

The first candidate to announce against McMath was Congressman Boyd Tackett. Trying to capitalize on United States Senator Joseph McCarthy's popularity, Tackett made his main issue McMath's veto of an anti-communist oath that the courts probably would have found unconstitutional anyway. Broadening the attack, Tackett demanded the firing of professors Harvalak and Grigeroeff at the University of Arkansas, saying that, "Even the prouncation [sic] of their names does not go hand in hand with the people in our midst."

The second major candidate to enter the field was Attorney General Ike Murry, who capitalized on his uncovering the alleged "mess in Little Rock." Sensing his chance for revenge, Frank Holt, who felt he had been robbed in 1948, entered the fray. Chancery Judge Francis Cherry, a political newcomer from Jonesboro with few statewide ties or liabilities, became the dark-horse entry.

The issues were obscured in part by the entertainment aspect. Ike Murry recruited country music star, the Duke of Paducah; Boyd Tackett, who flew over county seats and landed in a helicopter, brought in Hank

Williams Sr. and Minnie Pearl; Frank Holt enlisted Jimmy "You Are My Sunshine" Davis, a country and western singer later elected governor of Louisiana, and utilized the first drive-in headquarters. McMath brought out a new edition of the comic book, a rousing campaign song and counted heavily on a mammoth parade of his supporters.

However, it was Judge Cherry who introduced the major entertainment innovation in the race. Convinced by two Florida promoters that his limited campaign money would have the greatest impact if used on a massive radio "talkathon," Cherry talked for twenty-four straight hours over five Little Rock radio stations on July 2, 1952. Plugging "Dollars for Decency," he promised to answer any and all questions. This seeming frankness allowed his supporters to distribute every possible smear without Cherry himself having to endorse it. As a fascinated audience waited for him to tire, they heard "Is it true . . ." questions attacking McMath, his family and his administration. On the lighter side, Cherry sang "Happy Birthday" to children on request. He candidly discussed state problems without the usual vacuous rhetoric common to politicians. Sounding like an Arkansas Eisenhower and promising little but honest government and an end to serving liquor in the governor's mansion, Cherry repeated his "talkathon" in different parts of the state, although never again for twenty-four hours.

McMath led the ticket in the primary, but Cherry passed all other contenders and trailed the incumbent by a mere 9,000 votes. As McMath had less than one-third of the total vote (100,858 out of 329,050), and all of his opponents endorsed Cherry, the runoff was a foregone conclusion. Cherry won by nearly 100,000 votes. The election was especially bitter for McMath, who not only watched the big money shift to Cherry but also saw Senator John McClellan come from Washington to campaign for Judge Cherry and then take personal credit for his victory.

Conservative Interlude: The Cherry Administration

Cherry came into office as an enemy of the sales tax on feed, seed and fertilizer. Convinced that the state needed the money, however, he began his administration by vetoing the legislature's attempt to repeal the tax on those items. Drought conditions were putting considerable economic pressure on many hill farmers, and with poultry beginning to assume major importance, Cherry made many enemies by this unexpected veto.

The new governor also urged the adoption of a constitutional amendment requiring that all property be assessed at 100 percent of its market value. The state still relied primarily on the property tax for revenue, and assessment inequities were a state scandal. Cherry worked hard to get the measure on the ballot, but he dropped it when it got there. Voters feared any change in taxes, and those with the most to lose in tax modernization convinced the poor that there was a conspiracy to raise taxes.

Cherry also called welfare recipients "deadheads," dropped some 2,300 from the rolls, and suggested that every person receiving aid should sign a lien to the state on their property. His appointment of a Texan to run the state highway system and a Californian to head the State Hospital stirred resentment against "foreigners." Finally, AP&L rates went up by $3,900,000 even as drought conditions were worsening and unemployment was high. Cherry's biographer noted that the governor was, "essentially passive" in dealing with these problems, and this was not the quality needed to survive in Arkansas politics.

Sensing winds of disillusionment with Cherry, Orval Faubus, a Madison County newspaper owner, postmaster and McMath highway man, filed against the governor in the Democratic primary along with some lesser-known figures. Faubus was something of a rags-to-riches story. His father, a follower of Socialist

Eugene V. Debs, had been jailed for opposing United States participation in World War I.

Young Orval, raised in a log cabin near Combs in "borderline poverty and political radicalism," attended Huntsville High School and went from there to Commonwealth College in Mena. He worked as a fruit picker, lumber handler, hobo and school teacher during the Depression before being elected circuit clerk of Madison County in 1938 and again in 1940. At the onset of World War II, he enlisted as a private, rose to the rank of major and kept his name before the people by writing a newspaper column from the front.

Returning to Huntsville after the War, Faubus was appointed postmaster, bought the local newspaper and entered into state politics as a supporter of Sid McMath. He was described during this period as "always chewing a matchstick, wearing clothes that looked like Salvation Army castoffs and slicking his hair back with oil." But Faubus quietly built up a local following and statewide contacts. He emerged untarnished from the highway scandals although he was a commissioner and state highway director. Even so, few observers gave him a chance of overturning an incumbent governor seeking the customary second term.

Playing on rural fears of tax increases and citing his record on highways, Faubus and two other dissidents, Guy "Mutt" Jones and Gus McMillan, narrowly kept Cherry from getting a majority of the votes cast, forcing the incumbent into a runoff. In the runoff, Cherry raised the charge on television that Faubus's attendance at Commonwealth College tainted him with Communism. After first denying the charge clumsily, Faubus admitted that he had attended the school but asserted that he never paid tuition, attended classes or participated in school events. He said he went home as soon as he discovered the nature of the school.

Arkansas Gazette editor Harry Ashmore and Judge Edwin E. Dunaway crafted a denial speech for Faubus, who rushed in from campaigning, and read their work by flashlight en route to the television station. The *Gazette*, which had avoided gubernatorial politics since the days of Jeff Davis, denounced Cherry for using a McCarthy-type smear. Just how involved Faubus really was with Commonwealth College has intrigued historians, but Cherry's charge generated a sympathy vote for the poor-boy Faubus in the runoff. In an election marked by the usual fraudulent practices, Faubus polled 191,328 votes to 184,509 for Cherry. It was the first defeat for an incumbent first-term governor since 1926.

Little Rock Republican Mayor Pratt Remmel announced for governor after Cherry's political demise. Nephew of prominent Republican Harmon Remmel, he had been active in Republican circles and had considered running against incumbent Congressman Brooks Hays. He changed his mind after Cherry's defeat and entered the governor's race, backed by the assurance from many Cherry supporters that he would get their votes.

Remmel managed to visit every Arkansas county, promised a moral reformation and emphasized his religious values. He also assured incumbent Democratic appointees that they would be kept on in the event of his victory. Faubus ran scared in the general election, although he outpolled Remmel by 81,000 votes. Nevertheless, Remmel's 127,004 votes compared more than favorably with the 49,292 that Jefferson W. Speck had managed two years earlier and represented a rebirth for the moribund state Republican Party.

The 1954 Democratic primary also saw Sid McMath's challenge to incumbent Senator John McClellan, a match sparked by the bitterness left over from McClellan's active support of Cherry in the previous gubernatorial election. Calling McClellan the "Republican Senator from Arkansas," McMath castigated him for supporting the grant of off-shore oil rights to the states rather than to the nation, linked McClellan to AP&L and censured him for supporting the witch hunts of Joe McCarthy. Heavily financed, McClellan polled

The Thin Gray Line. *(Mendy, 1953) This photograph, taken after the widows and children of Arkansas's Confederate Veterans were dumped at Camp Robinson, suggests their displeasure with the move. Public outrage at the Cherry Administration helped elect Orval Faubus to the governor's office in 1952.* **Arkansas Gazette**

164,905 votes compared to 127,941 for McMath and 31,068 for other candidates. The incumbent ran up his largest margins in Delta counties, where McMath supporters charged that fraud was common and anti-McClellan votes had been manipulated.

Faubus: The First Term

The new governor inherited a difficult situation. Cherry's economies found Arkansas with the nation's lowest teacher salaries. Meanwhile, the post-war baby boom was beginning to put major stresses on schoolhouse capacities. The state's working population continued to decline, 200 patients were sleeping on the floor at the State Hospital, and the last widows of Confederate veterans were dying off rapidly in an overheated army barracks.

However, the most widely discussed issue had little to do with government services. Horse racing had been legalized at Hot Springs, and the franchise came up for renewal during Faubus's term. Gambling interests also wanted to develop dog racing at West Memphis. Considerable money was involved in each case, so much political jockeying took place. The day the State Racing Commission was to decide, Faubus fired all of the members he originally appointed. His new appointees renewed the existing franchise at Oaklawn but rejected the application for the dog track.

Faubus scored a popular victory on the utility issue. The AP&L rate increase that had damaged Cherry was rolled back, and consumers got a $9,000,000 refund. An attempted increase by Arkansas Louisiana Gas Co. (Arkla) fared no better, and $1,000,000 was returned to consumers. By combining industrial promotion with social justice, Faubus was able to build a strong record during his first term as governor. He confidently predicted that Arkansas was just about poised to enter the atomic age and become a diversified and prosperous state.

CONCLUSION

The question of black civil rights had been a threatening cloud on the political horizon during World War II and into the post-war period. Perhaps because blacks were leaving the state rapidly, attempts to insert the race issue directly into politics failed. Progressive rhetoric, devoid of racism, constituted the Arkansas politics of Bailey, McMath and Faubus, although not of Adkins or Laney.

The twentieth century increasingly was marked by economic and social shocks. The first of sufficient magnitude to be noticed by ordinary people was the Great Depression. During this event Arkansans had fallen back on their own local resources but soon found out they could not weather the storm without massive federal assistance. The second shock was World War II, not because it was a world war, but because it offered escape opportunities for all those who had come to feel that Arkansas had become a trap rather than a land of opportunity. Many left, and even those who stayed desired to share in the American standard of living. This was the challenge of the post-war decade, and one which, despite some notable efforts, was not met. The destruction of economic footings for family farmers gave rural children few viable choices other than flight, while the mechanization of agriculture displaced the landless laborers of the Delta. It was impossible to find enough factory jobs to take up the slack, and because of educational and health deficiencies, the working class was not prepared to assume new roles. Significant population loss hurt the South politically, and the North resented the arrival of often unskilled and uneducated people whose Southern ways of life ill fit Northern standards. The resulting social problems were still much in evidence half a century later.

Population displacement and loss affected every aspect of Arkansas life. Racially motivated incidents declined during the Great Depression, but an underlying belief in segregation remained strong in the white consciousness. It surfaced several times in World War II, and white Arkansans added Japanese to their list of undesirables. National tolerance for the South's institutional racism began to wane, and at least a few Arkansans recognized that trying times were ahead. The key question for Arkansas was whether the public's support for transforming Arkansas into a modernized state was worth sacrificing in order to maintain the racial status quo. It was not a question a majority of white Arkansans had ever considered or even wanted to think about. Perhaps had Arkansas not had the mind of a closed society on racial issues, the events of the following decade might have taken a different turn.

BIBLIOGRAPHIC ESSAY

Although critical in the state's development, the period 1940-1954 has begun to attract scholarly attention only recently. The only overview is Boyce Drummond, "Arkansas, 1940-1954" in *Historical Report of the Secretary of State,* III, 175-185. The significance of the war is emphasized in C. Calvin Smith, *War and Wartime Changes.*

The issue of civil liberties in wartime Arkansas warrants further study. Only the court decisions are available readily at present, with *Johnson* v. *State* being the leading case. H. L. Weinstock, "The Drought of 1944: Craighead County Goes Dry," *CrCHQ,* XXII (fall 1984) discusses Wartime liquor controversies. Little data can be found on Arkansas military participation in the War. A published biography is James L. Hudson, "Major Pierce McKennon: Arkansas's 'Boogie Woogie' Playing Air Ace," *AHQ* XXIII (spring 1964), 3-35. Frances Shiras, "Norfork Dam," *AHQ* IV (summer 1945), 150-158, discusses the history of a wartime project. Black Arkansans' struggle to regain voting rights awaits a study, but some reference to the first attacks on segregation can be found in Thomas E. Patterson, "History of the Arkansas Teachers Association," (Washington, 1981).

The story of the Japanese relocation program produced two articles: Ruth B. Bickers, "Japanese-American Relocation," *AHQ,* X (summer 1951), and William Cary Anderson,

"Early Reaction in Arkansas to the Relocation of Japanese in the State," *AHQ,* XXIII (autumn 1964), 195-211. See also, Deborah Gesensway and Mindy Roseman, *Beyond Words: Images from America's Concentration Camps* (Ithaca: Cornell University Press, 1987). German prisoners were the focus of Merrill R. Pritchett and William L. Shea, "The Afrika Corps in Arkansas, 1943-1946," *AHQ,* XXXVII (spring 1978, 3-22.

Little attention has been paid to wartime and post-war farming except in the gathering of farm statistics. However, Robert W. Harrison, "Clearing Land in the Mississippi Alluvial Valley," *AHQ,* 352-371, discusses one important aspect of the change. Milk production in the Cabot area was analyzed in J. M. Park, Jr., "The Evolution of an Industry," *AHQ,* XI (autumn 1952), 149-163. Robert L. Gatewood, *A Bicentennial History of Bradley County, Arkansas,* (Warren, 1976), offers a brief account of the pink tomato in that area.

Industrialization and promotion have attracted more attention. The promotional literature includes Marguerite Lyon, *Hurrah for Arkansas* (New York, 1947); Karr Shannon, *On a Fast Train Through Arkansas* (Little Rock, n. d.), and three works by Avantus Green, *With This We Challenge,* (Little Rock, 1945); *Look Who's Laughing,* (Little Rock, 1947), and *The Arkansas Challenge, a Bragging, Roasting, Swaggering, Toasting Handbook on the Wonder State,* (Little Rock, 1966). More realistic are the various economic reports, notably Morris Lamberson, *An Analysis of the Financing Experiences of New and Expanding Manufacturing Firms in Arkansas,* (University of Arkansas Industrial Research and Extension Center, 1972).

"Selfish Arkansas Power," a defense of business, appeared in *Fortune,* XLVI (October 1952), 127-206, and the comments in "Ten Prize Winning Essays by Arkansas High School Students," (Little Rock 1948), deserve notice. Various aspects of state government are treated in *Taxes and Government Services in Arkansas,* (University of Arkansas Industrial Research Center, 1956). Stinnett and Kennon, *All This and Tomorrow, Too* (Little Rock, 1951), show veiled hostility to the Ford Foundation Plan, but Robert A. Leflar, *The First Hundred Years: Centennial History of the University of Arkansas,* was cautiously optimistic.

Much attention has been given to politics. A general study invaluable for the South as a whole and Arkansas in particular is V. O. Key, Jr., *Southern Politics in State and Nation,* (New York, 1949). An overall view of Arkansas can be found in Boyce A. Drummond, "Arkansas Politics: A Study of a One-Party System," (Ph. D. diss., University of Chicago, 1957). Also revealing is *Investigation of Presidential, Vice Presidential, and Senatorial Campaign Expenditures, 1944,* Report of the Special Committee, 79th Congress, 1st Session, Senate, Report No. 101 (Washington, 1945). Some detail is given in Ben Laney, *A Report to the People of Arkansas, Our Stewardship in Public Office, 1945-1949,* (Little Rock, n. d.), and Senator John McClellan got national recognition with Milton MacKaye, "The Senate's New Investigator," *SEP,* CCXXVIII (August 13, 1955), 30-70. Of the men who dominated the era, Sid McMath received a laudatory biography in Jim Lester, *A Man for Arkansas: Sid McMath and the Southern Reform Tradition,* (Little Rock, 1976).

Arrival of Federal Troops in Little Rock, 1957 *Larry Obsitnik, an* Arkansas Gazette *photographer, caught the conflict between modernization and traditionalism in graphic form as federal troops cross the Arkansas River in the pre-dawn hours on their way to take up positions at Little Rock Central High School.* **Nina Obsitnik and the Arkansas Gazette**

Chapter XVII

The Conflict of Integration and Modernization

INTRODUCTION

The South underwent a second Reconstruction between 1954 and 1976. The Thirteenth, Fourteenth and Fifteenth Amendments to the United States Constitution began to be enforced seriously and uniformly for the first time, along with the federal civil rights laws passed during the first Reconstruction immediately after the Civil War and new laws passed in the 1960s. Collectively, the amendments and new laws guaranteed full citizenship and equal rights for black citizens. A reluctant national government began to enforce compliance.

The handwriting was on the wall for segregation in 1948 when President Harry S Truman desegregated the Army. Nevertheless, the South again fought a losing battle, comparable in some ways to the Civil War because defeat was inevitable. Aside from church bombings and assassinations, this time most of the battles were fought in federal courts and in the hearts and minds of those who had to adjust to the new order. New federal laws, enforced by a vastly expanded federal bureaucracy, came a decade after the initial court rulings under the Constitution and the old civil rights laws outlawing segregation. Surveys show most white Arkansans opposed treating blacks as equals, but integration always aroused less hostility in Arkansas than in the Deep South.

The crisis at Little Rock's Central High School marked the beginning of the end for segregated schools and produced circumstances that allowed Orval Faubus to become a six-term governor. At the end of the Faubus era, Winthrop Rockefeller captured the statehouse as the first Republican governor since 1874. The progressive resurgence exemplified by Rockefeller continued under his Democratic successors, interrupted only in 1980 by the one term of conservative Republican businessman Frank White. Two-party politics tentatively emerged for the first time in a century, although the old themes of personality continued to be uppermost for many voters as party affiliation and ideological identification remained casual.

ORVAL FAUBUS AND THE INTEGRATION CRISIS

Arkansas's road to the elusive goal of attaining the national average per capita income slowed from the mid-1950s to the mid-1960s when the emotional issue of racial integration sidetracked the state from its economic goals.

Desegregation Before 1954

Segregation came under vigorous attack during the 1930s in Congress, where the most debated issue was a national anti-lynching bill proposed by the NAACP. Southern hostility doomed the bill in Congress, but blacks did score some victories in the courts. Arthur W. Mitchell, a black Illinois congressman visiting Hot Springs, had been denied Pullman accommodations on the Rock Island Railroad even though Pullmans were available for whites. In *Mitchell* v. *United States* (1941), the United States Supreme Court held that this discrimination violated the Interstate Commerce Act. Other victories in the transportation field followed, and in 1955, the Interstate Commerce Commission ordered an end to segregation in interstate carriers and terminals.

In 1948, Arkansas finally decided to comply with *Missouri ex rel. Gaines* v. *Canada*, the 1938 United States Supreme Court decision mandating that separate college programs be equal. Unable to afford a law school for blacks, University of Arkansas authorities quietly let Silas Hunt, a black former GI, enter. Initial attempts to place him in a segregated cage marked *Colored* and deny him use of the library were met by faculty and student opposition and were abandoned quickly. Hunt died unexpectedly, but other blacks followed. Wiley Branton of Pine Bluff became a noted civil rights lawyer, serving as counsel for the state NAACP and executive director of the President's Council on Equal Opportunity. Edith Irby Jones was admitted at the same time to the University of Arkansas School of Medicine. The Arkansas State Board of Education announced plans in 1955 to end segregation in the state's other colleges.

The Brown Decision

As colleges were moving to comply with decisions concerning higher education, the Supreme Court was hearing arguments in the landmark case of *Brown* v. *The Board of Education of Topeka, Kansas* (1954). In a rare per curiam decision written by Eisenhower's recently appointed Chief Justice Earl Warren, the Court held that because "separate but equal" was intrinsically unequal, segregation was unconstitutional. A wave of hysterical protest arose in the Deep South against the Court, Earl Warren, the United Nations, President Eisenhower, the NAACP and Communists. Nearly all Southern senators and representatives, including those from Arkansas, signed the Southern Manifesto declaring that the Court had overstepped its authority by interfering with the South's social arrangements. Highway billboards proclaiming "Impeach Earl Warren" greeted travelers through Searcy and Pine Bluff for the next twenty years.

Booker T. Washington High School *(photographer unknown, ca. 1960) In the process of integration, school buildings once used by blacks, even if they were structurally adequate, were abandoned. Jonesboro's Booker T. Washington High School was one of the casualties.* **Author's Collection**

Meanwhile, newly vigilant blacks in Arkansas began agitating for implementation of the ruling. The first school system to integrate was Fayetteville in 1955, which had been forced by segregation laws to transport its black secondary students to Fort Smith sixty-three miles away. Fayetteville's integration led to a boycott against its football team by other Arkansas schools but caused no reaction from state officials. Such long-range busing of black children to segregated schools was not unusual. Black students from Hickory Plains in Prairie County were for many years bused past the white high school in Des Arc and on to an all-black school in Biscoe, twenty-seven miles each way.

Fayetteville's success was not repeated at Hoxie. This small Lawrence County community, located on the extreme northern edge of the black belt, had only twenty-five black pupils, a school building in near ruins and no funds. Prodded by Superintendent K. E. Vance, who believed in equal educational opportunity, the school board decided to proceed with integration, anticipating little local protest. However, Hoxie was within easy driving distance of the lower Delta. A small local protest led by Herbert Brewer soon involved segregationist attorney Amis Guthridge of Little Rock and Crossett fire-eater James D. Johnson. After threats of violence and a white boycott, the school board obtained a federal court injunction preventing further interference with the planned desegregation. Hoxie thus became the first Southern case involving federal officials. It also spurred Johnson into drafting a

Integration at Hoxie (Garland Studio, 1956) *This photograph of Ann Vance, Viola Tompkins and Rheamona Selvidge suggests that parents tended to be more upset with integration than the students themselves.*
Arkansas Gazette

proposed state constitutional amendment to nullify the *Brown* decision and segregation became a statewide political issue.

The Climate of Opinion

Nearly all white Arkansans were committed to white supremacy by habit or conviction, but few were extremists. Extremists began to organize in the aftermath of the *Brown* decision. Most vehement were the White Citizens Councils, whose Little Rock branch claimed 500 members. The Council's views were best expressed by Arkansas's most articulate segregationist, James D. Johnson. "Tall and lean and consumed by the fire of the old-time white religion," Johnson resurrected John C. Calhoun's long-discredited nullification doctrine

and made it Amendment 44 to the Arkansas Constitution. According to that amendment, the *Brown* decision was "Un-constitutional" and the state must interpose its sovereignty "to the end of nullification."

This was bad constitutional law and Law School Dean Robert A. Leflar termed the doctrine "a legal absurdity," but the absurdity became a part of the Arkansas Constitution in November 1956 by a vote of 185,374 to 146,064. Among the enforcement provisions was the clause that state officials who failed to carry out its mandates were to forfeit their offices and have no immunity from arrest. The Amendment remained in the Constitution as an embarrassment to the state until repealed in 1990, and even though it could not be enforced, it was used by civil rights attorneys to hang on the state the responsibility for maintaining a "history, pattern and practice of racial discrimination."

Segregationists in Arkansas were never united. Most extremists were from the Delta or the southern part of the state. However, many of the elite from those areas had long-standing ties of affection to black servants and opposed violence. Extremists often were rabid Negrophobes, and running throughout their rhetoric was a concern about sexual relations between the races. Hot Springs journalist Curt Copeland claimed integration was a plot to put "the nigger into your bedroom," and Johnson stated at Hoxie that, "If I send my child to an integrated school, I might see the day when I'll be bouncing a half-nigger on my knee and have him call me 'Grandpa.'"

The other part of the white community called themselves Southern moderates or gradualists. They were mostly middle-class whites who, through education and travel, had seen that the old system of segregation could not survive. Moderates did not support integration openly — that would have been social, economic and political suicide in Arkansas — but they did urge peaceful acceptance of change, sometimes because violence would interfere with economic development.

The Methodist and Presbyterian Churches made statements supporting peaceful change, and the Arkansas Human Relations Council was formed in Little Rock in 1954 with *Arkansas Gazette* editor Harry Ashmore as one of the prime movers. The Council provided one of few white-black forums in the state and it had branches in many smaller towns. Open supporters of integration were the few urban blacks who were members of such organizations as the NAACP or the Urban League. The president of the local chapter of the NAACP was a black minister, Reverend J. C. Crenshaw, and its most conspicuous leader was Mrs. Daisy Bates, the wife of black newspaperman L. C. Bates. White faculty members at Philander Smith College, Dr. George G.

Iggers and Dr. Lee Lorch, were active, and it became a matter of some embarrassment to the group that Lorch and his wife had ties to the American Communist Party.

Not all blacks supported the integration movement. Clifford H. Jones, editor of the black newspaper, the *Southern Mediator*, still believed in accommodation, and black teachers in segregated schools had well-justified fears for their jobs if black schools were closed.

The NAACP scored a few successes during the early 1950s. Blacks rejoined the Little Rock police force, and the "White" and "Colored" signs were removed from downtown drinking fountains. When the Little Rock crisis erupted, however, the NAACP bore the full force of segregationist hatred. A 1959 state law made it illegal for a public employee to be a NAACP member on the basis of the Arkansas Legislative Council's finding that the NAACP was "a captive of the international communist conspiracy."

The Politics of Segregation

Many whites believed that blacks did not want integration and thought segregation could be preserved for years despite the Supreme Court's ruling, especially if state services to blacks were upgraded. Therefore, many communities made a belated effort to achieve "separate but equal" facilities after 1954.

Governor Orval E. Faubus worked to increase black teacher salaries, supported integration of public transportation, increased social spending and appointed blacks to Democratic Party committees. However, his pollster, Eugene Newsom, found that 85 percent of voters opposed integration. Faubus tried to dodge the issue at first. He said in 1954 that integration was a local matter "with state authorities standing ready to assist in every way possible," and he promised to "remain free of prejudice, considerate of all." Thus Governor Faubus took no action when Fayetteville and Hoxie integrated.

Faubus was opposed for a second term in 1956 by radical segregationist James D. Johnson. Johnson denounced Orval "Fabalouse" for his moderation and alienated the voters with his rabid rhetoric. Faubus defeated Johnson in the primary and a Republican opponent in November. Even so, the governor had assured the voters that "no school board will be forced to mix races while I am governor."

In order to build political support for a large tax increase earmarked for badly needed state social programs, Faubus made a deal with legislators from heavily segregationist eastern Arkansas. A group went to Virginia to study that state's "massive resistance" plan and came back with a legislative package that the governor supported. New laws abolished compulsory school attendance, gave financial aid to districts threatened with court suits, required the NAACP to register and publish its membership and created a State Sovereignty Commission to wage war on the federal courts. One senator commented after the measures passed that, "If members of the Senate had voted their convictions, those bills wouldn't have gotten more than five votes." But conviction was swamped in a rising tide of white hysteria.

The United States Supreme Court ruled in a rehearing known as *Brown II* (1955) that segregation of schools needed to end with "all deliberate speed" under the supervision of federal district courts. Forrest City attorney Richard B. McCulloch, a leading segregationist, hoped that the new legislation he had helped draft would delay integration indefinitely. Meanwhile, the Little Rock NAACP had filed a suit in federal court to force local compliance with *Brown II*.

Governor Faubus sat in the middle, already planning to run for the ever-elusive third term. Once Faubus got his tax increase through the legislature, he showed little inclination to further the segregationist cause. The members of the State Sovereignty Commission went unappointed until a segregationist

lawsuit forced the governor to act, and when Van Buren desegregated under court order, Faubus said, "I do not believe that there is any action that could be taken that would supersede this authority."

Crisis at Central High School

Outposts of segregation had tumbled at Fayetteville, Hoxie and Van Buren, but only the desegregation of the capital city would be viewed as decisive proof that Arkansas was in compliance with the Supreme Court's ruling. Community leaders in Little Rock were ready to comply. Many observers at the time noted Little Rock's favorable racial environment. The city bus system had been desegregated voluntarily, and community leaders were openly discussing ending the dual education system. Osro Cobb, United States Attorney for the Eastern District of Arkansas in 1957, states in his *Memoirs* that counsel for the NAACP, Thurgood Marshall, told him that, "Central High School had been picked as a target for testing integration because the Little Rock community had exhibited a remarkable tolerance in race relations."

An initial plan calling for beginning integration in the early grades was scrapped. In its place, a few token blacks were to be sent to Central High School and a new high school, Hall, would be built in the fashionable western suburbs, leaving working-class children and their families to bear the brunt of social change. The local NAACP filed suit in *Aaron* v. *Cooper*, (1957) but the regional attorney mishandled the case in district court, and Judge John E. Miller, the former Arkansas United States senator who had prosecuted blacks in the Elaine race riot, upheld the district. It did little for local race relations when the school board's attorney made racial slurs about the NAACP and Daisy Bates. In the fall of 1957, Little Rock school integration was scheduled to take place under the token plan devised by

School Superintendent Virgil Blossom.

Integration was debated hotly during the summer months. Many agreed with *Arkansas Democrat* columnist Karr Shannon, whose views were collected and published as *Integration Decision Is Unconstitutional*. Robert E. Brown, head of the Capital Citizens Council, demanded that Governor Faubus prevent the scheduled integration. Citing the active intervention of Texas Governor Allan Shivers in stopping integration at Mansfield, Texas, Brown told Faubus, "you are immune to federal court orders." According to segregationist literature, Superintendent Blossom and the NAACP were planning for black boys to dance with white girls.

The climax of segregationist efforts came in late August when Georgia Governor Marvin Griffin and aide Roy Harris came to Little Rock to address a segregationist fund-raiser. Faubus put the two men up at the mansion, but only after receiving assurances that they would not embarrass him politically. Both said in their speeches that no integration had or ever would take place in Georgia. Strong leadership and the will of "every white man in Georgia" to defend "our cherished institutions" would defeat the attempt. At the mansion, the two governors discussed the merits of quail and duck hunting.

"I think my visit did make a little contribution to the unity of the people," Governor Griffin recalled later, and Superintendent Blossom said that Griffin's speech "had more to do with strengthening opposition than anything that happened." It left Governor Faubus on the spot for as he observed: "People are coming to me and saying if Georgia doesn't have integration why does Arkansas have it?"

Faubus made his first move six days later. In a meeting he requested with A. B. Caldwell, assistant for Civil Rights in the Criminal Division of the Justice Department (and a native Arkansan), Faubus said violence would occur if Central integrated on September 3. The federal reply was that maintaining law and order was a local affair unless there was direct interference with a federal court order.

Failing to get the redress that federal officials might have provided either by delaying integration or assuming responsibility for it, Faubus next had the segregationist Mothers' League of Central High School file suit in state chancery court to delay the opening of school. Faubus, the group's only witness, testified that gangs had been formed and gun sales were up, but teacher Elizabeth Huckaby said this "sounded to me more like fantasies from comic books than the behavior of the Little Rock adolescents." Faubus later claimed Superintendent Blossom provided the information, but an FBI investigation disproved the allegation. Chancellor Murray Reed granted the injunction, but the school board challenged the ruling in federal court. Judge Miller refused to decide the controversy, leaving United States District Judge Ronald N. Davies, a North Dakota jurist temporarily assigned to Arkansas, to make the decision. Judge Davies ordered that integration proceed as planned.

Winthrop Rockefeller, the Faubus-appointed head of the Arkansas Industrial Development Commission (AIDC), feared a violent confrontation would impede Arkansas's economic progress. When the tension heightened, he met with Faubus on September 1, but the meeting was inconclusive. In his book *Down From the Hills* (1980), Governor Faubus said that "Rockefeller wanted me to use my office and state powers to implement the federal court order."

Faubus countered with the question: "How can I assist the federal authorities when they are unprepared to do anything and whose official policy is to do nothing?" Faubus recalled that Rockefeller was not convinced:

[T]his did not deter him from his original position that I should use my office and state forces to implement the order. He emphasized the futility of opposing the federal government because of its overpowering might.

Faubus reported that Rockefeller persisted:

When he insisted that my best course was to implement the federal court order with state forces, I made a reply which was quoted in substance in the press as coming from "Mr. Rockefeller," I said, "If I should do now what you are suggesting, soon after the next election you would be working for Jim Johnson and his lieutenants."

Governor Faubus went on television that night to announce his dispatch of the National Guard to Central High School. His statement that the Guard "will not act as segregationists or integrationists, but as soldiers called to active duty to carry out their assigned tasks" made it unclear just what the governor intended. In Georgia, Roy Harris commented, "I sat there . . . just scratching my head and wondering if he called 'em out for us or agin us." Further complicating the situation, Faubus also sent troops to Horace Mann, the black high school.

The School Board asked the nine black children not to attend the opening day at Central, but Judge Davies reissued his integration order on September 3. The classic confrontation of the civil rights era occurred on September 4, 1957, when Arkansas National Guardsmen turned away seven of the nine black students at a side door of Central High School. Most of the press and an angry mob of whites were at the front door, and the two black students who arrived there received most of the attention. Elizabeth Eckford was the first to appear. "The niggers are coming! Get her! Lynch her!" cried members of the crowd as the young black girl in the starched white dress encountered the armed Guardsmen barring the door and a mob of some 1,000 persons. Television and newspaper photographs

caught this moment, one that put Little Rock on the map for the next thirty years. Governor Faubus said the whole affair was the fault of Communists represented locally by Mrs. Grace Lorch, who walked Elizabeth Eckford back to the bus stop.

Reaction was swift. Little Rock Mayor Woodrow Mann claimed that the governor's action was a "disgraceful political hoax" and that there was no threat of violence until the governor manufactured one. The *Arkansas Gazette*, heretofore supportive of Faubus, also was critical and on September 4, 1957, wrote its most famous editorial entitled "The Crisis Mr. Faubus Made."

Little Rock arose yesterday to gaze upon the incredible spectacle of an empty high school surrounded by National Guard troops called out by Governor Faubus to protect life and liberty against a mob that never materialized. . . .

Now it remains for Mr. Faubus to decide whether he intends to pose what could be the most serious constitutional question to face the national government since the Civil War. The effect of his action so far is to interpose his state office between the local School District and the United States Court. The government, as Judge Davies implied last night, now has no choice but to proceed against such interference or abandon its right to enforce its rulings and decisions.

Segregationists blamed the nation's press. In Faubus's words, Dr. Benjamin Fine, education writer for the *New York Times*, "created some problems on the school grounds which had to be handled," and Fine was charged with trying to bribe students to riot for the benefit of the press. Fine recalled that he was kicked and called a dirty Jew for helping Elizabeth Eckford get back to the bus.

With an unabashed Judge Davies continuing to issue orders and the National Guard still at Central, Congressman Brooks Hays helped arrange a conference between Faubus and President Dwight D. Eisenhower, who was then vacationing at a segregated Rhode Island country club. The two men had an inconclusive discussion. In *Down From the Hills,* Faubus stated that the president's remarks were in the nature of a lecture. "I got the definite impression that I had been called in for a lecture, just as a general would summon a lieutenant before him for a reprimand for an alleged transgression of military rules."

Faubus argued for a cooling off period and left the meeting believing that Eisenhower was amenable to a compromise but that his advisors, especially Attorney General Herbert Brownell, were not. On the Mike Wallace television show, Faubus defended his actions as those of a responsible state official just trying to keep the peace. Judge Davies concluded on September 20, 1957, that no threat of violence existed and enjoined the governor from further interference with court-ordered desegregation. Faubus's attorneys never heard the decision, having walked out of court halfway through the proceedings. But the governor removed the troops, leaving the city police to protect the school and then left the state to attend the Southern Governors' Conference.

The long-awaited violence finally materialized on September 23, 1957, "Black Monday." The black students were admitted, but school officials decided to send them home at noon because the crowd outside was swelling, with many coming from out of state. Once faced with an overt attack on federal authority, President Eisenhower took action.

Instead of following the usual procedure of sending in United States Marshals to enforce the court order, President Eisenhower ordered elements of the elite 101st Airborne Division of the United States Army sent to Little Rock from Fort Campbell, Kentucky, on September 24, 1957.

Federal troops remained in control of Central High School throughout most of the school year, although federalized National Guardsmen replaced the paratroopers in November 1957. Segregationists constantly exploited local resentment, charging on one occasion that soldiers spied on girls in the showers. The nine blacks were subjected to what Vice Principal Elizabeth Huckaby called "verbal abuse and sneak physical attacks."

Minnijean Brown observed that, "They throw rocks, they spill ink on your clothes, they call you 'nigger,' they just keep bothering you every five minutes." Brown, who fought back, called one girl "white trash" and was expelled. "One down and eight to go" became the new segregationist slogan.

Meanwhile, Arkansans increasingly were bombarded by segregationist propaganda. The *Arkansas Democrat,* which had taken a moderate stance in the beginning, opened its columns to segregationists and gained readers at the expense of the *Gazette.*

Religious Arkansans were assured by Dallas minister Reverend J. A. Lovell that segregation was Biblical, and another minister asserted that the Bible "is the original book on segregation and God the original segregationist." Of the state's major denominations, only the Missionary Baptists took a formal segregationist stand, calling the *Brown* decision "deplorable, unscriptural and not in harmony with previous decisions of that body, nor with the beliefs and purposes of God-fearing and democratic-minded men who at the first drafted the Constitution of the United States."

The school year ended in May 1958, and one of the nine, Ernest Green, received the first diploma awarded to a black at Central. Critics called it the $5,000,000 diploma, but it closed only the first act of the Little Rock drama.

The School Board returned to federal court during the summer, this time asserting that "conditions of chaos, bedlam and turmoil" made a thirty-month delay in desegregation necessary. In spite of a favorable ruling from United States District Judge Harry J. Lemley in *Aaron* v. *Cooper* (1958), the Supreme Court, in only the third special term in its history, curtly rejected the Board's argument. The Court said in an unusual decision signed by all nine justices that constitutional rights could not be "nullified openly and directly by state legislators or state executive officials nor nullified indirectly by them by evasive schemes for segregation."

The next move was up to Governor Faubus, now a segregationist hero. In the aftermath of *Cooper* v. *Aaron*, Faubus invoked the new School Closing Law and shut Little Rock's high schools for the 1958-59 school year. Little Rock voters endorsed the move a few weeks later with a tally of 19,470 to 7,561. Because of massive public discontent, football teams were allowed to play, but children were otherwise on their own. As public schools stood empty, private academies such as the segregationist Private School Corporation appealed all over the South for financial contributions. When the Presbyterian ministers of Arkansas called for the governor to reopen the schools and to undertake a program of Christian conciliation to restore order to public education, Governor Faubus stated in a press conference "that a large number of ministers in the Presbyterian church have been effectively brainwashed . . . [by] [t]he leftwingers and the Communists."

The high-water mark of the segregationist era came in the November election of 1958 when ophthalmologist Dr. Dale Alford, a staunch segregationist, resigned from the School Board to run as a write-in candidate against Congressman Brooks Hays. The best example in Arkansas of a Southern moderate, Hays earlier had defeated Amis Guthridge, the segregationist leader, in the Democratic primary. Voters were upset further and ready to find a scapegoat by the fall. Faubus put the weight of his political machine behind Alford,

and Dr. Alford referred to him as "our great and wonderful governor." Photographs of Hays with black religious leaders were circulated before the election; some election judges allowed voters to use stickers bearing Alford's name in marking their ballots. Alford won, and the "Great Purge" was underway.

Anyone known to be sympathetic to integration was subjected to obscene telephone calls and economic harassment during the crisis. Victims included members of the Arkansas Council on Human Relations. Some left the state, and those who stayed found themselves under police surveillance and believed that their telephones were tapped. Social activist Mamie Ruth Williams recalled such activities in 1992: "I didn't know what the Southwestern Bell telephone truck was doing parked down the street. I thought the neighbors had phone trouble." Governor Faubus claimed that proponents of integration were a Communist front and said:

> [T]hey are trying to stir up the Negro, telling him that he is being discriminated against. That group is dangerous. Some of these people are not so well known, but when we get through they'll be well known.

With the state police acting in conjunction with the segregationists, civil liberties ceased to have much meaning in Arkansas during the integration crisis. Locally, the NAACP was driven underground, Arkansas moderates were left weak and divided, and Orval Faubus became a six-term governor.

The next target for segregationists was the *Arkansas Gazette*. The paper published an anonymous letter on December 13, 1957, warning stores advertising in the *Gazette* to expect retaliation. Businesses hurried to capitulate to the segregationist threat as the paper lost 18 percent of its circulation and $1,000,000 in revenues even as it received the second Pulitzer Prize ever bestowed in

Arkansas. Although the *Gazette* survived and in time recovered, L. C. Bates's black paper folded when white firms withdrew their advertising.

Believing that a liberal view on race relations was tied to a liberal education, segregationists attacked the state's colleges. Act 10 of 1958 required every teacher to file as a condition of employment an annual affidavit listing every organization the person joined or supported. The object was to locate members of the American Civil Liberties Union (ACLU), the Urban League and the American Association of University Professors (AAUP), as well as those on the federal government's subversive list. The law was challenged in *Shelton* v. *Tucker* (1960) and found to violate the due process clause of the Fourteenth Amendment. That did not end the matter, however. A number of faculty members had been dismissed before the decision, and the University of Arkansas board refused to rehire them. The AAUP investigated the Fayetteville campus and placed it on its List of Censured Administrations in 1964, further damaging Arkansas's image. The University compromised with the dismissed faculty in 1968 and the censure was withdrawn. Dean Guerdon D. Nichols won the coveted Meiklejohn Award for Academic Freedom from the AAUP in 1960 for his opposition to Act 10.

The families of the Little Rock "nine" also were victims of segregationists' wrath. All were subjected to harassment, and many lost their jobs and left the state. Attorney General Bruce Bennett campaigned to drive the NAACP out of Arkansas and had Reverend Crenshaw and Mrs. Bates briefly under arrest. Following the publication of Bates's memoir, *The Long Shadow of Little Rock*, in 1962, Mrs. Bates had a large cross burned on her front lawn.

The great winner was Orval Faubus. His third term became a foregone conclusion, and he defeated Chris Finkbeiner and Lee Ward in the 1958 primary. Governor Faubus's Republican opponent, George W. Johnson,

polled barely 50,000 votes in the general election. Meanwhile, James D. Johnson, the most articulate of segregationists, became known as "Justice Jim" by winning a seat on the state Supreme Court.

The segregationist impulse peaked, however, and reaction set in. The Little Rock School Board resigned during the fall of 1958. After a hard-fought race in December, a new Board took over with three segregationists and three members representing a businessman's ticket. Paralysis resulted, leading segregationists to introduce a board-packing bill in the legislature that would allow the governor to appoint three additional members. According to the bill's sponsor, it was "a little on the dictatorial side, but we have no choice. The people voted the man [Faubus] back to do whatever he can to preserve their way of life."

The Little Rock PTA and a moderate group called the Women's Emergency Committee to Open Public Schools, which had formed in response to the crisis and the failure of the business establishment to provide leadership, lobbied against the measure, and it failed to pass.

The Women's Emergency Committee, which came to include 1,000 members, continued to lead the opposition to Governor Faubus. Composed primarily of white middle and upper class educated women, the Committee registered voters, arranged for rides to the polls, and at great personal and social sacrifice, became politically visible. Many had their friends from church, bridge clubs and the country clubs turn against them, but they persevered, taking over the leadership of the community from the men.

Adolphine Fletcher Terry, the daughter of prominent Little Rock businessman and banker, John G. Fletcher, who had run against Jeff Davis for governor; an 1898 graduate of Little Rock Peabody High School and 1902 graduate of Vassar; the sister of Pulitzer Prize winning poet John Gould Fletcher; wife of ex-Congressman, David D. Terry; and a formida-

Ted L. Lamb

Ted L. Lamb, who grew up on a farm near Alexander and graduated from Little Rock High School, was a successful advertising executive until he decided to run for the Little Rock School Board. Elected in December 1958, he lost 21 out of his 26 Arkansas advertising accounts over the next six months, largely because of a campaign of harassment directed at his clients. Lamb retrained as a lawyer and left for his family this account of one episode in the Little Rock school struggle. He died in 1984. In his unpublished memoirs, he recalled:

When we decided to open schools in early August of 1959, Dr. Malcolm Taylor declared that the school board was acting in an irresponsible manner, since we were unnecessarily exposing Little Rock children to the possibilities of a polio epidemic by putting them in close association during the heat of the summer months. Dr. Taylor was an osteopath and, only coincidentally, the then chairman of the local White Citizens Council. He reported this one afternoon and other members of the school board contacted Dr. Briggs and some other Little Rock physicians, who explained publicly to concerned mothers and fathers that they didn't think that opening schools would bear much medical relationship to polio, but that same night, I thought long and hard about what I could do to overcome this threat that had put natural fear in the hearts of mothers and fathers, so I set my alarm for 6:30 that morning, which would be 7:30 Pittsburgh time, and called Dr. Jonas Salk, who was then at the University of Pittsburgh, and identified myself and explained my problem.

Dr. Salk only the year before had won the Nobel Prize for medicine, with the discovery of the Salk vaccine. I asked Dr. Salk for a telegram and he said that he was pledged to the March of Dimes not to enter controversial subjects, although he was personally very sympathetic to my position. He offered me a statement from the Surgeon General of the United States, and I told him that if that was the best I could do, I would take it, but I'd rather have something from him.

Finally, Dr. Salk called me back about 8 o'clock in the morning and said that the March of Dimes people had told him that he could respond to an inquiry telegram from me, and I sent him a telegram inquiring as to the effects of opening schools on the possibility of creating a polio epidemic, and he responded by telegram that in his judgment it would have no effect, and that his vaccine was the only medical answer available. He told me on the phone that it wouldn't have a damn thing to do with it, and that, "the only way to keep those kids from coming down with polio was to shoot their butts full of my vaccine."

At any rate, we had a school board meeting that morning, and Dr. Taylor appeared, and made a public appeal as a physician for us not to act in such an irresponsible manner, that would potentially endanger the lives of the children in the community, and one or two board members said that they had talked to their family physicians, who didn't see any real threat, and I sat back in a sort of cat and mouse position, waiting till everybody had finished, and I turned to Everett Tucker, the president of the Board, and said, "Everett, I talked to a doctor friend of mine about it last night," and Tucker said, "I think we've heard all we want to on it, Ted. I don't think it's necessary to add any more fuel to the fire." And I said, "Well, I think you'll be interested in who I talked to."

And he said, "Well, who did you talk to?"

I said, "Well, I called a little Jewish doctor friend of mine in Pittsburgh," and Tucker responded with something like this, "Well, I don't think we have to go to Pittsburgh for any answers since we've heard from Barney Briggs and Sam Thompson here in Little Rock." I said, "Yeah, however, but my little Jewish doctor friend in Pittsburgh is named Jonas Salk, and I have a telegram here from him," which brought a stillness and hush over the entire proceedings, and the matter of the polio epidemic was never again raised by Dr. Taylor.

Source: Ted L. Lamb, "Chronicle of Events, Little Rock School Crisis," Private papers of Mrs. Ted L. Lamb

ble political and social force in her own right, opened her home, provided strong leadership and impeccable "old Little Rock" social and political connections for the Committee. She was the key member in the organization and had the ability and prestige to draw women into the group. Her home, the old Albert Pike mansion, provided the activists with a setting that could have come straight out of *Gone With the Wind.* In addition, the Committee threatened the use of even more powerful persuasion. A member of the committee, Jane Mendel, recalled that another outspoken leader encouraged members to deny their husband's conjugal rights unless they opposed Faubus and segregation. The Committee grew quickly and Jane Mendel, the head of a telephone chain of 122, built up the telephone contacts from 200 to 1,000 in one week. Vivian Brewer was the first president of the group. Despite its numbers, the Women's Emergency Committee was more influential than popular.

Among those who worked with the Committee, Ted L. Lamb, a two-term school board member, stood out, as one astute observer noted, "like a sore thumb in a city of cowardly people." Lamb survived attempted bombings, but lost his advertising business in the process. Practically alone among local leaders, he decried attempts to limit integration through evasive measures and predicted federal courts would one day be called upon to force real rather than token integration.

The moderate Board members walked out in May and segregationists, temporarily in control, announced the firing of forty-four teachers for "integrationist" activity and the appointment of Dr. Dale Alford's father, T. H. Alford, as superintendent. Galvanized by this move, the Stop This Outrageous Purge (STOP) committee endorsed the PTA's demand for a recall election, and the Committee to Retain Our Segregated Schools (CROSS) demanded the recall of the moderates.

The recall election on May 25, 1959, was a referendum on the year's events. Governor

Faubus, Congressman Alford and Mississippi Congressman John Bell Williams campaigned for the segregationists. The voting was heavy, and moderates regained control by a small margin. The Supreme Court ruled the next month in *Faubus* v. *Aaron* (1959) that the school-closing laws were unconstitutional, and this opened the way for schools to open in the fall.

Some extreme segregationists did not accept defeat. A series of dynamite explosions on Labor Day damaged School Board offices, the mayor's office and a city automobile parked in the fire chief's driveway. Ku Klux Klan member E. A. Lauderdale, Sr., a local lumberman and segregationist politician, was arrested and convicted of the crime, but his prison term was brief because Governor Faubus pardoned him. Emmett E. Miller, the founder and president of the Crittenden County Citizens Council, also was arrested for planting thirty sticks of dynamite at Philander Smith College.

The Moderate Reaction

Public opinion polls showed that the overwhelming majority of white Arkansans favored segregation, but the events of 1957-1958 tested the degree of their commitment. Historically, race relations in Little Rock had been good and educational opportunities there for blacks had been the best in the state. Because integration was not a social problem in those parts of the state with few or no black inhabitants, many whites were segregationists from habit rather than from conviction. There remained a hardcore of whites who thrived on racial antagonism. Many working-class whites had a long history of racial antagonism. One difficult Central student reported that he had been "fighting niggers" since age five.

Public opinion began to moderate with the reopening of the Little Rock public schools and the resort to violence by the extremists. Voters in 1960 overwhelmingly rejected a constitutional amendment similar to the School Closing Law. The measure, which carried the endorsement of the Citizens Council and of Governor Faubus at the last minute, failed in every county. Noting the winds of change, Faubus hastened to shorten his sails after his Republican opponent, Henry M. Britt of Hot Springs, polled 144,846 votes in 1960 — almost three times the total Republican vote of two years before. Meanwhile, desegregation proceeded apace by court order and without gubernatorial intervention. The Dollarway School District, the gateway to southeastern Arkansas, desegregated in 1960, and Pine Bluff followed two years later. By the fall of 1963, 390 blacks were attending previously all-white schools.

The Faubus Machine

As term after term mounted, Faubus was able to change the entire leadership of Arkansas government, primarily by appointing virtually all the members of every state board. He gained control over the powerful Arkansas Highway Commission and its vast patronage system. Forging close ties with machine politicians and special interests he once had opposed, Faubus became the manager of an intricate political network. By virtue of Faubus's complete mastery of the budget process over which he presided on an item-by-item basis, and using block rather than line item appropriations, not a single state expenditure or job hiring escaped his supervision. The General Assembly, customarily independent of the governor, voted nearly everything he wanted.

State services were expanded, schools and colleges received more financial support, and road construction improved the state's highways. Critics complained, however, that welfare benefits were manipulated politically. The State Police continued to be politicized, submitting regular reports after 1957 on

groups such as the NAACP, the Congress of Racial Equality, the Council on Foreign Relations and the Young Women's Christian Association. State employees suspected of involvement with these subversive groups were terminated or reprimanded.

Faubus learned how to work effectively with powerful economic interests that provided crucial financial backing. Among the most prominent was Wilton R. "Witt" Stephens. With his brother, Jackson or "Jack," Witt controlled Stephens Inc., the nation's tenth largest investment banking firm by 1977. Witt Stephens began as a speculator in drainage district bonds, invested heavily in municipal bonds and eventually became the head of Arkansas Louisiana Gas Co.

He served two terms in the legislature during the Faubus era and provided legislators with special rates at his motel, the Coachman's Inn. Four of the six state senators on the powerful Joint Budget Committee had obligations or ties to Stephens by 1977. Stephens acquired statewide influence during the Faubus years by investing in many local Arkansas banks and giving timely assistance to emerging Arkansas businesses such as Wal-Mart Inc.

The kind of political system Faubus erected was coming under increasing pressure by 1962. President John F. Kennedy challenged Americans to look at social problems. Civil rights bills in Congress kept piling up, frustrated only by the legislative maneuvers of Southern Democrats with seniority.

The 1962 gubernatorial election in Arkansas tested the Faubus machine against challenges from both the right and the left. Faubus had broken his ties to the extreme segregationists, boasting that, "If history records anything about my administration, it will be its humanity." The segregationists ran Dr. Dale Alford, who was no longer in Congress after Arkansas lost a congressional seat in 1960 because of a drop in state population. Alford's relations with Faubus had soured since 1958. Calling Faubus a toothless tiger in the integration struggle, Alford charged also that the governor had become the "tool of the bond dealers, wholesale whiskey dealers, gamblers, and large utility companies, and the corporation lawyers of Little Rock." Faubus responded that segregationists were too few in number to matter politically.

Another entry into the gubernatorial race was Faubus's old mentor, Sid McMath. Here, too, relations had become embittered. McMath was quoted as saying during the Little Rock crisis that, "The only mistake I made as governor was building that road [into Madison County] and letting Orval out." The dig hurt, and Faubus returned to it twenty years later with the observation that "so far, governors who can be charged with only one mistake during their tenure are nonexistent." McMath blamed Faubus for encouraging violence during the crisis by allowing his office to be "prostituted and used to pander prejudice." Invoking the chivalry of the Old South against the segregationists, McMath observed that, "I have never been able to visualize Jeb Stuart leading a raid on a high school or a synagogue with a satchel of dynamite."

McMath concentrated his spending on television in the 1962 campaign and emphasized that it was no accident that Arkansas Louisiana Gas Co. got regular rate increases when two of Faubus's appointees on the Public Service Commission were large stockholders in the company. In addition, he pointed out that the state put $40,000,000 on deposit in pet banks without receiving any interest.

Using the slogan "Keep Arkansas' Program of Proven Progress," Faubus hit all the rallies, barbecues and fish fries, shaking hands with voters and applying his folksy charm. One critic observed that Faubus's ability:

[T]o find common threads which united everyone's interests was nothing short of genius. Brother Faubus has learned how to mix homely analogies, trite sayings,

chauvinistic pleas, corny slogans, monstrous lies, and bellicose tactics into unsurpassed vote-getting speeches.

Like Jeff Davis before him, Faubus lived on denouncing the *Arkansas Gazette* and projected himself as the victim of a vast conspiracy involving Daisy Bates, the NAACP and Sid McMath.

Despite the disparate opposition, Faubus garnered more than half the votes with 208,996, compared to 83,473 for McMath and 82,815 for Alford. Faubus's power over Arkansas became complete with this victory and he had only token Democratic opposition in 1964 for his sixth and final term. The reformist impulse was reborn in the person of Winthrop Rockefeller and the vehicle of a revived Republican Party.

The Rockefeller Republicans

The Arkansas Rockefeller, as he came to be called in order to distinguish him from Nelson in New York and Jay in West Virginia, settled at Petit Jean after his spectacular divorce from Barbara "Bobo" Sears. His Winrock cattle operation became an international show place, attracting thousands of visitors, and he headed the AIDC by appointment of Governor Faubus. Rockefeller's initially friendly relations with Faubus soured during the Central High School crisis and led the former New Yorker into politics.

Rockefeller was unique as a politician, even for Arkansas. He was a large rambling man often incapable of coherent speech, much given to conspicuous consumption of alcohol and invariably late for appointments. Rockefeller shared little of the culture common to most Arkansans. He had a lot of money and he spent a lot of it improving the state, its cultural institutions and its image.

Rockefeller emerged in 1964 as a serious gubernatorial candidate, translating his money into scientific electioneering. His extensive use of pollsters, voter identification techniques and voter targeting told Rockefeller why he lost the election. Faubus, secure in his power, emphasized the sanctity of marriage, his opposition to the use of liquor at the governor's mansion and charged that Rockefeller had destroyed cemeteries in his farming operations. Even so, the Republican newcomer polled 254,561 votes compared to Faubus's 337,489, and Rockefeller set his sights on the 1966 race.

The 1966 contest started early with, among other things, a controversy about the election returns from Faubus's home county of Madison. Republicans charged election fraud, and county officials destroyed records before an inquiry could be made. When Rockefeller found that he had drawn only 14 percent of the black vote, he set out to register and organize blacks.

Meanwhile, the Faubus regime suffered a series of embarrassments. A young cartoonist, George Fisher, fixed the farkleberry bush as Faubus's symbol and made the governor famous for saying, "Just because I said it doesn't make it so." There was less laughter for investors in the politically connected and bankrupt Arkansas Loan and Thrift Co. of Van Buren. Attorney General Bruce Bennett was convicted later of criminal involvement in the tangled affairs of the concern. For whatever reason, Faubus's decision not to seek reelection in 1966 left the field unexpectedly wide open.

The 1966 Election

Faubus had not nurtured a successor, and one did not develop under his governance. Therefore, the 1966 Democratic primary replayed all the bitterness of the 1950s. The most colorful of candidates was James D. Johnson, now "Justice Jim," after serving on the state Supreme Court. Still the fanatical segregationist, he campaigned with a Bible in his hand and refused to shake hands with

blacks. Johnson also had little good to say about the other candidates. Dr. Dale Alford, an earlier ally, was a mere "specs peddler," Frank Holt, the scion of an old political family, was the "pleasant vegetable," and Brooks Hays, the veteran attempting a comeback, was a "putrid quisling." Businessman Raymond Rebsamen and Newport attorney Sam Boyce were the other major candidates. Johnson outpolled the rest in a bitter contest and defeated Holt by 5,000 votes in the runoff. But Johnson and extreme segregationists had captured the state Democratic Party too late in history.

By 1966, the Arkansas racial climate had changed from those early days when Johnson led the segregationists at the Battle of Hoxie. After black victories on the buses at Montgomery, Alabama, and at the lunch counters of Greenville, North Carolina, civil rights workers had invaded the South, undeterred by occasional murders in Mississippi, Alabama and Georgia. In contrast to the turmoil in the Deep South, Arkansas was relatively quiet. Freedom Riders were arrested in 1961 for attempting to integrate the Little Rock bus depot, and the cafeteria in the state Capitol remained segregated despite protests. Apparently many blacks did not consider Arkansas worth a struggle. When Amis Guthridge offered free bus tickets to the North, fifty-seven blacks accepted.

Some 200,000 marchers converged on Washington during the summer of 1963 demanding the passage of civil rights legislation. The assassination of President Kennedy in Dallas on November 22, 1963, brought Lyndon Johnson to power. A Texas New Deal Democrat, Johnson broke the power of the Southern bloc and declared a "War on Poverty."

Under Johnson's strong leadership, Congress passed the Civil Rights Act of 1964, ending segregation in all public facilities. One Arkansas response to this came from the *Arkansas Gazette*, which dropped its separate obituary page for blacks. The Federal Voting Rights Act came in 1965, though Arkansas was not one of the seven states covered by the law.

Arkansas did feel the effect of other reforms. The Twenty-fourth Amendment to the United States Constitution banned the poll tax from federal elections, and the United States Supreme Court removed it from local ones. The high court's ruling in *Baker* v. *Carr*, (1962) the first case challenging malapportioned legislative seats, was even more important to Arkansas. The one man-one vote rule that evolved obliterated Amendment 45 to the Arkansas Constitution that Arkansas voters had adopted in 1956 "to preserve present apportionment of state senators and existing senatorial districts." The transfer of power from the rotten boroughs of rural constituencies to the growing towns and suburbs weakened Old Guard conservative politics. Elements of the reform spirit could be found in Amendment 50 (1962), which permitted voting machines and Amendment 51 (1964), by which Arkansas voluntarily abandoned the poll tax.

The 1966 election of Rockefeller versus Johnson pitted the old against the new, the rural with the urban and the sophisticated with the bumpkin. Johnson made no attempt to be conciliatory toward moderate Democrats, and Republicans organized "Democrats for Rockefeller." In the end, Johnson's appeal to racism failed. One poll showed that, on the racial issue, 66 percent of the voters wanted "things as orderly as possible," and only 11 percent wanted to "fight with all forces."

Enough Democrats joined with the small traditional Republican vote and the newly enfranchised blacks to give Rockefeller a nearly 50,000-vote margin over Johnson in the first Republican victory since Reconstruction. Overt racism was dead in Arkansas politics and modern politicians knew that they had to take the black vote into account to win.

A NEW REFORM ERA

Beginning in 1966, Arkansas politics moved to a central position. Although critics accused reform leaders of the crime of "liberalism," the politics of the era in reality were rooted firmly in the progressive tradition and represented a renewed commitment to modernization. The Women's Emergency Committee had given many educated women their first taste of political activism, and many liked it, and remained active for the progressive point of view in other political causes. These women included, but were not limited to, Jane Mendel, Mamie Ruth Williams, Sara Murphy and Irene Samuel. Brownie Ledbetter was not part of the original Women's Emergency Committee, but later became politically active and followed in the Committee's footsteps with the Panel of American Women. Paradoxically, conservatism triumphed in national politics, first with Richard Nixon and then more strongly with Ronald Reagan.

The Rockefeller Years

Although Winthrop Rockefeller and running mate Lieutenant Governor Maurice "Footsie" Britt won in 1966, the legislature remained solidly Democratic with only a handful of Arkansas Republicans from the northwestern counties. There was little cooperation from the start. Rockefeller tried both reason and hospitality, but reason proved ineffective and hospitality backfired when the legislators and their families visiting Petit Jean pilfered towels and costly furnishings. Programs initiated from the governor's office were more the result of executive fiat than legislative cooperation.

Waiting on Rockefeller's desk when he took office was an Arkansas State Police investigation into the affairs of Arkansas prisons. Cummins and Tucker were already notorious in folk song and popular legend. Designed to be

"I'm Aimin' to Bring Him In!"
*Jon Kennedy's May 28, 1964,
Arkansas Democrat cartoon
addressed Winthrop Rockefeller's
efforts to build a two-party system
in Arkansas. Rockefeller argued
that one-party politics inevitably
led to cronyism and corruption.*
**University of Arkansas at Little
Rock.**

self-supporting, the prisons were worked by inmates, guarded by inmates and inmates were available to do favors for important political persons. The State Police report added that the system operated under conditions of brutality, extortion, murder, sadism and fraud. An amazed Rockefeller announced that, "We have probably the most barbaric prison system in the United States."

Rockefeller expected a strong public outcry to be followed by a commitment to alter the system after the report's release, but he reck- oned without a strong understanding of many Arkansans who believed that any progressive reforms would turn the prisons into a "country club for criminals." Many newspapers did take up the issue, but the legislature gave a stand- ing ovation to a prisoner who testified that he saw nothing wrong. Many in the general pub- lic felt that because criminals were sent to prison for punishment, it did not matter how they got it.

Undismayed, Rockefeller began reforming the system by importing outsider Tom Murton to run the prisons. Murton was convinced that the prisons were even worse than they were pictured. Giving credence to rumor of a secret prisoner burial ground, Murton unearthed an old pauper's cemetery as national television cameras and millions of viewers watched. There were enough real problems without robbing graveyards, and an irate Rockefeller replaced Murton with another reformer, Robert Sarver. In the absence of funding from the legislature, the most reformers could do was to eliminate the "Tucker telephone," (a hand-turned electric generator made from an old-fashioned crank phone attached to the genitalia), the strap and other instruments of torture.

During the 1960s, the United States Supreme Court began giving new meaning to the "cruel and unusual punishment" clause of the Fifth Amendment to the Constitution of the United States, and in 1970, the Arkansas prison system was found to be unconstitutional by United States District Judge J. Smith Henley. For the next thirteen years the prisons remained under federal supervision. Tom Murton published a book about his experiences in the Arkansas prisons, *Accomplices to the Crime: The Arkansas Prison Scandal* (1969) on which the Robert Redford film, *Brubaker,* was based.

To Rockefeller, prisons were only part of the problem. What Arkansas needed was a completely reorganized state government so that effective decision-making processes and modern budgeting could be implemented. The legislature balked, and Rockefeller's initial accomplishments consisted only of state funding for high school textbooks, a ban on granting driver's licenses to the legally blind, the state's first real minimum wage law and study commissions on prisons and the state Constitution.

One unintended product of this session was the passage of the Freedom of Information Act. Drafted by a group of journalists but passed largely because legislators distrusted Rockefeller, it became a cornerstone of responsible government. Meanwhile, the divided Democrats remained at odds with Rockefeller, whose comment on the legislature was, "I just wish the bastards would go home."

The 1968 Election

Democratic gubernatorial contenders in 1968 included Virginia Johnson, the wife of "Justice Jim;" Bruce Bennett, the former attorney general; moderate Ted Boswell; and Marion Crank, a former Speaker of the House perhaps tagged unfairly as the inheritor of the old Faubus machine. Crank led in the primary and defeated Virginia Johnson in the runoff. Rockefeller made much in the general election of the "Crank family plan" after it was revealed that the entire Crank family, including an eight-year-old daughter, had been on the state payroll during his legislative tenure. In defense of Crank, such arrangements were not unusual in a state that refused to pay its legislators sufficient compensation for their service. The two candidates met in an echo of the Kennedy-Nixon debates. Rockefeller, free from his occasional foot-in-mouth disease, won by 30,000 votes, again with his combination of urban moderates, blacks and traditional Republicans.

The 1968 election also demonstrated the selectivity of Arkansas voters. By that year, civil rights had taken a back seat to the War in Vietnam. Southerners generally supported the War, and draft resistance and student demonstrations had not yet become a part of the Arkansas scene. J. William Fulbright, chairman of the Senate Foreign Relations Committee, emerged as an anti-war hero in the United States Senate, arguing that America should choose to exercise its vast power only in places where its strategic interests were threatened. Employing logic and high style, Fulbright indefatigably repeated his thesis in *The Arrogance of Power* and in speeches.

Conservatives labeled him "Halfbright" and

J. W. Fulbright, John L. McClellan and Wilbur D. Mills

Arkansas's national political clout was at its all-time zenith in the 1960s and 1970s when powerful United States Senators John L. McClellan and J. William Fulbright and United States Representative Wilbur D. Mills represented Arkansas in Washington, D. C. All three amassed their enormous power through intelligence, political skill and seniority.

Wilbur D. Mills, a native of Kensett, Arkansas, almost went directly from Harvard Law School to county judge of White County. Elected to the United States House of Representatives from the Second Congressional District in 1938 at age 30, he rose to become chairman of the powerful House Ways and Means Committee, which writes the nation's tax laws. Perhaps the most important legislation to emerge from his committee was the 1965 Medicare Act. His knowledge of the ponderous revenue code was legendary, and he gauged the political winds of the Congress carefully enough to gain a reputation of near infallibility in backing tax legislation. Mills often was referred to as the second most important man in Washington because of his legislative influence, superseded only by the president. He retired in 1977, and pundits still say that no one in Washington has understood the United States Internal Revenue Code since. While Mills focused on national tax policy, he did not forget about his central Arkansas district, having obtained the financing for the numerous interstate links in the Little Rock area — 430, 440, and the one that bears his name — 630.

John L. McClellan was the "king of pork" for a state starved for infrastructure and capital development. A native of Sheridan, he was elected to the House in 1934 and then to the Senate in 1942, where he served until his death in late 1977. McClellan was a politician who knew that his constituents needed and cherished "bricks and mortar," and he satisfied their yearnings in his early political career by keeping the United States Army Corps of Engineers building flood control dams, including Blakely Mountain, which forms Lake Ouachita. As chairman of the Senate Appropriations Committee, he was able to team up with Oklahoma's United States Senator Robert Kerr to obtain the $1.2 billion needed to make the Arkansas River navigable for barges from the Port of Catoosa near Tulsa to the Mississippi River. The system is named for the two senators. McClellan also obtained the necessary funding to construct a new Veterans Administration hospital in Little Rock and renovate the old one at Fort Roots in North Little Rock. Both are now divisions of a single VA hospital named for McClellan.

McClellan first came to national prominence in the 1950s when, as chairman of the Permanent Subcommittee on Investigations, he conducted extensive televised hearings on labor racketeering. He was a former prosecutor, and one of his last accomplishments before his death was to play a key role in a comprehensive revision of the United States Criminal Code.

A crusty conservative, McClellan fended off the

accused him of treason. President George Benson of Harding College in Searcy led the opposition at home, and "Justice Jim" Johnson became Fulbright's bitter opponent in the 1968 primary. Fulbright never strayed from Southern orthodoxy in civil rights; Johnson had no expertise in foreign relations. Fulbright defeated Johnson in the primary and met Charles T. Bernard, a Republican businessman, in the general election. Bernard got scant help from Governor Rockefeller, for many of the Governor's Democratic supporters also were committed to Fulbright, and Rockefeller's moderate rhetoric clashed with that of the more conservative Bernard. Fulbright was returned to the Senate and continued his opposition to the Vietnam War.

The 1968 election year also included a hotly

J. W. Fulbright, John L. McClellan and Wilbur D. Mills

challenge of United States Representative David Pryor in 1972 in one of the state's classic political confrontations. Pryor recovered from his defeat to become governor of Arkansas for two terms and was elected in 1978 to McClellan's seat after his death.

United States Senator J. William Fulbright gave credibility to Arkansas. When their state was derided as a haven for hillbillies, Arkansans could point to Fulbright to give that the lie, for he was the epitome of the intelligent world statesman. Fulbright became just plain "Bill" when he came home to Arkansas to campaign. He was an All-Southwest Conference halfback at the University of Arkansas and won a Rhodes Scholarship in the 1920s. He became a law professor. He was one of the nation's youngest university presidents at age 34 when he was named to head his alma mater. In a move directed against his politically active mother Roberta, who owned the Fayetteville paper, the Northwest Arkansas Times, *Governor Homer Adkins fired Fulbright in 1941. Fulbright was elected to the United States House of Representatives the next year as a Democrat over Adkins's opposition and moved up to the United States Senate in 1945, where he served for 30 years.*

He made an indelible mark on Congressional and world history by sponsoring the Fulbright Act of 1946, which funded the exchange of university students between the United States and other countries. Thousands of scholars and internation-

al leaders emerged from this program, which was renewed continuously for more than 45 years.

Another noted contribution was his criticism of the Vietnam War in the 1960s and 1970s while serving as chairman of the Senate Foreign Relations Committee. His heavily publicized committee hearings were directed to exercising more control over presidential warmaking powers. His dignified and scholarly dissent through books such as Old Myths and New Realities *and* The Arrogance of Power *helped legitimize opposition to the War in the United States. His philosophies of what types of foreign intervention are in the national interest have become part of the popular political culture.*

Although all the Arkansas Congressional delegation signed the Southern Manifesto denouncing as unconstitutional the Brown *desegregation decision, it was Senator Fulbright who took the most national criticism for it. While racism was considered normal behavior by most Southern voters, many liberals believed that the urbane Fulbright had such intellectual superiority that they never forgave him for signing the Southern Manifesto.*

In reality, Fulbright would have been vulnerable in the late 1950s and nearly 1960s if he had deviated from white norms in this matter. By 1968 racial attitudes had changed and Republicans, busy registering black voters, tried to capitalize on Fulbright's lack of commitment to civil rights. This, in turn prepared the ground for Governor Dale Bumpers's defeat of Fulbright in 1974.

contested presidential race. Arkansas voters had stayed loyal to Democrats despite the Roman Catholicism of John F. Kennedy and the appeal of Barry Goldwater's conservatism. But the failure to win the War and a growing white backlash against civil rights fractured Democratic unity and undermined the chances of Democratic hopeful Hubert Humphrey. Republican Richard M. Nixon, a

former vice-president under Dwight D. Eisenhower, was the Republican candidate. Alabama Governor George Wallace, who ran on the American Party label, spoke for racism and white supremacy. The Wallace movement received support from former Governor Ben Laney and other old-line segregationists. Arkansas voters gave Wallace 235,637 votes, Nixon came in second with 189,062 and

Humphrey followed closely with 184,901.

Thus in one election, Arkansas voters reelected a liberal Republican governor, returned a Democratic "dove" to the Senate, and voted for an independent party presidential candidate philosophically incompatible with the first two. The election has fascinated political scientists ever since.

Rockefeller's Second Term

As the Vietnam War continued, Rockefeller moved into his second term by confronting the volatile mix of black militance and white backlash. Trouble erupted in Forrest City when black teacher and minister J. F. Cooley, who had modest hopes of improving local race relations, was fired by the white school board. This firing touched off a riot followed by a boycott of white-owned businesses and gave Memphis resident "Sweet Willie Wine" Watson a chance to demonstrate the new techniques of confrontation in a march from Forrest City to Little Rock.

At Hazen in Prairie County, Sweet Willie was met by local residents who, under the leadership of Mayor Jerry Screeton, donned black shirts and barricaded the streets intersecting the main street, U. S. Highway 70, with combines. Wine was escorted through the county without incident by Sheriff Socrates "Crate" Grady, who met him at the county line with a simple question: "Do your feet hurt, Willie?" Rockefeller and members of the Arkansas Council on Human Relations established some dialogue in Forrest City and defused the passions.

Another hot spot was Marianna in troubled Lee County, where 44.3 percent of all families lived below the poverty level. Federal funds helped create the Lee County Cooperative Clinic, which tried to improve the health of people living largely without medical services. The clinic stood as a symbol of emergent black pride, but to some area whites, it was a subversive center where a mass insurrection was

being planned. With the aid of United States Senator John McClellan, these whites tried to get the clinic closed as liberals and moderates sought to retain it. Marianna race relations deteriorated until blacks began a boycott in 1971 to publicize their grievances.

Governor Rockefeller continued to make good on his commitment to the black community. More blacks began to appear on state boards, including some politically important ones such as Pardons and Paroles, county welfare boards and state college boards. On August 1, 1967, Marion Taylor became the first black to join the Arkansas State Police. Conrad Pattillo, the brother of one of the "Little Rock nine," followed in 1969, and the numbers grew appreciably after 1973. In all, the number of blacks in state government rose from 608 to 1,225. After Reverend Martin Luther King was assassinated in Memphis on April 4, 1968, Rockefeller took part in an impromptu memorial service on the steps of the state Capitol.

Possessing little hypocrisy, Rockefeller had no use for the seamy casino gambling that flourished openly in Hot Springs despite state laws against it. Everyone in Arkansas knew it existed, and many politicians had run against it, only to back off once in office. Rockefeller had embarrassed Faubus on the issue, and he immediately sent the State Police to destroy slot machines and close clubs — permanently. Hypocrisy also surrounded Arkansas's liquor laws. Rockefeller supported the successful passage of a mixed-drink law during his second term.

Rockefeller began his Arkansas career promoting economic development. He tried without success as governor to interest the legislature in a campaign entitled "Arkansas is Worth Paying For," his slogan for promoting an ambitious tax program in 1969. The legislature rejected his proposal. Bypassing the legislature in order to seek more federal funds, Rockefeller caused Arkansas to become the first state covered by planning

Confiscated Slot Machines at Hot Springs *(Gene Prescott, 1967) Pulaski County Sheriff B. Frank Mackey is shown looking at slot machines seized in a raid on a Hot Springs club.* **Arkansas Gazette**

and development districts. When the legislature refused to fund a human resources council, Rockefeller paid the bills with his own money. Federal aid benefited the prisons and mental and public health programs. Additional funds came from drawing interest on state funds rather than leaving the money interest-free in favored banks.

Rockefeller broke his promise in 1970 and announced for a third term. Democrats were torn again by internal strife. Orval Faubus made his first comeback attempt and led the other seven candidates, but with only 36.4 percent of the vote. His runoff opponent was Charleston lawyer Dale Bumpers, who had surprised political observers by outpolling such better-known figures as Attorney General Joe Purcell and Speaker of the House Hayes McClerkin.

Faubus practiced his old style in the runoff and Bumpers used television to project him-self as moderate and progressive. Bumpers's 70,000-vote margin of victory indicated that a new era of politics and politicians had arrived. Rockefeller, deserted by Democratic moderates, spent at least $3,000,000 in vain in the general election, carrying only two heavily black counties.

Rockefeller and the End of the Second Reconstruction

Like the Republicans of the first Reconstruction, Rockefeller had come from the outside and attempted to change the old Arkansas. They had promoted railroads; he pushed industrialization and better agriculture. The first Republicans were defeated to a large extent, but Rockefeller succeeded: "I see a different place," he said in his farewell address to the legislature. The Rockefeller legacy to Arkansas was the rebirth of progressivism, for the next three governors carried on his vision for the state in that tradition.

For all the money he spent, however, Rockefeller did not revitalize the state Republican Party, even though the events of the 1957 crisis at Central High tragically had demonstrated the need for a strong two-party system to give rise to political debate on important social and political issues. Elsewhere in the South, Republicans tended to be middle-class conservatives from the suburbs.

Rockefeller, however, was a liberal Republican. Conservatives gradually moved into power within the G.O.P. after his defeat. Businessman John Paul Hammerschmidt defeated long-time Democratic Congressman James W. Trimble in 1966, thereafter making the Third Congressional District seat in northwestern Arkansas the state's Republican stronghold. An alliance of businessmen and Northern retirees kept Hammerschmidt in office, and conservatism proved politically viable in Fort Smith and part of central Arkansas. Thus the progressive legacy passed to the Democrats in Arkansas.

Catalysts for Change

The emergence of groups free to lobby for change lay behind the transformation of politics in the 1960s and early 1970s. Their freedom was not achieved easily. Dr. Albert Ellis, a well-known author and psychotherapist from New York, delivered a lecture in 1962 at the University of Arkansas entitled, "Reason and Emotion in Sex-Love Relationships," in which, according to newspaper accounts, he approved of premarital sexual relations. Governor Faubus's demand for the immediate firing of Ellis's sponsor led zoologist Richard V. Ganslen, Ph.D., who was also a noted authority on pole vaulting, to leave the state.

The University in reaction took steps to prevent future controversies. A speech entitled "Life in Bulgaria" was banned on campus but was given at the Methodist Student Center despite public pressure on Center minister Reverend James A. Loudermilk. Among those who supported the minister was Senator J. William Fulbright, who noted that "the right to hear as well as to speak freely about controversial subjects is a basic principle of our democratic society." University censorship in 1962 even reached the point that the school forbade the gubernatorial candidates to appear on campus.

With student discontent over the War in Vietnam rising, support for free speech and press broadened. A mimeographed underground newspaper appeared, and students protested until the speaker policy substantially was abandoned in 1965. In 1966, however, State Auditor Jimmie "Red" Jones refused to print the student poetry journal because of the presence of four scatological words: "I was raised in a Christian home where words that appear in these poems were never used." Although Dean R. S. Fairchild rejoined that, "the people who receive it have broad exposure to literature and are not squeamish," the journal had to be printed privately two years later. Student protests continued into the 1970s but died as the Vietnam War faded from view and the economic picture darkened.

The Fayetteville campus was not alone in experiencing difficulties. In 1967, the former agricultural high school in Jonesboro was named a university. Its president, Carl R. Reng, had close ties to the Faubus administration, and he watched his faculty closely for signs of disaffection. "Half of them live in fear," sociology professor John S. Osoinach observed, "and the other half in apathy."

Reng received a five-year contract from his Board just before Rockefeller took office, but things were not as simple as before with the regents that the governor appointed. Upset that faculty should protest the removal from the classroom of a pregnant instructor, Reng ordered several professors fired in 1970, including philosophy professor Bill L. Stroud,

Draft Board, Hot Springs (*photographer and date unknown*) *During the Vietnam War, the fates of young men rested in the hands of local draft boards composed of old white men.* **University of Arkansas**

a former Baptist minister active in the Jonesboro Council on Human Relations; historian Dr. Ronald Hayworth, the president of the local chapter of the AAUP; and political scientist and Republican Dr. Mary Susan Power. When some of the faculty protested, the purge list was expanded by forty-two names. A student protest followed, during which an abandoned building was set on fire. Both Stroud and Hayworth departed, but the others survived.

The longest-lived controversy was at the University of Arkansas at Little Rock (UALR). Historian Grant Cooper, Ph.D., a native son whose father was a prominent former Little Rock School Board member, admitted in 1974 to being a member of the obscure Progressive Labor Party and teaching from an economic determinist standpoint. "The Communist at UALR" controversy had the legislature threatening to cut off all funds to the school if Coop-

er were not fired. Cooper was discharged for incompetency, but the federal courts ordered him rehired, without tenure. Cooper, however, had moved to Texas and chose not to return.

In 1969, a diverse mixture of civil rights advocates, law professors and peace activists organized the state chapter of the American Civil Liberties Union (ACLU). One of the first cases involved the conviction in Arkadelphia of Mr. and Mrs. Joe Neal for "causing a disturbance on school property" after they spoke to a group of students and distributed antiwar "offensive literature designed to excite the emotions of students." The Neals appealed their banishment to the state Supreme Court. Jim Guy Tucker, a future attorney general, congressman and governor, argued their case in *Neal* v. *Still* (1970), the first ACLU victory in Arkansas. The ACLU had nearly 500 members and a full-time executive director by 1975.

March for Victory in Vietnam *(Gene Prescott, 1970)*
In the face of growing public dissatisfaction, Arkansas's
conservatives staged this victory rally in 1970. Reverend
Carl McIntire from Texas is pictured here with his
Bible. He is accompanied by Mrs. McIntire and
Reverend M. L. Moser, Jr. According to Moser, Arkansas
Senator J. William Fulbright, was the "chief
Communist spokesman in the United States."
Arkansas Gazette

A different catalyst for change was the Arkansas Community Organizations for Reform Now (ACORN), the creation of activist organizer Wade Rathke. ACORN sought to get the poor to speak for themselves on streets, housing, welfare, utilities and other public issues. ACORN's strategy was to use the politics of direct confrontation to make officials more cautious in adopting and implementing policy. Rathke eventually expanded his idea, modified the name by replacing Arkansas with American and moved the national headquarters to New Orleans.

One outlet for liberal sentiment was the *Arkansas Advocate*, a sometime monthly founded in 1972 by Rathke and published by a variety of owners for four years. Its columns presented the "new journalism" of personal opinion and offered an outlet for covering controversial topics unlikely to appear in established newspapers. The first issue, for example, carried reporter Martin Kirby's expose of the Haven of Healing Hope at Russellville, where senile patients discharged from the State Hospital were padlocked and drugged, largely without medical supervision. Subsequent issues explored the fate of a Jacksonville journalism teacher fired for letting her students criticize deteriorating restrooms, the death of a fifteen-year-old prisoner in the Mississippi County Penal Farm and an expose on the role of insurance men in Arkansas politics. Liberalism lost its voice with the demise of the *Advocate*, for only an occasional *Arkansas Times* article could be considered controversial.

The Proposed Constitution of 1970

The proposed Arkansas Constitution of 1970 was perhaps the best example of the progressive liberal spirit in the state. Serious students of government had long been aware of the archaic and restrictive limitations of the old 1874 document. But revision threatened too many entrenched interests until, in repugnance against Old Guard politics at the end of the Faubus era, the reformist spirit momentarily attained the upper hand.

A study commission headed by University of Arkansas Law Dean Robert A. Leflar not only summarized the problem in 1967 but submitted a completely revised draft document. The voters approved summoning a convention in 1968 and elected 100 delegates. Little interest was shown in many parts of the state, and a generally harmonious body with Leflar as president produced a more modern constitution. Most archaic provisions were deleted, local government was modernized, the executive branch was reorganized, municipal government was strengthened and state officers were given four-year terms.

Despite the support of virtually all of the state's press and professional organizations in 1970, voters defeated the constitution decisively. Local courthouse organizations led the attack, claiming that God had been left out and taxes would go up. That Winthrop Rockefeller, a supporter of the proposed document, was going down to defeat against Dale Bumpers did the cause little good.

Despite the defeat, many of the most significant provisions were adopted in various ways during the next twenty years. Executive reorganization was achieved through legislation supported by Governor Dale Bumpers. Amendment 55 revised county government in 1974 by making the quorum court a truly deliberative body. Finally, voters elected state constitutional officers to four-year terms beginning in 1986.

The Progressive Democrats

Dale Bumpers won from the legislature in 1971 many of the programs that Rockefeller had sought in vain. The reorganization of the executive branch from numerous small agencies into thirteen cabinet positions created a more modern executive system. State income tax rates were increased to allow the creation of new programs and more adequate funding for old ones. Voters responded to prosperity by authorizing the creation of community colleges (Amendment 52) and kindergartens (Amendment 53).

Bumpers won a second term handily in 1972, but Senator John McClellan encountered stiff primary opposition from Congressman David Pryor and reformer Ted Boswell. Pryor forced McClellan into a runoff, but the incumbent spent heavily in the closing days of the campaign and convinced enough voters that Pryor was a tool of big labor who favored

amnesty for draft dodgers. Senator McClellan was at his best in a television debate and squeaked through to victory.

The same year marked the pinnacle of the career of veteran Congressman Wilbur D. Mills. A "Draft Mills" committee entered his name in the New Hampshire Democratic presidential primary in 1972, spent nearly $100,000, but got only 3,508 votes or 4.1 percent of the total. Mills dropped out of the race, embarrassed by reports that milk producers and liquor interests had bankrolled his campaign.

Arkansas's most respected congressman, Wilbur Mills, suffered embarrassment when found in his car near the Tidal Basin in the company of Argentina stripper Fanne Fox in October 1973. Mills faced a strong challenge in 1974 from Republican unknown Judy Petty. Reelected, he again turned up with his stripper friend in a Boston nightclub. After admitting he was an alcoholic, Mills resigned his chairmanship of the influential Ways and Means Committee and did not seek reelection in 1976. He then turned his considerable talents to practicing law in Washington, D.C., and to speaking for Alcoholics Anonymous. He died in 1992.

Another illustrious political career halted in the 1970s was that of Senator J. William Fulbright. The highly popular Dale Bumpers opposed Fulbright in the Democratic primary in 1974. Running on his record as governor and using the same "smile and shoeshine" technique that worked so well four years earlier, Bumpers buried the incumbent with 65.2 percent of the vote.

Fulbright fell in part because he was perceived as having become too remote from Arkansas concerns as well as being the victim of one of Arkansas's most effective and popular politicians. His civil rights record deprived him of significant black support, and his opposition to Zionism led both local and national Jewish groups to contribute heavily to his defeat. Out of office, Fulbright remained in Washington to practice law and continued to be a much-quoted authority on American foreign policy and widely honored for his sponsorship of the Fulbright-Hays exchange program.

A third career that failed to flourish was Orval Faubus's. Bumpers's quest for the Senate and the absence of any heir apparent left the gubernatorial field wide open. In his second comeback attempt for governor, Faubus told voters in 1974 his record was that of a Progressive and promised to appoint blacks, women and young reformers to state positions. Witt Stephens supported David Pryor, and Faubus found himself attacking many of his old supporters. The old machine and the old magic failed, and a much-publicized divorce and remarriage hurt the image of the ex-governor. Pryor successfully defeated Faubus and Lieutenant Governor Bob Riley, a Ouachita Baptist College professor and disabled war veteran, without a runoff.

Under Pryor, the state began a retrenchment program. State government during the preceding administration had been founded on a prosperous economy and generous federal aid. The Arab oil embargo hit rural Arkansas hard, leading Pryor to call for dismantling or transferring many state programs to counties and reducing state taxes accordingly. He said in his inaugural address that if state expenses could be reduced, the home folks might be able to afford a new coon dog. Cartoonist George Fisher seized on the remark, making the coon dog a symbol for the Pryor administration.

In hard times accompanied by double-digit inflation, taxpayer resistance increased. Yet Arkansas's state services were so underfunded that Pryor found little support for his plan. In 1975, Pryor appointed Elsijane Trimble Roy as the first woman on the state Supreme Court. When she resigned in 1977 to become a federal judge, black civil rights lawyer George Howard was appointed to take her place. Judge Howard was appointed to the federal bench in 1980. Meanwhile, the efforts of segregationist James

D. "Justice Jim" Johnson to reclaim a court seat failed, and Johnson announced his retirement from politics. The last member of the old generation, Senator John L. McClellan, died in 1977. Kaneaster Hodges of Newport, a moderate, was appointed to serve out the remaining one year of McClellan's term.

Another reform-minded Democrat moved into the governor's mansion. Bill Clinton had emerged as a Party leader in 1974 when he came within 6,000 votes of unseating incumbent Third District Republican Congressman John Paul Hammerschmidt. Elected attorney general in 1976, Clinton continued the progressive record that Joe Purcell, Ray Thornton and Jim Guy Tucker had established in the aftermath of the Bruce Bennett scandals. Clinton carried the reform banner against a variety of other candidates in the 1978 gubernatorial race. With more than four times the financial support of his opponents combined and the endorsement of the AFL-CIO, the AEA and ACORN, Clinton won easily and swamped his Republican opponent, conservative Lynn Lowe of Texarkana, in the general election. Cartoonist George Fisher celebrated the nation's youngest governor, 32, by drawing him seated on a tricycle.

The 1978 senatorial race was a battle of moderates. In his quest for McClellan's former seat, Pryor was opposed by Ray Thornton and Jim Guy Tucker, who were both former attorneys general and congressmen. Because all three candidates were similar ideologically, they scrambled hard for support. Pryor was forced into a runoff with Tucker and won with 54.8 percent of the vote. Pryor easily defeated an unknown Republican in the general election.

Part of Pryor's success lay in his early identification with the needs of the elderly. He had undertaken an intensive investigation into nursing home management while in Congress. As the Arkansas population grew older, concerns of the aged became politically important and possibly accounted for his margin of victory.

The conservative temper of the times manifested itself in central Arkansas in the race for the congressional seat being vacated by Jim Guy Tucker. The Democratic primary ended in a bitter runoff between Doug Brandon of Little Rock and Cecil Alexander of Heber Springs. After Brandon won the primary, a number of prominent Alexander supporters lined up behind conservative Republican Ed Bethune of Searcy, whose victory in November gave Arkansas two Republican congressmen.

Arkansas voters overwhelmingly had supported Southerner Jimmy Carter during the 1976 presidential election. But the Carter administration's decision to locate Cuban refugees at Fort Chaffee proved a major political embarrassment to Governor Clinton. Rioting that some said was publicized heavily by the conservative Fort Smith press for political purposes stirred up the latent xenophobia of voters. Former Democrat and AIDC commissioner Frank White announced his conversion to Republicanism in 1980 and his candidacy against Clinton.

Clinton had other problems as well. A model jobs plan to cut firewood, abbreviated SAWER, spent some $40,000 for a minuscule amount of wood. In addition, the raising of auto and truck license fees in an effort to repair Arkansas's deteriorating highways produced a public outcry that White effectively exploited. Clinton should have been forewarned when idiosyncratic gubernatorial campaigner Monroe Schwartzlose, an elderly Cleveland County turkey farmer noted for inventing a cure for turkey sinus problems, drew 30 percent of the vote in the Democratic primary.

In a stunning upset, voters repudiated Clinton in November. Clinton thus joined Tom Terral and Francis Cherry as incumbent governors who failed to win second two-year terms. The state went on to give its vote to conservative Republican Ronald Reagan with only Dale Bumpers escaping the Republican sweep.

The Conservative Interlude

The 1980 election marked the high tide of the conservative resurgence. Republicans had failed to field strong candidates in congressional races. When Chuck Banks of Osceola launched a well-financed campaign in 1982 against First District incumbent Bill Alexander, voter disillusionment already had set in, and Alexander won by an unexpectedly large margin. But Banks had earned his spurs, and later was appointed United States Attorney for the Eastern District of Arkansas.

Frank White, the new Republican governor, stood in marked contrast to his Republican predecessor, Winthrop Rockefeller. A recent convert to Republicanism, he had few ties to the old Rockefeller Republicans but many connections with business Democrats. White's appointment of Orval Faubus as director of Veterans Affairs so angered many older Republicans that it seriously undermined his reelection bid in 1982.

In addition, Governor White signed but admitted not having read a controversial law mandating the teaching of "creation science" in the public schools. The law was challenged immediately in court, and cartoonist George Fisher put Darwin's monkey on White's back and a banana in his hand.

A chastened Bill Clinton said he had learned his lesson, and accompanied by his lawyer-wife Hillary Rodham, who took his last name rather than continuing to keep her own, he easily beat White in a 1982 rematch.

Further evidence that the conservative resurgence in Arkansas had passed could be found in the 1984 election. The popular Ronald Reagan was running for a second term as president against Walter Mondale, a Democrat identified with the liberal wing of the Party. Although the Moral Majority and other conservative groups were at the height of their power in shaping the political awareness of religious conservatives, Republicans were unable to capitalize politically. Woody Freeman, a Jonesboro businessman, failed to make headway against Clinton, and Republican Congressman Ed Bethune failed to unseat Senator David Pryor.

What did come to the fore in the 1984 election was a unique brand of populism put forth by Pulaski County Sheriff Tommy Robinson. Robinson had become notorious for his quarrels with county and state officials, staging antics that harkened to Jeff Davis and evoked the same wholehearted response from blue-collar voters. What had once been the "wool hat boys" had now become the pick-up truck crowd. At the same time, Robinson received large, virtually interest-free loans from ideologically friendly bankers. When Robinson decided to run for the Second District congressional seat in central Arkansas that Republican Congressman Ed Bethune was vacating, Secretary of State Paul Riviere, black businessman Thedford Collins and former Congressman Dale Alford all opposed him in vain.

Robinson went on to defeat Judy Petty, a conservative Republican state legislator from Little Rock and Jim Taylor, an unknown, who ran as an independent. The victorious Robinson, although nominally a Democrat, allied himself with conservative Republicans and often was at odds both personally and politically with other Arkansas Democrats. After a short career as a boll weevil Democrat, Robinson openly switched sides. In 1990, he left Congress to run as a Republican for governor. For the first time in recent Arkansas history, there was serious interest in the Republican primary. Sheffield Nelson, a poor boy who had risen to be Witt Stephens's pick as the head of Arkla and himself a recent convert, defeated Robinson even though the Stephenses' interests were allied with Robinson. Nelson could not overcome Clinton's popularity and the perpetual incumbent won yet another term.

In sharp contrast to the roistering Robinson was the metamorphosis of Dale Bumpers.

Bumpers had never been an issue-oriented campaigner. Once in the Senate, however, his public stands on a number of controversial issues offended many Arkansas conservatives. The new Bumpers spoke openly before often hostile audiences. He was a masterful speaker and acknowledged to be the best orator in the Senate. Although targeted for defeat by right-wing religious fundamentalist Reverend Jerry Falwell, Bumpers was spoken of as a possible presidential candidate in 1984 and 1988.

Despite statewide victories by a number of Progressive candidates, modernist successes were hard to achieve in the legislature. From the late 1950s to the early 1980s, the federal government provided assistance for highways, schools, hospitals, social programs, the arts and numerous other programs. Most of these programs were abandoned, frozen or reduced during the Reagan years. As federal incentives for improving the quality of Arkansas life dried up, state officials responded.

The first bold move was taken by Governor Clinton during his second term. Calling for a thorough study of Arkansas public schools, he appointed a commission headed by his wife, Hillary Rodham Clinton. The comission recommended raising teacher salaries, which usually ranked last or next to last among the states, setting standards that all school districts had to meet and testing teachers. Despite a stagnant economy, the legislature passed a 1 cent increase in the state sales tax to finance the improvements. Other Southern states tried harder, and by 1988, the governor renewed his call for a commitment to education, this time including the woefully underfunded state colleges and universities.

Clinton's second step, the Economic Development Program of 1985, aroused less controversy. Meanwhile, federal courts forced Arkansas customers to pay part of the costs of the Grand Gulf nuclear power plant at Port Gibson, Mississippi. The issue aroused some passions but did not become a political liability for Governor Clinton, who supported a negotiated settlement on Arkansas's share of the plant's costs.

In his 1989 legislative program, "Moving Arkansas Forward into the 21st Century," Clinton sounded the recurring progressive tocsin: "Either we invest more in human capital and develop our people's capacity to compete, or we are headed for a long term decline. If we don't, our economic future will almost certainly be more of what we have seen in the last decade: too much unemployment, wages too depressed, and too many young people leaving the Land of Opportunity in search of opportunity." But the forces of traditionalism remained strong.

The Structure of Arkansas Politics: A Retrospective

During most of the state's history, personality and machines rather than issues and strong political parties proved to be the mainsprings of the political process. Of these two forces, machine politics dominated more than personality. Despite repeated efforts to establish a two-party system, most Arkansas voters preferred only Republican presidential nominees. In the age of public relations, issues became television "sound bites." However, changes in laws and customs sent machine politics into decline.

The Politics of Rurality

The persistence of rural ways has been much in evidence in state politics. From 1890 to 1937, the state legislature refused to reapportion itself, although required to do so by the state Constitution. The United States Supreme Court's reapportionment rule, "one man one vote," further emphasized the declining rural influence. By 1984, 51.6 percent of the population lived in towns of 2,500 or more, and 40 percent lived in a Standard Metropolitan Statistical Area. Nevertheless, fourteen counties had no urban population at all, and

sixty-two counties were classified as more rural than urban.

Despite the urban statistical edge, rural ways remained powerful in politics. It was rural opposition to a motor license increase that led in part to Frank White's unseating of incumbent Bill Clinton in 1980. Rural forces kept Arkansas well supplied with school districts, although, in general, rural voters seemed to prefer roads to schools.

Most rural themes were more important in legislative affairs than in any other branch of government. Political trade-offs were the way bills became law, for in a state as short of money as Arkansas, no one major need could afford to be met unless everybody got a piece of the pie. In one state Senate election, the successful challenger charged that his opponent was a "statesman" who had failed to consider just how each vote would profit his county. The challenger went on to promise that, if elected, he would vote only for what benefited the county. A by-product of the politics of rurality was that intelligent discussion of the issues yielded to a few well-placed telephone calls or the consensus of the local coffee shop. State planning was almost impossible, and rural interests fought vigorously to prevent the passage of a comprehensive water code even though water shortages loomed.

Although the politics of rurality consisted mostly of inaction and opposition, rural forces actually sponsored much legislation relating to themes such as hunting laws and tax exemptions. The state Constitution banned local legislation in 1926, but in what was hardly an isolated instance, the General Assembly fifty-seven years later passed for the benefit of cattlemen "An Act to Require Landowners to Prevent Thistles from Going to Seed on Their Property," which then applied only to Benton and Washington Counties. On the whole, the legislature remained more friendly to rural interests than to any other lobbying force. Not surprisingly, the National

Conway County Sheriff Marlin Hawkins and Governor Orval Faubus at the Levy Day Rally in 1985. *(Kelly Quinn)* **Arkansas Gazette**

Rifle Association (NRA) exercised considerable power in legislative lobbies.

Modernization in the Counties

Throughout most of the twentieth century, counties have been "little kingdoms." Nationally, Arkansas counties ranked sixth in discretionary authority of finances, functions, personnel and structure. Within counties, however, power shifted as "Old Guard" politicians went into retirement.

Conway County Sheriff Marlin Hawkins was perhaps the last politician who ran his county. Hawkins got into a quarrel in the late 1960s with Morrilton newspaper editor Gene Wirges, who was backed by Winthrop Rocke-

feller. The resulting controversy and lawsuits did much to discredit the machine system.

Modernizing features after 1970 included Amendment 55 to the Arkansas Constitution, which ended the unchecked power of the county judge and created a meaningful quorum court, and Amendment 51, which established a permanent voter registration system. Federal criminal investigations on county buying practices sent a number of county judges to jail. In 1988, St. Francis County Sheriff Coolidge Conlee was convicted on gambling and racketeering charges and was featured on an ABC television network program, "20-20."

In addition, work by the League of Women Voters, the Election Laws Institute, the Institute of Politics and Government and a press armed with the Freedom of Information Act took most of the mystery out of elections. As one result, the political processes became more open to participation by minorities. By 1988, only a few of the smallest counties were still run by a "courthouse gang."

Local politics could be egalitiarian and democratic. As a student of Arkansas politics has observed, "That candidates often seek office under such nicknames as Junior and Bubba, Junebug and Jughead, nicely conveys the nonelitist nature of most local contests." Roughly similar conditions prevailed in Arkansas's 480 incorporated towns and cities.

Arkansas fully embraced democracy. At the state level, voters chose all the local and appellate judges as well as seven separate constitutional offices of state government, including the now minor position of state land commissioner. On the local level, few communities adopted the city manager form of government. By law, obsolete offices such as coroner, county surveyor and constable still had to be filled.

Yet given the meager pay and the potentially upsetting situations that could develop, it was not surprising that some difficulty existed in recruiting opponents. The town of Sherrill in Jefferson County, satisfied with its mayor and aldermen in 1978, simply stopped bothering to hold elections for ten years. "It's not the way it's supposed to go," the mayor commented, "but it's the way we do it."

Modernization in the Executive Branch

The unprecedented six terms (1955-67) served by Orval Faubus created, more than any constitutional amendment or legislative enactment, the modern office of governor. Executive reorganization during Bumpers' tenure confirmed what had become the practice. Although constitutionally weak, Arkansas governors function as super legislators in preparing their programs, chief admin-

istators of the state bureaucracy, handlers of emergencies, national intermediaries, promoters of economic development and a symbol of the state. After analyzing these functions, Diane Blair, the most recent student of Arkansas government, concluded that the executive branch was the most modernized in state government. However, salaries, fixed by the state Constitution, remained low and attempts to supplement pay through a variety of legal subterfuges cast a pall over the honesty of veteran public officials. Attorney General Steve Clark's gubernatorial bid in 1990 was short circuited and Clark forced to resign amid evidence that he had misreported his credit card charges.

Modernization in the Legislative Branch

By contrast, the legislature was the least modernized. Legislators remained underpaid, effectively limiting service to professionals or those owning their own businesses. Few women, and until 1973, no blacks sat in either the state House of Representatives or the state Senate. Seniority was important, and in contrast to the nineteenth century when the turnover rate stood at more than 80 percent, only about 20 percent of the members failed to be returned at election time after 1972.

Lobbyists dominated the legislative process. In the 1950s, Arkla displaced AP&L in dominance, so that by 1966, seventeen of the thirty-five state senators were on the company payroll. Every substantial economic interest was invariably well represented, and on occasion the state Capitol was flooded with the constituents of some moral issue. By the early 1970s, Diane Blair observed, lobbyists "swarmed on the chamber floors (and freqently joined in the voting), bills were scheduled or buried at whim through mysterious manipulations, committees and committee assignments were so numerous as to be meaningless, and whatever real business the legislature accomplished was worked out in late-night (and frequently liquorish) sessions in downtown hotel rooms." Lobbyists preferred incumbents, and special interest groups contributed generously to election campaigns. As a result, many laws gave special privileges and favors to powerful vested interests, often in the form of tax exemptions.

Not even the legislature could escape the reformist impulse, and after a 1972 study, the committee system was reformed. The Legislative Council, established in 1949, took an increasing role despite recurring questions concerning its constitutionality. The ethical problems proved to be more difficult to address. Arkansas's first ethics law, adopted in 1979, required only that legislators disclose their financial interests. When the legislature failed to adopt Governor Clinton's strengthened law in 1988, the voters, prodded by Common Cause and other reform groups, passed it as an initiated act.

The legislature remained hostile to innovation. Legislative Council members garnered much publicity in objecting to state contracts relating to sex education, modern dance and a political show on the Arkansas Educational Television Network. During the Rockefeller years, powerful Representative John Miller took offense at an art exhibit at the Capitol that contained "nekked women . . . with everything showing." Legislators also found offense with a Richard Allin and George Fisher cartoon book the *Southern Legislative Dictionary*, which accurately described southern speech. The book was banned from the state capitol gift shop. A proposal to fund school health clinics in 1989 was greeted by one legislator with the comment, "I will not turn these children over to their vile affections . . . We have gave up on Arkansas. We have gave up on the family."

Despite the real work done by the legislators, much public attention was focused on bills that gave some members a chance to strike out at social issues. Among those that received national publicity was one to locate and tax unmarried couples, and another to ban the backward masking of alleged "satanic messages" on rock records. The most expensive for Arkansas was the "Creation Science Law," which passed with little legislative investigation despite plain warnings of its unconstitutionality. The high cost of the Creation Science litigation curbed, at least temporarily, the flow of obviously unconstitutional legislation.

What the legislature did provide for Arkansas was color. In 1963, Representative Paul Van Dalsem of Perryville voiced his dislike of "frustrated" women to a civic club:

> We don't have any of these University Women [American Association of University Women] in Perry County, but I'll tell you what we do up there when one of our women starts poking around in something she doesn't know anything about. We get her an extra milk cow. If that don't work, we give her a little more garden to tend. And if that's not enough, we get her pregnant and keep her barefoot.

Women's rights groups all over the country seized on "barefoot and pregnant," using it to summarize male chauvinist attitudes. Local women had their revenge. In 1966, redistricting put portions of Little Rock in Van Dalsem's district and he failed to retain his seat. Van Dalsem was typical in many ways of rural or small-town legislators of that era. However, urban growth after 1970 resulted in new faces more likely to be younger, better educated, more careful in their speech, and occasionally, Republican. The defeat in 1990 of Senator Knox Nelson of Pine Bluff, who became the epitome of an effective old-time legislator, was heralded as the rebirth of the Arkansas legislature by those who believed Nelson had amassed enough power to block reforms of which he did not approve. Significantly, Governor Clinton was able to win major tax increases in the 1991 legislative session, including more funding for higher education and new money for highways.

Modernization in the Judicial Branch

In 1950, a state study commission gave up trying to discover how many courts actually were operating in the state. Luxora might hold a police court, it reported, "but this department has not been able to obtain confirmation of this fact." Justices of the peace still could hold court at that time, and some counties continued to maintain prison farms. The court system not only lacked in coherence, but it failed to respond to the broader challenges posed by constitutional law.

One example of the conflict between state practices and national standards came in the United States Supreme Court case of *Gent* v. *Arkansas* (1967). The Community Interest Committee in Pine Bluff, composed primarily of religious leaders, began an anti-pornography campaign, prosecuting a local newsstand owner who stocked *Gent, Swank* and a half-dozen other magazines that all had second-class mailing permits. Although convicted in state courts, the owner was acquitted by the Supreme Court, which held that pornography had to mean more than the disapproval of Pine Bluff ministers.

A second major case to reach the national tribunal was that of Little Rock biology teacher Susan Epperson, who challenged the anti-evolution law in *Epperson* v. *Arkansas* (1968). When Epperson complained that an assignment to teach biology required her to violate state law, Chancellor Murray O. Reed agreed, ruling that the statute violated the Fourteenth Amendment as well as the First Amendment guarantee of freedom of speech. The state Supreme Court reversed Reed without addressing any of the constitutional questions. When the case reached Washington, the

Supreme Court had no trouble concluding "fundamentalist sectarian conviction was and is the law's reason for existence." What bothered it more was that Arkansas's Supreme Court had failed to act.

Two factors retarded modernization. First, all Arkansas judges are elected. Sustaining the anti-evolution law probably was good politics. Second, most Arkansas judges were not familiar with constitutional law. As Diane Blair has noted, only sixteen cases involved constitutionality during the state Supreme Court's 1983-84 term. Judges were far more familiar with contracts and automobile negligence. In 1989, the Arkansas Bar Association called for the creation of an appointive system of choosing judges.

The nationalization of the Bill of Rights by the United States Supreme Court changed Arkansas practices in areas such as right to counsel, civil rights, search and seizure, confessions and prisoner rights. Following the recommendations of the Judiciary Commission Report of 1965, circuits were standardized. The greatly overworked state Supreme Court got relief when Amendment 58 in 1978 created a Court of Appeals. In national studies, Arkansas ranked high for judicial efficiency. Evidences of scandal and corruption were less common than in many other states.

Despite the improvements, Diane Blair's 1988 assessment was that the Arkansas courts "have been less touched by modern court reform movements than those of almost any other state in the country." Arkansas was one of only three states that still maintained a separate equity court system, and it ranked forty-ninth out of fifty in judicial professionalism.

Perhaps the most shocking omission was Arkansas's failure to provide for a system of juvenile justice. Under a law passed in 1911 and upheld in 1919, the county judge could turn juvenile case over to an appointed judge. In *Walker* v. *Arkansas Department of Human Services* (1987), a unanimous state Supreme Court found this system to be unconstitutional because the 1874 Constitution contained no reference to juvenile courts. In 1988, voters approved letting the legislature establish a juvenile court system. The state had come a long way since the days when Pulaski County Judge Arch Campbell was rumored to determine paternity suits by inspection of the ears of the reputed father and the child.

CONCLUSION

For more than the two decades after 1957, a little black schoolgirl blocked by the National Guard and threatened by a howling mob symbolized Arkansas to the people of the world. Yet for all the publicity, the Arkansas integration story was not as hate-filled or as bloody as it was elsewhere in the South. Governor Faubus, although assuming the role of a demagogue, eventually returned to a course of racial moderation. Support for Southern moderation won the *Arkansas Gazette* a Pulitzer Prize and made Winthrop Rockefeller a two-term Republican governor.

By the late 1960s, the progressive impulse was again dominant and remained the basic theme in Arkansas politics despite adverse economic conditions and entrenched provincialism. Arkansas's leaders tended to be far above the regional average, confounding those Americans who still thought of Arkansas in the hillbilly stereotype. But underneath the seeming triumph of modernization lay the pent-up frustrations of a people who were never completely at ease with progress. The appeal of Tommy Robinson, a politician from urban Little Rock, served to indicate that old resentments still flourished and might again displace the progressive facade of reason with something far more elemental and emotional.

BIBLIOGRAPHIC ESSAY

Contemporary events are the most difficult to write about dispassionately, and nothing in Arkansas history aroused more hard feelings than the desegregation crisis. The only overview is Dan Durning, "1954 to Present," *Historical Report of the Secretary of State* III (1978)

Many participants in the Little Rock crisis have had recourse to writing. Orval Faubus covered those years in *Down From the Hills,* (Little Rock, 1980); others include Dale and L'Moore Alford, *The Case of the Sleeping People (Finally Awakened by Little Rock School Frustration),* (Little Rock, 1959); Daisy Bates, *The Long Shadow of Little Rock — A Memoir,* (New York, 1962); Virgil T. Blossom, *It Has Happened Here,* (New York, 1959); Robert R. Brown, *Bigger Than Little Rock,* (Greenwich, Conn., 1959), and Elizabeth Huckaby, *Crisis at Central High, Little Rock, 1957-1958,* (Baton Rouge, 1980). Brooks Hays addressed the immediate issues in *A Southern Moderate Speaks,* (Chapel Hill, 1959), before completing his story in *Politics Is My Parish,* (Baton Rouge, 1981). A recent addition is *Osro Cobb: Memoirs of Historical Significance* (Little Rock, 1989).

Scholars have been equally busy. Tony Freyer, *The Little Rock Crisis; A Constitutional Interpretation,* (Westport, Conn., 1984) in addition to its legal insights is valuable for examining the FBI records. "*Numan v. Bartley, Looking Back at Little Rock,*" *AHQ,* XXV (Summer 1966), 101-116, was followed by his *The Rise of Massive Resistance: Race and Politics in the South During the 1950's* (Baton Rouge, 1969) Neil R. McMillen, "White Citizen Council and Resistance to School Desegregation in Arkansas," *AHQ,* XXX (Summer 1971), 95-122, is excellent, while David Wallace, "Orval Faubus: The Central Figure at Little Rock Central High School," *AHQ,* XXXIX (Winter 1980), 314-329, makes a case against the governor.

Higher education is treated in Leflar, "The First Hundred Years," and in Guerdon D. Nichols, "Breaking the Color Barrier at the University of Arkansas," *AHQ,* XXVII (Spring 1968), 3-21. The concentration on education has led to the neglect of other racial issues. Elaine McNeil, "White Members of a Biracial Voluntary Association in Arkansas," (Ph. D. Diss., University of Kansas, 1967), is an incomplete history of the Arkansas Council on Human Relations.

The Rockefeller years are sympathetically but by no means exhaustively discussed in John L. Ward, *The Arkansas Rockefeller,* (Baton Rouge, 1978). Some changes during that period are recorded in George D. Morgan, *Marianna — A Sociological Essay on an Eastern Arkansas Town* (Jefferson City, Mo.,1973) and by Juanita D. Sanford, *Poverty in the Land of Opportunity,* (Little Rock, 1978). The Arkansas prisons became the subject of a number of emotional treatments beginning with Dale Woodcock, *Ruled by the Whip,* (New York, 1969), which is grossly exaggerated. K. Wymand Keith, *Long Line Rider; The Cummins Prison Farm,* (New York, 1971) is impressionistic; Bruce Jackson, *Killing Time; Life in the Arkansas Penitentiary,* (New York, 1977) is a picture essay.

Many of the problems of contemporary Arkansas are addressed in the varied essays included in Walter Nunn, ed., *Readings in Arkansas Government,* (Little Rock, 1973). More recent is Diane D. Blair, *Arkansas Politics and Government,* (Univ. of Neb. Press, 1988). One study in federalism is Joel D. Barker, "The Arkansas Law on Obscenity and "*Gent* v. *Arkansas, AHQ,* XXXVII (Spring 1979), 44-73.

During the Vietnam conflict, Senator Fulbright became the focus of national attention. His most important writing was *The Crippled Giant: American Foreign Policy and Its Domestic Consequences,* (New York, 1972). Back home, critic James D. Bales of Searcy produced *Senator Fulbright's Secret Memorandum,* (Searcy, 1962). Fulbright inspired a number of biographers, none of whom had any familiarity with Arkansas: Haynes Johnson and Bernard M. Gwertzman, *Fulbright, The Dissenter,* (Garden City, N. Y., 1968), and Tristram Coffin, *Senator Fulbright, Portrait of a Public Philosopher,* (New York, 1966). Wilbur Mills inspired Annabel *"Fanne Foxe"* Battistella, *The Stripper and the Congressman,* (New York, 1975).

Mildred B. Cooper Memorial Chapel, Bella Vista, Arkansas. (Tod Swiecichowski, 1993) *Mildred B. Cooper was the wife of John A. Cooper, Sr., founder of Cooper Communities, Inc. This nondenominational chapel was dedicated on April 2, 1988, and was designed by the award winning architects E. Fay Jones and Maurice Jennings, Fayetteville, Arkansas.*

Chapter XVIII

Developing an Arkansas Culture

INTRODUCTION

Arkansans have worried about their national image, but the literature, music and art emanating from and about the state have been rich. These cultural expressions sometimes have played a pivotal role in defining the state, occasionally in harmony with political, social and economic developments, but more often at war with dominant trends in commenting, moralizing, satirizing and beautifying the state.

Arkansas's first book, *Laws of the Territory of Arkansas,* was published at Arkansas Post in 1821 by William E. Woodruff, but shortly after its publication Woodruff followed the territorial government and moved the *Arkansas Gazette* to Little Rock. Fittingly, this book, a compilation of the laws carried over from Missouri and those enacted by the territorial legislature in 1819 and 1820, caused a controversy when Crittenden, believing Woodruff had charged too much for the work, refused full payment.

ARKANSAS LITERATURE

The Spanish and French Period

Arkansas literature began with the fragmentary accounts left by the De Soto expedition, none of which possessed significant literary qualities. The early French accounts were similarly sparse. It was not until the late eighteenth century, when Captain Jean Bernard Bossu recorded his visits to the region, that the first largely Arkansas focused work appeared. Only a portion of his book dealt with the Quapaw, but that section lacked nothing in color. He recorded the words of Indian poet Rutel-Attekatoubemingo, who fell in love with Mlle. Manon Robert, a French lass of fourteen, whom he berated in twenty-eight verses for concealing her bosom from view. The lady's response was not recorded. Most of Bossu's narrative glorified his own exploits among Arkansas's "noble savages."

Three Early Travelers

In the absence of a native population capable of writing, the first accounts about Arkansas came from travelers. Many Americans and Europeans had a strong interest in the West, and travel books were a staple of publishers. Because emigrants looked to literature for clues about where to seek economic advancement, early accounts helped shape the development of the area. The Mississippi River was a major artery of travel, so it was not surprising that Arkansas received casual mention in dozens of accounts, with Mark Twain's *Life on the Mississippi* (1874) being the most famous. Twain noted that Helena

"occupies one of the prettiest situations on the Mississippi." Twain was less complimentary by 1884 when *Huckleberry Finn* was published for by that time Arkansas had become a literary metaphor for backwoods and violence.

Some daring and curious men began to forsake the broad Mississippi River to enter the turbulent currents of the Arkansas River by the early nineteenth century. Arkansas literature began in earnest with their arrival. Thomas Nuttall was the most comprehensive and fair of the early visitors. Born in England in 1786, Nuttall came to America at age twenty-three to study natural history. His travels took him all over the land, where he was credited with discovering and describing more plants than any other pioneer botanist except Asa Gray. The author of several volumes on American birds, Nuttall also taught six years at Harvard College.

Nuttall reached Arkansas by boat in 1819. After floating down the Mississippi he took the White River cutoff to the Arkansas River and continued to Arkansas Post. His book's title, *A Journal of Travels into the Arkansa Territory, During the Year 1819, With Occasional Observations on the Manner of the Aborigines* (1821), made it unclear whether the aborigines were the Quapaw Indians living around the Post or the white residents. Nor could one tell from his text:

> It is to be regretted that the widely scattered state of the population of this territory is but too favorable to the spread of ignorance and barbarism. The means of education are, at present, nearly proscribed, and the rising generation are growing up in mental darkness, like the French hunters who have preceded them, and who have almost forgot that they appertain to the civilized world.

Nuttall ascended the Arkansas River, passed the various pine bluffs, the big and little rocks, and stopped at Cadron (near present-day Conway), where he talked with the investors in this "speculation" town. Continuing up the River to Belle Point, he met with the Cherokee and Osage Indians, made a side trip south to the Red River, visited the hot springs and returned to Cadron, which had grown to four families. Nuttall was not impressed:

> A considerable concourse of travellers and some emigrants began to make their appearance at this imaginary town. The only tavern, very ill provided, was consequently crowded with all sorts of company. It contained only two tentable rooms, built of logs, with hundreds of crevices still left open, notwithstanding the severity of the season. Every reasonable and rational amusement appeared here to be swallowed up in dram-drinking, jockeying, and gambling; even our landlord, in defiance of the law, was often the ringleader of what was his duty to suppress.

Moving back down the Arkansas River in time to see Governor Miller's "I'll Try, Sir," keelboat, Nuttall witnessed the deliberations of the Superior Court in its first criminal case: the appeal from Thomas Dickinson's sentence of castration for the rape of his infant stepdaughter. Finally, Nuttall proceeded downstream to the Mississippi, ending his account with descriptions of life on the lower Mississippi. Nuttall typified the views of educated Americans, who preferred progress and civilization over the freer mode of living then in vogue in the territory. His prejudices became the standard for his successors.

Henry Rowe Schoolcraft was in Arkansas at almost the same time as Nuttall and produced two popular volumes about his trip. Born in New York in 1793, Schoolcraft combined a college education with a desire for western adventure that led him to head southwest

from St. Louis through the lead mining region into Arkansas. Two books, *A View of the Lead Mines* (1819) and *Journal of a Tour in the Interior of Missouri and Arkansas* (1821), emerged from his prolific pen, and they were followed by a series of works on Indian languages, his hunt for the origins of the Mississippi, and a number of poetic pieces.

Nuttall had seen a cross-section of Arkansas society, but Schoolcraft's activities were confined to the White River Valley area. He generally admired the scenery and was appalled by the people, writing that:

> Nothing could be more remote from the ideas we have attached to domestic comfort, neatness, or conveniency, without allusion to cleanliness, order, and the concomitant train of household attributes which make up the sum of human felicity in refined society.

Of the hunters living at Sugar Loaf Prairie, Schoolcraft noted that, "In manners, morals, customs, dress, contempt of labor and hospitality, the state of society is not essentially different from that which exists among the savages."

Like the abstemious Nuttall, Schoolcraft was appalled by what passed for a party: a cabin full of people drinking, dancing and singing all night.

The third great traveler to Arkansas was George William Featherstonhaugh (pronounced Fanshaw). This English-born geologist made an inspection for the federal government in 1834-1835, and the results were published scientifically by the government and in narrative form by the author under the title *Excursion Through the Slave States* (1844). The territorial period was in full glory and political violence had become almost a way of life by the time Featherstonhaugh arrived in Arkansas. This translator of Cicero refused to concede to the rough and tumble of Arkansas. Nuttall had moved by canoe and dugout and Schoolcraft by foot and horse, but Featherstonhaugh and his son tried to proceed by horse and carriage down the military road from southeastern Missouri to Little Rock and the Red River.

Featherstonhaugh expected the worst from the beginning. One resident along the route explained that many desperate men had settled there to rob and murder unsuspecting travelers. Towns were not any safer. Helena, he was assured, was where "negur runners, counterfeiters, horsestealers, murderers and sick like, took shelter agin the law." Featherstonhaugh and his son fortified themselves in their room each night, momentarily expecting attack. He investigated a reported murder one day, found a body, and supervised the burial. After other difficulties that included following advice on an alleged shortcut, they arrived in Little Rock at last.

He found that the capital was home to many "sportsmen," which he explained as "a designation by which all the bloods who live by faro and rouge et noir are known in Arkansas." The territory was home to:

[G]entlemen, who had taken the liberty
to imitate the signatures of other
persons; bankrupts, who were not
disposed to be plundered by their
creditors; homicides, horse-stealers, and
gamblers. . . .

The tone was set by the young bucks "who, never having had the advantages of good examples for imitation, had set up a standard of manners consisting of everything that was extravagantly and outrageously bad." One resident assured him that everyone was armed, and Featherstonhaugh described in detail the famous Bowie knife, named "from a conspicuous person of the fiery climate." He found William E. Woodruff one of the "most indefatigably industrious men of the territory," and Governor Pope, although out in the woods with a sow when he called, was "an

unaffected, worthy person," a judgment not shared by other contemporaries.

Leaving Little Rock, Featherstonhaugh stopped at a "sort of tavern" on the Saline River kept by "a sort of she Caliban" whose five forks were named Stump Handle, Crooky Prongs, Horny, Big Pewter and Little Pickey. He met Chester Ashley and a party of lawyers there who recounted tales of the legal circuit. After visiting Hot Springs, he went to Red River country in southwestern Arkansas. He was shocked at Jacob Barkman's by the contrast between the fine brick house and Mrs. Barkman, commonly called "she Bar." This daughter of a local hunter "chewed tobacco, she smoked a pipe, she drank whiskey, and cursed and swore as heartily as any backwoodsman, all at the same time." After returning to Little Rock, he departed southeast on the Arkansas River by steamboat and stopped at some of the plantations along the waterway. He especially was impressed with New Gascony, where he conversed in French with Mrs. Antoine Barraque, who had "French manners" although she was of Quapaw ancestry. Major Barraque accompanied the party to the Post, and Featherstonhaugh found him "a very intelligent and agreeable fellow-passenger." Featherstonhaugh's pleasant trip ended abruptly at the Post when the boat was boarded by a gang he described as vicious swindlers, all drunk and breathing foul oaths. Chief among them, he reported, was the United States Marshal for Arkansas, Elias Rector, "a man of mean stature, low and sottish in his manners, and as corrupt and reckless as it was possible for a human to be." The boat entered the Mississippi after passing Montgomery's Point — a "notorious place" — and left Arkansas via Chicot Point.

Featherstonhaugh developed the theory that Arkansas was corrupted by "the manners of the Gulf of Mexico," and that western lands were refuges for outlaws. Both problems would in time be resolved in favor of civilization through immigration, but in the meantime, "a great deal must be tolerated by the magistrates, for the truth is, they are only tolerated themselves upon that condition."

Washington Irving crossed the state while returning from a western tour, but his Arkansas experiences were unrecorded except for a short sketch of Arkansas Post entitled "The Creole Village." Few Americans shared Irving's interest in the old and traditional, and most came to believe that Arkansas was as described by Nuttall, Schoolcraft, and Featherstonhaugh. Just before the Civil War, the Powhatan *Advertiser* complained that the very name of Arkansas "conjures up to the benighted, misinformed stranger, the bloody bowie knife, assassins, cut throats and highway robbers." Junius Henri Browne observed in 1862 that, "The semi-barbarous condition of Arkansas has become proverbial." So it remained.

The Big Bear School

The Victorian middle-class prudery exemplified by Featherstonhaugh found its polar opposite in the Southwest humorists, a variegated group of rough-hewn frontier aristocrats rooted in the tradition of eighteenth-century novelists Smollett, Fielding and Sterne. Their writings emanated from "sporting" circles and frequently appeared in *Porter's Spirit of the Times*, a New York publication with a national audience. It was from this tradition that Arkansas was immortalized by Thomas Bangs Thorpe's "The Big Bear of Arkansas," satirized by Dr. Marcus Lafayette Byrn, and from which it produced its first native products in the writings of Charles Fenton Mercer Noland and Albert Pike.

Thomas Bangs Thorpe was born in Massachusetts in 1815 and settled in Louisiana in 1836. A prolific writer and also a painter, Thorpe used Arkansas as a literary backdrop, notably in his 1841 story, "The Big Bear of Arkansas." In this multi-level symbolic story, an old hunter regales a captive audience on a

steamboat with stories full of western exaggeration, beginning with the shooting of a forty-pound wild turkey: "On striking the ground he bust open behind, and the way the pound gobs of tallow rolled out of the opening was perfectly beautiful." But the hunter's centerpiece was the quest for the great eight-foot bear that he tracked unsuccessfully through all kinds of terrain. As preparations were being made for the last hunt, the mighty bruin came out of the woods and allowed himself to be shot. The old hunter could not rightly grasp the death's meaning, and concluded that, "My private opinion is, that that bar was an unhuntable bar, and died when his time come." Modern critics see a parable of the passing of the frontier in this story as well as similarities to William Faulkner's *The Bear.*

So popular did this tale become that William T. Porter, the editor of the *Spirit of the Times*, issued a collection of stories in 1843 named after Thorpe's piece, thus giving birth to the "Big Bear" school of humor. One corollary might be called the "Big Needle" school, because Marcus Lafayette Byrn used an Arkansas setting for the first of his many books, *The Life and Adventures of an Arkansaw Doctor* (1853). This book used much dialect, some medicine, and a heavy dose of swamp humor, notably in the case of one patient, dosed with ipecac who vomited twenty-two ears of green corn.

Thorpe actually lived in Louisiana and Byrn was a resident only briefly, but this type of writing soon was given ample representation through the works of Charles Fenton Mercer Noland and Albert Pike. Noland, a Virginia-born dropout from West Point, came to Batesville, where his father was the land office receiver. He studied law there with James Woodson Bates, entered politics as a Whig and began writing.

His major contribution to the *Spirit of the Times* was the creation of a frontier alter-ego, Pete Whetstone of Devil's Fork. Noland's use of backwoods vernacular was so successful

The Big Bear of Arkansaw *(Frank Ver Beck, 1898) This drawing was used to illustrate an Arkansas bear story by Albert Bigelow Paine. The fiddle the bear is playing is a reference to the Arkansas Traveler.* **Suzanne Kittrell Collection**

HORATIO DREW HIS BOW ACROSS THE STRINGS

that his readers were convinced that Whetstone was a real person. Census records do show a man with that name who left Arkansas for Texas after some years, but Noland's Pete was a literary device for expressing the author's opinions. Unlike Nuttall, Schoolcraft and Featherstonhaugh, Noland saw gambling, horse racing and hunting as the spice of life, properly topped by a good fight, frolic or drunk. Echoes of the eighteenth century's lustier ethos, as well as an oblique attack on Alfred W. Arrington, run throughout the stories:

Old aunt Peggy Simes told me t'other day, with a sorter smile, that the rattlesnake gals had out-fattened anything she ever saw; say she, what else could be expected when they make a circuit rider such a handsome young fellow. Let me tell one thing, "Pete," says she, "I am now seven and seventy years of age. I have been used to camp meetings all my life, and I never knew it to fail, that nine months after them, there was three times as many babies born as any other time of the year."

By electing Pete to the state legislature, Noland was able to use the familiar technique of taking the rustic to the city. Pete encountered his first "pe-anny," which he called a box full of horse teeth, and attended the theater and fancy dress balls, expressing Noland's strong Whig sentiments throughout.

The Whetstone stories are touched with good humor, but the author suffered greatly from tuberculosis, which eventually killed him. His best work was done during Arkansas's Flush Times, 1832-1840. Some critics have found him inferior to Thorpe and other Southwest humorists. Noland, living in Little Rock by the early 1850s, contributed reminiscences of early pioneers to the *Arkansas Gazette*. Arkansas had changed so much by then that he was seen as "the impersonation of a gone time, the impress of an age passed away, [the] living, moving, speaking record, and one that never gets musty at any age."

Albert Pike also was represented in Porter's *Big Bear* collection, but his writing career began before he came to Arkansas. The poetic "Hymns to the Gods," published in the highly esteemed *Blackwood's Magazine* in 1839, was written before his arrival and attracted favorable critical notice at a time when American poets were not regarded highly abroad. Pike's most celebrated lyrics in Arkansas were set to a common drinking song and they celebrated Elias Rector, that "fine Arkansas gentleman, Close to the Choctaw line," who "gets drunk once a week on whiskey and immediately sobers himself up completely on the very best of wine." Pike also wrote travel accounts and satires for the *Spirit of the Times*. Pike's erroneously reported death in 1858 led to a privately published volume of humorous verse entitled, *Life Wake of the Fine Arkansas Gentleman Who Died Before His Time*. His poetry had become sentimental verse heavily laced with morbidity by the 1860s, and he was most remembered in Arkansas for "Every Year:"

Life is a count of losses Every Year; For the weak are heavier crosses, Every Year Lost springs with sobs replying Unto weary Autumn's sighing, While those we love are dying, Every Year.

As with all Arkansas writers, Pike wrote only in his spare time. He edited the *Arkansas Advocate*, served in the Mexican War and Civil War, taught school and practiced law in one of the most versatile careers in history. He had built up a large law practice specializing in Indian claims by 1860 and erected Little Rock's most impressive surviving Greek Revival house. The Civil War destroyed his business, and Pike relocated in Washington, D.C., where he practiced law and became increasingly active in Masonry, culminating in 1872 with publication of the *Morals and Dogma of the Ancient and Accepted Scottish Rite of Freemasonry*.

Pike was the most celebrated of the state's early poets, but he was not the first. That honor went to Hewes Scull, the sheriff of Arkansas County from 1819 to 1823 and county clerk from 1830 to 1833. Scull was a native of Philadelphia who had come to Arkansas before the Louisiana Purchase. His two surviving poems, tributes to Christmas and Lafayette, have no Arkansas allusions. Little Rock was home to the short-lived Thomas J. Worthen, who was born about 1830 and died at age twenty-five. His "The Old Canoe" was reprinted widely in the nineteenth century. Finally, George P. Smoote, a lawyer and member of the secession convention, published *Song of the Mississippi* before his death in 1891.

Alfred W. Arrington's Desperadoes

In contrast to the writings of Noland and Pike, Alfred W. Arrington gave credence to the Featherstonhaugh view that Arkansas was a bloody land. Arrington began his curious career as a Methodist minister in North Carolina, renounced his faith, found it again in

Arkansas and lost it again. He settled in Fayetteville to practice law, and turned to literature after the Cane Hill lynchings of 1839. *The Desperadoes of the South-West* (1847) hardly cast Arkansas in a favorable light, and pursued by charges of adultery, Arrington moved to Texas and later Illinois.

His first novel was based on the romantic fiction of James Fenimore Cooper and William Gilmore Simms. Instead of measuring up to his mentors, however, Arrington became the precursor for the dime novels issued by yellow presses later in the century. A second work, *The Mathematical Harmonies of the Universe; The Rangers and Regulators of Tanaha* (1856), drew on his Washington County experiences, but otherwise it has been called "a typical romantic novel of the period."

The German Friedrich Gerstäcker followed Arrington in writing bloody fiction about Arkansas. Born of opera singers in 1816, young Gerstäcker was affected by a wanderlust that brought him to America. After touring, hunting, and living by his wits, he produced what in translation was called *Wild Sports in the Far West* in 1854.

Gerstäcker's perspective was based on rubbing shoulders with the common folk. Although a criminal element existed in Arkansas, he wrote: "I . . . have met with as honest and upright people as are to be found in any other part of the Union." In his novels, written in German and largely untranslated, Gerstäcker followed Arrington's lead and populated the frontier with dastardly villains. He returned for a visit after the Civil War but found his friends dead and the hunting sadly depleted.

Tall Tales

The writings of Gerstäcker were the most realistic and the least prejudiced of any outside observers. They stand in sharp contrast to the "tall tale" type of literature, the earliest example of which supposedly came from the pen of Colonel David Crockett that was published after his death in 1836 at the Alamo. Although of doubtful authenticity, the Crockett book used Arkansas as a backdrop for his feat of putting two bullets in the same spot on a target. Crockett had passed through the state, stopping at Little Rock for a banquet and a puppet show before moving on to Texas and destiny. He was not forgotten; folklorist Vance Randolph collected ten stories in which Crockett emerged as the mythical Great Hunter.

A second tall tale was a mythical boasting speech entitled, "Change the Name of Arkansas? Hell No!" Arising from the nineteenth century's confusion over the state's proper pronunciation, the speech circulated in a variety of mostly unpublished versions, each more ribald than the other, but all concluding, "but change the name of Arkansas? Hell, no!" So strongly was the tall tale tradition rooted in popular culture that folklorist Vance Randolph produced an entire collection *We Always Lie to Strangers* (1951).

The Arkansas Traveler

In between the conscious literary creations and the authorless folk tales stood the state's most enduring (and not too endearing) multimedia masterpiece, *The Arkansas Traveler*, consisting of a story, a tune and pictures. The story begins when a lost lawyer approaches a squatter's cabin sometime around 1836:

Traveler: Halloo, stranger.
Squatter: Hello yourself.
T: Can I get to stay all night with you?
S: No, sir, you can't git to.
T: Have you any spirits here?
S: Lots uv'em; Sal seen one last night by that ar ole hollar gum, and it nearly skeered her to death.
T: You mistake my meaning; have you any liquor?
S: Had some yesterday, but Ole Bose he

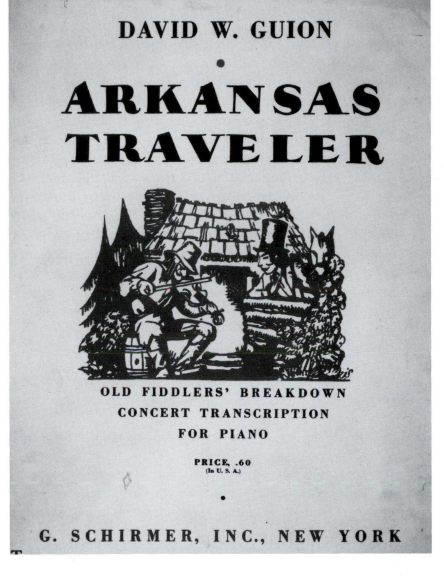

DAVID W. GUION

•

ARKANSAS TRAVELER

OLD FIDDLERS' BREAKDOWN
CONCERT TRANSCRIPTION
FOR PIANO

PRICE, .60
(In U. S. A.)

•

G. SCHIRMER, INC., NEW YORK

Arkansas Traveler *(artist unknown, 1929) The music, picture and story have endured, giving Arkansas its best known national symbol. David W. Guion, who recalled hearing the tune at cowboy dances and old fiddler contests, composed a number of popular Southern and Western songs.* **Author's Collection**

got in and lapped all uv it out'n the pot.

T: You don't understand; I don't mean pot liquor. I'm wet and cold and want some whiskey. Have you got any?

S: Oh, yes — I drunk the last this mornin.

The squatter fiddles an incomplete tune during this jagged dialogue. The exasperated traveler at last takes up the fiddle and finishes the tune to the squatter's amazement, and all is changed in a flash:

S: Stranger, tuck a half a duzen cheers and sot down. Sal, stir yourself round like a six-horse team in a mud hole. Go round in the hollar whar I killed that buck this mornin', and cut off some of the best pieces, and fotch it and cook it for me and this gentleman, d'rectly. Raise up the board under the head of the bed, and get the old black jug I hid from Dick, and git us some whiskey; I know thar's some left yit. Til, drive ole Bose out'n the bread-tray, then climb up in the loft, and git the rag that's got the sugar tied in it. Dick, carry the gentleman's hoss round under the shed, give him some fodder and corn; much as he kin eat.

Arkansas enthusiasts claim that the story began with the actual experiences of Colonel Sanford C. Faulkner, a Kentuckian who settled in Chicot County about 1831, served as head of the Columbia branch of the ill-fated Real Estate Bank, and experienced such events on Illinois Bayou or Bayou Macon in the company of A. H. Sevier, Archibald Yell, Chester Ashley, and William S. Fulton. Faulkner claimed he completed the tune and first told the story at the Anthony House in Little Rock.

At least twelve other versions exist, however. In Faulkner's version, the squatter is suspicious of strangers, short on words and sturdily independent. In other versions, the squatter is a low-class comic character who displays ignorance and poverty instead of self-sufficiency and independence. The tune was probably older than the story, and the pictures, drawn by Edward Payson Washburn just before his death in 1860, became the basis for popular Currier and Ives prints.

For many outsiders, the story, picture and music reflected actual living conditions in Arkansas even in the twentieth century. Disregarding the obvious point that the Traveler and the Squatter share a common tune and that their differences were resolved, Northerners came to regard all Arkansans as squatters. Thus, elitist Arkansans have tried to suppress the story, while the disaffected have gloried in it. One Northern immigrant, who left Arkansas in disgust in 1985 after nineteen "hellish months," could think of no worse thing to say than that the Arkansas Traveler "is still your image."

Patriotic Gore

The Civil War prompted one of the most extensive creative writing endeavors in modern history, one that involved all classes. That nineteenth century art form, the letter, flourished as both privates and generals wrote extensively. Those who took their "pen in hand" included one Van Buren County lad, Val Stark, whose Tennessee girlfriend prompted him to write that, "the rose is red/the stem is green/the time is parted that we hav [sic] seen. . . ." Another poet was Arkansas's premier war child, General Patrick Cleburne.

Those who could not write might sing, and new words were made up to old tunes in the camps. Several versions of "The Battle of Pea Ridge" circulated, and the text had become corrupted hopelessly by the time Vance Randolph wrote it down in the 1930s. Songs about bushwhackers were popular, and much heavy-handed humor was present in the popular Trans-Mississippi song, "The Brass-Mounted Army:"

Oh whiskey is monster
    that ruins great an' small
But in old Kerby's army
    Headquarters gets it all.
Oh how do you like the army?
    The brass-mounted army,
The high-fallutin' army,
    where eagle buttons rule?

The standard Civil War songs were popular. Soldiers passing through Clarksville early in the War were serenaded by girls singing "Dixie" "in its purity." Because "Dixie" was a minstrel tune, the words were neither pure nor patriotic. Albert Pike sought to improve the text. His version, stilted and romantic, cast the Southerners as "Southrons," and it might have become the national anthem if the South had won.

Arkansas Gazette editor C. C. Danley observed early in the War that history was in the making and urged participants to save the records of the struggle. Even as the Confederate cause sagged, U. M. Rose was sent to Richmond to copy records of Arkansas's participation. These were lost, but the first history appeared as early as 1864. Chaplain Washington L. Gammage published *The Camp, the Bivouac, and the Battlefield: Being the History of the Fourth Arkansas Regiment* in Selma,

Alabama. The Union side had better access to paper and a poignant and powerful story to tell. New Yorker A. W. Bishop put the Union version in print in 1863 under the title, *Loyalty on the Frontier, or Sketches of Union Men of the South-West*. William Baxter, who was the head of Arkansas College before the War, followed the next year with his more insightful, *Pea Ridge and Prairie Grove* (1864). After the Union occupation of Little Rock, J. William Demby spilled much of the political dirt in *The War in Arkansas* (1864).

A few Arkansas publications came after the War. Dr. Charles E. Nash offered biographical sketches in 1898 of Pat Cleburne and Thomas C. Hindman. William E. Woodruff, Jr., in *With the Light Guns in '61-65* (1903) reminisced about his days with the artillery. Privates Joe M. Scott (*Four Years' Service in the Southern Army*, 1897), Leander Stillwell (*The Story of a Common Soldier of Army Life in the Civil War*, 1920) and Thomas J. Estes, (*Early Days and War Times in Northern Arkansas*, 1928) had their say. The state chapters of the United Daughters of the Confederacy collected *Confederate Women of Arkansas* (1907). Studies of battles, leaders and commands began to appear about the time of the Civil War Centennial, and a number of diaries and collections of letters were published.

The Civil War also inspired poets. Deafmute John W. "Dummy" Woodward had his chess-by-mail game with David Walker interrupted and wrote a poem about the experience. The execution of David O. Dodd inspired numerous poets after the War. Fannie Borland Moores, the daughter of Senator Borland, was first, and Fred Allsopp followed with "David O. Dodd, The Nathan Hale of Arkansas."

Arkansas produced not a single significant example of plantation romanticism. However, old "mountain boomer" William Monks, in *History of Southern Missouri and Northern Arkansas* (1907), did recall an idealized agrarian world, unbuffeted by the whirlwinds of commodity prices, where the Arkansas Adam and Eve lived with simplicity and integrity. Monks perceived that the Northern victory involved more than just slavery and states' rights; industrial America was on the march and the nation's farmers and herdsmen were doomed.

The Civil War ended the days of gentlemen dilettantes. The last of the breed was William M. "Cush" Quesenbury. Born in Arkansas in 1822 and educated at St. Joseph's College at Bardstown, Kentucky, Quesenbury served in the Mexican War and made a trip to California before returning to Fayetteville, where he made the *Southwest Independent* the most quoted newspaper of its day. Quesenbury reflected in a droll and satiric way on the progress and problems of Arkansas and continued to write a column for the *Arkansas Gazette* after his paper suspended operation. He produced his memorable woodcuts in 1860 on the gubernatorial election. After service in the Confederate army and a stint editing a paper in Navasota, Texas, Quesenbury returned to Arkansas to teach at Cane Hill College. The obscurity of his last years was broken in 1878 when he read "Arkansas: A Pome" to the Arkansas Press Association. Subsequently printed, the poem was called: "[A] rhythmic satire on many of the follies and vices of the times peculiarly applicable to Arkansas life, together with a strange, weird medley of poetic thoughts, odd fancies and eccentric conceits." It ended with what has become the immortal line of all Arkansas-inspired poetry: "God loves not him that loves not Arkansas."

The New Arkansas Traveler

In Quesenbury's obituary, M. E. Benton, father of painter Thomas Hart Benton, called him typical of a class of good, true men who lived in the '40s and '50s in Tennessee, Kentucky, Arkansas and Missouri "with no care for the morrow, no desire to acquire wealth, bubbling up with great good humor, faithful to friends."

Typical of the dominant men in Arkansas, first in Reconstruction and then in the Gilded Age, were businessmen striving to acquire great wealth and eager to promote Arkansas. The *New Arkansas Traveler*, an 1876 recounting of a railroad junket for Northerners, sought to convince Americans that Arkansas was no longer the land of the squatter. Sandford Faulkner and his story had become an embarrassment, and ruined by the War, he eventually sold his prized violin. "The fiddling drinking squatter has sold out and moved to Indian Territory," one promotional tract proclaimed. But the old "Arkansas Traveler" refused to die. Inquisitive Yankees always could find someone able to play the tune, and a popular late nineteenth century potboiler melodrama, "Kit, the Arkansas Traveler," kept the name alive.

Opie Read

The writings of Opie Read were another reason the Arkansas Traveler failed to die and even took on a new lease on life. An impoverished child of the war years, Read came to Arkansas as an itinerant newspaperman, once running a newspaper out of a parked boxcar. He worked for a time on the *Arkansas Gazette*. He founded his own comic paper, *The Arkansas Traveler*, in 1882, and it soon became a forum for exposing "the boorishness of the backcountry for the edification of the city bred." Such a work was not popular in Gilded Age Arkansas, and Read moved the paper to Chicago, where it continued for several years.

Read also became a prolific writer of genteel romantic novels, of which three were set in Arkansas: *Len Gansett* (1889), *Emmet Bonlore* (1891) and *An Arkansas Planter* (1896). The first two glorified country editors, and the third addressed current controversies with a cast that included a planter who combined business acumen with antebellum hospitality, a friend given to the latter with none of the

former, a daughter determined to be a feminist and a bad white man who deluded hapless blacks who failed to recognize their best friends. Read also wrote in black dialect and the story, "An Arkansas Hanging," was told entirely from a black's point of view. Read never embraced the strident racism of the new twentieth century. As one of his black characters says:

> You counts de votes o' de white trash,
> but you doan' count mine, An now, ergin,
> Mr. Martin, let me ax you, is dat right?

As Read's rejection of strident modernism became more pronounced, his credo became, "to a thoughtful mind there is more of interest in decay than in progress." Denying that he had ever criticized Arkansas, he elaborated on his philosophy in a 1910 article:

> I would rather look out upon her rivers,
> Spring, Current and Eleven Point, the
> most beautiful streams I believe that flow
> in America; I would rather see the black
> bass strike at a ray of the rising sun,
> rather hear the dew-crested quail whirl
> over the gem-sprinkled meadowland;
> rather lie down beneath the wild crab tree
> in bloom, and listen to the mimic roar of
> the hummingbird — far rather than be
> jerked skyward in an elevator and
> commanded to look out from a tower upon
> the trade marvels that unpoetic "progress"
> has wrought. In Arkansas the Captains of
> Industry are remarkable men, tracking
> down flowers in waste places, erecting
> smokestacks; but I love the humorous old-
> timer, unconscious poet, lover of the
> woods, the friend of all men.

Such a philosophy found a ready acceptance at the turn of the century as Americans looked back nostalgically on their rural pasts. But the twentieth century's march to modernism by-passed Read, leaving him unread.

Octave Thanet

The obscurity that befell Read also over-whelmed his contemporary, Alice French. Born in New England and reared in the Midwest, she wrote under the pen name of Octave Thanet and wintered at Clover Bend in Lawrence County. The author of a large number of short stories, she used Arkansas material extensively. Most were of contemporary rural life along the Black River, but she also wrote "Trusty No. 49" about the convict-lease system in Arkansas. Of all Arkansas writers in the nineteenth century, she gave the best descriptions of scenery, studied the dialect in detail and made a determined effort to understand the minds of blacks, sharecroppers, women and farmers. A vigorous supporter of modernization, sanitation, cleanliness and other Northern causes, her attempts to romanticize a moonlight and magnolia past were few and ineffective. She ended her Arkansas career with the novel *By Inheritance* (1910), which advocated manual training for blacks and their strict obedience to the superior class of whites who were their best friends.

Victorian Prose and Poetry

In contrast to the self-proclaimed realism of French, a number of novelists opted for the romantic. John Breckinridge Ellis was the author of three such novels: *Arkansaw Cousins: A Story of the Ozarks* (1908), *Fran* (1912), and *The Little Fiddler of the Ozarks* (1913). Writing from Washington, Arkansas, Ruth McEnery Stuart created a fictional *Simpkinsville* populated with simple and kind-hearted folks. The most successful glorifier of the rustics was Harold Bell Wright, who wrote *Shepherd of the Hills* (1907), which inspired an outdoor drama near Branson, Missouri, and *The Calling of Dan Matthews* (1909). Both reflected understanding and sympathy for the declining ancient hill culture.

The same combination of the romantic and rustic dominated poetry. Arkansas possessed a small cult of women poets by the early twentieth century: Mrs. John T. Sifford, Zula Camille Vaughan and Mrs. Melcenia A. Caton. Most of their efforts glorified the Lost Cause, as did the work of Fay Hempstead, poet laureate of Masonry and a historian. Charles T. Davis was elected poet laureate by the state legislature and is remembered best for his widely printed tribute to a dead horse that "Goes racing on and upward, flecked with foam,/Bearing a Valkyrie and a hero home." Clio Harper, a Little Rock newspaperman, was the author of much light verse, and M. E. Dunaway offered a complete rustic philosophy in dialect. The Arkansas Authors and Composers Society was formed early in the century. Its president in 1919, Josee F. Cappleman, was thoroughly traditional in "The Old Darkey:"

> Aye, the Uncles and the Aunties, they
> are going fast,
> They're going With the by-gones soon to
> be, from the ole-time cabin door;
> And no more of "marse" and "missus"
> will there come to you and me.
> For the places now that know them will
> know them soon no more.

Slow Trains and Razorbacks

As middle-class Arkansans were laboring to bring the state into the mainstream, the national public was responding to a wave of joke books featuring Arkansas. Mark Twain had used the Arkansas metaphor in *Huckleberry Finn* (1885) and other writings, and newspapers printed jokes about the Memphis and Little Rock Railroad as early as 1870. Arkansas came to be seen as the home of the failure of technology, typified when Thomas W. Jackson published *On A Slow Train Through Arkansas: Funny Railroad Stories — All the Latest and Best Minstrel Jokes of the Day* in 1903. Little of the material actually related to Arkansas, but it inspired a host of imitators who were closer to the mark. One was Marion Hughes, whose *Three Years in Arkansas* (1904) carried a pictograph title showing three ears of corn, a can and a saw. Hughes, who also wrote *Why I am a Socialist* told of life in Hatton Gap at the time of the coming of the railroad. In addition to introducing the razorback hog into Arkansas heraldry, Hughes illustrated all of the different kinds of hogs, discoursing at length on their metaphysical properties and added a discourse on the seamier side of Hot Springs. Other humorists included George D. Beason, *I Blew in from Arkansas* (1908); Andrew Guy Chilton, *Through Arkansas on the Hog* (1908); Charles S. Hibler, *Down in Arkansas* (1902); George D. Biscoe, *Angel of Commerce; or Thirty Days with the Drummers of Arkansas* (1891); Taylor Beard, *The Arkansas Cracker Jack* (1905) and several volumes by Press Woodruff, "the Arkansaw humorist."

Arkansas boosters deplored this literature and counterattacked. *Three Years in Arkansas* prompted Mrs. Mary Hughes (no relation to Marion Hughes) to write *An Answer to Three Years in Arkansas* (1907), although she asserted "there is little honor in slaying a skunk."

The most determined defender of the state was Bernie Babcock. A widow with five children who started earning her living in 1898, she tried to return the humor in *The Man Who Lied on Arkansas and What It Got Him* (1909). Babcock was a prolific writer and carried a national reputation for her romantic tale, *The Soul of Ann Rutledge* (1919), about a supposed love of Abraham Lincoln. She edited the *Sketch Book*, a photographic, poetic, and prose magazine between 1906 and 1910 that avoided the controversial. The failure of the *Sketch Book* deterred others and limited cultural communication.

In 1931, Fred W. Allsopp published *The Folklore of Romantic Arkansas,* which provided a place for new myths designed to make

Arkansas look respectable. Allsopp continued the war against the joke books, commenting in 1931 that:

> Time has transformed a back-woods land
>   Into a busy, modern State.
> The Easy-going days are gone,
>   And sland'rous jests are out of date
> 'Bout Arkansas, Fair Arkansas.

However out of date, literature defending the state continued for another thirty years.

Modernism

World War I and its immediate aftermath brought radical changes to literature. The bourgeois values of the Victorian era were overturned, and the literature of the Jazz Age was marked by a strong sense of rebellion against conventionalities. Like china painting, the corpus of Victorian literature became outmoded.

Except for the short stories of Thyra Samter Winslow, Arkansas was almost devoid during the 1920s of any intellectual activity while Mississippi produced William Faulkner and North Carolina had Thomas Wolfe. T. S. Stribling, a popular Tennessee novelist, used the 1927 flood in Arkansas for the setting of *Backwater* (1930), featuring a conflict between a college-educated son and his bootlegger father. It was not a novel calculated to be embraced by Arkansas patriots.

John Gould Fletcher

The first modern figure in twentieth century literature, John Gould Fletcher, falls into several classifications and can be called a modernist, orientalist, regionalist, agrarian and imagist. A native of Little Rock who grew up in the old Albert Pike home, Fletcher dropped out of Harvard and went to Europe, where his first poems written in the then avant-garde Imagist style attracted wide

John Gould Fletcher and Charlie May Simon *(photographer and date unknown)*
Central Arkansas Library System

attention, including that of a powerful patron, Amy Lowell.

He ended his expatriate days during the 1930s and joined the Southern Agrarians at Nashville, writing one chapter in the manifesto *I'll Take My Stand* (1930). Fletcher was Arkansas's first Pulitzer Prize winner for his *Selected Poems* in 1939. His work increasingly featured Arkansas themes after 1930.

Fletcher wrote an ode to the state for its Centennial celebration in 1936, and he became increasingly aware of the plight of the rural poor after his marriage to author Charlie May Simon. His early poems are difficult

for readers unfamiliar with oriental symbolism, myth and philosophy, but contain many beautiful images reminiscent of oriental painting. His autobiography, *Life is My Song*, (1937) is a vivid recollection of his varied past and is remarkable for its honesty.

Fletcher wrote a history of the state entitled *Arkansas* in 1947. He worked hard to engraft the folk and the cause of the small farmer into a state history that previously had been largely elitist. Alone among the state's writers, Fletcher was not embarrassed by the Arkansas Traveler or the folk culture it represented. His wife, a noted children's book author, turned to realism in the *The Share-Cropper* (1937) and described her life with Fletcher in *Johnswood* (1953).

The Ozark Revival

As John Gould Fletcher was undergoing a transformation from trans-Atlantic poet to regionalist, others were discovering spiritual and financial solace in the Ozarks. The leader of the movement was Vance Randolph, who collected stories, songs and speech patterns as a folklorist and sold anything as a writer to keep himself afloat financially. Randolph was remarkably clear-sighted about his subject matter, but many who followed him in what might be called the "Eureka Springs School" missed the manure and flies.

By 1940, Randolph counted fifty-two novels, 210 short stories, seventy-five histories, thirty-one dialect studies, fifty music books and pamphlets, thousands of poems and two motion picture scripts. He found most of this work to be "pretty bad," and wrote, "It is a strange thing that so few people have been able to write dispassionately of the Ozark hill folk." Randolph's financial success came posthumously with *Pissing in the Snow*, a collection of the type of Ozark folk tales not considered appropriate generally for polite society. Many of these tales have been told for so long in Arkansas that families relate them as true family stories.

Randolph had called his pioneering study *The Ozarks — An American Survival of Primitive Society* (1931). The prolific Otto Ernest Rayburn concluded a decade later in *Ozark Country* (1941) that the work of the soil conservation agents, the National Forestry Service, the Civilian Conservation Corps and other New Deal agencies had taken the mountain men "to the end of his primitive trail of freedom and necessity forced him into the regimented road." As Ozark rurality faded, Rayburn's *Ozark Guide* series at least gave outsiders clues about where to look. By 1975, when Nancy McDo-

nough brought forth *Garden Sass: A Catalog of Arkansas Folkways*, the emphasis was on "practical advice in keeping traditional ways alive." Ernie Deane in *Ozarks Country* (1975) was simply nostalgic. Surveying the decline of the region, Paul Faris in his important photographic essay, *Ozark Log Cabin Folks: The Way They Were* (1983), retraced his 1949 quest for cabin folk and found that most of the sites had been abandoned.

The glorification of this provincial culture probably began with Charles J. Finger in *Ozark Fantasia* (1926). His successors, especially in the Eureka Springs School, wrote primarily for middle-class audiences and remained in the now nationally discredited genteel tradition. One early exponent was Charles Morrow Wilson, whose first Ozark novel was *Acres of Sky* (1930) and who used the Ozarks in his subsequent works. Romantic historical novels remained acceptable locally, but anything smacking of realism produced a violent public outcry from Arkansans worried about the state's image. "Certain loud-mouthed village patriots" consistently hounded Vance Randolph.

Murray Sheehan was a Fayetteville professor whose *Half-Gods* (1927) so closely resembled townfolk that he found it expedient to leave the state. Mary Medearis managed to be both realistic and popular in *Big Doc's Girl* (1942). The apotheosis of the Ozarks came in 1975 with Donald Harington's *The Architecture of the Arkansas Ozarks*, which was ranked one of the top ten novels of the year by the American Library Association. It was a comic masterpiece that surveyed the sweeping cultural changes that had overtaken the area with surprising accuracy and correct architectural detail, and it benefited from the author's own drawings. He continued the Ozark saga in *The Cockroaches of Stay More* (1989), this time from an insect's perspective. *The Choiring of the Trees* (1991) featured an *Arkansas Gazette* reporter as the heroine and the Arkansas state prison for much of the setting.

These books, several other novels and *Let Us Build Us a City* (1986) made Harington the inheritor of the Southern Agrarian tradition of anti-modernization.

Public interest in the Ozarks finally sparked a few natives to venture into print. The quality of writing varied, as did the educational backgrounds of the authors. John Q. Wolf's *Life in the Leatherwoods* (1974) doubtless benefited from editing by his son, a university professor. Wayman Hogue's *Back Yonder, An Ozark Chronicle* (1931) was one of the best. Although reminiscences could be inaccurate historically, self-serving and parochial, some told a pointed tale. Claude E. Johnson offered much good social description free from romantic embellishments, selective memory or self-congratulation in the *The Humorous History of White County, Arkansas* (1975).

Arkansas Gothic

The writings of William Faulkner revolutionized Southern literature and provided models for studies of social change and psychological introspection. His first imitator in Arkansas was Francis Irby Gwaltney, who explored small-town violence in *Yeller-Headed Summer* (1954). Gwaltney looked at the integration crisis in *A Moment of Warmth* (1957) and *The Number of Our Days* (1959). Corrupt state politics inspired *A Step in the River* (1960), a novel that drew heavily on Arkansas gubernatorial elections. Gwaltney became an English professor at Arkansas Tech University at Russellville and was a close friend of Norman Mailer. Unlike Mailer, he turned sentimental in his last work, *Idols and Axle Grease* (1974), which was a series of character sketches of hometown life in Charleston, some only barely fictionalized.

The central theme in Arkansas gothic writing was that Arkansas was the home of bumpkins (more recently known as "good ole boys") and bigots. These forces in Gwaltney's novels were at war with the more respectable element, which sought modernization and civilization. The modernizers usually won, but only at some personal and financial expense. Less optimistic but perhaps the single greatest achievement in the genre was *The Burning Season* (1974), a novel written by B. C. Hall, another professor at Arkansas Tech University. Set in an eastern Arkansas college town, the plot played off a fascist campus regime, a psychotic small town sheriff and a generous portion of sexual activity. Hall spared Arkansas and turned to Texas in his second work, *Keeper of the Feast* (1980). Baseball and Southern gothic might appear an unlikely combination, but Donald Hays managed the union convincingly in *The Dixie Association* (1984), offering an ample supply of bigots, bumpkins and baseball.

Nostalgia and Rebellion

Recalling childhood could lead either to nostalgia or rebellion. Maya Angelou identified the universality of this theme:

All of childhood's unanswered questions must finally be passed back to the town and answered here. Heroes and bogey men, values and dislikes, are first encountered and labeled in that early environment. In later years they change faces, places and maybe races, tactics, intensities and goals, but beneath those penetrable masks they wear forever the stocking-capped faces of childhood.

This inability to escape, combined with a desire to defy Thomas Wolfe and go home again, defined a significant portion of Arkansas literature.

Not surprisingly, the revolt theme played extensively in the writings of Arkansas blacks. William Pickens was first in *Bursting Bonds* (1923), but its most able exponent was Maya Angelou, whose *I Know Why the Caged Bird Sings* (1969), constitutes one of the major autobiographical studies of the black experience. The community of Stamps that she recalled so vividly hardly reflected favorably on Arkansas, for "segregation was so complete that most Black children didn't really, absolutely know what whites looked like . . . I remember never believing that whites were really real." A rebel during the Civil Rights era, Angelou gained acceptance. *I Know Why the Caged Bird Sings* was filmed for television, and she was the *Ladies Home Journal* "Woman of the Year" in 1975. Her works included volumes of poetry and further memoirs. She recited her politically correct poem of racial, sexual and political inclusion, "On the Pulse of Morning," at the inauguration of President William Jefferson Clinton on January 20, 1993.

Eldridge Cleaver was another Arkansas native whose *Soul on Ice* (1968), although devoid of specific Arkansas references, was considered essential reading during the Civil Rights era.

The identity crisis that blacks experienced also affected other minority groups. The Jewish experience dominated in Bette Greene's award-winning novel, *Summer of My German Soldier* (1973). Being Italian from Arkansas inspired Ben Piazza in *The Exact and Very Strange Truth* (1964).

What Maya Angelou did for the black experience was attempted for Arkansas women by Shirley Abbott. *Womenfolks: Growing Up Down South* (1983) described the author's own Arkansas childhood set in the historical context of Southern womanhood. In her case, this included a heritage divided between a Northern born father and country-raised mother, and town life in Hot Springs was balanced by trips to visit rural relatives. Like Angelou, Abbott wrote from a national perspective, including discussions of themes such as the servant problem and "that old-time religion," that more provincial writers delicately avoided. In her estimation, many girls trained to be Southern belles wanted to catch a "good ole

boy" and then lead lives full of vapid routine. There was no place for highly educated women in the stifling local atmosphere. Abbott observed, "The supply of female intellectuals, however skimpy the number may be, has always exceeded the demand." For her, freedom lay in flight to New York.

Her liberation from Arkansas did not bring happiness, and Abbott explored the inner strength that came from following the time-honored rituals. She worried that the day would come when families would forget to decorate graves or remember "the middle names of a second cousin's five children." Tradition and community were important in defining womanhood; "that history weighs on us and refuses to be forgotten by us, and that the worst poverty women — or men — can suffer is to be bereft of their past." In 1991, Shirley Abbott published a memoir about growing up in Hot Springs, Arkansas, *The Bookmaker's Daughter*.

Arkansas men had their champions, too. Bob Lancaster, in *Southern Strategy* (1981), drew heavily on the Arkansas Gothic for a novel set in Sheridan. His main theme was that the "good ole boys" were not so bad after all. This thesis also dominated Bill Terry's *The Watermelon Kid* (1984), a novel about a rowdy crew working the eastern Arkansas honkytonks in the 1950s.

Of these writers, Bob Lancaster in his non-fiction *The Jungles of Arkansas: A Personal History of the Wonder State* (1989) puts nostalgia for Arkansas's past in its proper place, with powerful and realistic essays about notable events in Arkansas's past, including the DeSoto expedition, LaSalle's luck, the end of slavery from the black point of view and hookworm eradication. It provides detailed support for Lancaster's conclusions about Arkansas history elsewhere: "Our history kicks like a mule and often smells like one."

The Thomas Wolfe theme that you can't go home again inspired a number of authors. In *Arkansas Adios* (1971), Earl Mac Rauch described Delta poverty in detail and suggested flight. The opposite view — that you have to come home — figured in *The Annunciation* (1983) by Ellen Gilchrist, who settled in Fayetteville. The heroine of her story found Arkansas to be "where a person could live a real life," drawing strength from the mountains. That life in the faraway city could never be good until childhood problems were resolved was the major theme of *The Girl in White Coat on the Delta Eagle* (1979) by Gary Youree, a native of Arkansas City.

Russell Murphy's *Spent* (1981) revolved around a journey whose denouement took place in Arkansas. Probably no writer used the Wolfe theme better than Hamburg native Charles Portis. In *Norwood* (1966), strength comes from the quest for the payment of a debt; in *Dog of the South* (1979), it arose from the Southerner's proverbial love of his automobile. Portis achieved his greatest popularity with *True Grit* (1968), a novel about the Indian Territory told convincingly in the first-person memories of its heroine, Mattie Ross of Dardanelle, Yell County, Arkansas, a girl bent on avenging her father's murder. Subsequently made into a motion picture starring John Wayne, *True Grit* probably ranked as the most popular Arkansas novel of the twentieth century.

Two of the state's best-known writers made their careers elsewhere but returned home, both physically and spiritually. Librarian, novelist and distinguished historian Dee Brown became best known for *Bury My Heart at Wounded Knee* (1970), the saga of the American Indian that sold a million copies and was translated into more than a dozen languages. Brown wrote more than twenty books, both fiction and nonfiction on the American West. After he retired to Arkansas, he wrote *The American Spa*, a history of Hot Springs and volumes of historical fiction.

Douglas C. Jones, who was born at Winslow and retired to Fayetteville, captured the public's imagination with *The Court Martial of George Armstrong Custer* (1976), a novel based on the hypothetical possibility that Custer survived his Little Big Horn encounter with the Sioux. After returning to Arkansas, Jones produced *Elkhorn Tavern* (1980), a romantic novel set during the Civil War; *Weedy Rough* (1981), a panegyric to Winslow, and *The Barefoot Brigade* (1982), based on Arkansas Confederates in Lee's army. That both Brown and Jones should come home and turn to Arkansas themes indicates the pull on the creative imagination that the state exercised.

Romantic novels continued to attract readers and inspire authors. Arkansas was home to Claud Garner, a Hope native who turned to writing after a checkered career. His most popular book, *Cornbread Aristocrat* (1950), described the life of Sam Houston. Janice Holt Giles was another popular romantic, and romanticism found a home in the children's books of Lois Lenski, Faith Y. Knoop and Bernie Babcock. Children's books could be realistic. Robbie Branscum of Big Flat used plots that ran the gamut of twentieth century family life in the backwoods and Bette Greene utilized the Delta as her background.

Poet's Poetry

Twentieth century journalism limited the market for local poets. Newspapers commonly published verse before 1920, and newspapermen Dan Hogan, Clio Harper and Fred W. Allsopp were among the active poets. After that time, papers seldom printed verse, and new poets no longer wrote verse that newspaper audiences could understand. Hence, the Poets' Roundtable was organized in 1931 and began producing annual volumes of verse in 1939 that were read largely by other poets. Much that appeared in those volumes was parochial and chauvinistic, but a modest poetry revival soon was underway. Glenn Ward Dresbach, a Eureka Springs bank president, was the Arkansas Poet of the Present in 1953. Rosa Zagnoni Marinoni, a native of Bologna, Italy, who lived in Fayetteville, experimented in new forms and was the poet laureate of the Arkansas Federation of Women's Clubs.

Northwest Arkansas also was home to Edsel Ford, whose objective was "to write good poetry and to write it in and of Arkansas." Ford's *Looking for Shiloh* won the Devins Memorial Award in 1968. The Delta produced Lily Peter of Marvell, a multi-talented poet, painter, photographer, musician and cotton planter, whose *The Great Riding* (1966) told the De Soto saga in verse.

Academics increasingly came to play a major role in Arkansas poetry. Marinoni was first. Her successor at Fayetteville was Hoxie native Miller Williams, winner of the Prix de Rome for literature and the director of the University of Arkansas Press. Williams's *Halfway from Hoxie* (1973) and his subsequent works included Arkansas themes. Younger poets included Frank Stafford, who produced twelve volumes of verse during his brief life. Stafford also founded the Lost Roads Press, which along with August House helped provide local outlets. C. D. Wright was the most active younger female, and no poet was more Arkansas-centered than Jack Butler, who asked: "Why can't you make flour from Johnson grass seed?" in *West of Hollywood* [Clark County]: *Poems from a Heritage* (1980). *The Kid Who Wanted to Be a Spaceman* (1984) was perhaps as relevant to the present as any Arkansas poet ever had been.

Perpetuating a Literary Culture

The attempt to nourish an Arkansas spirit by creating a magazine devoted to the state continually enticed entrepreneurs. Bernie Babcock's *Sketch Book* was the longest lived until the *Union Station Times* was founded by Allen Leveritt in 1973. Renamed the *Arkansas Times*, it found its audience in affluent middle-class readers especially interested in restaurants and entertainment. On May 9, 1992, it became a tabloid style weekly with its lead column titled "The Insider," brief news stories, occasional investigative pieces, numerous columns and sections by former

Gazette writers and George Fisher's editorial cartoons.

The perpetuation of a literary culture also benefited from local presses. Rose Publishing Company, Inc., founded in 1973, specialized in the publication of Arkansas textbooks, history and humor. August House explored the fiction and poetry market before it found its niche as a general interest regional publisher specializing in folkore. It also had success with cookbooks. The establishment of the University of Arkansas Press and the University of Central Arkansas Press greatly benefited writers. Arkansas consistently ranked last in the nation in libraries, but the state association's magazine, *Arkansas Libraries*, often features Arkansas writers and reviews their books.

The State Without a History

In contrast to the extensive list of fiction, historical writing languished. Robert Ward Johnson called on Arkansans in 1868 to develop a history lest the state's residents lack pride. Johnson's words were not heeded until John Hallum produced his *Biographical and Pictorial History of Arkansas* in 1887, which was valuable primarily for the biographies it included, some written by Albert Pike. Poet Fay Hempstead wrote the first school text in 1889 and followed it with a larger history in 1890 and a three-volume version containing solicited biographies in 1911. Apparently there was no market for a history without the memorial gimmick, because state archivist Dallas T. Herndon produced similar volumes in 1922 and 1947, as did David Y. Thomas in 1930.

All of these early histories concentrated on politics and the "best people," giving little attention to blacks, women, economic conditions or social problems. Unfootnoted, these books repeated numerous errors. Only the Thomas work included a few essays that touched controversial issues. The first scholarly book on Arkansas history was *Reconstruction in Arkansas, 1862-1874*

(1923) by Thomas S. Staples, long-time dean at Hendrix College. Begun as a dissertation at Columbia University under Professor William Dunning, Staples's book reinforced the Southern Democratic interpretation of Reconstruction as an economic, political and racial disaster. Although a long-time Arkansas fixture, Staples did no more work, and the first active historian was Fayetteville professor David Y. Thomas, actually a practicing political scientist. History can be controversial, and utility interests repeatedly tried to get him fired during the 1930s. His work included a history of the Civil War years published by the United Daughters of the Confederacy and scholarly articles in academic journals.

One major reason for the weakness of Arkansas historical writing lay in the loss of records that historians needed. The state had created the Arkansas History Commission, but had not supplied it with an adequate budget. The average annual expenditure by the state from 1936 to 1942 was a mere $6,605, which was $400 less than the 1922 appropriation. By comparison, the Barbers Examining Board received more than $10,000. The operation was so minuscule that it took the Library of Congress ten years to discover the archive's existence.

Meanwhile, archives hunters from Louisiana, Texas, and North Carolina invaded the state, taking away its legacy. The papers of Mrs. Daisy Bates ended up in Wisconsin, hampering local historians as Mrs. Bates remained here. What did not get sent away was often burned by families insensitive to historical documents. The Arkansas History Commission, which for so long struggled just to survive, benefited in 1954 when a small building was attached to its space in the Old State House. In 1979, the archives moved into modern facilities located in the Capitol Mall office complex. Adequate staffing remained a problem, especially in the budgetary cutbacks of the 1980s.

Most Southern state university libraries collected historical records, but the University of Arkansas at Fayetteville was so starved for funds that it did not begin an archives program until 1967, followed by the University of Arkansas at Little Rock in the early 1980s and the University of Central Arkansas in 1985. Other institutions received papers from time to time, but these were sometimes processed inadequately and stored improperly.

The absence of needed records meant that John Gould Fletcher had to rely more on intuition than on sound research in writing his one-volume adult history, *Arkansas*, in 1947. Many county records, although microfilmed in the 1980s, were found in a 1985 study to be housed and maintained poorly.

A second difficulty lay in publishing opportunities. The Arkansas Historical Association, founded at the beginning of the century, managed to produce four volumes before state funding stopped and the body died in 1918. No outlet existed until 1942, when the Association was reborn and began publishing the *Arkansas Historical Quarterly*. A related drawback was the absence of a university press because most commercial publishers were not interested in book-length Arkansas manuscripts. Before 1980, when the University of Arkansas Press was founded, Arkansas was the only Southern state without a nonprofit press.

Interest in Arkansas surged after World War II despite the difficulties. The *Quarterly* offered publishing opportunities as did an increasing number of county journals. Colleges began offering graduate instruction in history, which often involved thesis writing, and the University supported a doctoral program. Several small commercial firms tried to fill the market and both they and the University Press received assistance from the Arkansas Endowment for the Humanities.

The number of Arkansas-related works grew apace in the 1980s and 1990s, encompassing books for the general public as well as for the scholar's shelf. Topics ranged from Dan F. and Phyllis A. Morse, *Archeology of the Cen-*

tral Mississippi Valley (1983), a seminal work on pre-history, the equally important works on pre-territorial history by Judge Morris S. Arnold, *Unequal Laws Unto a Savage Race: European Legal Traditions in Arkansas, 1686-1836,* (1985) and *Colonial Arkansas 1686-1804: A Social and Cultural History* (1991) and a wealth of other studies, many of which are cited in the bibliographic essays. The publication by Timothy Donovan and Willard Gatewood of *Governors of Arkansas: Essays in Political Biography* (1981) led the way in what promises to be the systematic collection of basic reference sources long needed.

Although gaps remain to be filled and events will be subject to interpretation and reinterpretation, Arkansas studies have attracted scholarly attention and received popular support. If the old Arkansas image problem was the result of ignorance of the facts, then the problem will be solved. Robert Ward Johnson, writing in 1868, proposed a remedy for the image problem: "Let each citizen and soldier feel that the man who derides and traduces his state, or his best men, strikes him in the face." A better response is research and writing.

MUSIC IN ARKANSAS CULTURE

Washington Irving reported hearing an old French chanson during his stay in the state, and an awareness of music along with its use as a medium of cultural communication formed an important part of the Arkansas experience in a wide range of idioms. Not only did the French have a musical tradition, but the first American settlers carried their repertoire of folk songs and printed music into Arkansas.

A thin line divided folk songs from those of published origins in the nineteenth century, and perhaps no better example could be cited than that of the famous "Arkansas Traveler." Two composers, José, Tasso, a Cincinnati violinist, and Mose Case, a black itinerant guitarist from Indiana, published versions in the 1850s, probably based on a folk tune already in circulation.

The tune soon became recognized nationally and today remains one of the most frequently played pieces at country fiddle contests. The great Belgian violinist Henri Vieuxtemps played an elaborate variation of it, and other versions also flourished. An attempt to make a state song using the melody failed in 1949, but visitors to Hardy, Arkansas, could savor country cooking and a modernized version of the story and the tune at the Arkansaw Traveler Folk and Dinner Theater.

One sheet music version of the "Arkansas Traveler" was coupled in 1847 with the "Rackinsack Waltz." This second nickname, of uncertain origins, caught the public's fancy after the Mexican War and was much used by Northern soldiers during the Civil War. Both "The Arkansas Traveler" and Rackensack (the usual spelling) suggested the nineteenth century's image of Arkansas as a land of primitive pioneer conditions. The music reflecting that point of view became controversial in time in an Arkansas that was desperately eager to be accepted as "normal" by American standards.

Most Arkansas-related music did not carry the cultural implications of "The Arkansas Traveler" or the "Rackinsack Waltz." The first formally composed Arkansas song to be published was entitled "I am Near to Thee." It was written by Little Rock newspaperman John E. Knight, a native of Newburyport, Massachusetts, to music by Ben F. Scull, whose family had come to Arkansas from Pennsylvania. The song was published in Philadelphia by Lee and Walker in 1858 and was dedicated to Mary E. Woodruff.

A second early number and the first to be given an Arkansas related title was the "Fayetteville Polka," composed in 1856 by a former Sophie Sawyer student, Ferd Zellner. Arkansas poets and musicians thereafter turned out

Booth Campbell, Ruth Tyler and Fred Woodruff (*photographer unknown, ca. 1950*) *These three leading Ozark folk musicians were almost the last to learn their material from oral sources. Ruth Tyler wrote for the* Ozark Mountaineer *and was a leader in reviving the popularity of the dulcimer.* **University of Arkansas at Little Rock**

occasional songs descriptive of the state during the heyday of sheet music (1840-1950). This music was designed for the parlor piano and befitted the tastes of the middle class.

Three Composers: Joplin, Still and Price

Scott Joplin was the first major Arkansas figure in American musical history. Born in 1868 near the present site of Texarkana, he studied with his violinist father and played piano in honky-tonks and brothels. His travels took him to St. Louis by 1885 and from there to New York. By the turn of the century, he had become the preeminent figure in an essentially black musical idiom known as Ragtime.

Joplin's own piano playing was preserved on piano rolls, and he composed perhaps the first opera by a black composer, *Treemonisha*. Set in Reconstruction Arkansas to a libretto of his own devising, the opera celebrated the victory of education over superstition and ignorance. Although forgotten after his death in 1917, the opera received its first professional performance in 1975 as part of the Joplin revival touched off by the use of his music in the motion picture, *The Sting*.

Joplin's career was a triumph over adversity and helped prepare the way for the second black Arkansas composer, William Grant Still (1895-1978). Born in Mississippi and reared in Little Rock, Still received formal musical instruction from George Chadwick and Edgar Varése and also studied with black musician W. C. Handy in Memphis.

Still's formal composition instruction was merged with black idioms most successfully in 1930 in his Afro-American *Symphony*, the single most frequently performed major composition by an American black. Still went on to compose other symphonies, operas and chamber music as well as the theme music for the television shows "Perry Mason" and "Gunsmoke." He was also the first American black to conduct major symphony orchestras.

Still's female equivalent was Florence Price (1888-1953). Born in Little Rock, she was valedictorian of her high school class in 1903 and graduated three years later from the New England Conservatory of Music. An active composer, she became the first black woman to have her works performed by major orchestras. Despite living most of her life in the North, a few of her piano pieces, "Arkansas Jitter" and "From the Canebrakes," reflected her origins. None of the three composers received any recognition in segregated Arkansas.

The Struggle to Create Cultural Institutions

A poor state like Arkansas lacked almost every means of adequate support for the appreciation of the higher arts. Despite possessing "opera houses" in most larger towns, only Little Rock actually saw an occasional performance by touring companies. The Musical Coterie, the state's pioneer music club, was organized in 1893. The group sponsored the Little Rock appearance of opera singer Lillian Nordica at the Capitol Theatre ten years later at a cost of $3,000. Such events invariably lost money, and Arkansas was home to few rich underwriters.

Elsewhere, orchestras and other cultural institutions benefited greatly from the talents of immigrants, especially Germans. With its small foreign born population, Arkansas lacked such a pillar of support. Even so, Little Rock copied the Cincinnati May Festival beginning in 1912 by establishing a week of music in April. The second year was described as an "appalling failure from a financial point of view," but the festival endured for almost a decade. The sponsors imported singer Ernestine Schumann-Heink one year, and performing orchestras included those of St. Paul, St. Louis, Minneapolis and Walter Damrosch's New York Symphony. The week usually included a major choral work such as

Mary Lewis

"Mary Lewis," wrote Arkansas Democrat feature writer Kay Tallquist, "has beauty and compelling radiance of an inner light which warms into artistic harmony every discordant note of life." During the 1920s, she was the very embodiment of Arkansas's contribution to the "flapper" girls. But like a character from an F. Scott Fitzgerald story, beneath the facade lay another world.

Born into poverty in Hot Springs, Mary Lewis experienced a succession of fathers, escaped from an orphanage, and grew up in the slums. At about age six, she was rescued by Reverend and Mrs. W. S. Fitch. Mrs. Fitch recognized the potential in her voice and launched her on her career, singing, "Jesus Wants Me for a Sunbeam," in Judsonia. Repelled by the strictness of the Fitches' home life, Mary attracted the attention of H. F. Auten, the prominent Republican and real estate developer, who took her under his wing during her high school years. Auten decided boys meant more to Mary than singing, and propelled her into marrying Keene Lewis. After a few years, Mary walked out and ended up in California, singing in cafes and working in silent movies. Then she moved to New York to become a star in the Ziegfeld Follies while studying voice at night.

Convinced that she had a shot at an operatic career, Mary headed off for Europe, making her operatic debut and generating much publicity. After studying in Europe, she made her much publicized debut in 1925 in New York's Metropolitan Opera House. When she returned to Little Rock thereafter and sang "Home, Sweet Home," neither the singer nor the audience was dry-eyed. The most notable event in her career was her role in the premiere of Robert Vaughn Williams' opera, Hugh the Drover, which she subsequently recorded. Returning to America, she attracted more publicity than critical acclaim but can be heard with pleasure on the handful of records she recorded for RCA Victor.

A disastrous marriage to German baritone Michael Bohnen precipitated a decline in her fortunes. She lost battles with more than vocal

Mary Lewis and her husband, Robert C. Hague
(photographer and date unknown) **Author's Collection**

scales, and repeated alcoholic binges made managers reluctant to engage her. A much publicized plan to make a motion picture evaporated, and Mary was left penniless. In 1931, she married a Standard Oil executive and for a while her life seemed to turn around. She gave a number of well-received concerts, and once again ventured into a recording studio. Two of these sessions were satisfactory, but at the third, the producer recalled, "She arrived drunk—not with just a hangover, but really stoned. Not only was she unable to sing, but she kept breaking off to insult the musicians, who were playing faultlessly. I wish you could have heard her attempt a sustained high B— like a death-rattle."

Three years later she was dead. A colleague had the last word: "She was a touching enigma, evidently bent on destroying herself, in spite of her excelling gifts."

Mendelssohn's *Elijah* or *St. Paul*, but a concert performance of Gounod's *Faust* was ventured in 1917.

The new standards of "taste" in the Roaring Twenties were shaped by motion pictures, radio and phonographs. The revolt of youth against traditional values displaced the old cultural guardians, making appreciation of art forms less imperative for entrance into "society." Arkansans abandoned most of their cultural efforts and simply went to the movies.

The 1920s in Arkansas were notable mostly for the international activities of two native born daughters. The best known was Mary Lewis, a Hot Springs native, who left Little Rock for a career in the movies first and then went on Broadway in the *Ziegfeld Follies*. A second Arkansas celebrity was Mary McCormic of Belleville in Yell County, a graduate of Ouachita Baptist College, who sang in Paris and in Chicago. She, too, became involved in society affairs and failed to fulfill her early promise.

The weakness of Arkansas's cultural aspirations became apparent when composer Laurence Powell tried to make a living in the state. The English born Powell came to the University of Arkansas in 1927 and organized an orchestra. He moved to Little Rock in 1934 and repeated the process. Powell composed the music for the "Arkansas Centennial Ode" to words by John Gould Fletcher and interested himself in the state's rich folk music legacy. He left for Michigan in 1939, largely because of the low pay at Little Rock Junior College.

Charles J. Finger wrote of Powell in 1927 that "Arkansas has a conductor and composer within its borders, and if the state does not appreciate the man it deserves to lose him." Powell's departure delayed by two decades the establishment of a permanent orchestra staffed by professional musicians.

In the late 1940s, the Little Rock orchestra was revived and it became the Arkansas Symphony in 1970. It represented the state at the nation's Bicentennial in Washington, D.C., giving a concert that critic Paul Hume considered meritorious. The Symphony also supported a string quartet of full-time professionals that played extensively around the state. Fort Smith supported a community orchestra, and the University orchestra, reorganized in 1953, became the North Arkansas Symphony Orchestra.

Federal arts money in the late 1970s prompted the establishment of regional orchestras in the southern and northeastern sections of the state. The Arkansas Opera Theater was begun in the late 1970s when Blanche Thebom joined the UALR faculty, and it prospered under the leadership of Dr. Ann Chotard. Helena benefited from a free concert series that was so well funded that more famous performers visited there than anywhere else in the state. Arkansans could also point with pride to Sarah Caldwell from Fayetteville, who reestablished opera in Boston and conducted at the Metropolitan Opera in New York.

Arkansas cultural institutions rested on a narrow base of support. Although the legislature made the fiddle Arkansas's official musical instrument, string instruction was limited to a few metropolitan areas. The public schools offered only limited cultural enrichment, and budgetary restrictions severely limited the efforts of colleges and universities.

The Decline of Popular Participation

Most Arkansans heard music in the late nineteenth century either from readily available sheet music played at home on the piano or at city parks, town squares and picnics where local amateur bands performed. Home entertainment and community concerts died with the coming of the phonograph, motion pictures and radio. The coming of air-conditioning and television to the state in the 1950s also limited popular participation in the arts as people began to stay indoors and watch television for entertainment.

Gone too were lazy, hot summer evenings on the porch, spent telling stories of the past. Also gone was the easy informality of "visiting" as people forgot their manners and kept the television on when friends arrived. Different audiences continued to respond to a variety of musical legacies in spite of this, resulting in a growing cultural fragmentation. Interest in music did not decline, but instead became fragmented by age, income, race and cultural background. The cultural unity present in the Age of the Arkansas Traveler was lost, probably forever.

The Folk Music Legacy

A rich legacy of the past was preserved in folk songs in the isolated areas of the Ozarks and Ouachitas. The serious academic study of this culture began in England in the late nineteenth century and spread to America. Led by Vance Randolph, ballad hunters recorded hundreds of songs, some of them locally created and others of ancient British origin that had changed little through generations.

Arkansas was home to Fred Woodruff and dozens of other active folk singers, but Emma Dusenbury was the most famous. As John Gould Fletcher wrote of her, she lived "in a leaky-roofed, decaying cabin; . . . dressed in flour-sacked clothes, [and] whose repertory consisted of nearly a hundred ballads." A native of Georgia brought to Arkansas as a child in 1872, Dusenbury went blind a few years after her marriage and the birth of her invalid daughter, Ora. Left near Mena in extreme poverty, she attracted the attention of Laurence Powell, John Gould Fletcher and Vance Randolph and recorded 116 songs for the Library of Congress. Her moment of glory came when Powell brought her to Little Rock in 1936 to sing at the state's Centennial celebration.

Most middle-class Arkansans were reluctant to admit the existence of a folk culture and considered it a mark of poverty. What

many refused to acknowledge, other Americans came to cherish. Pockets of ruralia were disappearing by the 1950s, and a nostalgia for the simple past gripped the nation. It was in this altered context that James Morris, a fifty-year-old school superintendent at Snowball, adopted the name Jimmy Driftwood. After the success of his song, "The Battle of New Orleans," Driftwood made a career out of existing folk songs and his own compositions in a folk idiom.

His female counterpart was Almeda Riddle, a singing grandmother from the Heber Springs area, whose repertoire prompted a scholarly study. Mrs. Riddle performed until well into her eighties and treated her age with good humor, once noting at a concert at Hall High School that she was scheduled first on the program because of fear she might die before the program was completed. The popularity of these singers and the possibilities of promoting tourism spurred creation in 1973 of the Ozark Folk Center at Mountain View.

The Gospel Music Legacy

Gospel singing was related closely to folk music. Eugene Bartlett ran the Hartford Music Company, one of the foremost shape-note publishing houses in the South. Among its active composers were Luther G. Presley and L.O. Sanderson. Black Sister Rosetta Tharpe doubled as a "hot" guitarist. Singing schools, common in the nineteenth century, remained entrenched in rural areas, and local quartets continued to find appreciative audiences. Prominent performers included Al Green, a popular singer who turned to gospel music, and the Loving Sisters.

The Blues Legacy

The Arkansas Delta was home to many blues singers from 1920 to 1950. Historian Robert Palmer credited Charley Parton with popularizing this blend of traditional African music and American idioms. Invariably performed in honky-tonks, roadhouses and at picnics, blues music was counter-culture to the churches, and its lyrics often bordered on obscene. Emphasizing hard drinking and fast women, blues reflected the depressed state of consciousness of the blacks during the era of segregation.

Charley Parton and many of the early performers were from Mississippi, but all of these musicians visited Arkansas as they worked an area bounded by the Missouri Bootheel on the north and Louisiana in the south. Helena, "a little Chicago" from the period 1920 to 1950, was the blues capital of the Delta, especially after radio station KFFA created the "King Biscuit Time" program in 1941. Featured performers included Sonny Boy Williamson (Rice Miller), a native of Mississippi, and Robert Lockwood, who was born near Marvell. Williamson's picture appeared on sacks of meal, and radio stations KLCN in Blytheville and KXLR in Little Rock sponsored similar programs. *Deep Blues: A Musical and Cultural History of the Mississippi Delta* (1981) by Arkansan Robert Palmer is an invaluable reference on the Arkansas blues scene, particularly in Helena, as well as a literary classic, and a general reference on the "birth of the blues" in Mississippi Delta states.

Some of the early bluesmen from Arkansas were Robert "Washboard Sam" Brown, born in Walnut Ridge; his half-brother Bill Broonzy, who grew up near Pine Bluff; Albert "Sunnyland Slim" Luadrew, who moved to Helena from Mississippi; Robert Nighthawk (Robert Lee McCollum); Roosevelt Sykes of Helena; James "Peck" Curtis; George "Harmonica" Smith; Howlin' Wolf (Chester Arthur Burnett) and Bob Lowery from Shuler in Union County. Peetie Wheatstraw from Cotton Plant was one of the most popular singers during the 1930s, and Louis Jordan, a former student at Arkansas Baptist College, reached out to more sophisticated audiences in the next decade with his Tympany Five.

The underlying rebellion and despair at the heart of blues was present not only in words and music but in the performers themselves. Peetie Wheatstraw advertised himself as "The Devil's Son-in-law and High Sheriff of Hell." Heaven became Chicago, and most bluesmen gravitated in that direction by the 1950s. Their legacy was perpetuated by phonograph records, Wheatstraw alone recording some 160 titles between 1930 and 1941.

Black flight from the Delta led to a rapid decline of the blues in the 1950s. Most of the early performers were dead or retired by the 1960s when the civil rights struggles led to white interest in the blues. Blues became for some a musical symbol of the black experience and hence a valid part of Americana to be collected, studied and anthologized in the same manner as white folk music. The interest of the white community led to the founding of the Arkansas Blues Connection in Little Rock, which was an attempt to provide a forum for current performers. Blues continued to be a living art form to some extent. Calvin Levy's 1970 song "Cummins Prison" helped galvanize blacks to support Winthrop Rockefeller's prison reform program. Attempts to revitalize Helena's economy in the 1980s focused extensively on a blues festival.

Blues styles also entered the mainstream of white popular music during the 1960s. Sonny Boy Williamson played for six weeks at the Palladium in London and influenced an English group called the Beatles. Closer to home, a Memphis white boy named Elvis Presley blended blues, gospel and Tin Pan Alley music to create rock and roll in the 1950s. Young Presley's first appearances were in Arkansas honky-tonks, where local whites once stormed the stage and drove him off. A few years later, Presley took the nation by storm; in his wake, Helena native Conway Twitty (Harold Lloyd Jenkins) began his career as a rock and roll artist performing on Helena's KFFA.

The Country Music Legacy

Blues belonged exclusively to blacks and rock and roll was morally degenerate to many Arkansas whites. Many working and lower-middle-class persons found solace in the simple musical idiom and easy-to-understand lyrics of country music. Conway Twitty eventually moved into this field. Pioneers in the field included Patsy Montana (Rubye Blevins), the singing cowgirl, whose "I Want to Be a Cowboy's Sweetheart" was the first country song to sell a million copies; Jimmy Wakely, the "Singing Cowboy" of the 1940s; T. Texas Tyler (David Myrick) and Elton Britt (James Britt Baker), probably the greatest yodler.

Important groups included the Wilburn Brothers and the Browns, from which Jim Ed Brown long remained active. More recently, Glen Campbell came from Delight, Charlie Rich from Colt and Lefty Frizzell from El Dorado. Wayland Holifield was an important composer. A singer who sometimes addressed controversial themes was Johnny Cash, who was reared in the Dyess community during the Depression. The state legislature chartered the Arkansas Country Music Hall of Fame in 1985 and changed the name to Entertainers Hall of Fame in 1987.

Politicians discovered the appeal of country music with the voters in the 1940s. Minnie Pearl, the Duke of Paducah and other Nashville performers earned substantial amounts on the campaign trail. Country music sometimes mirrored the alienation of the working classes from middle-class insularity in 1960s and 1970s. The success of Johnny Cash, who gave some of his best performances at prisons, reflected the sense of frustration that had long been a feature of the blues.

The Rock and Roll Legacy

The social commentary explicitly present in blues, and sometimes implicitly present in country music, permeated nearly every aspect of the new music of the 1950s: rock and roll. One Arkansas group, Black Oak Arkansas, was led by Jim "Dandy" Mangrum and consisted of youths from the Black Oak community in Craighead County. It aroused great animosity from parents and cultural guardians but nevertheless kept close ties to the state. Mangrum's songs included "The Hills of Arkansas" and "When Electricity Came to Arkansas," hardly the standard material for an idiom mostly given to sex, drugs and juvenile wailings. Fundamentalist ministers railed against godlessness in music, several public record burnings received national publicity and Wal-Mart Discount stores removed "offensive" material in the conservative reaction of the 1980s.

Arkansas Music Today

The old Arkansas Traveler story describes a cultural situation where different social classes share a knowledge of the same tune. During the late nineteenth and early twentieth centuries, the public schools attempted to instill some elements of unity by teaching important songs from the nation's history, but these efforts were abandoned largely by the 1970s. Cultural fragmentation snowballed in the twentieth century and music became a marketable item controlled by international corporations whose chief concerns were in making money. All aspects of Arkansas's musical life were affected.

Geographic, cultural and educational forces imposed severe restraints on the prospects for classical music. Classical music remained the most expensive to produce, and Arkansas lacked a major metropolitan area or the great inherited wealth considered necessary generally to support adequately high culture. Folk music retained a limited appeal, but the Ozarks took second place to Appalachia as its home base. Folk music adherents remained split on an issue that surfaced in the 1970s when oldtimers insisted that all the songs already had been written. Blues, too, had a museum quality to it although white prejudice against the idiom declined noticeably. Country music reflected the tastes of many adults, but its center was in Nashville even if some claimed the Grand Ole Opry had its origins in Mammoth Spring. Rock and roll began as a youth revolt, but black children in the 1980s turned to rap music and in one school district fights broke out between supporters of "heavy metal" on the white side and rap on the other. Rock music, doubtless the most international-ized musical commodity, had by 1990 the least content identification with Arkansas.

ARKANSAS ART

Early Art Traditions

The first artists of Arkansas were the pre-historic Indians, who went beyond the practi-cal to incise their pots and create effigies. Arkansas was particularly rich in such arti-facts at one time, but a succession of out-of-state buyers and the crude recovery practices of "pothunters" have taken a heavy toll. Some fine examples are on display at area muse-ums, but many more are out of state, often in private collections.

The French left no artistic legacy: not even a house in the French colonial style commemo-rates their presence. The pioneer Americans brought a vigorous tradition of home crafts with them, notably in quilts, samplers and cov-erlets. Such items continue to be produced and form an important part of folk expression. Before manufactured products displaced local craftsmen, Arkansas was home to hundreds of cabinet makers, silversmiths, gunmakers and other artisans. One set of slave-made silver-ware reportedly exists in the state, and talent-ed slaves often worked as artisans. Even so, the frontier shifted so rapidly as transporta-tion improved that Arkansas artisans never had time to develop a local style comparable to Kentucky furniture. Log cabins could be con-

sidered a form of artistic expression, but none of the styles used in the state was indigenous. Gideon Shryock, the architect for the State Capitol, was from Kentucky and used the Greek Revival theme popular for public build-ings at the time.

Art meant portrait painting for most nine-teenth century Americans, and numerous lim-ners worked the state before the invention of photography. The Helena *Constitutional Jour-nal* carried an advertisement in 1836 for D. Myers, "Portrait & Ornamental Painter," who promised "a good resemblance warranted in all cases." The first to take up permanent res-idence was Henry C. Byrd, often erroneously called John Henry Byrd. Byrd painted the likenesses of hundreds of the state's notables as well as the first Arkansas nude. Chester Harding, best known for a life portrait of the aged Daniel Boone, was another active limner.

The First Painters

The first professional Arkansas-born artist was Edward Payson Washburn, the son of missionary Cephas Washburn. Born at Dwight Mission in 1831, he began painting in 1851. After eighteen months of study in New York, he returned to Arkansas, where he made the "Arkansas Traveler" immortal, supposedly using the children of Little Rock doctor R. L. Dodge as models.

The original painting now hanging at the Arkansas History Commission was mutilated by improper restoration, but it achieved national fame from the lithograph first pub-lished in 1859 by Leopold Grozelier of Boston, who specialized in quality work. The first edi-tion sold for $2.50 and inspired cheaper imita-tions, including one by Currier and Ives that sold for a quarter. By 1870, one version had adopted the "w" ending for *Arkansaw*, invok-ing the negative image that many persons in Arkansas resented. The full extent of Wash-burn's talents was never revealed, because he died in 1859.

Painting attracted a few amateurs, one of whom was the multi-talented William "Cush" Quesenbury. Quesenbury's work, nearly all in private possession or lost today, included a full-length self-portrait in hunting garb, a view of early Van Buren, a satirical drawing of Arkansas roads and a lithograph of Fayetteville Female Seminary. Quesenbury taught art at Cane Hill College during the 1870s. The deaf-mute Little Rock newspaperman J. W. "Dummy" Woodward was another amateur artist. His sketch of the state archives being moved to Hot Springs in 1862 is the only known Civil War drawing from the Confederate side.

The turbulent post-war years were not productive for the arts, but one of the most talked-about exhibits at the Philadelphia Exposition in 1876 was a butter sculpture, "The Dreaming Iolanthe," that artist Caroline S. Brooks had shipped from Helena packed on ice. Mrs. Brooks remained active in this unusual medium for several years. A contemporary of Brooks was Vinnie Ream, a Fort Smith sculptress, who rendered early busts of Abraham Lincoln and Arkansans Albert Pike and Elias C. Boudinot.

Small art colonies existed in Little Rock, Helena and a few other towns by the late nineteenth century. First the Aesthetic Club and then the Fine Arts Club offered forums in Little Rock, and active artists included Benjamin C. Brown, Mrs. Jenny Delongy Rice-Myrowitz, Mrs. Winfield S. Holt, Adrian Brewer, Mrs. Theodore Dubé, and Dea Carr Smith. A few of these artists attained more than local attention. Mrs. Myrowitz did a life-sized oil painting of Mrs. Jefferson Davis. Mrs. Holt, who studied in Paris and traveled extensively, drew several early Arkansans and Arkansas scenes. Mrs. Dubé opened one of the first studios in the state at Helena and specialized in murals and portraits. Art teachers included Dea Smith at Galloway College.

Arkansas artists reflected Southern middle-class tastes in both styles and subject matter. Patriotic scenes were much in demand.

The Arkansas Nude. John Henry Byrd painted the state's nude in 1857. Influenced by the Hudson River School, Byrd gave to his model an authentic Arkansas setting with an old oxbow lake. Byrd apparently painted this picture for his own pleasure and it long stayed in the family. **Arkansas Territorial Restoration**

Colonel V. Y. Cook had a large mural of General Forrest's cavalry erected in his house in Batesville. It was taken down later and moved to Mississippi. May Danaher did a portrait of David O. Dodd based on a war-time photograph. Mrs. Elmer Stuck decorated her dining room in Jonesboro with a mural in which each month was described with appropriate Bible verses. At the St. Louis World's Fair in 1905, Eula Spivey displayed "The Nileists," showing a little African "in abbreviated toilet sitting on the sunny shore of the Egyptian river with a large stork standing sedately near by." China painting was popular for young women from the upper classes. Modern scholars have seen it as the first wave of liberation for women.

Art appreciation remained limited in part because of the absence of galleries and museums. The works of some local artists were hung in the Little Rock public library about 1905. This inspired the first showing a few years later when the rooms of the Woman's Cooperative Association were used for a three-day exhibit. During the 1920s, the Fine Arts Club gave receptions to display new works. Such was the volume that the 1927 meeting of the Arkansas Federation of Women's Clubs devoted its El Dorado meeting to a display featuring Arkansas artists. The next year the Club opened the Fine Art Gallery in Little Rock. Meanwhile, the Arkansas Museum of Natural History opened on the third floor of the Pulaski County Courthouse with Mrs. Bernie Babcock in charge.

The early years of the century also were productive for Arkansas potteries. Stoneware was made even before the Civil War in Dallas County, and by the turn of the century, Arkansas could boast the Hot Springs Clay Products Company, the Ouachita Pottery Company, the Hot Springs Art Pottery, the Niloak Pottery in Benton and the Camark Pottery in Camden. In addition, art glass was manufactured in Fort Smith.

The Rise of Modern Art

The cultural revolution of the 1920s undermined the middle-class values in art even as it affected music and literature, and the Depression temporarily incapacitated the middle class. China painting became outmoded, and social realism came to the fore. The federal government's relief program in the 1930s included aid for artists. H. Louis Freund, the resident artist at Hendrix College from 1937 to 1946 and the most influential of Arkansas artists to break from the old Victorian restraints, worked for the Works Progress Administration. Mrs. Fern Knecht did a Public Works Administration mural in the Little Rock Public Library, and Charles Eames did

another in Helena.

The Depression indirectly aided art in Arkansas. The Fine Art Gallery had grown to hold 104 paintings, the oldest of which was *The Adoration of the Shepherds* by Giacomo da Ponte Bassano (1510-1592). Using a promise of city support, a $25,000 gift from Frederick W. Allsopp and federal money from the WPA, the Fine Arts Club built a Museum in the Art Deco style in MacArthur Park. This city museum became the Arkansas Arts Center (AAC) in the 1960s. With financial aid from Winthrop Rockefeller, it greatly expanded its facilities and began to acquire a more adequate collection, specializing in twentieth century American drawings.

Meanwhile, the Arkansas Watercolor Society held its first exhibit in 1937, and the Arkansas Ozarks became a major source of inspiration for Missouri native Thomas Hart Benton, one of the famous American painters of the twentieth century. Howard Simon, husband of writer Charlie May Simon, was a back-to-the-land artist who settled in the Ozarks before his divorce from Simon. His woodcuts illustrated the *Arkansas Gazette Centennial Edition* in 1936.

Dilettantes and hard-working professionals could make careers in art in Arkansas in the late nineteenth century, but most chose to do so elsewhere. Ben Brown, whose *Morning Light* was the first painting acquired by the Fine Arts Club, moved to California. Louis Betts, a prominent illustrator, began his career in Little Rock. His first painting (now at the AAC), was a portrait of music teacher Ferdinand Armellini that Betts traded for music lessons. Jim R. Shaver of Evening Shade achieved fame for his "Little Shavers" drawings in the 1920s.

Arkansas artists began a new round of activity in the post-World War II period. The most important was Carroll Cloar, born in Earle (Crittenden County) of mixed Quapaw ancestry. Cloar, who moved to Memphis, was featured in *Life* magazine. Many of his

Camark Pottery *(photographer and date unknown) Camark of Camden began producing art pottery but shifted to utilitarian ware in order to survive. By the 1980s, Arkansas ceramics began to be considered collector's items with Niloak pieces commanding the highest prices.* **University of Arkansas**

best paintings, often with Arkansas settings, were published in book form in *Hostile Butterflies, and Other Paintings* (1977). Like Thomas Hart Benton, Cloar was attracted to the people and the landscape of the state. One painting, *Angel in a Thornpatch*, showing the headstone of black Crittenden County planter George Berry Washington, alone and surrounded by cotton,

aptly symbolized the falling roles of blacks in eastern Arkansas.

Al Allen of the University of Arkansas at Little Rock and Ronald Roller Wilson of Pine Bluff had national reputations. Arkansas also offered several parallels to the primitivist Grandma Moses. One was Ruth Brigham, known as "Granny Chicken," whose *The Celebration of Big Flat, Arkansas* was used as the state's Heritage Week Poster in 1983. Another was Fennie Lou Spelce, whose works have been shown at the Arkansas Arts Center and in New York.

Support for the arts also emerged at the University of Arkansas, which began granting a Masters of Fine Arts degree in the 1940s. Evan Linquist became an active artist-printer at Arkansas State University. The cause of art education was furthered by the Arkansas Arts Center Artmobile that toured remote areas, and the Arkansas Arts Festival, held during the 1950s and 1960s in Little Rock, gave artists a chance to reach out to the public and display their wares. The Arkansas Arts Center, greatly enlarged in the 1960s and 1980s, provided gallery space for touring shows and increased its holdings. Pine Bluff, El Dorado and other larger towns opened galleries. The Arkansas Arts Council identified 172 arts organizations within the state by 1984, generating an economic impact estimated at $34,400,000.

A latent hostility remained, however. Little Rock police raided the West Seventh Street Gallery in 1965 and arrested the owner for possession of pre-Columbian Mexican Indian statues that someone thought obscene. State legislators on another occasion grew incensed about paintings of "nekked women," and repressive college administrators censored art films and books and tried to prohibit the use of models. A Henry Moore sculpture, *Large Standing Figure: Knife Edge,* in Little Rock's Metrocenter Mall, cost $185,000, perhaps the largest single investment in a work of art by any unit of Arkansas government.

Photography as Art

The decline of oils and watercolors in the early twentieth century coincided with the full artistic possibilities of the camera. The first photographers specialized in taking personal portraits, and no scenes pre-dating the Civil War are known to exist. A few pictures of Hele-na, DeValls Bluff and Little Rock were taken during the War, but line drawings were the favored way to convey outdoor activity. Great improvements in technology made photography a popular hobby and one that attracted women by the 1890s. Alice French at Clover Bend used Arkansas scenes in her 1893 book *Adventures in Photography*, and "art" photographs appeared in Bernie Babcock's magazine, *The Sketch Book.*

Every town boasted at least one photographer by 1900. Some, such as Emily Alquest at Paragould, showed considerable talent. The postcard craze early in the twentieth century produced a rich legacy of pictures. Some were formal views of towns and scenery, but others captured wrecks, disasters, family gatherings, hangings and lynchings. Spa photographers were particularly busy. At McLeod's Happy Hollow studio in Hot Springs, tourists could be photographed in a variety of settings, including a "Wild West Combination" or "Rustic and Comic Photos," one featuring a ride in an ox cart. Brownie cameras made the snapshot a middle-class necessity during the 1920s.

Photographers still made their rounds in rural areas, posing families in their best clothes standing in front of their homes. The Arkansas Arts Center eventually acquired the 3,150 photographs of Mike Disfarmer, a Heber Springs photographer. More recently, Andrew Kilgore's photographic exhibits, *We Drew A Circle,* and one on Fayetteville folk, have been acclaimed widely, as has the work of James S. McGinnis, a photographer at the University of Arkansas at Little Rock.

Most of the photographs documenting ordinary life in Arkansas came from programs connected with the federal government. National Forest Service officials were the first to record their activities. A number of photographs relating to levees, ditches and especially the great floods of 1927 and 1937 documented man and nature in the Delta. During the Great Depression, highly skilled photographers such as Russell Lee, Dorthea Lange,

(Arthur Keller, 1910) Hundreds of itinerant photographers worked the state. *If the customer wanted a studio effect, the photographer unrolled a canvas and posed the subjects. In this picture from the Mountain Home area, several things went wrong. The camera was too far back, revealing how such pictures were made. The possum that was presumably the object of the serenade decided not to cooperate, disrupting the picture.* **University of Central Arkansas**

Ben Shahn and Arthur Rothstein photographed the scenes that middle-class Arkansans preferred to ignore.

Dozens of books since World War II have used photographs effectively. The camera covered such topics as the state prisons, the conditions of the aged, the decline of rural ways, the variety of courthouses, the styles of architecture and the beauty of the land. Matt Bradley's painstaking work of the 1970s and 1980s best captured the essence of Arkansas life and was featured in *The National Geographic* and three books.

Arkansas Architecture

Arkansas never developed a particular style of architecture, but the state is rich in architectural examples. These range from log cabins and other vernacular styles to the prime work of professional architects. Architect Charles L. Thompson, whose firm Cromwell, Truemper, Levy, Parker and Woodsmall still operates, designed buildings in a variety of styles at the turn of the century, and many of them have been placed on the National Register of Historic Places.

Fayetteville was home to internationally famous architect Edward Durrell Stone, who kept close ties to the University and encouraged its architecture program. Formal instruction in architecture began at the University in 1946 under Van Buren native John G. Williams. Understaffed and underbudgeted like all University activities except sports, the degree program was not accredited until 1958. Even so, the school acquired a reputation early for creativity, and faculty member Cyrus A. Sutherland became one of the leaders in the historic preservation movement in the 1970s.

E. Fay Jones of Fay Jones and Maurice Jennings, Architects, Fayetteville, regional interpreters of organic architecture, became internationally famous for his design of Thorncrown Chapel, a nondenominational chapel of wood and glass, built in a natural wooded set-

ting near Eureka Springs. To preserve the natural setting around the chapel, Jones used only materials two workers could carry up the path to the site, no heavy machinery and no decorative ornaments. The small building, 24 feet wide by 50 feet long and 48 feet high, soars in the imagination, and was visited by over 300,000 people in 1992. Jones was awarded the Architects Gold Medal Award in 1990, the highest award of the American Institute of Architects, and in 1991, the American Institute of Architects voted Thorncrown Chapel the best American building since 1980. *The Architecture of E. Fay Jones* was published in 1992.

The Quapaw Quarter in Little Rock and Belle Grove in Fort Smith became focal points for much of the historic preservation work that began in the late 1960s.

Arkansas Cartoonists

In contrast to the rarified world of art and architecture, even the semi-literate could appreciate cartoons. The first political cartoons appeared in the *Gazette* in 1852 and may have been the work of Edward Payson Washburn. William Quesenbury's famous satire on the 1860 gubernatorial race was long remembered, and cartoons became a regular feature in the 1880s.

Cartoonists achieved considerable importance in the post-World War II era. The *Arkansas Democrat* boasted Jon Kennedy and John Deering. Their competition at the *Gazette* included Bill Graham and George E. Fisher. Fisher made a career of satirizing Orval Faubus and then did not spare his successors, or the Army Corps of Engineers on environmental issues. Cartooning was not limited to the capital. Ron Meyer, Mike Gauldin, Jan C. Gosnell, Roger C. Drebelbis and Roger Harvell earned solid local reputations. Arkansan Dan Glass became a nationally famous cartoonist for his *Betty Boop* series.

The Arkansas Arts Center Decorative Arts Museum *(Robert L. Coon, Jr., 1993) The former Albert Pike home is believed to have been built in 1840. The house was given to the City of Little Rock by Adolphine Fletcher Terry and her sister, Mary Fletcher Drennan in 1976. After Mrs. Terry died, the City took possession in 1981 and began renovations. The house opened as the Decorative Arts Museum in 1985.*

Future Prospects

Art, even folk art, requires money and leisure. All cultural activities received a big boost during the Great Society programs of the 1960s. Federal funding spurred the creation of the state Arts Council, the Arkansas Endowment for the Humanities and a host of community organizations. The Arkansas Historic Preservation Program catalogued more than 1,400 structures, 700 of which were listed on the National Register of Historic Places. Arkansas ranked twenty-eighth among the states in support of the arts, spending 32 cents per resident. Despite financial hard times and reduced federal support, a 1984 survey indicated "arts dollars" had increased 350 percent since 1978.

The artistic awakening of Arkansas was long delayed, and much remained to be accomplished. Arkansas showed such rapid percentage increases because the starting base was so low. Yet the positive signs were many. The old Albert Pike home, hallowed also for its occupation by John Gould Fletcher, Adolphine Fletcher Terry, a noted civic leader, and her husband, Congressman David D. Terry, became the Decorative Arts Museum, a satellite gallery of the Arkansas Arts Center. Public television, which by 1983 reached virtually every part of the state, offered outlets for local arts and music as well as current events programs. The 1980 census recorded 5,468 persons designated as artists.

The growth of artistic awareness led to a decline in provincialism, but it also produced a deemphasis on Arkansas subject matter. So-called "modern" or "contemporary" art generally eschewed all attempts at representation. Folk artists and some photographers remained committed to exploring the Arkansas heritage, but most art in Arkansas was not "Arkansas Art" in content.

CONCLUSION

The realms of literature, art and music have always been part of a broad Arkansas cultural complex. Yet salient Arkansas characteristics have emerged most strongly in literature and the architecture of E. Fay Jones and Maurice Jennings. A concern with local culture and an unwillingness to surrender totally to modernity can be found in all three areas. That state histories are written in the first place is evidence that the spirit survives. The vitality shown by the arts probably will continue. In fact, the real future of the state may lie in the liberation of the spirit, with literature, music and art becoming universal expressions of the *volkgeist* rather than esoteric anomalies.

BIBLIOGRAPHIC ESSAY

The best place to begin a study of Arkansas literature is by reading the books mentioned in the text. Useful poetry collections include Fred W. Allsopp, comp. and ed., *Poets and Poetry of Arkansas,* (Little Rock, 1933), and O. Coke, *The Scrapbook of Arkansas Literature,* (N.P., 1939) A new anthology is William M. Baker and Ethel C. Simpson, eds., *Arkansas in Short Fiction: Stories from 1841 to 1984,* (Little Rock, 1986). For analysis, James R. Masterson, *Tall Tales of Arkansaw,* (Boston, 1942) reprinted as *Arkansas Folklore,* (Little Rock, 1974) is perhaps the best book ever written about any aspect of Arkansas life. His inclusion of the ribald texts for the famous speech, "Change the Name of Arkansas? Hell, No!" makes this book second only to Vance Randolph's *Pissing in the Snow and Other Ozark Folktales* (Urbana, 1976) as the saltiest book in Arkansas literature.

The works of C. F. M. Noland have been collected in Leonard Williams, ed., *Cavorting on the Devil's Fork: The Pete Whetstone Letters of C. F. M. Noland* (Memphis, Tenn., 1979). Other early Arkansas stories can be found in

John Q. Anderson, *With the Bark On,* (Nashville, Tenn., 1967). One interesting analysis of the Big Bear is Katherine G. Simoneaux, *Symbolism in Thorpe's "The Big Bear of Arkansas,"* AHQ XXV (Autumn 1966), 240-247. The Arkansas Traveler has had many scholars on his trail, including Margaret S. Ross, "Sandford C. Faulkner," *AHQ,* XIV (Winter 1955), 301-314; Mary D. Hudgins, "Arkansas Traveler: A Multi-Parented Wayfarer," *AHQ,* XXX (Summer 1971), 145-160, and Robert L. Morris, "The Success of Kit, The Arkansas Traveler," *AHQ,* XXII (Winter 1963), 338-350. The most incredible of Arkansas authors is surveyed in Ted R. Worley, "The Story of Alfred W. Arrington," *AHQ* XIV (Winter 1955), 315-339.

Albert Pike's poems can be found in many collections, and his essays appear in Mark Keller and Thomas A. Belser, Jr., "Albert Pike's Contributions to the Spirit of the Times," *AHQ,* XXXVII (Winter 1978), 318-353. William Quesenbury's career is summarized briefly in Michael B. Dougan, "William Quesenbury: Poet of Arkansas," *PAPA* III (Summer, 1977), 1-7. Augustus J. Prahl, "Friedrich Gerstäcker, The Frontier Novelist," *AHQ,* XIV (Spring 1955), 43-50, is a brief survey of the prolific German. Additional materials include Anita and Evan B. Bukey, trans. and eds., "Arkansas After the War: From the Journal of Frederick Gerstäcker," *AHQ,* X (Spring, 1951), 1-36; Clarence Evans, trans. and ed., "Gerstäcker and the Konwells of White River Valley," *AHQ,* X (Spring, 1951) 1-36; and Clarence Evans and Liselotte Albrecht, trans. and eds., " Frederick Gerstäcker in Arkansas," *AHQ* V (Spring 1946), 39-57.

There are no surveys or studies on Civil War era writings, but Robert L. Morris, *Opie Read, American Humorist,* (New York, 1965), treats the state's most productive post-war writer. George McMichael, *Journey to Obscurity: The Life of Octave Thanet* (Lincoln, Neb., 1965), rescues Alice French from obscurity and Michael B. and Carol W. Dougan, eds., collected *By the*

Cypress Swamp: the Arkansas Stories of Octave Thanet (Little Rock, 1980). Ethel C. Simpson, ed., *Simpkinsville and Vicinity: The Arkansas Stories of Ruth McEnery Stuart,* (Fayetteville, 1983), fulfilled a similar role.

Treatments on the modern period are somewhat sparse. Michael B. Dougan, "Bumpkins and Bigots: The Arkansas Image in Fiction," *PAPA,* I (Summer, 1975), 5-14, is an overview. Robert Cochran, *Vance Randolph: An Ozark Life* (Urbana and Chicago, 1985) is a good introduction to one leading figure. Diane Rowland, "Arkansas Lives: Bernie Babcock's Turn-of-the-Century Diaries," *AL,* XXXVII (March 1980), performs a similar service for a colorful local writer. Although the works of John Gould Fletcher remain uncollected, Twayne included him in its authors' series: Edna B. Stephens, *John Gould Fletcher,* (New York, 1967). Thomas Cochran, "Arkansas Lives: The Strange Ride of Donald Harrington," *AL,* XXXVIII (December 1981), 27-31, treats a modern.

Instead of evaluating this literature, most critics have related it to the state's image problem. Examples include E. E. Dale, "Arkansas: The Myth and the State," *AHQ,* XII (Spring 1953), 8-29; William F. Lisenby, "A Survey of Arkansas's Image Problem," *AHQ,* XXX (Spring 1971), 60-71; E. J. Friedlander, 'The Miasmatic Jungles,' Reactions to H. L. Mencken's 1921 Attack on Arkansas," *AHQ,* XXXVIII (Spring 1979), 63-71; Lee A. Dew, "On a Slow Train Through Arkansaw—The Negative Image of Arkansas in the Early Twentieth Century," *AHQ,* XXXIX (Summer 1980), 125-135, and C. Fred Williams, "The Bear State Image: Arkansas in the Nineteenth Century," *AHQ,* XXXIX (Summer, 1980), 99-111.

Arkansas music has been covered unevenly. A good place to begin is James R. Rebworth, *A Directory of 132 Arkansas Composers,* (Fayetteville, 1979). Mary D. Hudgins. "Composer Laurence Powell in Arkansas," *AHQ,* XXXI (Summer 1972), 181-188, is one of the few articles on classical music.

The folk music of Arkansas has been collected by Vance Randolph, *Ozark Folksongs,* (Columbia, Mo., 1948) and more recently in Mary C. Parler, *An Arkansas Ballet Book,* (Fayetteville, 1963, reprinted, Norwood, Pa., 1975), and Roger D. Abrahams, ed., *A Singer and Her Songs, Almeda Riddle's Book of Ballads,* (Baton Rouge, 1970).

Black composers have attracted national attention. James Haskins and Kathleen Benson, *Scott Joplin* (New York, 1978), is a standard account. Robert Haas, ed., *William Grant Still and the Fusion of Culture in American Music,* (Los Angeles, 1972), treats broader issues and Still's "My Arkansas Boyhood," *AHQ,* XXVI (autumn, 1967), adds personal items. Barbara G. Jackson, "Florence Price, Composer," *BPM,* V (Spring 1977), 30-43, is an introduction.

American popular music and especially the blues recently have come under scholarly scrutiny. Two invaluable books are Robert Palmer, *Deep Blues,* (New York, 1981), and Phillip Kimball, *Harvesting Ballads,* (New York, 1984). Lorenzo Thomas, "For Bluesman Sonny Boy Williamson, Pass the Biscuits One More Time," *AT,* V (June 1979), 24-31, should not be missed. Johnny Cash, *Man in Black,* (Grand Rapids, 1975), tells an unusual story, and Richard Anderson, "Jimmy Driftwood: Poet Laureate with a Banjo," *AT,* VI (October 1979), 60-63, is laudatory.

Ralph Hudson in "Art in Arkansas," *AHQ,* III (Winter 1944) 299-350, wrote an adequate survey more than forty years ago, but no further general studies exist. Useful articles include Margaret Ross, "Arkansas Woman's Butter Sculpture is a Sensation at Philadelphia Exposition," *CrCHQ,* X (Summer, 1972), 20-23; Mary D. Hudgins, "Information Needed on Hot Springs Potteries," *REC,* XVII (1976), 75-76, and also her "More About a Twentieth Century Hot Springs Art Pottery," *REC,* XIX (1978), 50-53. Carroll Cloar, *Hostile Butterflies, and Other Paintings,* (Memphis, 1977), reproduces a number of this Crittenden County native's Arkansas scenes.

Construction of the Interstate 30 Bridge Over the Arkansas River at Little Rock *(photographer unknown, ca., 1959) The supremacy of the automobile was achieved when federal money made possible the building of interstate highways. Within ten years, passenger rail travel almost ceased in the state.* **University of Central Arkansas**

Chapter XIX

The Promise and Problems of Modernization

INTRODUCTION

"We were poor but we didn't know it. I thought we ate beans and squirrel because they were good," Mary Etta Grady of Beedeville remarked and thousands of other Arkansans echoed. Arkansans who lived during the Depression or grew up under its long shadow had experienced an event as cataclysmic to the twentieth century as the Civil War was for the nineteenth. Their experiences with absolute poverty contrasted sharply with the great American affluence after World War II and the relative poverty ameliorated by social programs. Shaped by their Depression era experiences, older Arkansans were unimpressed by statistics and often openly contemptuous of the problems of post-war Arkansans.

After World War II, the increasing availability of comparative economic statistics made it plain that Arkansas had far to go to

Arkansas Fishermen. *(Arthur Keller, ca. 1940) Four Mountain Home residents pose with their catch after a White River fishing expedition. Hunting and fishing remain a major part of Arkansas life, particularly for men. Note the dress of these fishermen.* **University of Central Arkansas**

catch up with the rest of the United States. Widely publicized rankings of the state covered everything from teen-age pregnancy to teacher salaries. Thus the harsh light of numbers replaced travelers' anecdotes or joke books as the main source of information about Arkansas.

Looked at over time, these rankings often reflected progress, both in absolute and comparative terms. Far too often, however, Arkansas did not fare well. "Thank God for Mississippi," was one popular response to some forty-ninth ranking, but during the late 1980s even Mississippi seemed to be reacting more vigorously in education, road-building and tourism than Arkansas to the challenges of the impending twenty-first century.

Traditionalists responded that statistics failed to show the intangibles best reflected in local pride, clean air, family ties and good hunting and fishing. The struggle between national standards, often called the "mainstream," and traditionalism intensified during the 1970s and 1980s as America entered what scholars called the post-industrial era. Having come late to the industrial age, Arkansas saw the promise of the "American dream" draw close to fulfillment and then begin to falter as the federal government sharply reduced its support of state governments in the Reagan era, particularly in social services. The theme of modernization versus traditionalism remained central to interpreting Arkansas life.

THE STRUGGLE FOR MODERNIZATION

Promise and Problems in Industry

Arkansas's drive toward reaching the national average income began with the New Deal. World War II narrowed the gap somewhat by bringing higher prices for farm products and new jobs in wartime industries. State and federal initiatives continued in the post-war era. Money from the federal government for dams, highways, drainage and military installations began to transform Arkansas.

Unless one owned land or a business, those who left Arkansas to help fight World War II or for a well-paying defense job had little economic reason to return to the state, and the 1940s and 1950s were decades of population decline. The peacetime draft proved to be a popular economic security valve for some who did return but found themselves displaced from the land by the rapid mechanization of agriculture.

Most of the installations the War spawned in Arkansas were downsized, dismantled, or sold to private industry, as with the aluminum plants in Hot Spring County. A naval ordnance built late in the War in Calhoun County across the Ouachita River from Camden sat vacant until sold to private interests in the 1970s. As Highland Industrial Park, it blossomed with high-tech defense contractors assembling battlefield weapons such as mobile rocket launchers.

On 15,000 acres deep in the piney woods of Jefferson County, workers at the Pine Bluff Arsenal had created, tested, stored, and designed defenses against deadly chemical weapons during World War II. Largely because the government could not figure out what to do with the weapons, the Arsenal's mission continued. By 1993, when the Department of Defense (as the former War Department had been renamed) decided incineration was the proper disposal method, the Pine Bluff Arsenal disclosed at a "media day" that it housed 12 percent of the nation's stockpile of nerve agents and gases and 90,281 obsolete rockets.

In 1971, 30 yellow-brick buildings on 496 acres of the Pine Bluff Arsenal site were dedicated to a wholly different use — saving lives — when President Richard M. Nixon established the National Center for Toxicological Research (NCTR). Administered by the Food and Drug Administration, NCTR employs hundreds of scientists and support personnel who use laboratory animals to assess the risk of various toxic exposures to humans.

The Korean War, as the first major confrontation of what came to be called the "Cold War," brought a stepped-up military presence to Arkansas. Blytheville changed from celebrating cotton to relying on the jobs created by nearby Eaker Air Force Base. The history of the Little Rock Air Force Base, actually located at Jacksonville, illustrated the importance of the domestic politics of the Cold War.

Other than roads, dams and the construc-

Little Rock Air Force Base

Jacksonville was the site of a fuse and detonation ordnance factory during World War II. The facility was shut down almost immediately after the War and part of the site was occupied by Reasor-Hill, a maker of agricultural chemicals. Local business leader Kenneth "Pat" Wilson, founder and chairman of the First Jacksonville Bank and Trust, was among those in central Arkansas who sensed that a "window of opportunity" existed for Arkansas because of the pent-up consumer demand that was fueling an unprecedented economic boom in the country. At the time, Wilson was thinking more in terms of the former fuse and detonation ordnance becoming a manufacturing complex that would spur the growth of his hometown of 2,000.

A much greater opportunity presented itself in 1951 when downtown Little Rock businessmen Harry W. Pfeifer Jr., Ike Teague and Everett C. Tucker, Jr., heard that the Air Force was looking for a bomber base site. The Arkansas Congressional delegation voiced an interest in having the bomber base in its state, and in October 1951, Brigadier General H. R. Maddux inspected Adams Field at Little Rock as a possible location. He found Adams Field was too small and not expandable but thought the metropolitan area could assimilate an air base.

Pfeifer, Tucker and the Chamber's defense installations committee chaired by Harvey D. Couch, Jr. preferred a location south of Little Rock at Wrightsville or Woodson. Maddux and five other military officers flew into Little Rock on January 7, 1952, to inspect the Wrightsville site, which was accessible only by horseback and mules.

"That wasn't as easy as I thought it would be," Pfeifer said of the horseback ride on returning home, his widow Raida Cohn Pfeifer said. The trip also was disappointing because the entourage found a gas pipeline traversing the site, automatically excluding it from consideration. The local leaders, however, persuaded Maddux to visit the 9,000 acres that had been the World War II fuse and detonator ordnance at Jacksonville, which was occupied at the time by several private industries. Wilson recalled standing on the far side of what became the base and listening as General Maddux proclaimed, "Boys, there's where we are going to build our runway, right in that valley."

Actually, central Arkansas leaders provided 7,500 acres for the base, and Tucker assembled a prospectus detailing the facts and figures on amenities in Little Rock and environs. The Pulaski County Citizens Council, often referred to as the Committee of 100, set a goal of raising $800,000 and achieved it in short order. An Arkansas Democrat newsboy gave 81 cents, all the money he had in his pocket, while Max Moses of Charles S. Stifft & Co., jewelers, left a blank check. In Washington, United States Representative Wilbur Mills proved invaluable. "We practically used Wilbur Mills's office as our headquarters," Wilson commented.

The Missouri Pacific Railway built a spur into the base to deliver jet fuel only to have Phillips Petroleum Company extend a pipeline from Conway, providing a cheaper source and cutting the railroad out. Construction began on the base in 1953, and within two years, ninety buildings were in progress. A severe housing shortage developed, and it took Congress two more years to appropriate money for quarters to house base personnel and their families.

tion of the Little Rock Air Force Base at Jacksonville during the Korean War, the chief tangible federal project was the McClellan-Kerr Navigation System on the Arkansas River, which opened officially in 1971. To make the River navigable for freight year-round from the Mississippi River to the Port of Catoosa near Tulsa, Oklahoma, the United States Army Corps of Engineers built seventeen locks and dams at a cost of $1.2 billion, and named it for its principal proponents, United States Senators John L. McClellan and Robert

Little Rock Air Force Base

Congressional approval allowed the Arkansas Highway Commission to start construction on a $1 million, twelve-mile, four-lane highway from Little Rock to Jacksonville, which was one of several road improvements Governor Sidney McMath had promised.

The officially named Little Rock Air Force Base (LRAFB) was activated on August 1, 1955, as a home to the Strategic Air Command, which was the United States' intercontinental nuclear bomber answer to the perceived threat from the Soviet Union. Missiles followed in 1960 when Titan II intercontinental ballistic sites (commonly called silos) were installed in central and north central Arkansas. At a silo near Searcy in 1963, fifty-three civilians who were making repairs died in an accidental fire.

The economic benefits of the military payroll in the beginning were estimated to be about $1.5 million (the equivalent of two Westinghouse plants). By 1980, the payroll climbed to $80 million. Total base population (military and civilian employees) reached a high of 16,832 in the mid-1980s, but declined as the Cold War became history.

Mercy missions have been an integral part of the LRAFB's work, ranging from a helicopter rescue of a Hot Springs family from a flash flood in 1964 to participating in the formal, organized United States effort in Somalia in 1993.

By 1992, with the downsizing of the military after the collapse of the Soviet Union and the end of the Cold War, total base population was 11,020, but the annual payroll was $188.4 million for military personnel and about $19 million for civilian and contract workers. In addi-tion, nearly 9,400 military retirees with annual income totaling $130 million lived in proximity to the base.

Although Arkansas lost Eaker Air Force Base at Blytheville and the Joint Readiness Training Command at Fort Smith's Fort Chaffee, the Little Rock base survived, largely because of its central location, relative newness, good relations with the city of Jacksonville, long primary runway (11,000 feet) and because it was the nation's only C-130 training center.

LRAFB was the last great industrial triumph for Little Rock's downtown business community. After 1957, business unity was fractured first by the passions of segregation and then by economic changes that arose as the building of interstate highways led to the rise of strip and regional shopping centers, displacing the traditional, close-knit Main Street elite. As a result, the Little Rock Air Force Base became a Jacksonville affair. Local merchants flew oversize American flags in catering to servicemen.

During the height of the Cold War, military bases served as symbols of American patriotism. In contrast to the distrust of the military common in the South after the Civil War and still evident early in the twentieth century, Southerners accepted the premises of the Cold War and endorsed the new militarism. For many males, especially in the rural areas, going into the military became a patriotic duty born of visceral admiration of gallantry and heroism, as well as an escape from the collapsing economy of the family farm. In those towns enriched by the presence of military bases, keeping those jobs took precedence over all other issues.

S. Kerr of Oklahoma. Those who assumed navigation would convert the Arkansas River Valley into another Ruhr Valley were to be disappointed, however. In its first year, 4,294,048 tons of freight were moved on the River. It took thirteen years for that figure to double to 8,521,210 tons in 1984, after which tonnage began slipping and was 7,915,037 in 1987.

Senator McClellan also brought the state a new regional Veterans Administration hospital with one division near the campus of the University of Arkansas for Medical Sciences

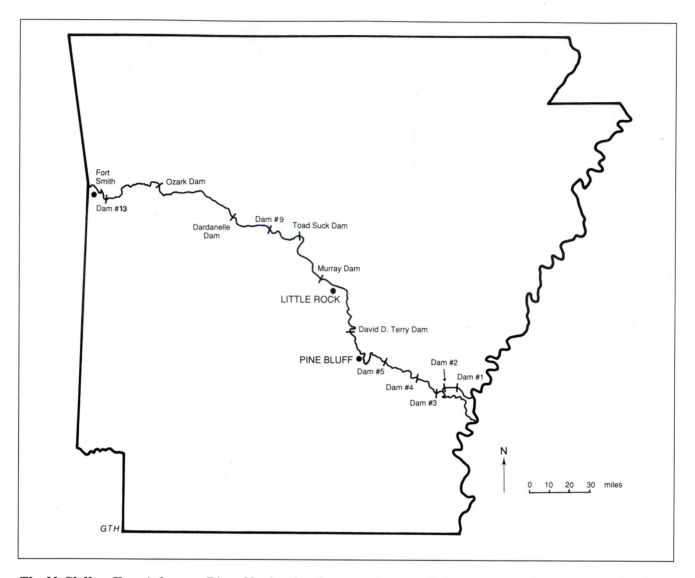

The McClellan-Kerr Arkansas River Navigation System. *Since completion in 1971 the Arkansas River has been navigable for freight year-round from the Mississippi River to Catoosa, Oklahoma.* **Gerald T. Hanson**

Campus and the other at the old Fort Roots facility in North Little Rock. The hospitals were completed in 1981, four years after Senator McClellan's death, and they also were named for him.

Federal aid to Arkansas declined rapidly in three short years in the 1970s with the 1974 defeat of United States Senator J. William Fulbright by Governor Dale Bumpers, the retirement of Wilbur Mills and the 1977 death of Senator McClellan. Thereafter, in the new political and economic climate of the 1980s, the federal government largely ignored Arkansas.

The state made substantial efforts in economic development, but they were never adequate to close the economic gap between it and other states. Amendment 49 to the Arkansas Constitution, adopted in 1958, permitted cities and counties to issue tax-free bonds to aid industrial plant construction. Under Act 9, future rent collected from plants could be used to guarantee bonds. Between 1960 and 1989, Arkansas county and city governments approved 109 bond issues valued at $42,834,350 under Amendment 49 and 867 bond issues valued at $2.2 billion under Act 9.

In addition to luring new industries, existing firms were allowed to use local borrowing power for expansion. The Crossett-based Georgia-Pacific Corporation was the beneficiary of a $75 million bond issue in 1967. Not every firm that came to Arkansas prospered. By 1989, companies had defaulted on twenty-five of the 149 bond issues sponsored by the Arkansas Industrial Development Commission (AIDC); however, new companies, sometimes several smaller ones, could be found to occupy plant space. As part of a larger tax change package in 1978, the federal government put a $10 million cap on tax-free bond issues.

As a measure of the success of industrialization, Arkansas had a higher percentage of its labor force in manufacturing in 1980 than the nation. Although American manufacturing eroded in the wake of the shift to a service-based economy and world competition in the labor market, Arkansas clung to the industrial model. The percentage of Arkansas's labor force engaged in manufacturing stood at 26.5 percent in 1988 compared to 18.4 percent nationally.

Arkansas's economic improvement during the 1960s and 1970s was achieved by attracting labor-intensive industries that needed a large unskilled, and preferably nonunion, labor force. As the mechanization of farming reduced the need for agricultural labor, industries absorbed some of the displaced workers. These plants, however, were precisely the kinds of industry that were hurt by economic developments in the 1980s. Mohawk Tire Company in Helena, a big catch in the 1950s, left in the late 1970s because it declined to retool to meet the competition from steel-belted radial tires. The Singer Sewing Machine Company in Trumann, a fixture for fifty years and the employer of 600, moved its operations to Mexico. A wood products company and firms making shock absorbers and hotel-motel fixtures were found for the abandoned space and replaced 450 of the lost jobs. The strong

dollar in the mid-1980s, coupled with the higher cost of American labor, led to the closing of shoe and textile plants unable to compete with cheap foreign imports. This trend peaked October 19, 1984, on what became known as "Black Friday" when three textile mills in Osceola and Morrilton closed abruptly, throwing 1,800 persons out of work.

Reynolds Metals Company and the Aluminum Company of America (Alcoa), mainstays of Arkansas's post-World War II economy, began phasing out some key operations in Saline, Hot Spring and Clark Counties in the 1980s. Finally, Reynolds shut its reduction plants in Jones Mill and Arkadelphia in 1985, putting 900 out of work, citing the depressed price of aluminum on the world market compared to its high operating costs. Alcoa closed its refinery in the same year with a loss of 350 jobs and reduced its mining operations as the quality of Arkansas bauxite continued to decline. Its chemical division, employing about 150, remained open, and Reynolds continued to operate its cable plant and continuous rolling mill with a combined workforce of 530.

Arkansas also weathered daily depressing reports about another historic industry — the Rock Island Lines, the country's twelfth largest railroad with more than 7,000 miles of track in thirteen states. It entered bankruptcy in 1975 and struggled to stay alive until forced into its grave at 129 years of age in 1980. Parts of the railroad were taken over by thriving competitors, the Missouri-Pacific Lines and the Cotton Belt Route of the Southern Pacific, but other sections became defunct. The thirty-five mile section of the old railroad between Danville and Perry was so vital to the poultry interests in western Arkansas that Continental Grain Company of Chicago leased it from the state Highway and Transportation Department and rehabilitated it with a federal grant.

Among those who mourned the passage of the Rock Island was *Arkansas Gazette* columnist Richard Allin, who wrote:

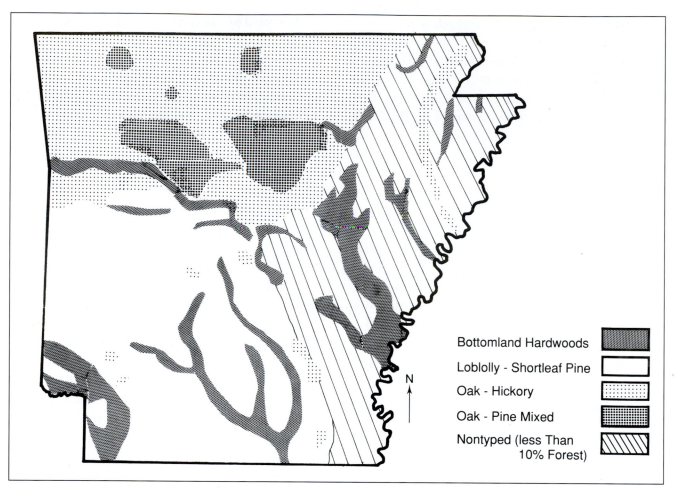

Vegetation Patterns. *Much of eastern Arkansas has had the natural forest removed. Farming has led to the clearing of trees. Along rivers, bottomland hardwood trees exist across the state. The Ozarks are covered with an oak-hickory forest. Pine trees are the dominant forest cover in the Ouachitas and in the Gulf Coastal Plain.* **Gerald T. Hanson**

When I was a mere tad, it was said that Newton County (Jasper) was the only county in Arkansas without railroad service. That, of course, was when many of the Ozark Mountain counties were threaded like pearls on the old May Never Arrive, the Missouri and North Arkansas. Now the counties in Arkansas that are without rail service have multiplied.

The erosion of some traditional manufacturing continued into the late 1980s as Fort Smith's largest employer, the Whirlpool Corporation, began moving some of its assembly lines to Mexico. Later, blaming a lack of orders for its refrigerators and freezers, Whirlpool began reducing its Fort Smith workforce from 5,000 to fewer than 3,000 in 1989.

A flood of higher-quality but cheaper Canadian lumber coincided with a severe national recession to send the Arkansas timber industry into a slump in 1982-84, during which production fell 10 percent. In the long run, however, total production of forest products increased 8 percent over the twenty-year period from 1965 to 1985, from fewer than 500 million cubic feet to 542 million cubic feet. The value of wood flowing from Arkansas's forests in 1985 reached $237 million, about half of it from lands owned by private industry.

Because of its relative stability, the importance of the timber industry declined as the state's economy became more diversified. This was reflected by these figures:

Private forest products industry 1965 1985

	1965	1985
Total employees	41,208	40,225
Jobs per 1,000 workers	69	41
Percentage of total manufacturing employees in Arkansas	31	19
Annual worker earnings (millions)	$188	$738

Arkansas's problems were compounded by the combination of government deregulation and greed that propelled the nation into a savings and loan crisis of monumental proportions, one that led to a $147 billion taxpayer bailout of the industry, with rumors of a $500 billion bailout, or more, yet to come. The crisis hit home early for Arkansas. In December 1986, the Federal Savings and Loan Insurance Corporation (FSLIC) closed and took over the state's second largest thrift, Pine Bluff-based FirstSouth. At least nine other savings and loans were to follow. Liquidation sometimes hit consumers hard when their home equity loans were called abruptly.

Slow and steady growth commands less media attention than the dramatic closing of large industrial plants. In truth, however, many losses of the 1980s were offset in part by the rise in Arkansas of several corporate giants, foreign investment, and the expansion of some existing facilities.

With wonderment and pride, Arkansans watched as Sam Walton of Bentonville built Wal-Mart, a national discount retail business that challenged and surpassed the industry leader, Sears, Roebuck & Co. Walton was listed by *Forbes* magazine as America's richest person, and he was ballyhooed by another business publication as the third wealthiest in the world behind two Japanese.

Arkansans reflected bemused pride as feisty Don Tyson built the business his father John had started in 1930 with a half load of hay and 5 cents in his pocket into the country's largest poultry processor by 1986 and the world's largest by 1989. *Successful Farming* reported in January 1987 that with $1.5 billion in sales, Tyson Foods was the largest "farm" in America. *Fortune* reported in 1985 that Tyson had the highest total return to investors in 1984 at 118.67 percent.

Arkansans learned in 1986 that there was a small quirk in all of this — a quirk in the federal tax code. Designed to help family farmers, the Internal Revenue code allowed any agri-related firm whose stock was controlled 50 percent or more by three or fewer families, to defer paying a large share of its taxes if it stocked up on feed and other inventory at the end of each year. In 1985, Tyson deferred $26 million or about three-quarters of its tax bill, dropping its effective tax rate to 6.1 percent. When President Ronald Reagan and the Congress undertook sweeping tax reform in 1986, Arkansas's United States Senators, Dale Bumpers and David Pryor, fought furiously to keep the golden egg from cracking. Bumpers made no apologies, pointing out that the break existed only so long as Tyson continued to expand.

Tyson was the largest but by no means the only major poultry firm in the state. In fact, the industry had some 84,000 workers (including growers) in 1989, of whom 13,000 were Tyson's, an annual payroll of $1.3 billion and a capital investment of more than $2 billion.

Trucking became big business with Arkansas Best Freight at Fort Smith, J. B. Hunt at Lowell and Arkansas Freightways leading the pack. TCBY grew into a national frozen yogurt chain. Dillard's, with a corporate style as somber as Wal-Mart was exuberant, acquired its way into the big leagues among department stores and built its headquarters on the banks of the Arkansas River

Sam Walton

In 1950, Sam Walton was a dispossessed five and dime store merchant who lost his lease in Newport, Arkansas, and decided to move to Bentonville. In 1984, Forbes magazine reported that he was the second richest man in America. What happened in between was the "Wal-Mart Way."

After relocating in Bentonville, Sam Walton discovered that the public liked discount stores. By offering a large variety of cheap merchandise and emphasizing volume sales, Wal-Mart grew to thirteen stores by 1961. After going public and issuing stock, the company really began to grow, so that by 1987, there were more than 1,000 stores and 160,000 plus employees.

Several key ingredients went into Wal-Mart's success. First founder Sam Walton called all the employees "associates" and used profit-sharing and work incentives to increase productivity. "Everything Wal-Mart does is enthusiastically done," he once commented, and one of his enthusiasms was holding down management costs. Although much of his early merchandise was cheap in quality as well as price, Walton began a "buy-American" campaign in the 1980s when national concern over imports began to be heard in middle America. Increasingly, name brand merchandise began to appear in the stores as Wal-Mart gradually changed from a lower-class to a middle-class shopping clientele. In addition, Sam's Wholesale Clubs made their appearance in the 1980s, and in what was called the "concept of the 1990s," Hypermarts, with three times the space of the average Wal-Mart, were planned for metropolitan areas.

By the 1980s, Sam Walton had become an American folk hero, the Arkansas Horatio Alger. More than 6,000 stockholders and employees attended the 1987 stockholders' meeting in Fayetteville's Barnhill Arena. Federal Transportation Secretary Elizabeth Dole praised Walton as "an entrepreneur of heroic stature" during a session that more nearly resembled a religious revival than a business meeting. Perhaps the greatest miracle of the age was for stockholders. Had one purchased 100 shares of Wal-Mart in October 1970 at the offering price of $16.50 per share, by May 1991 and nine stock-splits later, one would own 25,600 shares selling for approximately $41 a share and worth $1,049,600.

Wal-Mart was not without its critics. Many small-town merchants cannot compete with the arrival of a Wal-Mart. Invariably located on a by-pass or highway outside of town, Wal-Mart was commonly known as a "town-killer." Politically conservative and strongly opposed to unions, Walton paid his Searcy distribution center employees a lower wage rate than comparable employees outside Arkansas.

Until his death in 1992, Walton remained locally popular, drove a pickup truck, and was one of America's least known rich men. He never quit expanding his horizons. In 1987, he announced his intention to have stores coast to coast. Probably the key to his character is a dog story, for Walton had a bird dog named "Ol' Roy." When Ol' Roy died, Walton created a line of dog food commemorating a discount-store owner's best friend and joked that Ol' Roy was better at selling dog food than hunting birds.

Well displayed on Wal-Mart's shelves is Sam Walton, Made in America (New York, 1992); a more balanced view can be found in Sandra S. Vance and Roy V. Scott, "Sam Walton and Wal-Mart Stores, Inc. : A Study in Modern Southern Entrepreneurship," Journal of Southern History, LVIII (May 1992), 231-252.

---

in Little Rock. Systematics and Acxiom, both in central Arkansas, were the high-tech stars in banking computer software and direct mail marketing respectively.

Public relations executive Hugh Pollard

delighted in telling in 1986 about an associate who went to a party in Florida where he met a big-league stock broker. The broker became animated when he learned he was talking to an Arkansan and asked excitedly, "Wal-Mart,

Tyson, Dillard's, TCBY? Good Grief! What's going on back there?"

Pollard went on to write:

Needless to say, my associate returned to the Land of Opportunity with a real sense of pride — pride in our high-profile companies. And a heightened pride in our state. . . . Pride is something we've been rather short on for a long time. Razorback excellence in football and later basketball became a rallying point for the diverse areas of our state, and it was the closest thing we had to unity. But pride in a college athletic program is a slim thing around which to build long-term hope for the people, young and old.

Like the rest of the United States, Arkansas began receiving an influx of foreign investment in the 1970s and 1980s. Globalization of the economy was brought home most forcefully in late 1986 when Nucor-Yamato Steel Company, representing a 49 percent Japanese investment, located a specialty steel mill in agricultural Mississippi County. In return for 600 jobs, the county transformed a gravel road into a paved industrial access route to the plant and the state had to give a sales tax exemption on electricity and natural gas to Nucor, an exemption the 1987 General Assembly had to broaden to keep the playing field level when Razorback Steel at Newport demanded equal treatment.

Nucor-Yamato was not the first major Japanese investment in Arkansas. That came when Sanyo bought 75 percent of a television manufacturer in Forrest City in the late 1970s. The Japanese retained an American-style management team in an early effort to "do as the Romans do," and Sanyo was struggling to stay afloat by the mid-1980s. A Japanese firm also acquired the Excelsior Hotel in Little Rock and was promoting tours for Japanese that included a trip to the Southland dog races in West Memphis. By 1990, Arkansas had thirteen Japanese-owned companies.

In June 1989, Arkansas's industrial community welcomed its first Luxembourg member with word that TrefilARBED would locate a $70 million steel cord plant with 400 jobs at Pine Bluff, a result of a ten-year courtship by Jefferson County and state officials. On the other side of the state, N. V. Bakaert S. A. of Belgium began building a $200 million steel cord plant at Rogers, up the road from its steel wire factory at Van Buren. The TrefilARBED decision brought the number of European industrial investments in Arkansas to fifty-four. Other European investments — at least 129 of them — went into agricultural land. Ten companies had substantial Canadian investment.

On the whole, economic health was spotty, focused almost exclusively in central Arkansas and in what *Arkansas Gazette* editorial page director J. O. Powell dubbed the "string of pearls" — Benton, Washington, Crawford and Sebastian Counties in northwestern Arkansas. With Arkansas State University and a diversified industrial base, Jonesboro was the only oasis in the economic desert of eastern Arkansas, and Camden became southern Arkansas's greatest pocket of prosperity as the privately owned Highland Industrial Park lured defense contractors to the old World War II naval ordnance at East Camden.

Cheap energy was one post-war attraction of the Sun Belt states, and many Arkansas factories, especially the aluminum plants, were heavy power users. Although Arkansas had the reputation of being an oil and gas producing state, it was thoroughly outclassed in this respect by neighboring Oklahoma, Texas and Louisiana. They were energy exporters, but Arkansas was only 43 percent self-sufficient, primarily because of gas fields in the Arkoma Basin of western Arkansas. Oil production in Arkansas had peaked long ago — in 1925 — at 77.5 million barrels; slightly more than 13.6 million barrels were pumped in 1988.

As late as the mid-1950s, oil production was big business in southern Arkansas, and Lion Oil, founded in El Dorado in 1922, was the state's premier oil and gasoline refining company. It then was a $150 million company with a full-service refinery encompassing thousands of miles of pipeline, some 3,000 employees, a $16.5 million payroll, 900 producing wells and nearly 2,000 service stations across the South. The refinery turned out some 30,000 barrels of oil daily. Then the company went through three decades of ownership changes during which it was broken up as some parts were sold. The last Lion Oil station, located at Stifft Station in Little Rock, closed in the 1970s. When the refinery was scheduled for shutdown in 1984 after the bottom dropped out of the world oil market, a Mississippi multimillion dollar conglomerate called Ergon, Inc., teamed up with Arkansas investors to buy the refinery and put it back on its feet. By 1989, employment had resurged to 400 workers and a more efficient plant was producing 50,000 barrels of oil a day. Lion was the only major refinery in the state in 1989. A 7,000-barrel-a-day plant operated in nearby Norphlet and there was an even smaller one in the community of Crystal.

El Dorado also was home to the Murphy Oil Company, a multi-national corporation which drew its crude from points around the world. The company's net income for 1990 was $114 million and included natural gas, oil and real estate development. Its 1991 capital and exploration budget was $363 million.

The Arab oil embargo of 1973 sent the industrialized world reeling into double-digit inflation, but no one was hit harder than farmers who used propane heavily to fire irrigation pumps and the many rural residents who relied on it for cooking and heating. The price of propane soared from 22 cents a gallon before the embargo to 79 in 1989. The state's

woodlands resounded with the buzz of chainsaws as some hard-pressed homeowners returned to an old-fashioned energy source. Independent propane retailers suffered because the government froze propane prices until 1980, but not those the producers charged them.

In the 1960s, natural gas was used to generate 94 percent of the state's electricity. In 1971, however, the Arkansas Public Service Commission shocked AP&L by allowing Arkla, Inc., to cancel its long-term service contracts to the electric utility. AP&L already was building the Southwest's first nuclear power plant near Russellville. The first unit went into operation in December 1974. Meanwhile, AP&L proposed in 1973 to build the state's first coal-fired generating station, a four-unit plant at Redfield (Jefferson County) in conjunction with the electric cooperatives — a major change because of the bitter battles the two had fought from the 1930s through the 1950s. On the advice of the state Pollution Control and Ecology Department, the Commission allowed AP&L to build only two units at Redfield. The other two were built eventually at Newark in Independence County. Southwestern Electric Power Company also received the go-ahead for a coal-fired plant at Gravette (Benton County).

The costs of the stations and the skyrocketing prices of oil in the wake of the Arab embargo plus reduced consumption by a conservation-conscious public put AP&L on the brink of bankruptcy by the late 1970s. Arkansas received another shock when the courts ruled that rate-payers must pay 36 percent of the $3.4 billion that it cost a subsidiary of Entergy Corporation (formerly Middle South Utilities) to build the first unit of the Grand Gulf nuclear plant at Port Gibson, Mississippi, even though the power was not needed for years to come. Entergy was a holding company that included AP&L, Louisiana Power and Light, New Orleans Public Service and Mississippi Power and Light. Entergy halted construction on the second Grand Gulf unit when it was about 35 percent complete, but the utility reached an agreement with state officials in 1989 that its stockholders rather than ratepayers would absorb the $900 million cost.

By 1987, most of AP&L's rates were above the national average:

Cents per kilowatt hour

	Residential rate	Commercial rate	Industrial rate
National average	7.75	7.24	4.88
AP&L	7.98	6.6	5.4

AP&L served about 60 percent of Arkansas's population; 50 to 65 percent of its electricity came at any given time from nuclear generation and the balance from coal.

Arkansas mined coal, but it, too, was in decline, dropping from 2,277,157 tons in 1909 to only 150,000 tons in 1988. On an experimental basis in 1988, AP&L took lignite, a low-grade coal readily available in Arkansas, and blended it with the low-sulfur coal being imported from Wyoming for its Redfield plant. No lignite was mined in the state in 1989 because of litigation problems. Arkansas's lignite, lying in a band from central Arkansas to southwestern Arkansas, was much discussed during the energy crunch of the 1970s, but Sheffield Nelson, then president of Arkla, put the quality of the resource into perspective when he told a legislative committee that its BTU (British Thermal Unit) content made it little better than "high-grade dirt."

Arkansas's coal reserves were estimated at between 400 million and one billion tons. The proximity of the coal to the new McClellan-Kerr Arkansas River Navigation System would have opened exciting prospects, but the resource was anthracite with high sulfur content, and its use was limited by federal and state air quality standards.

Arkansas lost ground in rankings among twenty-nine so-called "high manufacturing" states listed by the Chicago accounting firm of Grant Thornton, dropping to sixteenth in 1989 from ninth in 1988. Slippage of this kind was all right with at least one newspaper editor, who pointed out that the rankings were based on low taxes, weak unions, low worker benefits, cheap energy cost and little business regulation. "[S]tates like Arkansas and South Dakota were always around the top but on economic performance consistently near the bottom. Prosperous states tended to flunk the business climate test," the *Gazette's* Ernest Dumas noted.

The prestigious Stanford Research Institute ranked the states on technology, the adaptability and skill of their people, and availability of capital in 1987. Arkansas and the rest of the Southwest flunked. Stanford found Arkansas ranked forty-fourth on the quality of science and engineering faculties, fiftieth in the percentage of its population with high school diplomas, forty-ninth in spending on public education and fiftieth in the percentage of those sixteen to twenty-four years old who were attending vocational schools or college.

Another obstacle to economic progress in Arkansas was the lack of venture capital. In part, the money was simply not there. In 1988, Arkansas had eighty-four national banks and 172 with state charters. The state's savings and loans, consisting of seven state-chartered institutions and twenty-seven federally insured thrifts, had assets of $6 billion in 1983 and only $6.35 billion in 1988.

More important than dollar amounts were attitudes. Journalist Harry Ashmore recalled that when he moved to Little Rock shortly after World War II, bankers were so conservative that they would only loan money to people who did not need it. In agricultural regions, banks loaned money to farmers in the spring and did little business for the rest of the year. Until a number of wildcat bankers entered the picture with deregulation in the mid-1980s, Arkansas attitudes were best summarized by

Clemson University professors William F. Sheirer and James C. Hite at a conference in Memphis in 1982:

> Upon one thing all observers agree. . . . the poverty of the South has greatly influenced policy and perceptions. What happens is that the presence of chronic poverty serves to deaden initiative and reinforce conservative attitudes on property rights. When relatively little is owned, people maintain a strong hold on what they have and tend not to risk losing that on innovative schemes.

The traditional approach to economic growth, snaring out-of-state plants with giveaways rather than fostering home-grown businesses and bolstering existing ones, received a scathing indictment from the Winthrop Rockefeller Foundation in a 1983 report entitled, *Twelve Obstacles to Economic Development.* Other negative factors cited included the state usury limit, which was raised by Amendment 60 in 1982, but was still restrictive; the low severance tax on natural resources (particularly gas) that cost the state at least $12 million in lost revenues, and a woefully deficient education system. In a 1987 follow-up, the Foundation reported some obstacles had been removed with adoption of four-year terms for constitutional officers, increased public awareness of the importance of education, an upgraded transportation system and better authority for local government financing. In other categories, the Foundation said Arkansas had regressed, especially in higher education and in the equity of its tax system. It called for an overhaul of the state Constitution. There was no action on its recommendation.

Promise and Problems in Agriculture

The 1970s and 1980s saw profound changes in Arkansas agriculture. Generations of school children had recited "cotton, corn and rice are Arkansas's main cash crops," but that was no longer true. Central to the change was the decline in the dominance of cotton. Instead of being grown in every county in the state as in 1900, cotton by 1988 was being cultivated in countable amounts in only twenty-five counties, most of them in the Delta, with production ranging from 270 bales in Little River County in southwestern Arkansas to 150,900 bales in Mississippi County. Mississippi County usually ranked first in cotton production, and Blytheville claimed to be the world's "Cotton Capital."

As late as 1962, cotton supplied as much as a third of Arkansas's farm income, but that dropped to 20 percent by the end of the 1980s. Cotton acreage and cotton revenue dropped steadily after World War II:

Cotton acreage	No. of bales	Total revenue
1948		
2,300,000	2,000,000	$295,000,000
1988		
675,000	1,000,000	265,000,000

Other crops took cotton's place. Soybeans led, reaping $618.2 million in 1985 to $516.8 million for rice. Soybeans, rice and wheat acreage increased dramatically in the postwar years. The long growing season permitted wheat to be double-cropped with soybeans.

1988 acreage	
Soybeans	3,250,000
Rice	1,200,000
Wheat	1,100,000
Cotton	675,000
Grain sorghum	360,000
Oats	35,000

Fish farming, totally dependent on pure groundwater, became a sizable industry in the Lonoke, Des Arc and Pine Bluff areas in the

Riceland Rice, Jonesboro *(photographer unknown, ca. 1965) Towering like medieval cathedrals over their towns, these grain elevators suggest the power of farmer-owned marketing cooperatives in modern Arkansas farming. The Jonesboro Grain Drying Cooperative, pictured here, had storage capacity for 3,000,000 bushels of rice; by 1989, the facility had been enlarged to hold 7,000,000 bushels. In 1988, Arkansas accounted for 40 percent of all rice grown in the United States and ranked first among the states in its production.* **Arkansas State University Museum**

1980s. Catfish farming brought in $22 million in 1988 while minnows for bait were even more profitable at $25 million to $28 million.

Arkansas also ranked number one in broiler chicken production, number four in turkeys and was among the top ten states in egg production. Most Arkansans did not realize that the value of all cattle and calves produced in the state in 1987 totaled $384 million. The value of hog production, which stood at $103.9 million in 1987, was expected to soar in the 1990s because of hundreds of new "pig parlors" both Tyson Foods and Cargill, Inc., installed with contract growers in northwest-

ern and southwestern Arkansas and the Arkansas River Valley in the late 1980s.

Livestock, which includes poultry, was about twice as important to Arkansas's economy as row crops. Preliminary cash receipts from farm marketings in 1987 totaled $2.9 billion. Of this, $1.9 billion or 66 percent was generated by livestock and livestock products with the remainder coming from the sale of crops.

Growing illegal marijuana replaced brewing illegal moonshine as a principal cash crop in the remote reaches of the Ozarks and Ouachitas in the 1970s and 1980s. The Arkansas

State Police, federal agents and local law enforcement officers pulled up and burned 118,352 plants in 1988 with each mature plant having a value of $1,000. Arkansas ranked fifth for marijuana-growing arrests and fourteenth among the states in the number of plants destroyed. What percentage of the crop was destroyed? State Police Lieutenant Doug Williams confessed there was no way of knowing.

The same combination of domestic policies and world economic forces that upset the industrial order created chaos in world commodity markets, and America's farm belt slipped into its worst depression since the 1930s during the first half of the 1980s. When generally high farm prices prevailed during the 1970s and the talk was of food shortages, farmers cleared new land, bought more acreage at inflated prices and invested heavily in equipment. To increase yield they expanded irrigation so that it covered some two million of the 7,500,000 acres harvested in 1982, and used pesticides extensively.

Over-production by the late 1970s led to falling world market prices, and the strong American dollar hurt exports. A ban on agricultural sales to Cuba especially hurt rice farmers. In 1979, Arkansas farmers reported a net income of $1 billion. The most severe drought on record in 1980 contributed to losses of $199 million, and despite better weather in 1981, losses totaled more than $300 million. Cash receipts were down 16 percent in 1983 as area banks involved with farm loans engaged in frantic struggles to stay afloat. A series of bank failures, mergers and reorganizations followed, and farmers found it increasingly difficult to finance their next year's crop. Forty-five farm implement dealers failed during the period and others were bought and merged, leaving only between seventy-five and 100 doing business in the state by 1989. At least thirteen grain elevators went into bankruptcy, sometimes taking the farmers' grain with them, and local retail sales declined.

Although fresh produce continued to find ready markets, the value of Arkansas's peach crop nosedived from nearly $5.5 million in 1979 to $1.6 million in 1987. Bradley County was once renowned for its pink tomatoes, but other less tasty but more shippable tomatoes were substituted. Hempstead County remained famous for its watermelons. Strawberries were a long-time staple, and blueberries began to make a strong appearance by the mid-1980s. Spinach disappeared from Arkansas fields by 1980, the victim of disease, but University of Arkansas research scientists made it possible for the crop to make a comeback try in the Arkansas River Valley in the late 1980s. Most fruit farmers complained about labor shortages. Peaches in the 1980s went unpicked in St. Francis County even though the county had the highest unemployment rate in the state.

Also beginning to blossom in the 1980s was a wine industry, even though the state was next-to-last in wine consumption. The industry took root in the state because hard-working German, Swiss and Italian immigrants settled in northwestern Arkansas where the climate and soil turned out to be excellent for raising grapes. Grapes were being produced in seventeen counties by 1989, but no one was keeping statistics on how much wine was being made or its value. Al Wiederkehr, head of the state's largest and best-known winery at Altus, noted that an entire year's production from his business probably would fit into just one of Gallo's storage tanks in California.

Land prices both rose and fell spectacularly from 1978 to 1987.

Average value per farm acre in Arkansas

1978	$619
1982	1,104
1983	972
1987	634

Despite the steep drop, Arkansas farmland value in 1987 was still well above the national average of $548 per acre.

The depression brought renewed concern for the survival of the so-called "family farm," but records show that the earlier mechanization of agriculture had been a far greater threat. Bad times were cushioned by the more varied crop base and rapid action by the federal government to prop up prices. Government payments were a good barometer of the economic woes of farmers.

Government payments to Arkansas farmers

1970	$87,700,000
1980	34,500,000
1982	119,300,000
1983	290,800,000
1984	209,500,000
1985	328,700,000
1987	313,700,000

Arkansas had 218,000 farms in 1910, and the number peaked at 254,000 in 1933 and 1934 during the height of the Great Depression. The number of farms slipped to 188,000, with an average size of 102 acres in 1950. By 1988, the figure fell to 47,000 farms and an average size of 319 acres.

The volatile 1980s convinced some eastern Arkansas farmers like Bart Turner of Marion and Jim Burton of Newport that they would have to learn to grow and sell high-value vegetables commercially for the fresh produce market if they were going to survive. However, most truck farming was in northwestern Arkansas. There was little financing and no infrastructure such as packing sheds and a marketing capability in eastern Arkansas. Convinced that these "alternative crops" could salvage eastern Arkansas farmers, the Clinton administration led Arkansas State University and the University of Arkansas Agricultural Experiment Station into a major initiative to help them by establishing a nonprofit marketing firm.

The slow decline in the value of the Ameri-can dollar in the late 1980s brought some relief to farmers, and cotton, soybeans and rice staged modest comebacks. Even so, Arkansas's farm sector faced a troubled future.

Promise and Problems in State Government

As the post-war economy boomed in the United States, Arkansas's per capita income rose slowly but steadily from a paltry 56 percent of the national average in 1950 to 62 percent in 1960 until it stalled at 77 percent in 1974 in the wake of double-digit inflation and stagnation spawned by the energy crisis. Then per capita income started to slide — down from 75 percent of the national average in 1982 to 74 percent in 1988 although the actual per capita dollars earned yearly grew to $12,147 in the six-year period. Throughout the post-war era, Arkansas played musical chairs near the bottom of the per capita income scale with such states as Alabama, West Virginia, Utah and Mississippi.

The early 1970s were the halcyon years: in 1974, the state unemployment rate was 5.2 percent, actually below the national rate of 5.6 percent. By early January 1983, Arkansas's unemployment rate had skyrocketed to 12.8 percent, and sixty-three of its seventy-five counties had unemployment rates of more than 10 percent. St. Francis County's rate eventually came dangerously close to 30 percent. The state's unemployment rate in June 1989 was 8.4 percent, more than three percentage points above the nation's. As always and in tune with the nation, minorities bore the brunt of joblessness in Arkansas. Their unemployment rate stood at 14.9 percent in June 1989, and it was a whopping 31.4 percent for black teen-agers.

With President Lyndon B. Johnson's "Great Society" and "War on Poverty," the federal government dramatically expanded domestically during the 1960s, but so did Arkansas's, and both flush and hard times

Mohawk Tire Dedication in Helena *(photographer unknown, ca. 1954) Governor Orval Faubus (holding the tire on the left), Winthrop Rockefeller (left), first chairman of the Arkansas Industrial Development Commission, and other dignitaries gather for what seemed to be a big industrial catch for Arkansas during the early 1960s. Unfortunately, the company decided against making radial tires, had problems with race relations and is now closed.* **Arkansas History Commission**

were reflected in the growth of state revenues and expenditures.

Orval Faubus, who served as governor from 1955 through 1966, benefited from a 1-cent sales tax increase early in his administration and a period of great national prosperity to swell state revenues. Many of Arkansas's social services entered the modern period and became firmly established during this period.

Faubus was followed as governor by Winthrop Rockefeller (1967-70), the first Republican governor since Reconstruction, who had many ambitious plans for expansion of state services. However, he was unable to get his tax program passed by a hostile legislature that feared the advent of a true two-

party system would result in Republican opponents for their seats.

Dale Bumpers, a reform Democrat, defeated Rockefeller in his attempt for a third term. At the beginning of his tenure (1971-74), he persuaded the legislature to revise the state income tax rates upward, and this coincided with a cornucopia of federal aid programs and another wave of national prosperity. As a result, total state revenues from all sources jumped 33 percent in two years and topped the billion-dollar mark for the first time. Bumpers enjoyed surpluses in state money, but his administration added new state services such as community colleges, kindergartens and free high school textbooks.

Shoe Workers in Jonesboro *(photographer unknown, ca. 1965) The shoe industry was a major employer for women in Arkansas until competition from cheaper foreign labor closed many factories in the 1970s.* **Arkansas State University Museum**

David Pryor (1975-78), the next governor, had Bumpers's inclinations to expand social services, but had the misfortune of encountering stagnant revenues because of a slowdown in the economy and declining federal aid dollars. He was forced to be little more than a caretaker governor.

Bill Clinton served one term as governor (1979-80), was defeated for reelection by Republican Frank White, and then regained his seat by beating White in 1982. He was in office through the rest of the 1980s and was re-elected for a fifth time in 1990. Under Clinton's leadership, the legislature increased the state sales tax by 1 percent in 1983 and half a percent in 1991, and gasoline

taxes also went up significantly during his administration. Most of the new revenue went into education, particularly for a long list of new education standards and a $4,000 salary increase for teachers.

Some of this increase in sales tax was offset by a large number of tax exemptions for various narrow business purposes passed with the influence of well-financed lobbyists. Another large setback in state revenues came with the sharp cuts in federal aid during the Ronald Reagan administration (1981-88). In fiscal 1981, Arkansas received $717.75 million in federal aid. The next year the figure plummeted to $612.6 million and did not exceed the pre-Reagan level until fiscal 1985. Between

1980 and 1989, federal aid dropped from 25.8 percent of total state and local government expenditures in Arkansas to 17.1 percent.

Realizing that President Reagan was planning to do away with the no-strings-attached giveaway to local governments called revenue sharing, the 1981 General Assembly — under Republican Frank White — gave Arkansas's cities and counties their first opportunity to enact 1-cent sales taxes. As of April 1, 1989, forty-four counties had adopted a sales tax by votes of their residents. One hundred and sixteen cities also had a 1-cent sales tax, and in fiscal 1988, the localities collected $129.7 million from this source.

In addition, most school districts had to increase their property tax millages to meet new education standards. Failure to meet the standards would result in consolidation of a school district with a neighbor. Numerous small districts voted themselves huge percentage increases in their taxes in order to survive, as well as to offer increased educational services to their children.

In spite of this unprecedented wave of state and local taxes, by fiscal 1987 Arkansas was only forty-eighth among the states in the amount of state and local taxes paid per capita. However, even Mississippi made a huge leap forward in the 1980s to thirty-ninth. Other states also were feeling the crunch of educational reform and the loss of federal funds, and they were making similar demands on their citizens. Of every $100 in personal income, Arkansans paid $9.42 in state and local taxes. Only Missouri ($9.11) and New Hampshire ($8.99) ranked lower.

In terms of ability to pay taxes based on income, Arkansas ranked thirty-fifth among the states in 1987. The state was high on "sin" taxes, ranking ninth in levies on cigarettes and twentieth on alcohol, but its fees were 91.4 percent of the national average, its corporate income taxes were 87.8 percent of the United States average, its property taxes only 57.9 percent of the national average and its

corporate license (franchise or privilege) taxes a mere 17.9 percent of the national average. "Texas loves to boast that it doesn't have an income tax, but what they don't talk about is their corporate license tax — they get $1 billion in revenues from that in a year," a Legislative Council statistician said scornfully. As for Arkansas, taxes weighed most heavily on those least able to pay and state tax laws were loaded with exemptions for special interests.

Promise and Problems in Cultural Modernization

Those persons embarrassed by Arkansas's historic national image believed that economic progress would pave the way for cultural modernization, thereby ridding Arkansas of its backward image. As in the past, public relations professionals were busy. Little Rock's Chamber of Commerce boasted in nationwide newspaper advertisements that "We're not New York, but neither are our prices." Using a base of 100, the American Chamber of Commerce Research Association said that in late 1988, the cost of living was 91.5 in Bentonville, 88.7 in Fayetteville and 88.2 in Jonesboro, compared to 160.3 in Nassau-Suffolk, New York and 127.1 in San Diego, California.

The state was active in promotion. The AIDC spent $3 million in 1985 on nine weekly full-page advertisements in *The Wall Street Journal*. Midway through the campaign, *The Journal* printed a map of the lower Mississippi River Valley on the front page and mislabeled Arkansas as Missouri, graphically illustrating one aspect of the problem.

In reality, national modernization trends were apparent in Arkansas. One could find restaurants in Arkansas offering French, Italian, German, Japanese, Middle-Eastern and several varieties of Chinese food and not all were located in Little Rock. State cultural institutions such as the Arkansas Symphony Orchestra, the Arkansas Arts Center, the

Arkansas Repertory Theatre, the Arkansas Opera Theater, Ballet Arkansas and the Little Rock Zoo had come into being or expanded greatly over the last two decades, and the construction of a $15 million Wildwood Center for the Performing Arts began in 1990 in western Pulaski County. More than a quarter of the state was served by public radio stations, although the legislature rejected plans to establish a state network similar to Mississippi's. Arkansas Educational Television Network (AETN), though chronically underfunded, occasionally hounded by displeased legislators, and plagued by recurring leadership voids, reached almost all of the state's counties from its studios in Conway and regional satellite stations.

Most cultural institutions in Arkansas were seriously undercapitalized. The most conspicuous example of weakness was the public library system. The first statewide movement for libraries began with federal assistance during the Depression. In 1940, libraries achieved the passage of Amendment 30 to the Arkansas Constitution authorizing a one-mill municipal tax. In 1946, Amendment 38 allowed counties to pass a one-mill library tax. These were great victories at the time, but the one-mill limit eventually became a source of weakness, giving libraries only the barest support. Voters in 1992 approved a constitutional amendment allowing the millage to be increased up to five mills after local approval at election. Federal funds raised standards, and state support increased during the Great Society days of the 1960s. By 1989, local library support varied from region to region.

Libraries were hit especially hard by the post-1973 energy crisis because both book and energy prices rose faster than income. Amendment 59 to the Arkansas Constitution, which mandated reassessment of property, also forced millage rollbacks if tax increases exceeded 10 percent, causing some libraries to lose money. Local campaigns to restore or raise the library tax often encountered strong resistance. In 1989, only nine counties were collecting full one-mill real and personal property taxes for the libraries serving them. Another twenty counties levied a full one-mill library tax against real property only. Voters in 1992 approved a constitutional amendment allowing voters to increase the millage up to five mills.

Excluding state and federal aid, Arkansas localities spent nearly $7.8 million to support their libraries in 1985, a per-capita expenditure of $3.41. This made Arkansas rank last among forty-five states that reported their spending that year. Mississippi ranked thirty-ninth at $5.65.

THE FOUR R'S AND ONE S OF ARKANSAS

The dominant theme of Southern history since the Civil War has been the surprising strength traditional folk culture has shown in withstanding the onslaughts of national modernization. The enduring features of folk culture contain the seeds of controversy. In elite or business circles throughout the century, there has been a deliberate effort to suppress or ignore Arkansas's salient features, even though many of the elite themselves have been imperfectly modernized. Despite local efforts and the impact of television and air-conditioning, strong elements of traditionalism remain. But most significantly for history, the South has been identified with the survival of four R's and one S: rurality, political reaction, religion, racism and sexism. Arkansas history always has been a battleground over these issues. During the Reagan era, traditionalism took heart from national political trends.

THE ENDURANCE OF RURALITY

Beginning in 1940, Arkansas lost population until the 1960s when the outflow of whites reversed. Blacks continued to become a smaller percentage of the population through

Census year	Total population	white	black	black percent	other
1940	1,949,387	1,445,084	482,578	24.7	725
1950	1,909,511	1,481,507	436,639	22.3	1,365
1960	1,786,272	1,395,703	388,787	21.7	1,782
1970	1,923,295	1,565,915	325,445	16.9	4,935
1980	2,286,435	1,890,322	373,768	16.3	22,345
1990	2,350,725	1,944,744	373,912	15.9	32,069

the 1990 census. Arkansas increased its overall population 18.9 percent in the 1970s, but this large growth rate dropped to 2.9 percent in the 1980s. The 1990 census showed 39 counties gained population but 36, mostly in the eastern and southern parts of the state where the bulk of the existing black population lived, continued to show losses.

The Rural Invasion of the Towns

The transformation in Arkansas life since 1940 affected how people lived as well as where they lived. Families moved primarily from farms into town, and by 1990, 51.6 percent of the state's population was classified as urban, living in communities of 2,500 or more. Within counties, towns grew at the expense of unincorporated areas. Many crossroads villages disappeared across the Ozarks and the Ouachitas. Farmers often sought to keep their land while working in town. This put new strains on the family because the wife often held a job, too. Abandoned farm houses sometimes were used for storage, but those in the Delta, especially the once-ubiquitous sharecropper cabins, were torn down and the sites planted in soybeans and rice.

Rural folks often carried their traditional ways into the urban environment. It became common to see cars, trucks and other equipment parked on what middle-class families considered to be the front lawn. City ordinances banning the burning of trash and the keeping of livestock often were ignored in the smaller cities. Some rural immigrants fought any progress that involved raising taxes, and many settled on the outskirts of cities and vigorously fought any annexation efforts. City ordinances regulating mobile homes occasioned fierce battles.

Given the harsh economics of the early 1980s and the growing isolation of rural Arkansas, some wondered why anyone elected to remain in the state's smallest communities. They did so by choice, according to Marshall newspaper editor Edward Tudor, who explained:

> They are hesitant to leave because of the city traffic, the much faster pace of life in the cities, and the fact that family, friends and community mean more to them than a new beginning in a strange place.

The Retirement Communities

Even as native Arkansans were moving to town, Northern immigrants began discovering retirement opportunities in Arkansas in the 1950s. Not all Americans wanted "sand and sun," and for those seeking four seasons, but a mild winter with sunshine, John A. Cooper offered Cherokee Village in Sharp County, Bella Vista in Benton County and Hot Springs Village in Garland County. These and Horseshoe Bend on the White River, Fairfield Bay on Greers Ferry Lake, and several smaller ventures competed in offering low taxes, freedom from crime, clean air and recreational activities. Better educated than the average Arkansan, the newcomers supported some forms of modernization. They raised the local per capita income and added a modernist element to local elections (several Ozark counties voted "wet" because of them) and volunteered for local charities.

On the other hand, because most retirees were without school-age or young adult children living with them, it was tough to sell the immigrants on education millages. For example, the major retirement community at Mountain Home rejected a proposed community college in 1974. Nearby Harrison in Boone County — less influenced by retirees — snapped it up with a local millage election. The immigrants also tended to care little about state affairs. Generally Republican in politics, they wholeheartedly supported Republican United States Congressman John Paul Hammerschmidt in northwestern Arkansas. Retirees voting straight-ticket Republican in 1984 turned out a woman state senator, Vada Sheid, even though she was a conservative Democrat and in age was "one of them."

Between retirees and the growing Reagan conservatism permeating the affluent suburbs in western Pulaski County, Republican strength reached a post-Reconstruction high in 1989 of eleven in the state House of Representatives and four in the Senate. Locally, most Republican officeholders were still to be found in northwestern Arkansas, with Benton County being the stronghold, though Saline County elected a Republican sheriff and White County a Republican county judge in 1988. The Party had thirty-four justices of the peace serving on county quorum courts in 1989.

The Northern immigrant's desire to put urban values in a rural setting and the retired farmer's effort to preserve rural living in town were manifestations of the age and found numerous examples in Arkansas life, including the lyrics to country music songs, local political animosities and family conflicts.

The "Back to the Land" Movement

During the late 1960s and early 1970s, some young Americans were lured to a rural existence because of philosophical objections to modernization. This "back to the land" movement was most evident in the Ozarks and typically called young people from outside the region who were indiscriminately called "hippies." Some came as individuals or in family units, but groups and communes also were found. These newcomers often aroused bitter hatred and old prejudices against subsistence farming, including charges that they were Soviet agents, committed sinful sexual practices, and were drug users. Those in the first wave in the late 1960s sought to raise their own food organically and market the surplus. Failing in this, some left, but those who stayed often had to find outside employment. Their relations with older settlers mellowed in time. "They are learning to adapt the old ways to the new," one speaker noted at the Ozark In-Migration Conference at Eureka Springs in 1976, and added, "They plant by the signs, never whittle toward themselves, never spit toward the wind — and heat their homes with solar panels."

The mix of "hippies," retirees and new factories made the Ozarks the fastest-growing section of the state. Between 1960 and 1975, Sharp County led the state with a population gain of 68 percent. Washington County grew by 60 percent, followed by Cleburne County with 53 percent, and even remote Newton County, which had lost population since 1900, added 14 percent and a pizza parlor. The 1980 census recorded a 78 percent increase for Baxter County in the 1970s, largely because of Mountain Home. The state growth rate overall dropped from 18.9 percent in the 1970s to 2.9 percent in the 1980s.

The lack of job and recreational opportunities, white racism and the over-abundance of mosquitoes were all cited as factors in the simultaneous loss of population in the Delta

Houseboat in Winter on the White River, Near Des Arc. *(ca. 1954) This serene river scene does not reveal how difficult life could be for those who made their living on the rivers of eastern Arkansas. Houseboats like this were cold in the winter and surrounded by mosquitoes in the summer. Most people who lived on riverboats year-round were hardy and independent long before anyone ever heard of the "back to the land" movement.* **Publisher's Collection**

where the main streets of some towns were desolate ghosts of prosperity. Helena's historic homes and businesses awaited discovery by preservationists from outside the state, and in 1986, it was possible to buy a well-preserved, double-brick Victorian cottage with a slate roof in Cotton Plant for as little as $10,000. Belated federal and regional attention was focused on the Delta in the late 1980s, and one by-product was the state's creation of the Delta Cultural Center in Helena. Opened in 1990 in a former railroad depot, the Center offered the prospect of promoting awareness of the Delta's cultural contributions to the state.

Rurality and Environmentalism

Protection of the environment was another controversial issue in Arkansas, one that challenged head-on the traditional ways of rural folks and divided modernizers.

The ecological battle started early in Arkansas when federal forestry officials tried in the early 1900s to stop the annual practice of burning the woods. It continued when urban sportsmen attempted to enforce hunting and fishing seasons in order to rebuild wildlife populations in the early 1940s. It shifted in the 1960s and later to a struggle to preserve free-flowing streams, to control and eliminate the disposal of hazardous and other wastes and to keep the national forests from being clear-cut and converted into pine plantations.

As America entered the age of disposable bottles and plastic wrapping, trash became a growing problem. The traditional methods consisted of dumping large items in gullies or streams and burning the rest in open dumps. At Williford in Sharp County, which for years held an old fiddlers' contest, the highway right-of-way south of town was a continually burning dump. Arkansas streams, which the state promoted to Northern tourists as pure and beautiful, often were repositories for old tires, beer cans and garbage. State and federal laws eventually were promulgated, and under duress from the state Pollution Control and Ecology Department, communities began establishing expensive monitored sanitary landfills. No resident wanted a landfill in the neighborhood, and hot political battles erupted. Even though Arkansans did not mind littering their own highways and streams, they certainly didn't want garbage from New York City and other states to be buried in "The Natural State" as proposed, and residents of Benton in Saline County and Chicot County voters told their public officials this in no uncertain terms when it was proposed in the late 1980s.

Hazardous wastes were another by-product of the industrialization process. Vertac, a pesticide manufacturer at Jacksonville, was the focus of the most publicity because its site and others in the city were contaminated by TCDD, commonly called dioxin, which was the most toxic man-made chemical compound known to scientists. By 1989, the federal Environmental Protection Agency had placed ten sites in Arkansas on its national list of locations to be cleaned up through its "Superfund."

Dam construction was another aspect of the environmental debate. The first major impoundments were built by AP&L on the

Hardwood Logs *(Gordon Smith, 1984) The size of these logs can be estimated by comparing them to the height of the woman, who is five feet and two inches tall. Bottomland hardwood forests such as the ones in Prairie County that produced these logs were a rare Arkansas resource by 1970 as most level land had been cleared for farming. This resulted in loss of environmental diversity, wildlife habitat and degradation of streams.* **Publisher's Collection.**

upper Ouachita River in the 1920s. These lakes, Hamilton and Catherine, had been joined by the 1970s by three large lakes on the White River — Norfork, Beaver and Bull Shoals — plus eight more in southwestern Arkansas and Greers Ferry Lake on the Little Red River, all built by the Army Corps of Engineers. Not including the pools created by locks and dams on the Arkansas River, Corps-built lakes covered 244,240 acres in Arkansas, of which Bull Shoals at 71,240 acres was the largest.

Some of the lakes supplied electricity but were primarily for flood control. Many farmers lost their ancestral lands, and in the case of Beaver Lake, a whole community disappeared under water. As these farmers and rural communities were being submerged, an entire leisure industry appeared that benefited adjacent towns such as Hot Springs, Cotter, Heber

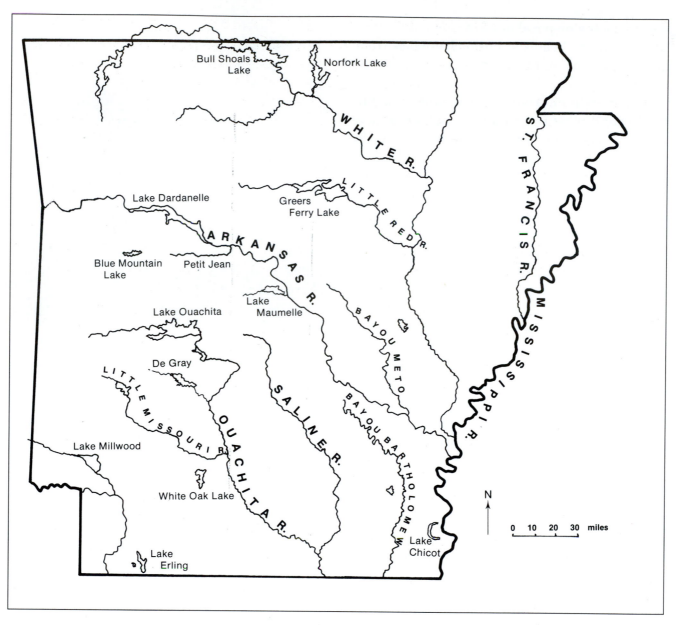

***Arkansas Lakes and Rivers.* Gerald T. Hanson**

Springs, Mountain Home and Rogers. Lakeside properties became prime real estate investments, and the northern lakes attracted many retirees. Lake Hamilton had boat traffic jams and a sewage problem caused in part by too many septic tanks. Later Corps lakes were protected from intense shoreline development by buffer strips that the government acquired. Promoters during the 1960s and 1970s encouraged the Corps to dam other free-flowing streams.

The Buffalo River was one of the major undammed streams in Arkansas. Running through the heart of the Ozarks, the Buffalo presented some of the most spectacular scenery in the state and was used heavily by fishermen and canoeists. The Corps planned a series of dams on the River, and promoters at Marshall formed the Buffalo River Improvement Association to support the dam. A map published in 1962 by *Reader's Digest* showed Lone Rock Lake already in place.

Dr. Neil Compton, M. D., of Bentonville created the Ozark Society to focus national attention to fight for preserving the Buffalo River. After floating the River, environmentalist William O. Douglas, a United States Supreme Court justice, called it "worth fighting to the death to preserve," and Interior Secretary Stewart L. Udall referred to it as a "national treasure." Painter Thomas Hart Benton, who often used Arkansas scenes in his internationally famous murals, added his endorsement to the campaign.

Some of the dam's supporters retaliated, and people floating the River were harassed. One party of lawyers and real estate agents, mistaken for Ozark Society members, was raided by local lawmen and deprived of its liquor. Other floaters encountered barbed wire and threats of physical abuse.

The running battle over the Buffalo eventually became a political issue. All Arkansas congressmen supported the dam, but Senators John L. McClellan and J. William Fulbright endorsed National Park Service status for the River. Perhaps the decisive blow to the dam was delivered when Governor Orval E. Faubus, born and reared in the hills of Madison County, sided with the environmentalists. Modern man, he said, needed a place where:

> [F]rogs of every size and kind join with unnumbered katydids to make the summer night musical for the tired camper seeking rest from social and political problems and the revered market place.

Congress made the Buffalo a national river in 1972.

Efforts to save the Cossatot River in the southwest proved less successful, though the state later acquired 4,230 acres along its wildest section as a park and natural area. Both Lee Creek and the North Fork of the Illinois Bayou near Russellville later were threatened by municipal water needs, but plans to dam the Strawberry River in northeastern Arkansas were shelved.

A second major controversy erupted in the Delta. Almost all of the region's streams had been ditched for drainage, and swampy wild areas were becoming converted to farmland. One partial exception was the lower Cache River and its principal tributary, Bayou DeView. By 1960, the upper Cache had become a series of barren drainage ditches that dumped water on the middle and lower sections, causing flooding during the rainy seasons. The channelization of the middle and lower sections would have allowed area farmers to clear and farm more land but at the cost of destroying one of the nation's prime duck wintering areas.

In the early 1970s, Pratt Remmel, Jr., organizer and president of the Arkansas Ecology Center at Little Rock, and his research assistant, Gale S. Eddins, and Richard S. Arnold, a Texarkana lawyer later appointed to the United States Eighth Circuit Court of Appeals, persuaded the national Environmental Defense Fund to challenge the project in court. The Arkansas Game and Fish Commission and the Arkansas Wildlife Federation entered the litigation on the side of the environmentalists. Senator Dale Bumpers and Dr. Rex Hancock, a Stuttgart dentist, also took up the fight and continued it for a decade in behalf of duck hunters. Although problems of local flooding and habitat destruction remain, the channelization plan was abandoned in 1981. The Cache controversy represented the first time that a state agency had joined with private groups in a modern environmental controversy and thus set an important precedent. The United States Fish and Wildlife Service targeted the middle and lower Cache River as a national wildlife refuge. It and The Nature Conservancy, a national private non-profit organization, began acquiring land toward this goal in the mid-1980s.

Balancing competing interests remained a problem. The publicity about the Buffalo

River soon resulted in wall-to-wall canoes and pollution problems. The National Park Service was undecided about whether it wanted to preserve the Park as a natural setting or whether evidence of historic development would be preserved. At first, the Park Service bought up the land and closed roads to allow the area to revert to wilderness. This policy was reversed in 1985, and limited land use and preservation of older buildings, many of them log houses, was permitted.

Arkansas had other successful environmental projects as well. In 1973, during the Bumpers administration, state legislation was signed into law creating the Arkansas Natural Heritage Commission to acquire and preserve unusual, threatened examples of the state's early-day environments — prairies, caves, glades, tupelo gum swamps, cliffs and seeps — with emphasis on protecting endangered plant and animal species. By 1989, the Commission had acquired forty-two natural areas totaling 12,000 acres. In 1987, the General Assembly doubled the real estate transfer tax and earmarked revenues from the increase, projected to be about $4 million annually, for protecting the cultural, historical and natural heritage of Arkansas.

In 1969, Weyerhaeuser Company bought nearly one million acres in southwestern Arkansas and southeastern Oklahoma and proceeded to clear-cut or strip all vegetation from thousands of acres at a time and replant them with pine seedlings. Although riled, Arkansans generally felt helpless to stop this because the land was privately owned. In 1985, the Ouachita National Forest released a long-range management plan in which even-aged management carried out exclusively through clear-cutting was proposed. Fearing that Weyerhaeuser's "tree farm mentality" was slopping over into the Forest, various conservation groups and a few individuals appealed the plan and forced it to be revised. The new version reduced clear-cutting by 50 percent and placed a substantial portion of the

reserve off-limits to all timber production in favor of recreation and wildlife, giving the conservationists another substantial victory.

The January 1993 Winrock International Institute for Agricultural Development publication *Seeds* used 1991 USDA figures to estimate that Arkansas raised 980 million chickens per year, produced 3.7 million eggs and 24 million turkeys annually. With the profits came problems.

For many observers, poultry litter and pig manure from large indoor poultry houses and pig "parlors" in northwestern Arkansas, the Arkansas River Valley and southwestern Arkansas posed the greatest environmental problems for the state. Cattle were less intensively raised generally so that problems with cow manure were less prominent, but the phosphorus contained in poultry, swine and cattle manure produced annually was the equivalent of a human population of 21 million in Arkansas. In addition, few Arkansans wanted a pig "parlor" on the farm next door.

This poultry litter provided a cheap source for fertilizer that enriched fields and helped advance the region's cattle industry. Two firms in Mulberry and Russellville mineralize chicken litter into an environmentally benign super organic fertilizer. University of Arkansas at Fayetteville experimenters found that this fertilizer produced great yields on marginal lands in eastern Arkansas, but the transportation costs to date have been prohibitive.

In the spring and summer of 1992 during Governor Bill Clinton's presidential bid, both state and national media pounded him for inaction on what he already had acknowledged was Arkansas's number one potential environmental problem — water pollution from chicken litter and hog manure. The national stories were particularly damaging because they exaggerated the problem and "gave the impression dead chickens were floating down the White River." The poultry industry tried to project a positive image but at the same time took steps to limit public knowledge.

Arkansas Game and Fish Commission Director Steve N. Wilson ordered that a story by former *Arkansas Gazette* environmental writer Caroline Decker on animal waste water pollution be pulled from the summer issue of the agency's magazine. Her story was a compilation of previously published material, but Wilson felt the timing would make it appear political. The article was published in the December 1992 issue of the magazine, and it did not make the poultry industry happy even then.

Meanwhile, state regulations for managing "liquid wastes" from hog farms, egg-laying operations and small dairies were adopted in the summer of 1992. The poultry industry made it clear, however, that it would not accept any state authority on chicken litter waste management. Many environmentalists believed that the only solution was to require by law the industries to pay as much attention to what came out of the backside of poultry and pigs as what went into the front end.

Arkansas as "A Natural"

Arkansas had extolled its natural features since the nineteenth century as a means of attracting tourist dollars. The first state park was built on Petit Jean Mountain in 1927, and by 1989, the state supported forty-five parks, twenty-nine of them with overnight facilities. The federal government maintained an equally extensive list of National Forest Recreation Areas and Army Corps of Engineers use areas. Blanchard Springs Caverns in Stone County, not fully explored until the 1960s, became one of the best underground attractions in the nation.

Travel and tourism became a $2.1 billion industry in 1988, supporting 47,469 workers and making it Arkansas's third largest dollar volume industry behind food and health services. The industry proved in 1989 that it was cohesive and determined to promote its own growth by persuading the General Assembly to enact a special 2-cent sales tax on hotel and motel rooms and admissions to tourist attractions with the revenues earmarked for promotion, designed in part to offset vigorous television campaigns by Tennessee, Oklahoma and Texas.

The Ozarks remained the chief lure, with a reborn Eureka Springs emerging from its long sleep to become a tourist center dominated by the *Christ of the Ozarks* statue and the Passion Play. Less successful was a theme park near Harrison called Dogpatch. In the Ouachitas, Hot Springs was hurt economically when illegal gambling was shut down by Governor Winthrop Rockefeller in 1967. New horseracing tracks in Louisiana, Oklahoma and Texas began to offer competition for Oaklawn Park, leading the 1989 legislature to give it a $3 million tax break. A local theme park, Magic Springs, experienced financial difficulties. By 1989, the once famous Bathhouse Row was nearly abandoned. The Fordyce Bath House became a museum and visitor center, and preservationists pointed to the opportunities presented by the city's fine Victorian architectural heritage.

Local festivals became the prime social promotion activities of the 1970s and 1980s. It seemed that any community with an agricultural product or unique feature or heritage to promote did just that, giving Arkansans and visitors an opportunity to sample everything from armadillo and coon to Bradley County pink tomatoes and Hope watermelons. Des Arc celebrated Steamboat Days, Mountain View celebrated mountain music and War Eagle had a nationally famous crafts fair. Fordyce saluted the Cotton Belt Railroad and Prescott asked "Which came first? The Chicken or the Egg?" and Dumas hailed "Ding Dong Daddy." Little Rock and North Little Rock used the Arkansas River at their doorsteps as focal points. The capital opened summer with Riverfest, attracting hundreds of thousands, and North Little Rock closed the season with Summerset. Among its other titles, Stuttgart probably could law claim to the crown as the "Festival Capital" of Arkansas. It held rice festivals, duck calling contests and farm equipment extravaganzas. In most areas of the state, local history as a means of promoting tourism remained an untapped resource.

Rurality and Education

Nowhere could the influence of rurality be demonstrated better than in education. The move to consolidate rural schools began in earnest in 1948 when Amendment 40 to the Arkansas Constitution and Initiated Act 1 reduced the number of school districts from about 3,000 to slightly fewer than 500 and mandated the creation of high schools available to all students. Consolidation and attrition dropped the number of districts to 324 by 1991, but other similarly rural Southern states reduced their numbers more. Louisiana had sixty-six districts, and even Georgia, second to Arkansas, had only 187. The excess of small districts produced inferior education, but the minimum standards enacted in 1983 made a step toward correcting this. Prairie County supported three school districts even though the total population was only 9,519 in 1989. The number of schools accredited by the North Central Association increased significantly between 1983 and 1989.

1983		*1989*	
Total schools	NCA accredited	Total schools	NCA accredited
Elementary			
647	170	615	232
Middle and junior high			
149	65	133	82
Senior high			
NA	155	344	166

These figures represented a 23 percent increase in the total number of NCA-accredited schools in a six-year period.

Education initially was a local responsibility, but state aid became increasingly important in the post-war period. In 1989, 60 percent of the money came from the state while local taxes supplied only 31 percent and the federal government 9 percent. The 1980 census showed that 41 percent of Arkansans eighteen years and older did not have a high school diploma and only 9 percent had a college degree. The state Literacy Office said that in 1986, 323,012 Arkansans read below the fifth grade level, which meant that 20 percent of the adult population was functionally illiterate. As discussed in Chapter 17, Governor Bill Clinton mobilized the state to improve its public schools and managed to cut the dropout rate in grades seven through twelve to 3.6 percent in 1987-88 and raise the college-going rate from 38.2 percent in 1982 to 44.5 percent in 1988.

Even before Clinton started his reform movement, Arkansas knew its education system was weak. Deficiencies were described mercilessly by a study commission headed by Professor Kern Alexander of the University of Florida in 1977. In spite of the presence on the Commission of a number of legislators, the General Assembly remained inactive. However, in *Du Press* v. *Alma School District* (1983), the state Supreme Court voided the old system of state aid as a denial of equal protection of the laws. The Quality Education Act of 1969, Associate Justice Darrell Hickman observed, "is meaningless so far as quality is concerned."

Arkansas schools subsequently were subjected to the minute examination of their defects in 1983 and 1984 by the Commission on Education Standards directed by Hillary Rodham Clinton, which was the basis for her husband's reform campaign. Aside from funding, the Commission found that athletics were over-emphasized in too many systems. School personnel sometimes were hired, promoted and fired for personal rather than professional reasons, though new grievance procedure

Last Day at the Morefield Post Office *(Clyde McGinnis, 1972) Mrs. Y. M. Mack, the postmistress, is shown canceling a stamp on the last day of this Independence County post office. Closing post offices marked the end of many rural communities.* **Independence County Historical Society**

laws promoted by the Arkansas Education Association tried to stop this. Little emphasis was placed on basic education, and students were assigned little or no homework. One tentative 1979 study showed that first-grade Arkansas children scored about the national average, but their scores fell in each succeeding year in the public school system until they were at only half the national average by the twelfth grade. The Commission recommended a long laundry list of minimum standards that were immensely popular with the voters, and they were adopted wholesale by the state Board of Education. The changes included maximum class sizes, counselors in all ele-

mentary schools and the offering of physics, art, global studies, two years of foreign language and chemistry in every high school.

Hundreds of communities debated whether local pride was worth substantial tax increases and whether the legislature could be induced to relax the new standards. However, the popularity of the standards allowed them to remain in place in spite of financial pressure to relieve the expenses they imposed. The threat of consolidation for failure to meet the standards galvanized many small districts into approving unprecedented millage increases. The Arkansas Business Council was so frustrated with the

Kappa Kappa Gamma Sorority Sisters *(photographer unknown, ca. 1950) These models of beauty and fashion were on their way to an all-white sorority tea in the early 1950s. University students met lifelong friends and business associates at such functions and formed racial attitudes that were unconscious and pervasive.*
University of Arkansas

large number of districts that it recommended in 1988 that the state Board of Education prepare a plan for consolidating schools for the 1989 legislative session and make its adoption a prerequisite for additional tax revenues going to public education. The Council also noted that the average school millage rate, which was 19 in 1985, had risen to 26 by 1988, but that state law only penalized those districts failing to achieve a millage rate of 16.

As public schools were consolidating in the twentieth century, institutions of higher education were expanding. The state acquired the Henderson-Brown campus in Arkadelphia from the Methodist Church in 1927 and named it Henderson State Teachers College. Powerful state Senator W. H. Abington forced the creation of the first designated junior college at Beebe. The former district agricultural high schools evolved from two-year to four-year status, a process often accompanied by name changes. As enrollments increased rapidly after World War II and then with the arrival of post-war baby-boom students, each legislative session became marked by bitter sectional rivalries about the distribution of money. The Jonesboro campus became Arkansas State University in 1967, and a new round of infighting ended only when every state college won the right to use university designation.

The expansion of regional schools weakened the University of Arkansas at Fayetteville. School enrollments dropped in the early 1980s and local legislators gave first priority to their regional schools. Arkansas State University managed to field creditable football teams and demanded the right to play the Razorbacks. Only after a bitter battle in the 1987 General Assembly was a bill mandating intrastate play defeated. Meanwhile, although the University of Arkansas possessed one of the finest athletic facilities in the nation, its chemistry building was obsolete and historic Old Main had to be vacated as unsafe in 1981 until private funds, some general revenues and college revenue bonds made it possible to start renovation in 1989.

Perhaps the greatest threat to the Fayetteville campus — or so it thought — came from the growth of an urban university in Little Rock, The state had assumed control of the financially troubled Little Rock University in 1969 and renamed it the University of Arkansas at Little Rock (UALR). Because of its location in a fast-growing urban area, enrollment soon exceeded 9,000, second only to the Fayetteville campus. In addition, Little Rock was home to the Medical Sciences campus, founded in 1879, and the Graduate Institute of Technology (GIT), founded in 1957 and incorporated into UALR in 1988. Little Rock won a signal victory in 1977 when the state established a second law school, although many considered it an expensive duplication. By the mid-1980s, however, UALR law school graduates regularly were out-performing those from Fayetteville on the Arkansas Bar examination.

In 1970, AM&N at Pine Bluff almost had to close its doors because of a lack of funds. This historically underfunded black school was saved by adding it to the University of Arkansas system, returning in effect to the relationship that had existed when the school was established in 1873. Financial collapse also hit the Monticello campus in 1972, and it, too,

became a part of the system. This added to the University's budget a needed forestry program that did not become accredited until 1985.

The state also created community colleges. Using studies that showed college attendance was based on accessibility, Governor Dale Bumpers and the legislature provided generous state assistance to operate the schools, provided the communities raised the taxes to build the facilities. Fort Smith Junior College already had become Westark Community College in 1965 and Phillips County operated a community college near Helena before the 1973 law. Additional schools were established at Forrest City, Harrison, Blytheville, Hot Springs, Mena and Rogers. Southern Arkansas University at Magnolia serviced El Dorado and East Camden with technical campuses and Arkansas State University ran the two-year Beebe campus that was designated as the State Technical Institute. The legislators initially were happy to divide funds because it satisfied so many local constituents. Difficulties arose when state money became short. A tongue-in-cheek proposal to erect a university at tiny Fox in Stone County touched off a legislative debate and enthusiasm waned.

Community colleges were both stepping stones for students to get to four-year institutions and centers for continuing education. Their chief advantage was that they offered educational opportunity close to home in a woefully undereducated state. Among the disadvantages were small libraries, lower academic standards and serious problems with academic freedom. In spite of the heightened accessibility, in 1988 Arkansas ranked forty-seventh among the states in percentage of its population enrolled in public and private higher education institutions.

A 1987 study by the state Department of Higher Education found that all ten of the state's two-year colleges had administrative costs above the national average of 14.3 percent, as did three of the University of

Arkansas's five campuses. Arkansas ranked fiftieth in tax dollars spent per student for higher education in 1983, but stood fifth in one survey and tenth in another in administrative expenses. Relative to the two-year campuses, a Department official said they generally were "much smaller than their peer institutions across the country and therefore do not have the economy of scale that a larger institution would experience."

Adjacent states made substantially greater commitments to higher education than Arkansas with Mississippi appropriations increasing by 28 percent — the largest in the country — Texas increasing by 21 percent, Oklahoma going from minus 9 percent to 8 percent and Kansas leaping to 17 percent.

With elementary and secondary education as the first priority, the percentage of dollars appropriated to higher education declined from 18.4 percent of general revenues to 17.3 percent from 1979 to 1988-89, but enrollments at the state-supported campuses were rising. Low black enrollment was a continuing concern, however, for only 9,117 blacks were enrolled in the fall of 1988, which was 12.9 percent of the student body — more than 4 percentage points below their proportionate share of the population.

To keep their doors open in the face of funding that did not keep pace with inflation and increasing enrollments, the campuses resorted to a series of tuition and fee increases. This was especially true after the 1989 General Assembly refused to enact Governor Clinton's tax increase package. Arkansas residents who had paid $305 a semester to attend Arkansas State University in 1979-80 received a bill in 1989-90 of $700 a semester. UA-Fayetteville went from $300 a semester to $724 during the same period, and UALR was at $710. Southern Arkansas University balked, saying an increase would price a college education out of the market for those in its area and kept its rate at $540 a semester, which was the lowest for any state four-year campus.

After the 1989 General Assembly failed to act, several leading faculty members left the state, including one at ASU who had won the Board of Higher Education's top teaching award and Dr. Allen Hermann, a physicist who had helped give UA-Fayetteville a world-class program on superconductivity. Their departures were well publicized, and in May 1989, the *Arkansas Democrat* reported that a scientific poll found that 61.3 percent of Arkansas adults supported increasing state funding for colleges and universities. In 1991, higher education finally got significant increases. Little of the money went into salaries, however, and faculty morale remained a serious problem on most state campuses.

Rural politics had much to do with the founding of twenty-four vocational-technical schools. Created during the Faubus era and located, as the Winthrop Rockefeller Foundation observed, on the basis of "political patronage in lieu of good planning," they were intended to train workers for the industrial age. However, the schools became obsolete when new technologies created more complex training needs and more expensive equipment. Politically, it proved impossible either to consolidate them or to fund them, as Governor Frank White suggested, by taking money away from the colleges.

The expansion of educational opportunity resulted in more Arkansas students attending college. In 1975, only 27.3 percent of the population aged eighteen to twenty-four was enrolled, compared to a national average of 40.6 percent. By 1988, 44 percent were attending, but the national average had risen to 55 percent.

As in the past, graduation time was leaving time. In 1985, thirty-nine out of forty-two graduates in the University of Arkansas's chemical engineering program left the state to find work. Although the percentage of the Arkansas population having four years of college increased from 4.8 to 9.7 percent between

1960 and 1980, national rates increased at a greater pace, leaving Arkansas last in the nation in percentage of college graduates.

Four private schools — Ouachita Baptist, John Brown, Harding and College of the Ozarks — followed the lead of the state colleges and designated themselves as universities. Hendrix College at Conway and Arkansas College at Batesville resisted the trend. Hendrix continued its academically challenging program, and Arkansas College became heir to several large bequests and greatly strengthened its program.

The twentieth-century erosion of the state's black community, along with the integration of previously all-white schools, kept Philander Smith, Shorter and Arkansas Baptist Colleges with small enrollments and in precarious financial condition.

Rurality and Health

The spotlight that the United States had always focused on youth began to dim in the late twentieth century because general sanitation and medical advances were extending life. In 1900, life expectancy was forty-six for men and forty-nine for women. The median age was 22.9, and three million people were sixty-five and older. The life expectancy in the United States in 1989 was seventy-two years for men and seventy-eight for women. The median age was 32.3, and there were thirty million people sixty-five and older — outnumbering teen-agers for the first time in the country's history. The gap was expected to widen as the post-World War II "baby boomers" aged.

Life expectancy in Arkansas wasn't much different from the national average in 1981 — 70.46 years for white males, 78.59 years for white females, 65 for black males and 73.77 years for black females. The median age in Arkansas was 30.6 years in 1980. What did differ significantly in Arkansas was the death rate because Arkansans had poorer health

than average Americans. The overall death rate in 1987 was 10.2 persons per thousand population compared to the national rate of 8.7. In part, this probably reflected that 14 percent of the state's population was sixty-five and older, ranking it in the top five states for proportionate percentage of aged population. This was attributable in part to the influx of retirees to the Ozarks to take advantage of the mild climate, relaxed rural pace of life, low property taxes, and abundant hunting and fishing opportunities.

The Wilbur D. Mills Freeway through central Little Rock was bounded by medical complexes, dominated by the Arkansas Children's Hospital, one of the best in the country; the University of Arkansas for Medical Sciences and its teaching hospital; the adjoining John L. McClellan Veterans Administration Medical Center; the State Hospital; the Catholic-operated St. Vincent Infirmary Medical Center, Doctors Hospital and a city within the city — the Baptist Medical System complex. Each offered some of the finest tertiary treatment available. Strong regional medical services were available at Searcy, Fort Smith, El Dorado, Jonesboro and Pine Bluff. Rural Arkansas, however, was a medical desert and becoming ever drier in the 1980s.

Under the Reagan administration, the difference in reimbursements widened to 50 percent between what urban and rural physicians received under Medicare and Medicaid. In an effort to contain skyrocketing medical costs, the government also devised a reimbursement system based on diagnostic related groups (DRGs) and treatment later was second-guessed by "peer review groups." As a result, many hospitals, most of them rural, could not even cover the costs of services given and there were repeated charges that those without medical insurance were being turned away. Eight rural hospitals closed in Arkansas between 1985 and 1989, and up to fifteen more were said to be in danger of meeting the same fate by 1990. Across the country, 280 rural hospitals closed between 1985 and 1988. Even the Baptist Medical System in Little Rock reported it had provided $42.1 million more in health care in 1988 than it was paid for under Medicare's reimbursement program for illnesses in DRGs. This was $12.6 million more than the $29.5 million that the medical center had written off under the DRG program the year before.

Seventy-two of Arkansas's seventy-five counties were designated by the Public Health Service to be medically underserved areas, and no relief was in sight in 1989. Arkansas's health care providers were concentrated in larger cities, especially in central and northwestern Arkansas, even though half the state's population was rural, and many of the greatest needs were in poor southern and eastern Arkansas counties with a high black population. Only 23 percent of the licensed physicians less than sixty years old and 24 percent of active registered nurses were practicing in the fifty-eight counties classified as rural although 49 percent of the population lived in them.

The number of uninsured rural Arkansans was 15 percent higher than the United States average and 24 percent above urban levels. Only a fourth of the rural poor qualified for Medicaid, compared to 43 percent of the poor in inner cities. About 14 percent of the rural population had an income level below poverty compared to a national poverty rate of 11 percent. Rural populations had greater distances to travel to get to services, yet public transportation was nonexistent.

Arkansas was one of the nation's poorest states in terms of physician service. The state Medical Board found in 1988 that Arkansas had 75 fewer physicians per 100,00 population than the national average — 138 Arkansas physicians per 100,000 compared to the United States rate of 213.

Rural areas presented far more chronic health problems than urban areas. Rural residents have higher rates than urban dwellers for infant and maternal mortality, chronic illness and disability and morbidity related to diabetes, cancer, high blood pressure, heart disease, stroke and lung disease. Between 1980 and 1985, low birth weight rates increased steadily and significantly in rural poor counties, with the 1985 rural rate nearly 30 percent higher than the national rate. Rural occupations are likely to be hazardous (farming, mining and timber), and therefore often produced higher injury rates.

Governor Dale Bumpers, himself the product of tiny Charleston in Franklin County, recognized a rural health care crisis in 1973 and persuaded the legislature to fund Area Health Education Centers (AHECs) through the University of Arkansas for Medical Sciences. Under AHECs, most medical students did some of their training at centers in Jonesboro, Pine Bluff, El Dorado, Texarkana and Fort Smith. A 1989 survey of 1,268 UAMS College of Medicine graduates from 1979 to 1988 found that 77 percent of them had remained in Arkansas to practice; 82 percent of former AHEC residents practiced in Arkansas. Ninety-three percent of former AHEC residents practiced in Arkansas areas other than Pulaski County. Even so, getting physicians and nurses to practice in rural areas was proving to be an intractable problem.

In one respect, Arkansas's rurality spared it the scourge of acquired immune deficiency syndrome (AIDS), the medical horror of the 1980s, which was transmitted sexually, by blood transfusion and by unsanitary needles used by drug addicts. Some 58,000 persons had died of AIDS nationally by 1989 but only 165 were in Arkansas.

THE REVIVAL OF POLITICAL REACTION

Post-World War II America went through conservative phases in the 1950s during the McCarthy era and in the Reagan years of the

1980s. Ideological conservatism was at a severe disadvantage in Arkansas because there was so little to conserve economically. The William F. Buckley style of intellectual conservatism was almost as rare as active members of the John Birch Society. Business conservatism in tax policies was more evident, and the state legislature was often the target of powerful organized special interests. The most conspicuous forms of conservatism, however, were rooted in the defense of cultural traditionalism and tended to focus on narrow and often symbolic issues such as abortion, school prayer, gay rights and Creation Science.

Given the rural and small-town backgrounds of most Arkansans, it was not surprising that many reacted negatively to the cultural changes of the 1960s and 1970s. Unquestioning patriotism made it difficult for many to accept criticism of the government during the Vietnam War. Most supported a strong role for the police and did not share the U. S. Supreme Court's concern with civil liberties.

The death penalty remained popular, and gubernatorial candidate Kim Hendren of Benton County promised if elected in 1980 to electrocute an inmate himself. In 1988, the legislature mandated that all capital punishment in Arkansas be carried out by lethal injection rather than by electrocution on "humane" grounds. Those convicted and sentenced to die before 1983 could choose electrocution or lethal injection. There were thirty-three prisoners on "death row" in Arkansas by mid-1989 and no executions had been carried out since January 1965. The media followed their efforts to die — or not to die — with unusual thoroughness. Eugene Simmons, convicted of the largest family mass killing in United States history in a shooting rampage in Russellville during the 1987 Christmas holidays, asserted he wanted to die but was thwarted by appeals from death penalty opponents. In the summer of 1990 he got his wish. The U. S.

Eighth Circuit Court of Appeals could be counted on to take a strongly critical look at death penalty cases. In 1992, Arkansas executed Barry Fairchild, whose retarded condition attracted national attention.

When the United States Supreme Court under Chief Justice Earl Warren greatly enlarged judicial protection for personal liberties, one manifestation in Arkansas was a youth revolt against restrictive school rules. The chief symbol became hair length. The rock musical *Hair* played in Arkansas only after federal District Judge G. Thomas Eisele, a Republican, overturned local attempts at censorship.

The youth revolution had arrived in Arkansas public schools. Virtually all male students soon began wearing their hair longer than the crewcut standard of the 1950s. Authorities resisted. Knickers were banned at Perryville, an American Legion baseball team found itself disqualified for hair length at Ozark and flared jeans led to students being suspended at Mountain View. Other cases erupted at Fort Smith, Huntsville, Nashville, Helena, Eureka Springs, Valley View and Hazen. The trial of one student at Piggott elicited the testimony of a teacher that Jesus Christ wore a crewcut. The courts invariably held that hairstyle was a part of the expression of personal freedom guaranteed by the Constitution, and schools were told that the disciplining of students had to follow standards of fairness and due process.

This revolution had interesting side effects in the larger towns, especially Little Rock, where the relaxing of dress codes and other nonacademic standards led parents to enroll students in private schools where stricter codes of dress and behavior applied. Such dress codes became so popular by the late 1980s that the Little Rock School District's Williams Elementary School, a magnet school, had dress codes that were voluntarily agreed to by students and parents as a condition of attendance.

The generation gap blossomed into open warfare at Eureka Springs. After steady population decline since 1900, the town staged a comeback in the 1960s through the investments of Reverend Gerald L. K. Smith, whose statue, *Christ of the Ozarks*, and Passion Play attracted many tourists. Smith, an anti-Semite, also published a magazine, *The Cross and the Flag*, devoted to exposing the workings of an alleged international Jewish conspiracy. The same town attributes that attracted Smith also inspired young "hippies" to settle there. The result was a battle for local control in which the police were conspicuous for their use of force and liberal definition of vagrancy. In a war of private violence against "deviates," one unintended victim whose long hair was shaved turned out to be the actor who portrayed Jesus in the Passion Play. Tempers cooled by the 1980s. The hippies who remained frequently became stable and successful members of the business community, and Eureka Springs became Arkansas's most culturally variegated small community, whose mayor in 1989 posed nude for the *Arkansas Times*.

Tolerance was less certain elsewhere. One losing party at first was a communal band of families known as the The Group, Inc., that came to Arkansas in 1968, settling at Greers Ferry. It set up a dinner theater, established a newspaper, formed the Optimist Club, and supported the Chamber of Commerce. Its members volunteered for the fire department and gave blood to the Red Cross.

In 1972, however, The Group decided to register and vote in an election in which its fifty votes would decide a hotly contested race that pitted those who favored tourism against those who liked things the way they were. The Property Owners Association claimed that The Group supported the radical Students for a Democratic Society (SDS) and planned to "put us in chains and enclose us and make us live in a commune." The Group's property burned mysteriously, rifle shots were fired at

members, and eventually an armed mob of leading citizens attacked its headquarters. State Police arrived to rescue the beleaguered members, and nine persons were arrested on night-riding charges under the old anti-Ku Klux Klan law. Sensing that its survival was problematical and fearing for the safety of members' children, The Group left Greers Ferry and settled in Little Rock, where it purposefully kept a low profile and encountered no violence.

The identity of The Group remained intact but its structure changed, founder Dixon Bowles said in the interview he gave for this book in July 1989. No longer a commune, The Group is now "a very big extended family" made up of individuals who pursued their own careers. Three had become lawyers, one a pathologist, three nurses with advanced degrees, one a molecular biologist, two criminologists, one a systems analyst, to name a few — and a woman mechanic. The families lived in individually owned homes on two blocks in Little Rock`s Quapaw Quarter, but their children attended The Group's state accredited school that had ten pupils and four full-time teachers at the time of the interview. Three products of this school graduated from college in 1989: one was *summa cum laude* and the others were *magna cum laude*, Bowles said.

The entity is "still the same in our minds," Bowles said. There was a lot of disappointment when the Greers Ferry effort ended, he recalled, "but fifteen years later, it's easy to take a positive view. The environment we have created here is superior to anything we could have anticipated doing there."

As vigilantes were forcing The Group out of Greers Ferry, the realtors of Mountain Home were in open conflict against the award-winning Baxter *Bulletin*. According to the realtors, news coverage of fires and accidents was detrimental to the community, and a picture of an outdoor privy (for which Arkansans incidentally ranked first in the nation) projected a bad image. They also objected to newspaper coverage of local controversies: "We believe the paper should wait until the matters have been discussed, ironed out, and then the paper should print the decision."

When the *Bulletin* refused to give in to a boycott, the Pine Bluff *Commercial* — another newspaper that occasionally offended some of its readers — called it the latest attempt to "Pravdaize the Arkansas press." Batesville *Daily Guard* columnist Paul Buchanan satirized the realtors this way: "We wonder how they stand on the publication of obituaries and losses suffered by the Mountain Home High School football and basketball teams."

The boycott soon fizzled, but newspapers in many communities refused to engage in controversy. When Star City editor Ross W. Dennis criticized Anita Bryant, a popular singer then engaged in a campaign against homosexuals, he was fired by the paper's owner. Champions of the newspaper's traditional watchdog role were especially critical of the chain-owned papers of Hot Springs, El Dorado, Camden, Texarkana and Magnolia. Critic Martin Kirby, editor of the *Arkansas Advocate*, complained about a lack of hard news in the papers, observing that the Palmer chain "doesn't know the difference between a newspaper and an advertising throwaway."

Advertising and politics had much to do with the newspaper war between the *Arkansas Democrat* and the *Arkansas Gazette* in the 1980s. After Walter Hussman, Jr., became the new owner of the *Democrat*, a poor quality, conservative, money losing newspaper in 1974, he proposed a joint operating agreement for the two papers. Hugh B. Patterson stated that *Gazette* owners refused because they believed that Little Rock could support only one quality newspaper, and they did not want to use *Gazette* revenues to subsidize the inferior *Democrat*.

Hussman renewed the ancient battle between the two papers by switching the *Democrat* from an afternoon to a morning newspaper in 1979 to go head-to-head with the politically liberal *Gazette* in the morning time slot. He used free classified advertising and expanded news coverage to compete. He continued the *Democrat's* conservative political stance.

After several years of eroding earnings, the *Gazette* counterattacked by filing an antitrust suit against the *Democrat*. The *Gazette* claimed among other things that the *Democrat* was using unfair business practices to subsidize the paper from other sources and was subsidizing corporate advertising. The *Gazette* lost its case in court. In late 1986, the *Gazette's* owners sold to the Gannett chain, believing that it had the necessary resources to dominate the market and the circulation war continued. Both papers increased their Sunday circulations to more than 200,000, and the *Gazette* continued to outstrip the *Democrat* in weekday sales.

Both papers were losing money, but Hussman, a life-long resident of Arkansas, was more willing to make the fight than the management of the out-of-state Gannett chain. The *Gazette's* new owners alienated many readers by trying to convert "the old gray lady" into something resembling the Gannett's *USA Today*. By the time the paper folded on October 18, 1991, it bore little resemblance to the paper J. N. Heiskell had forged during his heyday in the 1930s, 1940s and 1950s when it provided strong statewide coverage and ran the work of excellent local feature writers. Hussman bought the assets of the *Gazette*, styled his paper the *Arkansas Democrat-Gazette*, and added some of the less controversial writers from the *Gazette*. The *Democrat* effectively eliminated much hostility by acquiring the *Gazette's* comics.

Arkansas had enjoyed the increased local coverage resulting from the newspaper war, but across America competing newspapers had become almost extinct in markets the size of Arkansas's. The *Gazette's* demise ended more than a 172 year-old business and

726 full-time and 1,200 part-time jobs. It coincided with the end of an era when people relied on newspapers for knowledge of national and world events. In the new information age, most people got their national and international news from CNN. The loss of the *Gazette's* prestige also underscored the long-time fragmentation of the Arkansas newspaper market. Although both the *Democrat* and *Gazette* had put *Arkansas* on their masthead, neither paper commanded the full allegiance of Arkansas readers. Memphis papers were more common in the Delta, Tulsa and Springfield papers in the northwest, and Louisiana and Texas papers in the southern and western counties.

Hostility to the themes of modernization had political consequences. Legislators used their positions to attack schools dispensing birth control devices and sex education aimed at controlling acquired immune deficiency syndrome (AIDS).

School boards also were receptive to conservative pressures. After complaints from a few parents, the Conway School Board acted in 1989 to keep one teacher from using Pulitzer Prize-winning author William Manchester's United States history book, *The Glory and the Dream*, on the grounds it was outdated because it was written in 1974 and wasn't on the state-approved textbook list. Parents had objected to references in the book to Marilyn Monroe's sex appeal and President Harry Truman's profanity. After much debate the Board eventually retreated. A proposal for a school-based health clinic was rejected in DeValls Bluff when the opposition claimed the clinic would give students access to birth control, even though the state Health Department assured the school that it would not.

Most issues were local, but one conspicuous exception was the appearance in Arkansas of Peace Links, a women's peace advocacy group founded by Betty Bumpers, wife of the state's senior United States senator. Condemned on the floor of the Senate by Alabama Senator Jeremiah Denton as allegedly having Communist ties, Peace Links nevertheless created a chapter in every county. One Jonesboro art teacher who allowed her students to enter a peace art contest was reprimanded by school officials who said that peace was "controversial." In mid-1989, Peace Links closed its state headquarters, saying its mission was accomplished and it would rely in the future exclusively on volunteers. Peace became less controversial with the winding down of the Cold War.

THE RESURGENCE OF RELIGION

Closely allied with both rurality and reaction was conservative religion, especially of the evangelical fundamentalist sects. Opposed to modernization in church doctrine, they discovered another evil in the modernization of society and thus provided the leadership, rationale and money for attacks on modernism on a wide range of issues.

Liberal Religion under Attack

Many mainline Protestant denominations criticized the war in Vietnam, and during the 1960s, began to liberalize their stances on church dogma and social issues. More women appeared in positions of authority; new types of church services were instituted, often using aspects of popular culture, and a heightened commitment to social reform, civil rights, and political involvement could be heard from the pulpit. Many churchgoers did not approve when these trends reached Arkansas. As mainline churches moved away from their traditional moorings, some got their religion at home from the new television evangelists. Oral Roberts, the PTL Club, and others commanded the allegiance of thousands of Arkansans. Perhaps inspired by what they had seen on television, the evangelicals sometimes splintered old established churches, and pentecostal practices such as speaking in tongues and faith healing found a wider audience. Their popularity began to fade in the late 1980s, however, when at least two nationwide "televangelists" were discredited by sex and financial scandals and Roberts was widely ridiculed for his fund-raising tactics.

Nationally, the Southern Baptist Convention was locked in a bitter feud nominally about Biblical interpretation that divided Arkansas congregations. In 1989, a conservative group plotting to capture the presidency of the Arkansas Baptist State Convention was frustrated when a tape recording of their strategy meeting was made public. By 1991, conservatives were firmly in control of the national Convention, and Baptists reversed their traditional support for separation of church and state. Many Baptist-affiliated colleges took steps to preserve their academic independence, and within Arkansas the more moderate ministers made tentative steps toward moving out of the Convention. However, the Southern Baptists remained dominant among the mainline denominations in Arkansas, having 483,483 members at the end of 1988 with Methodists following at 160,525. Roman Catholics became more numerous at 67,608, which considerably outpaced the "regular" Presbyterians at 19,795.

Much religious ferment was expressed locally. In Jonesboro, long-time Methodist minister Reverend Worth Gibson seceded with a large minority of his congregation to form a separate church that later splintered again. Five Cumberland Presbyterian ministers, "slain by the Spirit," left to form new churches with pentecostal practices in 1980. The new churches often differed on doctrine, but nearly all shared a common political orientation, rejecting the Equal Rights Amendment, opposing equal legal rights for homosexuals, condemning abortion, supporting the death penalty and a strong national defense.

Morality Issues

Conservatives sometimes attempted to impose their moral values on the entire community. One controversial issue was teacher-led prayer and Bible reading in the public schools, which the Supreme Court had ruled violated the constitutional proscription against state-established religion. The practice continued in Arkansas from Gravette to Blytheville in proud and open defiance of the law. On occasion, parents who protested local practices were subjected to threatening calls and economic discrimination and their children were harassed in school. The controversial motion picture, *The Last Temptation of Christ,* could not be shown in Arkansas because of threats of violence. Liberal and conservative Protestant denominations agreed only on opposition to a state lottery and other forms of legalized gambling.

Some rural communities remained hostile to dancing. In voting to ban dancing at Glenwood (Pike County), one school board member observed, "Dancing is now something that preys on sexual desires in young people." Vilonia became the center of a bitter debate about school dances in 1982, and some youngsters who gathered around a jukebox in Trumann found themselves afoul of a city ordinance banning all dancing.

Liquor remained controversial. The 1969 legislature authorized the sale of liquor-by-the-drink on a local option basis, and cocktails were voted in by Pulaski and Garland Counties, the cities of Pine Bluff, Eureka Springs and Helena, and eventually by Wiederkehr Village in Altus, where dining and "wine-tasting" at the winery there were a part of its tourism business. The 1987 legislature, told by promoters that inability to sell cocktails on Sunday was hurting convention business, authorized localities with mixed-drink sales to vote on whether to allow liquor to flow on the Sabbath. By mid-1989, Pulaski and Garland Counties, Eureka Springs and Wiederkehr Village had said "yes."

Early Crop-Dusting *(photographer unknown, ca. 1950) The first cotton poison was lead arsenic applied by hand or by man and mule to fight boll weevils. Mechanical crop dusting began in the 1920s, and in this picture, John Hackleroad of Oil Trough is applying benzidine hexachloride from a homemade converted Willis Jeep.* **Independence County Historical Society**

The 1969 General Assembly also provided for the creation of private clubs in dry counties. It was argued that such clubs were necessary because out-of-state businessmen would never come to Arkansas without such facilities as a bar, and that by using the private club method, undesirables could be excluded. Although officially forty-five counties were legally dry in 1989, only seven (Crawford, Grant, Howard, Lafayette, Lincoln, Madison, Perry) did not have at least one private club, and "dry" Benton County, the heart of conservatism, had thirty-one. State Alcoholic Beverage Control officials called the dry counties with private clubs "moist." Fort Smith was a "wet" oasis in a dry Sebastian County, and Logan County was "wet" for nothing stronger than beer and native wines. Even in wet counties, some townships voted themselves dry, creating a "now you see it, now you don't" situation even in Pulaski County. To many Northern immigrants, private clubs were an unsatisfactory compromise, and places with many out-of-state retirees, such as Mountain Home and Eureka Springs, voted themselves wet.

A 1975 Fort Smith battle over booze was a good example of the contrast between the modernists' tolerance and the traditionalists' insistence on conformity. Led by a number of Baptist ministers, local drys sought to ban alcohol at the city auditorium. One member of the city's Board of Directors had rented the auditorium for an Episcopalian diocesan convention at which communion wine would be served. "Are you willing to discriminate against these people?" he asked. According to newspaper accounts, the ministers answered in the affirmative.

One bastion of traditionalism fell in 1982 when the state Supreme Court in *Handy Dan Improvement Center, Inc.* v. *Adams* struck down the state's "blue law." The sacredness of Sunday had been a feature of Arkansas law since statehood, and laws against Sunday work were repealed only after World War II. But in 1965, small-town merchants supported the passage of a law banning the sale of goods in fourteen different categories. Repeatedly violated and rarely enforced, the law finally came under court scrutiny and was found unconstitutionally vague. Clerks could not be expected to know which of the 70,000 articles available for sale fit into very broad and overlapping categories. "Pervasive confusion" at the cash register was unconstitutional. The state did not appeal, and soon most chain stores and malls in urban areas were open on Sunday afternoons. By contrast, in the small towns and rural areas where traditionalists dominated, stores — even Wal-Marts — remained closed.

Religion and Education

Many fundamentalists worried that the public schools had become instruments of "godless atheism." One issue that upset many parents was sex education. Certainly school children knew enough to make babies. In 1986, more than 470,000 babies were born nationwide to mothers under nineteen, and nearly half of those were in the South. The South also accounted for more than half the births to girls fifteen and under. Oddly enough, the number of births to females from ten to nineteen years old in Arkansas dropped from 1976 to 1987 — from 7,767 to 6,502 — but the number of illegitimate babies rose, from 3,030 to 1976 to 3,531 in 1987. Abortions by Arkansas teen-agers went from 868 in 1976, just three years after the United States Supreme Court's historic *Roe* v. *Wade* decision legalizing abortions in the first trimester, to 2,037 in 1987, an increase of nearly 135 percent. In 1985, Arkansas children aged ten to fourteen ranked sixth in the nation in live births, while those fifteen to nineteen ranked fifth. In addition, Arkansas teen-agers ranked thirteenth in reported cases of syphilis and fifteenth in gonorrhea.

Among seventeen Southern and border states, Arkansas was next to last in money spent in fiscal 1987 on Aid to Families with Dependent Children (AFDC), food stamps and Medicaid tied to teen pregnancies. Even Mississippi spent almost $126 million.

Citing these and other statistics, Governor Bill Clinton told the state:

> Hopelessness often pervades the lives of children at risk. By working to break that cycle of hopelessness, we not only address the problem of adole-scent pregnancy, but also address substance [drug and alcohol] abuse, delinquency, illiteracy and many other debilitating conditions. . . . If we do not begin our intervention early in children's lives and continue to work with children to enhance their prospects, we have failed.

Yet in many communities, school attempts to educate their charges led to heated confrontations with parents, and some teachers lost their jobs. The discovery of AIDS in the early 1980s gave a new urgency to sex education, and two public school programs — at Lincoln in conservative northwestern Arkansas and Turrell in the Delta — received Clinton's endorsement.

The governor also appointed a black pediatrician, Dr. Joycelyn Elders, as director of the state Department of Health, and she campaigned vigorously throughout the state in 1988 for the establishment of school-based health clinics that would dispense contraceptives. To clear up questions about the authority of schools to create such clinics, a bill was introduced in the 1989 General Assembly. Opponents led by Representatives Lacy Landers of Benton and Frank Willems of Paris succeeded in amending it so that school clinics would be banned from dispensing contraceptives. The bill's sponsors refused to accept the change, saying it would gut the purpose of the measure and jeopardize fourteen existing clinics that were providing birth control devices to sexually active teen-agers.

Arkansas had one program for early intervention with children at risk — Home Instruction Program for Pre-School Youngsters (HIPPY) — that received national acclaim. It was a home-based program for four-and five-year-olds in which parents were trained in techniques to promote language and problem-solving skills. Parents worked with their children for fifteen minutes a day, five days a week, thirty weeks a year for two years, and met twice monthly with HIPPY instructors and other parents.

Those who objected to sex education in the schools frequently disliked the content of science courses. Although Arkansas's Anti-Evolution Law had been struck down in 1968, Governor Frank White signed into law Act 590 entitled the "Balanced Treatment for Creation-Science and Evolution-Science Act" on March 19, 1981. White later admitted not having read the bill, and about fifteen minutes of discussion had preceded its adoption by the legislature.

The new law required that if a teacher mentioned Darwinian evolution in class, equal time had to be given to what the law defined as "creation-science." A national uproar greeted what an alliance of scientists, civil libertar-

ians, and mainline religious leaders called an attempt to teach the Book of Genesis as science. This alliance filed suit in federal court, and Judge William R. Overton presided over *McLean* v. *Arkansas Board of Education* (1982). Reminiscent of the famous Tennessee *Scopes* "monkey trial" of sixty years earlier, the case was commonly called *Scopes II*. Reporters came from all over the world for this first test case in the new battle between science and religion. Judge Overton held that the law violated the separation of church and state by requiring the teaching of a religion. Attorney General Steve Clark did not appeal, observing that few legal authorities believed the decision could be reversed by higher courts. The state's flirtation with state-established religion cost more than $400,000 in legal fees, and Clark's view was proven correct when the U. S. Supreme Court struck down a similar Louisiana law in *Edwards* v. *Aguillard* (1987).

Alarmed by this and other trends, fundamentalists led by state Representative Tim Hutchinson of Benton County pushed for and received legislative approval in 1985 of a law that allowed parents to educate their children at home provided the students could pass standardized tests. There were 518 children engaged in home schooling in 1985-86, the first year it was legal. Of those, 430 were tested and 81 percent passed. By 1987-88 the number of pupils in home schooling had grown to 1,132 and 84.5 percent of those tested passed. In the 1988-89 school year, 1,345 children were enrolled in home schools.

Cults and the End of the World

In the wake of the battles about modernization, some persons became involved actively in eschatology. The Zarepath Horeb Church retreated far into the hills of Marion County to prepare for the collapse of civilization. Heavily armed against an expected attack by urban blacks, members used a photograph of

Andrew Young, United Nations ambassador in the Carter administration, for target practice.

The Covenant, The Sword, and The Arm of the Lord (CSA) was another group with Arkansas connections, and it had affiliations with a neo-Nazi body called The Order that engaged in robbery and murder nationwide. After the death of a Missouri state trooper in 1985, authorities raided the Marion County headquarters of the CSA and discovered a large cache of illegal military weapons. An Arkansas state trooper died in the southwestern part of the state while trying to arrest a right-wing supporter. In June 1983, federal and local authorities stormed the Lawrence County hideout of Gordon Kahl, a member of the Posse Comitatus, a militant anti-tax group, who was wanted for the killing of two federal marshals in North Dakota. Both Kahl and Lawrence County Sheriff Gene Matthews died in the ensuing gun battle. The federal government invoked the Sedition Act among other charges against thirteen white supremacist leaders, but they were acquitted at a lengthy trial in Fort Smith in early 1988, after which defiant and free former Texas Ku Klux Klansman Louis Ray Beam ran up the Confederate flag and proclaimed "to hell with the federal government" in the shadow of the courthouse.

A different approach to the world's troubles took place in Grannis (Polk County) in 1975 when a group of families, convinced of the imminent end of the world, took their children out of school, quit their jobs, and quietly awaited the return of Jesus. State officials eventually intervened because the parents were violating truancy laws, and failure to keep up mortgage and car payments cost sect members many of their possessions. Arkansas was also home to Edgar C. Whisenart, a retired engineer, who published *88 Reasons Why the Rapture Will Be in 1988*. His book, which generated profits of more than $200,000, attracted national attention, although the dates he gave passed repeatedly

without the start of World War III and the subsequent nuclear winter. Religious extremists attracted media attention out of proportion to their numbers.

THE DECLINE OF RACISM

The view that the white race was superior in all regards to other races came under increasing public attack after 1960. Overt racism quietly disappeared from public view as blacks entered the political, economic and even social mainstreams. Such changes were not distributed equally by geographic location or age classification. Powerful resentments against blacks lurked beneath the surface.

Token Integration

True integration in the United States began with the 1954 United States Supreme Court decision that separate school systems for blacks and whites were inherently unequal. The next major step was the Civil Rights Act of 1964, which led to the disappearance of the "Whites Only" signs once common around Arkansas and the South. They disappeared so completely that when a Star City laundromat owner posted a new one in 1979, widespread state and regional attention was generated before the sign came down.

The dual school systems were phased out by 1973 in the holdout districts of eastern Arkansas, largely because of the threat that the federal government would withhold its contribution to school budgets. As a result of the dismantling of dual systems, it was usually the black school that was closed and the black teachers and administrators who suffered. By one estimate, three-fourths of the black administrators lost their jobs. Only seven black superintendents remained in 1989, located mostly in overwhelmingly black districts. Black teachers also gave up their separate organizational identity in 1969 when the black Arkansas Teachers Association

(ATA) merged with the Arkansas Education Association (AEA). But the number of black teachers rose considerably, from about 1,200 in 1970 to the full-time equivalent of 3,937 in 1989. The racial breakdown in Arkansas schools in 1988-89 was 74.8 percent white, 24 percent black (well above the percentage of blacks in the state's total population), and 1.2 percent other minorities.

In spite of the magnitude of the change, trouble was localized and for the most part short-lived. Black teachers at Chidester (Ouachita County) went to federal court to win their rehiring. The playing of "Dixie" aroused racial animosities in many districts. At Watson Chapel near Pine Bluff, 400 whites walked out after the song was dropped but returned to classes after the demonstration.

The combination of new laws and a young class of blacks no longer schooled in subservience created a tense racial climate in eastern Arkansas in the late 1960s and 1970s. Forrest City, Marianna, Earle, Parkin and Cotton Plant had scenes of violence, and two black churches in Texarkana fell victim to arson. By the 1980s, Madison, Cotton Plant, Benton and Little Rock had black mayors, and Forrest City High School reinstituted its prom.

Racial incidents still occurred. After a black girl was barred from participating in a school tennis tournament at a Forrest City country club because of her race, the 1989 General Assembly tried to see that this never happened again by enacting a law prohibiting school districts from scheduling functions at facilities that discriminate on the basis of race.

The overall success of integration was influenced heavily by geography; most school districts did not have to contend with busing for racial balance. By contrast, Little Rock had large concentrations of black populations in distinct housing patterns and government-supported housing projects. In order to integrate, the Little Rock district began busing in 1971. White flight followed, and the district went from being 74 percent white to 64 percent black in 1981. The district then sued the other two Pulaski County districts to force consolidation, and in 1984, federal Judge Henry Woods granted the request, only to be overturned on appeal, although the Eighth Circuit Court of Appeals did expand the Little Rock District's boundaries to the Little Rock city limits. Litigation resulted in mounting public discontent. In 1989, the three school districts, the blacks, and the state reached a settlement, but it caused enormous turmoil in the legislature. Wealthier families increasingly placed their children into private schools, and many incoming families carefully avoided buying homes in the Little Rock School District even as other members of the upper-middle class sought to send their children to the academically excellent Little Rock Central High School.

Behind Little Rock's problem was age-old discrimination in housing. In spite of federal laws, real estate agents continued to engage in subtle but racially selective buying and selling. Persisting white racism in many counties made it impossible to sell or rent to blacks in white neighborhoods.

Blacks discovered that new laws gave them legal remedies. Discrimination suits were filed in the 1970s against many major employers, including AP&L, Montgomery Ward, Missouri Pacific Lines, International Paper Company, and local employers such as Harris Hospital at Newport. Effective challenges were made against Helena's ward system for municipal elections and the exclusion of wage earners and blacks from jury duty. A new lawsuit challenging the majority vote to win a Democratic runoff primary was filed in federal court in 1989 by Sam Whitfield, who twice led the preferential primary for Phillips County judge but was defeated in the runoff. He said the white majority split their votes in the preferential primary but always united behind his white opponent in the runoff to deny him victory because he was black.

Most companies and communities partially acceded to black demands. Act 253 of 1973 deleted racial references to "the Black, Colored, or Negro Race or Malattoes [sic]" from state laws; among other things, this meant hospitals no longer needed to store blood by race as well as by type. Voters in 1990 by a narrow margin repealed Amendment 44, which although superseded by federal court decisions, had committed the state to a segregation policy since 1956. White resistance stiffened, however, as America moved from abolishing overt racism to attacking the more covert and insidious forms.

White Backlash

Black success in job discrimination suits and affirmative action programs led some whites to feel that blacks had gained an unfair advantage. School busing was another issue in the white backlash. A 1971 survey showed that 99.74 of those who responded opposed busing. In central Arkansas, Tommy Robinson won election to Congress in 1984 in part by denouncing federal Judge Henry Woods's order consolidating the Little Rock, Pulaski County, and North Little Rock School Districts. Ironically, as Pulaski County sheriff, Robinson had had more black deputies on his force than any of his predecessors and carried Little Rock's predominantly black wards in the election.

White racial attitudes were reinforced in 1985 when Governor Clinton's widely debated teacher testing program showed a black teacher failure rate significantly higher than that for whites. In addition, graduates of the predominantly black University of Arkansas at Pine Bluff showed a higher failure rate than those from mostly white schools. The resulting debate over cultural differences, testing biases, and methods of statistical reporting did little to advance the cause of civil rights.

Emerging Black Leadership

By the time blacks could enter fully into Arkansas life, their numbers had been diminished greatly by emigration, and Arkansas ranked twenty-second among the states in black population. Although blacks were an important voting element, and Arkansas ranked third in 1989 in the South in the number of black elected officials, black cultural aspirations remained underdeveloped. A black newspaper, the *Arkansas Tribune*, founded in 1973, survived only three months; the *State Press* of L. C. Bates was revived in 1983 but experienced financial difficulties.

Part of the problem was leadership. A cultural gap separated educated blacks from aged sharecroppers, unwed teen-age mothers and unemployed young males. The poor remained inarticulate, concerned with daily survival, and increasingly involved with drugs. Most successful black politicians were middle-class individuals who owed much of their success to white support. As in the past, many of the most able chose flight. Lloyd "Vic" Hackley, chancellor at the University of Arkansas at Pine Bluff, seemed destined for major roles but chose instead to depart for North Carolina in 1985.

The absence of cultural awareness and strong leadership left blacks divided and inadequately aware of their Arkansas heritage. Black civil rights lawyer John W. Walker reported widespread apathy by 1987. "What is lacking today is a cadre of younger people willing to push for more change," he said. Arkansas native Lou Brock, a Hall of Fame baseball player, commented that Arkansas was a good place to get out of, perhaps reflecting an attitude that was still prevalent among the state's black youth.

One of the black success stories of 1980s had important constitutional implications. The legislature had fulfilled the constitutional mandate of "one man one vote," but in Crittenden County had provided for a multi-member district thus effectively making the district's delegation all-white. In 1988, blacks challenged the system, and the federal district court agreed, splitting the district. The decision was upheld by the United States Supreme Court, and Ben McGee, a black businessman from Marion, defeated a veteran white incumbent.

McGee had served on the Arkansas State University Board of Trustees and was its chairman in 1981. He said his mission was:

> . . . to bring a message to black people. I
> have come through the system and I
> know it works. I used to pick cotton. It
> taught me humility, and that it's up to
> the individual . . . what he does with his
> life. You can do it. Let's forget the past
> and get going.

With the demeanor of a man born to politics, McGee did not let his freshman status intimidate him in the 1989 legislative session as he went to the well of the House to tell his colleagues about the facts of black life in the Delta, usually in defense of the bill to legalize school-based health clinics that could dispense contraceptives. He impressed *Arkansas Gazette* political columnist John Brummett, who hailed McGee as the possible leader the blacks had lacked among their small contingent in the House. But, Brummett added, he really should pay his taxes, a reference to McGee's ongoing battle with the state about his back taxes.

Robert "Say" McIntosh, a black Little Rock restaurateur, was considerably less sanguine than McGee about the system. One capital city newspaper editor steadfastly refused during the 1970s to acknowledge McIntosh's stunts designed to draw attention to perceived injustices against blacks and white hypocrisy until they became so bizarre that the editor had to capitulate. McIntosh cut down the Martin Luther King Memorial tree at the state capitol, dumped trash on a state official's desk, threw a piece of furniture at a judge, and

finally "crucified" himself on a cross in front of the Capitol. He also regularly fed breakfasts to hungry black school children, played "Black Santa" at Christmas, and attacked the system — usually Governor Clinton — in leaflets placed on windshields of cars parked throughout downtown Little Rock. Some thought McIntosh crazy, but others slowly came to the conclusion voiced by black lawyer Austin Porter, Jr., that McIntosh was "acting out" the frustrations that many blacks felt and what they would like to say but were afraid to.

It was McIntosh who triggered the incident in 1989 that reminded Arkansans that racism was still alive and put the state back on national television with that message. After the U. S. Supreme Court ruled in 1989 that flag burning as a political protest was a constitutionally protected right of free speech, McIntosh twice tried to burn a flag in a trash can on the Capitol steps. A fist fight blocked the first attempt and the second brought a near-riot as whites cried "Burn nigger" to him. *Arkansas Democrat* reporter Jamie Wise wrote:

> . . . for the first time in my 27 years of
> life, someone called me a nigger. . . . I
> was pushed, walked on, spat at and
> mistreated — all because of the color of
> my skin.

Black *Arkansas Gazette* columnist Deborah Mathis asked, "who among us can say honestly we didn't know it would happen?" because:

> Whites and blacks alike contend that
> race relations are better than they were
> a generation ago; if one walks into an
> office building, school, or restaurant, it
> certainly looks so. But looks can be
> deceiving. While actual hatred may be
> declining, something else has taken its
> place: festering resentment.

When the state and Little Rock announced it would provide up to 200 law enforcement officers to protect McIntosh on his third attempt to "exercise my rights" to burn the American flag, the activist backed off, saying he had made his point to all of America and never intended to burn the symbol anyway.

Having learned a bitter lesson in 1957, coalitions of business, civic, and religious leaders from both races were quick to form and denounce the racism while urging "dialogue" to keep emotions from escalating.

Clinton was not the first governor to have a black in his cabinet or to appoint blacks to major positions, but he went further — putting a black on every major board and on most less significant commissions, thus providing a growing cadre with leadership and administrative experience. Tommy Sproles of Little Rock became the first black to serve on the Game and Fish Commission with what he said was the assignment to represent the "typical average sportsman" rather than the wealthy ones. Rodney E. Slater of Jonesboro went on the powerful Highway Commission and became a tireless advocate for rebuilding the Delta. Little Rock City Manager Mahlon Martin was named director of the Department of Finance and Administration, where he served ably as the state's chief fiscal officer until becoming president of the Winthrop Rockefeller Foundation. The state's largest agency and the toughest to manage, the Department of Human Services, was directed by Walt Patterson, and Dr. Elders spread her message border to border and across the country as the Health Department director. Bob Nash was director of the Arkansas Development Finance Authority after serving several years as Clinton's economic development chief.

SEXISM: THE FAILURE OF THE EQUAL RIGHT'S AMENDMENT

The Equal Rights Amendment, the symbol of women's liberation in the 1970s, failed primarily because no Southern state would pass it, including Arkansas. The failure was not because of the rational legal argument that women already possessed equal rights under the U. S. Constitution, but because of prejudice against women. Each time the issue was introduced into the legislature it was sidetracked, usually amid merriment.

Supporters of the amendment pointed out that fifty of Arkansas's laws were inherently unequal, including one that prohibited women from working in coal mines. Another study revealed that women's pay was not the equal of men's in state-supported higher education. An "equality index" study in 1986 by two New England sociologists ranked Arkansas fourth from the bottom among the states and the District of Columbia but ahead of South Carolina, Alabama, and Mississippi. The legislature had eliminated most of the state's sexually discriminatory statutes by the late 1980s.

Sexist attitudes were well established in the public school system. Although more than 75 percent of teachers were females, only 16 percent of the principals and assistant principals were women in 1986. Women served as superintendents in only seven of the 329 school districts in 1989. More than half the superintendents had been coaches, an occupation not open to women until federal rules mandated women's sports opportunities.

Middle-class women became more politically active, often in such organizations as the League of Women Voters, a nonpartisan body that worked for election reform and disseminated political education information. The League usually commanded more respect than its size warranted — 653 members in 1989 in 12 counties.

A group calling itself FLAG (Family, Life, America, God) was organized in 1977 to fight ratification of the Equal Rights Amendment by Arkansas and to work for fundamentalist and conservative causes. Although associated with Eagle Forum, the national anti-ERA group, FLAG never took its name. Marilyn Sharp Simmons, FLAG's leader, said the

Arkansas Equal Rights Amendment (ERA) March *(Steve Keesee, 1978) Despite the presence in Arkansas of supporters for women's rights, militant feminism remained on the fringes of Arkansas life.* **Arkansas Gazette**

group was "truly grassroot — not that structured" and she did not know how many members it had. She said FLAG mailed 1,200-1,300 newsletters, mostly to churches, and "All I know is that when we put out the call, people show up."

In the legislature, Carolyn Pollan, a Fort Smith Republican businesswoman, and Gloria Cabe of Little Rock, a Democrat, represented different philosophical approaches, yet both served as evidence of increasing female involvement in politics and both supported the ERA.

In spite of this bi-partisan support, women remained at risk in male-dominated Arkansas. Changes in divorce, alimony and child custody laws often resulted in the victimization of women who remained unable to compete economically with men even though considered by the law to be equal. Arkansas laws offered woefully inadequate protection to women with abusive husbands, and the woman who was the victim of male aggression often found herself on trial. In 1991, when it was alleged that a group of Razorback basketball players took part in a group sexual experience inside the Bud Walton athletic dormitory in Fayetteville, disciplinary action was delayed until after the team was eliminated from the NCAA basketball tournament.

CONCLUSION

As a part of the 1976 celebration of the American Bicentennial, the NBC television show "Today" produced a tribute to each state. The Arkansas segment gave prominence to the Ozarks and featured the singing of Jimmy Driftwood. Many Arkansas viewers were outraged, and irate letters to the newspapers for the next month asserted that NBC should have shown the Arkansas Arts Center, the Arkansas Symphony Orchestra, and evidence of material progress instead of the ever-present hillbilly stereotype.

Eleven years later, Fayetteville journalism professor Roy Reed wrote a story for *TV Guide* on television-watching in the Ozarks that was accompanied by an illustration of a barefoot hillbilly with a black-and-white console television set on the front porch. Another storm of protest followed. Reed was even denounced editorially by the Fort Smith paper as a "sorry spokesman for the people of this state" who "milks the public teat as a taxpayer-supported professor." Reed, it added, "does a disservice to every promoter of progress and builder of bridges of understanding between his region and the rest of America." Ironically, it was not Reed's words but *TV Guide's* graphic that seemed to upset the people most.

The continual sensitivity by many people to any word, deed or picture that suggested Arkansas was in any way unusual or un-American has been an important part of the Arkansas Odyssey. But mixed with this sensitivity has been a proud defiance of world opinion. This book has sought to follow Arkansans through the ages in their search for an accurate portrait of the state.

In contrast to the saga of American history, which portrays the past as one success after another in pursuit of modernization, Arkansas has as its legacy a national reputation for having failed in modernization. As AIDC Director Frank White observed in 1976, "People everywhere think of us as Old South, perhaps hillbilly, rural, backward and most of all racist."

In reality, Arkansas history records both victories and defeats in the struggle between modernization and tradition. Modernization's successes have been most evident in matters economic and least present in cultural values. Incomplete modernization ultimately is reflected in a time lag between Arkansas and the rest of the nation, so that Arkansas represents America's yesterdays. In addition, the various geographic sections of the state have modernized at different rates, making generalizations risky and further confusing the national public.

Throughout Arkansas history, modernization has been controversial. Small farmers opposed creating state banks in 1837; proponents of localism repeatedly have denounced school consolidation; and modernization has been blamed for destroying the family, corrupting the youth and subverting the church. Because modernization is relative to time and place, people can be expected to disagree. Poet John Gould Fletcher struggled with these ambiguities in two poems, each of which offers insights on how individuals can come to terms with the Arkansas experience. His poetic tribute, "The Epic of Arkansas," written for the state's Centennial suggested adventure:

> Cease your fiddling and scraping, Draw
> up the latchstring, let the guests go
> home Tread out the smouldering fires,
> Snuff up the guttering candles;
> Tomorrow we shall ride beyond these
> hills To seek our star.

Yet, Fletcher had returned home to live out his life, and that theme, from "The Christmas Tree," is part of the Odyssey:

> Yet this at least I find is surely mine,
> After a long hard journey, and mighty
> cities seen: The pure sweet scent of a
> southern long-leafed pine, Dangling with
> chains and balls of glass and toys, Into
> my nostrils breathed, soft, rich, and
> clean.

BIBLIOGRAPHIC ESSAY

Historians have long recognized and tried to identify a central theme in Southern history. Every eminent Southern historian has offered a theory at one time or another and usually followed it by projecting the theme into the future. Two notable Arkansans, Professor C. Vann Woodward (a native of Vanndale in Cross County) in *The Burden of Southern History,* (Baton Rouge, 1960), and long-time journalist Harry S. Ashmore, *An Epitaph for Dixie,* (New York, 1958) have been among the most quoted. In general, historians have marshaled considerable evidence to support the notion that cultural continuity will insure the survival of Southern distinctiveness. By contrast, journalists and industrial promoters prefer to ignore themes such as racism, reaction, rurality, etc., which Francis Butler Simkins studied in *The Everlasting South,* (Baton Rouge, 1963)

To a large extent, research materials for this chapter consist of newspaper articles and personal experiences. However, state government increasingly issues documents and studies. For education, Kern Alexander, et. al., *Educational Equity; Improving School Finance in Arkansas,* (Little Rock, 1978) is thorough and devastating. The Governor's Commission on the Status of Women produced *The Status of Women in Arkansas,* (Little Rock, 1973). Business and industrial information, besides appearing in newspapers and government reports, has benefited from the founding in 1983 of the bi-weekly *Arkansas Business.* Its sesquicentennial issue, *150 Years of Arkansas Business, AB,* III (June 30, 1986), contained much good information and a realistic assessment of continuing problems.

A few books and other non-governmental sources are relevant for studying the present. Juanita Sandford, *Poverty in the Land of Opportunity* (Little Rock, 1978) touches on the underside of prosperity; the "Proceedings of the Conference on Ozark In-Migration," (N.P., n. d.) fortuitously recorded one aspect of the changes in the Ozarks. John Heuston, "The Battle — From One Man's Foxhole," *OSJ,* XVI (Autumn 1982), chronicles the struggle to save the Buffalo River. The definitive book is Neil Compton's book, *The Battle for the Buffalo River* (Fayetteville, 1992). The muckraking *Arkansas Advocate* published a wide range of articles in the early 1970s, including Martin Kirby, "Sins of the Palmer Media," *AAdv,* II

(Mar-Apr-May 1974). Those interested in the persistence of rural ways should consult Patricia A. Averill, "Can the Circle Be Unbroken: A Study of the Modernization of Rural Born Southern Whites Since World War I Using Country Music," (Ph. D. diss., University of Pennsylvania, 1975).

The image of Arkansas, which is probably more important than the reality, remains a topic of enduring interest. Bill Terry, "Arkansas in Search of an Image," *AT*, (September 1978), 36-39, and Bob Lancaster, "Bare Feet and Slow Trains," *AT*, XIII (June 1987), 34-41, 88-101, address current concerns that suggest there is an "Everlasting Arkansas."

Cartoonist George Fisher's Old Guard Resthome Contemplates Governor Bill Clinton's Campaign for President of the United States. (Arkansas Times, first issue as a weekly, May 7, 1992.) George Fisher's Old Guard Resthome for politicians has become a part of Arkansas folklore. The coon dog is Fisher's alter ego. From left to right, the Arkansas politicians featured are former Arkansas House Representative Marion Crank, ex-Congressman and ex-Pulaski County Sheriff Tommy Robinson, ex-Sheriff of Conway County Marlin Hawkins, Former Governor Frank White and Former Governor Orval E. Faubus.

Epilogue

On November 3, 1992, Americans selected Arkansas Governor Bill Clinton as their new president, but it was as William Jefferson Clinton that he was sworn in as the 42nd President of the United States on January 20, 1993. How a man who had always been just plain "Bill" became president was not only a personal saga of success, but also the apotheosis of Arkansas history.

Born in Hope, Arkansas, on August 19, 1946, as William Jefferson Blythe IV, soon after the death of his father in an automobile crash, young Bill had a troubled childhood. His widowed mother went to New Orleans, Louisiana, to train as a nurse, leaving Bill with his maternal grandfather in Hope. His grandfather ran a grocery store in a black neighborhood, and years later, when Clinton was campaigning for the presidency, he recalled that he learned respect for people of all races there.

After his mother became a nurse anesthetist and remarried, the family moved to Hot Springs, Arkansas. A step-brother, Roger, was born ten years later, and Bill changed his last name to Clinton to avoid confusion.

Young Clinton's political ambitions began early. While a delegate to Boy's Nation as a high school senior in 1963, Clinton visited the White House and shook hands with President John F. Kennedy. He later recalled that from that day on he knew he wanted to go into public service.

Clinton attended Georgetown University in Washington, D. C., majored in international relations, and worked on Senator J. William Fulbright's staff for the Senate Foreign Relations Committee. Awarded a Rhodes Scholarship, he studied at Oxford University in England from 1968 to 1970. Upon his return, he enrolled at the Yale University Law School where he met his future wife, Hillary Rodham of Park Ridge, Illinois, a Chicago suburb. A Wellesley graduate and student body president, she became the first Wellesley student invited to speak at her own graduation.

Clinton joined the faculty of the University of Arkansas Law School in Fayetteville in 1973, and the rest, as we say, is history. Through these early years, he accumulated some liabilities that would come back to haunt him in his 1992 presidential race. He admitted trying marijuana in England. His statement that he did not inhale was greeted with derision in the press. He successfully avoided being drafted into the Vietnam War. And after his marriage, there were charges that he had affairs with other women. Finally, he broke his promise to the Arkansas voters to be a full four-year governor when he announced his presidential bid.

On the positive side, Clinton received timely support from hardworking Friends of Bill or "Arkansas Travelers," who carried the early burden of the campaign in the New Hampshire primary and elsewhere. In addition, he raised $4 million from Arkansas friends alone, the largest per capita amount raised from any state for any candidate. Success in the primaries was followed by a strong attack on President Bush for ignoring the economy. Clinton urged health care reform and called for economic revitalization as well as deficit reduction.

Although Clinton garnered only 43 percent of the popular vote in the presidential race, he won a convincing victory in the Electoral College with 370 votes. Incumbent President George Bush, who a year earlier had appeared the invincible hero of Desert Storm, proved vulnerable on a variety of fronts. Hurt by a weak economy, and growing public criticism of the nation's political mood (whose anti-incumbency mood cost Arkansas two seemingly entrenched veteran Democrats, Congressman Bill Alexander and Beryl Anthony), Bush ran one of the weakest campaigns in recent political memory. Meanwhile, a newly invigorated Democratic Party pulled stray voters back to the fold, found surprising strength in the suburbs, and received with open arms the votes of women and gays forcefully driven out of the Republican Party at its Houston convention by Patrick Buchanan's call for a "religious war." Many disillusioned Republicans opted for Ross Perot, the most successful independent candidate since 1968.

For many Arkansas observers, Clinton's run for the presidency was also Arkansas's bid for national respectability as a state without an image problem. Certainly, the Republicans did their best to revive the old negatives. President Bush, by calling Arkansas "the lowest of the low," disparaged Clinton just for being from Arkansas. Some state residents responded by wearing buttons reading, "We Live Here Because We Elect to Live Here."

Ozark chic—barefoot and pregnant—surfaced, and after the election one Little Rock resident was quoted as observing, "We are definitely not barefoot and pregnant. What we are is Democratic and victorious." Although the Saint Paul Press (whose editor, Walker Lundy, played an important role in the collapse of the *Arkansas Gazette*), ran a story under the headline, "Arkansas: shoddy, vulgar, treacherous....," all culled from the definitions in the Dictionary of American Regional English, many reporters, who, it should be noted, saw only Little Rock, were impressed. Marlyn Schwartz of the Knight-Ridder/Tribune News Wire concluded, "Clinton's election as president of the United States is the biggest thing that's happened to Arkansas since the Civil War. Well, at least the biggest since Wal-Mart." Arkansans, she discovered, did wear shoes, and even (in Little Rock, at least) Ferragamos.

Meanwhile, many Arkansans rejected Clinton and his pragmatic liberalism. Local critics at the *Arkansas Democrat-Gazette* continued their vigorous assault on Clinton. Pulitzer Prize winning editorial writer Paul Greenberg, who had applied the term "Slick Willie" (originally a Little Rock restaurant) to Clinton, and John Robert Starr carried on a vigorous sniper attack on Clinton throughout the campaign. Dogmatically conservative, the paper even endorsed ultra-conservative Baptist minister Mike Huckabee, who garnered only 40 percent of the vote against liberal incumbent Senator Dale Bumpers.

While Clinton stood for a pragmatic liberalism with expanded roles for women and minorities, Texas Baptists stood outside his home church, Immanuel Baptist in Little Rock, during the campaign, calling for Clinton's expulsion. Although Immanuel stood by its choir member, conservative religious groups renewed their activities. One of Little Rock's most dynamic new churches, Fellowship Bible, demanded prayers in public schools, reaffirmed the traditional tenet that women could not share in church government and denounced the sins of homosexuality and abortion. Its individual members continued their boycott of the sons of families who subscribed to *Playboy* magazine. On January 17, 1993, a crowd estimated at from 10,000 to 20,000 took part in the annual March for Life anti-abortion protest. One of Clinton's legacies, the Governor's School for talented high school students, was under vigorous attack for exposing students to "dangerous" ideas. That Clinton received only 53 percent of the vote in Arkansas indicated to some how weak his triumph really was. Carrying this argument further, the election of President Bill Clinton represents the apotheosis and the end of Arkansas history. In the preface to this book, we argued that Arkansas history has been a constant struggle between the forces of modernization and those of traditionalism. Modernizers seemed cast in the role of the legendary Greek figure Sisyphus, doomed to carry the hard rock of modernization to the "Rock" only to have it roll all the way back to Benton County. However, a more recent scholarly theme proposed by conservative writer Francis Fukayama first in an 1989 article and then in a 1992 book, *The End of History and the Last Man*, is "the end of history." Fukayama did not mean that events had ceased, but rather that through the historical process liberal capitalism had won out over fascism on the right and communism on the left. Problems would, of course, remain, but they would be pragmatic rather than ideological.

The Arkansas variant on this thesis is that the election of Clinton means on the national scale that the old negative comments about Arkansas so long resented are dead. John Brummett argued that Clinton's victory put to rest at least the brutal legacy of September 1957 at Central High School. Modernization, albeit of Clinton's pragmatic, cautious sort, has won. This is not to say that anti-modernism is dead: Far from it, given the editorial direction of the *Arkansas Democrat-Gazette*, but Clinton's victory ushers Arkansas into the American mainstream, and while there may in the future be eddies, there can be no turning back from the drift of history.

Like the nation's cold warriors, caught suddenly without an enemy and thus deprived of purpose in their lives, we must face a dull future. For many, the end of history can also be found in the demise of the *Arkansas Gazette*, beloved by liberals and the paper conservatives loved to hate. The so-called merged version, the *Arkansas Democrat-Gazette*, has yet to be more than a Little Rock paper without state influence. Thousands who thought they could not live without the *Arkansas Gazette* have learned to do so.

Time and events may prove this epilogue to be misguided. An American high school history text written in the late nineteenth century concluded that England, Germany and other European countries would soon borrow our constitution and put an end to monarchy: Instead, World War I occurred.

William Quesenbury, the nineteenth century author of a heroic poem on the state, provides the fitting final curtain:

The song is sung — if such it may be called —
An unmethodical, rude, backwoods song
Discordantly discoursed or rather bawled: —
But be it what it may, it will not long
Remain in memories amid the throng
Of busy life pursuits, — a passing flaw
Upon the stream of time, — and, right or wrong,
From it one truth, a rock-truth, we may draw, —
'Tis this: GOD LOVES NOT HIM THAT LOVES NOT ARKANSAS!

A Chronology of Arkansas History

MAY 31, 1539	Hernando De Soto landed in Florida.
JUNE 19, 1541	De Soto crossed the Mississippi River into Arkansas.
MAY 21, 1542	De Soto died at the Indian village of Guachoya.
JULY 2, 1543	The remainder of the De Soto party departed, going down the Mississippi River.
MAY 17, 1673	Marquette and Joliet began their expedition.
JULY 1673	Marquette and Joliet arrived among the Quapaw and then turned back north.
MARCH 12, 1682	La Salle and Henri de Tonti arrived at the Quapaw villages near the mouth of the Arkansas River.
MARCH 13, 1682	La Salle took formal possession of Arkansas for the King of France.
APRIL 9, 1682	La Salle took formal possession of the mouth of the Mississippi River.
SPRING 1686	De Tonti established his trading post among the Quapaw.
MARCH 19, 1687	La Salle was killed by his own men in Texas.
MARCH 1700	Taensas temple destroyed by fire.
1716	One of John Law's companies was granted a charter to develop Louisiana.
DECEMBER 14, 1720	Bankruptcy forced John Law to flee France.
AUGUST 1721	Law's colonists arrived at Arkansas Post.

DECEMBER 1721	De la Harpe explored the Arkansas River.
NOVEMBER 1729	Father Paul Du Poisson was killed at Natchez.
MAY 10, 1749	Payah Matahah led an attack on Arkansas Post.
NOVEMBER 3, 1762	Louisiana was ceded by France to Spain in the Treaty of Fontainbleau.
FEBRUARY 2, 1778	Americans petitioned for sanctuary at Arkansas Post.
APRIL 17, 1783	Colbert unsuccessfully attacked Arkansas Post.
SEPTEMBER 3, 1783	The Treaty of Paris ending the Revolutionary War gave America the east bank of the Mississippi River.
OCTOBER 1, 1800	Napoleon forced Spain to sign the Treaty of San Ildefonso returning Louisiana to France.
APRIL 30, 1803	The Louisiana Purchase was consummated by the Treaty of Paris giving possession to the United States.
JUNE 27, 1806	The District of Arkansaw was created by the territorial legislature of Louisiana.
DECEMBER 16, 1811	The first shock of the New Madrid earthquake was felt.
DECEMBER 13, 1813	The Missouri territorial legislature created Arkansas County.
JUNE 1817	The first post office was established at Davidsonville in Lawrence County.
JULY 8, 1817	The Cherokee ceded part of their eastern lands in exchange for new land in northwestern Arkansas.
AUGUST 24, 1818	The Quapaw were forced to cede most of their Arkansas lands.
JULY 4, 1819	The Territory of Arkansas was created by Congress.
JULY 28, 1819	The first Arkansas territorial legislature met at Arkansas Post.
NOVEMBER 20, 1819	Arkansas held its first election, selecting a territorial delegate to Washington and members of the legislature.
NOVEMBER 20, 1819	William E. Woodruff published the first issue of the *Arkansas Gazette*.

MARCH 6, 1820	President Monroe signed the Missouri Compromise legislation.
MARCH 31, 1820	The steamboat *Comet* arrived at Arkansas Post, the first craft of its kind to navigate the Arkansas River.
SEPTEMBER 20, 1820	Construction began on Dwight Mission.
JUNE 1, 1821	The territorial capital was moved to Little Rock.
MARCH 22, 1822	The Eagle became the first steamboat to arrive in Little Rock.
JULY 27, 1826	The first steam sawmill in Arkansas was reported in operation at Helena.
OCTOBER 29, 1827	Robert Crittenden killed Henry W. Conway in a duel.
MAY 6, 1828	The Cherokee exchanged their Arkansas lands for holdings farther west. All Indian land titles now were formally extinguished.
NOVEMBER 4, 1834	The first theatrical performance was given in Little Rock.
JANUARY 4, 1836	The constitutional convention assembled in Little Rock.
JUNE 16, 1836	President Andrew Jackson signed the bill admitting Arkansas into the Union.
OCTOBER 26, 1836	Governor Conway signed the bill creating the Real Estate Bank.
NOVEMBER 2, 1836	The State Bank was chartered by the legislature.
DECEMBER 4, 1837	Speaker of the House John Wilson killed State Representative J. J. Anthony on the floor of the House.
JUNE 27, 1838	The first steam ferry on the Arkansas River went into operation at Little Rock.
NOVEMBER 21, 1838	The Masonic Grand Lodge of Arkansas was created by the state's four lodges.
OCTOBER 31, 1839	The Real Estate Bank suspended payment of its notes in specie. The State Bank adopted the same policy.
JANUARY 1, 1840	The Real Estate Bank illegally sold bonds for less than their face value (Holford Bonds). Both banks subsequently closed.
MAY 13, 1846	President Polk proclaimed the start of the Mexican War.

FEBRUARY 23, 1847	Colonel Archibald Yell was among those killed at the Battle of Buena Vista.
APRIL 5, 1849	The first party headed for the California Gold Rush left Arkansas from Fort Smith.
FEBRUARY 9, 1853	Congress granted alternate sections of land to aid in the building of the Cairo and Fulton Railroad.
SEPTEMBER 10, 1857	An Arkansas party headed west was massacred at Mountain Meadow by Mormons.
MARCH 4, 1859	School for the Blind at Arkadelphia was incorporated by the legislature.
FEBRUARY 5, 1861	Armed troops gathered to force the evacuation by the federal forces of the United states Arsenal in Little Rock.
MARCH 4, 1861	The Secession Convention met but rejected taking immediate action.
APRIL 12, 1861	Confederates in Charleston, South Carolina, opened fire on the federal garrison in Fort Sumter, thus beginning the Civil War.
APRIL 19, 1861	State troops commanded by Colonel Solon Borland seized Fort Smith.
MAY 6, 1861	The Convention adopted an ordinance of secession by a vote of sixty-nine to one.
AUGUST 10, 1861	The Arkansas army participated in the Confederate victory at Wilson's Creek (Oak Hills) near Springfield, Missouri.
MARCH 6-8, 1862	The Confederates lost the Battle of Pea Ridge (Elkhorn Tavern).
SEPTEMBER 22, 1862	President Abraham Lincoln issued the Emancipation Proclamation, portending the end of slavery in Arkansas, and the rest of the Confederacy.
DECEMBER 7, 1862	The Confederates lost the Battle of Prairie Grove.
JANUARY 11, 1863	The Union army and navy captured Arkansas Post.
JULY 4, 1863	The Confederates lost the Battle of Helena.
SEPTEMBER 1, 1863	The Union army occupied Fort Smith.

SEPTEMBER 10, 1863	The Union army captured Little Rock.
JANUARY 4, 1864	A Union constitutional convention met at Little Rock.
JANUARY 8, 1864	David O. Dodd was executed as a Confederate spy at Little Rock.
APRIL 18, 1864	Isaac Murphy was inaugurated governor under President Lincoln's reconstruction program.
APRIL 18, 1864	The Union army lost the Battle of Poison Spring.
APRIL 25, 1864	The Union army lost the Battle of Marks' Mills.
APRIL 30, 1864	Confederate forces failed to destroy General Steele's Army at the Battle of Jenkins' Ferry.
MAY 24, 1865	The last skirmish of the Civil War in Arkansas was fought at Monticello.
JANUARY 7, 1868	The Convention that wrote the Constitution of 1868 assembled in Little Rock.
JUNE 22, 1868	Arkansas was readmitted to the Union under the radical program of Reconstruction.
JULY 2, 1868	Powell Clayton was inaugurated governor.
SEPTEMBER 29, 1868	Former U. S. Representative and Confederate Major General Thomas C. Hindman was murdered in Helena.
OCTOBER 22, 1868	Republican Congressman James Hinds was murdered by the Ku Klux Klan at Indian Bay.
NOVEMBER 4, 1868	Ku Klux Klan violence led Governor Clayton to declare martial law in thirteen counties.
MARCH 27, 1871	The legislature created Arkansas Industrial University located at Fayetteville.
APRIL 11, 1871	The Little Rock & Memphis Railroad was completed.
AUGUST 3, 1872	Efforts began to organize chapters of a farmer organization called the National Grange.
FEBRUARY 10, 1873	The railroad from St. Louis to Texas was completed to Little Rock.

APRIL 15, 1874	Joseph Brooks, claiming to be the lawful governor of Arkansas, ousted Elisha Baxter, thus beginning the Brooks-Baxter War.
MAY 15, 1874	President U. S. Grant officially recognized Elisha Baxter as governor, thereby ending the war.
JULY 14, 1874	The fifth Arkansas Constitutional Convention assembled.
OCTOBER 13, 1874	The voters ratified the new constitution and elected a slate of Democrats to office, thus ending Reconstruction.
MAY 10, 1875	U. S. District Judge Isaac C. Parker arrived at Fort Smith to restore integrity to the court. He became known as the "Hanging Judge."
MARCH 3, 1877	President U. S. Grant signed an act creating the Hot Springs Reservation, which ended the legal battles over the Springs' ownership.
FEBRUARY 15, 1882	The Agricultural Wheel, a farmer-protest group, organized in Prairie County.
JANUARY 14, 1885	Voters approved the Fishback Amendment that repudiated paying the Holford Bonds illegally sold by the Real Estate Bank.
OCTOBER 15, 1885	The Agricultural Wheel merged with the Brothers of Freedom.
SEPTEMBER 6, 1888	Union Labor Party gubernatorial candidate C. M. Norwood was defeated amid charges of election fraud.
JANUARY 29, 1889	Republican congressional candidate John M. Clayton was murdered at Plumerville while investigating election frauds.
DECEMBER 1, 1890	The Confederate Soldiers' Home opened.
FEBRUARY 23, 1891	The Separate Coach Bill, Arkansas's first Jim Crow Law, was signed into law.
APRIL 25, 1898	Congress declared war on Spain.
JANUARY 13, 1899	A constitutional amendment passed by the voters created a railroad commission to curb abuses.
NOVEMBER 27, 1900	The cornerstone of the new state capitol was laid.
SEPTEMBER 5, 1904	Jeff Davis became the first governor elected to a third term.

DECEMBER 7, 1912	Governor George Donaghey pardoned more than 360 convicts in order to put an end to the convict-lease system.
FEBRUARY 6, 1915	The Newberry Law imposed statewide prohibition.
MARCH 7, 1917	Arkansas permitted women to vote in party primaries.
APRIL 6, 1917	America entered World War I.
NOVEMBER 19, 1917	A constitutional convention met in Little Rock.
JUNE 18, 1918	Lieutenant John McGavock Grider, a fighter pilot, was killed in action in France.
DECEMBER 14, 1918	The voters rejected the new proposed constitution.
OCTOBER 1-4, 1919	The Elaine Race Riot erupted in Phillips County.
JANUARY 10, 1921	S. T. Bussey's discovery of oil near El Dorado initiated the Arkansas oil boom.
JANUARY 10, 1921	The Ku Klux Klan held its first public initiation in a pasture near Little Rock.
FEBRUARY 18, 1922	WOK, the first radio station in Arkansas, went on the air in Pine Bluff.
JANUARY 26, 1923	The legislature decreed that Arkansas be "known and styled" as "The Wonder State."
MARCH 14. 1923	Little Rock's Broadway Bridge became the first concrete automobile bridge to span the Arkansas River.
OCTOBER 10, 1923	The Harrelson Road Act made highways a state responsibility.
DECEMBER 1924	Remmel Dam on the Ouachita River became the state's first large hydroelectric dam.
FEBRUARY 16, 1926	In *Brickhouse* v. *Hill*, the state Supreme Court ruled that a number of constitutional amendments previously believed to have been defeated had passed, including initiative and referendum, an enlarged Supreme Court and woman's suffrage.
APRIL 12, 1926	The state Supreme Court ruled that the amendment creating the office of lieutenant governor had passed.

APRIL 21, 1927   Flood waters on the Mississippi River broke through levees.

OCTOBER 6, 1928   Voters used initiative to pass an anti-evolution law.

OCTOBER 29, 1929   The stock market crash on Wall Street signaled the beginning of
                      the Great Depression.

NOVEMBER 17, 1930   The banking empire of A. B. Banks collapsed.

JANUARY 4, 1931   A food riot, triggered by the Drought of 1930, occurred in England
                      (Lonoke County).

NOVEMBER 9, 1932   Hattie Caraway became the first woman to be elected to a full term
                      in the U. S. Senate.

MARCH 4, 1933   Franklin Roosevelt became president, starting the New Deal.

AUGUST 24, 1933   The legislature legalized the sale of wine and beer.

NOVEMBER 24, 1933   The University of Arkansas Razorbacks football team won its first
                      Southwest Conference championship.

JULY 1934   The Southern Tenant Farmers Union organized at Tyronza.

JANUARY 15, 1935   Amendment 19 was adopted, giving Arkansas a highly restrictive
                      taxing system, requiring a three-fourths majority vote of the
                      legislature to increase existing taxes.

MARCH 23, 1935   The legislature legalized the sale of hard liquor.

MAY 22, 1936   The Dyess community, the first Arkansas agricultural resettlement
                      project, was dedicated.

JUNE 15, 1936   Arkansas celebrated the centennial of its statehood.

JANUARY 19, 1937   The Flood of 1937 struck eastern Arkansas.

DECEMBER 7, 1941   The Japanese attack on Pearl Harbor began American
                      participation in World War II.

NOVEMBER 7, 1944   Voters approved Amendment 34, "Freedom to Work," weakening
                      labor unions, and Amendment 35 creating the Arkansas Game and
                      Fish Commission.

NOVEMBER 2, 1948   Voters approved Amendment 49 removing the eighteen-mill limit
                      on school taxes and an act forcing some school consolidation.

JUNE 25, 1950	The Korean War began.
JULY 2, 1952	Gubernatorial candidate Francis Cherry talked for twenty-four hours on a Little Rock radio station.
NOVEMBER 4, 1952	Voters approved Amendment 42 (Mack-Blackwell) making the highway commission an independent agency.
MARCH 27, 1953	The legislature resolved officially that Arkansas was "The Land of Opportunity."
MAY 17, 1954	The United States Supreme Court rendered its decision in *Brown v. the Board of Education of Topeka, Kansas* invalidating school segregation.
JULY 11, 1955	Hoxie became the first school district in the Delta to integrate.
NOVEMBER 6, 1956	Voters approved Amendment 44, asserting that the state can block decisions of the United States Supreme Court.
SEPTEMBER 4, 1957	Governor Orval Faubus used the Arkansas National Guard to prevent integration at Little Rock's Central High School.
SEPTEMBER 24, 1957	United States paratroopers occupied Little Rock in order to enforce desegregation.
NOVEMBER 4, 1958	U. S. Representative Brooks Hays, a racial moderate, was defeated by write-in candidate Dale Alford, and Orval Faubus was elected to a third term.
NOVEMBER 3, 1964	Orval Faubus was elected to his sixth term as governor, and voters approved Amendment 52, permitting the establishment of junior colleges.
NOVEMBER 9, 1966	Arkansas voters elected Republican Winthrop Rockefeller as governor, reelected Democrat J. William Fulbright to the United States Senate and supported the Independent Party candidate, George Wallace, for president.
NOVEMBER 5, 1968	Amendment 53 authorized kindergartens.
DECEMBER 31, 1968	The McClellan-Kerr Arkansas River Navigation dedication declared the Arkansas River was open for shipping from its mouth to Catoosa (near Tulsa), Oklahoma.

JANUARY 7, 1969	A constitutional convention assembled to revise the 1874 constitution.
FEBRUARY 19, 1970	The Arkansas prison system was declared unconstitutional by U.S. District Judge J. Smith Henley.
NOVEMBER 3, 1970	Voters rejected the new proposed constitution.
NOVEMBER 5, 1974	Amendment 55 restructured county government by giving more power to the quorum court.
NOVEMBER 7, 1978	William Jefferson "Bill" Clinton is elected governor.
NOVEMBER 4, 1980	Frank White is elected governor.
NOVEMBER 2, 1982	William Jefferson "Bill" Clinton is elected governor.
JANUARY 6, 1982	In *McLean* v. *Arkansas Board of Education*, U. S. District Judge William Overton declared Arkansas's Creation Science Law unconstitutional.
JANUARY 18, 1984	Middle South Utilities planned to charge Arkansas electrical customers $3.5 billion to pay for the costs of the Grand Gulf nuclear power plant in Mississippi.
NOVEMBER 7, 1984	Voters approved a constitutional amendment giving statewide officials four-year terms of office.
1985	Controversy over Grand Gulf continues.
JUNE 14, 1986	Arkansas celebrates its sesquicentennial with a federal postage stamp depicting the Old State House.
JANUARY 15, 1987	Governor Bill Clinton proclaimed in behalf of the Parks and Tourism Department that Arkansas's new slogan is "The Natural State." The General Assembly has not officially changed the name from "The Land of Opportunity."
JANUARY 21, 1987	Arkansas juvenile justice "system" ruled unconstitutional by the state Supreme Court.
DECEMBER 1987	Ronald Gene Simmons became one of America's leading mass murderers by killing fourteen family members and two other individuals during the Christmas holidays in rural Pope County. He did not want to appeal his death sentence and was executed by lethal injection on June 25, 1990.

MAY 19, 1988	Arkansas reported 126 known cases of AIDS, including the first infected child.
SEPTEMBER 29, 1988	The Mississippi Delta Commission was created with the goal of investigating and improving Delta life.
JUNE 17, 1989	Arkansas savings and loans recorded a negative net worth of $1 billion as the crisis growing out of deregulation spread.
JUNE 18, 1990	John Edward Swindler became the first convicted murderer to be executed in Arkansas since January 24, 1964.
November 4, 1990	Attorney General Steve Clark resigned after being found guilty of theft of state property in his handling of expense account monies.
DECEMBER 4, 1990	Dr. Iben Browning's predicted earthquake for the New Madrid fault region led to a wave of hysteria called "Quakeamania" but failed to materialize.
NOVEMBER 9, 1990	Sheffield Nelson defeated United States Representative Tommy Robinson in the Republican primary but lost to Governor Clinton in the general election. Clinton, elected to his fifth term, carried through on his promise and danced in the streets of Fort Smith afterwards.
OCTOBER 18, 1991	The *Arkansas Gazette* published its last edition.
NOVEMBER 3, 1992	Governor Bill Clinton was elected President of the United States.

Publisher's Note

This book is the culmination of my twenty-one years of work publishing books in Arkansas. I started in 1973 after I submitted my own manuscript *Readings in Arkansas Government,* to twenty-six out-of-state publishers and received twenty-six rejection slips. The success of publishing the manuscript myself made me realize the great need for Arkansas materials. When I began, there was no book publisher in the state and few sources of material for Arkansas studies. Other publishers have entered the field since and I am gratified by the number of publications about the state that are now available from other presses. However, we remain the only publishing house that focuses exclusively on Arkansas studies.

Early on, I dedicated my efforts toward producing three history books for students of Arkansas history: one for elementary school, *Arkansas Heritage,* by Ruth Mitchell; one for secondary school, *The History of Arkansas* by Fred Berry and John Novak; and this book for the adult reader and college classrooms. Along the way, I have published several other books that I consider to be milestones in Arkansas studies, including *Arkansas Geography,* by Gerald Hanson and Hubert Stroud, and *Ozark Log Cabin Folks: the Way They Were,* by Paul Faris.

Arkansas Odyssey would not have been possible without the work of my wife, Gale Stewart, who took over the job when my spirits and energy were low, and who was the final editor of the work; the cheerful assistance of my executive editor, Mary Etta Madden, who worked long hours for low pay because as she said, she sort of likes the book business; and the financial assistance of my mother-in-law, Emma Jean Stewart, who assisted me when I had exhausted all other sources of capital. All of us are proud members of pioneer Arkansas families.

I also want to thank the authors of all the books published by Rose. These authors have persevered in spite of little public recognition, low pay and, more frequently, no pay, because of their love for Arkansas and dedication to its people.

— *Walter Nunn*

Appendix A

Counties

County Name	County Seat	Named For	Year Established
Arkansas County	DeWitt and Stuttgart	in honor of District of Arkansas	1813
Ashley County	Hamburg	Chester Ashley, U.S. senator	1848
Baxter County	Mountain Home	Elisha Baxter, governor	1873
Benton County	Bentonville	Thomas Benton, state senator	1836
Boone County	Harrison	Legends conflict. May be named for Daniel Boone, but some say it was a "boon" to create the county.	1869
Bradley County	Warren	Hugh Bradley, military captain and hero of War of 1812	1840
Calhoun County	Hampton	John C. Calhoun, senator from South Carolina	1850
Carroll County	Eureka Springs and Berryville	Charles Carroll, signer of the Declaration of Independence	1823
Chicot County	Lake Village	Point Chicot on the Mississippi River	1823
Clark County	Arkadelphia	Governor William Clark of Missouri Territory	1818
Clay County	Piggott and Corning	John Clayton, state senator	1873
Cleburne County	Heber Springs	Patrick Cleburne, Confederate general	1883
Cleveland County	Rison	President Grover Cleveland	1873
Columbia County	Magnolia	another name for America	1852
Conway County	Morrilton	Henry Conway, territorial delegate to Congress	1823
Craighead County	Jonesboro and Lake City	Thomas Craighead, state senator	1859
Crawford County	Van Buren	William Crawford, U.S. secretary of war	1820
Crittenden County	Marion	Robert Crittenden, territorial secretary of state	1825
Cross County	Wynne	Colonel David Cross of Fifth Arkansas Infantry, Confederate Army	1862
Dallas County	Fordyce	George Dallas, U.S. vice president	1845
Desha County	Arkansas City	Captain Benjamin Desha, hero of War of 1812	1838
Drew County	Monticello	Thomas Drew, governor	1846
Faulkner County	Conway	Sanford Faulkner, early settler	1873
Franklin County	Ozark and Charleston	Benjamin Franklin	1837
Fulton County	Salem	William Fulton, territorial governor	1842
Garland County	Hot Springs	Augustus Garland, governor	1873

Grant County	Sheridan	President U.S. Grant	1869
Greene County	Paragould	Nathaniel Greene, hero of War for Independence	1833
Hempstead County	Hope	Edward Hempstead, 1st delegate to Congress from Missouri Territory	1818
Hot Spring County	Malvern	named for local springs	1829
Howard County	Nashville	James Howard, state senator	1873
Independence County	Batesville	honor of independence of state	1820
Izard County	Melbourne	George Izard, territorial governor	1825
Jackson County	Newport	President Andrew Jackson	1829
Jefferson County	Pine Bluff	President Thomas Jefferson	1829
Johnson County	Clarksville	Benjamin Johnson, territorial judge	1833
Lafayette County	Lewisville	Marquis de Lafayette, hero of War for Independence	1827
Lawrence County	Walnut Ridge	Captain James Lawrence, hero of War of 1812	1815
Lee County	Marianna	General Robert E. Lee	1873
Lincoln County	Star City	President Abraham Lincoln	1871
Little River County	Ashdown	the Little River	1867
Logan County	Paris and Booneville	James Logan, early settler	1871
Lonoke County	Lonoke	from "Lone Oak"	1873
Madison County	Huntsville	President James Madison	1836
Marion County	Yellville	Francis Marion, hero of War for Independence	1835
Miller County	Texarkana	James Miller, territorial governor	1820
Mississippi County	Blytheville and Osceola	Mississippi River	1833
Monroe County	Clarendon	President James Monroe	1829
Montgomery County	Mount Ida	General Richard Montgomery, hero of War for Independence	1842
Nevada County	Prescott	state of Nevada	1871
Newton County	Jasper	Congressman Thomas Newton	1842
Ouachita County	Camden	Ouachita Mountains or the Ouachita River	1842
Perry County	Perryville	Commodore Oliver Perry, hero of War of 1812	1840
Phillips County	Helena	Sylvanus Phillips, early settler	1820
Pike County	Murfreesboro	Lieutenant Zebulon Pike, explorer	1833
Poinsett County	Harrisburg	Joel Poinsett, secretary of war	1838
Polk County	Mena	President James Polk	1844
Pope County	Russellville	John Pope, territorial governor	1829
Prairie County	Des Arc and DeValls Bluff	grand prairie country	1846
Pulaski County	Little Rock	Count Pulaski, hero of War for Independence	1818

Randolph County	Pocahontas	John Randolph, statesman of late 18th century	1835
Saline County	Benton	local salt works	1835
Scott County	Waldron	Andrew Scott, territorial judge	1833
Searcy County	Marshall	Richard Searcy, territorial judge	1838
Sebastian County	Greenwood and Fort Smith	William Sebastian, U.S. senator	1851
Sevier County	DeQueen	Ambrose Sevier, U.S. senator	1828
Sharp County	Ash Flat	Ephraim Sharp, state representative	1868
St. Francis County	Forrest City	St. Francis River	1827
Stone County	Mountain View	local hills	1873
Union County	El Dorado	honoring the Union of American States	1829
Van Buren County	Clinton	President Martin Van Buren	1833
Washington County	Fayetteville	President George Washington	1828
White County	Searcy	White River	1835
Woodruff County	Augusta	William Woodruff, founder of *Arkansas Gazette*	1862
Yell County	Danville and Dardanelle	Archibald Yell, governor	1840

Appendix B

Governors

Territorial Governors

James Miller 1819-1825

George Izard 1825-1829

John Pope 1829-1835

William Fulton 1835-1836

State Governors

James S. Conway 1836-1840

Archibald Yell .1840-1844

Thomas S. Drew 1844-1849

John S. Roane 1849-1852

Elias N. Conway 1852-1860

Henry M. Rector 1860-1862

Harris Flanagin 1862-1864

Isaac Murphy 1864-1868

Powell Clayton 1868-1871

Elisha Baxter 1873-1874

Augustus H. Garland 1874-1877

William R. Miller 1877-1881

Thomas J. Churchill 1881-1883

James H. Berry 1883-1885

Simon P. Hughes 1885-1889

James P. Eagle 1889-1893

William M. Fishback 1893-1895

James P. Clarke 1895-1897

Dan W. Jones 1897-1901

Jeff Davis 1901-1907

John S. Little 1907-1909

George W. Donaghey 1909-1913

Joseph T. Robinson 1913-

George W. Hays 1913-1917

Charles H. Brough 1917-1921

Thomas C. McRae 1921-1925

Tom J. Terral 1925-1927

John E. Martineau 1927-1928

Harvey Parnell 1928-1933

J. M. Futrell .1933-1937

Carl E. Bailey 1937-1941

Homer M. Adkins 1941-1945

Ben T. Laney .1945-1949

Sid McMath 1949-1953

Francis Cherry 1953-1955

Orval E. Faubus 1955-1967

Winthrop Rockefeller 1967-1971

Dale Bumpers 1971-1975

David Pryor .1975-1979

Bill Clinton 1979-1981

Frank White .1981-1983

Bill Clinton 1983-1992

Jim Guy Tucker 1992-1996

Mike Huckabee 1996-

Appendix C
Arkansas Population

Year	Total Population	White	Free Blacks	Slaves and After-1860 Foreign Born
1810	1,062[11]	924	—	138
1820	14,273[1]	12,579[1]	59[1]	1,617[1]
1830	30,388[2]	25,671[2]	141[2]	4,576[2]
1840	97,574[8]	77,174[8]	465[3]	19,935[4]
1850	209,897[5]	162,189[5]	608[5]	47,100[5]
1860	435,450[8]	324,191[8]	144[6]	111,115[7]
1870	484,471[8]	362,302[8]	122,169[8]	187[10]
1880	802,525[8]	591,859[8]	210,666[8]	328[10]
1890	1,128,179[8]	818,062[8]	309,117[8]	342[10]
1900	1,311,564[9]	944,708[9]	366,856[9]	128[9]
1910	1,574,449[10]	1,131,026[10]	442,891[10]	532[10]
1920	1,752,204[10]	1,279,757[12]	472,220[12]	227[12]
1930	1,854,482[13]	1,375,315[13]	478,463[13]	704[13]
1940	1,949,387[13]	1,446,084[14]	482,578[14]	725[14]
1950	1,909,511[15]	1,481,507[14]	426,639[14]	1,365[14]
1960	1,786,272[15]	1,395,703[14]	388,787[14]	1,782[14]
1970	1,923,295[15]	1,565,915[16]	352,445[16]	4,935[16]
1980	2,286,435	1,890,322	373,768	22,345
1990	2,350,725	1,944,744	373,912	32,069

[1]*Fourth Census, 1820 Book I* (Washington: Gales and Seaton, 1821), p. 41.

[2]*Abstract of the Return of the Fifth Census*, Document No. 263 (Washington: Duff Green, 1832), p. 43.

[3]U.S. Department of State, *Compendium of the Enumeration of the Inhabitants and Statistics of the United States*, from the Sixth Census (Washington: Thomas Allen, 1841) p. 93.

[4]*Ibid.*, p. 94.

[5]*Compendium of the Seventh Census or Statistical View of the United States, 1850* (Washington: J.D.B. DeBow, 1854), p. 194.

[6]*Eighth Census or Population of the United States in 1860* (Washington: Secretary of Interior, 1864), p. 15.

[7]*Ibid.*, p. 17.

[8]U.S. Treasury Department, *Statistical Abstract of the United States, 1900*, Document No. 2216 (New York: Johnston Reprint Corp., 1964), p. 8.

[9]U.S. Department of Commerce and Labor, Bureau of Statistics, *Statistical Abstract of the United States, 1910* (New York: Johnson Reprint Corp., 1970), p. 36.

[10]U.S. Department of Commerce, Bureau of Foreign and Domestic Commerce, *Statistical Abstract of the United States, 1920*, No. 43 (Washington: Government Printing Office, 1921), p. 35.

[11]*Ibid.*, p. 21.

[12]U.S. Department of Commerce, Bureau of Foreign and Domestic Commerce, *Statistical Abstract of the United States, 1930*, No. 52 (Washington: Government Printing Office, 1930), P. 12.

[13]U.S. Department of Commerce, Bureau of Census, *Statistical Abstract of the United States, 1942*, No. 64 (Washington: Government Printing Office, 1943), p. 13.

[14]U.S. Department of Commerce, Bureau of Census, *Statistical Abstract of the United States*, 1970. 91st Edition (Washington: Government Printing Office, 1970), P. 27.

[15]U.S. Department of Commerce, Bureau of Census, *1970 Census of Population, Volume 1 - Characteristics of the Population, Part 5 - Arkansas* (Washington: Government Printing Office, 1973), p. 7.

[16]*Ibid.*, p. 49.

Appendix D

Profile*
State of Arkansas

Geography

Arkansas is near the geographic and population centers of the United States; its borders adjoin Texas, Louisiana, Mississippi, Tennessee, Missouri and Oklahoma with the Mississippi River forming the state's eastern border.

It is located on the same latitude as Osaka, Japan, and North Africa.

Land Surface

137,591 square kilometers (53,124 square miles)

East

Alluvial valleys of the Arkansas and Mississippi Rivers, with agricultural land dominated by cotton, rice, and soybeans

North and West

Mountainous or coastal plains

South

Wildlife refuges and timberlands

Climate

Temperate with four seasons, long summers and short winters

Temperature

Annual maximum in Little Rock . . . . . . .73°F
Annual minimum in Little Rock . . . . . . .52°F

Humidity

Annual relative at noon in Little Rock 57%

Precipitation

Total annual in Little Rock . . . . .48"

Major Urban Centers 1990 Population

Little Rock-North Little Rock-
Jacksonville MSA 513,117
Fort Smith MSA 175,911
Pine Bluff MSA 85,487
Fayetteville-Springdale MSA 113,409
Texarkana MSA 120,132

Natural Resources

Water

Arkansas has over 283,000 hectares (699,293 acres) of surface water; over 800 billion liters of high quality ground water are contained in aquifers capable of yielding over 2,000 liters per minute.

Arkansas has a large network of navigable rivers with ports on the Mississippi, Arkansas and Ouachita rivers.

Timber

Forests cover 7.16 million hectares (17.69 million acres), or more than half of the state. Pine woods make up 42% and the rest is mixed hardwoods, mostly oak.

Timber growing, harvesting, management, transporting and processing are major industries in Arkansas.

Oil

Crude oil production is located in the southwest.

Total production . . . .8 million barrels (1990)
Reserves . . . . .60 million barrels

Natural Gas

Production . . . . .164 billion cubic feet (1990)

Reserves . . . . . .1,731 billion cubic feet (1990)

Coal and Lignite

Reserves . . . . . . .0.4 billion short tons (1990)

Minerals in Commercial Production

Bauxite (#1 in nation), bromine (#1 in world), cement rock, clay, gypsum, limestone, novaculite (only producer in nation), quartz crystals (#1 in nation), serpentine rock, shale, silica sand, syenite, tripoli, dimension stone, crushed stone, sand, gravel and slate

Minerals Present But Not In Production

Iron, manganese, diamond, copper, lead, zinc, silver, mercury, titanium, barite, vanadium, rare earths, phosphate rock, antimony and greensand

Business Highlights

Tourism

Tourists spent $2.5 billion in Arkansas in 1991; the Ozark and Ouachita Mountain regions are popular recreational areas.

Principal Industries

Manufacturing, agriculture, forestry and tourism

Principal Manufactured Goods

Chemicals, food products, lumber, paper, electric motors, furniture, home appliances, auto components, transformers, apparel, fertilizers, machinery, petroleum products, airplane parts and steel

Fortune 500

There are 219 Fortune 500 firms with operations in Arkansas. Four of the firms, Tyson's, Riceland Foods, Murphy Oil and Hudson Foods, Inc., are headquartered here. Five Fortune Service 500 companies are headquartered in Arkansas; Arkansas Best, Beverly Enterprises, Wal-Mart Stores, Dillard Depart-

ment Stores and J.B. Hunt Transport.

Principal Agricultural Products 1991

Rice
(#1 in nation) . . .66.8 million hundredweight
Wheat . . . . .20.5 million bushels
Soybeans . . . . .89.6 million bushels
Poultry
(#1 in nation) . . . . .980.2 million birds
Cotton . . . . .1,576,000 bales

Market

Within an 880-kilometer (550-mile) radius of Arkansas is a market of 103 million people (42% total U.S. population). Major market centers in the region include: Memphis, Chicago, Atlanta, Dallas, Fort Worth, Houston, Kansas City, Oklahoma City, New Orleans and St. Louis.

Transportation

Highways

Interstate
(4 or 5 lanes) . . . .872 kilometers (542 miles)
Primary
(4 or more lanes) .821 kilometers (510 miles)
Primary
(2 lanes) . . . . .7,562 kilometers (4,700 miles)

Truck Lines

There are 1,238 Interstate Commerce Commission regulated carriers in the state.

Railroads

Four major and 24 shortline railroad companies have a total of 4,023 kilometers (2,500 miles) of intrastate tracks; three of the rail systems are among the nation's largest: Burlington Northern, Southern Pacific/Cotton Belt and Union Pacific.

Airlines

Thirteen airlines (7 national-regional, 6 air taxi commuter) provide Arkansas with air freight and passenger service.

Airports

The state has 90 public use airports, with principal airports located at Little Rock, Hot Springs, Jonesboro, Harrison, Pine Bluff, Texarkana, Fort Smith and Fayetteville.

Waterways

1,853 kilometers (1,000 miles) of navigable waterways

Twelve cities have public terminals: Osceola, West Memphis, and Helena on the Mississippi River; Little Rock, North Little Rock, Pine Bluff, Dardanelle, Van Buren, Morrilton, and Fort Smith on the Arkansas River; and Camden and Crossett on the Ouachita River.

Barge shipping time from Little Rock to New Orleans is 6 days, 7 days from Little Rock to St. Louis.

Gross State Product (1989)

Manufacturing	25.0%
Finance, Insurance, and Real Estate	14.1%
Services	13.5%
Retail Trade	9.5%
Transportation, Communication, and Public Utilities	11.3%
Government	10.4%
Agriculture, Forestry and Fisheries	5.8%
Wholesale Trade	5.2%
Construction	4.2%
Mining	1.0%

Income and Wages

Per Capita Personal Income, USA, 1991 . . . . $19,092

Per Capita Personal Income, AR, 1991 . . . . $14,629

Arkansas ranked 47th in per capita income in 1991.

Manufacturing Average Hourly Earnings, USA 1991 . . . . $11.18

Manufacturing Average Hourly Earnings, AR, 1991 . . . . $8.81

Labor Force

Total Civilian Work Force (1991) . .1,118,000
Total Employment (1991) 1,036,000

Employment Distribution (1991)

Manufacturing	21.4%
Wholesale and Retail Trade	18.9%
Services	18.1%
Government	15.0%
Self-employed, Unpaid and Domestics	10.5%
Transportation and Public Utilities	5.1%
Agriculture	3.8%
Finance, Insurance, and Real Estate	3.5%
Construction	3.3%
Mining	0.4%

Financing Available

Municipal and County Industrial Revenue Bonds
General Obligation Bonds
State Loan/Guarantee Programs
Development Finance Corporations

Education

Twenty state and private four-year colleges/universities
Twelve two-year colleges
Six vocational-technical schools
Five technical institutes
Thirteen technical colleges

Foreign Trade Zones (FTZ)

Little Rock has an FTZ #14 in a new 104,000 sq. ft. building on 11.33 hectares (28.0 acres) and adjacent to a 404.7 hectare (1,000 acres) port and industrial park which has water, air, truck and rail transportation. An FTZ sub-zone was established for Sanyo Manufacturing Corporation in Forrest City.

*Compiled by and reproduced with permission of the Research Division, Arkansas Industrial Development Commission, One Capitol Mall, Little Rock, Arkansas 72201.

ARKANSAS MAP and
1990 CENSUS DATA

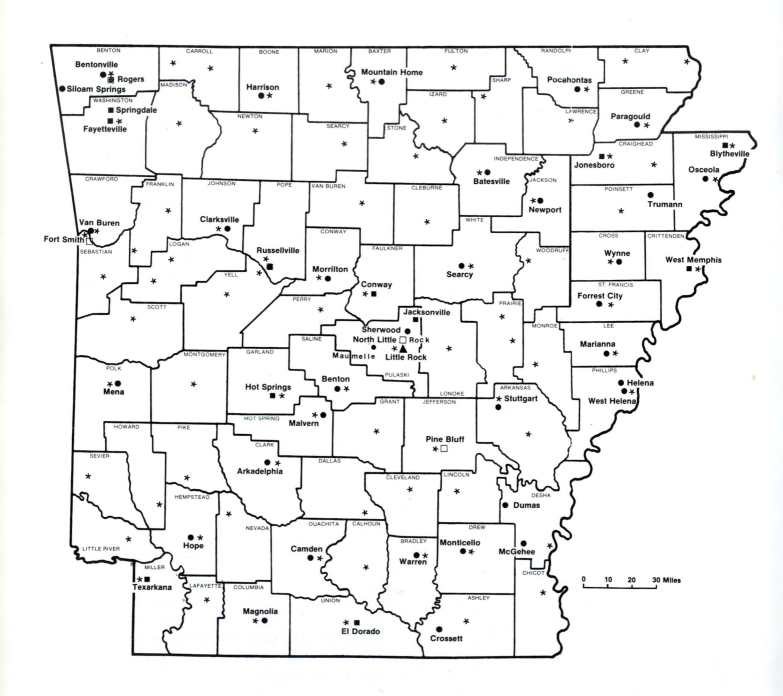

*County Seat
●   5,000 - 20,000
■ 20,000 - 50,000
☐ 50,000 - 100,000
▲ 100,000 and over

COUNTY	COUNTY SEAT	COUNTY	COUNTY SEAT
ARKANSAS	DeWitt, Stuttgart	LAWRENCE	Walnut Ridge
ASHLEY	Hamburg	LEE	Marianna
BAXTER	Mountain Home	LINCOLN	Star City
BENTON	Bentonville	LITTLE RIVER	Ashdown
BOONE	Harrison	LOGAN	Paris, Booneville
BRADLEY	Warren	LONOKE	Lonoke
CALHOUN	Hampton	MADISON	Huntsville
CARROLL	Eureka Springs, Berryville	MARION	Yellville
CHICOT	Lake Village	MILLER	Texarkana
CLARK	Arkadelphia	MISSISSIPPI	Osceola, Blytheville
CLAY	Piggott, Corning	MONROE	Clarendon
CLEBURNE	Heber Springs	MONTGOMERY	Mount Ida
CLEVELAND	Rison	NEVADA	Prescott
COLUMBIA	Magnolia	NEWTON	Jasper
CONWAY	Morrilton	OUACHITA	Camden
CRAIGHEAD	Jonesboro, Lake City	PERRY	Perryville
CRAWFORD	Van Buren	PHILLIPS	Helena
CRITTENDEN	Marion	PIKE	Murfreesboro
CROSS	Wynne	POINSETT	Harrisburg
DALLAS	Fordyce	POLK	Mena
DESHA	Arkansas City	POPE	Russellville
DREW	Monticello	PRAIRIE	Des Arc, De Valls Bluff
FAULKNER	Conway	PULASKI	Little Rock
FRANKLIN	Ozark, Charleston	RANDOLPH	Pocahontas
FULTON	Salem	ST. FRANCIS	Forrest City
GARLAND	Hot Springs	SALINE	Benton
GRANT	Sheridan	SCOTT	Waldron
GREENE	Paragould	SEARCY	Marshall
HEMPSTEAD	Hope	SEBASTIAN	Greenwood, Fort Smith
HOT SPRING	Malvern	SEVIER	De Queen
HOWARD	Nashville	SHARP	Ash Flat
INDEPENDENCE	Batesville	STONE	Mountain View
IZARD	Melbourne	UNION	El Dorado
JACKSON	Newport	VAN BUREN	Clinton
JEFFERSON	Pine Bluff	WASHINGTON	Fayetteville
JOHNSON	Clarksville	WHITE	Searcy
LAFAYETTE	Lewisville	WOODRUFF	Augusta
		YELL	Danville, Dardanelle

Gilchrist], 549

[An] Answer to Three Years in Arkansas [see also Mrs. Mary Hughes], 544

Anthony, Beryl, Jr., 626

Anthony, J.J., 92, 631

Anthony House, 113, 115, 260, 540

Anthony, Susan B., 338-339

Antioch Baptist Church (Little Rock), 374

Antiquarian and Natural History Society, 128

Anti-Saloon League, 345, 397

Appomattox Courthouse, 229

Aquixo, Indian town, 18, 20

Arbuckle, Colonel Matthew, 79

Archeology of the Central Mississippi Valley [see also Dan F. and Phyllis A. Morse], 551

Architecture
   antebellum, 55, 106-107, 114-115, 158; wattle and daub chimney photograph, 102; Wolf House photograph, 108
   Arkansas Post, 40, 47, 49-50, 54-55
   Great Depression, photograph, 414; photograph, 445
   modern, 566; photograph, 530
   Progressive era, 358-359

[The] Architecture of the Arkansas Ozarks [see also Donald Harington], 546

[The] Architecture of E. Fay Jones, 566

Area Health Education Centers (AHECs), 606

Argenta [see also North Little Rock], 283, 343

Arkadelphia [see also Blaketown], 56, 117, 211, 218, 221, 230, 242, 253, 275-276, 284-285, 401, 403, 517, 577, 602, 632, 642

Arkadelphia *Southern Standard,* 286, 288

Arkansea [see also Kappa], 24

Arkansas, state, map of first counties, 64; map of counties at statehood, 81; map of 1836 settlements, 111; map of counties in 1860, 178

Arkansas
   census, 47, 109, 281, 461, 476, 591-592
   Crowley's Ridge, 4-6, 290, 369; Indians, 12; "King Crowley" false artifact, 14
   Delta (Mississippi Alluvial Plain), 1-2, 4-7, 35, 81, 103-104, 107, 155, 273, 293, 348, 364, 387-389, 429-432, 462, 474, 557, 595; drawing, 41; photograph, 34
   geographic regions, map, xxxvi
   Gulf Coastal Plain, 1-4, 6, 288, 475; map, 578
   lakes and rivers, map, 596
   Ouachita Mountains, 1, 3, 5-6, 82, 103, 175, 189, 389, 557, 585-586, 592; in

Civil War, 225; Indians, 12-13; religion, 138; map, 578
   Ozark Mountains, 1-3, 5-7, 82, 103, 107, 172, 175, 189, 369, 388-389, 428, 462, 475, 557, 585-586, 592-593; in Civil War, 219-220, 222, 225, 231, 290, 293; Indians, 12-13, 16; religion, 138; map, 578; photograph, 444

Arkansas, town, 58-59; demise, 110

Arkansas, Confederate ram, artist's rendering, 192

Arkansas [see also John Gould Fletcher], 545, 551

Arkansas Adios [see also Earl Mac Rauch], 548

Arkansas Advocate, 72-74, 144, 537

Arkansas Advocate, (Rathke/Kirby), 518, 609

"Arkansas: A Pome" [see also William M. "Cush" Quesenbury], 541

Arkansas Agricultural and Industrial Commission, 441

Arkansas Agricultural and Mechanical College (A&M) [see also University of Arkansas at Monticello], 468

Arkansas Agricultural and Mechanical Journal, 289

Arkansas Anthracite Coal Company, 322

Arkansas Archeological Survey, *viii*

Arkansas Army, in Civil War, 198-199; disbanded, 202; drawing, 199; reestablished, 205, 207

Arkansas Arts Center, 562, 564, 567, 590, 621

Arkansas Arts Center Decorative Arts Museum see also Albert Pike Home and Pike-Fletcher-Terry House], 115; photograph, 567

Arkansas Arts Council, 564, 567

Arkansas Arts Festival, 564

Arkansas Association of Photographers, 357

Arkansas Association of Retail Lumber Dealers, 357

Arkansas Authors and Composers Society, 543

Arkansas Bankers Association, 395

Arkansas Banner, 93, 95, 145, 181-182

Arkansas Baptist, 169

Arkansas Baptist College [see also Baptist Institute], 276, 318, 404, 439, 558, 605

Arkansas Bar Association, 395, 527, 603

Arkansas Best Freight, 579

Arkansas "Black" (apple), 368

Arkansas Blues Connection, 558

Arkansas Business Council, 601-602

Arkansas Centennial, 441, 545, 557, 622, 636; photograph, 424

"Arkansas Centennial Ode," 556

Arkansas Central Railroad, 259

Arkansas Children's Hospital, 605

Arkansas City, 350, 359, 459, 642; photograph, 411

Arkansas College [see also Campbellites, College of the Ozarks], 139, 146

Arkansas College, 275, 541, 605; photograph, 405

Arkansas Community Organizations for Reform (ACORN), 518, 520

Arkansas Conference on Charities and Correction, 356

Arkansas Conference of Social Work, 484

Arkansas Corporation Commission, 437

Arkansas Council of Defense, 377

Arkansas Council on Human Relations, 497, 502, 514

Arkansas County, 4, 63, 122, 149, 155, 242, 254-255, 277, 292, 630, 642

Arkansas Country Music Hall of Fame [see also Arkansas Entertainers Hall of Fame], 559

[The] Arkansas Cracker Jack [see also Taylor Beard], 544

Arkansas Cumberland College, 275

Arkansas Deaf Mute Institute [see also Arkansas School for the Deaf], 254, 276

Arkansas Democrat, 182, 271, 273, 311, 314, 340, 372, 407, 441, 465, 499, 502, 555-566, 574, 604, 609-610, 618

Arkansas Democrat-Gazette, 361, 609-610, 626-627

Arkansas Department of Pollution Control and Ecology (ADPC&E), 582, 595

Arkansas Development Finance Authority (ADFA), 619

Arkansas Ecology Center, 597

Arkansas Economic Council (AEC), 478

Arkansas Education Association [see also Arkansas Teachers Association], 520, 601, 616

Arkansas Educational Television Network (AETN), 526, 591

Arkansas Electric Co-operative Corporation [see also electric cooperatives], 485

Arkansas Endowment for the Humanities, 551, 567

Arkansas Entertainers Hall of Fame, 559

Arkansas Farm Bureau Federation, 363, 472

Arkansas Federation of Women's Clubs, 340, 356-357, 549, 562

Arkansas First Light Artillery Battery, photograph, 223

Arkansas Free Enterprise Association, 482

Arkansas Funeral Directors Association, 350

Arkansas Gazette, vii, 59, 69-75, 77, 92, 100, 111, 115, 117, 119, 121, 122, 127,

Carroll Cloar